MW01706544

Practical Business Math Procedures

Custom Publishing

MCGRAW-HILL RYERSON LIMITED

Toronto Montréal Boston Burr Ridge, IL Dubuque, IA Madison, WI New York San Francisco
St. Louis Bangkok Bogotá Caracas Kuala Lumpur Lisbon London Madrid Mexico City Milan
New Delhi Santiago Seoul Singapore Sydney Taipei

Practical Business Math Procedures, First Canadian Edition, by Jeffrey Slater and Elena Skliarenko. ISBN 0-07-091663-2.
Published by McGraw-Hill, a business unit of the McGraw-Hill Companies, Inc., 1221 Avenue of the Americas, New York, NY, 10020.

Manager, Custom Learning Solutions: Jason Giles
Learning Solutions Custom Print Specialist: Corinne Mohr

ISBN-10: 0-07-109110-6
ISBN-13: 978-0-07-109110-7

Printed and bound in Canada

Table of Contents

***Practical Business Math Procedures*, First Canadian Edition,**
by Jeffrey Slater

Preface viii

Chapter 1 Whole Numbers: How To Dissect And Solve Word Problems. 1

Chapter 2 Fractions 35

Chapter 3 Decimals 67

Chapter 4 Powers and Roots 91

Chapter 5 Solving for the Unknown: Basic Linear Equations: A How-To Approach For Solving Equations 99

Chapter 6 Percents and Their Applications 121

Chapter 7 Ratios and Proportions 159

Chapter 8 Banking. 171

Chapter 9 Discounts: Trade and Cash 195

Chapter 10 Markups and Markdowns: Insight Into Perishables; Cost-Profit-Volume And Breakeven Analysis. 229

Chapter 11 Payroll. 265

Chapter 12 Simple Interest 297

Chapter 13 Promissory Notes, Simple Discount Notes, and the Discount Process 317

Chapter 14 Compound Interest: Present Value; Future Value; Equivalent Payments; Effective, Nominal, And Equivalent Interest Rates 331

Chapter 15 Annuities and Sinking Funds 355

Table of Contents

Chapter 16 The Cost of Home Ownership 383

Chapter 17 Business Statistics. 395

Appendix A 419

Glossary 429

Index 439

PREFACE

Welcome to the First Canadian Edition of *Practical Business Math Procedures*! As the name implies, this textbook is designed to provide complete coverage of practical business applications of math. Getting a postsecondary education isn't easy. Students often work full-time to put themselves through school and this textbook was developed to give students every opportunity for success. Slater supports student learning by providing clear explanations including detailed, step-by-step examples; complete coverage at the appropriate level; student-oriented pedagogical tools such as the Chapter Organizer and Reference Guide; a focus on real business applications; anticipation of student difficulties; and unsurpassed teaching support materials.

FEATURES OF THE FIRST CANADIAN EDITION

The First Canadian Edition, carefully written and developed for Canadian students with different backgrounds, focuses on the support and encouragement of learning, in order to provide students with a solid foundation for further courses in business statistics, accounting, marketing, economics, and more. Concepts are presented as clearly as possible, and examples and exercises are given. Using carefully selected examples, the book explains when, where, and why students will use their acquired skills. It is organized in a logical and teachable fashion, with unique and motivating pedagogy. Methods of computing and of solving problems are presented step by step, with formulas, articles, photos, and Internet projects.

LEARNING UNIT OBJECTIVES

The Learning Unit Objectives let students know what they can expect to learn in each chapter, and allow them to refer to the particular pages where these objectives are addressed.

> **LEARNING UNIT OBJECTIVES**
>
> **LU 7–1: Ratios: Basic Concepts**
> - Set up ratios (p. 160).
> - Perform operations with ratios (p. 160).
> - Applications: Allocate values according to a ratio (p. 161).
>
> **LU 7–2: Proportions: Basic Concepts**
> - Use the cross-multiplication rule (p. 162).
> - Applications: Solve problems involving proportions (p. 162).
> - Applications: Allocate according to a ratio (p. 162).
> - Applications: Use proportions in currency conversion (p. 163).

CHAPTER OPENERS

The chapter openers introduce students to the chapters' topics and explain the business applications of the new material. Students can see the real-world applications of business math through articles, Web sites, and advertisements, which make the topics relevant to them.

REAL-WORLD EXAMPLES

Interesting applications and illustrations of the text material are extensively integrated into the text.

Ratios can compare two or more values. For example, in this clipping of an advertisement for one of Edmonton's Chinese Buffets, the ratio of prices for dinners for two, for three, and for five people will be respectively $15.95 : $23.50 : $40.50.

Ratios have properties similar to those of equations. Multiplication or division of all ratio members by the same number will not change the meaning of the ratio. Thus, ratios can be reduced to lowest terms by dividing all the members by a common factor:

$$12:6:3 = 4:2:1$$
$$18:9:3 = 6:3:1$$
$$100:50:25 = 4:2:1$$
$$63:36 = 7:4$$
$$27:13:44 = \frac{27}{31}:\frac{13}{31}:\frac{44}{31}$$

Ratios on the left side are said to be **equivalent ratios** to the ratios on the right side.

KEY FORMULAS

Formulas used for the first time are boxed and numbered for easy reference. In addition, these key formulas are listed on the text's Online Learning Centre.

SIMPLE INTEREST FORMULA

To calculate simple interest, we use the following **simple interest formula:**

$$\text{Simple Interest } (I) = \text{Principal } (P) \times \text{Rate } (r) \times \text{Time } (t)$$
$$I = P \times r \times t \qquad \textbf{(12.2)}$$

KEY CONCEPTS

Important concepts unique to the study of business math are set apart from the text and highlighted for easy reference and review. Explanations are given in a step-by-step format that is easy to follow and remember, followed by relevant examples.

OPPOSITE PROCESS RULE

If an equation indicates a process such as addition, subtraction, multiplication, or division, solve for the unknown or variable by using the opposite process. For example, if the equation process is addition, solve for the unknown by using subtraction.

PRACTICE QUIZZES

A short quiz punctuates each Learning Unit, and allows students to practise the skills they have just learned. The worked-out solutions at the end of the chapter provide immediate feedback on students' understanding of the Units.

LU 6–2 PRACTICE QUIZ

Solve for portion:

1. 38% of 900. **2.** 60% of $9,000.

Solve for rate (round to nearest tenth percent as needed):

3. 430 is ______ % of 5,000. **4.** 200 is ______ % of 700.

Solve for base (round to the nearest tenth as needed):

5. 55 is 40% of ______ . **6.** 900 is $4\frac{1}{2}$% of ______ .

Solve the following (Blueprint Aids are shown in the solution; you might want to try some on scrap paper):

7. Five out of 25 students in Professor Ford's class received an "A" grade. What percent of the class *did not* receive the "A" grade?

8. Abby Biernet has yet to receive 60% of her lobster order. Abby received 80 lobsters to date. What was her original order?

9. The typical sales fee for a real estate agent is 2.5%. How much will an agent receive from the sale of a $400,000 home?

Blueprint Aid Boxes

Blueprint Aids are designed to help students navigate word problems. They show students how to begin the problem-solving process, get them actively involved in dissecting the problem, show them visually what has to be done before calculating, and provide a structure to use. In addition, with each Blueprint Aid, a **Step Approach** is provided that offers an alternative method for solving the problem, allowing students to select the method that best suits them.

Word Problem Situation 5: Calculating Unit and Dollar Sales (Cost per Unit) When Total Units Are Not Given Andy sold watches ($9) and alarm clocks ($5) at a flea market. Total sales were $287. People bought 4 times as many watches as alarm clocks. How many of each did Andy sell? What were the total dollar sales of each?

BLUEPRINT AID

Unknown(s)	Variable(s)	Price	Relationship
Unit sales:			
Watches	4*C*	$9	36*C*
Clocks	*C*	5	+ 5*C*
			$287 total sales

MATHEMATICAL STEPS

$36C + 5C = 287$

$\frac{41C}{41} = \frac{287}{41}$

$C = 7$

7 clocks

4(7) = 28 watches

EXPLANATION

Number of watches times $9 sales price plus number of alarm clocks times $5 equals $287 total sales.

CHECK

7($5) + 28($9) = $287

$35 + $252 = $287

$287 = $287

STEP APPROACH

STEP 1. In this problem we are talking about sales of two items: clocks and watches. Sales of watches exceeded the sales of clocks by four times. So sales of watches are expressed in terms of sales of clocks.

STEP 2. *C:* Number of clocks sold

4*C:* Number of watches sold

Revenue from sales of watches was: $4C \times 9$

Revenue from sales of clocks was: $C \times 5$

Total revenue was: $287

$C = ?$

$4C = ?$

STEP 3. $36C + 5C = 287$

STEP 4. $41C = 287$

$C = 7$

$4C = 28$

STEP 5. Verify the answer. Always substitute the values into the original formula. The left side must equal the right side.

Left Side		*Right Side*
9 × 28 + 7 × 5	=	287
252 + 35	=	287
287	=	287

THE ANSWER IS CORRECT

Chapter Organizer and Reference Guides

Each chapter ends with a Chapter Organizer and Reference Guide, which is an overview that provides students with a complete set of notes on the topics covered in the chapter. Key points, formulas, examples, and vocabulary are included all with page references. This tool is also useful for exam preparation.

CHAPTER ORGANIZER AND REFERENCE GUIDE

Topic	Key point, procedure, formula	Example(s) to illustrate situation
Converting decimals to percents, p. 135	1. Move decimal point two places to right. If necessary, add zeros. This rule is also used for whole numbers and mixed decimals. 2. Add a percent symbol at end of number.	.81 = .81. = 81% .008 = .00.8 = .8% 4.15 = 4.15. = 415%

Critical Thinking Discussion Questions

The Critical Thinking Discussion Questions, which follow the Chapter Organizer and Reference Guide, are designed to get students to think about the larger picture and the "whys" of business math. They go beyond the typical questions by asking students to explain, define, and create.

CRITICAL THINKING DISCUSSION QUESTIONS

1. Explain the difference between a variable and a constant. What would you consider your monthly car payment—a variable or a constant?
2. How does the opposite process rule help solve for the variable in an equation? If a Mercedes costs 3 times as much as a Saab, how could the opposite process rule be used? The selling price of the Mercedes is $60,000.
3. What is the difference between Word Problem Situations 5 and 6 in Learning Unit 5–2? Show why the more expensive item in Word Problem Situation 6 is assigned to the variable first.

END-OF-CHAPTER PROBLEMS

At the end of each chapter is a comprehensive set of Drill Problems and Word Problems, similar to those found throughout the chapter. There are also Challenge Problems, which let students stretch their understanding and ability to solve more complex problems. The problem section concludes with a Summary Practice Test that covers all the Learning Objectives in the chapter. The answers for the odd-numbered Drill and Word Problems, and for all Challenge Problems and Summary Practice Test Questions, are located in Appendix A.

END-OF-CHAPTER PROBLEMS

DRILL PROBLEMS

Express each of the ratios in the lowest terms:

7–1. **a.** 115 : 125 : 130 **b.** 25 : 225 : 1,225

7–2. **a.** 0.10 : 0.25 : 0.40 **b.** 0.36 : 0.66 : 0.72 : 0.42

7–3. **a.** 100 : 200 : 1,000 **b.** 300 : 30 : 900

WORD PROBLEMS

Set up a ratio for the following problems:

7–16. Peter, Oleg and Sunir entered into a partnership. Peter invested $2,000, Oleg $3,500, and Sounir $2,500. What was the ratio of their investments?

7–17. At a college athletic competition, John came first with a result of 13.5 seconds, Paul was next with a result of 13.8 seconds, Ying came third with a

CHALLENGE PROBLEMS

7–25. Mr. Percival exchanged CDN$2,000 in U.S. funds before his flight to Florida. After three days in Florida he travelled to Italy. Mr. Percival exchanged the remaining US$1,200 for Euros and in a week returned to Canada with €300 in his wallet. How much American funds did Mr. Percival get for CDN$2,000? How much in Euros did he have flying to Italy? How much money will he get back in Canadian funds in Canada upon his return? Use the current exchange rates.

SUMMARY PRACTICE TEST

Express terms of the ratios as whole numbers and reduce ratios to the lowest terms: (p. 161)

1. 1.52 : 7 **2.** 3.45 : 2.85 : 9.005

3. $\frac{3}{7} : \frac{5}{63}$ **4.** 4.5 : 3.4 : 9

Solve the proportions for the unknown values. Round to two decimals: (p. 162)

5. $d : 150 = 430 : 180$ **6.** $380 : 75 : c = a : 120 : 48$

7. Jimmy has noticed that if he increases the time he spends studying at home, his marks go up in the same ratio. Last semester Jimmy spent 2 hours studying at home every workday, and his average was 3.6. How many hours per day must Jimmy study to get a 4.0 average? (p. 162)

Business Math Scrapbook

At the end of each chapter, clippings from newspapers, magazines, and Web pages are presented with Projects that give students the chance to put their new math skills to work.

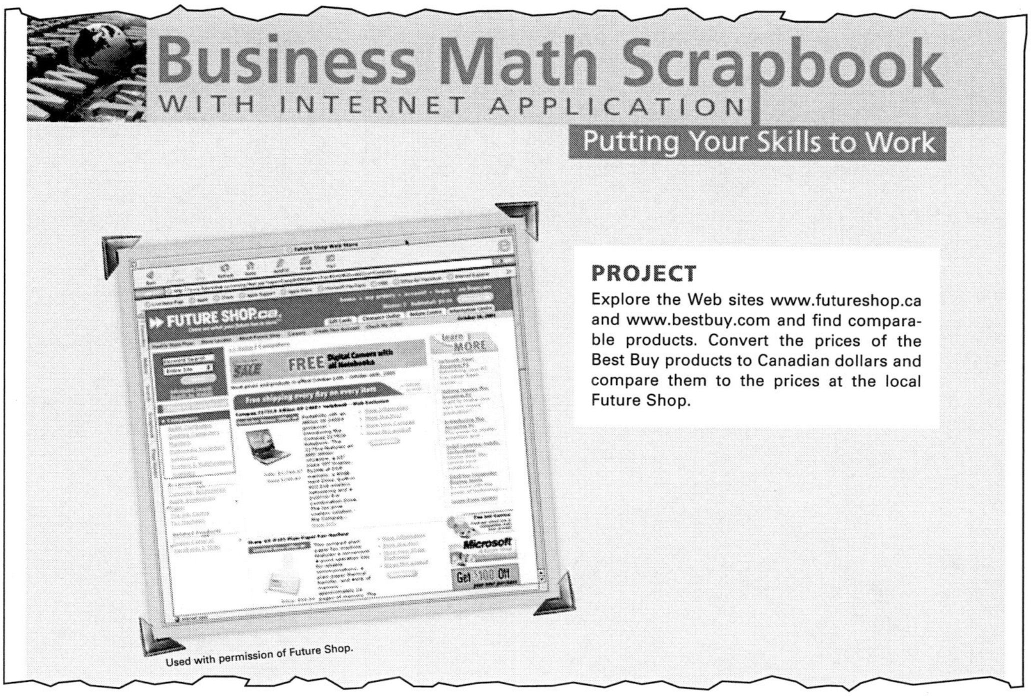

SUPERIOR SERVICE

Service takes on a whole new meaning with McGraw-Hill Ryerson and *Practical Business Math Procedures.* More than just bringing you the textbook, we have consistently raised the bar of innovation and educational research—both in business math and in education in general. These investments in learning and the education community have helped us to understand the needs of students and educators across the country, and allowed us to foster the growth of truly innovative, integrated learning.

Integrated-Learning

i-Learning ADVANTAGE McGraw-Hill Ryerson

Your *integrated*-Learning Sales Specialist is a McGraw-Hill Ryerson representative who has the experience, product knowledge, training, and support to help you assess and integrate any of the below-noted products, technology, and services into your course for optimum teaching and learning performance. Whether it's how to use our Test Item File, how to help your students improve their grades, or how to put your entire course online, your *i*-Learning Sales Specialist is there to help you do it. Contact your local *i*-Learning Sales Specialist today to learn how to maximize all of McGraw-Hill Ryerson's resources!

i-Learning Services Program

McGraw-Hill Ryerson iLearning Services Program

McGraw-Hill Ryerson offers a unique *i*Services package designed for Canadian faculty. Our mission is to equip providers of higher education with superior tools and resources required for excellence in teaching. For additional information visit www.mcgrawhill.ca/highereducation/eservices.

Teaching, Technology & Learning Conference Series

The educational environment has changed tremendously in recent years, and McGraw-Hill Ryerson continues to be committed to helping you acquire the skills you need to succeed in this new milieu. Our innovative Teaching, Technology & Learning Conference Series brings together faculty from across Canada with 3M Teaching Excellence award winners to share teaching and learning best practices in a collaborative and stimulating environment. Preconference workshops on general topics, such as teaching large classes and technology integration, will also be offered. We will also work with you at your own institution to customize workshops that best suit the needs of your faculty at your institution.

Research Reports into Mobile Learning and Student Success

These landmark reports, undertaken in conjunction with academic and private sector advisory boards, are the result of research into the challenge professors face in helping students succeed and the opportunities that new technology presents to impact teaching and learning.

SUPPLEMENTS

INSTRUCTOR SUPPLEMENTS

Instructor's Resource CD-ROM

This comprehensive resource contains all the necessary instructor supplements, including:

Instructor's Manual

This manual contains the complete solutions to all exercises in the text.

Test Item File

This resource contains individual chapter tests, a sample final exam, and true/false, multiple choice, and short answer questions. The answers to all questions are given, along with a difficulty rating.

Microsoft® PowerPoint® Lecture Slides

These full-colour slides include chapter objectives, definitions of key terms, graphics, and additional examples. Instructors can use them to enhance their lectures and add material of their own.

Instructor's Online Learning Centre (OLC)

Online LearningCentre

The OLC, at www.mcgrawhill.ca/college/slater, includes a password-protected Web site for instructors. The site offers downloadable supplements and access to PageOut, the McGraw-Hill Ryerson Web site development centre.

ALEKS

ALEKS (Assessment and Learning in Knowledge Spaces) is an artificial intelligence based system, which, acting much like a human tutor, can provide individualized assessment, practice, and learning. By assessing the student's learning, ALEKS focuses clearly on what the student is ready to learn next and helps him or her master the course content more quickly and clearly. You can visit ALEKS at www.business.aleks.com, or contact your local *i*-Learning Specialist for more information.

PageOut

PageOut

Create a custom course Website with PageOut, free with every McGraw-Hill Ryerson textbook.

Visit www.mhhe.com/pageout to create a Web page for your course using our resources. PageOut is the McGraw-Hill Ryerson Web site development centre. This Web page generation software is free to adopters and is designed to help faculty create an online course, complete with assignments, quizzes, links to relevant Web sites, lecture notes, and more—all in a matter of minutes.

In addition, content cartridges are available for course management systems, such as WebCT and Blackboard. These platforms provide instructors with user-friendly, flexible teaching tools. Please contact your local McGraw-Hill Ryerson *i*-Learning Sales Specialist for details.

STUDENT SUPPLEMENTS

STUDENT SOLUTIONS MANUAL *007-092210-1*

The Student Solutions Manual, prepared by Dr. Elena Skliarenko of Seneca College of Applied Arts and Technology, contains step-by-step solutions for several examples of every kind of problem in the text. It also contains a student progress chart that allows students to keep a record of their progress.

STUDENT ONLINE LEARNING CENTRE (OLC)

This electronic learning aid, located at www.mcgrawhill.ca/college/slater, offers a wealth of materials, including multiple-choice quizzes, fill-in-the-blank quizzes, Excel templates, annotated Web links, word problems, and much more!

ACKNOWLEDGMENTS

Comments and suggestions that have been invaluable to the development of the First Canadian Edition were provided by a variety of reviewers, and a debt of gratitude is owed to the following educators:

Chris Kellman	*British Columbia Institute of Technology*
Donald J. Wheeler	*College of the North Atlantic*
Sue Whissell	*Cambrian College of Applied Arts and Technology*
Felix Ernst	*Camosun College*
Ivo Kvarda	*Confederation College*
Evelyn Taylor	*Fanshawe College*
Marge White	*Medicine Hat College*
Baden Connolly	*Nova Scotia Community College*
Dianne Morden	*St. Clair College*
John Cavaliere	*Sault College*
Betty Pratt	*Seneca College of Applied Arts and Technology*
Nancy Kingsbury	*Sheridan Institute of Technology and Advanced Learning*

Thanks also to those academic experts and contributors who participated in the development of the U.S.-published Seventh Edition, upon which this adaptation is based.

Many thanks go to my family for their patience and encouragement. I would also like to thank my friends Annie Mishchenko and Vera Kaploun for their advice and support during the writing process.

A special thank you must be given to John Giquere, Sault College for his vigilant efforts as the Technical Reviewer of the text and solutions.

Finally, I wish to thank the staff at McGraw-Hill Ryerson. This includes Cathy Koop, Senior Sponsoring Editor; Lynn Fisher, Executive Sponsoring Editor; Kamilah Reid Burrell, Developmental Editor; Kim Verhaeghe, Marketing Manager; Kelly Dickson, Editorial Services Manager; Jaime Duffy, Supervising Editor; Andrée Davis, Production Coordinator; Gail Ferreira, Interior Design; and others I do not know personally who made important contributions.

Dr. Elena Skliarenko

Whole Numbers:

How to Dissect and Solve Word Problems

1

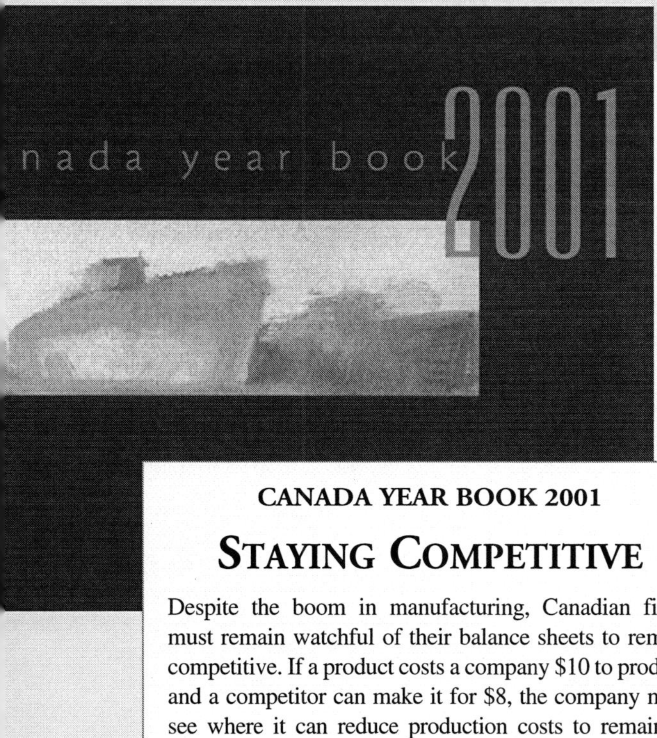

CANADA YEAR BOOK 2001

Staying Competitive

Despite the boom in manufacturing, Canadian firms must remain watchful of their balance sheets to remain competitive. If a product costs a company $10 to produce and a competitor can make it for $8, the company must see where it can reduce production costs to remain in business. Staying competitive often involves adopting manufacturing technology, allowing companies to churn out products more quickly and at lower cost. As a growing number of Canadian firms take this route, many have boosted their production capacities with machinery and equipment, exploiting the latest technological advances.

Manufacturers began to increase their investments in machinery and equipment substantially in 1994. That year, they spent almost $12 billion, representing an increase of over 20% from the year before. In 1995 and 1996, manufacturers spent just under $14 billion on machinery and equipment, and by 1998 spending exceeded $17 billion. In 1999, investment fell by $75 million, though the investment total still topped $17 billion.

Source: Statistics Canada 2002.

LEARNING UNIT OBJECTIVES

LU 1–1: Reading, Writing, and Rounding Whole Numbers

- Use place values to read and write numeric and verbal whole numbers (p. 3).
- Round whole numbers to the indicated position (p. 4).
- Use a Blueprint Aid for dissecting and solving a word problem (p. 6).

LU 1–2: Adding and Subtracting Whole Numbers

- Add whole numbers; check and estimate addition computations (p. 8).
- Use properties of addition (p. 10).
- Subtract whole numbers; check and estimate subtraction computations (p. 10).

LU 1–3: Multiplying and Dividing Whole Numbers

- Multiply whole numbers; check and estimate multiplication computations (p. 12).
- Use properties of multiplication (p. 14).
- Divide whole numbers; check and estimate division computations (p. 14).

LU 1–4: Order of Operations

- BEDMAS; PEMDAS (p. 17).
- Calculator use (p. 18).

People of all ages make personal business decisions based on the answers to number questions. Numbers also determine most of the business decisions of companies. For example, click on your computer and go to the Web site of a company such as eBay and note the importance of numbers in the company's business decision-making process.

The following *Wall Street Journal* clipping illustrates how McDonald's fast-food chain plans to increase its profit numbers by changing its business strategy.

Will Big Mac Find New Sizzle In Shoes, Videos?

By Jennifer Ordonez
Staff Reporter of The Wall Street Journal

McDonald's Corp. wants to supersize its brand name.

Led by a new brand-extension executive, the burger giant is quietly developing or expanding several lines of McDonald's-brand consumer goods. Already, German consumers are buying McDonald's-brand ketchup, and for some time American parents have been picking up McKids clothing and shoes at Wal-Mart stores. Under consideration now are McDonald's-brand snacks and other packaged goods, as well as a line of McDonald's books and videos.

"A few years from now, people will say, 'I remember when McDonald's was a restaurant,"' says Peter Oakes, a restaurant analyst for Merrill Lynch Global Securities who has caught wind of the strategy and is preparing a report on it. "Why not do something more than just sponsor Saturday morning cartoons?"

Jack Greenberg

McDonald's has yet to announce the strategy, whose initial thrust will likely be overseas. But a year ago it created a new executive position—vice president for corporate strategy—to explore ways of extending the McDonald's brand. Mats Lederhausen, who holds the title, reports directly to Chief Executive Jack Greenberg.

Source: © 2000 Dow Jones & Company, Inc.

Companies often follow a general problem-solving procedure to arrive at a change in company policy. Using McDonald's as an example, the following steps illustrate this procedure:

Step 1.	State the problem(s).	The restaurant business is very competitive. A new strategy is needed that broadens the scope of sales and results in a continued increase in profits.
Step 2.	Decide on the best method(s) to solve the problem(s).	Create new products (ketchup; McKids clothing and shoes) with McDonald's brand name.
Step 3.	Does the solution make sense?	Test-market new products overseas (ketchup). Sell McKids clothing and shoes at Wal-Mart.
Step 4.	Evaluate results.	All test markets will be evaluated before worldwide distribution begins.

Have you seen the new H. L. Heinz Company's green ketchup? McDonald's-brand ketchup was introduced in Germany to compete with the Heinz ketchup—the number one seller of ketchup in Germany. How well is McDonald's-brand ketchup performing in the Heinz market? As you may expect, a spokesperson for Heinz answers, "Not very well. Consumers tell us ours is better." The driving force behind McDonald's desire to add new products such as ketchup to its brand name is higher profit numbers.

Your study of numbers begins with a review of basic computation skills that focuses on speed and accuracy. You may think, "But I can use my calculator." Even if your instructor allows you to use a calculator, you still must know the basic computation skills. You need these skills to know what to calculate, how to interpret your calculations, how to make estimates to recognize errors you made in using your calculator, and how to make calculations when you do not have a calculator. (How to use a calculator is explained on the Web site for this book at www.mcgrawhill.ca/college/slater.)

The Canadian numbering system is the **decimal system** or *base 10 system.* Your calculator gives the ten single-digit numbers of the decimal system—0, 1, 2, 3, 4, 5, 6, 7, 8, and 9. The centre of the decimal system is the **decimal point.** When you have a number with a decimal point, the numbers to the left of the decimal point are **whole numbers** and the numbers to the right of the decimal point are decimal numbers (discussed in Chapter 3). When you have a number *without* a decimal, the number is a whole number and the decimal is assumed to be after the number.

This chapter discusses reading, writing, and rounding whole numbers; adding and subtracting whole numbers; and multiplying and dividing whole numbers.

LEARNING UNIT 1–1
READING, WRITING, AND ROUNDING WHOLE NUMBERS

RESIDENTIAL VALUES BY TYPE OF INVESTMENT, 1ST QUARTER (dollars), 2001–2002

Geography	Type of investment	2001/01	2002/01
Canada	**Total residential investment**	**8,580,482,000**	**9,874,245,000**
Newfoundland and Labrador	Total residential investment	93,165,000	109,292,000
Prince Edward Island	Total residential investment	29,197,000	33,776,000
Nova Scotia	Total residential investment	225,971,000	262,684,000
New Brunswick	Total residential investment	157,615,000	182,939,000
Quebec	Total residential investment	1,496,840,000	1,829,549,000
Ontario	Total residential investment	3,967,195,000	4,308,396,000
Manitoba	Total residential investment	172,055,000	203,401,000
Saskatchewan	Total residential investment	154,934,000	178,139,000
Alberta	Total residential investment	1,152,814,000	1,405,542,000
British Columbia	Total residential investment	1,107,478,000	1,334,882,000
Yukon	Total residential investment	11,745,000	10,200,000
Northwest Territories	Total residential investment	5,878,000	10,701,000
Nunavut	Total residential investment	5,593,000	4,748,000

Source: Statistics Canada, "Residential Values, by Type of Investment, 1st Quarter ($'s)," *Building Permits Survey.* Adapted from the Statistics Canada CANSIM database (cansim2.statcan.ca), Table 026-0013.

We often use whole numbers in business calculations. For example, look at Statistics Canada clipping "Residential values by type of investment, 1st quarter (dollars), 2001–2002." Note that in the first quarter of 2002, total residential investments in Canada increased to $9,874,245,000. From the information in this Unit, you will learn that you can read this numeric whole number "nine billion, eight hundred seventy-four million, two hundred forty-five thousand." Now let's begin our study of whole numbers.

READING AND WRITING NUMERIC AND VERBAL WHOLE NUMBERS

The decimal system is a *place-value system* based on the powers of 10. Any whole number can be written with the ten digits of the decimal system because the position, or placement, of the digits in a number gives the value of the digits.

To determine the value of each digit in a number, we use a place-value chart (Figure 1.1) that divides numbers into named groups of three digits, with each group separated by a comma. To separate a number into groups, you begin with the last digit in the number and insert commas every three digits, moving from right to left. This divides the number into the named groups (units, thousands, millions, billions, trillions) shown in the place-value chart. Within each group, you have a ones, tens, and hundreds place.

In Figure 1.1, the numeric number 1,605,743,891,412 illustrates place values. When you study the place-value chart, you can see that the value of each place in the chart is 10 times the value of the place to the right. We can illustrate this by analyzing the last four digits in the number 1,605,743,891,412:

$$1{,}412 = (1 \times 1{,}000) + (4 \times 100) + (1 \times 10) + (2 \times 1)$$

So we can also say that in the number 745, the "7" means seven hundred (700); in the number 75, the "7" means 7 tens (70).

FIGURE 1–1
Whole number place-value chart

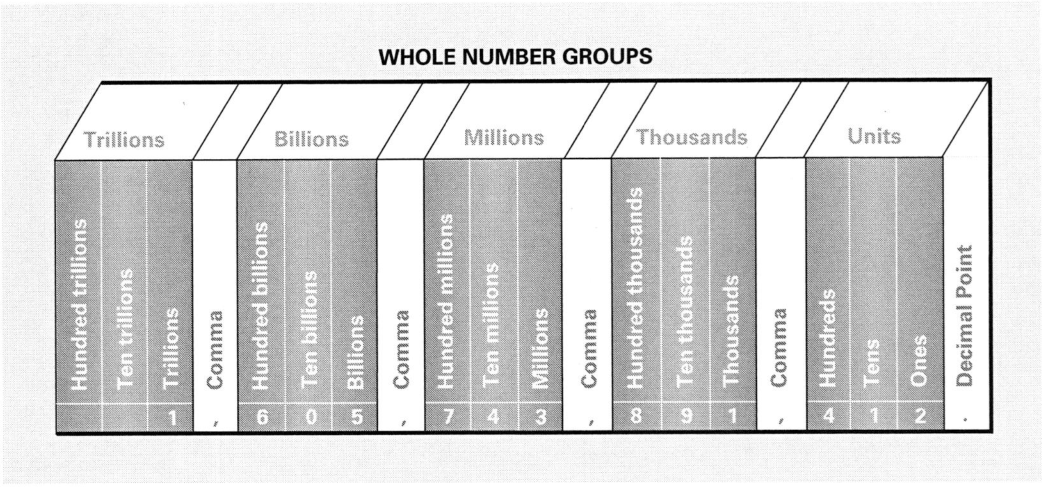

To read and write a numeric number in verbal form, you begin at the left and read each group of three digits as if it were alone, adding the group name at the end (except the last units group and groups of all zeros). Using the place-value chart in Figure 1.1, the number 1,605,743,891,412 is read "one trillion, six hundred five billion, seven hundred forty-three million, eight hundred ninety-one thousand, four hundred twelve." You do not read zeros. They fill vacant spaces as placeholders so that you can correctly state the number values. Also, the numbers twenty-one to ninety-nine must have a hyphen. And most important, when you read or write whole numbers in verbal form, do not use the word *and*. In the decimal system, *and* indicates the decimal, which we discuss in Chapter 3.

By reversing the above process of changing a numeric number to a verbal number, you can use the place-value chart to change a verbal number to a numeric number. Remember that you must keep track of the place value of each digit. The place values of the digits in a number determine its total value.

Rounding Whole Numbers

Many of the whole numbers you read and hear are rounded numbers. Government statistics are usually rounded numbers. The financial reports of companies also use rounded numbers. All rounded numbers are *approximate* numbers. The more rounding you do, the more you approximate the number.

Rounded whole numbers are used for many reasons. With rounded whole numbers you can quickly estimate arithmetic results, check actual computations, report numbers that change quickly such as population numbers, and make numbers easier to read and remember.

Numbers can be rounded to any identified digit place value, including the first digit of a number (rounding all the way). To round whole numbers, use the following three steps:

ROUNDING WHOLE NUMBERS

Step 1. Identify the place value of the digit you want to round.

Step 2. If the digit to the right of the identified digit in Step 1 is 5 or more, increase the identified digit by 1 (round up). If the digit to the right is less than 5, do not change the identified digit.

Step 3. Change all digits to the right of the rounded identified digit to zeros.

EXAMPLE 1
Round 9,362 to the nearest hundred.

STEP 1. 9,362 — The digit 3 is in the hundreds place value.

STEP 2. The digit to the right of 3 is 5 or more (6). Thus, 3, the identified digit in Step 1, is now rounded to 4. You change the identified digit only if the digit to the right is 5 or more.

9,462

STEP 3. 9,400 — Change digits 6 and 2 to zeros, since these digits are to the right of 4, the rounded number.

By rounding 9,362 to the nearest hundred, you can see that 9,362 is closer to 9,400 than to 9,300.

EXAMPLE 2
Round 67,951 to the nearest thousand.

STEP 1. 67,951 — The digit 7 is in the thousands place value.

STEP 2. Digit to the right of 7 is 5 or more (9). Thus, 7, the identified digit in Step 1, is now rounded to 8.

68,951

STEP 3. 68,000 — Change digits 9, 5, and 1 to zeros, since these digits are to the right of 8, the rounded number.

By rounding 67,951 to the nearest thousand, you can see that 67,951 is closer to 68,000 than to 67,000.

Now let's look at **rounding all the way.** To round a number all the way, you round to the first digit of the number (the leftmost digit) and have only one nonzero digit remaining in the number.

EXAMPLE 3
Round 7,843 all the way.

STEP 1. 7,843 — Identified leftmost digit is 7.

STEP 2. Digit to the right of 7 is greater than 5, so 7 becomes 8.

8,843

STEP 3. 8,000 — Change all other digits to zeros.

Rounding 7,843 all the way gives 8,000.

Remember that rounding a digit to a specific place value depends on the degree of accuracy you want in your estimate. For example, 24,800 rounds all the way to 20,000 because the digit to the right of 2 is less than 5. This 20,000 is 4,800 less than the original 24,800. You would be more accurate if you rounded 24,800 to the place value of the identified digit 4, which is 25,000.

We can use the Statistics Canada graph "Beer Production in Canada in January–April 2002 (litres)" to illustrate rounding to the nearest thousand.

BEER PRODUCTION IN CANADA IN JANUARY–APRIL 2002 (LITRES)

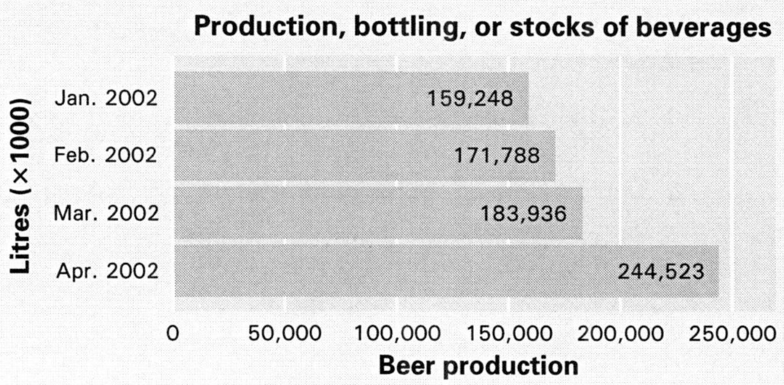

Source: "Production, Bottling or Stock of Beverages." Adapted from the Statistics Canada CANSIM database (cansim2.statcan.ca), Table 203-0019.

Note that production in January is 159,248 litres and in February 171,788 litres. Round these numbers to the nearest thousand as shown above and you can say "In January Canada produced 159,000 litres of beer and in February 172,000 litres." Numbers rounded to the nearest thousand can either be relatively less than the actual number, as in January, or a little more than the actual number, as in February.

Before concluding this Unit, let's look at how to dissect and solve a word problem.

How to Dissect and Solve a Word Problem

As a student, your author found solving word problems difficult. Not knowing where to begin after reading the word problem caused the difficulty. Today, students still struggle with word problems as they try to decide where to begin.

Solving word problems involves *organization* and *persistence.* Recall how persistent you were when you learned to ride a two-wheel bike. Do you remember the feeling of success you experienced when you rode the bike without help? Apply this persistence to word problems. Do not be discouraged. Each person learns at a different speed. Your goal must be to *finish the race* and experience the success of solving word problems with ease.

To be organized in solving word problems, you need a plan of action that tells you where to begin—a Blueprint Aid. Like a builder, you will refer to this Blueprint Aid constantly until you know the procedure. The Blueprint Aid for dissecting and solving a word problem looks like this:

Blueprint Aid for Dissecting and Solving a Word Problem

THE FACTS (What is given)	SOLVING FOR? (Variable/unknown value)	STEPS TO TAKE (And formulas to use)	KEY POINTS

Follow the same procedure every time you deal with a word problem.

Step 1. First read the problem to get a sense of the topic and the given information. For example, the problem may involve rounding of whole numbers or defining percent change of price increase.

Step 2. Read the problem slowly again, and identify what data is given. Label each item of the data and select a variable for the unknown quantity. Write down the given information in labelled form in the first and second columns of the Blueprint Aid.

Step 3. Create any diagrams, drawings, or figures that illustrate the problem or help you to visualize the process described.

Step 4. Insert into the third column the basic information you must know or calculate before solving the problem. Often, this column will contain formulas and equations that reflect what you know or would like to find out. For example, in the third column you might convert word information into mathematical equations. Then, in the last column, insert all issues and comments that may reinforce key points for you.

Step 5. Solve the equation and check your answer. Write the answer as a statement.

It's time now to try your skill at using the action plan and the Blueprint Aid for dissecting and solving a word problem.

THE WORD PROBLEM On the 100th anniversary of Tootsie Roll Industries, the company reported sharply increased sales and profits. Sales reached one hundred ninety-four million dollars and a record profit of twenty-two million, five hundred fifty-six thousand dollars. The company president requested that you round the sales and profit figures all the way.

Study the following Blueprint Aid and note how we filled in the columns with the information in the word problem. You will find the organization of the Blueprint Aid most helpful. Be persistent! You *can* dissect and solve word problems! When you are finished with the word problem, make sure the answer seems reasonable.

THE FACTS	SOLVING FOR?	STEPS TO TAKE	KEY POINTS
S: Sales: One hundred ninety-four million dollars. *P: Profit:* Twenty-two million, five hundred fifty-six thousand dollars.	Sales and profit rounded all the way. $S_{rounded} = ?$ $P_{rounded} = ?$	Express each verbal form in numeric form. Identify leftmost digit in each number. $S = \$194{,}000{,}000$ $P = \$22{,}556{,}000$	Rounding all the way means only the leftmost digit will remain. All other digits become zeros.

STEPS TO SOLVING PROBLEM

1. Convert verbal to numeric.
   S: One hundred ninety-four million dollars → $194,000,000
   P: Twenty-two million, five hundred fifty-six thousand dollars → $ 22,556,000
2. Identify leftmost digit of each number.
   $194,000,000 $22,556,000
3. Round.
   $200,000,000 $20,000,000

$S_{rounded} = \$200{,}000{,}000$ $P_{rounded} = \$20{,}000{,}000$

Note that in the final answer, $200,000,000 and $20,000,000 have only one nonzero digit.

Remember that you cannot round numbers expressed in verbal form. You must convert these numbers to numeric form.

Now you should see the importance of the information in the third column of the Blueprint Aid. When you complete your Blueprint Aids for word problems, do not be concerned if the order of the information in your boxes does not follow the order given in the text boxes. Often you can dissect a word problem in more than one way.

LU 1–1 PRACTICE QUIZ

At the end of each Learning Unit, you can check your progress with a Practice Quiz. If you had difficulty understanding the Unit, the Practice Quiz will help identify your area of weakness. Work the problems on scrap paper. Check your answers with the worked-out solutions that follow the quiz. Ask your instructor about specific assignments and the materials available on the OLC for each chapter Practice Quiz. A complete set of drill and word problems follows each chapter.

1. Write in verbal form:
   a. 7,948 **b.** 48,775 **c.** 814,410,335,414
2. Write in numeric form each of the following verbal expressions:
   a. Four and a half million **b.** Two and a quarter million
   c. Three hundred fifty-five million **d.** Seven hundred million
   e. Eleven billion **f.** One hundred fifty-two thousand three hundred forty-three
3. Round the following numbers as indicated:

Nearest ten	Nearest hundred	Nearest thousand	Rounded all the way
a. 92	**b.** 745	**c.** 8,341	**d.** 4,752

4. Kellogg's reported its sales as five million, one hundred eighty-one thousand dollars. The company earned a profit of five hundred two thousand dollars. What would the sales and profit be if each number were rounded all the way? (*Hint:* You might want to draw the Blueprint Aid since we show it in the solution.)

LEARNING UNIT 1–2
ADDING AND SUBTRACTING WHOLE NUMBERS

> **CANADA YEAR BOOK 2001**
>
> **EMPLOYMENT AND UNEMPLOYMENT**
>
> In 1999, the Canadian labour force comprised more than 15.7 million individuals from a population of nearly 24 million aged 15 and older. Roughly 14.5 million were employed while almost 1.2 million were classified as unemployed—either looking for work, on temporary layoff or about to start a job.
>
> Following years of rising unemployment in the early 1990s, the number of jobs grew steadily near the end of the decade. This period of growth was capped by a strong performance in 1999, as the number of people with jobs grew by 427,000 or 3.0% over the previous year.

Source: Statistics Canada 2002.

Everybody is interested in what the current employment situation is, what the movements in labour market are, and what the trends in previous years were. The clipping from *Canada Year Book 2001* shows that out of 15,700,000 individuals who were considered to be part of the labour force in 1999, 14,500,000 were employed and 1,200,000 were not.

Difference between labour force and employed individuals:

Labour force	15,700,000
Employed	− 14,500,000
	1,200,000

In 1999 the number of people with jobs grew by 427,000:

Old number of employed	
	+ 427,000

This Unit teaches you how to manually add and subtract whole numbers. When you least expect it, you will catch yourself automatically using this skill.

ADDITION OF WHOLE NUMBERS

To add whole numbers, you unite two or more numbers called **addends** to make one number called a **sum,** *total,* or *amount.* The numbers are arranged in a column according to their place values—units above units, tens above tens, and so on. Then, you add the columns of numbers from top to bottom. To check the result, you re-add the columns from bottom to top.

ADDING WHOLE NUMBERS

Step 1. Align the numbers to be added in columns according to their place values, beginning with the units place at the right and moving to the left (Figure 1.1).

Step 2. Add the units column. Write the sum below the column. If the sum is more than 9, write the units digit and carry the tens digit.

Step 3. Moving to the left, repeat Step 2 until all place values are added.

EXAMPLE

Adding top to bottom ↓		Checking bottom to top ↑
	2 1 1	
	1,362	
	5,913	
	8,924	
	+ 6,594	
	22,793	

Alternate check
Add each column as a separate total and then combine. The end result is the same.

1,362
5,913
8,924
+ 6,594
13
18
26
20
22,793

HOUSEHOLD SPENDING, SUMMARY-LEVEL CATEGORIES IN CANADA, 2000, AVERAGE EXPENDITURE (DOLLARS)

Household expenditure summary-level categories	2000	Rounded all the way
Total expenditure	55,834	52,900*
Total current consumption	39,385	
Food	6,217	6,000†
Shelter	10,498	10,000
Household operation	2,516	3,000
Household furnishings and equipment	1,557	2,000
Clothing	2,351	2,000
Transportation	7,576	8,000
Health care	1,357	1,000
Personal care	740	700
Recreation	3,165	3,000
Reading materials and other printed matter	275	300
Education	826	800
Tobacco products and alcoholic beverages	1,218	1,000
Games of chance (net)	261	300
Miscellaneous expenditures	827	800
Personal taxes	12,012	10,000
Personal insurance payments and pension contributions	3,135	3,000
Gifts of money and contributions	1,302	1,000
Total		52,900

**Note:* The final answer has more than one nonzero number, since the total is not rounded all the way.

†Rounding all the way means each number has only one nonzero digit.

Source: "Household Spending, Summary-Level Categories in Canada in 2000. Average Expenditure ($'s)." Adapted from the Statistics Canada CANSIM database (cansim2.statcan.ca), Table 203-0001.

How to Quickly Estimate Addition by Rounding All the Way

In Learning Unit 1–1, you learned that rounding whole numbers all the way gives quick arithmetic estimates. Using the Statistics Canada clipping "Household spending, summary-level categories in Canada, 2000," note that each number is rounded all the way, but that the total is not. Remember that rounding all the way is no substitute for the actual computations; but it is helpful in making fast, commonsense estimates and decisions.

You may use rounding skills for estimating your answers for word problems. It is essential that at the end of your calculations you be able to find out whether the answer is reasonable.

For example, your accommodation costs this month were: $475 rent, $123 utilities, $52 telephone bill, and $47 Rogers cable. What are your total expenses for this month?

To find the exact answer, you will add all four values:

$$475 + 123 + 52 + 47 = 697$$

To find an approximate answer (estimate), use rounding skills:

$$480 + 120 + 50 + 50 \approx 700$$

$697 \approx 700$, so this means your answer was reasonable.

Approximating your answer is very important, as it is very easy to press the wrong key on your calculator and get a seriously wrong answer. You can also use this method to get a quick idea of the result.

Horizontal and Vertical Addition

Frequently, companies must use both horizontal and vertical additions. For example, manufacturers often need weekly production figures of individual products and a weekly total of all products. Today, many companies use computer spreadsheets to determine various manufacturing figures. The following example shows you how to do horizontal and vertical addition manually.

EXAMPLE

PRODUCTION REPORT: UNITS PRODUCED

	Monday		Tuesday		Wednesday		Thursday		Friday		Total
Sneakers	400	+	300	+	170	+	70	+	450	=	1,390
Boots	650	+	180	+	190	+	210	+	220	=	1,450
Loafers	210	+	55	+	98	+	112	+	310	=	785
Totals	1,260	+	535	+	458	+	392	+	980	=	3,625

Besides production reports, payroll records often require horizontal and vertical addition.

The totals of the vertical and horizontal columns check to the grand total of 3,625.

Commutative and Associative Laws of Addition

- ☐ Switching the order of numbers being added does not affect the final result.
  $a + b = b + a$
- ☐ Regrouping the numbers does not affect the final result.
  $(a + b) + c = a + (b + c)$

For example,

a. $3 + 7 = 7 + 3$

b. $(2 + 5) + 7 = 2 + (5 + 7)$
$7 + 7 = 2 + 12$
$14 = 14$

c. Referring to the problem with accommodation costs the order of costs being added does not change the total amount of dollars, which you must pay at the end of the month:

$$475 + 123 + 52 + 47 = (123 + 475) + (47 + 52) = (123 + 47) + (475 + 52) = \$697$$

Subtraction of Whole Numbers

Subtraction is the opposite of addition. Addition unites numbers; subtraction takes one number away from another number. In subtraction, the top (largest) number is the **minuend.** The number you subtract from the minuend is the **subtrahend,** which gives you the **difference** between the minuend and the subtrahend.

SUBTRACTING WHOLE NUMBERS

Step 1. Align the minuend and subtrahend according to their place values.

Step 2. Begin the subtraction with the units digits. Write the difference below the column. If the units digit in the minuend is smaller than the units digit in the subtrahend, borrow 1 from the tens digit in the minuend. One tens digit is 10 units.

Step 3. Moving to the left, repeat Step 2 until all place values in the subtrahend are subtracted.

Example

The following item from Statistics Canada illustrates subtraction of whole numbers:

PRODUCTION OF NEW MOTOR VEHICLES BY MOTOR VEHICLE MANUFACTURERS ASSOCIATION OF CANADA, MONTHLY (UNITS)

Vehicle type	2002		
	January	February	March
Total, motor vehicles	177,603	208,987	209,184

Source: Statistics Canada.

In March, total motor vehicles production was 197 units (cars) more than in February. You can use subtraction to arrive at the 197 difference:

	10 17 8 0 7 14				
~~Cars~~	20~~9~~,~~184~~	← Minuend (the larger number)	**Check** ~~Cars~~	208,987
	− 208,987	← Subtrahend		+ 197
~~Cars~~	197	← Difference	~~Cars~~	209,184

Note how "borrowing" occurs in the example above. Starting at the rightmost column of the minuend and subtrahend, you can see that you cannot subtract 7 in the subtrahend from 4 in the minuend. You must borrow from the 8 to the left in the minuend. The 8 becomes 7, and you must borrow again from 1 to the left so you can subtract 8 in the subtrahend from 17 to get 9 in the difference. This means that 1 in the minuend becomes 0, and you must borrow from the 9 to the left to get 10 so you can subtract the 9 to the left in the subtrahend from 10 in the minuend. This gives 1 in the difference—197 cars is the difference between the subtrahend 208,987 cars and the minuend 209,184 cars, as proved in the check at the right. Checking subtraction requires adding the difference (197 cars) to the subtrahend (208,987 cars) to arrive at the minuend (209,184 cars). The Motor Vehicle Manufacturers Association of Canada produced 197 cars more in March 2002 than in February 2002.

How to Dissect and Solve a Word Problem

Accurate subtraction is important in many business operations. In Chapter 8 we discuss the importance of keeping accurate subtraction in your chequebook balance. Now let's check your progress by dissecting and solving a word problem.

THE WORD PROBLEM Hershey's produced 25 million Kisses in one day. The same day, the company shipped 4 million to Japan, 3 million to France, and 6 million throughout the North America. At the end of that day, what is the company's total inventory of Kisses? What is the inventory balance if you round the number all the way?

THE FACTS	SOLVING FOR?	STEPS TO TAKE	KEY POINTS
P: Produced: 25 million. *J: Shipped:* Japan, 4 million. *F: France,* 3 million. *A: North America,* 6 million.	Total Kisses left in inventory. Inventory balance rounded all the way. $\text{Balance}_r = ?$	Total Kisses produced − Total Kisses shipped = Total Kisses left in inventory. $\text{Balance} = P - (J + F + A)$	Minuend − Subtrahend = Difference. Rounding all the way means rounding to last digit on the left.

STEPS TO SOLVING PROBLEM

1. Calculate the total Kisses shipped.

$$\begin{array}{r} 4{,}000{,}000 \\ 3{,}000{,}000 \\ +\,6{,}000{,}000 \\ \hline 13{,}000{,}000 \end{array}$$

2. Calculate the total Kisses left in inventory.

$$\begin{array}{r} 25{,}000{,}000 \\ -\,13{,}000{,}000 \\ \hline 12{,}000{,}000 \end{array}$$

3. Rounding all the way.

   $\text{Balance}_r = 10{,}000{,}000$

Identified digit is 1. Digit to right of 1 is 2, which is less than 5. *Answer:* 10,000,000.

LU 1–2 PRACTICE QUIZ

1. Add by totalling each separate column:

$$\begin{array}{r} 8{,}974 \\ 6{,}439 \\ +\,6{,}941 \\ \hline \end{array}$$

2. Estimate by rounding all the way (do not round the total of estimate) and then do the actual computation:

$$\begin{array}{r} 4{,}241 \\ 8{,}794 \\ +\,3{,}872 \\ \hline \end{array}$$

3. Subtract and check your answer:

$$\begin{array}{r} 9{,}876 \\ -4{,}967 \\ \hline \end{array}$$

4. Jackson Manufacturing Company projected its year 2003 furniture sales at $900,000. During 2003, Jackson earned $510,000 in sales from major clients and $369,100 in sales from the remainder of its clients. What is the amount by which Jackson over- or underestimated its sales? Use the Blueprint Aid, since the answer will show the completed Blueprint Aid.

LEARNING UNIT 1–3
MULTIPLYING AND DIVIDING WHOLE NUMBERS

A. Ramey/PhotoEdit

Let's assume that the annual cost of living in London is $122,168 and in Singapore $119,040. The difference between living in London and living in Singapore is $3,128 ($122,168 − $119,040). If you lived in London for 3 years, it would cost you $9,384 more to live in London. You can get this number by multiplying $3,128 times 3. If you take the $9,384 and divide it by 3, you will get $3,128.

This Unit will sharpen your skills in two important arithmetic operations—multiplication and division. These two operations frequently result in knowledgeable business decisions.

Multiplication of Whole Numbers—Shortcut to Addition

From calculating your 3-year living expenses in London, you know that multiplication is a *shortcut to addition:*

$3,128 × 3 = $9,384 or $3,128 + $3,128 + $3,128 = $9,384

Before learning the steps used to multiply whole numbers with two or more digits, you must learn some multiplication terminology.

Note in the following example that the top number (number we want to multiply) is the **multiplicand.** The bottom number (number doing the multiplying) is the **multiplier.** The final number (answer) is the **product.** The numbers between the multiplier and the product are **partial products.** Also note how we positioned the partial product 20,900. This number is the result of multiplying 418 by 50 (the 5 is in the tens position). On each line in the partial products, we placed the first digit directly below the digit we used in the multiplication process.

Example

	418	← Top number (multiplicand)		
	× 52	← Bottom number (multiplier)		
Partial products	836		2 × 418 =	836
	20,900		50 × 418 =	+ 20,900
	21,736	← Product answer →		21,736

We can now give the following steps for multiplying whole numbers with two or more digits:

MULTIPLYING WHOLE NUMBERS WITH TWO OR MORE DIGITS

Step 1. Align the multiplicand (top number) and multiplier (bottom number) at the right. Usually, you should make the smaller number the multiplier.

Step 2. Begin by multiplying the right digit of the multiplier with the right digit of the multiplicand. Keep multiplying as you move left through the multiplicand. Your first partial product aligns at the right with the multiplicand and multiplier.

Step 3. Move left through the multiplier and continue multiplying the multiplicand. Your partial product right digit or first digit is placed directly below the digit in the multiplier that you used to multiply.

Step 4. Continue Steps 2 and 3 until you have completed your multiplication process. Then add the partial products to get the final product.

Checking and Estimating Multiplication

We can check the multiplication process by reversing the multiplicand and multiplier and then multiplying. Let's first estimate 52 × 418 by rounding all the way.

EXAMPLE

Estimate		Actual
50	←	52
× 400	←	× 418
20,000		416
		52
		20 8
		21,736

By estimating before actually working the problem, we know our answer should be about 20,000. When we multiply 52 by 418, we get the same answer as when we multiply 418 × 52—and the answer is about 20,000. Remember, if we had not rounded all the way, our estimate would have been closer. If we had used a calculator, the rounded estimate would have helped us check the calculator's answer. Our commonsense estimate tells us our answer is near 20,000—not 200,000.

Before you study the division of whole numbers, you should know (1) the multiplication shortcut with numbers ending in zeros and (2) how to multiply a whole number by a power of 10.

MULTIPLICATION SHORTCUT WITH NUMBERS ENDING IN ZEROS

Step 1. When zeros are at the end of the multiplicand or the multiplier, or both, disregard the zeros and multiply.

Step 2. Count the number of zeros in the multiplicand and multiplier.

Step 3. Attach the number of zeros counted in Step 2 to your answer.

EXAMPLE

65,000	65	3 zeros	No need to multiply rows of zeros.
× 420	× 42	+ 1 zero	65,000
	1 30	4 zeros	× 420
	26 0		00 000
	27,300,000		1 300 00
			26 000 0
			27,300,000

MULTIPLYING A WHOLE NUMBER BY A POWER OF 10

Step 1. Count the number of zeros in the power of 10 (a whole number that begins with 1 and ends in one or more zeros such as 10, 100, 1,000, and so on).

Step 2. Attach that number of zeros to the right side of the other whole number to obtain the answer. Insert comma(s) as needed every three digits, moving from right to left.

EXAMPLE

$99 \times 10 = 99\underline{0} = \boxed{990}$ ← Add 1 zero

$99 \times 100 = 9{,}9\underline{00} = \boxed{9{,}900}$ ← Add 2 zeros

$99 \times 1{,}000 = 99{,}\underline{000} = \boxed{99{,}000}$ ← Add 3 zeros

When a zero is in the centre of the multiplier, you can do the following:

EXAMPLE

658	$3 \times 658 =$	1,974
$\times$ 403	$400 \times 658 =$	+263,200
1 974		**265,174**
263 2□		
265,174		

Commutative, Associative, and Distributive Laws of Multiplication

- □ Switching the order of any numbers being multiplied does not affect the final result.
  $a \times b = b \times a$
- □ Regrouping the numbers does not affect the final result.
  $(a \times b) \times c = a \times (b \times c)$
- □ To multiply a number (factor) by a group of numbers that are being added or subtracted, it is necessary to multiply that number (factor) by each number in the group.
  $a(b + c) = ab + ac$

For example,

a. $3 \times 7 = 7 \times 3$

b. $(2 \times 5) \times 7 = 2 \times (5 \times 7)$
$10 \times 7 = 2 + 35$
$70 = 70$

c. $3(7 - 4) = 3 \times 7 - 3 \times 4 = 21 - 12 = 9$
$5(8 + 4) = 5 \times 8 + 5 \times 4 = 40 + 20 = 60$

DIVISION OF WHOLE NUMBERS

Division is the reverse of multiplication and a timesaving shortcut related to subtraction. For example, in the introduction to this Learning Unit, you determined that it would cost \$9,384 more to live 3 years in London compared to living 3 years in Singapore. If you subtract \$3,128 (the difference between living 3 years in London and 3 years in Singapore) three times from \$9,384, you would get zero. You can also multiply \$3,128 times 3 to get \$9,384. Since division is the reverse of multiplication, you can say that \$9,384 ÷ 3 = \$3,128.

Division can be indicated by the common symbols ÷ and $\overline{)\quad}$, or by the bar — in a fraction and the forward slant / between two numbers, which means the first number is divided by the second number. Division asks how many times one number (**divisor**) is contained in another number (**dividend**). The answer, or result, is the **quotient.** When the divisor (number used to divide) doesn't divide evenly into the dividend (number we are dividing), the result is a **partial quotient,** with the leftover amount the **remainder** (expressed as fractions in later chapters). The following example illustrates *even division* (this is also an example of *long division* because the divisor has more than one digit).

EXAMPLE

```
                18    ←— Quotient
Divisor ——→ 15)270    ←— Dividend
               15
               120
               120
```

This example divides 15 into 27 once with 12 remaining. The 0 in the dividend is brought down to 12. Dividing 120 by 15 equals 8 with no remainder; that is, even division. The following example illustrates *uneven division with a remainder* (this is also an example of *short division* because the divisor has only one digit).

EXAMPLE

```
  24 R1   ←— Remainder
7)169
  14
   29         Check
   28           (7     ×    24)    +      1      =    169
    1         Divisor × Quotient + Remainder = Dividend
```

Note how doing the check gives you assurance that your calculation is correct. When the divisor has one digit (short division) as in this example, you can often calculate the division mentally as illustrated in the following examples:

EXAMPLE

```
  108          16 R6
8)864        7)118
```

Next, let's look at the value of estimating division.

Estimating Division

Before actually working a division problem, estimate the quotient by rounding. This estimate helps check the answer. The example that follows is rounded all the way. After you make an estimate, work the problem out and check your answer by multiplication.

EXAMPLE

```
      36 R111       Estimate        Check
138)5,079                 50          138
    4 14          100)5,000         × 36
      939                             828
      828                            4 14
      111                           4,968
                                    + 111   ←— Add remainder
                                    5,079
```

Now let's turn our attention to division shortcuts with zeros.

Division Shortcuts with Zeros

The original artwork for a 1954 "Peanuts" daily comic strip sold for $10,800. If a group of 10 investors paid $10,800 for the comic strip artwork, what did each investor pay?

$$\begin{array}{r} \$1{,}080 \\ 10\overline{)\$10{,}800} \end{array} \leftarrow \text{Amount each investor pays}$$

The steps that follow explain the shortcut used in the above division.

DIVISION SHORTCUT WITH NUMBERS ENDING IN ZEROS

Step 1. When the dividend and divisor have ending zeros, count the number of ending zeros in the divisor.

Step 2. Drop the same number of zeros in the dividend as in the divisor, counting from right to left.

Note the following examples of division shortcut with numbers ending in zeros. Since two of the symbols used for division are ÷ and $\overline{)\quad}$, our first examples show the zero shortcut method with the ÷ symbol.

EXAMPLE

One ending zero

Dividend		**Divisor**				
95,000	÷	10	→ 95,00~~0~~	=	9,500	Drop 1 zero in dividend
95,000	÷	100	→ 95,0~~00~~	=	950	Drop 2 zeros
95,000	÷	1,000	→ 95,~~000~~	=	95	Drop 3 zeros

In a long division problem with the $\overline{)\quad}$ symbol, you again count the number of ending zeros in the divisor. Then drop the same number of ending zeros in the dividend and divide as usual.

EXAMPLE

$6{,}5\underline{00}\overline{)88{,}0\underline{00}}$ ← Drop 2 zeros → $65\overline{)880}$

$$\begin{array}{r} 13 \text{ R}35 \\ 65\overline{)880} \\ \underline{65} \\ 230 \\ \underline{195} \\ 35 \end{array}$$

You are now ready to practise what you learned by dissecting and solving a word problem.

How to Dissect and Solve a Word Problem

The Blueprint Aid that follows will be your guide to dissecting and solving the following word problem.

THE WORD PROBLEM Dunkin' Donuts sells to four different companies a total of $3,500 worth of doughnuts per week. What is the total annual sales to these companies? What is the yearly sales per company? (Assume each company buys the same amount.) Check your answer to show how multiplication and division are related.

THE FACTS	SOLVING FOR?	STEPS TO TAKE	KEY POINTS
S_w: *Sales per week:* \$3,500. *n: Companies:* 4. *m: Number of weeks per year:* 52.	Total annual sales to all four companies. Yearly sales per company. $S = ?$	Sales per week × Weeks in year (52) = Total annual sales. Total annual sales ÷ Total companies = Yearly sales per company. $S = S_w \times m \div n$	Division is the reverse of multiplication.

STEPS TO SOLVING PROBLEM

1. Calculate total annual sales, $S_w \times m$ — \$3,500 × 52 weeks = **\$182,000**
2. Calculate yearly sales per company, $S_w \times m \div n$ — \$182,000 ÷ 4 = **\$45,500**

   $S = \$45,500$

Check
\$45,500 × 4 = \$182,000

It's time to try the Practice Quiz.

LU 1–3 PRACTICE QUIZ

1. Estimate the actual problem by rounding all the way, work the actual problem, and check:

Actual	Estimate	Check
3,894 × 18		

2. Multiply:

   77,000
   × 1,800

3. Multiply by shortcut method:

   95 × 10,000

4. Divide by rounding all the way, complete the actual calculation, and check, showing remainder as a whole number.

   26)5,325

5. Divide by shortcut method:

   4,000)96,000

6. Assume General Motors produces 960 Chevrolets each workday (Monday through Friday). If the cost to produce each car is \$6,500, what is General Motors' total cost for the year? Check your answer.

LEARNING UNIT 1–4
ORDER OF OPERATIONS

When making several payments at the bank, buying tickets for the whole family, paying debts, making partial payments, preparing business plans, or calculating monthly budgets, people must perform different mathematical operations: adding, multiplying, dividing, subtracting. Knowledge of properties of these operations is useful and simplifies long strings of calculations.

Whenever a chain of operations must be performed it should be done in a certain order; otherwise, the result will most probably be wrong.

Acronyms useful for remembering this order are **BEDMAS** and **PEMDAS**. They mean basically the same thing:

B Brackets			**P** Parentheses
E Exponents			**E** Exponents
D Division **M** Multiplication	}	from left to right	{ **M** Multiplication **D** Division
A Addition **S** Subtraction	}	from left to right	{ **A** Addition **S** Subtraction

To memorize the second acronym, you may use the phrase: "**P**lease **E**xcuse **M**y **D**ear **A**unt **S**ally."

EXAMPLE

$55 \times (5 - 4) \div 11$

If you perform all the operations from the left to right without applying any rules of PEMDAS/BEDMAS you will get 271/11, which is the wrong answer. If you perform the operations in the right order the correct answer will be 5.

Most modern calculators are programmed according to PEMDAS/BEDMAS rules and will do operations in the correct order even if you enter them blindly from left to right. However, to make sure you give your calculator the right commands, you must not forget to insert brackets. For the expression above, press the following keys:

55, multiplication key, left bracket key, 5, subtraction key, 4, right bracket key, division key, 11, and finally equal sign key

55 [×] [( ] 5 [−] 4 [ )] [÷] 11 [=] 5

Such a calculator will first perform operations in brackets, then powers, then all multiplication and division operations in order from left to right, and only then perform all addition and subtraction operations in the same order—from left to right. And you should do the same in your manual calculations.

EXAMPLE

Calculate the following without a calculator:

$50 - 6 \times 5 + (6 - 2)^2 \div 8$

1. Perform operations in brackets:

   $6 - 2 = 4 \rightarrow 50 - 6 \times 5 + 4^2 \div 8$

2. Do powers:

   $4^2 = 16 \rightarrow 50 - 6 \times 5 + 16 \div 8$

3. Perform multiplication and division in order from left to right:

   $6 \times 5 = 30$

   $16 \div 8 = 2 \rightarrow 50 - 30 + 2$

4. And at last perform addition and subtraction in order from left to right:

   $50 - 30 = 20$

   $20 + 2 = 22$

5. The answer is 22.

   Now, perform all these operations with help of your calculator, as a one-step calculation:

   $50 - 6 \times 5 + (6 - 2)^2 \div 8$

   Press calculator keys in the following order:

   50, subtraction key, 6, multiplication key, 5, addition key, left bracket key, 6, subtraction key, 2, right bracket key, power key, 2, division key, 8, equal sign key

   50 [−] 6 [×] 5 [+] [( ] 6 [−] 2 [ )] [y^x] 2 [÷] 8 [=] 22

LU 1–4 PRACTICE QUIZ

1. Perform the operations in the right order and calculate the answer of the following expressions:
   a. $1 + 15 \div 3 - 2^2$
   b. $(9 - 4) \times 3 \div 5 + (25 - 14) \div 3$
   c. $(155 - 75) \div 4 + (225 - 75) \div 50$
   d. $[(12 - 9) + (14 - 11)]^3$

2. Perform the following operations with the help of your calculator as a one-step calculation:
   a. $[(10 - 8)^3 - (6 + 5 - 4)]^{11} + 9$
   b. $663{,}355 - 4{,}762 + 12 \times 367$

CHAPTER ORGANIZER AND REFERENCE GUIDE

Topic	Key point, procedure, formula	Example(s) to illustrate situation
Reading and writing numeric and verbal whole numbers, p. 3	Placement of digits in a number gives the value of the digits (Figure 1.1). Commas separate every three digits, moving from right to left. Begin at left to read and write number in verbal form. Do not read zeros or use *and*. Hyphenate numbers twenty-one to ninety-nine. Reverse procedure to change verbal number to numeric.	462 → Four hundred sixty-two 6,741 → Six thousand, seven hundred forty-one
Rounding whole numbers, p. 4	1. Identify place value of the digit to be rounded. 2. If digit to the right is 5 or more, round up; if less than 5, do not change. 3. Change all digits to the right of rounded identified digit to zeros.	643 to nearest ten 4 in tens place value. / 3 is not 5 or more. Thus, 643 rounds to 640.
Rounding all the way, p. 5	Round to first digit of number. One nonzero digit remains. In estimating, you round each number of the problem to one nonzero digit. The final answer is not rounded.	468,451 → 500,000 The 5 is the only nonzero digit remaining.
Adding whole numbers, p. 8	1. Align numbers at the right. 2. Add units column. If sum more than 9, carry tens digit. 3. Moving left, repeat Step 2 until all place values are added. Add from top to bottom. Check by adding bottom to top or adding each column separately and combining.	$\begin{array}{r} {}^{1}\ \ \\ 65 \\ +47 \\ \hline 112 \end{array}$ $\begin{array}{r} 12 \\ +10 \\ \hline 112 \end{array}$ Checking sum of each digit
Commutative Law, p. 10	$a + b = b + a$	$10 + 15 = 15 + 10$
Associative Law, p. 10	$(a + b) + c = a + (b + c)$	$(25 + 5) + 10 = 25 + (5 + 10)$

(*continues*)

CHAPTER ORGANIZER AND REFERENCE GUIDE (CONTINUED)

Topic	Key point, procedure, formula	Example(s) to illustrate situation
Subtracting whole numbers, p. 10	1. Align minuend and subtrahend at the right. 2. Subtract units digits. If necessary, borrow 1 from tens digit in minuend. 3. Moving left, repeat Step 2 until all place values are subtracted. Minuend less subtrahend equals difference.	5 18 685 −492 193 **Check** 193 +492 685
Multiplying whole numbers, p. 12	1. Align multiplicand and multiplier at the right. 2. Begin at the right and keep multiplying as you move to the left. First partial product aligns at the right with multiplicand and multiplier. 3. Move left through multiplier and continue multiplying multiplicand. Partial product right digit or first digit is placed directly below digit in multiplier. 4. Continue Steps 2 and 3 until multiplication is complete. Add partial products to get final product. **Shortcuts:** (a) When multiplicand or multiplier, or both, end in zeros, disregard zeros and multiply; attach same number of zeros to answer. If zero in centre of multiplier, no need to show row of zeros. (b) If multiplying by power of 10, attach same number of zeros to whole number multiplied.	223 × 32 446 6 69 7,136 a. 48,000 × 40 → 48 × 4 = 1,920,000 ← 4 zeros (3 zeros + 1 zero) 524 × 206 3 144 104 8 107,944 b. 14 × 10 = 140 (attach 1 zero) 14 × 1,000 = 14,000 (attach 3 zeros)
Commutative Law, p. 14	$a \times b = b \times a$	$2 \times 3 = 3 \times 2$
Associative Law, p. 14	$(a \times b) \times c = a \times (b \times c)$	$(4 \times 2) \times 5 = 4 \times (2 \times 5)$
Distributive Law, p. 14	$a \times (b + c) = ab + ac$	$3 \times (a + 4) = 3a + 12$
Dividing whole numbers, p. 14	1. When divisor is divided into the dividend, the remainder is less than divisor. 2. Drop zeros from dividend right to left by number of zeros found in the divisor. Even division has no remainder; uneven division has a remainder; divisor with one digit is short division; and divisor with more than one digit is long division.	1. 14)76 = 5 R6 70 6 2. $5{,}000 \div 100 = 50 \div 1 = 50$ $5{,}000 \div 1{,}000 = 5 \div 1 = 5$
BEDMAS, p. 18	1. Brackets; 2. Exponents (power); 3. Division; 4. Multiplication; 5. Addition; 6. Subtraction	$2 + 3 \times 4 - 5 = 2 + 12 - 5 = 9$ $(2 + 3) \times 4 - 5 = 5 \times 4 - 5 = 15$
PEMDAS, p. 18	1. Parentheses; 2. Exponents (power); 3. Multiplication; 4. Division; 5. Addition; 6. Subtraction	$3^2 \times 4 - 5 \times 2 = 9 \times 4 - 10 = 36 - 10 = 26$ $3^2 \times (4 - 5) \times 2 = 3^2 \times 1 \times 2 = 9 \times 2 = 18$
Calculator use, p. 18	Perform all operations with the help of your calculator as a one-step calculation.	$(6{,}784 + 345^2 \div 10 - 654 \times 18 - 189) \times 2 = 13{,}451$

(continues)

CHAPTER ORGANIZER AND REFERENCE GUIDE (CONCLUDED)

Key terms	Addends, p. 8 BEDMAS, p. 18 Decimal point, p. 3 Decimal system, p. 3 Difference, p. 10 Dividend, p. 14 Divisor, p. 14 Minuend, p. 10	Multiplicand, p. 12 Multiplier, p. 12 Partial products, p. 12 Partial quotient, p. 15 PEMDAS, p. 18 Product, p. 12 Quotient, p. 14 Remainder, p. 15	Rounding all the way, p. 5 Subtrahend, p. 10 Sum, p. 8 Whole number, p. 3

CRITICAL THINKING DISCUSSION QUESTIONS

1. List the four steps of the decision-making process. Do you think all companies should be required to follow these steps? Give an example.
2. Explain the three steps used to round whole numbers. Pick a whole number and explain why it should not be rounded.
3. How do you check subtraction? If you were to attend a movie, explain how you might use the subtraction check method.
4. Explain how you can check multiplication. If you visit a local supermarket, how could you show multiplication as a shortcut to addition?
5. Explain how division is the reverse of multiplication. Using the supermarket example, explain how division is a timesaving shortcut related to subtraction.

END-OF-CHAPTER PROBLEMS

DRILL PROBLEMS

Add the following:

1–1. $79 + 33$

1–2. $820 + 491$

1–3. $99 + 99$

1–4. $66 + 92$

1–5. $6{,}251 + 7{,}329$

1–6. $59{,}481 + 51{,}411 + 70{,}821$

1–7. $78{,}159 + 15{,}850 + 19{,}681$

Subtract the following:

1–8. $87 - 19$

1–9. $80 - 42$

1–10. $287 - 199$

1–11. $8{,}900 - 7{,}200$

1–12. $9{,}800 - 8{,}900$

1–13. $1{,}622 - 548$

Multiply the following:

1–14. 55×8

1–15. 510×61

1–16. 900×300

1–17. 677×503

1–18. 309×850

1–19. 450×280

Divide the following by short division:

1–20. $4\overline{)324}$ **1–21.** $9\overline{)810}$ **1–22.** $4\overline{)164}$

Divide the following by long division. Show work and remainder.

1–23. $6\overline{)520}$ **1–24.** $62\overline{)8{,}915}$

Add the following without rearranging:

1–25. 78 + 109 **1–26.** 1,055 + 88 **1–27.** 666 + 950 **1–28.** 1,011 + 17

1–29. Add the following and check by totalling each column individually without carrying numbers:

Check

  8,539
  6,842
+ 9,495

Estimate the following by rounding all the way and then do actual addition:

1–30. **Actual** **Estimate**

  7,700
  9,286
+ 3,900

1–31. **Actual** **Estimate**

  6,980
  3,190
+ 7,819

Subtract the following without rearranging:

1–32. 190 − 66 **1–33.** 950 − 870

1–34. Subtract the following and check answer:

  591,001
− 375,956

Multiply the following horizontally:

1–35. 13 × 8 **1–36.** 84 × 8 **1–37.** 27 × 8 **1–38.** 17 × 6

Divide the following and check by multiplication:

1–39. $45\overline{)876}$ **Check**

1–40. $46\overline{)1{,}950}$ **Check**

1–41. Add the following columns horizontally and vertically:

PRODUCTION REPORT

	Monday	Tuesday	Wednesday	Thursday	Friday
Software packages	450	92	157	24	40
Laptops	490	75	44	77	30
Video	325	82	22	44	18
Computer monitors	66	24	51	66	50

Using data in Problem 1–41, answer the following:

1–42. What was the total difference in production on Monday versus Friday?

1–43. If two weeks ago production was 7 times the total of this report, what was total production?

Complete the following:

1–44.

  9,200
− 1,510
−   700

1–45.

  3,000,000
−   769,459
−   68,541

1–46. Estimate the following problem by rounding all the way and then do the actual multiplication:

Actual	**Estimate**
870	
× 81	

Divide the following by the shortcut method:

1–47. $1{,}000\overline{)850{,}000}$ **1–48.** $100\overline{)70{,}000}$

1–49. Estimate the actual problem by rounding all the way and do the actual division:

Actual	**Estimate**
$695\overline{)8{,}950}$	

ADDITIONAL DRILL PROBLEMS

1–50. Express the following numbers in verbal form:

a. 7,954
b. 160,501
c. 2,098,767
d. 58,003
e. 50,025,212,015

1–51. Write in numeric form:

a. Eighty thousand, one hundred eighty-one _____
b. Fifty-eight thousand, three _____
c. Two hundred eighty thousand, five _____
d. Three million, ten _____
e. Sixty-seven thousand, seven hundred sixty _____

1–52. Round the following numbers:

a. To the nearest ten:

42 _______ 379 _______ 855 _______ 5,981 _______ 206 _______

b. To the nearest hundred:

9,664 _______ 2,074 _______ 888 _______ 271 _______ 75 _______

c. To the nearest thousand:

21,486 _______ 621 _______ 3,504 _______ 9,735 _______

1–53. Round off each number to the nearest ten, nearest hundred, and nearest thousand; then round all the way. (Remember that you are rounding the original number each time.)

	Nearest ten	**Nearest hundred**	**Nearest thousand**	**Round all the way**
a. 4,752				
b. 70,351				
c. 9,386				
d. 4,983				
e. 408,119				
f. 30,051				

1–54. Name the place position (place value) of the underlined digit.

a. $8{,}\underline{3}48$

b. $\underline{9}{,}734$

c. $3\underline{4}7{,}107$

d. $7\underline{2}3$

e. $2\underline{8}{,}200{,}000{,}121$

f. $7\underline{0}6{,}359{,}005$

g. $27{,}\underline{5}63{,}530$

1–55. Add by totalling each separate column:

a.	**b.**	**c.**	**d.**	**e.**	**f.**	**g.**	**h.**
599	43	493	36	716	535	751	75,730
142	58	826	76	458	107	378	48,531
	96		43	397	778	135	15,797
			24	139	215	747	
				478	391	368	

1–56. Estimate by rounding all the way, then add the actual numbers:

a.	**b.**	**c.**	**d.**	**e.**	**f.**
580	1,470	475	442	2,571	10,928
971	7,631	837	609	3,625	9,321
548	4,383	213	766	4,091	12,654
430		775	410	928	15,492
506		432	128		

1–57. Estimate by rounding all the way, then subtract the actual numbers:

a.	**b.**	**c.**	**d.**	**e.**	**f.**
81	91	68	981	622	1,125
− 42	− 33	− 59	− 283	− 328	− 913

1–58. Subtract and check:

a.	**b.**	**c.**	**d.**	**e.**	**f.**
4,947	3,724	474,820	50,000	65,003	15,715
− 4,362	− 2,138	− 85,847	− 21,762	− 24,987	− 3,503

1–59. In the following sales report, total the rows and the columns, then check that the grand total is the same both horizontally and vertically.

Salesperson	**Region 1**	**Region 2**	**Region 3**	**Total**
a. Becker	$5,692	$7,403	$3,591	
b. Edwards	7,652	7,590	3,021	
c. Graff	6,545	6,738	4,545	
d. Jackson	6,937	6,950	4,913	
Total				

1–60. In the following problems, first estimate by rounding all the way, then work the actual problems and check:

	Actual	**Estimate**	**Check**
a.	151 × 14		
b.	4,216 × 45		

c. 52,376
× 309

d. 3,106
× 28

1–61. Multiply (use the shortcut when applicable):

a. 4,072 × 100

b. 5,100 × 40

c. 76,000 × 1,200

d. 93 × 100,000

1–62. Divide by rounding all the way; then do the actual calculation and check showing the remainder as a whole number.

Actual	Estimate	Check
a. $8\overline{)7{,}709}$		
b. $26\overline{)5{,}910}$		
c. $151\overline{)3{,}783}$		
d. $46\overline{)19{,}550}$		

1–63. Divide by the shortcut method:

a. $200\overline{)5{,}400}$ b. $50\overline{)5{,}650}$ c. $1{,}200\overline{)43{,}200}$ d. $17{,}000\overline{)510{,}000}$

WORD PROBLEMS

1–64. Statistics Canada reports that production of selected types of cars in the first quarter of 2002 was as follows:

Vehicle type	January 2002	February 2002	March 2002
Chrysler, total cars	11,323	20,044	21,295
General Motors, total cars	33,073	48,287	46,139

a. What is the total amount of cars produced by Chrysler?

b. Compare production of Chrysler and General Motors. Which company produced more cars in the first quarter of 2002 and by how much?

1–65. In August 2002 a real estate agent prepared for his client information about prices for semidetached houses in a certain area of Toronto. The lowest price was two hundred sixty-five thousand, eight hundred dollars. The highest price was three hundred eighteen thousand dollars. In numerical form, what was the price range for semidetached houses in the selected area?

1–66. Three years ago, Eva Dempster bought four condominiums as investment properties at $120,000, $125,000, $140,000, and $150,000. This year she sold her condos at present market prices for $143,800, $157,000, $168,900, and $182,500 respectively.

a. What total revenue did Eva get from sale of these properties?

b. What was her total profit?

1–67. A Toronto local newspaper advertises a seasonal mattress sale. A twin-size set with a regular price of $299 is on sale for $145 and a queen-size Simmons set with a regular price of $1,255 is on sale for $529. How much will a family with three children save if they are going to buy three twin sets and one queen set during the sale?

1–68. Banking.com plans a company picnic. A pizza (provided by Pizza Hut) will serve 6 people. If the company expects 960 people to attend, how many pizzas will they need? Each pizza costs $10. What is the total cost of the pizzas?

1–69. NTB Tires bought 910 tires from its manufacturer for $36 per tire. What is the total cost of NTB's purchase? If the store can sell all the tires at $65 each, what will be the store's gross profit, or the difference between its sales and costs (Sales − Costs = Gross profit)?

1–70. Media Metrix (an Internet measurement firm) compared the visits to the top five retail Web sites for

U.S. Thanksgiving week ending November 26, 2000 as follows:

Rank/site	Average daily unique visitors
1. Amazon.com	1,527,000
2. Mypoints.com	1,356,000
3. Americangreetings.com	745,000
4. Bizrate.com	503,000
5. Half.com	397,000

What was the average number of visits for the top five?

1–71. Jose Gomez bought 4,500 shares of Microsoft stock. He held the stock for 6 months. Then Jose sold 180 shares on Monday, 270 shares on Tuesday and again on Thursday, and 800 shares on Friday. How many shares does Jose still own? The average share of the stock Jose owns is worth $52 per share. What is the total value of Jose's stock?

1–72. On May 2, 2001, Associated Press Online stated that New York is going after the bank account of pardoned financier Marc Rich. The tax commissioner announced he was going after Marc Rich in the amount of twenty-six million, nine hundred thousand dollars in back taxes; thirteen million, five hundred thousand in penalties; and ninety-seven million, four hundred thousand in interest. In numerical terms, what is the total amount?

1–73. At Blue Bay Community College, Alison Wells received the following grades in her online accounting class: 90, 65, 85, 80, 75, and 90. Alison's instructor, Professor Clark, said he would drop the lowest grade. What is Alison's average?

1–74. Lee Wills, professor of business, has 18 students in Accounting I, 26 in Accounting II, 22 in Introduction to Computers, 23 in Business Law, and 29 in Introduction to Business. What is the total number of students in Professor Wills' classes? If 12 students withdraw, how many total students will Professor Wills have?

1–75. Ben Hill bought a new truck. On Ben's first trip, he drove 2,200 kilometres and used 550 litres of gas. How many kilometres per litre did Ben travel on his new truck? How much gas does his truck consume per 100 kilometres? On Ben's second trip he drove 800 kilometres and used 216 litres. What is the difference in litres per 100 kilometres between Ben's first and his second trip?

1–76. Staples reduced its $390 Palm Pilot by $45. What is the new selling price of the Palm Pilot? If Staples sold 1,200 Palm Pilots at the new price, what were the store's Palm Pilot's dollar sales?

1–77. Chapters.indigo.ca has 289 business math texts in inventory. During one month, the online bookstore ordered and received 1,855 texts; it also sold 1,222 on the Web. What is the bookstore's inventory at the end of the month? If each text costs $59, what is the end-of-month inventory cost?

1–78. Para Paint Company produced 2,115,000 cans of paint in August. Para sold 2,011,000 of these cans. If each can cost $18, what were Para's ending inventory of paint cans and its total ending inventory cost?

1–79. Trinity College has 30 faculty members in the business department, 22 in psychology, 14 in English, and 169 in all other departments. What is the total number of faculty at Trinity College? If each faculty member advises 30 students, how many students attend Trinity College?

1–80. Hometown Buffet had 90 customers on Sunday, 70 on Monday, 65 on Tuesday, and a total of 310 on Wednesday to Saturday. How many customers did Hometown Buffet serve during the week? If each customer spends $9, what were the total sales for the week?

If Hometown's Buffet had the same sales each week, what were the sales for the year?

1–81. Longview Agency projected its year 2004 sales at $995,000. During 2004, the agency earned $525,960 sales from its major clients and $286,950 sales from the remainder of its clients. How much did the agency overestimate its sales?

1–82. Mark Morrison works at Canadian Tire. His gross earnings were $60,000 last year before tax deductions. From Mark's total earnings, his company subtracted $15,547 for federal income taxes, $1,673 for the government pension plan, and $858 for Employment Insurance. What was Mark's actual, or net, pay for the year?

1–83. The Bay received the following invoice amounts from suppliers. How much does the company owe?

	Per item
22 paintings	$210
39 rockers	75
40 desk lamps	65
120 coffee tables	155

1–84. Jole Company produces beach balls and it operates three shifts. It produces 5,000 balls per shift on shifts 1 and 2. On shift 3, the company can produce 6 times as many balls as on shift 1. Assume a 5-day workweek. How many beach balls does Jole produce per week and per year?

1–85. The results for the last math test were as follows:

Number of students	Mark (out of 100)
5	50
7	65
8	70
3	75
5	85
4	90
2	95

What was the class average for the test? Use a calculator.

1–86. Moe Brink has a $900 balance in his chequebook. During the week, Moe wrote the following cheques: rent, $350; telephone, $44; food, $160; and entertaining, $60. Moe also made a $1,200 deposit. What is Moe's new chequebook balance?

1–87. MVP, an athletic sports shop, bought and sold the following merchandise:

	Cost	Selling price
Tennis rackets	$2,900	$ 3,999
Tennis balls	70	210
Bowling balls	1,050	2,950
Sneakers	+ 8,105	+ 14,888

What was the total cost of merchandise bought by MVP? If the shop sold all its merchandise, what were the sales and the resulting gross profit (Sales − Costs = Gross profit)?

1–88. Excel John Purcell, the bookkeeper for Midland Real Estate, and his manager are concerned about the company's telephone bills. Last year the company's average monthly phone bill was $134. John's manager asked him for an average of this year's phone bills. John's records show the following:

January	$134	July	$128
February	160	August	123
March	120	September	129
April	125	October	125
May	130	November	122
June	159	December	141

What is the average of this year's phone bills? Did John and his manager have a justifiable concern?

1–89. On May 24, 2001, Associated Press reported that bankruptcy filings were up for the first three months of the year. Filings reached 366,841 in the January–March period, the highest ever for a first quarter, up from 312,335 a year earlier. How much was the increase in quarterly filings?

1–90. Excel On Monday, Wang Hardware sold 15 paintbrushes at $3 each, 6 wrenches at $5 each, 7 bags of grass seed at $3 each, 4 lawnmowers at $119 each, and 28 cans of paint at $8 each. What were Wang's total dollar sales on Monday?

1–91. While redecorating, Paul Smith went to Home Depot and bought 125 square metres of commercial carpet. The total cost of the carpet was $3,000. How much did Paul pay per square metre?

1–92. Washington Construction built 12 ranch houses for $115,000 each. From the sale of these houses, Washington received $1,980,000. How much gross profit (Sales − Costs = Gross profit) did Washington make on the houses?

The four partners of Washington Construction split all profits equally. How much will each partner receive?

ADDITIONAL WORD PROBLEMS

1–93. Ken Lawler was shopping for a laptop computer. He went to three different Web sites and found the computer he wanted at three different prices. At Web site A the price was $2,115, at Web site B the price was $1,990, and at Web site C the price was $2,050. What is the approximate price Ken will have to pay for the computer? Round to the nearest thousand. (Just one price.)

1–94. Amy Parker had to write a cheque at the bookstore when she purchased her books for the new semester. The total cost of the books was $384. How will she write this amount in verbal form on her cheque?

1–95. Matt Schaeffer was listening to the news and heard that steel production last week was one million, five hundred eighty-seven thousand tonnes. Express this amount in numeric form.

1–96. Jackie Martin is the city clerk and must go to the aldermen's meetings and take notes on what is discussed. At last night's meeting, they were discussing repairs for the public library, which will cost three hundred seventy-five thousand, nine hundred eighty-five dollars. Write this in numeric form as Jackie would.

1–97. A government survey revealed that 25,963,400 people are employed as office workers. To show the approximate number of office workers, round the number all the way.

1–98. Bob Donaldson wished to present his top student with a certificate of achievement at the end of the school year in 2004. To make it appear more official, he wanted to write the year in verbal form. How did he write the year?

1–99. Nancy Morrissey has a problem reading large numbers and determining place value. She asked her brother to name the place value of the 4 in the number 13,542,966. Can you tell Nancy the place value of the 4? What is the place value of the 3?

The 4 is in the ______________ place.

The 3 is in the ______________ place.

1–100. Bill Blue owes $5,299 on his car loan, plus interest of $462. How much will it cost him to pay off this loan?

1–101. Sales at Rich's Convenience Store were $3,587 on Monday, $3,944 on Tuesday, $4,007 on Wednesday, $3,890 on Thursday, and $4,545 on Friday. What were the total sales for the week?

1–102. Sault Variety Store sold $5,000 worth of lottery tickets in the first week of August; it sold $289 less in the second week. How much were the lottery ticket sales in the second week of August?

1–103. A truck weighed 9,550 pounds when it was empty. (1 pound = about 0.45 kilograms.) After being filled with rubbish, it was driven to the dump where it weighed in at 22,347 pounds. How much did the rubbish weigh (in pounds)?

1–104. Lynn Jackson had $549 in her chequing account when she went to the bookstore. Lynn purchased an accounting book for $62, the working papers for $28, a study guide for $25, and a mechanical pencil for $5. After Lynn writes a cheque for the entire purchase, how much money will remain in her chequing account?

1–105. A new hard-body truck is advertised with a base price of $6,986 delivered. However, the window sticker on the truck reads as follows: tinted glass, $210; automatic transmission, $650; power steering, $210; power brakes, $215; safety locks, $95; air conditioning, $1,056. Estimate the total price, including the accessories, by rounding all the way and *then* calculating the exact price.

1–106. Four different stores are offering the same make and model of camcorder:

Store A	Store B	Store C	Store D
$1,285	$1,380	$1,440	$1,355

Find the difference between the highest price and the lowest price. Check your answer.

1–107. A Xerox XC830 copy machine has a suggested retail price of $1,395. The net price is $649. How much is the discount on the copy machine?

1–108. Jeanne Francis sells provincial lottery tickets in her variety store. If Jeanne's Variety Store sells 385 lottery tickets per day, how many tickets will be sold in a 7-day period?

1–109. Calgary Oil Company employs 100 people who are eligible for profit sharing. The financial manager has announced that the profits to be shared amount to $64,000. How much will each employee receive?

1–110. John Duncan's employer withheld $4,056 in income taxes from his pay for the year. If equal deductions are made each week, what is John's weekly deduction?

1–111. Anne Domingoes drives a Volvo that gets 550 kilometres per tank of 55 litres of gasoline. How many kilometres can she travel on 25 litres of gas?

1–112. How many 8 centimetre pieces of yellow ribbon can be cut from a spool of ribbon that contains 6 metres (1 metre = 100 centimetres)?

1–113. The number of commercials aired per day on a local television station is 672. How many commercials are aired in 1 year?

1–114. The computer department at City College purchased 18 computers at a cost of $2,400 each. What was the total price for the computer purchase?

1–115. Net income for Goodwin's Partnership was $64,500. The five partners share profits and losses equally. What was each partner's share?

1–116. Ben Krenshaw's supervisor at the construction site told Ben to divide a load of 1,423 bricks into stacks containing 35 bricks each. How many stacks will there be when Ben has finished the job? How many "extra" bricks will there be?

CALCULATOR USE PRACTICE PROBLEMS

1–117. Use your calculator to perform one-step calculations.

a. $[(2{,}332 - 2{,}323)^2 - (848 - 840)^2]^3$

b. $7{,}849 + 864 \times 5^3 - 11^4$

c. $(84 + 92) \div 4^2$

d. $5{,}893 - 1{,}635 + 2^{16} - 10{,}000$

CHALLENGE PROBLEMS

1–118. On June 1, 2001, *USA Today* compared financial contributions that the tobacco industry gave to political parties in the 1999–2000 election. The total dollar amount was eight million, four hundred thousand, with the following companies in the top five:

1. Philip Morris—three million, four hundred fifty thousand, one hundred thirty-nine.
2. UST Inc.—one million, five hundred eighty-eight thousand, three hundred fifty-four.
3. RJ Reynolds Tobacco—nine hundred ninety-one thousand, four hundred twenty-seven.
4. Brown & Williamson Tobacco—nine hundred seventy-nine thousand, seven hundred thirty-two.

5. Loews Corp.—two hundred eighty-five thousand, fifty.

(a) In verbal form, what was the total dollar amount contributed by the top five tobacco companies? **(b)** In numerical form, what is the difference between the total dollar amount contributed by the tobacco industry and the dollar amount contributed by the top five tobacco companies? **(c)** What was Philip Morris' average monthly contribution? Round your answer to the nearest hundred thousand.

1–119. Pat Valdez is trying to determine her 2004 finances. Pat's actual 2003 finances were as follows:

Income:		Assets:		
Gross income	$69,000	Chequing account	$ 1,950	
Interest income	450	Savings account	8,950	
Total	$69,450	Auto	1,800	
		Personal property	14,000	
Expenses:		Total	$26,700	
Living	$24,500			
Insurance premium	350	Liabilities:		
Taxes	14,800			
Medical	585	Note to bank	4,500	
Investment	4,000	Net worth	$22,200	(= $26,700 −$4,500)
Total	$44,235			

Net worth = Assets − Liabilities
(own) (owe)

Pat believes her gross income will double in 2004 and her interest income will decrease $150. She plans to reduce her 2004 living expenses by one-half. Pat's insurance company wrote a letter announcing that insurance premiums would triple in 2004. Her accountant estimates her taxes will decrease $250 and her medical costs will increase $410. Pat also hopes to cut her investment expenses by one-fourth. Pat's accountant projects that her savings and chequing accounts will each double in value. On January 2, 2004, Pat sold her automobile and began to use public transportation. Pat forecasts that her personal property will decrease by one-seventh. She has sent her bank a $375 cheque to reduce her bank note. Could you give Pat an updated list of her 2004 finances? If you round all the way each 2003 and 2004 asset and liability, what will be the difference in Pat's net worth?

SUMMARY PRACTICE TEST

1. Translate the following verbal forms to numbers and add. (p. 3)

a. Four thousand, five hundred ninety-four

b. Eight million, twelve

c. Seventeen thousand, five hundred ninety-four

2. Express the following number in verbal form. (p. 3)

7,944,581

3. Round the following numbers. (p. 3)

Nearest ten	Nearest hundred	Nearest thousand	Round all the way
a. 58	**b.** 583	**c.** 8,280	**d.** 19,876

4. Estimate the following actual problem by rounding all the way, work the actual problem, and check by adding each column of digits separately. (pp. 5, 9)

Actual	Estimate	Check
2,251		
7,899		
+ 8,498		

5. Estimate the following actual problem by rounding all the way and then do the actual multiplication. (pp. 5, 13)

Actual	Estimate
8,492	
× 706	

6. Multiply the following by the shortcut method. (p. 13)
$844,582 \times 1,000 =$

7. Divide the following and check the answer by multiplication. (p. 14)

Check

$38\overline{)9,900}$

8. Divide the following by the shortcut method. (p. 14)
$3,000 \div 30$

9. Gracie Lee bought a $79 calculator that was reduced to $28. Gracie gave the clerk a $100 bill. What change will Gracie receive? (p. 8)

10. Joe Smith plans to buy a $19,900 P.T. Cruiser with an interest charge of $1,100. Joe figures he can afford a monthly payment of $650. If Joe must pay 30 equal monthly payments, can he afford the van? (p. 14)

11. Jon Ree has the propane tank at his home filled 14 times per year. The tank has a capacity of 150 gallons. (1 gallon = about 3.79 litres.) Assume **(a)** the price of propane fuel is $2 per gallon and **(b)** the tank is completely empty each time Jon has it filled. What is Jon's average monthly propane bill? Complete the following Blueprint Aid for dissecting and solving the word problem. (p. 14)

THE FACTS	SOLVING FOR?	STEPS TO TAKE	KEY POINTS

Steps to solving problem

12. Perform a one-step calculation. (p. 17)
$[(115 - 11.3)^2 - (12.5 - 5 - 4^2) - 3,548] \times 2$

SOLUTIONS TO PRACTICE QUIZZES

LU 1–1

1. **a.** Seven thousand, nine hundred forty-eight
b. Forty-eight thousand, seven hundred seventy-five
c. Eight hundred fourteen billion, four hundred ten million, three hundred thirty-five thousand, four hundred fourteen

2. **a.** 4,500,000 **b.** 2,250,000 **c.** 355,000,000 **d.** 700,000,000 **e.** 11,000,000,000 **f.** 152,343

3. **a.** 92 ≈ 90 **b.** 745 ≈ 700 **c.** 8,341 ≈ 8,000 **d.** 4,752 ≈ 5,000

4. Kellogg's sales and profit:

THE FACTS	SOLVING FOR?	STEPS TO TAKE	KEY POINTS
S: Sales: Five million, one hundred eighty-one thousand dollars. *P: Profit:* Five hundred two thousand dollars.	Sales and profit rounded all the way. $S_{\text{rounded}} = ?$ $P_{\text{rounded}} = ?$	Express each verbal form in numeric form. Identify leftmost digit in each number. $S = 5,181,000$ $P = 502,000$	Rounding all the way means only the leftmost digit will remain. All other digits become zeros.

Steps to solving problem

1. Convert verbal to numeric.
   S: Five million, one hundred eighty-one thousand → \$5,181,000
   P: Five hundred two thousand → \$502,000
2. Identify leftmost digit of each number.
   \$5,181,000   \$502,000
3. Round.
   \$5,000,000   \$500,000

$S_{rounded}$ = \$5,000,000 $P_{rounded}$ = \$500,000

LU 1–2

1.

```
   14
   14
  2 2
  20
 ------
 22,354
```

2.

Estimate	Actual
4,000	4,241
9,000	8,794
+ 4,000	+ 3,872
17,000	16,907

3.

	Check
9,876	4,909
−4,967	+4,967
4,909	9,876

4. Jackson Manufacturing Company over- or underestimated sales:

THE FACTS	SOLVING FOR?	STEPS TO TAKE	KEY POINTS
PS: Projected 2003 sales: \$900,000. *MC: Major clients:* \$510,000. *OC: Other clients:* \$369,100.	How much were sales over- or underestimated? $S_{o/u}$ = ?	Total projected sales − Total actual sales = Over- or underestimated sales. $S_{o/u} = PS - (MC + OC)$	Projected sales (minuend) − Actual sales (subtrahend) = Difference.

Steps to solving problem

1. Calculate total actual sales.
   MC + *OC*
   \$510,000
   + 369,100
   \$879,100
2. Calculate over- or underestimated sales.
   PS − (*MC* + *OC*)
   \$900,000
   − 879,100
   \$ 20,900 (overestimated)

$S_{o/u}$ = \$20,900

LU 1–3

1.

Estimate	Actual	Check	
4,000	3,894	8 × 3,894 =	31,152
× 20	× 18	10 × 3,894 =	+38,940
80,000	31 152		70,092
	38 94		
	70,092		

2. 77 × 18 = 1,386 + 5 zeros = 138,600,000

3. 95 + 4 zeros = 950,000

4. Rounding

$$\begin{array}{r} 166 \text{ R}20 \\ 30\overline{)5{,}000} \\ \underline{3\,0} \\ 2\,00 \\ \underline{1\,80} \\ 200 \\ \underline{180} \\ 20 \end{array}$$

Actual

$$\begin{array}{r} 204 \text{ R}21 \\ 26\overline{)5{,}325} \\ \underline{5\,2} \\ 125 \\ \underline{104} \\ 21 \end{array}$$

Check

$$\begin{array}{r} 26 \times 204 = \ 5{,}304 \\ \underline{+\ \ 21} \\ 5{,}325 \end{array}$$

5. Drop 3 zeros $= 4\overline{)96}$ = 24

6. General Motors' total cost per year:

THE FACTS	SOLVING FOR?	STEPS TO TAKE	KEY POINTS
n_d: *Cars produced each workday:* 960. *d*: *Workweek:* 5 days. $d = 5$ *c*: *Cost per car:* \$6,500. *m*: *Number of weeks per year:* 52.	Total cost per year. $C_{total} = ?$	Cars produced per week × 52 = Total cars produced per year. $n_d \times d \times m$ Total cars produced per year × Total cost per car = Total cost per year. $C_{total} = n_d \times d \times m \times C$	Whenever possible, use multiplication and division shortcuts with zeros. Multiplication can be checked by division.

Steps to solving problem

1. Calculate total cars produced per week. $n_d \times d$ — $5 \times 960 = 4{,}800$ cars produced per week
2. Calculate total cars produced per year. $n_d \times d \times m$ — $4{,}800$ cars $\times$ 52 weeks $= 249{,}600$ total cars produced per year
3. Calculate total cost per year. $C_{total} = n_d \times d \times m \times c$ — $249{,}600$ cars $\times$ \$6,500 $=$ \$1,622,400,000
   (multiply $2{,}496 \times 65$ and add zeros)
   $C_{total} = \$1{,}622{,}400{,}000$

Check

\$1,622,400,000 ÷ 249,600 = \$6,500 (drop 2 zeros before dividing)

LU 1–4

1. a. $1 + 15 \div 3 - 2^2 = 1 + 15 \div 3 - 4 = 1 + 5 - 4 = 2$

b. $(9 - 4) \times 3 \div 5 + (25 - 14) \div 3 = 5 \times 3 \div 5 + 9 \div 3 = 3 + 3 = 6$

c. $(155 - 75) \div 4 + (225 - 75) \div 50 = 80 \div 4 + 150 \div 50 = 20 + 30 = 50$

d. $[(12 - 9) + (14 - 11)]^3 = (3 + 3)^3 = 6^3 = 216$

2. a. [( ] [( ] 10 [−] 8 [ )] [y^x] 3 [−] [( ] 6 [+] 5 [−] 4 [ )] [ )] [y^x] 11 [+] 9 [=] 10

The answer is 10.

b. 663,355 [−] 476 [y^x] 2 [+] 12 [×] 367 [=] 444,183

The answer is 441,183.

Business Math Scrapbook

WITH INTERNET APPLICATION

Putting Your Skills to Work

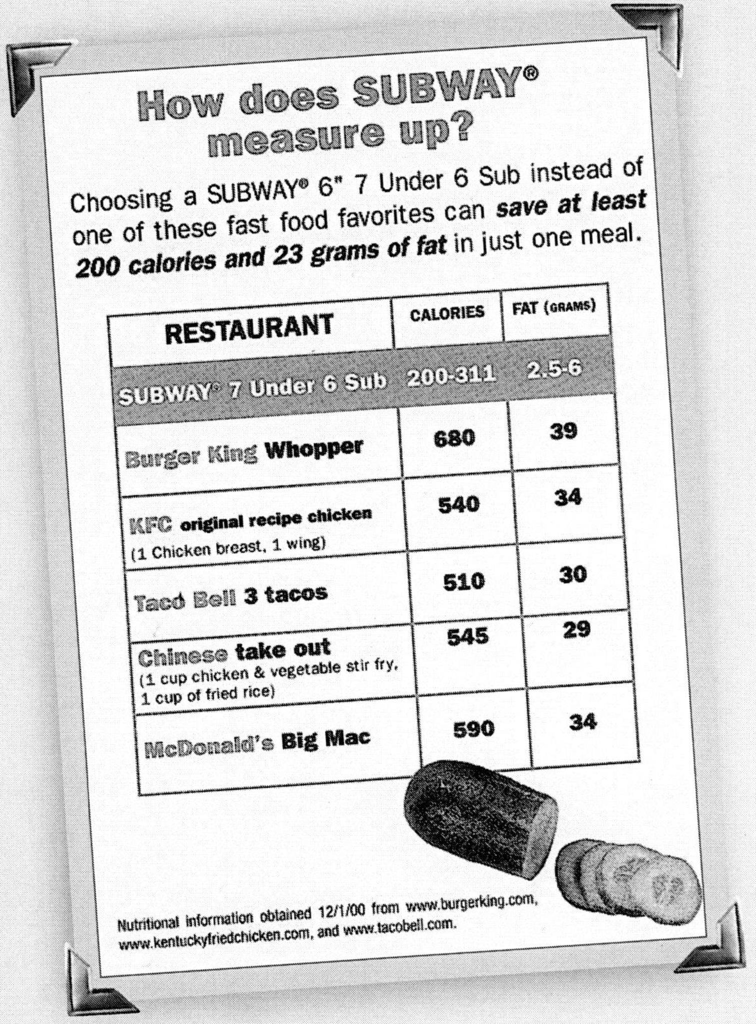

How does SUBWAY® measure up?

Choosing a SUBWAY® 6" 7 Under 6 Sub instead of one of these fast food favorites can ***save at least 200 calories and 23 grams of fat*** in just one meal.

RESTAURANT	CALORIES	FAT (GRAMS)
SUBWAY® 7 Under 6 Sub	200-311	2.5-6
Burger King **Whopper**	680	39
KFC **original recipe chicken** (1 Chicken breast, 1 wing)	540	34
Taco Bell **3 tacos**	510	30
Chinese **take out** (1 cup chicken & vegetable stir fry, 1 cup of fried rice)	545	29
McDonald's **Big Mac**	590	34

Nutritional information obtained 12/1/00 from www.burgerking.com, www.kentuckyfriedchicken.com, and www.tacobell.com.

PROJECT A

Show the mathematical advantage that Subway has over one of its competitors.

Go to the Web to see how Subway measures up today compared to the table shown. Update the table.

PROJECT B

Imagine as office manager for a company the budget for office furniture improvements this year is $11,300. The 24 employees (including you) have decided you should first replace the chairs in each of their offices. Go to www.staples.ca and select a chair from their catalogue you'd like in your own office. Round prices to the nearest dollar—for instance use $280 for $279.99.

Calculate how much 24 of those chairs would cost (ignore sales tax and delivery charges). Is $11,300 enough? If so, how much money do you have left? If not, how much more money do you need?

Fractions

2

Big Retailers Try to Speed Up Checkout Lines

By EMILY NELSON
Staff Reporter of THE WALL STREET JOURNAL

Imagine simply piling your groceries into a shopping cart, pushing it to a gate, swiping a credit-card and going on your way. Or having a store employee with a portable scanner greet you in line, and hand you a tally while you wait.

Mass-market retailers are testing these and other technologies to bring their checkout lines into the 21st century. At a time when Internet rivals offer shopping with no lines at all, retailers face more pressure than ever to speed customers along and eliminate big bottlenecks that take up precious selling space.

Many are also realizing that "register rage"—customer irritation over long lines and slow clerks—can be a real threat to business.

Studies show that eighty-three out of a hundred $\left(\frac{83}{100}\right)$ women and ninety-one out of a hundred $\left(\frac{91}{100}\right)$ men say long lines prompted them to stop patronizing a particular store.

LEARNING UNIT OBJECTIVES

LU 2–1: Types of Fractions and Conversion Procedures

- Recognize the three types of fractions and apply their properties (p. 36).
- Convert improper fractions to whole or mixed numbers and mixed numbers to improper fractions (p. 37).
- Convert fractions to lowest and highest terms (p. 38).

LU 2–2: Addition and Subtraction of Fractions

- Add like and unlike fractions (p. 41).
- Find the least common denominator (LCD) by inspection and prime numbers (p. 41).
- Subtract like and unlike fractions (p. 44).
- Add and subtract mixed numbers with the same or different denominators (pp. 43, 44).

LU 2–3: Multiplication and Division of Fractions

- Multiply and divide proper fractions and mixed numbers (p. 47).
- Use the cancellation method in the multiplication and division of fractions (p. 48).

LU 2–4: Using a Calculator

- Use a calculator in operations with fractions and mixed numbers (p. 50).
- Convert improper fractions into mixed numbers (p. 50).
- Add and subtract like and unlike fractions and mixed numbers (p. 50).
- Multiply and divide fractions and mixed numbers (p. 50).

Those M&M's® you have been calling "Plain" all these years have now received the name they deserve—Milk Chocolate M&M's®. These candies still come in different colours—yellow, red, blue, orange, brown, and green. Do you know how many of each colour are in a bag of M&M's®? You probably have never stopped to sort the colours and count them.

The 47.9 gram bag of M&M's® shown here contains 55 M&M's®. In this bag, you will find the following colours:[1]

18 yellow   9 blue   6 brown   10 red   7 orange   5 green

The number of yellow candies in a bag might suggest that yellow is the favourite colour of many people. Since this is a business math text, however, let's look at the 55 M&M's® in terms of fractional arithmetic.

Of the 55 M&M's® in the 47.9 gram bag, 5 are green, so we can say that 5 parts of 55 represent green candies. We could also say that 1 out of 11 is green. Are you confused?

For many people, fractions are difficult. If you are one of these people, this chapter is for you. First you will review the types of fractions and the fraction conversion procedures. Then you will gain a clear understanding of the addition, subtraction, multiplication, and division of fractions.

LEARNING UNIT 2–1
TYPES OF FRACTIONS AND CONVERSION PROCEDURES

> ### Advanced Technology in the Food Processing Industry
>
> About 90% of companies in the food processing sector, the nation's third-largest manufacturing industry, used at least one of 61 advanced technologies in 1998. About 30% used more than 10.
>
> **Six out of every 10** of these enterprises reported that these technologies improved the texture or appearance of their products, their shelf life, or their convenience for consumers. In addition, more than 70% of plants reported that the new technologies had improved food safety, and about 45% said they had also improved nutritional levels of their products.
>
> The food processing industry employs about 200,000 workers, accounting for just **over one-tenth** of total manufacturing sector employment. In 1998, the gross domestic product of this industry was $14.5 billion, or 11% of the total manufacturing gross domestic product. The sector produces food products ranging from meat and milk through to frozen pizzas and highly processed meat products.
>
> **Four out of every 10** companies reported in 1998 that they had solid plans to upgrade their technologies with new, more advanced technologies within three years.

Source: Statistics Canada, *Advanced Technology in the Canadian Food Processing Industry*, 88-518-XPE, 88-518-XIE. The publication is now available (88-518-XPE, $45; 88-518-XIE, $33).

This chapter explains the parts of whole numbers called **fractions.** With fractions you can divide any object or unit—a whole—into a definite number of equal parts. For example, the bag of 55 M&M's® shown at the beginning of this chapter contains 6 brown candies. If you eat only the brown ones, you have eaten 6 parts of 55, or 6 parts of the whole bag. We can express this in the following fraction:

$$\frac{6}{55}$$

6 is the **numerator,** or top of the fraction. The numerator describes the number of equal parts of the whole bag that you ate.

55 is the **denominator,** or bottom of the fraction. The denominator gives the total number of equal parts in the bag of M&M's®.

Before reviewing the arithmetic operations of fractions, you must recognize the three types of fractions described in this Unit. You must also know how to convert fractions to a workable form.

Types of Fractions

The article from Statistics Canada illustrates what a tremendous impact advanced technologies play in the food processing industry of Canada. Six out of every 10, or six-tenths $\left(\frac{6}{10}\right)$ of enterprises which used advanced technologies, reported positive change in product appearance, shelf life, or convenience for customers. Four out of 10, or four-tenths $\left(\frac{4}{10}\right)$ of surveyed companies, announced their plans to upgrade their technologies within three years. These positive trends are taking place in the nation's third-largest manufacturing industry, which employs about 200,000 workers, accounting for just over one-tenth $\left(\frac{1}{10}\right)$ of total manufacturing sector employment.

[1]The colour ratios currently given are a sample only used for educational purposes. They do not represent the manufacturer's colour ratios.

To describe current situation with innovations in food processing industry of Canada authors used numeric data, which included proper fractions $\frac{6}{10}$, $\frac{4}{10}$, and $\frac{1}{10}$.

PROPER FRACTIONS

A **proper fraction** has a value less than 1; its numerator is smaller than its denominator.

EXAMPLES $\frac{1}{10}, \frac{1}{12}, \frac{1}{3}, \frac{4}{7}, \frac{9}{10}, \frac{12}{13}, \frac{18}{55}$

IMPROPER FRACTIONS

An **improper fraction** has a value equal to or greater than 1; its numerator is equal to or greater than its denominator.

EXAMPLES $\frac{13}{13}, \frac{7}{6}, \frac{15}{14}, \frac{22}{19}$

MIXED NUMBERS

A **mixed number** is the sum of a whole number greater than zero and a proper fraction.

EXAMPLES $4\frac{1}{7}, 5\frac{9}{10}, 8\frac{7}{8}, 33\frac{5}{6}, 139\frac{9}{11}$

$\frac{3}{5}$ — 3: *Numerator:* Number above the fraction bar; —: *Fraction bar*; 5: *Denominator:* Number below the fraction bar

Conversion Procedures

In Chapter 1 we worked with two of the division symbols (÷ and $\overline{)\quad}$). The horizontal line (or the diagonal) that separates the numerator and the denominator of a fraction also indicates division. The numerator, like the dividend, is the number we are dividing into. The denominator, like the divisor, is the number we use to divide. Then, referring to the 6 brown M&M's® in the bag of 55 M&M's® $\left(\frac{6}{55}\right)$ shown at the beginning of this Unit, we can say that we are dividing 55 into 6, or 6 is divided by 55. Also, in the fraction $\frac{3}{4}$, we can say that we are dividing 4 into 3, or 3 is divided by 4.

Working with the smaller numbers of simple fractions such as $\frac{3}{4}$ is easier, so we often convert fractions to their simplest terms. In this unit we show how to convert improper fractions to whole or mixed numbers, mixed numbers to improper fractions, and fractions to lowest and highest terms.

Converting Improper Fractions to Whole or Mixed Numbers

Business situations often make it necessary to change an improper fraction to a whole number or mixed number. You can use the following steps to make this conversion:

CONVERTING IMPROPER FRACTIONS TO WHOLE OR MIXED NUMBERS

Step 1. Divide the numerator of the improper fraction by the denominator.

Step 2. **a.** If you have no remainder, the quotient is a whole number.

b. If you have a remainder, the whole number part of the mixed number is the quotient. The remainder is placed over the old denominator as the proper fraction of the mixed number.

EXAMPLES

$$\frac{15}{15} = 1 \qquad \frac{16}{5} = 3\frac{1}{5} \qquad \begin{array}{r} 3\ R1 \\ 5\overline{)16} \\ \underline{15} \\ 1 \end{array}$$

Converting Mixed Numbers to Improper Fractions

By reversing the procedure of converting improper fractions to mixed numbers, we can change mixed numbers to improper fractions.

CONVERTING MIXED NUMBERS TO IMPROPER FRACTIONS

Step 1. Multiply the denominator of the fraction by the whole number.
Step 2. Add the product from Step 1 to the numerator of the old fraction.
Step 3. Place the total from Step 2 over the denominator of the old fraction to get the improper fraction.

EXAMPLE

$$6\frac{1}{8} = \frac{(8 \times 6) + 1}{8} = \frac{49}{8}$$ ← Note that the denominator stays the same.

Converting (Reducing) Fractions to Lowest Terms

When solving fraction problems, you always reduce the fractions to their lowest terms. This reduction does not change the value of the fraction. For example, in the bag of M&M's®, 5 out of 55 were green. The fraction for this is $\frac{5}{55}$. If you divide the top and bottom of the fraction by 5, you have reduced the fraction to $\frac{1}{11}$ without changing its value. Remember, we said in the chapter introduction that 1 out of 11 M&M's® in the bag of 55 M&M's® represents green candies. Now you know why this is true.

To reduce a fraction to its lowest terms, begin by inspecting the fraction, looking for the largest whole number that will divide into both the numerator and the denominator without leaving a remainder. This whole number is the **greatest common divisor,** which cannot be zero. When you find this largest whole number, you have reached the point where the fraction is reduced to its **lowest terms.** At this point, no number (except 1) can divide evenly into both parts of the fraction.

REDUCING FRACTIONS TO LOWEST TERMS BY INSPECTION

Step 1. By inspection, find the largest whole number (greatest common divisor) that will divide evenly into the numerator and denominator (does not change the fraction value).
Step 2. Now you have reduced the fraction to its lowest terms, since no number (except 1) can divide evenly into the numerator and denominator.

EXAMPLE

$$\frac{24}{30} = \frac{24 \div 6}{30 \div 6} = \frac{4}{5}$$

Using inspection, you can see that the number 6 in the above example is the greatest common divisor. When you have large numbers, the greatest common divisor is not so obvious. For large numbers, you can use the following step approach to find the greatest common divisor:

STEP APPROACH FOR FINDING GREATEST COMMON DIVISOR

Step 1. Divide the smaller number (numerator) of the fraction into the larger number (denominator).
Step 2. Divide the remainder of Step 1 into the divisor of Step 1.
Step 3. Divide the remainder of Step 2 into the divisor of Step 2. Continue this division process until the remainder is a 0, which means the last divisor is the greatest common divisor.

EXAMPLE

STEP 1 **STEP 2**

$$\frac{24}{30} \rightarrow 24\overline{)30}\ \ 1,\ \ 30-24=6 \rightarrow 6\overline{)24}\ \ 4,\ \ 24-24=0 \qquad \frac{24 \div 6}{30 \div 6} = \frac{4}{5}$$

Reducing a fraction by inspection is to some extent a trial-and-error method. Sometimes you are not sure by what number you should divide the top (numerator) and bottom (denominator) of the fraction. The following reference table on divisibility tests will be helpful. Note that to reduce a fraction to lowest terms might result in more than one division.

	2	3	4	5	6	10
Will divide evenly into number if:	Last digit is 0, 2, 4, 6, 8.	Sum of the digits is divisible by 3.	Last two digits can be divided by 4.	Last digit is 0 or 5.	The number is even and the sum of the digits is divisible by 3.	The last digit is 0.
Examples	$\frac{12}{14} = \frac{6}{7}$	$\frac{36}{69} = \frac{12}{23}$ $3 + 6 = 9 \div 3 = 3$ $6 + 9 = 15 \div 3 = 5$	$\frac{140}{160} = \frac{1(40)}{1(60)}$ $= \frac{35}{40} = \frac{7}{8}$	$\frac{15}{20} = \frac{3}{4}$	$\frac{12}{18} = \frac{2}{3}$	$\frac{90}{100} = \frac{9}{10}$

Converting (Raising) Fractions to Higher Terms

Later, when you add and subtract fractions, you will see that sometimes fractions must be raised to **higher terms.** Recall that when you reduced fractions to their lowest terms, you looked for the largest whole number (greatest common divisor) that would divide evenly into both the numerator and the denominator. When you raise fractions to higher terms, you do the opposite and multiply the numerator and the denominator by the same whole number. For example, if you want to raise the fraction $\frac{1}{4}$, you can multiply the numerator and denominator by 2.

EXAMPLE

$$\frac{1}{4} \times \frac{2}{2} = \frac{2}{8}$$

The fractions $\frac{1}{4}$ and $\frac{2}{8}$ are **equivalent** in value. By converting $\frac{1}{4}$ to $\frac{2}{8}$, you only divided it into more parts.

Let's suppose that you have eaten $\frac{4}{7}$ of a pizza. You decide that instead of expressing the amount you have eaten in 7ths, you want to express it in 28ths. How would you do this?

To find the new numerator when you know the new denominator (28), use the steps that follow.

RAISING FRACTIONS TO HIGHER TERMS WHEN DENOMINATOR IS KNOWN

Step 1. Divide the *new* denominator by the *old* denominator to get the common number that raises the fraction to higher terms.

Step 2. Multiply the common number from Step 1 by the old numerator and place it as the new numerator over the new denominator.

EXAMPLE

$$\frac{4}{7} = \frac{?}{28}$$

STEP 1. Divide 28 by 7 = 4.

STEP 2. Multiply 4 by the numerator 4 = 16.

Result:

$$\frac{4}{7} = \frac{16}{28} \qquad \left(\textit{Note}\text{: This is the same as multiplying } \frac{4}{7} \times \frac{4}{4}.\right)$$

Note that the $\frac{4}{7}$ and $\frac{16}{28}$ are equivalent in value, yet they are different fractions.

Property of Fractions

Multiplication or division of numerator and denominator of a common fraction by the same nonzero number does not change the value of the fraction. These fractions are said to be equivalent.

$$\frac{3}{5} = \frac{3}{5} \times \frac{4}{4} = \frac{3 \times 4}{5 \times 4} = \frac{12}{20}$$

EXAMPLE

It is the same as multiplying or dividing by 1:

$$\frac{4}{4} = 1$$

$$\frac{44}{60} \div \frac{4}{4} = \frac{44 \div 4}{60 \div 4} = \frac{11}{15}$$

Now try the following Practice Quiz to check your understanding of this Unit.

LU 2–1 PRACTICE QUIZ

1. Identify the type of fraction—proper, improper, or mixed:

   a. $\frac{4}{5}$ **b.** $\frac{6}{5}$ **c.** $19\frac{1}{5}$ **d.** $\frac{20}{20}$

2. Convert to a mixed number (do not reduce):

   $\frac{160}{9}$

3. Convert the mixed number to an improper fraction:

   $9\frac{5}{8}$

4. Find the greatest common divisor by the step approach and reduce to lowest terms:

   a. $\frac{24}{40}$ **b.** $\frac{91}{156}$

5. Convert to higher terms:

   a. $\frac{14}{20} = \frac{\quad}{200}$ **b.** $\frac{8}{10} = \frac{\quad}{60}$

LEARNING UNIT 2–2
ADDITION AND SUBTRACTION OF FRACTIONS

ONLY ONE-FIFTH OF ON-LINE SALES ARE TO CONSUMERS OR HOUSEHOLDS

… The dollar value of business-to-consumer sales rose 59.0% to \$2.3 billion in 2001. … Business-to-business sales also rose sharply—39.5% to \$8.1 billion.

The retail trade sector accounted for 25% of the business-to-consumer market in 2001, the largest share, followed by the information and cultural industries (11%), manufacturing (11%) and wholesale trade (10%).

Sales to consumers accounted for 84% of Internet sales from the arts, entertainment and recreation sector, and 63% for the accommodation and food services sector.

Source: Statistics Canada, 2002.

This clipping from Statistics Canada tells that only one-fifth $\left(\frac{1}{5}\right)$ of online sales are made to households and consumers.

Since the value of all online sales is $\frac{5}{5}$, you can determine how much of the sales was to businesses by subtracting the numerator of $\frac{1}{5}$ from the numerator of $\frac{5}{5}$, which is $\frac{4}{5}$. You can make this subtraction because you are working with *like fractions*—fractions with the same denominators. Then you can prove that you are correct by adding the numerators of the fractions $\frac{1}{5}$ and $\frac{4}{5}$ to get the initial value of $\frac{5}{5}$.

In this Unit you learn how to add and subtract fractions with the same denominators (**like fractions**) and fractions with different denominators (**unlike fractions**). We have included how to add and subtract mixed numbers with the instructions for the addition and subtraction of fractions.

Addition of Fractions

When you add two or more quantities, they must have the same name or be of the same denomination. You cannot add 6 dollars and 3 Euros unless you change the denomination of one or both quantities. You must either make the dollars into Euros or the Euros into dollars. The same principle also applies to fractions. That is, to add two or more fractions, they must have a **common denominator.**

Adding Like Fractions

In our "On-Line Sales" clipping at the beginning of this Unit we stated that because the fractions had the same denominator, or a common denominator, they were *like fractions.* Adding like fractions is similar to adding whole numbers.

ADDING LIKE FRACTIONS

Step 1. Add the numerators and place the total over the original denominator.

Step 2. If the total of your numerators is the same as your original denominator, convert your answer to a whole number; if the total is larger than your original denominator, convert your answer to a mixed number.

EXAMPLE

$$\frac{1}{7}+\frac{4}{7}=\frac{5}{7}$$

The denominator, 7, shows the number of pieces into which some whole was divided. The two numerators, 1 and 4, tell how many of the pieces you have. So if you add 1 and 4, you get 5, or $\frac{5}{7}$.

Adding Unlike Fractions

Since you cannot add *unlike fractions* because their denominators are not the same, you must change the unlike fractions to *like fractions*—fractions with the same denominators. To do this, find a denominator that is common to all the fractions you want to add. Then look for the **least common denominator (LCD).**[2] The LCD is the smallest nonzero whole number into which all denominators will divide evenly. You can find the LCD by inspection or with prime numbers.

FINDING THE LEAST COMMON DENOMINATOR (LCD) BY INSPECTION The example that follows shows you how to use inspection to find an LCD (this will make all the denominators the same).

EXAMPLE

$$\frac{3}{7}+\frac{5}{21}$$

Inspection of these two fractions shows that the smallest number into which denominators 7 and 21 divide evenly is 21. Thus, 21 is the LCD.

You may know that 21 is the LCD of $\frac{3}{7}+\frac{5}{21}$, but you cannot add these two fractions until you change the denominator of $\frac{3}{7}$ to 21. You do this by building (raising) the equivalent of $\frac{3}{7}$, as explained in Learning Unit 2–1. You can use the following steps to find the LCD by inspection:

STEP 1. Divide the new denominator (21) by the old denominator (7): $21 \div 7 = 3$.

STEP 2. Multiply the 3 in Step 1 by the old numerator (3): $3 \times 3 = 9$. The new numerator is 9.

Result:

$$\frac{3}{7}=\frac{9}{21}$$

Now that the denominators are the same, you add the numerators.

$$\frac{9}{21}+\frac{5}{21}=\frac{14}{21}=\frac{2}{3}$$

Note that $\frac{14}{21}$ is reduced to its lowest terms $\frac{2}{3}$. Always reduce your answer to its lowest terms.

[2]Often referred to as the *lowest common denominator.*

You are now ready for the following general steps for adding proper fractions with different denominators. These steps also apply to the following discussion on finding LCD by prime numbers.

ADDING UNLIKE FRACTIONS

Step 1. Find the LCD.
Step 2. Change each fraction to a like fraction with the LCD.
Step 3. Add the numerators and place the total over the LCD.
Step 4. If necessary, reduce the answer to lowest terms.

FINDING THE LEAST COMMON DENOMINATOR (LCD) BY PRIME NUMBERS When you cannot determine the LCD by inspection, you can use the prime number method. First you must understand prime numbers.

PRIME NUMBERS

A **prime number** is a whole number greater than 1 that is only divisible by itself and 1. The number 1 is not a prime number.

EXAMPLES

2, 3, 5, 7, 11, 13, 17, 19, 23, 29, 31, 37, 41, 43

Monster Prime Number Is Discovered by Scientists

EAGAN, Minn. (AP) – Computer scientists crunching numbers at the outer limits of numeration say they've stumbled on the largest-known prime number.

Primes are whole numbers, like 3, 5, 17, 23 and so on, that are evenly divisible only by one and themselves. This one, at 378,632 digits, would fill up 12 newspaper pages in standard type. Mathematicians would express the number as two to the 1,257,787th power minus one.

Source: © 1996 Dow Jones & Company, Inc.

Note that the number 4 is not a prime number. Not only can you divide 4 by 1 and by 4, but you can also divide 4 by 2.

The largest example of a prime number given in the list of examples above contains two digits. The *Wall Street Journal* clipping "Monster Prime Number Is Discovered by Scientists" states that computer scientists stumbled on the largest known prime number—a number with 378,632 digits.

Now let's see how to use prime numbers to find the LCD.

EXAMPLE

$$\frac{1}{3}+\frac{1}{8}+\frac{1}{9}+\frac{1}{12}$$

STEP 1. Copy the denominators and arrange them in a separate row.

3 8 9 12

STEP 2. Divide the denominators in Step 1 by prime numbers. Start with the smallest number that will divide into at least two of the denominators. Bring down any number that is not divisible. Keep in mind that the lowest prime number is 2.

2 / 3 8 9 12
3 4 9 6

Note: The 3 and 9 were brought down, since they were not divisible by 2.

STEP 3. Continue Step 2 until no prime number will divide evenly into at least two numbers.

Note: The 3 is used, since 2 can no longer divide evenly into at least two numbers.

2 / 3 8 9 12
2 / 3 4 9 6
3 / 3 2 9 3
1 2 3 1

STEP 4. To find the LCD, multiply all the numbers in the divisors (2, 2, 3) and in the last row (1, 2, 3, 1).

$\boxed{2 \times 2 \times 3} \times \boxed{1 \times 2 \times 3 \times 1} = 72$ (LCD)

Divisors × Last row

STEP 5. Raise each fraction so that each denominator will be 72 and then add fractions.

$$\frac{24}{72} + \frac{9}{72} + \frac{8}{72} + \frac{6}{72} = \frac{47}{72}$$

$\frac{1}{3} = \frac{?}{72}$ $72 \div 3 = 24$ $24 \times 1 = 24$

$\frac{1}{8} = \frac{?}{72}$ $72 \div 8 = 9$ $9 \times 1 = 9$

The above five steps used for finding LCD with prime numbers are summarized as follows:

FINDING LCD FOR TWO OR MORE FRACTIONS

Step 1. Copy the denominators and arrange them in a separate row.
Step 2. Divide the denominators by the smallest prime number that will divide evenly into at least two numbers.
Step 3. Continue until no prime number divides evenly into at least two numbers.
Step 4. Multiply all the numbers in divisors and last row to find the LCD.
Step 5. Raise all fractions so each has a common denominator and then complete the computation.

Adding Mixed Numbers

The following steps will show you how to add mixed numbers:

ADDING MIXED NUMBERS

Step 1. Add the fractions (remember that fractions need common denominators, as in the previous section).
Step 2. Add the whole numbers.
Step 3. Combine the totals of Steps 1 and 2. Be sure you do not have an improper fraction in your final answer. Convert the improper fraction to a whole or mixed number. Add the whole numbers resulting from the improper fraction conversion to the total whole numbers of Step 2. If necessary, reduce the answer to lowest terms.

EXAMPLE
Using prime numbers to find LCD of example

```
2 / 20 5 4
2 / 10 5 2
5 /  5 5 1
     1 1 1
```

$2 \times 2 \times 5 = 20$ LCD

$$4\frac{7}{20} \quad 6\frac{3}{5} \quad +7\frac{1}{4}$$

$$4\frac{7}{20} \quad 6\frac{12}{20} \quad +7\frac{5}{20}$$

$\frac{3}{5} = \frac{?}{20}$

$20 \div 5 = 4$

$\times 3$

12

STEP 1. → $\frac{24}{20} = 1\frac{4}{20}$

STEP 2. $= 17$

STEP 3. → $= 18\frac{4}{20} = 18\frac{1}{5}$

ADDING MIXED NUMBERS AS IMPROPER FRACTIONS

Step 1. Convert mixed numbers into improper fractions with the same LCD.
Step 2. Perform addition.
Step 3. Convert the result back into a mixed number.

EXAMPLE

$3\frac{3}{4} + 1\frac{3}{4}$

STEP 1. $3\frac{1}{4} = \frac{12+3}{4} = \frac{15}{4}$ $\quad 1\frac{3}{4} = \frac{4+3}{4} = \frac{7}{4}$

STEP 2. $\frac{15}{4} + \frac{7}{4} = \frac{22}{4} = \frac{11}{2}$

STEP 3. $\frac{11}{2} = 5\frac{1}{2}$

SUBTRACTION OF FRACTIONS

The subtraction of fractions is similar to the addition of fractions. This section explains how to subtract like and unlike fractions and how to subtract mixed numbers.

Subtracting Like Fractions

To subtract like fractions, use the steps that follow.

SUBTRACTING LIKE FRACTIONS

Step 1. Subtract the numerators and place the answer over the common denominator.
Step 2. If necessary, reduce the answer to lowest terms.

EXAMPLE

$\frac{9}{10} - \frac{1}{10} = \frac{8 \div 2}{10 \div 2} = \frac{4}{5}$

STEP 1 **STEP 2**

Subtracting Unlike Fractions

Now let's learn the steps for subtracting unlike fractions.

SUBTRACTING UNLIKE FRACTIONS

Step 1. Find the LCD.
Step 2. Raise the fraction to its equivalent value.
Step 3. Subtract the numerators and place the answer over the LCD.
Step 4. If necessary, reduce the answer to lowest terms.

EXAMPLE

$$\begin{array}{r} \frac{5}{8} \\ -\frac{2}{64} \\ \hline \end{array} \qquad \begin{array}{r} \frac{40}{64} \\ -\frac{2}{64} \\ \hline \frac{38}{64} = \frac{19}{32} \end{array}$$

By inspection, we see that LCD is 64.

Thus 64 ÷ 8 = 8 × 5 = 40.

Subtracting Mixed Numbers

When you subtract whole numbers, sometimes borrowing is not necessary. At other times, you must borrow. The same is true of subtracting mixed numbers.

SUBTRACTING MIXED NUMBERS

When Borrowing Is Not Necessary

Step 1. Subtract fractions, making sure to find the LCD.

Step 2. Subtract whole numbers.

Step 3. Reduce the fraction(s) to lowest terms.

When Borrowing Is Necessary

Step 1. Make sure the fractions have the LCD.

Step 2. Borrow from the whole number.

Step 3. Subtract the whole numbers and fractions.

Step 4. Reduce the fraction(s) to lowest terms.

EXAMPLE

Where borrowing is not necessary:

$$\begin{array}{r} 6\frac{1}{2} \\ -\frac{3}{8} \\ \hline \end{array}$$

Find LCD of 2 and 8. LCD is 8.

$$\begin{array}{r} 6\frac{4}{8} \\ -\frac{3}{8} \\ \hline 6\frac{1}{8} \end{array}$$

EXAMPLE

Where borrowing is necessary:

$$\begin{array}{rrr} 3\frac{1}{2} = & 3\frac{2}{4} = & 2\frac{6}{4}\left(\frac{4}{4}+\frac{2}{4}\right) \\ -1\frac{3}{4} = & -1\frac{3}{4} = & -1\frac{3}{4} \\ \hline & & 1\frac{3}{4} \end{array}$$

LCD is 4.

Since $\frac{3}{4}$ is larger than $\frac{2}{4}$, we must borrow 1 from the 3. This is the same as borrowing $\frac{4}{4}$. A fraction with the same numerator and denominator represents a whole. When we add $\frac{4}{4} + \frac{2}{4}$, we get $\frac{6}{4}$. Note how we subtracted the whole number and fractions, being sure to reduce the final answer if necessary.

SUBTRACTING MIXED NUMBERS AS IMPROPER FRACTIONS

Step 1. Convert mixed numbers into improper fractions with the same LCD.

Step 2. Perform subtraction.

Step 3. Convert the result back into a mixed number.

EXAMPLE

$3\frac{1}{4} - 1\frac{3}{4}$

STEP 1. $3\frac{1}{4} = \frac{12+1}{4} = \frac{13}{4}$ $\quad 1\frac{3}{4} = \frac{4+3}{4} = \frac{7}{4}$

STEP 2. $\frac{13}{4} - \frac{7}{4} = \frac{6}{4} = \frac{3}{2}$

STEP 3. $\frac{3}{2} = 1\frac{1}{2}$

How to Dissect and Solve a Word Problem

Let's now look at how to dissect and solve a word problem involving fractions.

THE WORD PROBLEM The Albertson grocery store has $550\frac{1}{4}$ total square metres of floor space. Albertson's meat department occupies $115\frac{1}{2}$ square metres, and its deli department occupies $145\frac{7}{8}$ square metres. If the remainder of the floor space is for groceries, what square-metrage remains for groceries?

THE FACTS	SOLVING FOR?	STEPS TO TAKE	KEY POINTS
S: Total square-metrage: $550\frac{1}{4}\ m^2$ *M: Meat department:* $115\frac{1}{2}\ m^2$ *D: Deli department:* $145\frac{7}{8}\ m^2$	Total square-metrage for groceries. $G = ?$	Total floor space − Total meat and deli floor space = Total grocery floor space. $G = S - (M + D)$	Denominators must be the same before adding or subtracting fractions. $\frac{8}{8} = 1$ Never leave improper fraction as final answer.

STEPS TO SOLVING PROBLEM

1. Calculate total square-metrage of the meat and deli departments.

$$\text{Meat: } M = 115\frac{1}{2} = 115\frac{4}{8}$$
$$\text{Deli: } D = +145\frac{7}{8} = +145\frac{7}{8}$$
$$(M + D) = 260\frac{11}{8} = 261\frac{3}{8}\ m^2$$

2. Calculate total grocery square-metrage.

$$S = 550\frac{1}{4} = 550\frac{2}{8} = 549\frac{10}{8} \rightarrow \left(\frac{2}{8} + \frac{8}{8}\right)$$
$$-(M + D) = -261\frac{3}{8} = -261\frac{3}{8} = -261\frac{3}{8}$$
$$S - (M + D) = 549\frac{10}{8} - 261\frac{3}{8} = 288\frac{7}{8}\ m^2$$

Check

$$261\frac{3}{8} + 288\frac{7}{8} = 549\frac{10}{8} = 550\frac{2}{8} = 550\frac{1}{4}\ m^2$$

Note how the above Blueprint Aid helped to gather the facts and identify what we were looking for. To find the total square-metrage for groceries, we first had to sum the areas for meat and deli. Then we could subtract these areas from the total square-metrage. Also note that in Step 1 above, we didn't leave the answer as an improper fraction. In Step 2, we borrowed from the 550 so that we could complete the subtraction.

LU 2–2 PRACTICE QUIZ

1. Find LCD by the division of prime numbers:
   12, 9, 6, 4
2. Add and reduce to lowest terms if needed:
   a. $\frac{3}{40} + \frac{2}{5}$ **b.** $2\frac{3}{4} + 6\frac{1}{20}$
3. Subtract and reduce to lowest terms if needed:
   a. $\frac{6}{7} - \frac{1}{4}$ **b.** $8\frac{1}{4} - 3\frac{9}{28}$ **c.** $4 - 1\frac{3}{4}$
4. Computerland has $660\frac{1}{4}$ total square metres of floor space. Three departments occupy this floor space: hardware, $201\frac{1}{8}$ square metres; software, $242\frac{1}{4}$ square metres; and customer service, ____ square metres. What is the total square-metrage of the customer service area? You might want to try a Blueprint Aid, since the solution will show a completed Blueprint Aid.

LEARNING UNIT 2–3
MULTIPLICATION AND DIVISION OF FRACTIONS

Coconutty "M&M's"® Brownies

6 squares (1 ounce each) semi-sweet chocolate
½ cup (1 stick) butter
¾ cup granulated sugar
2 large eggs
1 tablespoon vegetable oil
1 teaspoon vanilla extract
1¼ cups all-purpose flour
3 tablespoons unsweetened cocoa powder
1 teaspoon baking powder
½ teaspoon salt
1½ cups "M&M's"® Chocolate Mini Baking Bits, divided
Coconut Topping (recipe follows)

Source: © 2000 Mars, Incorporated.

The following recipe for Coconutty "M&M's"® Brownies makes 16 brownies. What would you need if you wanted to triple the recipe and make 48 brownies?

Preheat oven to 350°F. Grease 8 × 8 × 2 inch pan; set aside. In small saucepan combine chocolate, butter, and sugar over low heat; stir constantly until smooth. Remove from heat; let cool. In bowl beat eggs, oil, and vanilla; stir in chocolate mixture until blended. Stir in flour, cocoa powder, baking powder, and salt. Stir in 1 cup "M&M's"® Chocolate Mini Baking Bits. Spread batter in prepared pan. Bake 35 to 40 minutes or until toothpick inserted in centre comes out clean. Cool. Prepare a coconut topping. Spread over brownies; sprinkle with $\frac{1}{2}$ cup "M&M's"® Chocolate Mini Baking Bits.

In this Unit you learn how to multiply and divide fractions.

MULTIPLICATION OF FRACTIONS

Multiplying fractions is easier than adding and subtracting fractions because you do not have to find a common denominator. This section explains the multiplication of proper fractions and the multiplication of mixed numbers.

MULTIPLYING PROPER FRACTIONS[3]

Step 1. Multiply the numerators and the denominators.

Step 2. Reduce the answer to lowest terms or use the cancellation method.

First let's look at an example that results in an answer that we do not have to reduce.

EXAMPLE

$$\frac{1}{7} \times \frac{5}{8} = \frac{5}{56}$$

In the next example, note how we reduce the answer to lowest terms.

EXAMPLE

$$\frac{5}{1} \times \frac{1}{6} \times \frac{4}{7} = \frac{20}{42} = \frac{10}{21}$$ Keep in mind $\frac{5}{1}$ is equal to 5.

We can reduce $\frac{20}{42}$ by the step approach as follows:

$$20\overline{)42} = 2 \text{ R } 2 \quad (42 - 40 = 2) \qquad 2\overline{)20} = 10 \quad (20 - 20 = 0)$$

We could also have found the greatest common divisor by inspection.

$$\frac{20 \div 2}{42 \div 2} = \frac{10}{21}$$

[3]You would follow the same procedure to multiply improper fractions.

As an alternative to reducing fractions to lowest terms, we can use the **cancellation** technique. Let's work the previous example using this technique.

EXAMPLE

$$\frac{5}{1} \times \frac{1}{\underset{3}{\cancel{6}}} \times \frac{\overset{2}{\cancel{4}}}{7} = \frac{10}{21}$$

2 divides evenly into 4 twice and into 6 three times.

Note that when we cancel numbers, we are reducing the answer before multiplying. We know that multiplying or dividing both numerator and denominator by the same number gives an equivalent fraction. So we can divide both numerator and denominator by any number that divides them both evenly. It doesn't matter which we divide first. Note that this division reduces $\frac{10}{21}$ to its lowest terms.

Multiplying Mixed Numbers

The following steps explain how to multiply mixed numbers:

MULTIPLYING MIXED NUMBERS

Step 1. Convert the mixed numbers to improper fractions.
Step 2. Multiply the numerators and denominators.
Step 3. Reduce the answer to lowest terms or use the cancellation method.

EXAMPLE

$$2\frac{1}{3} \times 1\frac{1}{2} = \frac{7}{\underset{1}{\cancel{3}}} \times \frac{\overset{1}{\cancel{3}}}{2} = \frac{7}{2} = 3\frac{1}{2}$$

STEP 1 STEP 2 STEP 3

DIVISION OF FRACTIONS

When you studied whole numbers in Chapter 1, you saw how multiplication can be checked by division. The multiplication of fractions can also be checked by division, as you will see in this section on dividing proper fractions and mixed numbers.

Dividing Proper Fractions

The division of proper fractions introduces a new term—the **reciprocal.** To use reciprocals, we must first recognize which fraction in the problem is the divisor—the fraction that we divide by. Let's assume the problem we are to solve is $\frac{1}{8} \div \frac{2}{3}$. We read this problem as "$\frac{1}{8}$ divided by $\frac{2}{3}$." The divisor is the fraction after the division sign (or the second fraction). The steps that follow show how the divisor becomes a reciprocal.

DIVIDING PROPER FRACTIONS

Step 1. Invert (turn upside down) the divisor (the second fraction). The inverted number is the *reciprocal.*
Step 2. Multiply the fractions.
Step 3. Reduce the answer to lowest terms or use the cancellation method.

Do you know why the inverted fraction number is a reciprocal? Reciprocals are two numbers that when multiplied give a product of 1. For example, 2 (which is the same as $\frac{2}{1}$) and $\frac{1}{2}$ are reciprocals because multiplying them gives 1.

EXAMPLE

$\frac{1}{8} \div \frac{2}{3} \qquad \frac{1}{8} \times \frac{3}{2} = \frac{3}{16}$

Dividing one fraction by another is the same as multiplying the first fraction by the reciprocal of the other.

Dividing Mixed Numbers

Now you are ready to divide mixed numbers by using improper fractions.

DIVIDING MIXED NUMBERS

Step 1. Convert all mixed numbers to improper fractions.

Step 2. Invert the divisor (take its reciprocal) and multiply. If your final answer is an improper fraction, reduce it to lowest terms. You can do this by finding the greatest common divisor or by using the cancellation technique.

EXAMPLE

$8\frac{3}{4} \div 2\frac{5}{6}$

STEP 1. $\frac{35}{4} \div \frac{17}{6}$

STEP 2. $\frac{35}{\not{4}_{2}} \times \frac{\not{6}^{3}}{17} = \frac{105}{34} = 3\frac{3}{34}$ Here we used the cancellation technique.

HOW TO DISSECT AND SOLVE A WORD PROBLEM

THE WORD PROBLEM Jamie Slater ordered $5\frac{1}{2}$ cords of oak. The cost of each cord is \$150. He also ordered $2\frac{1}{4}$ cords of maple at \$120 per cord. Jamie's neighbour, Al, said that he would share the wood and pay him $\frac{1}{5}$ of the total cost. How much did Jamie receive from Al?

Note how we filled in the Blueprint Aid columns. We first had to find the total cost of all the wood before we could find Al's share—$\frac{1}{5}$ of the total cost.

THE FACTS	SOLVING FOR?	STEPS TO TAKE	KEY POINTS
Cords ordered: *C:* $5\frac{1}{2}$ at \$150 per cord. *M:* $2\frac{1}{4}$ at \$120 per cord. *Al's cost share:* *A:* $\frac{1}{5}$ the total cost.	What will Al pay Jamie? $A = ?$	Total cost of wood × $\frac{1}{5}$ = Al's cost. $A = \frac{1}{5}(C + M)$	Convert mixed numbers to improper fractions when multiplying. Cancellation is an alternative to reducing fractions.

STEPS TO SOLVING PROBLEM

1. Calculate the cost of oak. $C = 5\frac{1}{2} \times \$150 = \frac{11}{\not{2}_{1}} \times \not{\$150}^{\$75} = \$825$

2. Calculate the cost of maple. $M = 2\frac{1}{4} \times \$120 = \frac{9}{\not{4}_{1}} \times \not{\$120}^{\$30} = +270$

   $C + M = \qquad \overline{\$1,095}$ (total cost of wood)

3. What Al pays. $A = \frac{1}{\not{5}_{1}} \times \not{\$1,095}^{\$219} = \$219$

LU 2-3 PRACTICE QUIZ

1. Multiply (use cancellation technique):

   a. $\frac{4}{8} \times \frac{4}{6}$ **b.** $35 \times \frac{4}{7}$

2. Multiply (do not use cancelling; reduce by finding the greatest common divisor):

   $\frac{14}{15} \times \frac{7}{10}$

3. Complete the following. Reduce to lowest terms as needed.

   a. $\frac{1}{9} \div \frac{5}{6}$ **b.** $\frac{51}{5} \div \frac{5}{9}$

4. Jill Estes bought a mobile home that was $8\frac{1}{8}$ times as expensive as the home her brother bought. Jill's brother paid $16,000 for his mobile home. What is the cost of Jill's new home?

LEARNING UNIT 2–4
USING A CALCULATOR

Many formulas and operations are already preprogrammed in your calculator. Different calculators have different functions with certain keys assigned to them. To process operations with fractions and mixed numbers you will need to have a button [ab/c] on your calculator. Using this button you will be able to easily perform multiplication, division, addition, subtraction and other operations involving fractions and mixed numbers. Most calculators, for example Sharp Scientific calculators, have the button [ab/c].

To become a specialist in your professional area you still have to understand and apply algebraic methods. This will give you an advantage in your career development, provide you with flexibility in problem solving, and strengthen your mathematical skills.

It is possible to solve most of the problems in this textbook both ways: algebraically and with the assistance of your calculator.

HOW TO USE THE [ab/c] BUTTON

To insert a fraction or a mixed number you need to follow these steps.

For example, you are preparing to work with $5\frac{3}{4}$. Press 5, then [ab/c]. You have inserted whole part of the number. On your screen you will see **5 r**. Press 3, and then again [ab/c]. You have inserted the numerator. Now on your screen you will have **5 r 3 r**. Press 4. You have inserted the denominator. And **5 r 3 r 4** will appear on your screen. Calculator is ready to work with the mixed number $5\frac{3}{4}$.

If you want to work with a fraction, for example $\frac{5}{6}$, you enter the fraction into your calculator in the same manner.

Press 5 and then the "magic" button [ab/c]. Press 6. You have inserted your fraction and you can see **5 r 6** on your screen. Your calculator is ready to work with this fraction.

You can use the "magic" button [ab/c] *for conversion of improper fractions into a mixed number.*

EXAMPLE

Convert $\frac{72}{47}$ into a mixed number.

Insert the given improper fraction in your calculator.

72 [ab/c] 47

Press the equal button [=] and you will get **1 r 25 r 47.** Convert it into standard form and you will get $1\frac{25}{47}$.

To illustrate the use of a calculator for operations with fractions and mixed numbers, examples from pages 42, 45, and 47 will be repeated here as Examples 1, 2, and 3 respectively.

EXAMPLE 1

$\frac{1}{3} + \frac{1}{8} + \frac{1}{9} + \frac{1}{12}$

Enter the given fractions and add them in sequence.

1 [ab/c] 3 + 1 [ab/c] 8 + [ab/c] + 1 [ab/c] 9 + 1 [ab/c] + 12 = 47 r 72

Now you have to convert the result into standard form. Start converting from right to left. 72 is your denominator and 47 is your numerator. There is no whole part of the number, so your result is a fraction.

The answer for the problem is proper fraction $\frac{47}{72}$.

EXAMPLE 2

$6\frac{1}{2} - \frac{3}{8}$

Enter the given numbers in sequence from left to right and subtract them.

6 [ab/c] 1 [ab/c] 2 − 3 [ab/c] 8 = 6 r 1 r 8

Convert the result into standard form. Perform conversion from right to left.

Denominator is 8, numerator is 1, and the whole part is 6. Your result is $6\frac{1}{8}$.

EXAMPLE 3

$\frac{5}{1} \times \frac{1}{6} \times \frac{4}{7}$

Insert the given fractions in sequence and multiply them.

5 [ab/c] 1 × 1 [ab/c] 6 × 4 [ab/c] 7 = 10 r 21

Convert the result into standard form and you will get $\frac{10}{21}$.

LU 2-4 PRACTICE QUIZ

Perform the operations using a calculator:

1. $\frac{1}{3} + \frac{4}{7} + \frac{8}{15} + 1\frac{2}{3} + \frac{16}{87}$

2. $\frac{1}{8} \times \frac{5}{165} + \frac{3}{14}$

3. $\frac{17}{125} \div \frac{13}{15} - \frac{1}{7}$

Convert the improper fraction into a mixed number:

4. $\frac{39}{14}$

CHAPTER ORGANIZER AND REFERENCE GUIDE

Topic	Key point, procedure, formula	Example(s) to illustrate situation
Types of fractions, p. 36	*Proper:* Value less than 1; numerator smaller than denominator. *Improper:* Value equal to or greater than 1; numerator equal to or greater than denominator. *Mixed:* Sum of whole number greater than zero and a proper fraction.	$\frac{3}{5}, \frac{7}{9}, \frac{8}{15}$ $\frac{14}{14}, \frac{19}{18}$ $6\frac{3}{8}, 9\frac{8}{9}$
Fraction conversions, p. 37	*Improper to whole or mixed:* Divide numerator by denominator; place remainder over *old* denominator. *Mixed to improper:* $\frac{\text{Whole number} \times \text{Denominator} + \text{Numerator}}{\text{Old denominator}}$	$\frac{17}{4} = 4\frac{1}{4}$ $4\frac{1}{8} = \frac{32+1}{8} = \frac{33}{8}$
Reducing fractions to lowest terms, p. 38	1. Divide numerator and denominator by largest possible divisor (does not change fraction value). 2. When reduced to lowest terms, no number (except 1) will divide evenly into both numerator and denominator.	$\frac{18 \div 2}{46 \div 2} = \frac{9}{23}$
Step approach for finding greatest common denominator, p. 38	1. Divide smaller number of fraction into larger number. 2. Divide remainder into divisor of Step 1. Continue this process until no remainder results. 3. The last divisor used is the greatest common divisor.	$\frac{15}{65}$ → $65 \div 15 = 4$; 60; remainder 5 $15 \div 5 = 3$; 15; remainder 0 5 is greatest common divisor.
Raising fractions to higher terms, p. 39	Multiply numerator and denominator by same number. Does not change fraction value.	$\frac{15}{41} = \frac{?}{410}$ $410 \div 41 = 10;\ 10 \times 15 = 150$
Properties of fractions, p. 40	Multiplication or division of numerator and denominator of a common fraction by the same nonzero number does not change the value of the fraction. These fractions are called equivalent.	$\frac{1}{3} \times \frac{3}{3} = \frac{3}{9} \times \frac{5}{5} = \frac{15}{45} \times \frac{2}{2} = \frac{30}{90}$ $\frac{100}{550} \div \frac{10}{10} = \frac{10}{55} \div \frac{5}{5} = \frac{2}{11}$
Adding and subtracting like and unlike fractions, p. 41	When denominators are the same (like fractions), add (or subtract) numerators, place total over original denominator, and reduce to lowest terms. When denominators are different (unlike fractions), change them to like fractions by finding LCD using inspection or prime numbers. Then add (or subtract) the numerators, place total over LCD, and reduce to lowest terms.	$\frac{4}{9} + \frac{1}{9} = \frac{5}{9}$ $\frac{4}{9} - \frac{1}{9} = \frac{3}{9} = \frac{1}{3}$ $\frac{4}{5} + \frac{2}{7} = \frac{28}{35} + \frac{10}{35} = \frac{38}{35} = 1\frac{3}{35}$
Prime numbers, p. 42	Whole numbers larger than 1 that are only divisible by itself and 1.	2, 3, 5, 7, 11
LCD by prime numbers, p. 42	1. Copy denominators and arrange them in a separate row.	$\frac{1}{3} + \frac{1}{6} + \frac{1}{8} + \frac{1}{12} + \frac{1}{9}$

(*continues*)

CHAPTER ORGANIZER AND REFERENCE GUIDE (CONTINUED)

TOPIC	KEY POINT, PROCEDURE, FORMULA	EXAMPLE(S) TO ILLUSTRATE SITUATION
	2. Divide denominators by smallest prime number that will divide evenly into at least two numbers. 3. Continue until no prime number divides evenly into at least two numbers. 4. Multiply all the numbers in the divisors and last row to find LCD. 5. Raise fractions so each has a common denominator and complete computation.	2 / 3 6 8 12 9 2 / 3 3 4 6 9 3 / 3 3 2 3 9 1 1 2 1 3 $2 \times 2 \times 3 \times 1 \times 1 \times 2 \times 1 \times 3 = 72$
Adding mixed numbers, p. 43	1. Add fractions. 2. Add whole numbers. 3. Combine totals of Steps 1 and 2. If denominators are different, a common denominator must be found. Answer cannot be left as improper fraction.	$1\frac{4}{7} + 1\frac{3}{7}$ Step 1: $\frac{4}{7} + \frac{3}{7} = \frac{7}{7}$ Step 2: $1 + 1 = 2$ Step 3: $2\frac{7}{7} = 3$
Adding mixed numbers as improper fractions, p. 43	1. Convert mixed numbers into improper fractions with same LCD. 2. Perform addition. 3. Convert result back into mixed number.	$\frac{7+4}{7} + \frac{7+3}{7} = \frac{11+10}{7} = \frac{21}{7} = 3$
Subtracting mixed numbers, p. 44	1. Subtract fractions. 2. If necessary, borrow from whole numbers. 3. Subtract whole numbers and fractions if borrowing was necessary. 4. Reduce fractions to lowest terms. If denominators are different, a common denominator must be found.	$12\frac{2}{5} - 7\frac{3}{5}$ $11\frac{7}{5} - 7\frac{3}{5}$ $= 4\frac{4}{5}$ Due to borrowing $\frac{5}{5}$ from number 12 $\frac{5}{5} + \frac{2}{5} = \frac{7}{5}$ The whole number is now 11.
Subtracting mixed numbers as improper fractions, p. 45	1. Convert mixed numbers into improper fractions with same LCD. 2. Perform subtraction. 3. Convert result back into mixed number.	$\frac{60+2}{5} - \frac{35+3}{5} = \frac{62-38}{5} = \frac{24}{5} = 4\frac{4}{5}$
Multiplying proper fractions, p. 47	1. Multiply numerators and denominators. 2. Reduce answer to lowest terms or use cancellation method.	$\frac{4}{\cancel{7}_1} \times \frac{\cancel{7}^1}{9} = \frac{4}{9}$
Multiplying mixed numbers, p. 48	1. Convert mixed numbers to improper fractions. 2. Multiply numerators and denominators. 3. Reduce answer to lowest terms or use cancellation method.	$1\frac{1}{8} \times 2\frac{5}{8}$ $\frac{9}{8} \times \frac{21}{8} = \frac{189}{64} = 2\frac{61}{64}$
Dividing proper fractions, p. 48	1. Invert divisor. 2. Multiply. 3. Reduce answer to lowest terms or use cancellation method.	$\frac{1}{4} \div \frac{1}{8} = \frac{1}{\cancel{4}_1} \times \frac{\cancel{8}^2}{1} = 2$
Dividing mixed numbers, p. 49	1. Convert mixed numbers to improper fractions. 2. Invert divisor and multiply. If final answer is an improper fraction, reduce to lowest terms by finding greatest common divisor or using the cancellation method.	$1\frac{1}{2} \div 1\frac{5}{8} = \frac{3}{2} \div \frac{13}{8}$ $= \frac{3}{\cancel{2}_1} \times \frac{\cancel{8}^4}{13}$ $= \frac{12}{13}$

(*continues*)

CHAPTER ORGANIZER AND REFERENCE GUIDE (CONCLUDED)

Topic	Key point, procedure, formula	Example(s) to illustrate situation
Using calculator to perform operations with fractions and mixed numbers, p. 50	1. Convert improper fractions into mixed numbers. 2. Perform algebraic operations. 3. Convert results into standard form, in sequence from right to left.	$\frac{15}{8}$ = 15 ab/c 8 = 1 r 7 r 8 Answer is $1\frac{7}{8}$. $2\frac{3}{4} - 1\frac{8}{9}$ = 2 ab/c 3 ab/c 4 − 1 ab/c 8 ab/c 9 = 31 r 36 Answer is $\frac{31}{36}$. $3\frac{1}{4} \times 2\frac{1}{2} + \frac{13}{8}$ = 3 ab/c 1 ab/c 4 × 2 ab/c 1 ab/c 2 + 13 ab/c 8 = 9 r 3 r 4 Answer is $9\frac{3}{4}$.
Key terms	Cancellation, p. 48 Common denominator, p. 41 Denominator, p. 36 Equivalent, p. 39 Fraction, p. 36 Greatest common divisor, p. 38	Higher terms, p. 39 Improper fraction, p. 37 Least common denominator (LCD), p. 41 Like fractions, p. 40 Lowest terms, p. 38 Mixed numbers, p. 37 Numerator, p. 36 Prime numbers, p. 42 Proper fractions, p. 37 Reciprocal, p. 48 Unlike fractions, p. 40

Note: For how to dissect and solve a word problem, see page 49.

CRITICAL THINKING DISCUSSION QUESTIONS

1. What are the steps to convert improper fractions to whole or mixed numbers? Give an example of how you could use this conversion procedure when you eat at Pizza Hut.
2. What are the steps to convert mixed numbers to improper fractions? Show how you could use this conversion procedure when you order doughnuts at Tim Hortons.
3. What is the greatest common divisor? How could you use the greatest common divisor to write an advertisement showing that 35 out of 60 people prefer tea to coffee?
4. Explain the step approach for finding the greatest common divisor. How could you use the tea-coffee example in Question 3 to illustrate the step approach?
5. Explain the steps of adding or subtracting unlike fractions. Using a ruler, measure the heights of two different-size cans of food and show how to calculate the difference in height.
6. What is a prime number? Using the two cans in Question 5, show how you could use prime numbers to calculate the LCD.
7. Explain the steps for multiplying proper fractions and mixed numbers. Assume you went to Staples (a stationery superstore, also known as Business Depot). Give an example showing the multiplying of proper fractions and mixed numbers.

END-OF-CHAPTER PROBLEMS

DRILL PROBLEMS

Identify the following types of fractions:

2–1. $\frac{1}{9}$ **2–2.** $12\frac{5}{7}$ **2–3.** $\frac{16}{11}$

Convert the following to mixed numbers:

2–4. $\frac{58}{7}$ **2–5.** $\frac{921}{15}$

Convert the following to improper fractions:

2–6. $8\frac{9}{10}$ **2–7.** $19\frac{2}{3}$

Reduce the following to the lowest terms. Show how to calculate the greatest common divisor by the step approach.

2–8. $\frac{16}{38}$ **2–9.** $\frac{44}{52}$

Convert the following to higher terms:

2–10. $\frac{7}{8} = \frac{\quad}{80}$

Determine the LCD of the following **(a)** by inspection and **(b)** by division of prime numbers:

2–11. $\frac{3}{4}, \frac{7}{12}, \frac{5}{6}, \frac{1}{5}$ **Check**

Inspection

2–12. $\frac{5}{6}, \frac{7}{18}, \frac{5}{9}, \frac{2}{72}$ **Check**

Inspection

2–13. $\frac{1}{4}, \frac{3}{32}, \frac{5}{48}, \frac{1}{8}$ **Check**

Inspection

Add the following and reduce to lowest terms:

2–14. $\frac{4}{9} + \frac{2}{9}$ **2–15.** $\frac{3}{7} + \frac{4}{21}$ **2–16.** $6\frac{1}{8} + 4\frac{3}{8}$ **2–17.** $6\frac{3}{8} + 9\frac{1}{24}$ **2–18.** $9\frac{9}{10} + 6\frac{7}{10}$

Subtract the following and reduce to lowest terms. Use both your calculator and the algebraic method.

2–19. $\frac{11}{12} - \frac{1}{12}$ **2–20.** $14\frac{3}{8} - 10\frac{5}{8}$ **2–21.** $12\frac{1}{9} - 4\frac{2}{3}$

Multiply the following and reduce to lowest terms. Do not use the cancellation technique for these problems. Use your calculator to check results.

2–22. $17 \times \frac{4}{2}$ **2–23.** $\frac{5}{6} \times \frac{3}{8}$ **2–24.** $8\frac{7}{8} \times 64$

Multiply the following. Use the cancellation technique.

2–25. $\frac{4}{10} \times \frac{30}{60} \times \frac{6}{10}$

2–26. $3\frac{3}{4} \times \frac{8}{9} \times 4\frac{9}{12}$

Divide the following and reduce to lowest terms. Use the cancellation technique as needed.

2–27. $\frac{12}{9} \div 4$

2–28. $18 \div \frac{1}{5}$

2–29. $4\frac{2}{3} \div 12$

2–30. $3\frac{5}{6} \div 3\frac{1}{2}$

ADDITIONAL DRILL PROBLEMS

2–31. Identify the type of fraction—proper, improper, or mixed number:

a. $\frac{14}{9}$ **b.** $\frac{26}{27}$ **c.** $\frac{29}{27}$ **d.** $9\frac{3}{11}$ **e.** $\frac{18}{5}$ **f.** $\frac{30}{37}$

2–32. Convert to a mixed number:

a. $\frac{29}{4}$ **b.** $\frac{137}{8}$ **c.** $\frac{27}{5}$ **d.** $\frac{29}{9}$ **e.** $\frac{71}{8}$ **f.** $\frac{43}{6}$

2–33. Convert the mixed number to an improper fraction:

a. $7\frac{1}{5}$ **b.** $12\frac{3}{11}$ **c.** $4\frac{3}{7}$ **d.** $20\frac{4}{9}$ **e.** $10\frac{11}{12}$ **f.** $17\frac{2}{3}$

2–34. Tell whether the fractions in each pair are equivalent or not:

a. $\frac{3}{4}$ $\frac{9}{12}$ ________ **b.** $\frac{2}{3}$ $\frac{12}{18}$ ________ **c.** $\frac{7}{8}$ $\frac{15}{16}$ ________

d. $\frac{4}{5}$ $\frac{12}{15}$ ________ **e.** $\frac{3}{2}$ $\frac{9}{4}$ ________ **f.** $\frac{5}{8}$ $\frac{7}{11}$ ________

g. $\frac{7}{12}$ $\frac{7}{24}$ ________ **h.** $\frac{5}{4}$ $\frac{30}{24}$ ________ **i.** $\frac{10}{26}$ $\frac{12}{26}$ ________

2–35. Find the greatest common divisor by the step approach and reduce to lowest terms:

a. $\frac{36}{42}$ **b.** $\frac{30}{75}$ **c.** $\frac{74}{148}$ **d.** $\frac{15}{600}$ **e.** $\frac{96}{132}$ **f.** $\frac{84}{154}$

2–36. Convert to higher terms:

a. $\frac{8}{10} = \frac{\quad}{70}$ **b.** $\frac{2}{15} = \frac{\quad}{30}$ **c.** $\frac{6}{11} = \frac{\quad}{132}$ **d.** $\frac{4}{9} = \frac{\quad}{36}$ **e.** $\frac{7}{20} = \frac{\quad}{100}$ **f.** $\frac{7}{8} = \frac{\quad}{560}$

2–37. Find the least common denominator (LCD) for each of the following groups of denominators using the prime numbers:

a. 8, 16, 32 **b.** 9, 15, 20 **c.** 12, 15, 32 **d.** 7, 9, 14, 28

2–38. Add and reduce to lowest terms or change to a mixed number if needed:

a. $\frac{2}{7} + \frac{3}{7}$ **b.** $\frac{5}{12} + \frac{8}{15}$ **c.** $\frac{7}{8} + \frac{5}{12}$ **d.** $7\frac{2}{3} + 5\frac{1}{4}$ **e.** $\frac{2}{3} + \frac{4}{9} + \frac{1}{4}$

2–39. Subtract and reduce to lowest terms:

a. $\frac{5}{9} - \frac{2}{9}$ **b.** $\frac{14}{15} - \frac{4}{15}$ **c.** $\frac{8}{9} - \frac{5}{6}$ **d.** $\frac{7}{12} - \frac{9}{16}$ **e.** $33\frac{5}{8} - 27\frac{1}{2}$

f. $9 - 2\frac{3}{7}$ **g.** $15\frac{1}{3} - 9\frac{7}{12}$ **h.** $92\frac{3}{10} - 35\frac{7}{15}$ **i.** $93 - 57\frac{5}{12}$ **j.** $22\frac{5}{8} - 17\frac{1}{4}$

2–40. Multiply (use cancellation technique):

a. $\frac{6}{13} \times \frac{26}{12}$ **b.** $\frac{3}{8} \times \frac{2}{3}$ **c.** $\frac{5}{7} \times \frac{9}{10}$ **d.** $\frac{3}{4} \times \frac{9}{13} \times \frac{26}{27}$ **e.** $6\frac{2}{5} \times 3\frac{1}{8}$

f. $2\frac{2}{3} \times 2\frac{7}{10}$ **g.** $45 \times \frac{7}{9}$ **h.** $3\frac{1}{9} \times 1\frac{2}{7} \times \frac{3}{4}$ **i.** $\frac{3}{4} \times \frac{7}{9} \times 3\frac{1}{3}$ **j.** $\frac{1}{8} \times 6\frac{2}{3} \times \frac{1}{10}$

2–41. Multiply (do not use cancelling; reduce by finding the greatest common divisor):

a. $\frac{3}{4} \times \frac{8}{9}$ **b.** $\frac{7}{16} \times \frac{8}{13}$

2–42. Multiply or divide as indicated:

a. $\frac{25}{36} \div \frac{5}{9}$ **b.** $\frac{18}{8} \div \frac{12}{16}$ **c.** $2\frac{6}{7} \div 2\frac{2}{5}$ **d.** $3\frac{1}{4} \div 16$

e. $24 \div 1\frac{1}{3}$ **f.** $6 \times \frac{3}{2}$ **g.** $3\frac{1}{5} \times 7\frac{1}{2}$ **h.** $\frac{3}{8} \div \frac{7}{4}$

i. $9 \div 3\frac{3}{4}$ **j.** $\frac{11}{24} \times \frac{24}{33}$ **k.** $\frac{12}{14} \div 27$ **l.** $\frac{3}{5} \times \frac{2}{7} \div \frac{3}{10}$

WORD PROBLEMS

2–43. For wrapping her Christmas presents, Jane bought $\frac{1}{3}$ metre of red ribbon, $\frac{1}{2}$ metre of purple ribbon, and $\frac{3}{4}$ metre of blue ribbon. How many metres of ribbon did Jane buy?

2–44. Pete Rowe bought a new hand-held computer at Future Shop for \$399. The manufacturer offers a rebate of $\frac{1}{3}$ off the selling price. How much did Pete pay after the rebate?

2–45. The Bay pays Paul Lose \$125 per day to work in security at the airport. Paul became ill on Monday and went home after $\frac{1}{5}$ of a day. What did he earn on Monday? Assume no work, no pay.

2–46. Brian Summers visited Gold's Gym and lost $2\frac{1}{4}$ pounds in week 1, $1\frac{3}{4}$ pounds in week 2, and $\frac{5}{8}$ pound in week 3. (1 pound = about 0.45 kilograms.) What is the total weight loss for Brian (in pounds)?

2–47. Joy Lee, who works at Putnam Investments, received a cheque for \$1,600. She deposited $\frac{1}{4}$ of the cheque in her Royal Bank account. How much money does Joy have left after the deposit?

2–48. Pete Hall worked the following hours as a manager for News.com: $12\frac{1}{4}$, $5\frac{1}{4}$, $8\frac{1}{2}$, and $7\frac{1}{4}$. How many total hours did Pete work?

2–49. The June 2001 *Woodsmith* magazine tells how to build a country wall shelf. Two side panels are $\frac{3}{4} \times 7\frac{1}{2} \times 31\frac{5}{8}$ inches long. (1 inch = about 2.54 centimetres.) **(a)** What is the total length of board you will need? **(b)** If you have a board $74\frac{1}{3}$ inches long, how much of the board will remain after cutting?

2–50. Lester bought a piece of property in Huntsville, Ontario. The sides of the land measure $115\frac{1}{2}$ m, $66\frac{1}{4}$ m, $106\frac{1}{8}$ m, and $110\frac{1}{4}$ m. Lester wants to know the perimeter (sum of all sides) of his property. Can you calculate the perimeter for Lester?

2–51. A group of six students travelled to Italy. The weight of their luggage respectively was $32\frac{1}{4}$ kg; $24\frac{1}{3}$ kg; $30\frac{3}{4}$ kg; $16\frac{3}{4}$ kg; $45\frac{1}{6}$ kg; $28\frac{1}{7}$ kg. What is the average weight of the luggage per person?

2–52. From Home Depot, Pete Wong ordered $\frac{6}{7}$ of a tonne of crushed rock to make a patio. If Pete used only $\frac{3}{4}$ of the rock, how much crushed rock remains unused?

2–53. At a Wal-Mart store, a Coke dispenser held $170\frac{1}{3}$ litres of pop. During working hours, $49\frac{1}{4}$ litres were dispensed. How many litres of Coke remain?

2–54. Katie Kaminski bought a home from Century 21 in Vancouver, B.C. that is $7\frac{1}{2}$ times as expensive as the home her parents bought. Katie's parents paid $16,000 for their home. What is the cost of Katie's new home?

2–55. Ajax Company charges $150 per cord of wood. If Bill Ryan orders $3\frac{1}{2}$ cords, what will his total cost be?

2–56. Learning.com bought 90 pizzas at Pizza Hut for their holiday party. Each guest ate $\frac{1}{6}$ of a pizza and there was no pizza left over. How many guests did Learning.com have for the party?

2–57. Marc, Steven, and Daniel entered into an Internet partnership. Marc owns $\frac{1}{9}$ of Dot.com, and Steven owns $\frac{1}{4}$. What part does Daniel own?

2–58. Lionel Sullivan works for Burger King. He is paid time-and-a-half for Sundays. If Lionel works on Sunday for 6 hours at a regular pay of $8 per hour, what does he earn on Sunday?

2–59. Hertz pays Al Davis, an employee, $125 per day. Al decided to donate $\frac{1}{5}$ of a day's pay to his church. How much will Al donate?

2–60. Excel A trip from Toronto to Algonquin Provincial Park will take you $2\frac{3}{4}$ hours. Assume you have travelled $\frac{1}{11}$ of the way. How much longer will the trip take?

2–61. Excel Michael, who loves to cook, makes apple cobbler (serves 6) for his family. The recipe calls for $1\frac{1}{2}$ pounds of apples, $3\frac{1}{4}$ cups of flour, $\frac{1}{4}$ cup of margarine, $2\frac{3}{8}$ cups of sugar, and 2 teaspoons of cinnamon. Since guests are coming, Michael wants to make a cobbler that will serve 15 (or increase the recipe $2\frac{1}{2}$ times). How much of each ingredient should Michael use?

2–62. In Mr. Thistleswith's garden, two cherry trees are $3\frac{1}{3}$ metres high, two apple trees are $2\frac{1}{2}$ metres high, a plum tree is $2\frac{3}{4}$ metres high, and a pear tree is $3\frac{1}{5}$ metres high. What is the average height of the trees in Mr. Thistleswith's garden?

2–63. A marketing class at Maritime Community College conducted a viewer preference survey. The survey showed that $\frac{5}{6}$ of the people surveyed preferred DVDs to videotapes. Assume 2,400 responded to the survey. How many favoured using traditional tapes?

2–64. The price of a new Ford Explorer has increased to $1\frac{1}{4}$ times its earlier price. If the original price of the Ford Explorer was $28,000, what is the new price?

2–65. Chris Rong felled a tree that was 65 metres long. Chris decided to cut the tree into pieces $3\frac{1}{4}$ metres long. How many pieces can Chris cut from this tree?

2–66. Tempco Corporation has a machine that produces $12\frac{1}{2}$ baseball gloves each hour. In the last 2 days, the machine has run for a total of 22 hours. How many baseball gloves has Tempco produced?

2–67. McGraw-Hill publishers stores some of its inventory in a warehouse that has 14,500 square feet (about 1,347 square metres) of space. Each book requires $2\frac{1}{2}$ square feet of space. How many books can McGraw-Hill keep in this warehouse?

2–68. Alicia, an employee of Tim Hortons, receives $23\frac{1}{4}$ days per year of vacation time. So far this year she has taken $3\frac{1}{8}$ days in January, $5\frac{1}{2}$ days in May, $6\frac{1}{4}$ days in July, and $4\frac{1}{4}$ days in September. How many more days of vacation does Alicia have left?

2–69. Amazon.ca offered a new portable colour TV for $250 with a rebate of $\frac{1}{5}$ off the regular price. What is the final cost of the TV after the rebate?

2–70. Shelly Van Doren hired a contractor to refinish her kitchen. The contractor said the job would take $49\frac{1}{2}$ hours. To date, the contractor has worked the following hours:

Monday	$4\frac{1}{4}$
Tuesday	$9\frac{1}{8}$
Wednesday	$4\frac{1}{4}$
Thursday	$3\frac{1}{2}$
Friday	$10\frac{5}{8}$

How much longer should the job take to be completed?

ADDITIONAL WORD PROBLEMS

2–71. On July 2, 2001, you received a special ad from Home Depot stating that a $\frac{3}{4}$ inch × 10 feet (about 1.9 centimetres × 3 metres) piece of PVC piping is on sale for \$1.39. You plan to install the PVC piping in your basement. The measurements you have calculated include pieces with a total length of $11\frac{3}{4}$ feet, $15\frac{3}{8}$ feet, and $8\frac{5}{16}$ feet. **(a)** What is the total length of piping needed? **(b)** If you purchased a total of 40 feet of piping, how much piping will you have left over?

2–72. Loblaws plans a big sale on apples and received 950 crates from the wholesale market. Loblaws will bag these apples in plastic. Each plastic bag holds $\frac{1}{8}$ of a crate. If Loblaws has no loss to perishables, how many bags of apples can be prepared?

2–73. Police monitored the speed of cars on a city road. The measurements were as follows:

Number of cars	3	4	10	11	7	15	3	2
Speed, km/h	$50\frac{1}{3}$	$51\frac{1}{2}$	$53\frac{3}{4}$	$54\frac{1}{2}$	$56\frac{1}{3}$	$57\frac{2}{5}$	59	$62\frac{1}{4}$

What was the average speed of the cars observed?

2–74. A local Papa Gino's conducted a food survey. The survey showed that $\frac{1}{9}$ of the people surveyed preferred eating pasta to hamburger. If 5,400 responded to the survey, how many actually favoured hamburger?

2–75. Tamara, Jose, and Milton entered into a partnership that sells men's clothing on the Web. Tamara owns $\frac{3}{8}$ of the company, and Jose owns $\frac{1}{4}$. What part does Milton own?

2–76. Olga works 40 hours per week developing five projects. She spends $\frac{1}{5}$ of her time on project one, $\frac{1}{4}$ on project two, $\frac{1}{20}$ on project three, $\frac{1}{8}$ on project four, and the rest of her time on project five. How much time does Olga spend on each of the projects during the week?

2–77. A trailer carrying supplies for a Taco Bell from Toronto to Kingston will take $3\frac{1}{4}$ hours. If the truck travelled $\frac{1}{5}$ of the way, how much longer will the trip take?

2–78. Land Rover has increased the price of a Discovery II by $\frac{1}{5}$ from the original price. The original price of the Discovery II was \$30,000. What is the new price?

2–79. Linda spends $\frac{1}{2}$ of her salary to pay for her mortgage and $\frac{1}{3}$ of her salary to pay her bills. If her annual salary is \$42,000, how much money does Linda have remaining for her personal needs and savings?

2–80. Ken drove to college in $3\frac{1}{4}$ hours. How many quarter-hours is that? Show your answer as an improper fraction.

2–81. Mary looked in the refrigerator for a dozen eggs. When she found the box, only 5 eggs were left. What fractional part of the box of eggs was left?

2–82. At a recent meeting of a local Boosters Club, 17 of the 25 members attending were men. What fraction of those in attendance were men?

2–83. By weight, water is two parts out of three parts of the human body. What fraction of the body is water?

2–84. Three out of five students who begin college will continue until they receive their degree. Show in fractional form how many out of 100 beginning students will graduate.

2–85. Tina and her friends came in late to a party and found only $\frac{3}{4}$ of a pizza remaining. In order for everyone to get some pizza, she wanted to divide it into smaller pieces. If she divides the pizza into twelfths, how many pieces will she have? Show your answer in fractional form.

2–86. Sharon and Spunky noted that it took them 35 minutes to do their exercise routine. What fractional part of an hour is that? Show your answer in lowest terms.

2–87. Norman and his friend ordered several pizzas, which were all cut into eighths. The group ate 43 pieces of pizza. How many pizzas did they eat? Show your answer as a mixed number.

2–88. Dan Lund took a cross-country trip. He drove $5\frac{3}{8}$ hours on Monday, $6\frac{1}{2}$ hours on Tuesday, $9\frac{3}{4}$ hours on Wednesday, $6\frac{3}{8}$ hours on Thursday, and $10\frac{1}{4}$ hours on Friday. Find the total number of hours Dan drove in the first 5 days of his trip.

2–89. Sharon Parker bought 20 m of material to make curtains. She used $4\frac{1}{2}$ m for one bedroom window, $8\frac{3}{5}$ m for another bedroom window, and $3\frac{7}{8}$ m for a hall window. How much material did she have left?

2–90. Molly Ring visited a local gym and lost $2\frac{1}{4}$ kg the first weekend and $6\frac{1}{8}$ kg in weeks 2, 3, and 4. What is Molly's total weight loss?

2–91. Bill Williams had to drive $46\frac{1}{4}$ km to work. After driving $28\frac{5}{6}$ km he noticed he was low on gas and had to decide whether he should stop to fill the gas tank. How many more kilometres does Bill have to drive to get to work?

2–92. Alpa's Lumber Yard purchased $52\frac{1}{2}$ cords of lumber on Monday and $48\frac{3}{4}$ cords on Tuesday. It sold $21\frac{3}{8}$ cords on Friday. How many cords of lumber remain at Alpa's Lumber Yard?

2–93. At Arlen Oil Company, where Dave Bursett is the service manager, it took $42\frac{1}{3}$ hours to clean five boilers. After a new cleaning tool was purchased, the time for cleaning five boilers was reduced to $37\frac{4}{9}$ hours. How much time was saved?

2–94. Mary Smith plans to make 12 meatloafs to store in her freezer. Each meatloaf requires $2\frac{1}{4}$ kg of ground beef. How much ground beef does Mary need?

2–95. Judy Carter purchased a real estate lot for \$24,000. She sold it 2 years later for $1\frac{5}{8}$ times as much as she had paid for it. What was the selling price?

2–96. Lynn Clarkson saw an ad for a camcorder that cost \$980. She knew of a discount store that would sell it to her for a markdown of $\frac{3}{20}$ off the advertised price. How much is the discount she can get?

2–97. To raise money for their club, the members of the Marketing Club purchased 68 bushels of popcorn to resell. (A bushel represents a volume of about 0.04 cubic metres.) They plan to repackage the popcorn in bags that hold $\frac{2}{21}$ of a bushel each. How many bags of popcorn will they be able to fill?

2–98. Richard Tracy paid a total of \$375 for stocks costing $\$9\frac{3}{8}$ per share. How many shares did he purchase?

2–99. While training for a marathon, Kristin Woods jogged $7\frac{3}{4}$ km per hour for $2\frac{2}{3}$ hours. How many kilometres did Kristin jog?

2–100. On a map, 1 cm represents 240 km. How many kilometres are represented by $\frac{3}{8}$ of a centimetre?

CHALLENGE PROBLEMS

2–101. In one of the provinces, the government wants to allot $\frac{1}{6}$ of the total PST collections to public education. The total PST collected is \$2,472,000. How much will go to education?

2–102. Ikea offers you a parts list for an entertainment centre project. Included in the parts list were the following:

Two $\frac{3}{4} \times 15\frac{7}{8} \times 59\frac{1}{2}$ cm side panels

Three $\frac{3}{4} \times 15\frac{7}{8} \times 35\frac{7}{8}$ cm shelves

Two $\frac{3}{4} \times 15\frac{7}{8} \times 17\frac{9}{16}$ cm shelf/partition

The $\frac{3}{4} \times 15\frac{7}{8}$ cm wood comes in 2 m lengths.

a. What is the total length of material needed?

b. How many 2 m lengths must be purchased?

c. How many centimetres will be left over?

2–103. Jack MacLean has entered into a real estate development partnership with Bill Lyons and June Reese. Bill owns $\frac{1}{4}$ of the partnership, while June has a $\frac{1}{5}$ interest. The partners will divide all profits on the basis of their fractional ownership.

The partnership bought 900 acres of land and plans to subdivide each lot into $2\frac{1}{4}$ acres. (An acre is about 0.4 hectares.) Homes in the area have been selling for \$240,000. By time of completion, Jack estimates the price of each home will increase by $\frac{1}{3}$ of the current value. The partners sent a survey to 12,000 potential customers to see whether they should heat the homes with oil or gas. One-fourth of the customers responded by indicating a 5-to-1 preference for oil. The partnership estimates its profit per home will be $\frac{1}{8}$ the selling price of each home.

From the above, please calculate the following:

a. Number of homes to be built.

b. Selling price of each home.

c. **(1).** Number of people responding to survey.

(2). Number of people desiring oil.

d. Amount of profit Jack will receive from the sale of homes.

SUMMARY PRACTICE TEST

Identify the following types of fractions. (p. 36)

1. $7\frac{9}{10}$ **2.** $\frac{3}{7}$ **3.** $\frac{12}{11}$

4. Convert the following to a mixed number. (p. 37)

$$\frac{138}{5}$$

5. Convert the following to an improper fraction. (p. 38)

$$7\frac{3}{4}$$

6. Calculate the greatest common divisor of the following by the step approach and reduce to lowest terms. (p. 38)

$$\frac{98}{140}$$

7. Convert the following to higher terms. (p. 39)

$$\frac{11}{33} = \frac{?}{264}$$

8. Find the LCD of the following by using prime numbers. Show your work. (p. 42)

$$\frac{1}{4} + \frac{1}{7} + \frac{1}{2} + \frac{1}{14}$$

9. Subtract the following. (p. 44)

$$\begin{array}{r} 14\frac{7}{9} \\ -\ 8\frac{5}{6} \\ \hline \end{array}$$

Complete the following using the cancellation technique. (p. 48)

10. $\frac{9}{14} \times \frac{2}{4} \times \frac{4}{6}$ **11.** $7\frac{3}{8} \times \frac{16}{19}$ **12.** $\frac{3}{4} \div 3$

13. A trip to Regina from Medicine Hat will take you $8\frac{1}{2}$ hours. If you have travelled $\frac{1}{5}$ of the way, how much longer will the trip take? (p. 48)

14. Chairs.com produces 310 beanbag chairs per hour. If the machine runs $40\frac{1}{2}$ hours, how many chairs will the machine produce? (p. 48)

15. A taste-testing survey of Nature Foods showed that $\frac{2}{5}$ of the people surveyed preferred the taste of soy milk to regular milk. If 60,000 people were in the survey, how many favoured soy milk? How many chose regular milk? (p. 47)

16. Lori Sharpe, an employee of Orillia Rent-A-Car, worked $7\frac{1}{4}$ hours on Monday, $4\frac{1}{4}$ hours on Tuesday, $8\frac{1}{2}$ hours on Wednesday, $8\frac{1}{4}$ hours on Thursday, and 8 hours on Friday. How many total hours did Lori work during the week? (p. 43)

17. Clairol offered a $\frac{1}{4}$ rebate on its \$20 hair dryer. Melissa bought a Clairol hair dryer. What did Melissa pay after the rebate? (p. 47)

SOLUTIONS TO PRACTICE QUIZZES

LU 2–1

1. **a.** Proper
   b. Improper
   c. Mixed
   d. Improper

2. $17\frac{7}{9}$

$$\begin{array}{r} 17 \\ 9\overline{)160} \\ \underline{9} \\ 70 \\ \underline{63} \\ 7 \end{array}$$

3. $\dfrac{(9 \times 8) + 5}{8} = \dfrac{77}{8}$

4. **a.**

$$\begin{array}{r} 1 \\ 24\overline{)40} \\ \underline{24} \\ 16 \end{array} \rightarrow \begin{array}{r} 1 \\ 16\overline{)24} \\ \underline{16} \\ 8 \end{array} \rightarrow \begin{array}{r} 2 \\ 8\overline{)16} \\ \underline{16} \\ 0 \end{array}$$

8 is greatest common divisor.

$$\frac{24 \div 8}{40 \div 8} = \frac{3}{5}$$

b.

$$\begin{array}{r} 1 \\ 91\overline{)156} \\ \underline{91} \\ 65 \end{array} \rightarrow \begin{array}{r} 1 \\ 65\overline{)91} \\ \underline{65} \\ 26 \end{array} \rightarrow \begin{array}{r} 2 \\ 26\overline{)65} \\ \underline{52} \\ 13 \end{array} \rightarrow \begin{array}{r} 2 \\ 13\overline{)26} \\ \underline{26} \\ 0 \end{array}$$

13 is greatest common divisor.

$$\frac{91 \div 13}{156 \div 13} = \frac{7}{12}$$

5. **a.** $\begin{array}{r} 10 \\ 20\overline{)200} \end{array}$ $\quad 10 \times 14 = 140 \quad \dfrac{14}{20} = \dfrac{140}{200}$

   b. $\begin{array}{r} 6 \\ 10\overline{)60} \end{array}$ $\quad 6 \times 8 = 48 \quad \dfrac{8}{10} = \dfrac{48}{60}$

LU 2–2

1.

$$\begin{array}{r|rrrr} 2 & 12 & 9 & 6 & 4 \\ 2 & 6 & 9 & 3 & 2 \\ 3 & 3 & 9 & 3 & 1 \\ & 1 & 1 & 1 & 1 \end{array}$$

LCD = $2 \times 2 \times 3 \times 1 \times 3 \times 1 \times 1 = 36$

2. **a.** $\dfrac{3}{40} + \dfrac{2}{5} = \dfrac{3}{40} + \dfrac{16}{40} = \dfrac{19}{40}$

$$\left(\frac{2}{5} = \frac{?}{40} \quad 40 \div 5 = 8 \quad 8 \times 2 = 16\right)$$

b.

$$\begin{array}{r} 2\frac{3}{4} \\ +\,6\frac{1}{20} \\ \hline \end{array} \qquad \begin{array}{r} 2\frac{15}{20} \\ +\,6\frac{1}{20} \\ \hline 8\frac{16}{20} = 8\frac{4}{5} \end{array}$$

$$\frac{3}{4} = \frac{?}{20}$$

$20 \div 4 = 5$

$5 \times 3 = 15$

3. a.
$$\frac{6}{7} = \frac{24}{28}$$
$$-\frac{1}{4} = -\frac{7}{28}$$
$$\frac{17}{28}$$

b.
$$8\frac{1}{4} = 8\frac{7}{28} = 7\frac{35}{28} \leftarrow \left(\frac{28}{28} + \frac{7}{28}\right)$$
$$-3\frac{9}{28} = -3\frac{9}{28} = -3\frac{9}{28}$$
$$4\frac{26}{28} = 4\frac{13}{14}$$

c.
$$3\frac{4}{4}$$ Note how we showed the 4 as $3\frac{4}{4}$.
$$-1\frac{3}{4}$$
$$2\frac{1}{4}$$

4. Computerland's total square-metrage for customer service:

THE FACTS	SOLVING FOR?	STEPS TO TAKE	KEY POINTS
Total square-metrage: $S = 660\frac{1}{4}$ m² *Hardware:* $H = 201\frac{1}{8}$ m² *Software:* $W = 242\frac{1}{4}$ m²	Total square-metrage for customer service. $C = ?$	Total floor space − Total hardware and software floor space = Total customer service floor space. $C = S - (H + W)$	Denominators must be the same before adding or subtracting fractions.

Steps to solving problem

1. Calculate the total square-metrage of hardware and software.

$$H \quad 201\frac{1}{8} = 201\frac{1}{8} \text{ (hardware)}$$
$$+W \quad +242\frac{1}{4} = +242\frac{2}{8} \text{ (software)}$$
$$443\frac{3}{8}$$

2. Calculate the total square-metrage for customer service.

$$660\frac{1}{4} = 660\frac{2}{8} = 659\frac{10}{8} \text{ (total square-metrage)}$$
$$-443\frac{3}{8} = -443\frac{3}{8} = -443\frac{3}{8} \text{ (hardware plus software)}$$
$$216\frac{7}{8} \text{ m}^2 \text{ (customer service)}$$

LU 2–3

1. a. $\frac{\overset{1}{\cancel{2}}}{\ldots}$ $\frac{\cancel{4}}{\cancel{8}} \times \frac{\cancel{4}}{\cancel{6}} = \frac{1}{3}$ (4/8 reduced to 2/2 → 1/1; 4/6 reduced to 1/3)

b. $\overset{5}{\cancel{35}} \times \frac{4}{\underset{1}{\cancel{7}}} = 20$

2. $\frac{14}{15} \times \frac{7}{10} = \frac{98 \div 2}{150 \div 2} = \frac{49}{75}$

$$98\overline{)150} = 1,\ 150 - 98 = 52 \rightarrow 52\overline{)98} = 1,\ 98 - 52 = 46 \rightarrow 46\overline{)52} = 1,\ 52 - 46 = 6 \rightarrow 6\overline{)46} = 7,\ 46 - 42 = 4 \rightarrow 4\overline{)6} = 1,\ 6 - 4 = 2 \rightarrow 2\overline{)4} = 2,\ 4 - 4 = 0$$

3. a. $\frac{1}{9} \times \frac{6}{5} = \frac{6 \div 3}{45 \div 3} = \frac{2}{15}$ b. $\frac{51}{5} \times \frac{9}{5} = \frac{459}{25} = 18\frac{9}{25}$

4. Total cost of Jill's new home:

THE FACTS	SOLVING FOR?	STEPS TO TAKE	KEY POINTS
J: Jill's mobile home: $8\frac{1}{8}$ as expensive as her brother's. *B: Brother paid:* $16,000.	Total cost of Jill's new home. *J* = ?	$8\frac{1}{8}$ × Total cost of Jill's brother's mobile home = Total cost of Jill's new home. $J = \frac{1}{8} \times B$	Cancelling is an alternative to reducing.

Steps to solving problem

1. Convert $8\frac{1}{8}$ to a mixed number. $\frac{65}{8}$

2. Calculate the total cost of Jill's home. $J = \frac{65}{\cancel{8}_1} \times \cancel{\$16{,}000}^{\$2{,}000} = \$130{,}000$

LU 2–4

1. 1 ab/c 3 + 4 ab/c 7 + 8 ab/c 15 + 1 ab/c 2 ab/c 3 + 16 ab/c 87 = 3 r 293 r 1015

Answer: $3\frac{293}{1{,}015}$

2. 1 ab/c 8 × 5 ab/c 165 + 3 ab/c 14 = 403 r 1848

Answer: $\frac{403}{1{,}848}$

3. 17 ab/c 125 ÷ 13 ab/c 15 – 1 ab/c 7 = 32 r 2275

Answer: $\frac{32}{2{,}275}$

4. 39 ab/c 14 = 2 r 11 r 14

Answer: $2\frac{11}{14}$

Business Math Scrapbook

WITH INTERNET APPLICATION

Putting Your Skills to Work

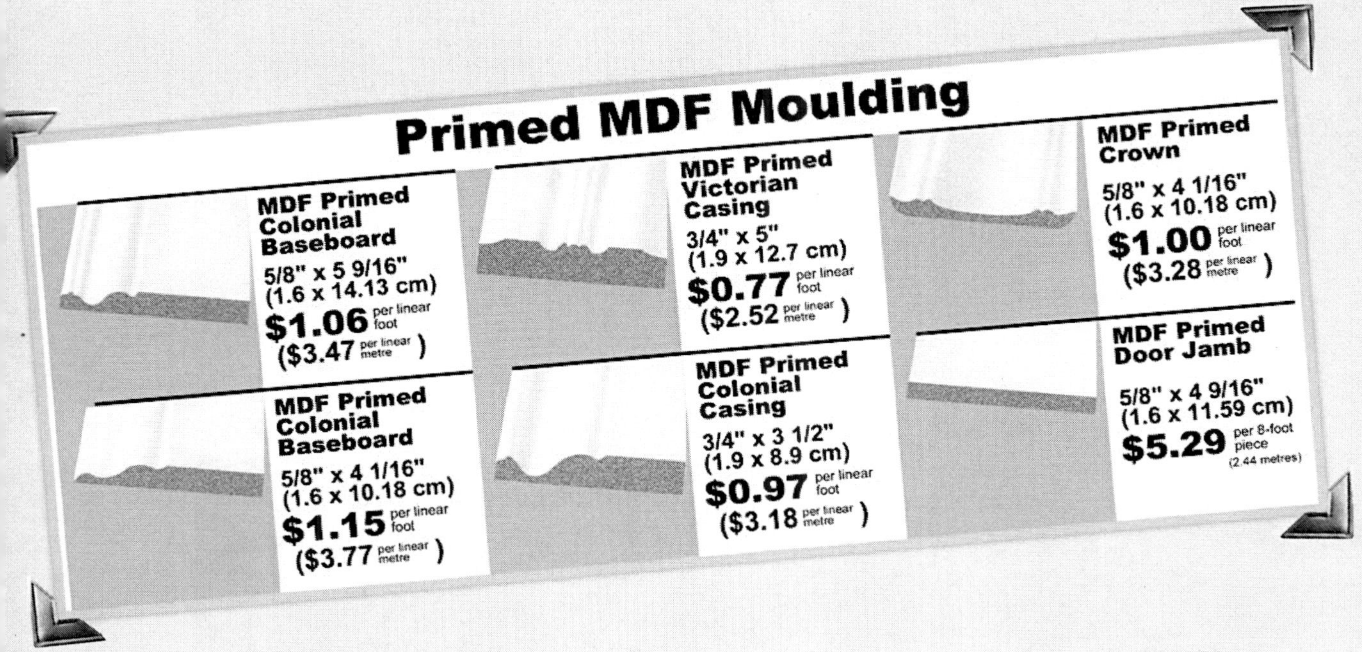

PROJECT A

Home building supply centres often advertise different types of MDF Mouldings. What is the difference in dimensions of moulding styles? Visit Web sites of your local Home Hardware and RONA and evaluate the selection of mouldings offered by them. Please note that some measurements are shown in feet and inches. Convert them into metres and centimetres. (1 foot = 0.3048 metre, 1 inch = 2.54 centimetres.)

Decimals

3

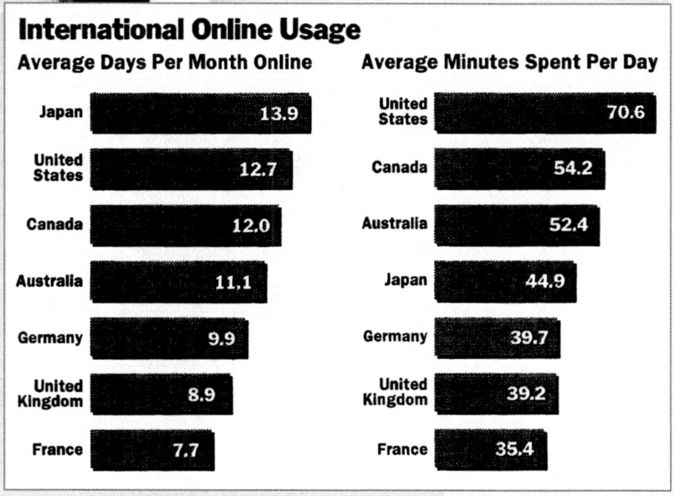

Source: Media Metrix (www.mediametrix.com). © 2000 Dow Jones & Company, Inc.

LEARNING UNIT OBJECTIVES

LU 3–1: Rounding Decimals; Fraction and Decimal Conversions

- Explain the place values of whole numbers and decimals; round decimals (p. 68).
- Convert decimal fractions to decimals, proper fractions to decimals, mixed numbers to decimals, and pure and mixed decimals to decimal fractions (p. 70).

LU 3–2: Adding, Subtracting, Multiplying, and Dividing Decimals

- Add, subtract, multiply, and divide decimals (p. 73).
- Complete decimal applications in foreign currency (p. 75).
- Multiply and divide decimals by shortcut methods (p. 76).

LU 3–3: Using a Calculator to Perform Operations with Decimals

- Converting fractions to decimals and decimals to fractions (p. 78).
- Adding, subtracting, multiplying, and dividing decimals (p. 78).

In Chapter 2 you learned about fractions. As you probably know, prior to the year 2001, all stock exchange quotes were given in fractional terms. However, beginning in 2001, all stock exchange quotes are expressed in decimals. This means that a stock such as IBM will be now quoted at $110.55.

Chapter 2 introduced the 47.9 gram bag of M&M's® shown in Table 3.1. Note that in the table we give the fractional breakdown of the six colours in the 47.9 gram bag and express the values in decimals. We have rounded the decimal equivalents to the nearest hundredth.

This chapter is divided into three Learning Units. The first Unit discusses rounding decimals, converting fractions to decimals, and converting decimals to fractions. The second Unit shows you how to add, subtract, multiply, and divide decimals, along with some shortcuts for multiplying and dividing decimals. Added to this Unit is a global application of decimals dealing with foreign exchange rates. The third Unit illustrates how to use a calculator for operations with decimals.

One of the most common uses of decimals occurs when we spend dollars and cents, which is a *decimal number.* A **decimal fraction,** then, is a decimal number with digits to the right of a *decimal point,* indicating that decimals, like fractions, are parts of a whole that are less than one. Thus, we can interchange the terms *decimals* and *decimal numbers.* Remembering this will avoid confusion between the terms *decimal, decimal number,* and *decimal point.*

LEARNING UNIT 3–1
ROUNDING DECIMALS; FRACTION AND DECIMAL CONVERSIONS

Remember to read the decimal point as *and.*

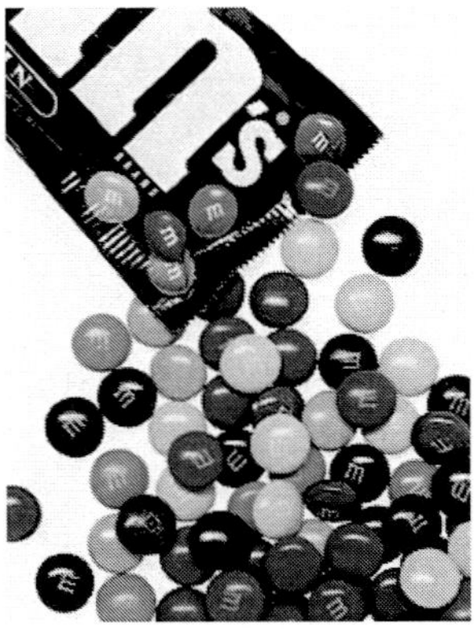

TABLE 3–1
ANALYZING A BAG OF M&M'S®

Colour*	Fraction	Decimal
Yellow	$\frac{18}{55}$	.33
Red	$\frac{10}{55}$	.18
Blue	$\frac{9}{55}$	.16
Orange	$\frac{7}{55}$	.13
Brown	$\frac{6}{55}$	.11
Green	$\frac{5}{55}$	.09
Total	$\frac{55}{55} = 1$	1.00

*The colour ratios currently given are a sample used for educational purposes. They do not represent the manufacturer's colour ratios.

In Chapter 1 we stated that the **decimal point** is the centre of the decimal numbering system. So far we have studied the whole numbers to the left of the decimal point and the parts of whole numbers called fractions. We also learned that the position of the digits in a whole number gives the place values of the digits (Figure 1.1). Now we will study the position (place values) of the digits to the right of the decimal point (Figure 3.1). Note that the words to the right of the decimal point end in *ths.*

You should understand the relationship of the place values of the digits on either side of the decimal point. If you move a digit to the left of the decimal point by place (ones, tens, and so on), you *increase* its value 10 times for each place. If you move a digit to the right of the decimal point by place (tenths, hundredths, and so on), you *decrease* its value 10 times for each place. This is why the decimal point is the centre of the decimal system.

FIGURE 3–1
Decimal place-value chart

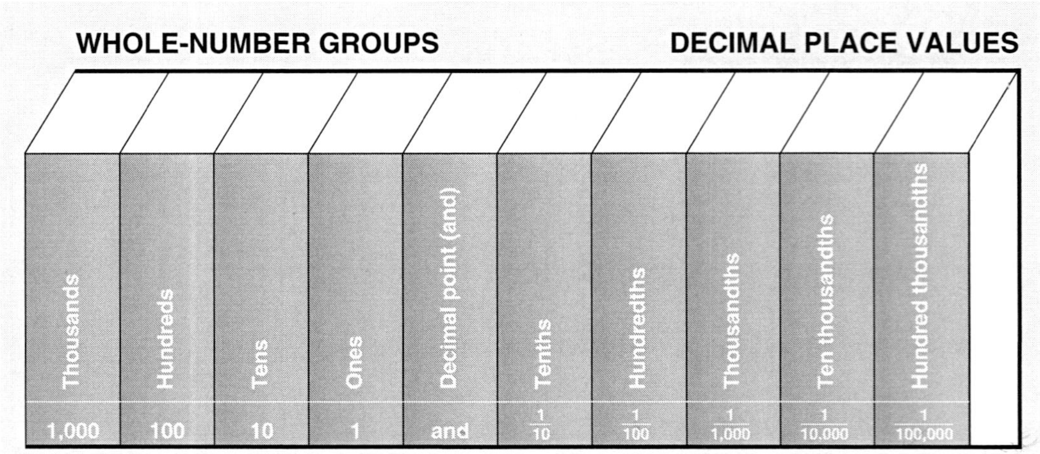

EXAMPLES

$.04 → The 4 is in the hundred*ths* place value.

1.527 → The 5 is in the ten*ths* place value.

2.8394 → The 4 is in the ten thousand*ths* place value.

.33 → The thirty-three hundred*ths* represents the yellow M&M's® in our bag of 55.

49.7 g → The forty-nine grams and seven ten*ths* of another gram is the weight of our bag of M&M's®.

Do you recall from Chapter 1 how you used a place-value chart to read or write whole numbers in verbal form? To read or write decimal numbers, you read or write the decimal number as if it were a whole number. Then you use the name of the decimal place of the last digit as given in Figure 3.1. For example, you would read or write the decimal .0796 as "seven hundred ninety-six ten thousandths" (the last digit, 6, is in the ten thousandths place).

To read a decimal with four or fewer whole numbers, you can also refer to Figure 3.1. For larger whole numbers, refer to the whole-number place-value chart in Chapter 1 (Figure 1.1). For example, from Figure 3.1 you would read the number 126.2864 as "one hundred twenty-six and two thousand eight hundred sixty-four ten thousandths." Remember that the *and* is the decimal point.

Now let's round decimals. Rounding decimals is similar to the rounding of whole numbers that you learned in Chapter 1.

ROUNDING DECIMALS

From Table 3.1, you know that the 49.7 gram bag of M&M's® introduced in Chapter 2 contained $\frac{18}{55}$, or .33, yellow M&M's®. The .33 was rounded to the nearest hundredth. **Rounding decimals** involves the following steps:

ROUNDING DECIMALS TO A SPECIFIED PLACE VALUE

Step 1. Identify the place value of the digit you want to round.

Step 2. If the digit to the right of the identified digit in Step 1 is 5 or more, increase the identified digit by 1. If the digit to the right is less than 5, do not change the identified digit.

Step 3. Drop all digits to the right of the identified digit.

Let's practise rounding by using the $\frac{18}{55}$ yellow M&M's® that we rounded to .33 in Table 3.1. Before we rounded $\frac{18}{55}$ to .33, the number we rounded was .3272727.

EXAMPLE

Round .3272727 to nearest hundredth.

Step 1. .3272727 The identified digit is 2, which is in the hundredths place (two places to the right of the decimal point).

Step 2. → The digit to the right of 2 is more than 5 (7). Thus, 2, the identified digit in Step 1, is changed to 3.

.3372727

Step 3. .33 Drop all other digits to the right of the identified digit 3.

We could also round the .3272727 M&M's® to the nearest tenth or thousandth as follows:

Tenth	or	Thousandth
.3272727 → .3		.3272727 → .327

OTHER EXAMPLES

Round to nearest dollar:	$166.39 →	$166
Round to nearest cent:	$1,196.885 →	$1,196.89
Round to nearest hundredth:	$38.563 →	$38.56
Round to nearest thousandth:	$1,432.9981 →	$1,432.998

The rules for rounding can differ with the situation in which rounding is used. For example, have you ever bought one item from a supermarket produce department that was marked "3 for $1" and noticed what the cashier charged you? One item marked "3 for $1" would not cost you $33\frac{1}{3}$ cents rounded to 33 cents. You will pay 34 cents. Many retail stores round to the next cent even if the digit following the identified digit is less than $\frac{1}{2}$ of a penny. In this text we round on the concept of 5 or more.

FRACTION AND DECIMAL CONVERSIONS

In business operations we must frequently convert fractions to decimal numbers and decimal numbers to fractions. This section begins by discussing three types of fraction-to-decimal conversions. Then we discuss converting pure and mixed decimals to decimal fractions.

Converting Decimal Fractions to Decimals

From Figure 3.1 you can see that a decimal fraction (expressed in the digits to the right of the decimal point) is a fraction with a denominator that has a power of 10, such as $\frac{1}{10}$, $\frac{17}{100}$, and $\frac{23}{1,000}$. To convert a decimal fraction to a decimal, follow these steps:

CONVERTING DECIMAL FRACTIONS TO DECIMALS

Step 1. Count the number of zeros in the denominator.

Step 2. Place the numerator of the decimal fraction to the right of the decimal point the same number of places as you have zeros in the denominator. (The number of zeros in the denominator gives the number of digits your decimal has to the right of the decimal point.) Do not go over the total number of denominator zeros.

Now let's change $\frac{3}{10}$ and its higher multiples of 10 to decimals.

EXAMPLES

Verbal form	Decimal fraction	Decimal	Number of decimal places to right of decimal point
a. Three tenths	$\frac{3}{10}$	.3	1
b. Three hundredths	$\frac{3}{100}$	.03	2
c. Three thousandths	$\frac{3}{1,000}$	.003	3
d. Three ten thousandths	$\frac{3}{10,000}$	.0003	4

Note how we show the different values of the decimal fractions above in decimals. The zeros after the decimal point and before the number 3 indicate these values. If you added zeros after the number 3, you do not change the value. Thus, the numbers .3, .30, and .300 have the same value. So 3 tenths of a pizza, 30 hundredths of a pizza, and 300 thousandths of a pizza are the same total amount of pizza. The first pizza is sliced into 10 pieces. The second pizza is sliced into 100 pieces. The third pizza is sliced into 1,000 pieces. Also, we didn't need to place a zero to the left of the decimal point.

Converting Proper Fractions to Decimals

Recall from Chapter 2 that proper fractions are fractions with a value less than 1. That is, the numerator of the fraction is smaller than its denominator. How can we convert these proper fractions to decimals? Since proper fractions are a form of division, it is possible to convert proper fractions to decimals by carrying out the division.

> **CONVERTING PROPER FRACTIONS TO DECIMALS**
>
> **Step 1.** Divide the numerator of the fraction by its denominator. (If necessary, add a decimal point and zeros to the number in the numerator.)
>
> **Step 2.** Round as necessary.

EXAMPLES

$\frac{3}{4} = 4\overline{)3.00}$ = .75

```
   .75
4)3.00
  2 8
   20
   20
```

$\frac{3}{8} = 8\overline{)3.000}$ = .375

```
   .375
8)3.000
  2 4
   60
   56
    40
    40
```

$\frac{1}{3} = 3\overline{)1.000}$ = .333

```
   .333
3)1.000
   9
   10
    9
    10
     9
     1
```

Note that in the last example $\frac{1}{3}$, the 3 in the quotient keeps repeating itself (never ends). We call this a **repeating decimal.** The short bar over the last 3 means that the number endlessly repeats.

Converting Mixed Numbers to Decimals

A mixed number, you will recall from Chapter 2, is the sum of a whole number greater than zero and a proper fraction. To convert mixed numbers to decimals, use the following steps:

> **CONVERTING MIXED NUMBERS TO DECIMALS**
>
> **Step 1.** Convert the fractional part of the mixed number to a decimal (as illustrated in the previous section).
>
> **Step 2.** Add the converted fractional part to the whole number.

EXAMPLE

$8\frac{2}{5}$ = (**Step 1**)

```
   .4
5)2.0
  2 0
```

(**Step 2**) $8 + .4 =$ 8.4

Now that we have converted fractions to decimals, let's convert decimals to fractions.

Converting Pure and Mixed Decimals to Decimal Fractions

A **pure decimal** has no whole number(s) to the left of the decimal point (.43, .458, and so on). A **mixed decimal** is a combination of a whole number and a decimal. An example of a mixed decimal follows.

EXAMPLE

737.592 = Seven hundred thirty-seven and five hundred ninety-two thousandths

Note the following conversion steps for converting pure and mixed decimals to decimal fractions:

CONVERTING PURE AND MIXED DECIMALS TO DECIMAL FRACTIONS

Step 1. Place the digits to the right of the decimal point in the numerator of the fraction. Omit the decimal point. (For a decimal fraction with a fractional part, see examples **c** and **d** below.)

Step 2. Put a 1 in the denominator of the fraction.

Step 3. Count the number of digits to the right of the decimal point. Add the same number of zeros to the denominator of the fraction. For mixed decimals, add the fraction to the whole number.

EXAMPLES

If desired, you can reduce the fractions in Step 3.

	Step 1	Step 2	Places	Step 3
a. .3	$\frac{3}{\ }$	$\frac{3}{1}$	1	$\frac{3}{10}$
b. .24	$\frac{24}{\ }$	$\frac{24}{1}$	2	$\frac{24}{100}$
c. $.24\frac{1}{2}$	$\frac{245}{\ }$	$\frac{245}{1}$	3	$\frac{245}{1{,}000}$

Before completing Step 1 in example **c**, we must remove the fractional part, convert it to a decimal ($\frac{1}{2}$ = .5), and multiply it by .01 (.5 × .01 = .005). We use .01 because the 4 of .24 is in the hundredths place. Then we add .005 + .24 = .245 (three places to right of the decimal) and complete Steps 1, 2, and 3.

	Step 1	Step 2	Places	Step 3
d. $.07\frac{1}{4}$	$\frac{725}{\ }$	$\frac{725}{1}$	4	$\frac{725}{10{,}000}$

In example **d,** be sure to convert $\frac{1}{4}$ to .25 and multiply by .01. This gives .0025. Then add .0025 to .07, which is .0725 (four places), and complete Steps 1, 2, and 3.

	Step 1	Step 2	Places	Step 3
e. 17.45	$\frac{45}{\ }$	$\frac{45}{1}$	2	$17 + \frac{45}{100} = 17\frac{45}{100}$

Example **e** is a mixed decimal. Since we substitute *and* for the decimal point, we read this mixed decimal as "seventeen and forty-five hundredths." Note that after we converted the .45 of the mixed decimals to a fraction, we added it to the whole number 17.

LU 3–1 PRACTICE QUIZ

Write the following as a decimal number.

1. Four hundred eight thousandths

Name the place position of the identified digit:

2. 6.8241 (arrow under 8) **3.** 9.3942 (arrow under 9)

Round each decimal to place indicated:

	Tenth	Thousandth
4. .62768	**a.**	**b.**
5. .68341	**a.**	**b.**

Convert the following to decimals:

6. $\frac{9}{10{,}000}$ **7.** $\frac{14}{100{,}000}$

Convert the following to decimal fractions (do not reduce):

8. .819 **9.** 16.93 **10.** $.05\frac{1}{4}$

Convert the following fractions to decimals and round answer to nearest hundredth:

11. $\frac{1}{6}$ **12.** $\frac{3}{8}$ **13.** $12\frac{1}{8}$

LEARNING UNIT 3–2
ADDING, SUBTRACTING, MULTIPLYING, AND DIVIDING DECIMALS

THE IMPACT OF FREE TRADE

International trade grabbed the headlines of many Canadian newspapers in the early 1990s. The focus, of course, was on the liberalization of our trade relations with the United States. Seeking to open up the continent to increased tariff-free trade and investment, Canada and the United States established the North American Free Trade Agreement, which entered into force on January 1, 1994.

Though it is difficult to isolate the precise effects of any trade agreement on economic growth, NAFTA's numbers are compelling: by the fifth anniversary of the agreement, Canada's merchandise trade with the United States and Mexico had vaulted 80% and 100%, respectively. By 1999, trade in goods and services between Canada and the United States totaled $622.7 billion—an average of $1.7 billion of business crossing our border every single day. The dominance of the United States in our trade statistics is striking: all told, in 1998 the United States bought over four-fifths of our exports and produced three-quarters of our imports.

Source: Adapted from Statistics Canada, *Canada Year Book*, March 2001, Catalogue No. 11-402.

Did you know that Canada, the United States, and Mexico are members of NAFTA? This agreement was signed to reduce or eliminate tariffs on goods and services being traded and to facilitate trade among these countries. The result of implementation of NAFTA is a better realization of country-participants' full potential and more efficient integration in the North American economy. The clipping from Statistics Canada shown here illustrates successful results of NAFTA's activity. By the fifth anniversary of the agreement, trade in goods and services between Canada and the United States stood at $622.7 billion—or $1.7 billion of business crossing the border every day. This number was obtained by dividing the total annual amount of trade in dollars by 365—the number of days in a year—and rounding further.

In this Learning Unit we will learn how to perform algebraic operations with decimal numbers.

ADDITION AND SUBTRACTION OF DECIMALS

Since you know how to add and subtract whole numbers, to add and subtract decimal numbers you have only to learn about the placement of the decimals. The following steps will help you:

ADDING AND SUBTRACTING DECIMALS

Step 1. Vertically write the numbers so that the decimal points align. You can place additional zeros to the right of the decimal point if needed without changing the value of the number.

Step 2. Add or subtract the digits starting with the right column and moving to the left.

Step 3. Align the decimal point in the answer with the above decimal points.

EXAMPLES

Add 4 + 7.3 + 36.139 + .0007 + 8.22.

Whole number to the right of the last digit is assumed to have a decimal. → 4.0000

Extra zeros have been added to make calculation easier.

```
  4.0000
  7.3000
 36.1390
   .0007
  8.2200
 -------
 55.6597
```

Subtract 45.3 − 15.273.

```
    2910
  45.300
− 15.273
 -------
  30.027
```

Subtract 7 − 6.9.

```
  6 10
  7.0
− 6.9
 ----
  .1
```

MULTIPLICATION OF DECIMALS

The multiplication of decimal numbers is similar to the multiplication of whole numbers except for the additional step of placing the decimal in the answer (product). The steps that follow simplify this procedure.

MULTIPLYING DECIMALS

Step 1. Multiply the numbers as whole numbers ignoring the decimal points.
Step 2. Count and total the number of decimal places in the multiplier and multiplicand.
Step 3. Starting at the right in the product, count to the left the number of decimal places totalled in Step 2. Place the decimal point so that the product has the same number of decimal places as totalled in Step 2. If the total number of places is greater than the places in the product, insert zeros in front of the product.

EXAMPLES

```
           8.52   (2 decimal places)
Step 1   × 6.7    (1 decimal place)   Step 2
          5 964
          51 12
         ------
         57.084
Step 3
```

```
   2.36    (2 places)
 × .016    (3 places)
   1416
   236
 ------
 .03776    Need to add zero
```

DIVISION OF DECIMALS

If the divisor in your decimal division problem is a whole number, first place the decimal point in the quotient directly above the decimal point in the dividend. Then divide as usual. If the divisor has a decimal point, complete the steps that follow.

DIVIDING DECIMALS

Step 1. Make the divisor a whole number by moving the decimal point to the right.
Step 2. Move the decimal point in the dividend to the right the same number of places that you moved the decimal point in the divisor (Step 1). If there are not enough places, add zeros to the right of the dividend.
Step 3. Place the decimal point in the quotient above the new decimal point in the dividend. Divide as usual.

EXAMPLE

Step 3

$$2.5\overline{)32.8.00}$$

Quotient: 13.12

Step 1   Step 2

```
      1 3.12
2.5)32.8.00
    25
    7 8
    7 5
      3 0
      2 5
        50
        50
```

Stop a moment and study the above example. Note that the quotient does not change when we multiply the divisor and the dividend by the same number. This is why we can move the decimal point in division problems and always divide by a whole number.

Canada–Mexico–United States Merchandise Trade Reconciliation

Canada and the United States participate in data exchange, in which the export statistics of each country are derived from the counterpart import data; therefore, there are no unexplained differences in their trade statistics. However, differences in the official trade statistics of Canada and Mexico and of the United States and Mexico are sizeable. Mexico's import trade statistics exceeded Canada's export statistics by $1.1 billion in 1996 and by $1.4 billion in 1997. The difference in northbound trade between Mexican export figures and Canadian import figures was $3.1 billion in 1996 and $4.0 billion in 1997.

COMPARISON OF MEXICAN AND CANADIAN TRADE STATISTICS

	1996 Southbound trade	1997 Southbound trade	1996 Northbound trade	1997 Northbound trade
	$ millions			
Mexican statistics	2,377	2,725	2,962	2,986
Canadian statistics	1,258	1,328	6,035	7,019
Difference	1,119	1,397	(3,073)	(4,033)

The reconciliation study identified indirect trade as the main source of discrepancy between Canada and Mexico in both directions of trade.

Source: Adapted in part from Statistics Canada, "Canada–Mexico–United States Merchandise Trade Reconciliation, 1996 to 1997," *The Daily*, August 3, 2000, available www.statcan.ca/Daily/English/000803/d000803b.htm, accessed December 30, 2003.

Decimal Applications in Foreign Currency

If you look at the Statistics Canada clipping "Canada–Mexico–United States Merchandise Trade Reconciliation" shown here, you will be able to follow the contents and understand how the difference was obtained. The question is: How is it possible to compare data of three countries, if Mexico operates in pesos, Canada in Canadian dollars, and the United States in American dollars?

The table Key Currency Cross Rates gives us exchange rates between currencies.

Major currencies, which are used in international trade, are usually represented in Key Currency Cross Rates tables, such as Table 3.2.

Any number in the table body shows how many units of the currency in the row heading is equivalent to one unit of the currency in the column heading. For example, per U.S. dollar (abbreviated US$1) you can purchase 122 Yen, 1.002 Euro, or 1.558 Canadian dollars (abbreviated C$1.558). From the fifth column you can determine

TABLE 3–2
KEY CURRENCY CROSS RATES, AFTERNOON, NOVEMBER 5, 2002

Currency	Per US$ N/A	Per Yen 6:19 p.m.	Per Euro 6:19 p.m.	Per C$ 6:02 p.m.	Per U.K. £ 5:35 p.m.	Per Aust $ 6:09 p.m.	Per SFranc 5:54 p.m.
US$	1	0.008199	0.9983	0.6418	1.562	0.5606	0.6831
Yen	122	1	121.8	78.28	190.5	68.37	83.31
Euro	1.002	0.008213	1	0.6429	1.565	0.5616	0.6842
C$	1.558	0.01277	1.555	1	2.434	0.8734	1.064
U.K. £	0.6402	0.005249	0.6391	0.4109	1	0.3589	0.4373
Aust $	1.784	0.01463	1.781	1.145	2.786	1	1.218
Sfranc	1.464	0.012	1.462	0.9397	2.287	0.8207	1

how many units of different currencies you may purchase per Canadian dollar: US$0.6418; Aust $1.145; Euro 0.6429. The Euro is a new common currency, which is used in 12 countries of the European Union: Germany, France, Italy, Austria, Spain, Portugal, Greece, Ireland, Belgium, Finland, Netherlands, and Luxembourg.

To illustrate how to use a Key Currency Cross Rates table, let's find out the amount of Swiss francs that C$750 could have purchased on the afternoon of November, 5, 2002.

C$1 could purchase Sfranc 0.9397, so C$750 would purchase respectively Sfranc 704.78 ($750 \times 0.9397 = 704.775$)

To compare prices in different countries, you need to convert these prices into the same currency. For example, suppose you did some research and found out that a Dell computer costs C$5,570.35 in Canada and that the same model costs US$3520.45 in the United States. Where will you get a better deal? To compare these prices it is necessary to convert them into the common currency. Let's compare them in Canadian dollars. US$1 can purchase C$1.558. So US$3,520.45 will be equivalent of C$5,484.86 ($1.558 \times 3{,}520.45$). The Canadian price is $85.49 higher ($5,570.35 − $5,484.86), so you will get a better deal in the United States.

Multiplication and Division Shortcuts for Decimals

The shortcut steps that follow show how to solve multiplication and division problems quickly involving multiples of 10.

SHORTCUTS FOR MULTIPLES OF 10

Multiplication

Step 1. Count the zeros in the multiplier.

Step 2. Move the decimal point in the multiplicand the same number of places to the right as you have zeros in the multiplier.

Division

Step 1. Count the zeros in the divisor.

Step 2. Move the decimal point in the dividend the same number of places to the left as you have zeros in the divisor.

In multiplication, the answers are *larger* than the original number.

EXAMPLE

If the art collector's average trip cost $252.59, what is the total value of 100 trips?

$252.59 × 100 = $25,259. (2 places to the right)

OTHER EXAMPLES

$6.89 \times 10 = 68.9$ (1 place to the right)

$6.89 \times 100 = 689.$ (2 places to the right)

$6.89 \times 1{,}000 = 6{,}890.$ (3 places to the right)

In division, the answers are *smaller* than the original number.

EXAMPLES

$6.89 \div 10 = .689$ (1 place to the left)

$6.89 \div 100 = .0689$ (2 places to the left)

$6.89 \div 1{,}000 = .00689$ (3 places to the left)

$6.89 \div 10{,}000 = .000689$ (4 places to the left)

Next, let's dissect and solve a word problem.

How to Dissect and Solve a Word Problem

THE WORD PROBLEM May O'Mally went to Sears to buy wall-to-wall carpet. She needs 101.3 square metres for downstairs, 16.3 square metres for the upstairs bedrooms, and 6.2 square metres for the halls. The carpet cost \$14.55 per square metre. The padding cost \$3.25 per square metre. Sears quoted an installation charge of \$6.25 per square metre. What was May O'Mally's total cost?

By completing the following Blueprint Aid, we will slowly dissect this word problem. Note that before solving the problem, we gather the facts, identify what we are solving for, and list the steps that must be completed before finding the final answer, along with any key points we should remember. Let's go to it!

THE FACTS	SOLVING FOR?	STEPS TO TAKE	KEY POINTS
S_1: *Carpet needed:* 101.3 sq. m; S_2: 16.3 sq. m; S_3: 6.2 sq. m. C_1: *Costs:* Carpet, \$14.55 per sq. m; C_2: padding, \$3.25 per sq. m; C_3: installation, \$6.25 per sq. m.	Total cost of carpet $C_{total} = ?$	Total square metres × Cost per square metre = Total cost $C_{total} = (S_1 + S_2 + S_3) \times (C_1 + C_2 + C_3)$	Align decimals. Round answer to nearest cent.

STEPS TO SOLVING PROBLEM

1. Calculate the total number of square metres.

$$\begin{array}{r} 101.3 \\ 16.3 \\ 6.2 \\ \hline \end{array}$$

$S_1 + S_2 + S_3 =$ 123.8 square metres

2. Calculate the total cost per square metre.

$$\begin{array}{r} \$14.55 \\ 3.25 \\ 6.25 \\ \hline \end{array}$$

$C_1 + C_2 + C_3 =$ \$24.05

3. Calculate the total cost of carpet.

123.8 × \$24.05 = **\$2,977.39**

$C_{total} = (S_1 + S_2 + S_3) \times (C_1 + C_2 + C_3)$ $\qquad C_{total} =$ \$2,977.39

It's time to check your progress.

LU 3–2 PRACTICE QUIZ

1. Rearrange vertically and add: 14, .642, 9.34, 15.87321
2. Rearrange and subtract: 28.1549 − .885
3. Multiply and round the answer to the nearest tenth: 28.53 × 17.4
4. Divide and round to the nearest hundredth: 2,182 ÷ 2.83

Complete by the shortcut method:

5. 14.28 × 100
6. 9,680 ÷ 1,000
7. 9,812 ÷ 10,000
8. Could you help Mel decide which product is the "better buy"?

Dog food A	**Dog food B**
\$9.01 for 1.815 kg	\$7.95 for 1.418 kg

   Round to the nearest cent as needed.
9. At Avis Rent-A-Car, the cost per day to rent a medium-size car is \$39.99 plus 29 cents per kilometre. What is the charge to rent this car for 2 days if you drive 602.3 km? You might want to complete a Blueprint Aid since the solution will show a completed one.
10. A trip to Mexico cost 6,000 pesos. What would this be in U.S. dollars? Check your answer.

LEARNING UNIT 3–3
USING A CALCULATOR TO PERFORM OPERATIONS WITH DECIMALS

In the previous chapter we were introduced to the "magic" button [ab/c], which helps us to perform operations with fractions and mixed numbers, to convert improper fractions into mixed numbers, and to add, subtract, multiply, and divide them.

We can use the same "magic" button when we need to convert a fraction or a mixed number into a decimal. For example, to convert $1\frac{3}{4}$ into a decimal, you can follow these steps:

Step 1.	Enter $1\frac{3}{4}$ in your calculator. 1 [ab/c] 3 [ab/c] 4 → 1 r 3 r 4
Step 2.	Press the equal sign button [=].
Step 3.	Press the "magic" button [ab/c] → 1.75.

To convert a decimal number into a mixed number or fraction, follow these steps:

Step 1.	Enter the decimal number in your calculator.
Step 2.	Press the equal sign button.
Step 3.	Press the "magic" button [ab/c].

EXAMPLE

To convert 1.75 back to a mixed number, enter 1.75 in your calculator, press the "equal sign" button and then the [ab/c] button. 1.75 [=ab/c] → 1 r 3 r 4 → $1\frac{3}{4}$

Division, multiplication, subtraction and addition for decimal numbers are performed in the same way as for whole numbers. The only difference is that you have to insert a decimal point after the whole part of your number.

EXAMPLE

Use your calculator to evaluate the following expression:

$1.35 + 22.43 \times 6.1 - 2.3 \times 13.89$

Insert numbers and operations in order from left to right and press equal sign button. The answer will be 106.226.

CHAPTER ORGANIZER AND REFERENCE GUIDE

TOPIC	**KEY POINT, PROCEDURE, FORMULA**	**EXAMPLE(S) TO ILLUSTRATE SITUATION**
Identifying place value, p. 68	$10, 1, \frac{1}{10}, \frac{1}{100}, \frac{1}{1{,}000}$, etc.	.439 in thousandths place value
Rounding decimals, p. 69	1. Identify place value of digit you want to round. 2. If digit to right of identified digit in Step 1 is 5 or more, increase identified digit by 1; if less than 5, do not change identified digit. 3. Drop all digits to right of identified digit.	.875 rounded to nearest tenth = .9 ↖ Identified digit

(continues)

CHAPTER ORGANIZER AND REFERENCE GUIDE (CONTINUED)

Topic	Key point, procedure, formula	Example(s) to illustrate situation
Converting decimal fractions to decimals, p. 70	1. Decimal fraction has a denominator with multiples of 10. Count number of zeros in denominator. 2. Zeros show how many places are in the decimal.	$\frac{8}{1,000} = .008$ $\frac{6}{10,000} = .0006$
Converting proper fractions to decimals, p. 71	1. Divide numerator of fraction by its denominator. 2. Round as necessary.	$\frac{1}{3}$ (to nearest tenth) = .3
Converting mixed numbers to decimals, p. 71	1. Convert fractional part of the mixed number to a decimal. 2. Add converted fractional part to whole number.	$6\frac{1}{4} = 6 + \frac{1}{4} = .25 + 6 = 6.25$
Converting pure and mixed decimals to decimal fractions, p. 71	1. Place digits to right of decimal point in numerator of fraction. 2. Put 1 in denominator. 3. Add zeros to denominator, depending on decimal places of original number. For mixed decimals, add fraction to whole number.	.984 (3 places) 1. $\frac{984}{}$ 2. $\frac{984}{1}$ 3. $\frac{984}{1,000}$
Adding and subtracting decimals, p. 73	1. Vertically write and align numbers on decimal points. 2. Add or subtract digits, starting with right column and moving to the left. 3. Align decimal point in answer with above decimal points.	Add 1.3 + 2 +.4 1.3 2.0 .4 3.7 Subtract 5 − 3.9 $\overset{4}{\not5}.\overset{10}{\not0}$ −3.9 1.1
Multiplying decimals, p. 74	1. Multiply numbers, ignoring decimal points. 2. Count and total number of decimal places in multiplier and multiplicand. 3. Starting at right in the product, count to the left the number of decimal places totalled in Step 2. Insert decimal point. If number of places greater than space in answer, add zeros.	2.48 (2 places) ×0.18 (3 places) 1 984 2 48 .04464
Dividing a decimal by a whole number, p. 74	1. Place decimal point in quotient directly above the decimal point in dividend. 2. Divide as usual.	1.1 42)46.2 42 42 42

(*continues*)

CHAPTER ORGANIZER AND REFERENCE GUIDE (CONCLUDED)

Topic	Key point, procedure, formula	Example(s) to illustrate situation
Dividing if the divisor is a decimal, p. 74	1. Make divisor a whole number by moving decimal point to the right. 2. Move decimal point in dividend to the right the same number of places as in Step 1. 3. Place decimal point in quotient above decimal point in dividend. Divide as usual.	14.2 2.9)41.39 29 123 116 79 58 21
Shortcuts on multiplication and division of decimals, p. 76	When multiplying by 10, 100, 1,000, and so on, move decimal point in multiplicand the same number of places to the right as you have zeros in multiplier. For division, move decimal point to the left.	$4.85 \times 100 = 485$ $4.85 \div 100 = .0485$
Converting a mixed number into a decimal using a calculator, p. 78	1. Enter the mixed number in your calculator. 2. Press the "equal sign" button. 3. Press [ab/c].	1. 2 [ab/c] 5 [ab/c] 7 → 2 r 5 r 7 2. [=] 3. [ab/c] → **2.714285714**
Converting a decimal number into a mixed number using a calculator, p. 78	1. Insert a decimal number in your calculator. 2. Press the "equal sign" button. 3. Press [ab/c].	1. 3.25 2. [=] 3. [ab/c] → 3 r 1 r 4 → $3\frac{1}{4}$
Adding, subtracting, multiplying, dividing decimals using a calculator, p. 78	Insert numbers and operations in order from left to right and press the "equal sign" button.	$5.5 \times 4.3 \div 2.1 + 7.2 = 18.46190476$
Key terms	Decimal fraction, p. 68 Decimal point, p. 68 Mixed decimal, p. 71 Pure decimal, p. 71	Repeating decimal, p. 71 Rounding decimals, p. 69

Note: For how to dissect and solve a word problem, see page 77.

CRITICAL THINKING DISCUSSION QUESTIONS

1. What are the steps for rounding decimals? Federal income tax forms allow the taxpayer to round each amount to the nearest dollar. Do you agree with this?

2. Explain how to convert fractions to decimals. If 1 out of 20 people buys a Land Rover, how could you write an advertisement in decimals?

3. Explain why .07, .70, and .700 are not equal. Assume you take a family trip to Quebec City that covers 800 km. Show that $\frac{8}{10}$ of the trip, or .8 of the trip, represents 640 km.

4. Explain the steps in the addition or subtraction of decimals. Visit a car dealership and find the difference between two sticker prices. Be sure to check each sticker price for accuracy. Should you always pay the sticker price?

END-OF-CHAPTER PROBLEMS

DRILL PROBLEMS

Identify the place value for the following:

3–1. 9.55682 (arrow under 6)   **3–2.** 162.891 (arrow under 9)

Round the following as indicated:

	Tenth	Hundredth	Thousandth
3–3. .9482			
3–4. .7481			
3–5. 6.9245			
3–6. 6.8415			
3–7. 6.5555			
3–8. 75.9913			

Round the following to the nearest cent:

3–9. \$2,011.669   **3–10.** \$4,892.046

Convert the following types of decimal fractions to decimals (round to nearest hundredth as needed). Use a calculator to check your answer.

3–11. $\frac{7}{100}$ **3–12.** $\frac{4}{10}$ **3–13.** $\frac{91}{1,000}$ **3–14.** $\frac{910}{1,000}$ **3–15.** $\frac{64}{100}$ **3–16.** $\frac{979}{1,000}$ **3–17.** $14\frac{91}{100}$

Convert the following decimals to fractions. Do not reduce to lowest terms.

3–18. .6   **3–19.** .62   **3–20.** .006   **3–21.** .0125
3–22. .609   **3–23.** .825   **3–24.** .9999   **3–25.** .7065

Convert the following to mixed numbers. Do not reduce to lowest terms. Use a calculator to check your answer.

3–26. 8.2   **3–27.** 28.48   **3–28.** 6.025

Write the decimal equivalent of the following:

3–29. Four thousandths   **3–30.** Three hundred three and two hundredths
3–31. Eighty-five ten thousandths   **3–32.** Seven hundred seventy-five thousandths

Rearrange the following and add:

3–33. .115, 10.8318, 4.7, 802.4811   **3–34.** .005, 2,002.181, 795.41, 14.0, .184

Rearrange the following and subtract. Use a calculator to check your answer.

3–35. $9.2 - 5.8$ **3–36.** $7 - 2.0815$ **3–37.** $3.4 - 1.08$

Estimate by rounding all the way and multiply the following (do not round final answer):

3–38. 6.24×3.9 **Estimate**   **3–39.** $.413 \times 3.07$ **Estimate**   **3–40.** 675×1.92 **Estimate**   **3–41.** $4.9 \times .825$ **Estimate**

Divide the following and round to the nearest hundredth:

3–42. $.8931 \div 3$ **3–43.** $29.432 \div .0012$ **3–44.** $.0065 \div .07$
3–45. $7,742.1 \div 48$ **3–46.** $8.95 \div 1.18$ **3–47.** $2,600 \div .381$

Convert the following to decimals and round to the nearest hundredth:

3–48. $\frac{1}{8}$ **3–49.** $\frac{1}{25}$ **3–50.** $\frac{5}{6}$ **3–51.** $\frac{5}{8}$

Complete these multiplications and divisions by the shortcut method (do not do any written calculations):

3–52. 96.7 ÷ 10 **3–53.** 258.5 ÷ 100 **3–54.** 8.51 × 1,000 **3–55.** .86 ÷ 100

3–56. 9.015 × 100 **3–57.** 48.6 × 10 **3–58.** 750 × 10 **3–59.** 3,950 ÷ 1,000

3–60. 8.45 ÷ 10 **3–61.** 7.9132 × 1,000

ADDITIONAL DRILL PROBLEMS

3–62. Write in decimal:

a. Forty-three hundredths
b. Seven tenths
c. Nine hundred fifty-three thousandths
d. Four hundred one thousandths
e. Six hundredths

3–63. Round each decimal to the place indicated:

a. .4326 to the nearest thousandth
b. .051 to the nearest tenth
c. 8.207 to the nearest hundredth
d. 2.094 to the nearest hundredth
e. .511172 to the nearest ten thousandth

3–64. Name the place position of the underlined digit:

a. .8<u>2</u>6
b. .91<u>4</u>
c. 3.<u>1</u>169
d. 53.17<u>5</u>
e. 1.017<u>4</u>

3–65. Convert to fractions (do not reduce):

a. .83 ____________ **b.** .426 ____________ **c.** 2.516 ____________

d. $.62\frac{1}{2}$ ____________ **e.** 13.007 ____________ **f.** $5.03\frac{1}{4}$ ____________

3–66. Convert to fractions and reduce to lowest terms:

a. .4 **b.** .44 **c.** .53 **d.** .336 **e.** .096 **f.** .125
g. .3125 **h.** .008 **i.** 2.625 **j.** 5.75 **k.** 3.375 **l.** 9.04

3–67. Convert the following fractions to decimals and round your answer to the nearest hundredth:

a. $\frac{1}{8}$ **b.** $\frac{7}{16}$ **c.** $\frac{2}{3}$ **d.** $\frac{3}{4}$ **e.** $\frac{9}{16}$ **f.** $\frac{5}{6}$ **g.** $\frac{7}{9}$ **h.** $\frac{38}{79}$

i. $2\frac{3}{8}$ **j.** $9\frac{1}{3}$ **k.** $11\frac{19}{50}$ **l.** $6\frac{21}{32}$ **m.** $4\frac{83}{97}$ **n.** $1\frac{2}{5}$ **o.** $2\frac{2}{11}$ **p.** $13\frac{30}{42}$

3–68. Rearrange vertically and add:

a. 4.83 + 6.2 + 12.005 + 1.84 **b.** 1.0625 + 4.0881 + .0775
c. .903 + .078 + .17 + .1 + .96 **d.** 3.38 + .175 + .0186 + .2

3–69. Rearrange and subtract:

a. .86 − .43 **b.** .885 − .069 **c.** 11.67 − .935 **d.** 261.2 − 8.08

3–70. Multiply and round to the nearest tenth:

a. 13.6 × .02 **b.** 1.73 × .069 **c.** 400 × 3.7 **d.** 0.025 × 5.6

3–71. Divide and round to the nearest hundredth:

a. 13.869 ÷ .6 **b.** 1.0088 ÷ .14 **c.** 18.7 ÷ 2.16 **d.** 15.64 ÷ .34

3–72. Complete by the shortcut method:

a. 6.87 × 1,000 **b.** 927,530 ÷ 100 **c.** 27.2 ÷ 1,000 **d.** .21 × 1,000
e. 347 × 100 **f.** 347 ÷ 100 **g.** .0021 ÷ 10 **h.** 85.44 × 10,000
i. 83.298 × 100 **j.** 23.0109 ÷ 100

WORD PROBLEMS

As needed, round answers to the nearest cent.

3–73. In preparation for a demonstration for a new Internet dot.com, 1,200 seats were set up. During the demonstration, 80 seats were vacant. In decimals to nearest hundredth, show how many seats were filled.

3–74. Al Fox got 6 hits out of 11 at-bats. What was his batting average to the nearest thousandths place?

3–75. On May 22, 2001, the *Chicago Sun-Times* reported that Amazon.com had dropped from its high for the last 52 weeks of $58.88 a share to $14.72 a share. You purchased 125 shares at the 52-week high. **(a)** What was your purchasing price? **(b)** What is the current selling price? **(c)** How much of a loss will you sustain if you sell your stock today?

3–76. Jane Lee purchased 18.49 metres of ribbon for the annual fair on the eBay auction site. Each metre cost 79 cents. What was the total cost of the ribbon before shipping charges?

3–77. Douglas Noel went to Home Depot and bought 4 doors at $42.99 each and 6 bags of fertilizer at $8.99 per bag. What was the total cost to Douglas? If Douglas had $300 in his pocket, what does he have left to spend?

3–78. The stock of Intel has a high of $30.25 today. It closed at $28.85. How much did the stock drop from its high?

3–79. Ed Weld is travelling by car to a convention in Nova Scotia. His company will reimburse him $.39 per kilometre. If Ed travels 906.5 km, how much will Ed receive from his company?

3–80. Mark Ogara rented a truck from Avis Rent-A-Car for the weekend (2 days). The base rental price was $29.95 per day plus $14\frac{1}{2}$ cents per kilometre. Mark drove 410.85 km. How much does Mark owe?

3–81. On August 4, 2000, the *Daily Mail* wrote that Unilever had a sales profit of 1.16 billion in U.K. pounds and 10.3 billion in U.K. pounds in sales. How much would each be in Canadian dollars (use table in text)?

3–82. Pete Allan bought a scooter on the Web for $99.99. He saw the same scooter in the mall for $108.96. How much did Pete save by buying on the Web?

3–83. Russell is preparing the daily bank deposit for his coffee shop. Before the deposit, the coffee shop had a chequing account balance of $3,185.66. The deposit contains the following cheques:

No. 1	$ 99.50	No. 3	$8.75
No. 2	110.35	No. 4	6.83

Russell included $820.55 in cash with the deposit. What is the coffee shop's new balance, assuming Russell writes no new cheques?

3–84. On July 23, 2000, the *New York Times* compared amusement park admission prices in Florida. The admission price to Orlando Science Center's planetarium, which includes a show, is $14.25 for adults, $13.25 for seniors, and $11 for children. You are visiting your grandparents in the United States and they plan to take the entire family to the planetarium. The members include 2 grandparents, 2 adults, and 2 children ages 4 and 10. What will be the total cost to attend the planetarium?

3–85. Randi went to Rona to buy wall-to-wall carpeting. She needs 110.8 square metres for downstairs, 31.8 square metres for the halls, and 161.9 square metres for the bedrooms upstairs. Randi chose a shag carpet that costs $14.99 per square metre. She ordered foam padding at $3.10 per square metre. The carpet installers quoted Randi a labour charge of $3.75 per square metre. What will the total job cost Randi?

3–86. Art Norton bought 4 new Aquatred tires at Goodyear for $89.99 per tire. Goodyear charged $3.05 per tire for mounting, $2.95 per tire for valve stems, and $3.80 per tire for balancing. If Art paid no sales tax, what was his total cost for the 4 tires?

3–87. Excel Shelly is shopping for laundry detergent, mustard, and canned tuna. She is trying to decide which of two products is the better buy. Using the following information, can you help Shelly? Please convert ounces into grams first. (1 oz = 28.35 g.)

Laundry detergent A	Mustard A	Canned tuna A
$2.00 for 37 ounces	$.88 for 6 ounces	$1.09 for 6 ounces
Laundry detergent B	**Mustard B**	**Canned tuna B**
$2.37 for 38 ounces	$1.61 for $12\frac{1}{2}$ ounces	$1.29 for $8\frac{3}{4}$ ounces

3–88. Roger bought season tickets to professional basketball games. The cost was $945.60. The season package included 36 home games. What is the average price of the tickets per game? Round to the nearest cent. Marcelo, Roger's friend, offered to buy 4 of the tickets from Roger. What is the total amount Roger should receive?

3–89. A nurse was to give her patients a 1.32-unit dosage of a prescribed drug. The total remaining units of the drug at the hospital pharmacy were 53.12. The nurse has 38 patients. Will there be enough dosages for all her patients?

3–90. Audrey Long went to Japan and bought an animation cell of Mickey Mouse. The price was 25,000 yen. What is the price in Canadian dollars? Check your answer.

ADDITIONAL WORD PROBLEMS

3–91. On Monday, the stock of IBM closed at $88.95. At the end of trading on Tuesday, IBM closed at $94.65. How much did the price of stock increase from Monday to Tuesday?

3–92. Tie Yang bought season tickets to the Blue Jays for $698.55. The season package included 38 games. What is the average price of the tickets per performance? Round to nearest cent. Sam, Tie's friend, offered to buy 4 of the tickets from Tie. What is the total amount Tie should receive?

3–93. Morris Katz bought 4 new tires at Goodyear for $95.49 per tire. Goodyear also charged Morris $2.50 per tire for mounting, $2.40 per tire for valve stems, and $3.95 per tire for balancing. Assume no tax. What was Morris's total cost for the 4 tires?

3–94. Gasoline is sold for US$1.60 per gallon in Detroit and for C$0.72 per litre in Windsor. Where is gas cheaper, and by how much? Use the exchange rate from Table 3.2. Note that 1 gallon = 3.785 litres.

3–95. Steven is travelling to a computer convention by car. His company will reimburse him $.29 per kilometre. If Steven travels 890.5 km, how much will he receive from his company?

3–96. Gracie went to Home Depot to buy wall-to-wall carpeting for her house. She needs 104.8 square metres for downstairs, 17.4 square metres for halls, and 165.8 square metres for the upstairs bedrooms. Gracie chose a shag carpet that costs $13.95 per square metre. She ordered foam padding at $2.75 per square metre. The installers quoted Gracie a labour cost of $5.75 per square metre in installation. What will the total job cost Gracie?

3–97. The *National Mortgage News* dated March 5, 2001 revealed a month-by-month breakdown of business activity in private mortgage insurance (PMI). For the last six months of 2000, amounts expressed in millions were as follows: December, $16.8; November, $13.5; October, $12.9; September, $18.3; August, $15.1; and July $11.9. **(a)** What was the total dollar (in millions) activity? **(b)** What was the average per month? Round to the nearest million.

3–98. Alan Angel got 2 hits in his first 7 times at bat. What is his average to the nearest thousandths place?

3–99. Bill Breen earned $1,555, and his employer calculated that Bill's total tax deduction should be $118.9575. Round this deduction to the nearest cent.

3–100. At the local college, .566 of the students are men. Convert to a fraction. Do not reduce.

3–101. The average television set is watched 2,400 hours a year. If there are 8,760 hours in a year, what fractional part of the year is spent watching television? Reduce to lowest terms.

3–102. On Saturday, the employees at the Newfoundland Fish Company work only $\frac{1}{3}$ of a day. How could this be expressed as a decimal to nearest thousandths?

3–103. A Thunder Bay cinema has 610 seats. At a recent film screening there were 55 vacant seats. Show as a fraction the number of filled seats. Reduce as needed.

3–104. Michael Sullivan was planning his marketing strategy for a new product his company had produced. He was fascinated to discover that

Rhode Island, the smallest state in the United States, was only twenty thousand, five hundred seven ten millionths the size of the largest state, Alaska. Write this number in decimal form.

3–105. Canadian Moose Company purchased a new manufacturing plant, located on 2 hectares of land, for a total price of $2,250,000. The accountant determined that $\frac{3}{7}$ of the total price should be allocated as the price of the building. What decimal portion is the price of the building? Round to the nearest thousandth.

3–106. John Sampson noted his odometer reading of 17,629.3 at the beginning of his vacation. At the end of his vacation the reading was 20,545.1. How many kilometres did he drive during his vacation?

3–107. Jeanne Allyn purchased 12.25 metres of ribbon for a craft project. The ribbon cost 37¢ per metre. What was the total cost of the ribbon?

3–108. Leo Green wanted to find out the gas kilometrage for his company truck. When he filled the gas tank, he wrote down the odometer reading of 9,650.7. The next time he filled the gas tank the odometer reading was 10,393.4. He looked at the gas pump and saw that he had taken 70.3 litres of gas. Find the gas kilometrage (litres per 100 kilometres) for Leo's truck. Round to the nearest tenth.

3–109. At Halley's Rent-a-Car, the cost per day to rent a medium-size car is $35.25 plus 37¢ a kilometre. What would be the charge to rent this car for 1 day if you drove 205.4 km?

3–110. A trip to Disneyland costs C$6,000. What is this in U.S. dollars? Check your answer. Use the following exchange rate: US$1 = C$0.75.

3–111. If a commemorative gold coin weighs 7.842 grams, find the number of coins that can be produced from 116 grams of gold. Round to the nearest whole number.

CHALLENGE PROBLEMS

3–112. The following items were charged in Germany to your bank credit card:

1. McDonalds, Baden-Baden, Germany	€15.32
2. Shell, Karlsruhe, Germany	25.20
3. Little Caesars, Karlsruhe, Germany	16.52
4. B&B, Triberg, Germany	79.08
5. Shell, Triberg, Germany	14.90
6. Shell, Munich, Germany	14.39
7. B&B, Munich, Germany	82.87

a. Using the currency exchange rates in Table 3.2 in this chapter, find the amount you should be charged for each item.

b. What should your total bill be? Check your answer.

3–113. Jill and Frank decided to take a long weekend in New York. City Hotel has a special getaway weekend for $79.95. The price is per person per night, assuming double occupancy. The hotel has a minimum two-night stay. For this price, Jill and Frank will receive $50 credit toward their dinners at City's Skylight Restaurant. Also included in the package is a $3.99 credit per person toward breakfast for two each morning.

Since Jill and Frank do not own a car, they plan to rent one. The car rental agency charges $19.95 a day with an additional charge of $.22 a mile and $1.19 per gallon of gas used. The gas tank holds 24 gallons.

From the following facts, calculate the total expenses of Jill and Frank in Canadian dollars (round all answers to nearest hundredth or cent as appropriate). Assume no taxes. Use the exchange rates from Table 3.2.

Car rental (2 days):	
Beginning odometer reading	4,820
Ending odometer reading	4,940
Beginning gas tank: $\frac{3}{4}$ full.	
Gas tank on return: $\frac{1}{2}$ full.	
Tank holds 24 gallons.	
Dinner cost at Skylight	$182.12
Breakfast for two:	
Morning No. 1	24.17
Morning No. 2	26.88

SUMMARY PRACTICE TEST

1. Add the following by translating the verbal form to the decimal equivalent. (p. 69)

Excel

Five hundred thirty-eight and nine hundred three thousandths

Seventeen and fifty-eight hundredths

Three and three thousandths

Seventy-four hundredths

Two hundred three and nine tenths

Convert the following decimal fractions to decimals. (p. 70)

2. $\frac{6}{10}$ **3.** $\frac{6}{100}$ **4.** $\frac{6}{1,000}$

Convert the following to proper fractions or mixed numbers. Do not reduce to lowest terms. (p. 71)

5. .4 **6.** 8.95 **7.** .951

Convert the following fractions to decimals (or mixed decimals) and round to the nearest hundredth as needed. (p. 71)

8. $\frac{1}{7}$ **9.** $\frac{2}{7}$ **10.** $4\frac{5}{8}$ **11.** $\frac{1}{8}$

12. Rearrange the following and add. (p. 73)
6.4, 8.92, 9.481, 181.0832, 82.95

13. Subtract the following and round to the nearest tenth. (p. 73)
13.891 − 3.59

14. Multiply the following and round to the nearest hundredth. (p. 74)
7.3891 × 14.831

15. Divide the following and round to the nearest tenth. (p. 74)
118,555 ÷ 5.28

Complete the following by the shortcut method. (p. 76)

16. 86.33 × 1,000

17. 7,055,189.781 × 100

18. The average pay of employees is $610.99 per week. Garth earns $630.58 per week. How much is Garth's pay over the average? (p. 74)

19. Prudential reimburses Al $.33 per kilometre. Al submitted a travel log for a total of 1,610.8 kilometres. What will Prudential pay Al? Round to the nearest cent. (p. 74)

20. Jose Roy bought 2 new car tires from Goodyear for $99.55 per tire. Goodyear also charged Jose $3.88 per tire for mounting, $1.95 per tire for valve stems, and $5.10 per tire for balancing. What is Jose's final bill? (p. 74)

21. Could you help Bernie decide which of the following products is cheaper per 100 grams? Convert ounces to grams. (1 oz = 28.35 g.) (p. 74)

Canned fruit A	**Canned fruit B**
$.58 for 4 ounces	$.71 for $4\frac{3}{4}$ ounces

22. Bee Paul bought a watch in Italy for 178 Euro. What is this in Canadian dollars? (p. 75)

23. Disney stock traded at a high of $42.85 and closed at $40.55. How much did the stock fall from its high? (p. 73)

SOLUTIONS TO PRACTICE QUIZZES

LU 3–1

1. .408 (3 places to right of decimal)
2. Hundredths
3. Thousandths
4. **a.** .6 (identified digit 6—digit to right less than 5)
   b. .628 (identified digit 7—digit to right greater than 5)
5. **a.** .7 (identified digit 6—digit to right greater than 5)
   b. .683 (identified digit 3—digit to right less than 5)
6. .0009 (4 places)
7. .00014 (5 places)
8. $\frac{819}{1{,}000}\left(\frac{819}{1 + 3 \text{ zeros}}\right)$
9. $16\frac{93}{100}$
10. $\frac{525}{10{,}000}\left(\frac{525}{1 + 4 \text{ zeros}} \quad \frac{1}{4} \times .01 = .0025,\ 0.0025 \times .05 = .0525\right)$
11. .16666 = .17
12. .375 = .38
13. 12.125 = 12.13

LU 3–2

1.

```
  14.00000
    .64200
   9.34000
  15.87321
  --------
  39.85521
```

2.

```
  28.1549
 −  .8850
 --------
  27.2699
```

3.

```
     28.53
  ×  17.4
  --------
    11 412
   199 71
   285 3
  --------
   496.422 ≃ 496.4
```

4.

```
          771.024  = 771.024 ≃ 771.02
  2.83)218200.000
       1981
       ----
        2010
        1981
        ----
         290
         283
         ---
           7 00
           5 66
           ----
           1 340
           1 132
           -----
```

5. 14.28 = 1,428 **6.** 9680. = 9.680 **7.** 9812. = .9812

8. **A:** $9.01 ÷ 1.815 = $4.96 **B:** $7.95 ÷ 1.418 = $5.61 Buy A.

9. Avis Rent-A-Car total rental charge:

THE FACTS	SOLVING FOR?	STEPS TO TAKE	KEY POINTS
C_1 = Cost per day, \$39.99. C_2 = 29 cents per km. D = Drove 602.3 km. n = 2-day rental.	Total rental charge. $C_{total} = ?$	Total cost for 2 days' rental + Total cost of driving = Total rental charge $C_{total} = n \times C_1 + D \times C_2$	In multiplication, count the number of decimal places. Starting from right to left in the product, insert decimal in appropriate place. Round to nearest cent.

Steps to solving problem

1. Calculate total costs for 2 days' rental. $n \times C_1 = \$39.99 \times 2 = \$79.98$
2. Calculate the total cost of driving. $D \times C_2 = \$.29 \times 602.3 = \$174.667 = \$174.67$
3. Calculate the total rental charge.

$$\begin{array}{r} \$\ 79.98 \\ +\ 174.67 \\ \hline C_{total} = \$254.65 \end{array}$$

10. $6{,}000 \times \$.10857 = \$651.42$

Check $\$651.42 \times 9.2110 = 6{,}000.23$ pesos due to rounding

Business Math Scrapbook

WITH INTERNET APPLICATION

Putting Your Skills to Work

Figuring Out the Tab

We asked five restaurants to tell us the ingredients of one of their entrees, and what they cost the restaurants wholesale. Then we bought the ingredients at the grocery store. The results:

RESTAURANT	DISH	INGREDIENTS	MENU PRICE	GROCERY STORE PRICE	WHOLESALE PRICE
Carmine's New York, NY	Zuppa di mussels	1 pound mussels with tomato sauce	**$12**	$3.15	$2.25–$2.50
Heaven on Seven Chicago, Ill.	Grilled Louisiana Gulf shrimp and Andouille sausage on bed of white rice (comes with a choice of cup of soup, gumbo or salad)	6 shrimp (about 6.5–7 ounces), 2.5 ounces andouille sausage, 6 ounces white rice, plus sauce and seasoning, and 1 cup of soup	**$18.95**	$9.00	$6.39
Grill 23 and Bar Boston, Mass.	Grilled swordfish	12 ounces swordfish	**$24.50**	$9.00	$4.50–$7.50
Docks New York, NY	Grilled tuna with steamed red potatoes and coleslaw	10 ounces tuna, 8 ounces potatoes, 5 ounces coleslaw	**$20.50**	$8.15	$6.55
Pinot Bistro Los Angeles, Calif.	Farm chicken with a roasted garlic glaze and Pinot fries	12 ounces chicken, 10 ounces french fries	**$15.95**	$3.00	$4.08

PROJECT A

For each restaurant, calculate the difference between the menu price and the grocery store price.

Go to the Web and find a restaurant of interest to you. Does the restaurant provide complete menus online? What will it cost you to order dinner for a family of four from Monday to Friday? Provide key details to support your answer.

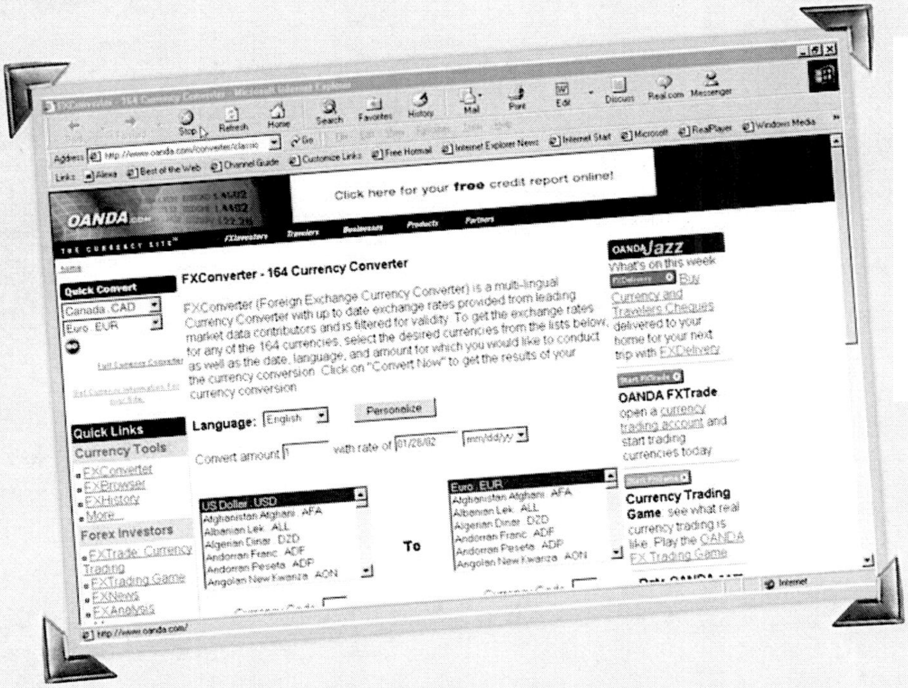

PROJECT B

Go to www.oanda.com/converter/classic. Find today's exchange rate from dollars to German marks by converting $1 to marks. Use this value to find how many marks $5,000 is worth. Confirm your answer by using the currency calculator.

CUMULATIVE REVIEW

A WORD PROBLEM APPROACH—CHAPTERS 1–3

1. The top rate at the Waldorf Towers Hotel in New York is US$390. The top rate at the Ritz Carlton in Boston is US$345. If John spends 9 days at the hotel, how much can he save if he stays at the Ritz? (p. 12)
2. Robert Half Placement Agency was rated best by 4 to 1 in an independent national survey. If 250,000 responded to the survey, how many rated Robert Half the best? (p. 44)
3. Of the 63.2 million people who watch professional football, only $\frac{1}{5}$ watch the commercials. How many viewers do not watch the commercials? (p. 44)
4. AT&T advertised a 10-minute call for $2.27. MCI WorldCom's rate was $2.02. Assuming Bill Splat makes forty 10-minute calls, how much could he save by using MCI WorldCom? (p. 74)
5. Paul earns C$42,000 per year. He has received an offer from Buffalo for an annual salary of US$30,000. Is the offered salary better than the present one? What will be the difference in Paul's income in Canadian dollars if he accepts the offer? (p. 75)
6. Cassandra returned from Europe with Euro 465 left after her holidays. How much in Canadian funds will she receive at the bank? (p. 75)
7. Lillie Wong bought 4 new Firestone tires at $82.99 each. Firestone also charged $2.80 per tire for mounting, $1.95 per tire for valves, and $3.15 per tire for balancing. Lillie turned her 4 old tires in to Firestone, which charged $1.50 per tire to dispose of them. What was Lillie's final bill? (p. 73)
8. Tootsie Roll Industries bought Charms Company for $65 million. Some analysts believe that in 4 years the purchase price could rise to 3 times as much. If the analysts are right, how much did Tootsie Roll save by purchasing Charms immediately? (p. 12)
9. Today the average business traveller will spend almost $50 a day on food. The breakdown is dinner, $22.26; lunch, $10.73; breakfast, $6.53; tips, $6.23; and tax, $5.98. If Clarence Donato, an executive for Honeywell, spends only $.3\overline{3}$ of the average, what is Clarence's total cost for food for the day? If Clarence wanted to spend $\frac{1}{3}$ more than the average on the next day, what would be his total cost on the second day? Round to the nearest cent. (pp. 74, 47)

   Be sure you use the fractional equivalent in calculating $.3\overline{3}$.

Powers and Roots

4

The Chateaus' two-storey homes range between 3,138 to 5,041 sq. ft. The various plans include a study or office to accommodate the needs of an executive family, and sprawling rooms that allow for great decorating versatility. The new coach house designs range from 3,691 sq. ft. up to 4,749 sq. ft. and provide additional living space above the garage.

Source: *New Homes and Condos for sale*, vol. 10, no. 23: 19.

LEARNING UNIT OBJECTIVES

LU 4–1: Powers and Operations with Powers

- Understand basic concept of powers and terms: powers, exponents, base, and coefficient (p. 92).
- Evaluate and simplify expressions with powers (p. 92).
- Apply rules of operations with powers (p. 93).

LU 4–2: Roots and Operations with Roots

- Understand basic concept of roots and terms: roots, base, radical, radicand, index (p. 95).
- Evaluate and simplify expressions with roots and fractional exponents (p. 95).
- Apply rules of operations with roots (p. 95).

LU 4–3: Use of a Calculator

- Evaluate expressions with exponents and roots with calculator (p. 95).

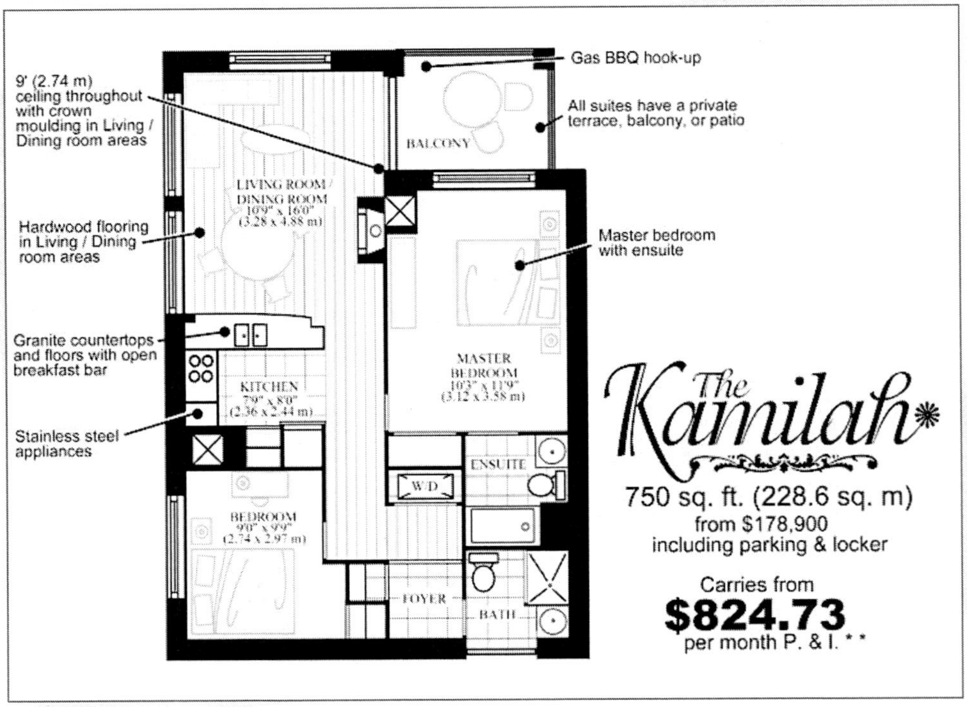

In the advertisement for new condos shown here, you will notice reference to "sq. ft.," which means "square feet" or ft^2. Areas of condos or homes can be measured either in square feet* or in square metres (m^2). These are sums of the areas of all the rooms, which are calculated as the product of the width and the length of a room.

For example, the area of a bedroom is $9 \text{ ft} \times 9.9 \text{ ft} = 89.1 \text{ ft}^2$. As you see, "ft" appears twice as a factor in the multiplication. The number of times the unit of measurement appears as a factor is equal to the exponent in the product. Thus, $\text{ft} \times \text{ft} = \text{ft}^2$.

*Despite the fact that Canada has switched to the metric system of measurement, the real estate and construction industries still use the imperial system in many cases. To convert, simply remember that 1 foot = .3048 metres, and 1 square foot = .0929 square metres.

LEARNING UNIT 4–1
POWERS AND OPERATIONS WITH POWERS

Power is the number of times a value appears as a factor of itself in a product. For example, $3 \times 3 = 3^2$; $6 \times 6 \times 6 \times 6 = 6^4$; $7 \times 7 \times 7 = 7^3$. You might also say a power is an expression with a *base* and an *exponent.* The exponent indicates how many times the base is multiplied by itself.

In the expression 7^3 → 7 is the **base** of a power
3 is the **exponent**
7^3 is the **power**

When you multiply a number by itself, you get it as a factor twice and it will be the square of the original number: $3 \times 3 = 3^2$. The expression 3^2 is read "3 squared" or "3 to the second power" or "second power of three" or "3 to the power of two." 6^4 is read "6 to the 4th power" or "4th power of 6."

If you multiply a variable by itself, you get the square of the variable: $Y \times Y = Y^2$. In this case, *Y* is the base, 2 is the exponent, and 1 is the coefficient. You may recall that when the coefficient preceding a variable is positive 1, we omit it and write down only the variable.

Consider the expression $4x^3$. The base is *x*, the exponent is 3, and the coefficient is 4. The exponent, 3, indicates how many times the base, *x*, was used as a factor of itself. So

$4x^3 = 4 \times x \times x \times x$. To evaluate the expression $4x^3$ when the value of x is given, you must first find the value of x^3 and then multiply that result by 4. This is because according to BEDMAS/PEMDAS rules, you must perform exponent operations prior to multiplication.

For the same reason, brackets have priority. If the expression were written $(4x)^3$, you would have to perform the operation in brackets first and then cube the result.

EXAMPLE

Calculate the value of $(5Y)^4$, when $Y = 3$.

1. Calculate $5Y = 5 \times 3 = 15$.
2. Evaluate 15 to the power of 4, like this: $15 \times 15 \times 15 \times 15 = 50{,}625$.

Operations with powers also obey special rules, as we will see in the next sections.

MULTIPLICATION OF POWERS

To multiply powers with a common base, it is necessary to maintain the base and add the exponents together:

$$A^m \times A^n = A^{m+n}$$

EXAMPLE

$$2^3 \times 2^{15} = 2^{3+15} = 2^{18}$$

$$\left(\frac{1}{3}\right)^3 \times \left(\frac{1}{3}\right)^7 \times \left(\frac{1}{3}\right)^{11} = \left(\frac{1}{3}\right)^{3+7+11} = \left(\frac{1}{3}\right)^{21}$$

$$(1 + a) \times (1 + a)^3 \times (1 + a)^5 = (1 + a)^{1+3+5} = (1 + a)^9$$

DIVISION OF POWERS

To divide powers with a common base, it is necessary to maintain the base and subtract the exponent of the divisor (denominator) from the exponent of the dividend (numerator):

$$\frac{a^m}{a^n} = a^{m-n}$$

EXAMPLE

$$5^6 \div 5^3 = \frac{5 \times 5 \times 5 \times \cancel{5} \times \cancel{5} \times \cancel{5}}{\cancel{5} \times \cancel{5} \times \cancel{5}} = 5^3$$

or $\quad 5^6 \div 5^3 = 5^{6-3} = 5^3$

RAISING A POWER TO A POWER

To raise a power to a power, it is necessary to maintain the base and multiply the exponents:

$$(a^m)^n = a^{mn}$$

EXAMPLE

$$(5^3)^4 = 5^{3\times4} = 5^{12}$$

$$\left[\left(\frac{1}{2}\right)^{15}\right]^4 = \left(\frac{1}{2}\right)^{15\times4} = \left(\frac{1}{2}\right)^{60}$$

$$(x^3)^2 = x^6$$

Please note that raising a negative number (base) to an even power gives a positive result and raising a negative number (base) to an odd power gives a negative result.

EXAMPLE

$$(-2)^2 = (-2) \times (-2) = +4$$

$$(-2\ )^3 = (-2) \times (-2\ ) \times (-2) = -8$$

Raising to the Power of 0

Raising any number or expression to the power of zero always equals 1:

$B^0 = 1;\quad (xy)^0 = 1;\quad \left(\frac{a}{b}\right)^0 = 1$

Example

$$\left(\frac{a^3b^5 - c^{23}}{ab - c^{16}}\right)^0 = 1$$

$$3^0 = 1$$

Raising to a Negative Power

Raising any number to a negative power is equivalent to 1 divided by the same number raised to the same power, except that the power is positive:

$$(a)^{-n} = \frac{1}{a^n}$$

Example

$$(12)^{-2} = \frac{1}{12^2} \qquad (1+i)^{-4} = \frac{1}{(1+i)^4}$$

$$\left(\frac{a}{b}\right)^{-3} = \frac{1}{\left(\frac{a}{b}\right)^3} = \left(\frac{b}{a}\right)^3$$

Raising a Product or Quotient to a Power

To raise a product to a power it is necessary to raise each factor to the power and multiply the results (the power is distributed to each factor):

$(ab)^n = a^n \times b^n$

To raise a quotient to a power it is necessary to raise the dividend and the divisor:

$$\left(\frac{a}{b}\right)^n = \frac{a^n}{b^n}$$

Example

$$\left(\frac{1}{2}\right)^3 = \frac{1^3}{2^3} = \frac{1}{8}$$

$$(5a)^4 = 5^4 \times a^4 = 625a^4$$

LU 4–1 Practice Quiz

1. Identify the base, exponent, and power in each of the following expressions:
   a. 5^7 b. $(ax)^3$

Simplify and evaluate the following expressions:

2. $\left(\frac{3}{4}\right)^4$
3. $(2x)^5$
4. $\frac{a^6b^4c^5}{a^3b^2}$
5. $(123z)^0$

LEARNING UNIT 4–2
ROOTS AND OPERATIONS WITH ROOTS

Root is the opposite of the power operation. If a power is expressed in exponential form, the base will be the root of the expression and an exponent will indicate the **power of the root.**

$9 = 3^2$ → 3 is the square root of 9

$256 = 4^4$ → 4 is the fourth root of 256

$8x^3 = (2^3x)^3 = (2x)^3$ → $(2x)$ is the (third power) cube root of $8x^3$

A root of an M power is a number or an expression which when multiplied by itself M times will equal this number or expression. The sign $\sqrt{}$, which expresses the root, is called the **radical.**

$\sqrt{81} = \sqrt[2]{81} = \sqrt[2]{9^2} = \pm 9$

$\sqrt[4]{81} = \sqrt[4]{3^3} = 3$

In this expression, "2," which indicates the power of the root, is called the **index;** the "81" under the radical sign is called the **radicand.** "9" is the **square root** of 81.

In square roots, the index "2" is usually omitted. Every positive number has two square roots, one positive and one negative.

Radicals can be also expressed in exponential form, as a power with a fractional exponent. In this case, the denominator of the fraction is the index.

$a^{m/n} = \sqrt[n]{a^m}$

$a^{1/n} = \sqrt[n]{a^1} = \sqrt[n]{a}$

EXAMPLE

$8^{1/3} = \sqrt[3]{8} = \sqrt[3]{2^3} = 2$

LU 4–2 PRACTICE QUIZ

Identify the radical, the radicand and the index:

1. $\sqrt[4]{64}$

2. Evaluate the following expressions:

a. $\sqrt{16}$ **b.** $\sqrt{x^2}$

3. Present in the exponential form:

a. $\sqrt{81}$ **b.** $\sqrt{x^3}$

LEARNING UNIT 4–3
USE OF A CALCULATOR

To evaluate powers or roots you can use a calculator. On the key panel of a calculator the power function may be represented by either [y^x] or [^].

Press the keys in the following sequence:

Base, power key, exponent, equal sign key

EXAMPLE

Evaluate 3^{15}.

3 [y^x] 15 [=] 14,348,907

To evaluate an expression, first simplify it and then evaluate. You can also use brackets to evaluate an expression in one step.

For example:

$$\left[\left(\frac{2}{3}\right)^5\right]^3$$

[(( ] 2 [÷] 3 [ )] [y^x] 5 [ )] 3 [=] 0.0022836583

To evaluate roots, present the radical in exponential form and perform the power operation with a fractional exponent.

$\sqrt{16} = 16^{1/2}$

Remember to use brackets for a fractional exponent!

16 [y^x] [( ] 1 [÷] 2 [ ) =] 4

There is another way to evaluate a radical with the help of a calculator. Instead of using brackets for a fractional exponent, you can calculate the decimal equivalent of the fraction and insert it after the power key.

$16^{1/2} = 16$ [y^x] .5 [=] 4

EXAMPLE

$25^{3/2} = 25^{1.5} = 125$

$\sqrt[7]{475^4} = 475^{4/7} = 475^{.5714285714} = 33.84848268$

Never round the intermediate result—if you round it, the final result will be different! In this case, this means you should keep all the decimals in the exponent. For example, let's try rounding the exponent .5714285714 to two decimals, which gives .57. Then:

475 [y^x] .57 = 33.55176393

The difference between this value and the more precise one in the above example is about .3.

LU 4–3 PRACTICE QUIZ

Use a calculator to evaluate the following:

1. $45^{1/4}$
2. $\sqrt{196}$
3. $\sqrt{.000125}$

CHAPTER ORGANIZER AND REFERENCE GUIDE

TOPIC	KEY POINT, PROCEDURE, FORMULA	EXAMPLE(S) TO ILLUSTRATE SITUATION
Power, p. 92	The number of times a value appears as a factor of itself in the product. Power is expressed by a base and an exponent. The exponent indicates how many times the base is multiplied by itself.	In the expression 7^3 7 is the **base;** 3 is the **exponent;** 7^3 is the **power.**
Multiplication of powers, p. 93	To multiply powers with a common base, keep the base and add the exponents together.	$3^4 \times 3^5 = 3^9$

(continues)

CHAPTER ORGANIZER AND REFERENCE GUIDE (CONCLUDED)

TOPIC	KEY POINT, PROCEDURE, FORMULA	EXAMPLE(S) TO ILLUSTRATE SITUATION
Division of powers, p. 93	To divide powers with a common base, keep the base and subtract the exponent of the divisor (denominator) from the exponent of the dividend (numerator).	$9^8 \div 9^4 = 9^4$
Raising to a power, p. 93	To raise a power to a power, keep the base and multiply the exponents.	$(2^3)^4 = 2^{12}$
Raising to a zero power, p. 94	Raising any number or expression to the power of zero makes it equal 1.	$1{,}364{,}598^0 = 1$
Raising to a negative power, p. 94	Raising any number to a negative power is equivalent to 1 divided by the base raised to the same power, except that the power is positive.	$9^{-2} = \frac{1}{9^2}$
Raising product and quotient to a power, p. 94	To raise a product to a power, raise each factor to the power and multiply the results (the power is distributed to each factor).	$(3d)^4 = 3^4d^4 = 81d^4$
Root, p. 95	To raise a quotient to a power, raise the dividend and the divisor to the power.	$\left(\frac{5}{4}\right)^3 = \frac{5^3}{4^3}$
	A root is the result of reversing a power operation.	$\sqrt[3]{64}$ 3 is the **index;** 64 is the **radicand;** $\sqrt{}$ is the **radical** sign.
	A radical can be expressed in exponential form as a power with a fractional exponent.	$\sqrt{25} = 25^{1/2}$
Calculator use, p. 95	Remember to use brackets for fractional exponents.	$3^{(3/4)}$
	To find a root, put the radical into exponential form and perform the power operation with the fractional exponent.	$\sqrt{49} = 49^{1/2}$
	It is possible to calculate a decimal equivalent of fractional exponent and calculate the power with it.	$\sqrt{49} = 49^{1/2} = 49^{.5}$
Key terms	Base, p. 92 Exponent, p. 92 Index, p. 95	Power, p. 92 Power of the root, p. 95 Radical, p. 95 Radicand, p. 95 Root, p. 95 Square root, p. 95

CRITICAL THINKING DISCUSSION QUESTIONS

1. What are the steps to calculate a root using a calculator? Give an example.
2. How can you perform power operations with a fractional exponent using a calculator? Give an example.
3. Explain why all areas are expressed in square units. Give examples.
4. Discuss how powers and roots are used in business.
5. Explain why any number to the power 0 is always equal to 1.

END-OF-CHAPTER PROBLEMS

DRILL PROBLEMS

Using a calculator evaluate each of the following, correct to three decimals.

4–1. $\sqrt{256}$ **4–2.** $\sqrt{564.987}$ **4–3.** $\sqrt{.00654}$ **4–4.** $\sqrt{5{,}678}$ **4–5.** $\sqrt[15]{1.096873}$

4–6. $\sqrt[10]{2.67893}$ **4–7.** $\sqrt[12]{31{,}567}$

Calculate each of the following:

4–8. $4{,}123^{.98}$ **4–9.** $35.7^{1/3}$ **4–10.** $.0657^{.75}$ **4–11.** $18^{-1/8}$

4–12. $.0126^{-1/3}$ **4–13.** $(1 - 2.56^{-21})/.08$ **4–14.** $568/(3 + 24^{-5})$

SOLUTIONS TO PRACTICE QUIZZES

LU 4–1

1. Identify base, exponent, and power in the following expressions:
   a. 5^7 is the power; 7 is the exponent; 5 is the base
   b. $(ax)^3$ is the power; 3 is the exponent; ax is the base

Simplify and evaluate the following expressions:

2. $\left(\frac{3}{4}\right)^4 = \frac{3^4}{4^4} = \frac{81}{256} = .32$

3. $(2x)^5 = 2^5x^5 = 32x^5$

4. $\frac{a^6b^4c^5}{a^3b^2} = a^{6-3}b^{4-2}c^5 = a^3b^2c^5$

5. $(123z)^0 = 1$

LU 4–2

Identify the radical, the radicand and the index:

1. $\sqrt[4]{64}$ ← The radical 4 is the index and 64 is the radicand

2. Evaluate the following expressions:
   a. $\sqrt{16} = \sqrt{4^2} = 4$ **b.** $\sqrt{x^2} = x$

3. Present in the exponential form:
   a. $\sqrt{81} = 81^{1/2}$ **b.** $\sqrt{x^3} = x^{3/2}$

LU 4–3

1. $45^{1/4} = 45$ [yˣ] $(1 \div 4) = 2.59002$

2. $\sqrt{196} = 196$ [yˣ] $(1 \div 2) = 196$ [yˣ] $.5 = 14$

3. $\sqrt{.000125} = .000125$ [yˣ] $.5 = 0.0111803399$

Solving for the Unknown: Basic Linear Equations

A How-To Approach for Solving Equations

5

Not Too Deep

India rates low in Internet penetration, compared with the rest of its region (in millions)

	NET USERS	ADULT POP.	USERS AS PCT. OF ADULT POP.
Singapore	1.2	3.4	36.2%
Australia	4.1	15.4	26.3
Taiwan	4.0	17.7	22.8
Hong Kong	1.2	5.9	19.7
S. Korea	6.8	37.8	17.9
Japan	17.7	109.2	16.2
China	8.3	964.9	0.9
INDIA	1.8	695.8	0.3

If Singapore increases its Net users by three times, will Singapore's users be more than Taiwan's users?

LEARNING UNIT OBJECTIVES

LU 5–1: Solving Equations for the Unknown: Basic Linear Equations

- Explain the basic procedures used to solve equations for the unknown (p. 101).
- List the five rules and the mechanical steps used to solve for the unknown in seven situations; know how to check the answers (verification) (p. 102).

LU 5–2: Solving Word Problems for the Unknown

- List the steps for solving word problems (p. 105).
- Complete Blueprint Aids to solve word problems; verify the solutions (p. 106).

The *MacLean's* clipping "Patents and Rodents" states that due to the Supreme Court decision that higher life forms such as mice cannot be patented, Canadian biotech companies may consider heading for more favourable jurisdictions. According to the article, in a four-year period the number of companies leaving increased from 227 to 400. What was the increase in the number of Canadian biotech companies? This value is unknown, and we must find it. To solve this word problem we will apply the step approach.

Step 1. Let's read the problem once again and write what is given in the top left corner of our notebook. The number of firms has increased *from* 227. This means that the initial or old value is 227. The number of firms has increased *to* 400. This means that the new value is 400. We must now find the amount of change.

Step 2. Let's assign variables to known and unknown values and translate the English language into math. Initial/old value is V_o; new value is V_n; and the unknown value is X. Now, we can write down the problem in the following form:

$V_o = 227$

$V_n = 400$

$X = ?$

Step 3. Let's think of a formula that will help us find the solution. The amount of the change equals the new value minus the old value:

$$X = V_n - V_o$$

Step 4. Substitute the known values into the formula:

$$X = 400 - 227 = 173$$

Write the answer in full sentence form.

The number of Canadian biotech companies voting has increased *by* 173 companies.

Step 5. Verify the answer. Substitute the values for the variables. Always use the original formula.

Associated Press, John Hopkins University/Keith Weller

PATENTS AND RODENTS

Does a genetically engineered mouse qualify for the same patent protection as, say, a hand-held computer? Not as far as the Supreme Court of Canada is concerned. In its long-anticipated, and ethically and morally charged ruling, the court decided that higher life forms—such as Harvard University's so-called OncoMouse which was at the heart of the case—cannot be patented.

Canada now stands almost alone—and biotechnologists aren't happy. The United States, Japan and much of Europe have long extended patent rights over the OncoMouse. Some critics now worry about brain drain as Canadian biotech companies may consider heading for more favourable jurisdictions. Between 1997 and 2001, the number of such firms in Canada increased from 227 to more than 400. Annual revenues reported by the sector's public companies now exceed $1.5 billion, a 160 per cent increase.

Learning Unit 5–1 explains how to solve for unknowns in equations. In Learning Unit 5–2 you learn how to solve for unknowns in word problems. When you complete these Units, you will not have to memorize as many formulas to solve business and personal math applications. Also, with the increasing use of computer software, a basic working knowledge of solving for the unknown has become necessary.

LEARNING UNIT 5–1

SOLVING EQUATIONS FOR THE UNKNOWN: BASIC LINEAR EQUATIONS

The following heading appeared in a *Wall Street Journal* article:

Calculating Retirement? It's No Simple Equation

Source: © 2000 Dow Jones & Company, Inc.

Many of you are familiar with the terms *variables* and *constants.* If you are planning to prepare for your retirement by saving only what you can afford each year, your saving is a *variable.* However, if you plan to save the same amount each year, your saving is a *constant.* This unit explains the importance of mathematical variables and constants when solving equations.

Basic Equation-Solving Procedures

Equation

Expression on the left side	=	Expression on the right side
$5b - 7$	=	$4b + 3$
$6x$	=	18
$4(a + 3)$	=	$-11(2a - 1)$
$3x + 2$	=	$5x - 2$

Do you know the difference between a mathematical expression, an equation, and a formula? A mathematical **expression** is a meaningful combination of numbers and letters called *terms.* Operational signs (such as + or −) within the expression connect the terms to show a relationship between them. For example, $6 + 2$ or $6A - 4A$ are mathematical expressions. An **equation** is a mathematical statement with an equal sign showing that a mathematical expression on the left equals the mathematical expression on the right. Mathematical expressions on both sides of the equal sign are called **members of an equation.** An equation has an equal sign; an expression does not have an equal sign. A **formula** is an equation that expresses in symbols a general fact, rule, or principle. Formulas are shortcuts for expressing a word concept. For example, in Chapter 12 you will learn that the formula for simple interest is Interest (I) = Principal (P) × Rate (R) × Time (T). This means that when you see $I = P \times R \times T$, you recognize the simple interest formula. Now let's study basic equations.

As a mathematical statement of equality, equations show that two numbers or groups of numbers are equal. For example, $6 + 4 = 10$ shows the equality of an equation. Equations also use letters as symbols that represent one or more numbers. These symbols, usually a letter of the alphabet, are **variables** that stand for a number. We can use a variable even though we may not know what it represents. For example, $A + 2 = 6$. The variable A represents the number or **unknown** (4 in this example) for which we are solving. We distinguish variables from numbers, which have a fixed value. Numbers such as 3 or −7 are **constants** or **knowns,** whereas A and $3A$ (this means 3 times the variable A) are variables. So we can now say that variables and constants are *terms of mathematical expressions.*

Usually in solving for the unknown, we place variable(s) on the left side of the equation and constants on the right. The following rules for variables and constants are important.

VARIABLES AND CONSTANTS RULES

1. If no number is in front of a letter, it is a 1: $B = 1B$; $C = 1C$.
2. If no sign is in front of a letter or number, it is a +: $C = +C$; $4 = +4$.

You should be aware that in solving equations, the meaning of the symbols +, −, ×, and ÷ has not changed. However, some variations occur. For example, you can also write $A \times B$ (A times B) as $A \bullet B$, $A(B)$, or AB. Also, A divided by B is the same as A/B. If an equation contains only one variable, it is called an **equation in one unknown.** If this unknown is in the first power, the equation is called a **linear equation.** The four equations shown in the margin are linear equations in one unknown. In each of these equations, the left member equals the right member. In the first equation, $5b - 7 = 4b + 3$. The expression $5b - 7$ is the left member and $4b + 3$ is the right member of the equation. They are equal.

To solve an equation for an unknown variable is to present the equation in such a form that the unknown variable with coefficient positive one (1) will be on the left side of the equal sign and all the other members of the equation on the right.
$x = 3a + 4$
$y = 85$

To **solve an equation** means to find the value of unknown variable or to find the **root** or the **solution of the equation.** To solve an equation for an unknown variable means to present it in such a form that the unknown variable with positive coefficient 1 will be on the left side of the equal sign and all other members on the right side. In other words, to find the solution or root of an equation is to find a replacement value for the unknown, which when substituted for the unknown variable will make the equation true.

EXAMPLE

$3x + 2 = 5x - 2$

In this equation the solution is $x = 2$, because when we substitute 2 for x, the two members of equation will still be equal.

Left side: $3 \times 2 + 2 = 8$

Right side: $5 \times 2 - 2 = 8$

Left side equals right side: $8 = 8$

This process of checking an equation is called **verification.**

Remember that to solve an equation, you must find a number that can replace the unknown in the equation and make it a true statement. Now let's take a moment to look at how we can change verbal statements into variables.

Verbal Statement	Variable *A* (age)
Dick's age 8 years ago	$A - 8$
Dick's age 8 years from today	$A + B$
Four times Dick's age	$4A$
One-fifth Dick's age	$A/5$

Assume Dick Hersh, an employee of Nike, is 50 years old. Let's assign Dick Hersh's changing age to the symbol A. The symbol A is a variable.

To visualize how equations work, think of the old-fashioned balancing scale shown in Figure 5.1. The pole of the scale is the equal sign. The two sides of the equation are the two pans of the scale. In the left pan or left side of the equation, we have $A + 8$; in the right pan or right side of the equation, we have 58. To solve for the unknown (Dick's present age), we isolate or place the unknown (variable) on the left side and the numbers on the right. We will do this soon. For now, remember that to keep an equation (or scale) in balance, we must perform mathematical operations (addition, subtraction, multiplication, and division) to *both* sides of the equation.

FIGURE 5–1
Equality in equations

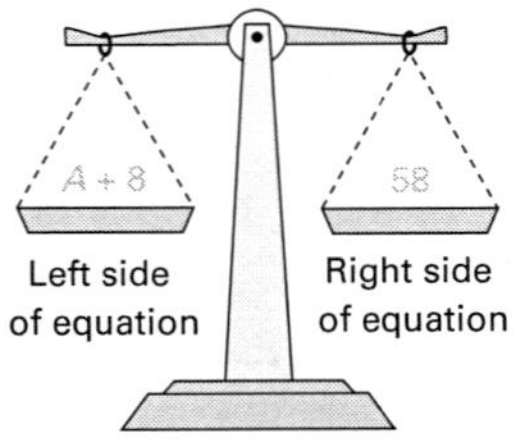

Dick's age in 8 years will equal 58.

SOLVING FOR THE UNKNOWN RULE

Whatever you do to one side of an equation, you must do to the other side.

If you change both sides of an equation in the same way, the meaning of the equation will remain the same.

If you change both sides of an equation in the same way, you will get **equivalent equations,** equations that have the same root.

EXAMPLE

$5b - 7 = 4b + 3$ and $b - 7 = 3$ are equivalent equations, because they have the same solution or root: $b = 10$. The equations $6x = 18$ and $2x = 6$ are also equivalent.

HOW TO SOLVE FOR UNKNOWNS IN EQUATIONS

This section presents seven drill situations and the rules that will guide you in solving for unknowns in these situations. We begin with two basic rules—the opposite process rule and the equation equality rule.

OPPOSITE PROCESS RULE

If an equation indicates a process such as addition, subtraction, multiplication, or division, solve for the unknown or variable by using the opposite process. For example, if the equation process is addition, solve for the unknown by using subtraction.

EQUATION EQUALITY RULE

You can add the same quantity or number to both sides of the equation and subtract the same quantity or number from both sides of the equation without affecting the equality of the equation. You can also divide or multiply both sides of the equation by the same quantity or number (*except zero*) without affecting the equality of the equation.

To check (verify) your answer(s), substitute your answer(s) for the letter(s) in the equation. The sum of the left side should equal the sum of the right side.

Drill Situation 1: Subtracting Same Number from Both Sides of Equation

EXAMPLE

$A + 8 = 58$
Dick's age A plus 8 equals 58.

Mathematical steps

$$\begin{array}{rcl} A + 8 & = & 58 \\ -8 & & -8 \\ \hline A & = & 50 \end{array}$$

Explanation

8 is subtracted from *both* sides of equation to isolate variable A on the left.

Check

$50 + 8 = 58$
$58 = 58$

These two equations are called "equivalent" equations.

Note: Since the equation process used *addition,* we use the opposite process rule and solve for variable A with *subtraction.* We also use the equation equality rule when we subtract the same quantity from both sides of the equation.

Drill Situation 2: Adding Same Number to Both Sides of Equation

EXAMPLE

$B - 50 = 80$
Some number B less 50 equals 80.

Mathematical steps

$$\begin{array}{rcl} B - 50 & = & 80 \\ +50 & & +50 \\ \hline B & = & 130 \end{array}$$

Explanation

50 is added to *both* sides to isolate variable B on the left.

Check

$130 - 50 = 80$
$80 = 80$

Equivalent equations

Note: Since the equation process used *subtraction,* we use the opposite process rule and solve for variable B with *addition.* We also use the equation equality rule when we add the same quantity to both sides of the equation.

Drill Situation 3: Dividing Both Sides of Equation by Same Number

EXAMPLE

$7G = 35$
Some number G times 7 equals 35.

Mathematical steps

$$7G = 35$$

$$\frac{\cancel{7}G}{\cancel{7}} = \frac{35}{7}$$

$$G = 5$$

Explanation

By dividing both sides by 7, G equals 5.

Check

$7(5) = 35$
$35 = 35$

Equivalent equations

Note: Since the equation process used *multiplication,* we use the opposite process rule and solve for variable G with *division.* We also use the equation equality rule when we divide both sides of the equation by the same quantity.

Drill Situation 4: Multiplying Both Sides of Equation by Same Number

EXAMPLE

$\frac{V}{5} = 70$

Some number V divided by 5 equals 70.

Mathematical steps	Explanation
$\frac{V}{5} = 70$	By multiplying both sides by 5, V is equal to 350.
$5\left(\frac{V}{5}\right) = 70(5)$	
$V = 350$	

Check

$\frac{350}{5} = 70$

$70 = 70$

Equivalent equations

Note: Since the equation process used *division,* we use the opposite process rule and solve for variable V with *multiplication.* We also use the equation equality rule when we multiply both sides of the equation by the same quantity.

Drill Situation 5: Equation That Uses Subtraction and Multiplication to Solve Unknown

MULTIPLE PROCESSES RULE

When solving for an unknown that involves more than one process, do the addition and subtraction before the multiplication and division.

EXAMPLE

$\frac{H}{4} + 2 = 5$

When we divide unknown H by 4 and add the result to 2, the answer is 5.

Mathematical steps	Explanation
$\frac{H}{4} + 2 = 5$	1. Move constant to right side by subtracting 2 from both sides.
$\frac{H}{4} + 2 - 2 = 5 - 2$	2. To isolate H, which is divided by 4, we do the opposite process and multiply 4 times *both* sides of the equation.
$\frac{H}{4} = 3$	
$4\left(\frac{H}{4}\right) = 4(3)$	
$H = 12$	

Check

$\frac{12}{4} + 2 = 5$

$3 + 2 = 5$

$5 = 5$

Equivalent equations

Drill Situation 6: Using Parentheses in Solving for Unknown

PARENTHESES RULE

When equations contain parentheses (which indicate grouping together), you solve for the unknown by first multiplying each item inside the parentheses by the number or letter just outside the parentheses. Then you continue to solve for the unknown with the opposite process used in the equation. Do the additions and subtractions first; then the multiplications and divisions.

EXAMPLE

	Mathematical steps	Explanation
$5(P - 4) = 20$ The unknown P less 4, multiplied by 5 equals 20.	$5(P - 4) = 20$ $5P - 20 = 20$ $+20 \quad +20$ $\frac{5P}{5} = \frac{40}{5}$ $P = 8$	1. Parentheses tell us that everything inside parentheses is multiplied by 5. Multiply 5 by P and 5 by -4. 2. Add 20 to both sides to isolate $5P$ on left. 3. To remove 5 in front of P, divide both sides by 5 to result in P equals 8. **Check** $5(8 - 4) = 20$ $5(4) = 20$ $20 = 20$

Drill Situation 7: Combining Like Unknowns

LIKE UNKNOWNS RULE

To solve equations with like unknowns, you first combine the unknowns and then solve with the opposite process used in the equation.

EXAMPLE

	Mathematical steps	Explanation
$4A + A = 20$	$4A + A = 20$ $\frac{5A}{5} = \frac{20}{5}$ $A = 4$	To solve this equation: $4A + 1A = 5A$. Thus, $5A = 20$. To solve for A, divide both sides by 5, leaving A equals 4.

Before you go to Learning Unit 5–2, let's check your understanding of this Unit.

LU 5–1 PRACTICE QUIZ

1. Write equations for the following (use the letter Q as the variable). Do not solve for the unknown.
   a. Nine less than one-half a number is fourteen.
   b. Eight times the sum of a number and thirty-one is fifty.
   c. Ten decreased by twice a number is two.
   d. Eight times a number less two equals twenty-one.
   e. The sum of four times a number and two is fifteen.
   f. If twice a number is decreased by eight, the difference is four.
2. Solve the following:
   a. $B + 24 = 60$ b. $D + 3D = 240$ c. $12B = 144$
   d. $\frac{B}{6} = 50$ e. $\frac{B}{4} + 4 = 16$ f. $3(B - 8) = 18$

LEARNING UNIT 5–2
SOLVING WORD PROBLEMS FOR THE UNKNOWN

On the first day of your business math class, you count 29 students in the class. A week later, 11 additional students had joined the class. The semester ended with 35 students in attendance. How many students dropped out of class? You can solve this unknown as follows:

29 students started the class + 11 students joined the class = 40 total students
40 total students − 35 students completed the class = 5 students dropped the class

Whether you are in or out of class, you are continually solving word problems. In this Unit we give you a road map showing you how to solve word problems with unknowns by using a Blueprint Aid. We have already used the step approach to solve word problems in the earlier chapters and in Learning Unit 5–1. In Chapters 1 through 3, we also presented Blueprint Aids for dissecting and solving word problems. Now the Blueprint Aid focuses on solving for the unknown.

We look at six different situations in this Unit. Be patient and *persistent.* The more problems you work, the easier the process becomes. Note how we dissect and solve each problem in the Blueprint Aids. Do not panic! Repetition is the key. Now let's study the five steps.

SOLVING WORD PROBLEMS FOR UNKNOWNS

Step 1. Carefully read the entire problem. You may have to read it several times. In the left corner of your notebook write what is given.

Step 2. Ask yourself: "What is the problem looking for?" Assign variables to known and unknown values. If the problem has more than one unknown, try to represent the second unknown in terms of the first. For example, if the problem has two unknowns, and you decide to call one of them Y, the second unknown might be called $4Y$ if you are told in the problem that it is four times the first unknown. You have translated English into mathematical terms.

Step 3. Think of a formula that will help you find a solution. Visualize the relationships between unknowns and variables. Set up an equation that expresses these relationships.

Step 4. Substitute the known values into the formula and find the unknown.

Step 5. Check (verify) the answer to see if it is accurate.

Bill Aron/PhotoEdit

The Flagging Division ...

A snapshot of the Disney Stores

- **NUMBER OF STORES:** 740
- **STORE VISITORS:** 250 million annually
- **LOCATIONS:** 11 countries including Britain, Australia and Japan
- **PRODUCTS:** Toys, costumes, apparel, jewelry, accessories, videos and games, among others
- **PRODUCT PLANS:** Each store will have 1,800 product offerings, down from 3,400 in the past. Focus on adults will be narrowed to sleepwear and parenting products.

Source: © 2000 Dow Jones & Company, Inc.

Word Problem Situation 1: Number Problems From the *Wall Street Journal* clip "The Flagging Division," you can determine that Disney Stores reduced its product offerings by 1,600. Disney now has 1,800 product offerings. What was the original number of product offerings?

BLUEPRINT AID

Unknown(s)	Variable(s)	Relationship*
Original number of product offerings	P	$P - 1{,}600$ = New offerings New offerings = 1,800

*This column will help you visualize the equation before setting up the actual equation.

MATHEMATICAL STEPS

$$\begin{aligned} P - 1{,}600 &= 1{,}800 \\ + 1{,}600 &\quad + 1{,}600 \\ P &= 3{,}400 \end{aligned}$$

EXPLANATION

The original offerings less 1,600 = 1,800. Note that we added 1,600 to both sides to isolate P on the left. Remember, $1P = P$.

CHECK

$3{,}400 - 1{,}600 = 1{,}800$

$1{,}800 = 1{,}800$

STEP APPROACH

STEP 1. Read the problem, and in the top left corner of your notebook write in brief form what is given.

New offerings after reduction = 1,800
Amount of reduction = 1,600
Original number of product offerings = ?

STEP 2. Assign variables to known and unknown values.

New offerings after reduction: B
Amount of reduction: A
Original number of product offerings: P
Rewrite the given information, using variables.

$B = 1{,}800$
$A = 1{,}600$
$P = ?$

STEP 3. Think of a formula that will help find the solution.

Original number − Amount of reduction = New number

$P - A = B$

To find the original number P, we must add the amount of reduction A and the new number B.

$P = B + A$

STEP 4. Substitute the values into the formula.

$P = 1{,}800 + 1{,}600$
$P = 3{,}400$

STEP 5. Verify the answer. Always substitute the values into the original formula.

$P - A = B$

The left side must equal the right side.

Left Side	=	*Right Side*
3,400 − 1,600	=	1,800
1,800	=	1,800

THE ANSWER IS CORRECT

Word Problem Situation 2: Finding the Whole When Part Is Known A local Burger King budgets $\frac{1}{8}$ of its monthly profits on salaries. Salaries for the month were $12,000. What were Burger King's monthly profits?

BLUEPRINT AID

Unknown(s)	Variable(s)	Relationship
Monthly profits	P	$\frac{1}{8}P$ Salaries = $12,000

MATHEMATICAL STEPS

$$\frac{1}{8}P = \$12{,}000$$

$$8\left(\frac{P}{8}\right) = \$12{,}000(8)$$

$$P = \$96{,}000$$

EXPLANATION

$\frac{1}{8}P$ represents Burger King's monthly salaries. Since the equation used division, we solve for P by multiplying both sides by 8.

CHECK

$\frac{1}{8}(\$96{,}000) = \$12{,}000$

$\$12{,}000 = \$12{,}000$

STEP APPROACH

STEP 1. Read the problem, and in the top left corner of your notebook write in brief form what is given.

Salaries for the month = $12,000
Salaries = $\frac{1}{8}$ of monthly profits
Monthly profits = ?

STEP 2. Assign variables to known and unknown values.

Salaries for the month: D
Monthly profits: P

$D = \frac{1}{8}$ of P

Rewrite the given information, using variables.

$D = \$12{,}000$
$D = \frac{1}{8} \times P$
$P = ?$

STEP 3. Think of a formula that will help find the solution.

$D = \frac{1}{8} \times P$
$P = D \div \left(\frac{1}{8}\right)$ (Use property of multiplications of fractions)
$P = D \times 8 = 8D$

STEP 4. Substitute the values into the formula.

$P = 8 \times 12{,}000$
$P = 96{,}000$

STEP 5. Verify the answer. Always substitute the values into the original formula.

$D = \frac{1}{8} \times P$

The left side must equal the right side.

Left Side	=	*Right Side*
12,000	=	$\frac{1}{8} \times 96{,}000$
12,000	=	12,000

THE ANSWER IS CORRECT

Word Problem Situation 3: Difference Problems ICM Company sold 4 times as many computers as Ring Company. The difference in their sales is 27. How many computers of each company were sold?

BLUEPRINT AID

Unknown(s)	Variable(s)	Relationship
ICM Ring	$4C$ C	$4C$ $-C$ 27

Note: If problem has two unknowns, assign the variable to smaller item or one who sells less. Then assign the other unknown using the same variable. *Use the same letter.*

MATHEMATICAL STEPS

$4C - C = 27$

$\frac{3C}{3} = \frac{27}{3}$

$C = 9$

Ring = 9 computers
ICM = 4(9)
= 36 computers

EXPLANATION

The variables replace the names ICM and Ring. We assigned Ring the variable C, since it sold fewer computers. We assigned ICM $4C$, since it sold 4 times as many computers.

CHECK

36 computers
− 9
27 computers

STEP APPROACH

STEP 1. Read the problem, and in the top left corner of your notebook write in brief form what is given. In this problem we are talking about two companies, ICM and Ring. ICM has sold four times more than Ring. In other words, the sales of ICM are expressed in terms of those of Ring.

Difference in their sales = 27
Sales of each company = ?

STEP 2. Assign variables to known and unknown values.

Sales of Ring = X
Sales of ICM = Y (Sales of ICM is $4 \times X$)
Difference in sales = $(Y - X)$
$Y = ?$
$X = ?$

Rewrite the given information, using variables.

$Y - X = 27$

STEP 3. Think of a formula, and visualize the relationships between the variables and unknowns.

Express Y in terms of X: $Y = 4X$
Substitute this expression in the formula: $4X - X = 27$

STEP 4. To find X (sales of the Ring company) we need to combine the like terms:

$3X = 27$
and then divide both parts of the equation by 3:
$X = 9$

To find Y (sales of ICM company) substitute the value of X into the formula $Y = 4X$.

$Y = 4 \times 9$
$Y = 36$

STEP 5. Verify the answer. Always substitute the values into the original formula.

$Y - X = 27$

The left side must equal the right side.

Left Side	=	*Right Side*
39 − 9	=	27
27	=	27

THE ANSWER IS CORRECT

Word Problem Situation 4: Calculating Unit Sales Together Barry Sullivan and Mitch Ryan sold a total of 300 homes for Regis Realty. Barry sold 9 times as many homes as Mitch. How many did each sell?

BLUEPRINT AID

Unknown(s)	Variable(s)	Relationship
Homes sold: B. Sullivan M. Ryan	$9M$ M	$9M$ $+M$ 300 homes

MATHEMATICAL STEPS

$9M + M = 300$

$\frac{10M}{10} = \frac{300}{10}$

$M = 30$

Ryan: 30 homes
Sullivan: 9(30) = 270 homes

EXPLANATION

We assigned Mitch M, since he sold fewer homes.
We assigned Barry $9M$, since he sold 9 times as many homes.
Together Barry and Mitch sold 300 homes.

CHECK

30 + 270 = 300

STEP APPROACH

STEP 1. Read the problem, and in the top left corner of your notebook write in brief form what is given. In this problem we are talking about two sales agents, Barry and Mitch. Together they have sold 300 homes. Barry has sold nine times as many homes as Mitch has. In other words, Barry's sales are expressed in terms of Mitch's sales.

STEP 2. M: Number of homes Mitch has sold
B: Number of homes Barry has sold
$M = ?$
$B = ?$
$B + M = 300$

STEP 3. Think of a formula, and visualize the relationship between the variables and unknowns.

Express B in terms of M: $B = 9 \times M$
Substitute this expression into the formula: $9M + M = 300$

STEP 4. To find M (Mitch's sales) we need to combine the like terms.

$10M = 300$ and then divide both parts of the equation by 10
$M = 30$

To find B, substitute the value of M into the formula $B = 9M$.

$B = 9 \times 30$
$Y = 270$

STEP 5. Verify the answer. Always substitute the values into the original formula.

$B + M = 300$

The left side must equal the right side.

Left Side	=	*Right Side*
270 + 30	=	300
300	=	300

THE ANSWER IS CORRECT

Word Problem Situation 5: Calculating Unit and Dollar Sales (Cost per Unit) When Total Units Are Not Given Andy sold watches ($9) and alarm clocks ($5) at a flea market. Total sales were $287. People bought 4 times as many watches as alarm clocks. How many of each did Andy sell? What were the total dollar sales of each?

BLUEPRINT AID

Unknown(s)	Variable(s)	Price	Relationship
Unit sales:			
Watches	$4C$	$9	$36C$
Clocks	C	5	$+ 5C$
			$287 total sales

MATHEMATICAL STEPS

$36C + 5C = 287$

$$\frac{41C}{41} = \frac{287}{41}$$

$C = 7$

7 clocks

$4(7) = 28$ watches

EXPLANATION

Number of watches times $9 sales price plus number of alarm clocks times $5 equals $287 total sales.

CHECK

7($5) + 28($9) = $287

$35 + $252 = $287

$287 = $287

STEP APPROACH

STEP 1. In this problem we are talking about sales of two items: clocks and watches. Sales of watches exceeded the sales of clocks by four times. So sales of watches are expressed in terms of sales of clocks.

STEP 2. C: Number of clocks sold
$4C$: Number of watches sold
Revenue from sales of watches was: $4C \times 9$
Revenue from sales of clocks was: $C \times 5$
Total revenue was: $287
$C = ?$
$4C = ?$

STEP 3. $36C + 5C = 287$

STEP 4. $41C = 287$
$C = 7$
$4C = 28$

STEP 5. Verify the answer. Always substitute the values into the original formula. The left side must equal the right side.

Left Side	=	*Right Side*
$9 \times 28 + 7 \times 5$	=	287
$252 + 35$	=	287
287	=	287

THE ANSWER IS CORRECT

Word Problem Situation 6: Calculating Unit and Dollar Sales (Cost per Unit) When Total Units Are Given Andy sold watches ($9) and alarm clocks ($5) at a flea market. Total sales for 35 watches and alarm clocks were $287. How many of each did Andy sell? What were the total dollar sales of each?

BLUEPRINT AID

Unknown(s)	Variable(s)	Price	Relationship
Unit sales:			
Watches	W*	$9	$9W$
Clocks	$35 - W$	5	$+ 5(35 - W)$
			$287 total sales

*The more expensive item is assigned to the variable first only for this situation to make the mechanical steps easier to complete.

MATHEMATICAL STEPS

$9W + 5(35 - W) = 287$

$9W + 175 - 5W = 287$

$4W + 175 = 287$

$- 175 \quad - 175$

$$\frac{4W}{4} = \frac{112}{4}$$

$W = 28$

Watches = 28

Clocks = 35 − 28 = 7

EXPLANATION

Number of watches (W) times price per watch plus number of alarm clocks times price per alarm clock equals $287. Total units given was 35.

CHECK

28($9) + 7($5) = $287

$252 + $35 = $287

$287 = $287

STEP APPROACH

STEP 1. In this problem, once again we are speaking about sales of two items: clocks and watches.

STEP 2. W: number of watches sold
$35 - W$: number of clocks sold
Revenue from sales of watches was: $9 \times W$
Revenue from sales of clocks was: $5 \times (35 - W)$
Total revenue was: $287
$W = ?$
$(35 - W) = ?$

STEP 3. $9W + 5(35 - W) = 287$

STEP 4. $9W + 175 - 5W = 287$
$4W + 175 = 287$
$4W = 287 - 175$
$4W = 112$
$W = 28$
$35 - W = 35 - 28 = 7$

STEP 5. Verify the answer. The left side must equal the right side.

Left Side	=	*Right Side*
$9 \times 28 + 7 \times 5$	=	287
$252 + 35$	=	287
287	=	287

THE ANSWER IS CORRECT

Why did we use $35 - W$? Assume we had 35 pizzas (some cheese, others meatball). If I said that I ate all the meatball pizzas (5), how many cheese pizzas are left? Thirty? Right, you subtract 5 from 35. Think of $(35 - W)$ as meaning one number.

Note in Word Problem Situations 5 and 6 that the situation is the same. In Word Problem Situation 5, we were not given total units sold (but we were told which sold better). In Word Problem Situation 6, we were given total units sold, but we did not know which sold better.

Now try these six types of word problems in the Practice Quiz. Do it in either way: complete Blueprint Aids or follow steps for solving word problems with the unknown(s).

LU 5–2 PRACTICE QUIZ

Situations

1. An L. L. Bean sweater was reduced \$30. The sale price was \$90. What was the original price?
2. Kelly Doyle budgets $\frac{1}{8}$ of her yearly salary for entertainment. Kelly's total entertainment bill for the year is \$6,500. What is Kelly's yearly salary?
3. Micro Knowledge sells 5 times as many computers as Morse Electronics. The difference in sales between the two stores is 20 computers. How many computers did each store sell?
4. Susie and Cara sell stoves at Elliott's Appliances. Together they sold 180 stoves in January. Susie sold 5 times as many stoves as Cara. How many stoves did each sell?
5. Pasquale's Pizza sells meatball pizzas (\$6) and cheese pizzas (\$5). In March, Pasquale's total sales were \$1,600. People bought 2 times as many cheese pizzas as meatball pizzas. How many of each did Pasquale sell? What were the total dollar sales of each?
6. Pasquale's Pizza sells meatball pizzas (\$6) and cheese pizzas (\$5). In March, Pasquale's sold 300 pizzas for \$1,600. How many of each did Pasquale's sell? What was the dollar sales price of each?

CHAPTER ORGANIZER AND REFERENCE GUIDE

Properties of equations	Key points, procedures, formulas	Examples
If you change both sides of the equation in the same way, you will get equivalent equations, p. 102	Add the same number to both members of an equation. Subtract the same value from both members of an equation. Multiply or divide both members by the same number/value.	$4X = 8$ $4X + 2 = 10$ $(8 + 2 = 10)$ $15Y + 3 = 8$ $15Y + 3 - 3 = 8 - 3 = 5$ $15Y = 5$ $15Y = 5$ (÷ by 5) $3Y = 1$ $15Y = 5$ (× by 4) $60Y = 20$

Solving for unknowns from basic equations	Mathematical steps to solve unknowns	Key point(s)
Situation 1: Subtracting same number from both sides of equation, p. 103	$D + 10 = 12$ $\quad - 10 = -10$ $D = 2$	Subtract 10 from both sides of equation to isolate variable D on the left. Since equation used addition, we solve by using opposite process—subtraction.
Situation 2: Adding same number to both sides of equation, p. 103	$L - 24 = 40$ $\quad + 24 = +24$ $L = 64$	Add 24 to both sides to isolate unknown L on left. We solve by using opposite process of subtraction—addition.

(continues)

CHAPTER ORGANIZER AND REFERENCE GUIDE (CONTINUED)

Solving for unknowns from basic equations	Mathematical steps to solve unknowns	Key point(s)
Situation 3: Dividing both sides of equation by same number, p. 103	$6B = 24$ $\frac{6B}{6} = \frac{24}{6}$ $B = 4$	To isolate *B* by itself on the left, divide both sides of the equation by 6. Thus, the 6 on the left cancels—leaving *B* equal to *4*. Since equation used multiplication, we solve unknown by using opposite process—division.
Situation 4: Multiplying both sides of equation by same number, p. 104	$\frac{R}{3} = 15$ $3\left(\frac{R}{3}\right) = 15(3)$ $R = 45$	To remove denominator, multiply both sides of the equation by 3—the 3 on the left side cancels, leaving *R* equal to 45. Since equation used division, we solve unknown by using opposite process—multiplication.
Situation 5: Equation that uses subtraction and multiplication to solve for unknown, p. 104	$\frac{B}{3} + 6 = 13$ $-6 \quad -6$ $\frac{B}{3} = 7$ $3\left(\frac{B}{3}\right) = 7(3)$ $B = 21$	1. Move constant 6 to right side by subtracting 6 from both sides. 2. Isolate *B* by itself on left by multiplying both sides by 3.
Situation 6: Using parentheses in solving for unknown, p. 104	$6(A - 5) = 12$ $6A - 30 = 12$ $+30 = +30$ $\frac{6A}{6} = \frac{42}{6}$ $A = 7$	Parentheses indicate multiplication. Multiply 6 times *A* and 6 times −5. Result is 6*A* − 30 on left side of the equation. Now add 30 to both sides to isolate 6*A* on left. To remove 6 in front of *A*, divide both sides by 6, to result in *A* equal to 7. Note that when deleting parentheses, we did not have to multiply the right side.
Situation 7: Combining like unknowns, p. 105	$6A + 2A = 64$ $\frac{8A}{8} = \frac{64}{8}$ $A = 8$	6*A* + 2*A* combine to 8*A*. To solve for *A*, we divide both sides by 8.

Solving for unknowns from word problems (step approach)	Assigning variables and defining formulas (translation from English into math)	Solution and verification
Step 1. Carefully read the entire problem. You may have to read it several times. In the left corner of your notebook write what is given. **Step 2.** Ask yourself: "What is the problem looking for?" Assign variables to known and unknown values. If the problem has more than one unknown, represent the second unknown in terms of the same variable. For example, if the problem has two unknowns, *Y* is one unknown. The second	1. The sum of two numbers is 60. The first number is twice as big as the second. Find both numbers. 2. The sum of two numbers is 180. The first number is 5 units greater then $\frac{3}{4}$ of the second. What are the numbers?	1. First number is *A*. Second number is *B*. A is twice *B*: $A = 2B$ $A + B = 60$ Substitute for *A* its equivalent value 2*B*: $2B + B = 60$ $3B = 60$ $B = 20$ $2B = A = 40$ Verify: **LS = RS** $40 + 20 = 60$ $60 = 60$

(*continues*)

CHAPTER ORGANIZER AND REFERENCE GUIDE (CONTINUED)

Solving for Unknowns from Word Problems (Step Approach)	Assigning Variables and Defining Formulas (Translation from English into Math)	Solution and Verification
unknown might be $4Y$ (four times the first unknown). You have translated English into math. **Step 3.** Think of a formula, which will help find the solution. Visualize the relationship between unknowns and variables. Set up an equation to solve for unknown(s). **Step 4.** Substitute the known values into the formula and find the unknowns. **Step 5.** Check (verify) the answer to see if it is accurate. p. 106		2. The first number is A, the second is B. $A = \frac{3}{4}B + 5$ $A + B = 180$ Substitute for A its equivalent value: $B + \frac{3}{4}B + 5 = 180$ $1\frac{3}{4}B = 175$; $1.75B = 175$ $B = 100$; $A = 80$ Verify: **LS = RS** $80 + 100 = 180$

Solving for Unknowns from Word Problems	Blueprint Aid	Mathematical Steps to Solve Unknown with Check	Solution and Verification
Situation 1: Number problems, p. 107 U.S. Air reduced its airfare to California by \$60. The sale price was \$95. What was the original price?	**Unknown(s):** Original price; **Variable(s):** P; **Relationship:** P − \$60 = Sale price; Sale price = \$95	$P - \$60 = \$95$ $+60 \quad +60$ $P = \$155$ **Check** $\$155 - \$60 = \$95$ $\$95 = \$95$	S = Sale price = \$95 D = Amount of discount = \$60 $P = ?$ $P - D = S$ $P = S + D$; $P = 60 + 95 = 155$ $P = 155$ Verify: **LS = RS** $155 - 60 = 95$ $95 = 95$
Situation 2: Finding the whole when part is known, p. 107 K. McCarthy spends $\frac{1}{8}$ of her budget for school. What is the total budget if school costs \$5,000?	**Unknown(s):** Total budget; **Variable(s):** B; **Relationship:** $\frac{1}{8}B$; School = \$5,000	$\frac{1}{8}B = \$5,000$ $8\left(\frac{B}{8}\right) = \$5,000(8)$ $B = \$40,000$ **Check** $\frac{1}{8}(\$40,000) = \$5,000$ $\$5,000 = \$5,000$	B − Total budget $\frac{1}{8}B$ − Spendings = \$5,000 $\frac{1}{8}B = 5,000$ $B = \frac{5,000}{\left(\frac{1}{8}\right)} = 5,000 \times 8 = 40,000$ Verify: **LS = RS** $\frac{1}{8} - 40,000 = 5,000$ $5,000 = 5,000$
Situation 3: Difference problems, p. 108 Moe sold 8 times as many suitcases as Bill. The difference in their sales is 280 suitcases. How many suitcases did each sell?	**Unknown(s):** Suitcases sold: Moe; Bill. **Variable(s):** Moe $8S$; Bill S. **Relationship:** $8S$ − S = 280 suitcases	$8S - S = 280$ (Bill) $\frac{7S}{7} = \frac{280}{7}$ $S = 40$ (Bill) $8(40) = 320$ (Moe) **Check** $320 - 40 = 280$ $280 = 280$	Bill's sales − S; Moe's sales = $8S$ $8S - S$ = Difference = 280 $S = ?$ $8S = ?$ $8S - S = 280$; $7S = 280$; $S = 40$ $8S = 320$ Verification: **LS = RS** $8 \times 40 - 40 = 280$ $280 = 280$

(continues)

CHAPTER ORGANIZER AND REFERENCE GUIDE (CONCLUDED)

Solving for unknowns from word problems	Blueprint aid	Mathematical steps to solve unknown with check	Solution and verification

Situation 4: Calculating unit sales, p. 108

Moe sold 8 times as many suitcases as Bill. Together they sold a total of 360. How many did each sell?

Blueprint aid

Unknown(s)	Variable(s)	Relationship
Suitcases sold:		
Moe	$8S$	$8S$
Bill	S	$+ S$
		360 suitcases

Mathematical steps to solve unknown with check

$8S + S = 360$

$\frac{9S}{9} = \frac{360}{9}$

$S = 40$ (Bill)

$8S = 320$ (Moe)

Check

$320 + 40 = 360$

$360 = 360$

Solution and verification

Bill's sales = S;
Moe's sales = $8S$
$S + 8S = 360$
= Total sales in units
$S = ?\ 8S = ?$
$S + 8S = 360$; $9S = 360$; $S = 40$
$8S = 320$
Verification:
LS = RS
$40 + 320 = 360$
$360 = 360$

Situation 5: Calculating unit and dollar sales (cost per unit) when *total units not given*, p. 109

Blue Furniture Company ordered sleepers ($300) and nonsleepers ($200) that cost $8,000. Blue expects sleepers to outsell nonsleepers 2 to 1. How many units of each were ordered? What were dollar costs of each?

Blueprint aid

Unknown(s)	Variable(s)	Price	Relationship
Sleepers	$2N$	$300	$600N$
Nonsleepers	N	200	$+200N$
			$8,000 total cost

Mathematical steps to solve unknown with check

$600N + 200N = 8{,}000$

$\frac{800N}{800} = \frac{8{,}000}{800}$

$N = 10$ (nonsleepers)

$2N = 20$ (sleepers)

Check

$10 \times \$200 = \$2{,}000$

$20 \times \$300 = \ \ 6{,}000$

$\$8{,}000$

Solution and verification

N = Sales of nonsleepers,
$2N$ = Sales of sleepers
$200N + 300 \times 2 \times N = 8{,}000$
= Total cost; $N = ?\ 2N = ?$
$600N + 200N = 8{,}000$
$800N = 8{,}000$; $N = 10$; $2N = 20$
Verification:
LS = RS
$200 - 10 + 300 \times 20 = 8{,}000$
$2{,}000 + 6{,}000 = 8{,}000$
$8{,}000 = 8{,}000$

Situation 6: Calculating unit and dollar sales (cost per unit) when *total units given*, p. 109

Blue Furniture Company ordered 30 sofas (sleepers and nonsleepers) that cost $8,000. The wholesale unit cost was $300 for the sleepers and $200 for the nonsleepers. How many units of each were ordered? What were dollar costs of each?

Blueprint aid

Unknown(s)	Variable(s)	Price	Relationship
Unit cost:			
Sleepers	S	$300	$300S$
Nonsleepers	$30 - S$	200	$+200\ (30 - S)$
			$8,000 total cost

*Note: When the total units are given, the higher-priced item (sleepers) is assigned to the variable first. This makes the mechanical steps easier to complete.

Mathematical steps to solve unknown with check

$300S + 200(30 - S) = 8{,}000$

$300S + 6{,}000 - 200S = 8{,}000$

$100S + 6{,}000 = 8{,}000$

$-6{,}000 \quad -6{,}000$

$\frac{100S}{100} = \frac{2{,}000}{100}$

$S = 20$

Nonsleepers $= 30 - 20$

$= 10$

Check

$20(\$300) + 10(\$200) = \$8{,}000$

$\$6{,}000 + \$2{,}000 = \$8{,}000$

$\$8{,}000 = \$8{,}000$

Solution and verification

S = Sleepers ordered
$30 = S$ = Nonsleepers ordered
$300S + 200(30 - S)$
$= 8{,}000$ = Total cost
$S = ?\ 30 - S = ?$
$300S + 6{,}000 - 200S = 8{,}000$
$100S + 6{,}000 = 8{,}000$
$100S = 2{,}000$; $S = 20$
$30 - S = 30 - 20 = 10$
Verification:
LS = RS
$300 \times 20 + 200 \times 10 = 8{,}000$
$6{,}000 + 2{,}000 = 8{,}000$
$8{,}000 = 8{,}000$

Key terms

Constants, p. 101	Formula, p. 101	Solution of an equation, p. 102
Equation, p. 101	Knowns, p. 101	Solve an equation, p 102
Equivalent equations, p. 102	Linear equation, p. 101	Unknown, p. 101
Equation in one unknown, p. 101	Members of equation, p. 101	Variables, p. 101
Expression, p. 101	Root of equation, p. 102	Verification, p. 102

CRITICAL THINKING DISCUSSION QUESTIONS

1. Explain the difference between a variable and a constant. What would you consider your monthly car payment—a variable or a constant?
2. How does the opposite process rule help solve for the variable in an equation? If a Mercedes costs 3 times as much as a Saab, how could the opposite process rule be used? The selling price of the Mercedes is $60,000.
3. What is the difference between Word Problem Situations 5 and 6 in Learning Unit 5–2? Show why the more expensive item in Word Problem Situation 6 is assigned to the variable first.

Visit the text website at www.mcgrawhill.ca/college/slater

END-OF-CHAPTER PROBLEMS

DRILL PROBLEMS (FIRST OF THREE SETS)

Solve the unknown from the following equations:

5–1. $H + 15 = 70$ **5–2.** $B + 29 = 75$ **5–3.** $N + 50 = 290$ **5–4.** $Q - 60 = 850$

5–5. $5Y = 75$ **5–6.** $\frac{P}{6} = 92$ **5–7.** $8Y = 96$ **5–8.** $\frac{N}{16} = 5$

5–9. $4(P - 9) = 64$ **5–10.** $3(P - 3) = 27$

DRILL PROBLEMS (SECOND OF THREE SETS)

Solve the unknown in the following equations:

5–11. $6B = 420$ **5–12.** $7(A - 5) = 63$ **5–13.** $\frac{N}{9} = 7$

5–14. $18(C - 3) = 162$ **5–15.** $9Y - 10 = 53$ **5–16.** $7B + 5 = 26$

DRILL PROBLEMS (THIRD OF THREE SETS)

Solve the unknown from the following equations:

5–17. $B + 82 - 11 = 190$ **5–18.** $5Y + 15(Y + 1) = 35$

5–19. $3M + 20 = 2M + 80$ **5–20.** $20(C - 50) = 19{,}000$

ADDITIONAL DRILL PROBLEMS

5–21. Write equations for the following situations. Use N for the unknown number. Do not solve the equations.

a. Three times a number is 70.
b. A number increased by 13 equals 25.
c. Seven less than a number is 5.
d. Fifty-seven decreased by 3 times a number is 21.
e. Fourteen added to one-third of a number is 18.
f. Twice the sum of a number and 4 is 32.
g. Three-fourths of a number is 9.
h. Two times a number plus 3 times the same number plus 8 is 68.

5–22. Solve for the unknown number:

a. $B + 12 = 38$ **b.** $29 + M = 44$ **c.** $D - 77 = 98$

d. $7N = 63$ **e.** $\frac{X}{12} = 11$ **f.** $3Q + 4Q + 2Q = 108$

g. $H + 5H + 3 = 57$ **h.** $2(N - 3) = 62$ **i.** $\frac{3R}{4} = 27$

j. $E - 32 = 41$ **k.** $5(2T - 2) = 120$ **l.** $12W - 5W = 98$

m. $49 - X = 37$ **n.** $12(V + 2) = 84$ **o.** $7D + 4 = 5D + 14$

p. $7(T - 2) = 2T - 9$

WORD PROBLEMS (FIRST OF THREE SETS)

5–23. Excel The *Omaha World-Herald,* on January 23, 2001, ran an article titled "Lending Agency Convicted of Predatory Lending Practices." A loan company took the title to an elderly Bellevue widow's home by paying taxes of about \$22,200. The market value of the house is $3\frac{1}{2}$ times the tax. What was the market value? Round to the nearest ten thousands.

5–24. A statistician compared the price of a 1955 Ford Thunderbird to that of a 2002 Ford Thunderbird. The 2002 Thunderbird's price is \$34,595. This is 13 times as much as the selling price for the 1955 Thunderbird. What was the selling price of the 1955 Ford Thunderbird? (Round to the nearest hundred.)

5–25. Joe Sullivan and Hugh Kee sell cars for a Ford dealer. Over the past year, they sold 300 cars. Joe sells 5 times as many cars as Hugh. How many cars did each sell?

5–26. Excel Nanda Yueh and Lane Zuriff sell homes for ERA Realty. Over the past 6 months they sold 120 homes. Nanda sold 3 times as many homes as Lane. How many homes did each sell?

5–27. Dots sells T-shirts ($2) and shorts ($4). In April, total sales were $600. People bought 4 times as many T-shirts as shorts. How many T-shirts and shorts did Dots sell? Check your answer.

5–28. Dots sells 250 T-shirts ($2) and shorts ($4). In April, total sales were $600. How many T-shirts and shorts did Dots sell? Check your answer. *Hint:* Let S = Shorts.

WORD PROBLEMS (SECOND OF THREE SETS)

5–29. On a flight from Vancouver to Toronto, Charter Airlines reduced its Internet price $130. The sale price was $299.50. What was the original price?

5–30. Fay, an employee at the Gap, budgets $\frac{1}{5}$ of her yearly salary for clothing. Fay's total clothing bill for the year is $8,000. What is her yearly salary?

5–31. Bill's Roast Beef sells 5 times as many sandwiches as Pete's Deli. The difference between their sales is 360 sandwiches. How many sandwiches did each sell?

5–32. A researcher compared the number of calories for the food sold by several fast-food chains. McDonald's "Big N' Tasty with Cheese" has almost 600 calories. This is 4 times as many as are in the "McSalad Shaker Chef Salad." How many calories are in the salad?

5–33. Computer City sells batteries ($3) and small boxes of pens ($5). In August, total sales were $960. Customers bought 5 times as many batteries as boxes of pens. How many of each did Computer City sell? Check your answer.

5–34. Staples sells cartons of pens ($10) and rubber bands ($4). Leona ordered a total of 24 cartons for $210. How many cartons of each did Leona order? Check your answer. *Hint:* Let P = Pens.

WORD PROBLEMS (THIRD OF THREE SETS)

5–35. On December 7, 2000, the *Chicago Sun-Times* ran an article comparing major media ad outlays in the millions of dollars (TV, print, radio, outdoor). In the year 2003, the expected outlay in North America will be $168.6. This is $1\frac{1}{4}$ times more than was spent in 1999. What was the total dollar outlay (in millions) during 1999? Round to nearest tenth.

5–36. At General Electric, shift $1\frac{1}{4}$ produced 4 times as much as shift 2. General Electric's total production for July was 5,500 jet engines. What was the output for each shift?

5–37. Ivy Corporation gave 84 people a bonus. If Ivy had given 2 more people bonuses, Ivy would have rewarded $\frac{2}{3}$ of the workforce. How large is Ivy's workforce?

5–38. Jim Murray and Phyllis Lowe received a total of $50,000 from a deceased relative's estate. They decided to put $10,000 in a trust for their nephew and divide the remainder. Phyllis received $\frac{3}{4}$ of the remainder; Jim received $\frac{1}{4}$. How much did Jim and Phyllis receive?

5–39. The first shift of GME Corporation produced $1\frac{1}{2}$ times as many lanterns as the second shift. GME produced 5,600 lanterns in November. How many lanterns did GME produce on each shift?

5–40. Wal-Mart sells thermometers ($2) and hot-water bottles ($6). In December, Wal-Mart's total sales were $1,200. Customers bought 7 times as many thermometers as hot-water bottles. How many of each did Wal-Mart sell? Check your answer.

5–41. Ace Hardware sells cartons of wrenches ($100) and hammers ($300). Howard ordered 40 cartons of wrenches and hammers for $8,400. How many cartons of each are in the order? Check your answer.

ADDITIONAL WORD PROBLEMS

5–42. A blue denim shirt at the Gap was marked down $15. The sale price was $30. What was the original price?

Unknown(s)	Variable(s)	Relationship

5–43. Goodwin's Corporation found that $\frac{2}{3}$ of its employees were vested in their retirement plan. If 124 employees are vested, what is the total number of employees at Goodwin's? Use the step approach. Verify your answer.

5–44. Eileen Haskin's utility and telephone bills for the month totalled $180. The utility bill was 3 times as much as the telephone bill. How much was each bill?

Unknown(s)	Variable(s)	Relationship

5–45. Ryan and his friends went to the golf course to hunt for golf balls. Ryan found 15 more than $\frac{1}{3}$ of the total number of golf balls that were found. How many golf balls were found if Ryan found 75 golf balls? Use the step approach. Verify your answer.

5–46. Linda Mills and Sherry Somers sold 459 tickets for the Advertising Club's raffle. If Linda sold 8 times as many tickets as Sherry, how many tickets did each one sell?

Unknown(s)	Variable(s)	Relationship

5–47. Jason Mazzola wanted to buy a suit at Giblee's. Jason did not have enough money with him, so Mr. Giblee told him he would hold the suit if Jason gave him a deposit of $\frac{1}{5}$ of the cost of the suit. Jason agreed and gave Mr. Giblee $79. What was the price of the suit? Use the step approach. Verify your answer.

5–48. Peter sold watches ($7) and necklaces ($4) at a flea market. Total sales were $300. People bought 3 times as many watches as necklaces. How many of each did Peter sell? What were the total dollar sales of each?

Unknown(s)	Variable(s)	Price	Relationship

5–49. Peter sold watches ($7) and necklaces ($4) at a flea market. Total sales for 48 watches and necklaces were $300. How many of each did Peter sell? What were the total dollar sales of each?

Unknown(s)	Variable(s)	Price	Relationship

5–50. A 3,000 piece of direct mailing cost $1,435. Printing cost is $550, about $3\frac{1}{2}$ times the cost of typesetting. How much did the typesetting cost? Round to the nearest cent.

Unknown(s)	Variable(s)	Price	Relationship

5–51. In 2003, Tony Rigato, owner of MRM, saw an increase in sales to $13.5 million. Rigato states that since 2000, sales have more than tripled. What were his sales in 2000? Use the step approach. Verify your answer.

CHALLENGE PROBLEMS

5–52. Jack Barney and Michelle Denny sold a total of 450 home entertainment centres at Circuit City. Jack sold 2 times as many units as Michelle. Michelle had $97,500 in total sales, which was $1\frac{1}{2}$ times as much as Jack's sales. **(a)** How many units did Michelle sell? **(b)** How many units did Jack sell? **(c)** What was the total dollar amount Jack sold? **(d)** What was the average amount of sales for Jack? **(e)** What was the average amount of sales for Michelle? Round both averages to the nearest dollar.

5–53. Bessy has 6 times as much money as Bob, but when each earns $6, Bessy will have 3 times as much money as Bob. How much does each have before and after earning the $6?

SUMMARY PRACTICE TEST

1. Railway Company reduced its round-trip first-class ticket price from Toronto to Montreal by $95. The sale price was $205.99. What was the original price? (p. 107)
2. Al Ring is an employee at Amazon.ca. He budgets $\frac{1}{6}$ of his salary for clothing. If Al's total clothing for the year is $9,000, what is his yearly salary? (p. 107)
3. A local Best Buy sells 6 times as many DVDs as Future Shop. The difference between their sales is 150 DVDs. How many DVDs did each sell? (p. 107)
4. Working at Sharper Image, Joy Allen and Flo Ring sold a total of 900 scooters. Joy sold 4 times as many scooters as Flo. How many did each sell? (p. 108)
5. Kitchen Etc. sells sets of pots ($19) and dishes ($13) at a local charity. On the Canada Day weekend, Kitchen Etc.'s total sales were $1,780. People bought 4 times as many pots as dishes. How many of each did Kitchen Etc. sell? Check your answer. (p. 108)
6. Dominos sold a total of 1,300 small pizzas ($7) and hamburgers ($9) during the Super Bowl. How many of each did Dominos sell if total sales were $11,000? Check your answer. (p. 108)

SOLUTIONS TO PRACTICE QUIZZES

LU 5–1

1. **a.** $\frac{1}{2}Q - 9 = 14$ **b.** $8(Q + 31) = 50$ **c.** $10 - 2Q = 2$

d. $8Q - 2 = 21$ **e.** $4Q + 2 = 15$ **f.** $2Q - 8 = 4$

2. **a.**
$$\begin{aligned} B + 24 &= 60 \\ -24 &\quad -24 \\ B &= \boxed{36} \end{aligned}$$

b.
$$\frac{\cancel{4}D}{\cancel{4}} = \frac{240}{4}$$
$$D = \boxed{60}$$

c.
$$\frac{\cancel{12}B}{\cancel{12}} = \frac{144}{12}$$
$$B = \boxed{12}$$

d.
$$\cancel{6}\left(\frac{B}{\cancel{6}}\right) = 50(6)$$
$$B = \boxed{300}$$

e.
$$\begin{aligned} \frac{B}{4} + 4 &= 16 \\ -4 &\quad -4 \\ \frac{B}{4} &= 12 \\ \cancel{4}\left(\frac{B}{\cancel{4}}\right) &= 12(4) \\ B &= \boxed{48} \end{aligned}$$

f.
$$\begin{aligned} 3(B - 8) &= 18 \\ 3B - 24 &= 18 \\ +24 &\quad +24 \\ \frac{\cancel{3}B}{\cancel{3}} &= \frac{42}{3} \\ B &= \boxed{14} \end{aligned}$$

LU 5–2

1.

Unknown(s)	Variable(s)	Relationship
Original price	P^*	$P - \$30 =$ Sale price Sale price $= \$90$

*P = Original price.

MATHEMATICAL STEPS

$$\begin{aligned} P - \$30 &= \$90 \\ +30 &\quad +30 \\ P &= \boxed{\$120} \end{aligned}$$

STEPS 1. & 2. *P:* Original price
D: Amount of reduction/discount = $30
S – Sale price = $90

STEP 3. $P - D = S$

STEP 4. $P - 30 = 90$
$P = 90 + 30$
$P = 120$

STEP 5. Verify the answer. The left side must equal the right side.

Left Side = *Right Side*
120 − 30 = 90
90 = 90

THE ANSWER IS CORRECT

2.

Unknown(s)	Variable(s)	Relationship
Yearly salary	S^*	$\frac{1}{8}S$ Entertainment = $6,500

*S = Salary.

MATHEMATICAL STEPS

$$\frac{1}{8}S = \$6{,}500$$
$$\cancel{8}\left(\frac{S}{\cancel{8}}\right) = \$6{,}500(8)$$
$$S = \boxed{\$52{,}000}$$

STEPS 1. & 2. *S:* Yearly salary = ?
$\frac{1}{8}S$: Entertainment budget
$\frac{1}{8}S = \$6{,}500$

STEP 3. $\frac{1}{8}S = 6{,}500$

STEP 4. $S = 6{,}500 \div \left(\frac{1}{8}\right)$
$S = 6{,}500 \times 8 = 52{,}000$

STEP 5. Verify the answer. The left side must equal the right side.

Left Side = *Right Side*
$\frac{1}{8} \times 52{,}000 = 6{,}500$
6,500 = 6,500

THE ANSWER IS CORRECT

3.

Unknown(s)	Variable(s)	Relationship
Micro	$5M$*	$5M$
Morse	M	$-\ M$
		20 computers

*M = Computers.

MATHEMATICAL STEPS

$5M - M = 20$

$\frac{\not{4}M}{\not{4}} = \frac{20}{4}$

$M = 5$ (Morse)

$5M = 25$ (Micro)

STEPS 1. & 2. M: Morse's sales

$5M$: Micro sales

$5M - M$: Difference in sales = 20

$M = ?$

$5M = ?$

STEP 3. $5M - M = 20$

STEP 4. $4M = 20$

$M = 5$

$5M = 25$

STEP 5. Verify the answer. The left side must equal the right side.

Left Side	=	*Right Side*
25 − 5	=	20
20	=	20

THE ANSWER IS CORRECT

4.

Unknown(s)	Variable(s)	Relationship
Stoves sold:		
Susie	$5C$*	$5C$
Cara	C	$+\ C$
		180 stoves

*C = Stoves.

MATHEMATICAL STEPS

$5C + C = 180$

$\frac{\not{6}C}{\not{6}} = \frac{180}{6}$

$C = 30$ (Cara)

$5C = 150$ (Susie)

STEPS 1. & 2. C: Cara's sales

$5C$: Susie's sales

$C + 5C$: Total sales in units = 180

STEP 3. $C + 5C = 180$

STEP 4. $6C = 180$

$C = 30$

$5C = 150$

STEP 5. Verify the answer. The left side must equal the right side.

Left Side	=	*Right Side*
30 + 150	=	180
180	=	180

THE ANSWER IS CORRECT

5.

Unknown(s)	Variable(s)	Price	Relationship
Meatball	M	$6	$6M$
Cheese	$2M$	5	$+\ 10M$
			$1,600 total sales

MATHEMATICAL STEPS

$6M + 10M = 1{,}600$

$\frac{\not{16}M}{\not{16}} = \frac{1{,}600}{16}$

$M = 100$ (meatball)

$2M = 200$ (cheese)

CHECK

$(100 \times \$6) + (200 \times \$5) = \$1{,}600$

$\$600 + \$1{,}000 = \$1{,}600$

$\$1{,}600 = \$1{,}600$

STEPS 1. & 2. M: Sales of meatball pizzas

$2M$: Sales of cheese pizzas

$6M + 5 \times 2M$: Total sales in $ = $1,600

$M = ?$

$2M = ?$

STEP 3. $6M + 10\ M = 1{,}600$

STEP 4. $16M = 1{,}600$

$M = 100$

$2M = 200$

STEP 5. Verify the answer. The left side must equal the right side.

Left Side	=	*Right Side*
6 × 100 + 5 × 200	=	1,600
1,600	=	1,600

THE ANSWER IS CORRECT

6.

Unknown(s)	Variable(s)	Price	Relationship
Unit sales:			
Meatball	M*	\$6	$6M$
Cheese	$300 - M$	5	$+5(300 - M)$
			\$1,600 total sales

*We assign the variable to the most expensive to make the mechanical steps easier to complete.

MATHEMATICAL STEPS

$$6M + 5(300 - M) = 1{,}600$$
$$6M + 1{,}500 - 5M = 1{,}600$$
$$M + 1{,}500 = 1{,}600$$
$$-1{,}500 \quad -1{,}500$$
$$M = 100$$

Meatball = 100

Cheese = 300 − 100 = 200

CHECK

100(\$6) + 200(\$5) = \$600 + \$1,000
= \$1,600

STEPS 1. & 2. *M:* Sales of meatball pizzas
$300 - M$: Sales of cheese pizzas
$6M + 5(300 - M)$: Total sales in \$ = \$1,600
$M = ?$
$300 - M = ?$

STEP 3. $6M + (300 - M) = 1{,}600$

STEP 4. $6M + 1{,}500 - 5M = 1{,}600$
$M + 1{,}500 = 1{,}600$
$M = 100$
$2M = 200$

STEP 5. Verify the answer. The left side must equal the right side.

Left Side	= *Right Side*
$6 \times 100 + 5 \times (300 - 100)$	= 1,600
1,600	= 1,600

THE ANSWER IS CORRECT

Business Math Scrapbook

WITH INTERNET APPLICATION

Putting Your Skills to Work

Eager in the East

Top five advertisers in Vietnam, January through June.

COMPANY	PRODUCT	AD SPENDING (millions)
Unilever	Soap and shampoo	$10.70
Coca-Cola	Soft drinks	1.80
Procter & Gamble	Soap and shampoo	1.40
PepsiCo	Soft drinks	0.96
LG Group	Televisions	0.95

Source: ACNielsen estimates

Source: © 2000 Dow Jones & Company, Inc.

PROJECT A

If Coca-Cola increases its advertising spending in Vietnam by 3 times for the next 6 months, what will it spend for the year?

Go to the Coca-Cola Web site and try to determine what Coca-Cola is spending on advertising today.

Goodyear to Cut Total of 650 Jobs At U.K. Facility

By Patricia Davis
Staff Reporter of The Wall Street Journal

Goodyear Tire & Rubber Co. said it will discontinue commercial truck-tire and mold production at the Dunlop Tyres U.K. plant in Birmingham, England, resulting in the loss of 650 jobs there.

The Akron, Ohio, company will integrate truck-tire and mold production within its recently completed joint venture with **Sumitomo Rubber Industries** Ltd. in Europe, which makes the Dunlop brand. Truck-tire production will be moved to joint-venture plants in the U.K., Germany and France. Mold production will shift to Goodyear's facility in Luxembourg.

The company said the action will result in substantial cost savings and synergies for the Goodyear and Dunlop joint venture.

Source: © 2000 Dow Jones & Company, Inc.

PROJECT B

If the total number of employees at Goodyear's Birmingham plant were 11,581 after the layoff, what was the total employment before the layoff?

Go to the Goodyear Web site to see how their business is doing today.

Juice Processors Make a Bet on India's Market

By Rasul Bailay
Staff Reporter of The Wall Street Journal

NEW DELHI—Breakfast in India rarely includes orange juice. Most people prefer their wake-up tea with milk and believe that citrus and milk mixed in the same meal are bad for the stomach and sour a person's mood. And later in the day, most Indians would rather stop at an open-air stall than buy a bottle or carton from a supermarket.

Despite these cultural hurdles, juice processors are betting they have identified a potentially profitable niche and their products, appearing in stores nationwide, are aimed at India's growing middle class.

"The market is in its infancy," says Abhay Manglik, country manager at Tropicana Beverages Co., the local unit of Bradenton, Fla.-based Tropicana Products Inc. "But the potentials are huge. We expect the Indian market to grow at least five times by the year 2002."

Source: © 2000 Dow Jones & Company, Inc.

PROJECT C

If the total market for orange juice in India is $35 million, what should the Indian market grow to in the year 2002?

Go to the Web and look up New Delhi. Try to find other cultural differences that may affect business corporations.

Percents and Their Applications

6

It's Payback Time

MAYBE YOU SPENT a lot of money remodeling your house. But will you get it all back when it's time to sell? Below, a look at what percentage of their costs various remodeling jobs tend to pay back:

Michael Sloan

PROJECT	COST	AVERAGE PAYBACK
Add bathroom	\$5,000 to \$12,000	92%
Major kitchen remodeling	\$9,000 to \$25,000	90
Add a family room	\$30,000	86
Add a fireplace	\$1,500 to \$3,000	75
Build a deck	\$6,000	73
Remodel home office	\$8,000	69
Replace windows	\$6,000	68 to 74
Build a pool	\$10,000 and up	44
Install or upgrade landscaping	\$1,500 to \$15,000	30 to 60
Finish basement	\$3,000 to \$7,000	15

Source: © 2001 Dow Jones & Company, Inc.

LEARNING UNIT OBJECTIVES

LU 6–1: Definition and Conversions

- Defining and understanding the percent operation (p. 122).
- Conversions (p. 123).

LU 6–2: Applications: Portion Formula

- List and define the key elements of the portion formula (p. 127).
- Solve for one unknown of the portion formula, when the other two key elements are given (p. 127).

LU 6–3: Applications: Percent Change: Percent of Increase/Decrease

- Calculate the rate of percent decreases and increases (p. 131).

LU 6–4: Applications: Taxes

- Goods and Services Taxes (GST) (p. 135).
- Provincial Sales Taxes (PST) (p. 136).
- Property Tax (p. 137).

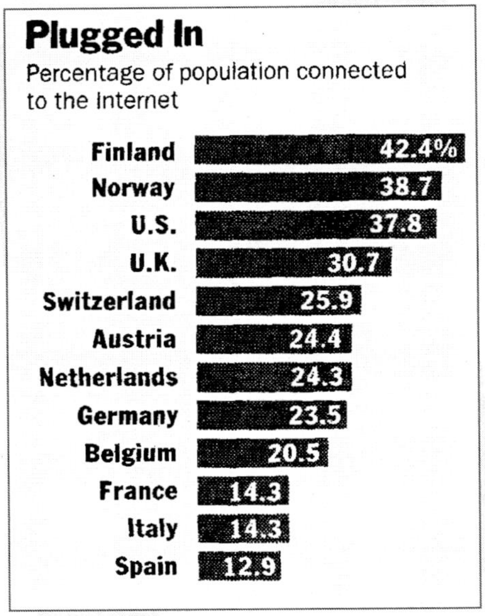

Source: © 2000 Dow Jones & Company, Inc.

Companies frequently use percents to express various decreases and increases between two or more numbers, or to express only a decrease or increase. For example, note the *Wall Street Journal* clipping "Plugged In." It expresses business numbers in terms of percents. The article reports that Finland had the highest percentage of population connected to the Internet—42.4%. This means that in Finland, 42 people out of 100 people are connected to the Internet.

To understand percents, you should first understand the meaning of percent, the conversion relationship between decimals, percents, and fractions as explained in Learning Unit 6–1. Then, in Learning Units 6–2, 6–3, and 6–4 you will be ready to apply percents to personal and business events.

LEARNING UNIT 6–1
DEFINITION AND CONVERSIONS

When we described parts of a whole in previous chapters, we used fractions and decimals. Percents also describe parts of a whole. The word *percent* means per 100. The percent symbol (%) indicates hundredths (that is, it stands for an operation—division by 100). **Percents** are the result of expressing numbers as part of 100. Thus, as stated above, the 42.4% of the population in Finland connected to the Internet is 42 out of 100 people $\left(\frac{42}{100}\right)$.

Percents can provide some revealing information. Do you know how many people actually make purchases on the Internet? The *Wall Street Journal* clipping "Online Activities" answers this question. Note that 88.7%, or 89 out of 100 online users $\left(\frac{89}{100}\right)$, send e-mail messages, but only 26.9%, or 27 online users out of 100 $\left(\frac{27}{100}\right)$, make purchases.

Online Activities

Entertainment doesn't yet rank high among what Internet users do online. The percentage of users doing each at least three times in previous three months:

Send e-mail	**88.7%**	Visit reference sites	**40.7%**
Go to World Wide Web	**85.1%**	Read newspapers and magazines	**33.8%**
Use search-engine sites	**77.8%**	View stock quotes	**27.7%**
Visit company/product sites	**52.0%**	Make purchases	**26.9%**
Do research about product purchases	**47.4%**	Visit sports sites	**23.8%**
Look up weather information	**46.6%**	Participate in chat	**23.0%**

Source: © 2000 Dow Jones & Company, Inc.

Let's return to the M&M's® example from Chapter 2. In Table 6.1, we use our bag of 55 M&M's® to show how fractions, decimals, and percents can refer to the same parts of a whole. For example, the bag of 55 M&M's® contained 18 yellow M&M's®. As you can see in Table 6.1, the 18 yellow candies in the bag of 55 can be expressed as a fraction $\left(\frac{18}{55}\right)$, decimal (.33), and percent (32.73%).

Michelle Burgess/Stock Boston

TABLE 6–1
ANALYZING A BAG OF M&M'S®

Colour	Fraction	Decimal (hundredth)	Percent (hundredth)
Yellow	$\frac{18}{55}$	.33	32.73%
Red	$\frac{10}{55}$	.18	18.18
Blue	$\frac{9}{55}$	.16	16.36
Orange	$\frac{7}{55}$	.13	12.73
Brown	$\frac{6}{55}$	.11	10.91
Green	$\frac{5}{55}$	.09	9.09
Total	$\frac{55}{55} = 1$	1.00	100.00%

Note: The colour ratios currently given are a sample used for educational purposes. They do not represent the manufacturer's colour ratios.

In this Unit we discuss converting decimals to percents (including rounding percents), percents to decimals, fractions to percents, and percents to fractions. You will see when you study converting fractions to percents why you should first learn how to convert decimals to percents.

Converting Decimals to Percents

Some 65% of Online Shoppers Bolt at the Checkout Point; E-tailers Try to Keep Them

This heading appeared above an article in the *Wall Street Journal.* Note that when making purchases online, 65 out of 100 online shoppers become discouraged and leave the purchase site. This means that only 35 out of 100 people complete their online shopping.

If the heading of the article stated the 65% as a decimal (.65), could you give its equivalent in percent? The decimal .65 in decimal fraction is $\frac{65}{100}$.[1] As you know, percents are the result of expressing numbers as a part of 100, so $65\% = \frac{65}{100}$. You can now conclude that $.65 = \frac{65}{100} = 65\%$. This leads to the following conversion steps:

CONVERTING DECIMALS TO PERCENTS

Step 1. Move the decimal point two places to the right. You are multiplying by 100. If necessary, add zeros. This rule is also used for whole numbers and mixed decimals.

Step 2. Add a percent symbol at the end of the number.

Examples

.65 = .65. = 65%

.8 = .80. = 80% — Add 1 zero to make two places.

8 = 8.00. = 800% — Add 2 zeros to make two places.

.425 = .42.5 = 42.5%

.007 = .00.7 = .7%

2.51 = 2.51. = 251%

Caution: One percent means 1 out of every 100. Since .7% is less than 1%, it means $\frac{7}{10}$ of 1%—a very small amount. Less than 1% is less than .01. To show a number less than 1%, you must use more than two decimal places and add 2 zeros. Example: .7% = .007.

[1]This is explained in Chapter 3.

Rounding Percents

When necessary, percents should be rounded. Rounding percents is similar to rounding whole numbers. Use the following steps to round percents:

ROUNDING PERCENTS

Step 1. When you convert from a fraction or decimal, be sure your answer is in percent before rounding.
Step 2. Identify the specific digit. If the digit to the right of the identified digit is 5 or greater, round up the identified digit.
Step 3. Delete digits to right of the identified digit.

For example, Table 6.1 shows that the 18 yellow M&M's® rounded to the nearest hundredth percent is 32.73% of the bag of 55 M&M's®. Let's look at how we arrived at this figure.

When using a calculator, you press 18 ÷ 55 %. This allows you to do right to percent, avoiding the decimal step.

Step 1.	$\frac{18}{55} = .3272727 = 32.72727\%$	Note that the number is in percent! Identify the hundredth percent digit.
Step 2.	32.73727%	Digit to the right of the identified digit is greater than 5, so the identified digit is increased by 1.
Step 3.	32.73%	Delete digits to the right of the identified digit.

Converting Percents to Decimals

Colas Duke It Out

2000 Market Share

	Coke Classic	Pepsi-Cola
Market share	20.4%	13.6%
Unit cases sold (billions)	2.03	1.36
Volume growth	+0.5%	−1.0%

Source: © 2001 Dow Jones & Company, Inc.

The *Wall Street Journal* clipping "Colas Duke It Out" states that in 2000 the volume growth of Coke Classic increased +0.5%. This percent is less than 1%. You will learn in the paragraph and steps that follow how to convert percents to decimals. The first example below the steps shows you how to convert the + 0.5% to a decimal. Our third example returns to the 65% of online shoppers that leave the checkout point and shows you how to state the 65% in decimal.

To convert percents to decimals, you reverse the process used to convert decimals to percents. The definition of percent states that $65\% = \frac{65}{100}$. The fraction $\frac{65}{100}$ can be written in decimal form as .65. You can conclude that $65\% = \frac{65}{100} = .65$. This leads to the following conversion steps:

CONVERTING PERCENTS TO DECIMALS

Step 1. Drop the percent symbol.
Step 2. Move the decimal point two places to the left. You are dividing by 100. If necessary, add zeros.

Examples

Note that when a percent is less than 1%, the decimal conversion has at least two leading zeros before the whole number .005.

.5% = .00.5 = .005 (Add 2 zeros to make two places.)

5% = .05. = .05 (Add 1 zero to make two places.)

65% = .65. = .65

82.4% = .82.4 = .824

824.4% = 8.24.4 = 8.244

Now we must explain how to change fractional percents such as $\frac{1}{5}\%$ to a decimal. Remember that fractional percents are values less than 1%. For example, $\frac{1}{5}\%$ is $\frac{1}{5}$ of 1%. Fractional percents can appear singly or in combination with whole numbers. To convert them to decimals, use the following steps:

CONVERTING FRACTIONAL PERCENTS TO DECIMALS

Step 1. Convert a single fractional percent to its decimal equivalent by dividing the numerator by the denominator. If necessary, round the answer. Keep the % sign.

Step 2. If a fractional percent is combined with a whole number (mixed fractional percent), convert the fractional percent first. Then combine the whole number and the fractional percent.

Step 3. Drop the percent symbol; move the decimal point two places to the left (this divides the number by 100).

EXAMPLES

$\frac{1}{5}\% = .20\% = .00.20 = .0020$

$\frac{1}{4}\% = .25\% = .00.25 = .0025$

$7\frac{3}{4}\% = 7.75\% = .07.75 = .0775$

$6\frac{1}{2}\% = 6.5\% = .06.5 = .065$

Think of $7\frac{3}{4}\%$ as

$7\% = .07$

$+\ \frac{3}{4}\% = +.0075$

$7\frac{3}{4}\% = .0775$

CONVERTING FRACTIONS TO PERCENTS

When fractions have denominators of 100, the numerator becomes the percent. Other fractions must be first converted to decimals; then the decimals are converted to percents.

CONVERTING FRACTIONS TO PERCENTS

Step 1. Divide the numerator by the denominator to convert the fraction to a decimal.

Step 2. Move the decimal point two places to the right; add the percent symbol.

EXAMPLES

$\frac{3}{4} = .75 = .75. = 75\%$ $\quad \frac{1}{5} = .20 = .20. = 20\%$ $\quad \frac{1}{20} = .05 = .05. = 5\%$

CONVERTING PERCENTS TO FRACTIONS

Using the definition of percent, you can write any percent as a fraction whose denominator is 100. Thus, when we convert a percent to a fraction, we drop the percent symbol and write the number over 100, which is the same as multiplying the number by $\frac{1}{100}$. This method of multiplying by $\frac{1}{100}$ is also used for fractional percents.

CONVERTING A WHOLE PERCENT (OR A FRACTIONAL PERCENT) TO A FRACTION

Step 1. Drop the percent symbol.

Step 2. Multiply the number by $\frac{1}{100}$.

Step 3. Reduce to lowest terms.

EXAMPLES

$76\% = 76 \times \frac{1}{100} = \frac{76}{100} = \frac{19}{25}$ $\quad \frac{1}{8}\% = \frac{1}{8} \times \frac{1}{100} = \frac{1}{800}$

$156\% = 156 \times \frac{1}{100} = \frac{156}{100} = 1\frac{56}{100} = 1\frac{14}{25}$

Sometimes a percent contains a whole number and a fraction such as $12\frac{1}{2}\%$ or 22.5%. Extra steps are needed to write a mixed or decimal percent as a simplified fraction.

CONVERTING A MIXED OR DECIMAL PERCENT TO A FRACTION

Step 1. Drop the percent symbol.
Step 2. Change the mixed percent to an improper fraction.
Step 3. Multiply the number by $\frac{1}{100}$.
Step 4. Reduce to lowest terms.

Note: If you have a mixed or decimal percent, change the decimal portion to fractional equivalent and continue with Steps 1 to 4.

EXAMPLES

$$12\frac{1}{2}\% = \frac{25}{2} \times \frac{1}{100} = \frac{25}{200} = \frac{1}{8}$$

$$12.5\% = 12\frac{1}{2}\% = \frac{25}{2} \times \frac{1}{100} = \frac{25}{200} = \frac{1}{8}$$

$$22.5\% = 22\frac{1}{2}\% = \frac{45}{2} \times \frac{1}{100} = \frac{45}{200} = \frac{9}{40}$$

LU 6–1 PRACTICE QUIZ

Convert to percents (round to the nearest tenth percent as needed);

1. .6666 ______ **2.** .832 ______ **3.** .004 ______ **4.** 8.94444 ______

Convert to decimals (remember, decimals representing less than 1% will have at least 2 leading zeros before the number):

5. $\frac{1}{4}\%$ ______ **6.** $6\frac{3}{4}\%$ ______ **7.** 87% ______ **8.** 810.9% ______

Convert to percents (round to the nearest hundredth percent):

9. $\frac{1}{7}$ ______ **10.** $\frac{2}{9}$ ______

Convert to fractions (remember, if it is a mixed number, first convert to an improper fraction):

11. 19% ______ **12.** $71\frac{1}{2}\%$ ______ **13.** 130% ______ **14.** $\frac{1}{2}\%$ ______ **15.** 19.9% ______

LEARNING UNIT 6–2
APPLICATIONS: PORTION FORMULA

The bag of M&M's® we have been studying contains Milk Chocolate M&M's®. M&M/Mars also makes Peanut M&M's® and some other types of M&M's®. To study the application of percents to problems involving M&M's®, we make two key assumptions:

1. Total sales of Milk Chocolate M&M's®, Peanut, and other M&M's® chocolate candies are $400,000.
2. Eighty percent of M&M's® sales are Milk Chocolate M&M's®. This leaves the Peanut and other M&M's® chocolate candies with 20% of sales (100% − 80%).

80% M&M's®		20% M&M's®		100%
Milk Chocolate M&M's®	+	Peanut and other chocolate candies	=	Total sales ($400,000)

A key point to remember is that rate is usually expressed in percent units (%). To find a rate,

$$R = \frac{\text{Portion}}{\text{Base or initial value}} \times 100\%$$

$$R = \frac{P}{B} \times 100\% \quad \textbf{(6.2)}$$

always think of a fraction with the base or initial value in the denominator. You can easily rearrange the rate formula to find the other values: base and portion.

Before we begin, you must understand the meaning of three terms—*base, rate,* and *portion.* These terms are the key elements in solving percent problems.

- **Rate (*R*).** The **rate** is a percent, decimal, or fraction that indicates the part of the base that you must calculate. The percent symbol often helps you identify the rate. For example, Milk Chocolate M&M's® currently account for 80% of sales. So the rate is 80%. Remember that 80% is also $\frac{4}{5}$, or .80.
- **Base (*B*).** The **base** is the beginning whole quantity or value (100%) with which you will compare some other quantity or value. Often the problems give the base after the word *of.* For example, the whole (total) sales of M&M's®—Milk Chocolate M&M's, Peanut, and other M&M's® chocolate candies—are $400,000.
- **Portion (*P*).** The **portion** is the amount or part that results from the base multiplied by the rate. For example, total sales of M&M's® are $400,000 (base); $400,000 times .80 (rate) equals $320,000 (portion), or the sales of Milk Chocolate M&M's®.

To help you remember what base is, associate it with words: initial value, whole quantity, value before change, original number, old value, total value, etc. Rearranging Formula 6.2, you can find the value of the base this way when the rate and the portion are given:

$$\text{Base} = \frac{\text{Portion}}{\text{Rate}}$$

$$B = \frac{P}{R} \quad \textbf{(6.3)}$$

A key point to remember is that portion is a number and not a percent. In fact, the portion can be larger than the base if the rate is greater than 100%. Key words associated with the idea of portion are: percentage, new number, amount of change.

Portion may be found by rearranging Formula 6.2:

$$\text{Portion} = \text{Base} \times \text{Rate}$$

$$P = B \times R \quad \textbf{(6.4)}$$

Solving Percents with the Portion Formula

In problems involving portion, base, and rate, we give two of these elements. You must find the third element. Remember the following key formula:

$$\boxed{\text{Portion } (P) = \text{Base } (B) \times \text{Rate } (R)} \quad \textbf{(6.1)}$$

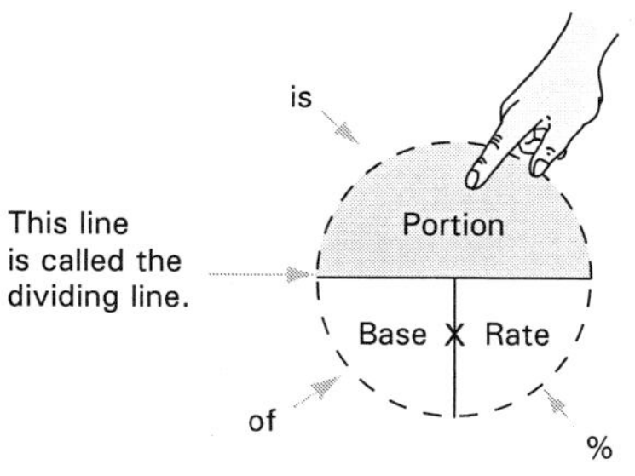

To help you solve for the portion, base, and rate, this Unit shows pie charts. The shaded area in each pie chart indicates the element that you must solve for. For example, since we shaded portion in the pie chart at the left, you must solve for *portion.* To use the pie charts, put your finger on the shaded area (in this case portion). The formula that remains tells you what to do. So in the pie chart at the left, you solve the problem by multiplying base by the rate. Note the circle around the pie chart is broken since we want to emphasize that portion can be larger than base if rate is greater than 100%. The horizontal line in the pie chart is called the dividing line, and we will use it when we solve for base or rate.

The following example summarizes the concept of base, rate, and portion. Assume that you received a small bonus check of $100. This is a gross amount—your company did not withhold any taxes. You will have to pay 20% in taxes.

Base: 100%—whole. Usually given after the word *of*—but not always.	**Rate:** Usually expressed as a percent but could also be a demical or fraction.	**Portion:** A number—not a percent and not the whole.
$100 bonus check	20% taxes	$20 taxes

First decide what you are looking for. You want to know how much you must pay in taxes—the portion. How do you get the portion? From the portion formula Portion (*P*) = Base (*B*) × Rate (*R*), you know that you must multiply the base ($100) by the rate (20%). When you do this, you get $100 × .20 = $20. So you must pay $20 in taxes.

Let's try our first word problem by taking a closer look at the M&M's® example to see how we arrived at the $320,000 sales of Milk Chocolate M&M's® given earlier. We will be using Blueprint Aids to help dissect and solve each word problem.

Solving for Portion

THE WORD PROBLEM Sales of Milk Chocolate M&M's® are 80% of the total M&M's® sales. Total M&M's® sales are $400,000. What are the sales of Milk Chocolate M&M's®?

THE FACTS	SOLVING FOR?	STEPS TO TAKE	KEY POINTS
R: Milk Chocolate M&M's® sales: 80%. *B: Total M&M's® sales:* $400,000.	*P:* Sales of Milk Chocolate M&M's®.	Identify key elements. *Base:* $400,000. *Rate:* .80. *Portion:* ? $P = ?$ Portion = Base × Rate. $P = B \times R$	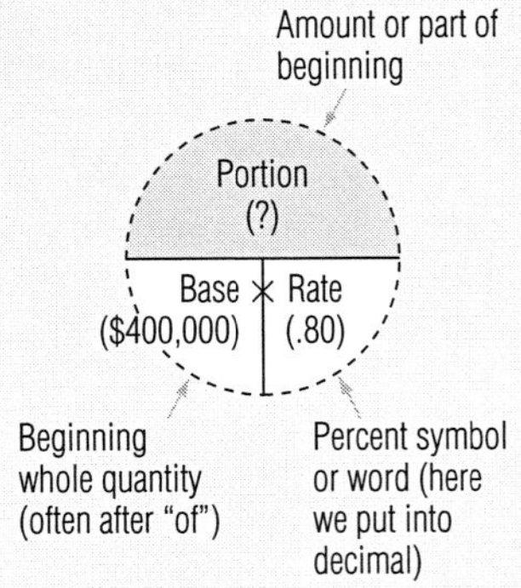 Portion and rate must relate to same piece of base.

STEPS TO SOLVING PROBLEM

1. Set up the formula. Portion = Base × Rate $P = B \times R$ (6.4)
2. Calculate portion (sales of Milk Chocolate M&M's®).

$$P = \$400{,}000 \times .80$$

$$P = \$320{,}000$$

In the first column of the Blueprint Aid, we gather the facts. In the second column, we state that we are looking for sales of Milk Chocolate M&M's®. In the third column, we identify each key element and the formula needed to solve the problem. Review the pie chart in the fourth column. Note that the portion and rate must relate to the same piece of the base. In this word problem, we can see from the solution below the Blueprint Aid that sales of Milk Chocolate M&M's® are $320,000. The $320,000 does indeed represent 80% of the base. Note here that the portion ($320,000) is less than the base of $400,000 since the rate is less than 100%.

Now let's work another word problem that solves for the portion.

THE WORD PROBLEM Sales of Milk Chocolate M&M's® are 80% of the total M&M's® sales. Total M&M's® sales are $400,000. What are the sales of Peanut and other M&M's® chocolate candies?

THE FACTS	SOLVING FOR?	STEPS TO TAKE	KEY POINTS
R_1: Milk Chocolate M&M's® sales: 80%. *B: Total M&M's® sales:* $400,000.	*P:* Sales of Peanut and other M&M's® chocolate candies.	Identify key elements. *B: Base:* $400,000. *R: Rate:* .20 (100% − 80%). *Portion:* ? $P = ?$ Portion = Base × Rate. $R = 100\% - R_1$ $P = B \times R$	If 80% of sales are Milk Chocolate M&M's, then 20% are Peanut and other M&M's® chocolate candies. 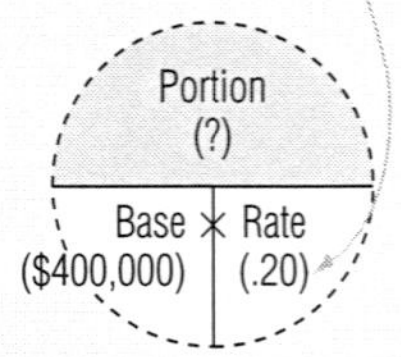 Portion and rate must relate to same piece of base.

STEPS TO SOLVING PROBLEM

1. Set up the formula. Portion = Base × Rate $P = B \times R$ (6.4)
2. Calculate portion (sale of Peanut and other M&M's® chocolate candies). $P = \$400{,}000 \times .20$

$P = \$80{,}000$

In the previous Blueprint Aid, note that we must use a rate that agrees with the portion so the portion and rate refer to the same piece of the base. Thus, if 80% of sales are Milk Chocolate M&M's®, 20% must be Peanut and other M&M's® chocolate candies (100% − 80% = 20%). So we use a rate of .20.

In Step 2, we multiplied $400,000 × .20 to get a portion of $80,000. This portion represents the part of the sales that were *not* Milk Chocolate M&M's®. Note that the rate of .20 and the portion of $80,000 relate to the same piece of the base—$80,000 is 20% of $400,000. Also note that the portion ($80,000) is less than the base ($400,000) since the rate is less than 100%.

Take a moment to review the two Blueprint Aids in this section. Be sure you understand why the rate in the first Blueprint Aid was 80% and the rate in the second Blueprint Aid was 20%: $R = (100\% - R_1)$.

Solving for Rate

THE WORD PROBLEM Sales of Milk Chocolate M&M's® are $320,000. Total M&M's® sales are $400,000. What is the percent of Milk Chocolate M&M's® sales compared to total M&M's® sales?

THE FACTS	SOLVING FOR?	STEPS TO TAKE	KEY POINTS
P: Milk Chocolate M&M's® sales: $320,000. *B: Total M&M's® sales:* $400,000.	Percent of Milk Chocolate M&M's® sales to total M&M's® sales. $R = ?$	Identify key elements. *Base:* $400,000. *Rate:* ? $R = ?$ *Portion:* $320,000 $\text{Rate} = \frac{\text{Portion}}{\text{Base}}$ $R = \frac{P}{B}$ (6.2)	Since portion is less than base, the rate must be less than 100%. 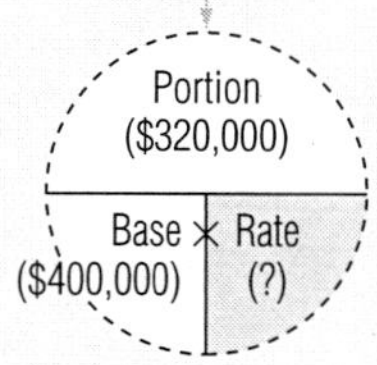 Portion and rate must relate to the same piece of base.

STEPS TO SOLVING PROBLEM

1. Set up the formula. $\text{Rate} = \frac{\text{Portion}}{\text{Base}}$ $R = \frac{P}{B}$ (6.2)
2. Calculate rate (percent of Milk Chocolate M&M's® sales). $R = \frac{\$320{,}000}{\$400{,}000}$

$R = 80\%$

Note that in this word problem, the rate of 80% and the portion of $320,000 refer to the same piece of the base.

THE WORD PROBLEM Sales of Milk Chocolate M&M's® are $320,000. Total sales of Milk Chocolate M&M's, Peanut, and other M&M's® chocolate candies are $400,000.

What percent of Peanut and other M&M's® chocolate candies are sold compared to total M&M's® sales?

THE FACTS	SOLVING FOR?	STEPS TO TAKE	KEY POINTS
P_1: Milk Chocolate M&M's® sales: $320,000. *B: Total M&M's® sales:* $400,000.	Percent of Peanut and other M&M's® chocolate candies sales compared to total M&M's® sales.	Identify key elements. *Base:* $400,000. *Rate:* ? $R = ?$ *Portion:* $80,000 $(P = B - P_1)$ ($400,000 − $320,000). $\text{Rate} = \frac{\text{Portion}}{\text{Base}}$ $R = \frac{P}{B}$ (6.2)	Represents sales of Peanut and other M&M's® chocolate candies. 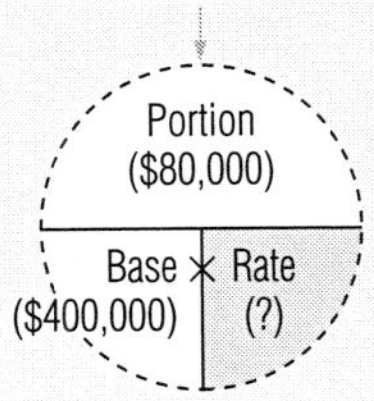 When portion becomes $80,000, the portion and rate now relate to same piece of base.

STEPS TO SOLVING PROBLEM

1. Set up the formula. $\text{Rate} = \frac{\text{Portion}}{\text{Base}}$ $R = \frac{P}{B}$ (6.2)

2. Calculate rate. $R = \frac{\$80,000}{\$400,000}$ ($400,000 − $320,000)

$R = 20\%$

The word problem asks for the rate of candy sales that are *not* Milk Chocolate M&M's. Thus, $400,000 of total candy sales less sales of Milk Chocolate M&M's® ($320,000) allows us to arrive at sales of Peanut and other M&M's® chocolate candies ($80,000). The $80,000 portion represents 20% of total candy sales. The $80,000 portion and 20% rate refer to the same piece of the $400,000 base. Compare this Blueprint Aid with the Blueprint Aid for the previous word problem. Ask yourself why in the previous word problem the rate was 80% and in this word problem the rate is 20%. In both word problems, the portion was less than the base since the rate was less than 100%.

Now we go on to calculate the base. Remember to read the word problem carefully so that you match the rate and portion to the same piece of the base.

Solving for Base

THE WORD PROBLEM Sales of Peanut and other M&M's® chocolate candies are 20% of total M&M's® sales. Sales of Milk Chocolate M&M's® are $320,000. What are the total sales of all M&M's®?

THE FACTS	SOLVING FOR?	STEPS TO TAKE	KEY POINTS
R_1: Peanut and other M&M's® chocolate candies sales: 20%. *P: Milk Chocolate M&M's® sales:* $320,000.	Total M&M's® sales. $B = ?$	Identify key elements. *B: Base:* $B = ?$ *Rate:* .80 $R = (100\% - R_1)$ (100% − 20%) *Portion*: $320,000 $\text{Base} = \frac{\text{Portion}}{\text{Rate}}$ $B = \frac{P}{R}$ (6.3)	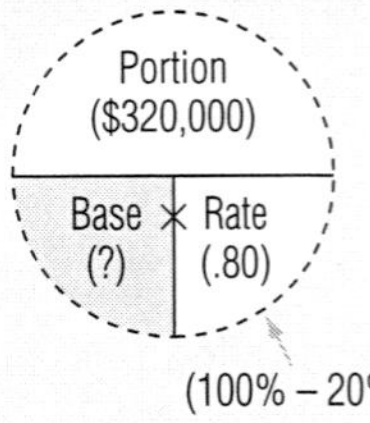 Portion ($320,000) and rate (.80) do relate to the same piece of base.

STEPS TO SOLVING PROBLEM

1. Set up the formula. $\text{Base} = \dfrac{\text{Portion}}{\text{Rate}}$ $B = \dfrac{P}{R}$ (6.3)

2. Calculate the base. $B = \dfrac{\$320{,}000}{.80}$ ← $320,000 is 80% of base

$B = \$400{,}000$

Note that we could not use 20% for the rate. The $320,000 of Milk Chocolate M&M's® represents 80% (100% − 20%) of the total sales of M&M's®. We use 80% so that the portion and rate refer to same piece of the base. *Remember that the portion ($320,000) is less than the base ($400,000) since the rate is less than 100%.*

LU 6–2 PRACTICE QUIZ

Solve for portion:

1. 38% of 900.   2. 60% of $9,000.

Solve for rate (round to nearest tenth percent as needed):

3. 430 is _______ % of 5,000.   4. 200 is _______ % of 700.

Solve for base (round to the nearest tenth as needed):

5. 55 is 40% of _______.   6. 900 is $4\frac{1}{2}$% of _______ .

Solve the following (Blueprint Aids are shown in the solution; you might want to try some on scrap paper):

7. Five out of 25 students in Professor Ford's class received an "A" grade. What percent of the class *did not* receive the "A" grade?
8. Abby Biernet has yet to receive 60% of her lobster order. Abby received 80 lobsters to date. What was her original order?
9. The typical sales fee for a real estate agent is 2.5%. How much will an agent receive from the sale of a $400,000 home?
10. Estatesavers Agency offers their clients a special program whereby the client will pay the agent only half the typical sales fee. How much will a sales agent receive in this case from the sale of a $400,000 home?
11. Using the information from Problems 9 and 10, calculate what percent of the sales fee the client will save with Estatesavers Agency.

LEARNING UNIT 6–3
APPLICATIONS: PERCENT CHANGE: PERCENT OF INCREASE/DECREASE

Darren Hick

In the advertisement shown here you can see that a real estate agency is offering its clients a much lower rate for a sales fee. The agency has decreased the typical listing fee of 2.5% to 1.25%, which would allow clients to save $5,000 on the sale of a $400,000 home.

The amount of savings as a portion or amount of change in a sales fee can be determined using portion Formula 6.4, but in this case instead of R (rate), we will use percent change R_c: 2.5% − 1.25% = 1.25%, where R_o is the initial or old rate of 2.5% and R_n the new rate of 1.25%.

Our adjusted formula will be:

$$P = (0.025 - 0.0125) \times 400{,}000 = 5{,}000$$

$$P = (R_o - R_n) \times B$$

← Percent change

Let's consider another example of percent change, selected from the business magazine *Maclean's*. The clipping here reports on recent changes in the population of Canada; it indicates an increase in the Chinese-speaking population by 18%.

> ## LINGUISTIC MOSAIC
>
> According to Statistics Canada, between 1996 and 2001 the number of people listing Chinese as their mother tongue grew by almost 18 percent, to 872,400 or 2.9 percent of Canada's population. English speakers remained in first place, although the percentage had dropped to 59.1 from 59.8, with French speakers in second place at 22.9 percent. Chinese was third, Italian fourth, German fifth and Punjabi sixth.
>
> Source: 2002, *Maclean's*.

We can find initial number B of Chinese speakers in 1996 by using the portion formula. The new number P for the Chinese-speaking population is 872,400. New rate after the change R_n is 118% (old or initial rate R_o 100% + Percent of change R_c 18%).

$$B = \frac{P}{R_n} \quad \begin{matrix}\leftarrow \text{New number} \\ \leftarrow \text{New rate}\end{matrix}$$

$$B = \frac{872{,}400}{1.18} = 739{,}322$$

Now, let's assume that we don't know the amount of percent change and try to use portion formula to determine the percent of increase R_c in the Chinese-speaking population.

In this case the initial number B will be 739,322 people. The new number P will be 872,400 people.

A key point is that the order of new and old numbers in numerator is very important. It determines the sign of the percent change. A negative sign indicates a decrease in quantity and a positive sign indicates an increase.

$$\text{Rate } (R_c) = \frac{\text{Portion}}{\text{Base}} \quad \begin{matrix}\leftarrow \text{Difference between new and initial (old) numbers} \\ \leftarrow \text{Initial (old) number}\end{matrix}$$

$$R_c = \frac{(P - B)}{B} \quad \text{or} \quad R_c = \frac{(V_n - V_o)}{V_o}$$

$$R_c = \frac{(872{,}400 - 739{,}322)}{739{,}322} = 0.18 \quad \text{or} \quad 18\%$$

The Chinese-speaking population has increased by 18%, as indicated in the clipping.

$$\text{Percent change} = \frac{(\text{New value} - \text{Old (initial) value})}{\text{Old (initial) value}} \times 100\% \quad \text{or} \quad \frac{\text{Amount of change}}{\text{Old (initial) value}}$$

V_n: New/final value
V_o: Old/Initial value
R_c: Percent change
$(V_n - V_o)$: Amount of change (increase or decrease)

If the **amount of change** is positive, the quantity increases in size and the percent change is also positive. If the amount of change is negative, the quantity decreases and the percent change is also negative.

$$R_c = \frac{(V_n - V_o)}{V_o} \times 100\% \tag{6.5}$$

Calculation of the **percent increase** or **percent decrease** may also be done in steps.

Rate of Percent Decrease

> **CALCULATING PERCENT DECREASES AND INCREASES**
>
> **Step 1.** Find the difference between amounts (such as airline fares).
>
> **Step 2.** Divide Step 1 by the original amount (the base): $R = P \div B$. Be sure to express your answer in percent.

Next you are ready for an example of calculating the rate of percent increase using M&M's®.

Rate of Percent Increase

THE WORD PROBLEM Sheila Leary went to her local supermarket and bought the bag of M&M's®. The bag gave its weight as 521.6 grams, which was 15% more than a regular one-pound (453.6 gram) bag of M&M's®. Sheila, who is a careful shopper, wanted to check and see if she was actually getting a 15% increase. Let's help Sheila dissect and solve this problem.

THE FACTS	SOLVING FOR?	STEPS TO TAKE	KEY POINTS
V_n: *New bag of* 521.6 g *M&M's®*: 15% increase in weight. V_o: *Original bag of M&M's®*: 453.6 g	Checking percent increase of 15%. $R_c = ?$	Identify key elements. *Base:* 453.6 g *Rate:* ? *Portion:* 68 g $\begin{pmatrix} 521.6 \\ -453.6 \\ \hline 68\text{ g} \end{pmatrix}$ $\text{Rate}_c = \frac{\text{Portion}}{\text{Base}}$ $= \frac{(V_n - V_o)}{V_o}$	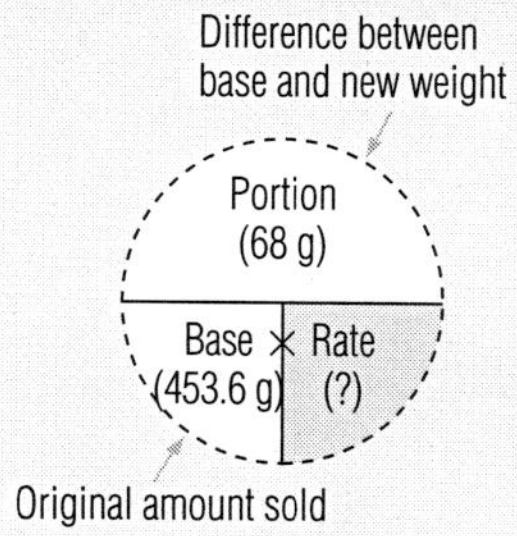

STEPS TO SOLVING PROBLEM

1. Set up the formula. $\text{Rate}_c = \frac{\text{Portion}}{\text{Base}} \quad R_c = \frac{(V_n - V_o)}{V_o} = \frac{(521.6 - 453.6)}{453.6} = .1499$

2. Calculate the rate. $R_c = \frac{+68\text{ g}}{453.6\text{ g}}$ ← Difference between base and new weight ← Old weight equals 100%.

$R = 15\%$ increase

The new weight of the bag of M&M's® is really 115% of the old weight:

$$\begin{array}{rcl} 453.6\text{ g} = & 100\% & \\ +\ 68\ \ \text{g} & +\ 15 & \\ \hline 521.6\text{ g} = & 115\% & = 1.15 \end{array}$$

We can check this by looking at the following pie chart:

Portion = Base × Rate

521.6 g = 453.6 g × 1.15

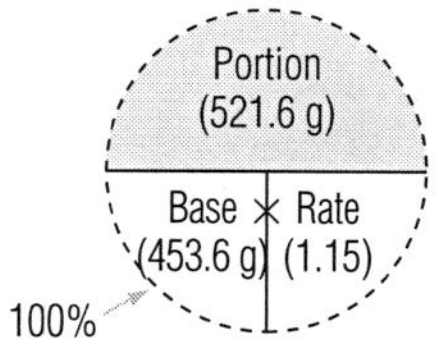

Why is the portion greater than the base? Remember that the portion can be larger than the base only if the rate is greater than 100%. Note how the portion and rate relate to the same piece of the base—521.6 grams is 115% of the base (453.6 grams).

Let's see what could happen if M&M/Mars has an increase in its price of sugar. This is an additional example to reinforce the concept of percent decrease.

THE WORD PROBLEM The increase in the price of sugar caused the M&M/Mars company to decrease the weight of each one-pound (453.6 gram) bag of M&M's® to 340.2 grams. What is the rate of percent decrease?

THE FACTS	SOLVING FOR?	STEPS TO TAKE	KEY POINTS
V_o: 453.6 g *bag of M&M's®* V_n: Reduced to 340.2 g	Rate of percent decrease. $R_c = ?$	Identify key elements. *Base:* 453.6 g *Rate$_c$:* ? *Portion:* 113.4 g $(V_n - V_o)$ (340.2 − 453.6) g $\text{Rate}_c = \frac{\text{Portion}}{\text{Base}}$ $R_c = \frac{(V_n - V_o)}{V_o}$	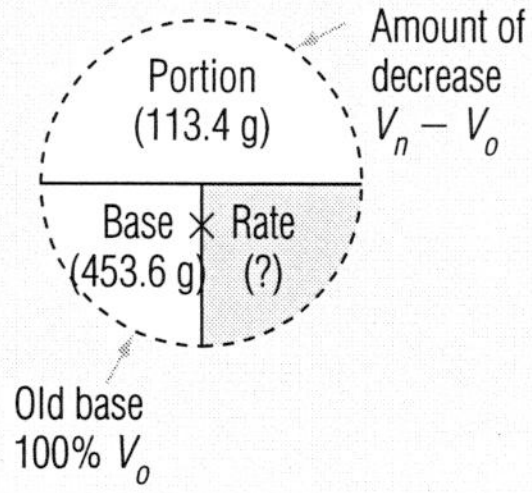

STEPS TO SOLVING PROBLEM

1. Set up the formula. $\text{Rate}_c = \frac{\text{Portion}}{\text{Base}} = \frac{(V_n - V_o)}{V_o} = \frac{340.2 - 453.6}{453.6} = -.25$

2. Calculate the rate. $R = \frac{113.4\text{ g}}{453.6\text{ g}}$

$R = 25\%$ decrease

The new weight of the bag of M&M's® is 75% of the old weight:

$$\begin{array}{rcr} 453.6\text{ g} & = & 100\% \\ -113.4\text{ g} & & -\ 25 \\ \hline 340.2\text{ g} & = & 75\% \end{array}$$

We can check this by looking at the following pie chart:

Portion = Base × Rate

340.2 g = 453.6 g × .75

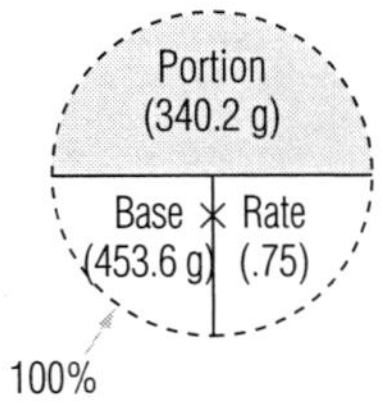

Note that the portion is smaller than the base because the rate is less than 100%. Also note how the portion and rate relate to the same piece of the base—340.2 grams is 75% of the base (453.6 grams).

LU 6–3 PRACTICE QUIZ

1. In 2003, Tim Hortons Company had $300,000 in doughnut sales. In 2004, sales were up 40%. What are Tim Hortons sales for 2004?
2. The price of an Apple computer dropped from $1,600 to $1,200. What was the percent decrease?
3. In 1982, a ticket to the Kingston cost $14. In 2003, a ticket cost $50. What is the percent increase to the nearest hundredth percent?
4. This week's price for 1 litre of gas is $.699. This is 2% lower than last week. What was the price of gas last week?

LEARNING UNIT 6–4
APPLICATIONS: TAXES

Darren Hick

What makes the biggest dent in your pocketbook—Goods and Service Tax, Provincial Sales Tax, property tax, or income tax? If you said "income tax," you are wrong. Property taxes or sales taxes—and almost always both—do the greatest damage to your finances.

In Canada there are two levels of government taxes, federal and provincial, on sales of goods and services to the final customers. In this Unit you will learn how to calculate these taxes, and also property taxes. To avoid confusion we will explain and demonstrate calculations of each of these taxes separately.

Northern Lights telecom

Account Statement

Account Number 416 555 4324
Bill Date March 18, 2004

Previous charges	Last statement	55.17
	Payment received 03/03/04	55.17 cr
	Adjustments	.00
	Balance forward	.00
Current charges	Monthly services (03/18/04–04/17/04)	50.90
	GST	3.57
	PST	4.08
	Total current charges	58.55
	Total amount due	**58.55**

Please pay promptly upon receipt of account statement. To avoid a late payment charge, please ensure your payment is received on or before April 17, 2004.

Darren Hick

FEDERAL GOODS AND SERVICES TAX (GST)

The **Goods and Services Tax (GST)** is a value-added tax, which is levied by the federal government on nearly all goods and services in Canada. GST payable is remitted to a special federal government authority called the Receiver General for Canada. Only educational, health, and financial services are subject to exemption from GST.

GST is calculated as 7% of all taxable goods and services. It is usually computed electronically by the new cash register systems and scanners or forwarded to you as a separate position on monthly bills. However, it is important to know how sellers calculate sales tax manually.

For example, on the telephone bill shown at the beginning of this section, you can see a separate entry for GST of \$3.57. This amount is 7% of \$50.90, which is the current monthly service charge.

You can calculate it using the portion formula. You want to find the amount of GST as a portion P. The rate R is 7% and the current monthly service charge is the base $B = \$50.90$.

$$P = B \times R$$

Substituting the values of the variables you can calculate GST as P:

$$P = 50.9 \times .07 = 3.57$$

On some receipts you will get a report of total sales with GST as a separate position, as shown in Figure 6.2. Total sales was \$44.41, including GST \$2.91. In this case \$44.41 includes 7% GST and represents a new value that is 107% (100% + 7%) of the initial value of the actual price.

FIGURE 6–2

ZERO TOUCH CAR WASH
3660 DUFFERIN STREET
DOWNSVIEW ON

01 OCT 02 09:07 TRANS NO. 288929
5033-01 GST 891281057

PRODUCT	UTY/L	PRICE	AMOUNT
REGULAR	60 925	0.729	44.41*
GST INC IN FUEL			\$2.91
TOTAL			\$44.41

To find the actual value of the sale price, we can use the portion formula:

$$P = \$44.41; \qquad R = 1.07; \qquad B = ?$$

$$B = \frac{44.41}{1.07} = 41.50$$

So the actual sale amount was \$41.50. To verify this answer, let's check it against the data on the receipt. The final sales amount including GST was \$44.41. The amount of GST was \$2.91. Actual sales are the difference between these two values:

$$\text{Actual sales} = \text{Final sales} - \text{Amount of GST} = \$44.41 - \$2.91 = \$41.50$$

Calculating Actual Sales

Managers often use the cash register to get a summary of their total sales for the day. The total sales figure includes the sales tax. So the sales tax must be deducted from the total sales. To illustrate this, let's assume the total sales for the day were $40,000, which included a 7% sales tax. What were the actual sales?

$$\boxed{\text{Actual sales} = \frac{\text{Total sales}}{1 + \text{Tax rate}}}$$

Hint: $40,000 is 107% of actual sales.

$$\text{Actual sales} = \frac{\$40{,}000}{1.07} = \$37{,}383.18$$

Total sales

100% sales
+ 7% tax
107% → 1.07

Thus, the store's actual sales were $37,383.18. The actual sales plus the tax equal $40,000.

Check

$37,383.18 × .07 =	$ 2,616.82	sales tax
	+ 37,383.18	actual sales
	$ 40,000.00	total sales including sales tax

EXAMPLE OF CALCULATING TAXES ON DISCOUNTED PRICES

Selling price of a Sears battery	$32.00	Shipping charge	$3.50
Trade discount to local garage	10.50	Sales tax	7%

Manual calculation

$32.00 − $10.50 = $ 21.50	taxable
+ 3.50	shipping
25.00	
× .07	
$ 1.75	tax
+ 25.00	taxable
$ 26.75	total price with tax and shipping

Check

100% is base + 7% is tax = 107%

1.07 × $25.00 = $26.75

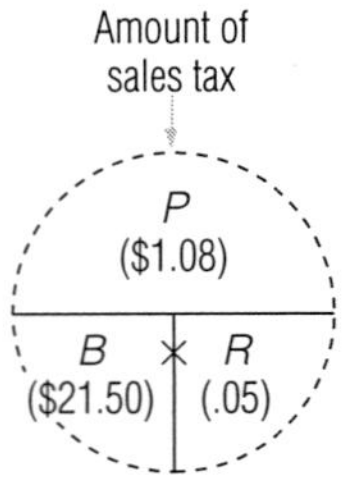

$21.50 + $1.08 = $22.58
(sale) (tax amount)

In this example, note how the trade discount is subtracted from the selling price before any cash discounts are taken. If the buyer is entitled to a 6% cash discount, it is calculated as follows:

.06 × $21.50 = $1.29

PROVINCIAL SALES TAX (PST)

Provincial Sales Tax (PST) is levied on sales to the final customers and varies from province to province. Out of all Canadian provinces, only Alberta and the Northwest Territories have exemptions for PST. In Prince Edward Island and in Quebec, provincial taxes are calculated as a percent of sales price plus GST, that is, PST = PST% × (Sales price + GST).

PST rates are represented in the following table:

Alberta	British Columbia	Manitoba	Northwest Territories	Nunavut	Ontario	PEI	Quebec	Saskatchewan	Yukon Territory
0%	7%	7%	0%	0%	8%	10%	7.5%	6%	0%

In New Brunswick, Nova Scotia, Newfoundland, and Labrador, the Harmonized Sales Tax (HST), which is a combined GST and PST of 15%, is applied.

The telephone bill presented at the beginning of this section was issued in the province of Ontario, where 8% of PST is levied. The PST of $4.08 is 8% of $50.90, which is the current monthly service charge. Applying the portion formula, we can calculate the amount of PST manually.

EXAMPLE

On June 1, Angel Rowe bought a fur coat for a retail price of $5,000. GST is 7% with a PST of 8%. Her total cost is as follows:

	$5,000	
+	350	GST (.07 × $5,000)
+	400	PST (.08 × $5,000)
	$5,750	

Let's check your progress with a Practice Quiz.

LU 6–4 PRACTICE QUIZ

1. From the following shopping list, calculate the total PST (food items are excluded from PST, which is 8%):

Chicken	$6.10	Orange juice	$1.29	Shampoo	$4.10
Lettuce	$ .75	Laundry detergent	$3.65		

PROPERTY TAX

"Property" Can Have Two Meanings

Both subject to property tax:

1. **Real property**—land, building, etc.
2. **Personal property**—possessions like jewellery, autos, furniture, etc.

When you own property, you must pay **property tax.** In this Unit we listen in on a conversation between a property owner and a tax assessor.

Defining Assessed Value

Bill Adams was concerned when he read in the local paper that the property tax rate had been increased. Bill knows that the revenue the town receives from the tax helps pay for fire and police protection, schools, and other public services. However, Bill wants to know how the town set the new rate and the amount of the new property tax.

Bill went to the town assessor's office to get specific details. The assessor is a local official who estimates the fair market value of a house. Before you read the summary of Bill's discussion, note the following formula:

$$\text{Assessed value} = \text{Assessment rate} \times \text{Market value} \qquad \textbf{(6.6)}$$

Bill: What does **assessed value** mean?

Assessor: *Assessed value* is the value of the property for purposes of computing property taxes. We estimated the market value of your home at $210,000. In our town, we assess property at 30% of the market value. Thus, your home has an assessed value of $63,000 ($210,000 × .30). Usually, assessed value is rounded to the nearest dollar.

Bill: I know that the **tax rate** multiplied by my assessed value ($63,000) determines the amount of my property tax. What I would like to know is how did you set the new tax rate?

DETERMINING THE TAX RATE

Assessor: In our town first we estimate the total amount of revenue needed to meet our budget. Then we divide the total of all assessed property into this figure to get the *tax rate.* The formula looks like this:

$$\text{Tax rate} = \frac{\text{Budget needed}}{\text{Total assessed value}} \qquad \textbf{(6.7)}$$

(*Note:* Regarding assessed value, remember that exemptions include land and buildings used for educational and religious purposes and the like.)

Our town budget is $125,000, and we have a total assessed property value of $1,930,000. Using the formula, we have the following:

$$\frac{\$125{,}000}{\$1{,}930{,}00} = \$.0647668 = .0648 \text{ tax rate per dollar}$$

Note that the rate should be rounded up to the indicated digit, *even if the digit is less than 5.* Here we rounded to the nearest ten thousandth.

HOW THE TAX RATE IS EXPRESSED

Assessor: We can express the .0648 tax rate per dollar in the following forms:

By percent	Per $100 of assessed value	Per $1,000 of assessed value	In mills
6.48% (Move decimal two places to right.)	$6.48 (.0648 × 100)	$64.80 (.0648 × 1,000)	64.80 $\left(\frac{.0648}{.001}\right)$

A **mill** is $\frac{1}{10}$ of a cent or $\frac{1}{1{,}000}$ of a dollar (.001). To represent the number of mills as a tax rate per dollar, we divide the tax rate in decimal by .001.

HOW TO CALCULATE PROPERTY TAX DUE[2]

Assessor: The following formula will show you how we arrive at your property tax:

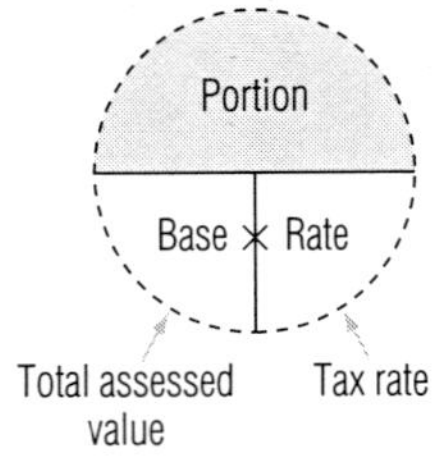

Total property tax due (Portion)	=	Tax rate (Rate)	×	Total assessed value (Base)
$4,082.40	=	.0648	×	$63,000

We can use the other forms of the decimal tax rate to show you how the property tax will not change even when expressed in various forms:

By percent	Per $100	Per $1,000	Mills		
6.48% × $63,000 = $4,082.40	$\frac{\$63{,}000}{\$100} = 630$ 630 × $6.48 = $4,082.40	$\frac{\$63{,}000}{\$1{,}000} = 63$ 63 × $64.80 = $4,082.40	Property tax due = Mills × .001 × Assessed value = 64.80 × .001 × $63,000 = $4,082.40	or	Property tax due $= \frac{\text{Mills}}{1{,}000} \times$ Assessed value $= \frac{64.80}{1{,}000} \times \$63{,}000$ = $4,082.40

Property tax is an annual tax paid by owners of real estate. At the end of every year, property owners receive information about their property assessment, which serves as a basis for calculation of their property tax for next year.

For example, in Ontario a special institution called the Municipal Property Assessment Corporation (mpac) is responsible for property assessments. They use three different methods based on three criteria:

- The selling price for a residential property
- The generated rental income for office or business property
- The cost of its replacement for an industrial property

Each method also considers the location of a property, the size and quality of the building, and features that might add to or take away from a property's value.

---

[2] Please note that in the U.S., unlike in Canada, some states have credits available to reduce what the homeowner actually pays. For example, 42 out of 50 states give tax breaks to people over age 65. In Alaska, the state's homestead exemption reduces the property tax of a $168,000 house from $1,512 to $253.

According to the mpac form, property taxes are calculated using an assessed value, a municipal tax rate, and an education tax rate set by the province. The formula is:

- Assessed value × Municipal tax rate = Amount of municipal property tax
- Assessed value × Education tax rate = Amount of education property tax
- Municipal property tax + Education property tax = The owner's property tax

The most frequently used formula for the calculation of property tax is: product of assessed value of the property and decimal equivalent of the mill rate (a mill is one-tenth of a cent, or one-thousandth of a dollar):

$$\text{Property tax} = \frac{\text{Mills}}{1{,}000} \times \text{Assessed value of the property} \qquad \textbf{(6.8)}$$

Now it's time to try the Practice Quiz.

LU 6–4 PRACTICE QUIZ (CONTINUED)

2. From the following facts: (1) calculate assessed value of Bill's home; (2) calculate the tax rate for the community in decimal (to nearest ten thousandths); (3) convert the decimal to **(a)** %, **(b)** per $100 of assessed value, **(c)** per $1,000 of assessed value, and **(d)** in mills (to nearest hundredth); and (4) calculate the property tax due on Bill's home in decimal, per $100, per $1,000, and in mills.

Given

Assessed market value	40%	Total budget needed	$ 176,000
Market value of Bill's home	$210,000	Total assessed value	$1,910,000

CHAPTER ORGANIZER AND REFERENCE GUIDE

Topic	Key point, procedure, formula	Example(s) to illustrate situation
Converting decimals to percents, p. 123	1. Move decimal point two places to right. If necessary, add zeros. This rule is also used for whole numbers and mixed decimals. 2. Add a percent symbol at end of number.	.81 = .81. = 81% .008 = .00.8 = .8% 4.15 = 4.15. = 415%
Rounding percents, p. 124	1. Answer must be in percent before rounding. 2. Identify specific digit. If digit to right is 5 or greater, round up. 3. Delete digits to right of identified digit.	Round to nearest hundredth percent. $\frac{3}{7}$ = .4285714 = 42.85714% = 42.86%
Converting percents to decimals, p. 124	1. Drop percent symbol. 2. Move decimal point two places to left. If necessary, add zeros. For fractional percents: 1. Convert to decimal by dividing numerator by denominator. If necessary, round answer. 2. If a mixed fractional percent, convert fractional percent first. Then combine whole number and fractional percent. 3. Drop percent symbol, move decimal point two places to left.	.89% = .0089 95% = .95 195% = 1.95 $8\frac{3}{4}$% = 8.75% = .0875 $\frac{1}{4}$% = .25% = .0025 $\frac{1}{5}$% = .20% = .0020

(*continues*)

CHAPTER ORGANIZER AND REFERENCE GUIDE (CONTINUED)

<table>
<tr><th>TOPIC</th><th>KEY POINT, PROCEDURE, FORMULA</th><th>EXAMPLE(S) TO ILLUSTRATE SITUATION</th></tr>
<tr><td>Converting fractions to percents, p. 125</td><td>1. Divide numerator by denominator.
2. Move decimal point two places to right; add percent symbol.</td><td>$\frac{4}{5} = .80 = 80\%$</td></tr>
<tr><td>Converting percents to fractions, p. 125</td><td>Whole percent (or fractional percent) to a fraction:
1. Drop percent symbol.
2. Multiply number by $\frac{1}{100}$.
3. Reduce to lowest terms.
Mixed or decimal percent to a fraction:
1. Drop percent symbol.
2. Change mixed percent to an improper fraction.
3. Multiply number by $\frac{1}{100}$.
4. Reduce to lowest terms.
If you have a mixed or decimal percent, change decimal portion to fractional equivalent and continue with Steps 1 to 4.</td><td>$64\% \rightarrow 64 \times \frac{1}{100} = \frac{64}{100} = \frac{16}{25}$
$\frac{1}{4}\% \rightarrow \frac{1}{4} \times \frac{1}{100} = \frac{1}{400}$
$119\% \rightarrow 119 \times \frac{1}{100} = \frac{119}{100} = 1\frac{19}{100}$
$16\frac{1}{4}\% \rightarrow \frac{65}{4} \times \frac{1}{100} = \frac{65}{400} = \frac{13}{80}$
$16.25\% \rightarrow 16\frac{1}{4}\% = \frac{65}{4} \times \frac{1}{100}$
$= \frac{65}{400} = \frac{13}{80}$</td></tr>
<tr><td>Solving for portion ("new number, percentage, amount of change"), p. 128</td><td>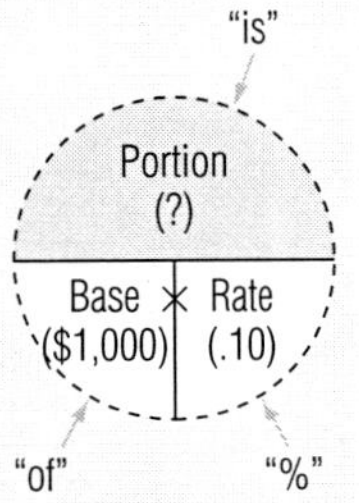

$P = B \times R$</td><td>10% of Mel's paycheque of $1,000 goes for food. What portion is deducted for food?
$B = \$1,000 \quad R = .10.$
$\$100 = \$1,000 \times .10$
$P = \$1,000 \times .10 = \$100$
Note: If question was "What amount does not go for food?" the portion would have been:
$\$900 = \$1,000 \times .90$
$(100\% - 10\% = 90\%)$</td></tr>
<tr><td>Solving for rate, p. 129</td><td>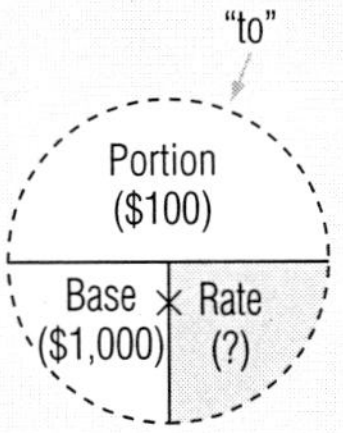

Think of a rate formula as a fraction with the base in the denominator.
$R = \frac{P}{B}$</td><td>Assume Mel spends $100 for food from his $1,000 paycheque. What percent of his cheque is spent on food?
$P = \$100 \quad B = \$1,000$
$R = ?$
$\frac{\$100}{\$1,000} = .10 = 10\%$
$R = \frac{\$100}{\$1,000} = .10 \rightarrow 10\%$
Note: Portion is less than base since rate is less than 100%.</td></tr>
<tr><td>Solving for base ("initial value, whole quantity, value before change, original number, old value, total value"), p. 130</td><td>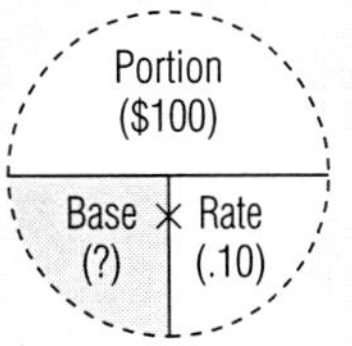

$B = \frac{P}{R}$</td><td>Assume Mel spends $100 for food, which is 10% of his paycheque. What is Mel's total pay?
$B = ? \quad P = \$100 \quad R = .10$
$\frac{\$100}{.10} = \$1,000$
$B = \frac{\$100}{.10} = \$1,000$</td></tr>
</table>

(continues)

CHAPTER ORGANIZER AND REFERENCE GUIDE (CONTINUED)

Topic	Key point, procedure, formula	Example(s) to illustrate situation
Calculating percent decreases and increases, p. 132	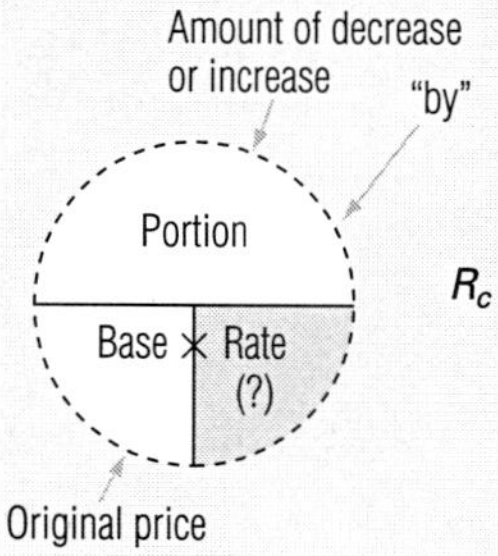 $R_c = \frac{(V_n - V_o)}{V_o} \times 100\%$	Stereo, \$2,000 original price. V_o Stereo, \$2,500 new price. V_n $\frac{\$500}{\$2{,}000} = .25 = 25\%$ increase $R_c = \frac{(\$2{,}500 - \$2{,}000)}{\$2{,}000} = .25$ 25% increase **Check** \$2,000 × 1.25 = \$2,500 *Note:* Portion is greater than base since rate is greater than 100%. 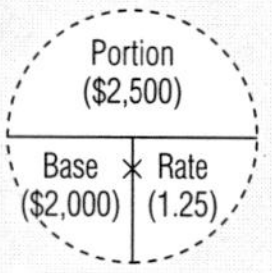 "Positive sign" that there was an increase in quantity.
Goods and Services Tax (GST), p. 135	GST is not calculated on trade discounts. Shipping charges, etc., also are not subject to sales tax. Actual sales $= \frac{\text{Total sales}}{1 + \text{Tax rate}}$ Cash discounts are calculated on sale price before GST is added on.	Calculate sales tax: Purchased 12 bags of mulch at \$59.40; 10% trade discount; 7% GST. \$59.40 − \$5.94 = \$53.46 \$53.46 × .07 \$3.74 GST Any cash discount would be calculated on \$53.46.
Provincial Sales Tax (PST), p. 136	PST is calculated separately from GST and is an additional tax. It is based as a percent of the selling price. Rate for PST will vary.	Jewellery........... \$4,000 retail price GST .... 7% PST..................... 10% \$4,000 + 280 sales tax + 400 excise tax \$4,680
Assessed value, p. 137	Assessment rate × Market value	\$100,000 house; rate, 30%; \$30,000 assessed value.
Tax rate, p. 137	$\frac{\text{Budget needed}}{\text{Total assessed value}} = \text{Tax rate}$ (Round rate up to indicated digit even if less than 5.)	$\frac{\$800{,}000}{\$9{,}200{,}000} = .08695 = .0870$ tax rate per \$1
Expressing tax rate in other forms, p. 138	1. Percent: Move decimal two places to right. Add % sign. 2. Per \$100: Multiply by 100. 3. Per \$1,000: Multiply by 1,000. 4. Mills: Divide by .001.	1. .0870 = 8.7% 2. .0870 × 100 = \$8.70 3. .0870 × 1,000 = \$87 4. $\frac{.0870}{.001} = 87$ mills

(*continues*)

CHAPTER ORGANIZER AND REFERENCE GUIDE (CONCLUDED)

Topic	Key point, procedure, formula	Example(s) to illustrate situation	
Calculating property tax, p. 138	$\text{Total property tax due} = \text{Tax rate} \times \text{Total assessed value}$ Various forms: 1. Percent × Assessed value 2. Per \$100: $\frac{\text{Assessed value}}{\$100} \times \text{Rate}$ 3. Per \$1,000: $\frac{\text{Assessed value}}{\$1{,}000} \times \text{Rate}$ 4. Mills: Mills × .001 × Assessed value or $\frac{\text{Mills}}{1{,}000} \times \text{Assessed value}$	*Example:* Rate, .0870 per \$1; \$30,000 assessed value 1. (.087)8.7% × \$30,000 = \$2,610 2. $\frac{\$30{,}000}{\$100} = 300 \times \$8.70 = \$2{,}610$ 3. $\frac{\$30{,}000}{\$1{,}000} = 30 \times \$87 = \$2{,}610$ 4. $\frac{.0870}{.001} = 87$ mills 87 mills × .001 × \$30,000 = \$2,610 $\frac{87 \text{ mills}}{1{,}000} \times \$30{,}000 = \$2{,}610$	
Key terms	Amount of change, p. 132 Assessed value, p. 137 Base, p. 127 Goods and Services Tax (GST), p. 135 Mill, p. 138 Percent decrease, p. 132	Percent increase, p. 132 Percents, p. 122 Personal property, p. 137 Portion, p. 127 Property tax, p. 137	Provincial Sales Tax (PST), p. 136 Rate, p. 127 Real property, p. 137 Tax rate, p. 137

CRITICAL THINKING DISCUSSION QUESTIONS

1. In converting from a percent to a decimal, when will you have at least two leading zeros before the whole number? Explain this concept, assuming you have 100 bills of \$1.
2. Explain the steps in rounding percents. Count the number of students who are sitting in the back half of the room as a percent of the total class. Round your answer to the nearest hundredth percent. Could you have rounded to the nearest whole percent without changing the accuracy of the answer?
3. Define portion, rate, and base. Create an example using Canada's Wonderland to show when the portion could be larger than the base. Why must the rate be greater than 100% for this to happen?
4. How do we solve for portion, rate, and base? Create an example using Roots Clothing sales to show that the portion and rate do relate to the same piece of the base.
5. Explain how to calculate percent decreases or increases. Many years ago, comic books cost 10 cents a copy. Visit a bookshop or newsstand. Select a new comic book and explain the price increase in percent compared to the 10-cent comic. How important is the rounding process in your final answer?
6. Explain Goods and Services Tax and Provincial Sales Tax. Should all provinces have the same tax rate for Provincial Sales Tax?
7. Explain how to calculate actual sales when the GST was included in the sales figure. Is a GST necessary?
8. How is assessed value calculated? If you think your value is unfair, what could you do?
9. What is a mill? When we calculate property tax in mills, why do we use .001 in the calculation?

END-OF-CHAPTER PROBLEMS

DRILL PROBLEMS (First of Two Sets)

Convert the following decimals to percents:

6–1. .74
6–2. .861
6–3. .7
6–4. 8.00
6–5. 3.561
6–6. 6.006

Convert the following percents to decimals:

6–7. 4%
6–8. 14%
6–9. $64\frac{3}{10}\%$
6–10. 75.9%
6–11. 119%
6–12. 89%

Convert the following fractions to percents (round to the nearest tenth percent as needed):

6–13. $\frac{1}{12}$
6–14. $\frac{1}{400}$
6–15. $\frac{7}{8}$
6–16. $\frac{11}{12}$

Convert the following to fractions and reduce to lowest terms:

6–17. 5%
6–18. $18\frac{1}{2}\%$
6–19. $31\frac{2}{3}\%$
6–20. $61\frac{1}{2}\%$
6–21. 6.75%
6–22. 182%

Solve for the portion (round to the nearest hundredth as needed): Excel

6–23. 6% of 120
6–24. 125% of 4,320
6–25. 25% of 410
6–26. 119% of 128.9
6–27. 17.4% of 900
6–28. 11.2% of 85
6–29. $12\frac{1}{2}\%$ of 919
6–30. 45% of 300
6–31. 18% of 90
6–32. 30% of 2,000

Solve for the base (round to the nearest hundredth as needed):

6–33. 170 is 120% of __________
6–34. 36 is .75% of __________
6–35. 50 is .5% of __________
6–36. 10,800 is 90% of __________
6–37. 800 is $4\frac{1}{2}\%$ of __________

Solve for rate (round to the nearest tenth percent as needed):

6–38. __________ of 80 is 50
6–39. __________ of 85 is 92
6–40. __________ of 250 is 65
6–41. 110 is __________ of 100
6–42. .09 is __________ of 2.25
6–43. 16 is __________ of 4

Solve the following problems. Be sure to show your work. Round to the nearest hundredth or hundredth percent as needed:

6–44. What is 180% of 310?
6–45. 66% of 90 is what?
6–46. 40% of what number is 20?
6–47. 770 is 70% of what number?
6–48. 4 is what percent of 90?
6–49. What percent of 150 is 60?

Complete the following table:

Product	Sales in millions 2004	2005	Amount of decrease or increase	Percent change (to nearest hundredth percent as needed)
6–50. Scooters	$380	$410		
6–51. DVD players	$ 50	$ 47		

DRILL PROBLEMS (SECOND OF TWO SETS)

Calculate the following:

	Retail selling price	Sales tax (5%)	Excise tax (9%)	Total price including taxes
6–52.	$900			
6–53.	$1,500			

Calculate the actual sales since the sales and sales tax were rung up together; assume a 6% sales tax (round your answer to the nearest cent):

6–54. $90,000 **6–55.** $26,000

Calculate the assessed value of the following pieces of property:

	Assessment rate	Market value	Assessed value
6–56.	40%	$180,000	
6–57.	80%	$210,000	

Calculate the tax rate in decimal form to the nearest ten thousandth:

	Required budget	Total assessed value	Tax rate per dollar
6–58.	$920,000	$39,500,000	

Complete the following:

	Tax rate Per dollar	In percent	Per $100	Per $1,000	Mills
6–59.	.0956				
6–60.	.0699				

Compute the amount of property tax due to the nearest cent for each situation:

	Tax rate	Assessed value	Amount of property tax due
6–61.	40 mills	$65,000	
6–62.	$42.50 per $1,000	$105,000	
6–63.	$8.75 per $100	$125,000	
6–64.	$94.10 per $1,000	$180,500	

ADDITIONAL DRILL PROBLEMS

6–65. Convert the following to percents (round to the nearest tenth of a percent if needed):

a. .08 ________ % **b.** .875 ________ %

c. .009 ________ % **d.** 8.3 ________ %

e. 5.26 ________ % **f.** 6 ________ %

g. .0105 ________ % **h.** .1180 ________ %

i. 5.0375 ________ % **j.** .862 ________ %

k. .2615 ________ % **l.** .8 ________ %

m. .025 ________ % **n.** .06 ________ %

6–66. Convert the following to decimals (do not round):

a. 37% ________ **b.** .09% ________

c. 4.7% ________ **d.** 9.67% ________

e. .2% ________ **f.** $\frac{1}{4}\%$ ________

g. .76% ________ **h.** 110% ________

i. $12\frac{1}{2}\%$ ________ **j.** 5% ________

k. .004% ________ **l.** $7\frac{5}{10}\%$ ________

m. $\frac{3}{4}\%$ ________ **n.** 1% ________

6–67. Convert the following to percents (round to the nearest tenth of a percent if needed):

a. $\frac{7}{10}$ ________ % **b.** $\frac{1}{5}$ ________ %

c. $1\frac{5}{8}$ ________ % **d.** $\frac{2}{7}$ ________ %

e. 2 ________ % **f.** $\frac{14}{100}$ ________ %

g. $\frac{1}{6}$ ________ % **h.** $\frac{1}{2}$ ________ %

i. $\frac{3}{5}$ ________ % **j.** $\frac{3}{25}$ ________ %

k. $\frac{5}{16}$ ________ % **l.** $\frac{11}{50}$ ________ %

m. $4\frac{3}{4}$ ________ % **n.** $\frac{3}{200}$ ________ %

6–68. Convert the following to fractions in simplest form:

a. 40% ________ **b.** 15% ________

c. 50% ________ **d.** 75% ________

e. 35% ________ **f.** 85% ________

g. $12\frac{1}{2}\%$ ________ **h.** $37\frac{1}{2}\%$ ________

i. $33\frac{1}{3}\%$ ________ **j.** 3% ________

k. 8.5% ________ **l.** $5\frac{3}{4}\%$ ________

m. 100% ________ **n.** 10% ________

6–69. Complete the following table by finding the missing fraction, decimal, or percent equivalent:

	Fraction	Decimal	Percent		Fraction	Decimal	Percent
a.	________	.25	25%	**h.**	$\frac{1}{6}$	$.16\overline{6}$	________
b.	$\frac{3}{8}$	________	$37\frac{1}{2}\%$	**i.**	________	$.083\overline{3}$	$8\frac{1}{3}\%$
c.	$\frac{1}{2}$	.5	________	**j.**	$\frac{1}{9}$	________	$11\frac{1}{9}\%$
d.	$\frac{2}{3}$	________	$66\frac{2}{3}\%$	**k.**	________	.3125	$31\frac{1}{4}\%$
e.	________	.4	40%	**l.**	$\frac{3}{40}$	.075	________
f.	$\frac{3}{5}$	.6	________	**m.**	$\frac{1}{5}$	________	20%
g.	$\frac{7}{10}$	________	70%	**n.**	________	1.125	$112\frac{1}{2}\%$

6–70. Fill in the amount of the base, rate, and portion in each of the following statements:

a. The Johnsons spend $1,000 a month on food, which is $12\frac{1}{2}\%$ of their monthly income of $8,000.

Base ________ Rate ________ Portion ________

b. Rocky Norman got a $15 discount when he purchased a new camera. This was 20% off the sticker price of $75.

Base ________ Rate ________ Portion ________

c. Mary Burns got a 12% senior citizens discount when she bought a $7 movie ticket. She saved $0.84.

Base ________ Rate ________ Portion ________

d. Arthur Bogey received a commission of $13,500 when he sold the Brown's house for $225,000. His commission rate is 6%.

Base ________ Rate ________ Portion ________

e. Leo Davis deposited $5,000 in a certificate of deposit (CD). A year later he received an interest payment of $450 which was a yield of 9%.

Base ________ Rate ________ Portion ________

f. Grace Tremblay is on a diet that allows her to eat 1,600 calories per day. For breakfast she had 600 calories, which is $37\frac{1}{2}\%$ of her allowance.

Base ________ Rate ________ Portion ________

6–71. Find the portion; round to the nearest hundredth if necessary:

a. 7% of 74 ________ **b.** 12% of 205 ________ **c.** 16% of 630 ________

d. 7.5% of 920 ________ **e.** 25% of 1,004 ________ **f.** 10% of 79 ________

g. 103% of 44 ________ **h.** 30% of 78 ________ **i.** .2% of 50 ________

j. 1% of 5,622 ________ **k.** $6\frac{1}{4}\%$ of 480 ________ **l.** 150% of 10 ________

m. 100% of 34 ________ **n.** $\frac{1}{2}\%$ of 27 ________

6–72. Find the rate; round to the nearest tenth of a percent as needed:

a. 30 is what percent of 90? ________ **b.** 6 is what percent of 200? ________

c. 275 is what percent of 1,000? ________ **d.** .8 is what percent of 44? ________

e. 67 is what percent of 2,010? ________ **f.** 550 is what percent of 250? ________

g. 13 is what percent of 650? ________ **h.** $15 is what percent of $455? ________

i. .05 is what percent of 100? ________ **j.** $6.25 is what percent of $10? ________

6–73. Find the base; round to the nearest tenth as needed:

a. 63 is 30% of ________ **b.** 60 is 33% of ________ **c.** 150 is 25% of ________

d. 47 is 1% of ________ **e.** $21 is 120% of ________ **f.** 2.26 is 40% of ________

g. 75 is $12\frac{1}{2}\%$ of ________ **h.** 18 is 22.2% of ________ **i.** $37.50 is 50% of ________

j. 250 is 100% of ________

6–74. Find the percent of increase or decrease. Round to nearest tenth percent as needed:

	Last year	This year	Amount of change	Percent of change
a.	5,962	4,378		
b.	$10,995	$12,250		
c.	120,000	140,000		
d.	120,000	100,000		

WORD PROBLEMS (FIRST OF FIVE SETS)

6–75. At a local McDonald's, a survey showed that out of 6,000 customers eating lunch, 1,500 ordered Diet Coke with their meal. What percent of customers ordered Diet Coke?

6–76. What percent of customers in Problem 6–75 did not order Diet Coke?

6–77. Homebuyers who don't make a down payment of at least 20% may be required to take out mortgage insurance from Canada Mortgage and Housing Corporation (CMHC). On a $200,000 loan, the premiums can cost more than $100 per month. What would be the minimum down payment on a $200,000 loan to avoid CMHC insurance?

6–78. Wally Chin, the owner of an Shell station, bought a used Ford pickup truck, paying $2,000 as a down payment. He still owes 80% of the selling price. What was the selling price of the truck?

6–79. Maria Fay bought 4 Aquatread tires at a local Goodyear store. The salesperson told her that her gas consumption would decrease by 6%. Before this purchase, Maria was getting 10.7 L/100 km. What should her kilometrage be with the new tires?

6–80. Pete Lavoie went to Bay Bloor Radio and bought a Sony CD player. The purchase price was $350. He made a down payment of 30%. How much was Pete's down payment?

6–81. Assume that in the year 2003, 800,000 people attended the Christmas Eve celebration at Walt Disney World. In 2004, attendance for the Christmas Eve celebration is expected to increase by 35%. What is the total number of people expected at Walt Disney World for this event?

6–82. Pete Smith found in his attic a Woody Woodpecker watch in its original box. It had a price tag on it for $4.50. The watch was made in 1949. Pete brought the watch to an antiques dealer and sold it for $35. What was the percent of increase? Round to the nearest hundredth percent.

6–83. In 2004, the price of a Dell computer rose to $1,200. This is 8% more than the 2003 price. What was the old selling price? Check your answer.

6–84. Christie's Auction sold a painting for $24,500. It charges all buyers a 15% premium of the final bid price. How much did the bidder pay Christie's?

WORD PROBLEMS (SECOND OF FIVE SETS)

6–85. Out of 6,000 college students surveyed, 600 responded that they do not eat breakfast. What percent of the students do not eat breakfast?

6–86. What percent of college students in Problem 6–85 eat breakfast?

6–87. Alice Hall made a $3,000 down payment on a new Ford Explorer wagon. She still owes 90% of the selling price. What was the selling price of the wagon?

6–88. On May 30, 2001, Associated Press Online provided information from a fiscal analyst stating that during the past 20 years, the average after-tax income of the wealthiest 1% of Americans had grown from $263,700 to $677,900. What was the percent increase? Round to the nearest percent.

6–89. Jim and Alice Lange, employees at Wal-Mart, have put themselves on a strict budget. Their goal at year's end is to buy a boat for $15,000 in cash. Their budget includes the following:

40% food and lodging	20% entertainment	10% educational

Jim earns $1,900 per month and Alice earns $2,400 per month. After one year, will Alice and Jim have enough cash to buy the boat?

6–90. The price of a Fossil watch dropped from $49.95 to $30. What was the percent decrease in price? Round to the nearest hundredth percent.

6–91. The Royal Ontario Museum estimated that 64% of all visitors came from within the province. On Saturday, 2,500 people attended the museum. How many attended the museum from out of province?

6–92. Staples pays George Nagovsky an annual salary of $36,000. Today, George's boss informs him that he will receive a $4,600 raise. What percent of George's old salary is the $4,600 raise? Round to the nearest tenth percent.

6–93. In 2003, Dairy Queen had $550,000 in sales. In 2004, Dairy Queen's sales were up 35%. What were Dairy Queen's sales in 2004?

6–94. Blue Valley College has 600 female students. This is 60% of the total student body. How many students attend Blue Valley College?

6–95. Dr. Grossman was reviewing his total accounts receivable. This month, credit customers paid $44,000, which represented 20% of all receivables (what customers owe) due. What was Dr. Grossman's total accounts receivable?

6–96. Timothy bought a new fridge and paid $1,500 at the cash register. What was the cost of the fridge before the tax? What was the amount of taxes (GST and PST) paid?

6–97. The price of an antique doll increased from $600 to $800. What was the percent of increase? Round to the nearest tenth percent.

6–98. Borders bookstore ordered 80 marketing books but received 60 books. What percent of the order was missing?

WORD PROBLEMS (THIRD OF FIVE SETS)

6–99. At a Christie's auction in London (U.K.), the auctioneer estimated that 40% of the audience was from within the country. Eight hundred people attended the auction. How many out-of-country people attended?

6–100. Referring to increased mailing costs, the May 14, 2001 *Advertising Age* commented "Magazines Go Postal over Rate Hike." The new rate will cost publishers $50 million; this is 12.5% more than they paid the previous year. How much did it cost publishers last year? Round to the nearest hundreds.

6–101. In 2004, Jim Goodman, an employee at PharmaPlus, earned $45,900, an increase of 17.5% over the previous year. What were Jim's earnings in 2003? Round to the nearest cent.

6–102. The *National Mortgage News,* dated February 5, 2001, reported on the number of applications received by Mortgage Insurance Companies of America. For the year 2000, application volume declined by 7% to l,625,415. What had been the previous year's application volume?

6–103. In 2004, the price of a business math text rose to $80. This is 5% more than the 2003 price. What was the old selling price? Round to the nearest cent.

6–104. Web Consultants, Inc. pays Alice Rose an annual salary of $48,000. Today, Alice's boss informs her that she will receive a $6,400 raise. What percent of Alice's old salary is the $6,400 raise? Round to nearest tenth percent.

6–105. Earl Miller, a lawyer, charges Lee's Plumbing, his client, 25% of what he can collect for Lee from customers whose accounts are past due. The attorney also charges, in addition to the 25%, a flat fee of $50 per customer. This month, Earl collected $7,000 from three of Lee's past-due customers. What is the total fee due to Earl?

6–106. Petco ordered 100 dog calendars but received 60. What percent of the order was missing?

6–107. Blockbuster Video uses MasterCard. MasterCard charges $2\frac{1}{2}$% on net deposits (credit slips less returns). Blockbuster made a net deposit of $4,100 for charge sales. How much did MasterCard charge Blockbuster?

6–108. In 2003, Internet Access had $800,000 in sales. In 2004, Internet Access sales were up 45%. What are the sales for 2004?

WORD PROBLEMS (FOURTH OF FIVE SETS)

6–109. Saab Corporation raised the base price of its popular 900 series by $1,200 to $33,500. What was the percent increase? Round to the nearest tenth percent.

6–110. The PST rate is 8% and the GST rate is 7%. If Jim bought a new Buick and paid a sales tax of $3,600, what was the cost of the Buick before the tax?

6–111. Puthina Unge bought a new Compaq computer system on sale for $1,800. It was advertised as 30% off the regular price. What was the original price of the computer? Round to the nearest dollar.

6–112. John O'Sullivan has just completed his first year in business. His records show that he spent the following in advertising:

Newspaper	$600	Radio	$650
Yellow Pages	700	Local flyers	400

What percent of John's advertising was spent on the Yellow Pages? Round to the nearest hundredth percent.

6–113. In 2004, Levin Furniture plans to ship furniture overseas for a sales volume of $11.2 million, an increase of 40% from that in 2003. What was the sales volume in 2003?

6–114. Abby Kaminsky sold her ski house at Blue Mountain in Collingwood for $35,000. This sale represented a loss of 15% off the original price. What was the original price Abby paid for the ski house? She also paid 5% commission to her sales agent. How much money did Abby receive for her ski house at the end? Round your answer to the nearest dollar.

6–115. Out of 4,000 colleges surveyed, 60% reported that they are starting new programs for students. How many schools are not starting new programs?

6–116. Refinishing your basement at a cost of $45,404 would add $18,270 to the resale value of your home. What percent of your cost is recouped? Round to the nearest percent.

6–117. A major airline laid off 4,000 pilots and flight attendants. If this was a 12.5% reduction in the workforce, what was the size of the workforce after the layoffs?

6–118. Assume 450,000 people line up on the streets to see the Santa Claus Parade in 2003. If attendance is expected to increase 30%, what will be the number of people lined up on the street to see the 2004 parade?

WORD PROBLEMS (FIFTH OF FIVE SETS)

6–119. Abby Kaminsky went to Precision Equipment and bought an $800 Stairmaster that is subject to a 7% GST and an 8% PST. What is the total amount Abby paid?

6–120. Don Chather bought a new computer for $1,995. This included a 15% HST. What is the amount of HST and the selling price before the tax?

6–121. The "We Are Against Smoking" group proposed a cigarette tax increase. If this proposition becomes a law, the tobacco tax would rise to $1.26 per pack. If a package of cigarettes sells for $3, what percent of this price is tax?

6–122. In the community of Revere, the market value of a home is $180,000. The assessment rate is 30%. What is the assessed value?

6–123. The January 8, 2001 issue of *Arkansas Business* reported on tax increases. The Arkansas sales and use tax rate increased from 4.625% to 5.125%. Claudia McClain recently purchased a Ford Explorer for $28,600. **(a)** What was the amount of sales tax Claudia paid? **(b)** How much would she have saved before the increase?

6–124. Lois Clark bought a ring for $6,000. She must still pay a 15% HST. The jeweller is shipping the ring, so Lois must also pay a $40 shipping charge. What is the total purchase price of Lois's ring?

6–125. Canadian Blue Bay County needs $700,000 from property tax to meet its budget. The total value of assessed property in Blue Bay is $110,000,000. What is the tax rate of Blue Bay? Round to the nearest ten thousandth. Express the rate in mills.

6–126. Bill Shass pays a property tax of $3,200. In his community, the tax rate is 50 mills. What is Bill's assessed value?

6–127. The home of Bill Burton is assessed at $80,000. The tax rate is 18.50 mills. What is the tax on Bill's home?

6–128. A local newspaper reported on a school district losing funds on two local businesses because of proposed reduced property tax assessments. Bake Line Products is seeking to have its property reassessed from the $2.27 million, at which it's now valued, to $1.98 million. The owners of the Golf Centre hope to have their property reassessed from $848,730 to $593,575. The current tax rate is .0725. How much will the district lose if both requests are granted? Round to the nearest ten thousands.

6–129. Bill Blake pays a property tax of $2,500. In his community, the tax rate is 55 mills. What is Bill's assessed value? Round to the nearest dollar.

6–130. On March 20, 2001, the *Saint Paul Pioneer Press* reported on property taxes based on square footage. A new comparative property tax study by the executive director of a Minneapolis group of landlords showed that the Wells Fargo Center in downtown Minneapolis pays four times the taxes of the Wells Fargo Center in downtown Denver. The property tax rate for Minneapolis is $8.73 a square foot, and the Denver rate is $2.14 a square foot. If 3,500 square feet is occupied at each location, what is the difference paid in property taxes?

ADDITIONAL WORD PROBLEMS

6–131. In 2004, Mutual of New York reported an overwhelming 70% of its new sales came from existing clients. What fractional part of its new sales came from existing clients? Reduce to simplest form.

6–132. Six hundred ninety corporations and design firms competed for the Industrial Design Excellence Award (IDEA) in 2004. Twenty were selected as the year's best and received gold awards. Show the gold award winners as a fraction; then show what percent of the entrants received gold awards. Round to the nearest tenth of a percent.

6–133. In the first half of 2004, stock prices in the Standard & Poor's 500-stock index rose 17.5%. Show the increase in decimal form.

6–134. In the recent banking crisis, many banks were unable to cover their bad loans. Citicorp, the nation's largest real estate lender, was reported as having only enough reserves to cover 39% of its bad loans. What fractional part of its loan losses was covered?

6–135. Dave Mattera spent his vacation in Las Vegas. He ordered breakfast in his room, and when he went downstairs to the coffee shop, he discovered that the same breakfast was much less expensive. He had paid 1.884 times as much for the breakfast in his room. What was the percent of increase for the breakfast in his room?

6–136. Putnam Management Company of Boston recently increased its management fee by .09%. What is the increase as a decimal? What is the same increase as a fraction?

6–137. Joel Black and Karen Whyte formed a partnership and drew up a partnership agreement, with profits and losses to be divided equally after each partner receives a $7\frac{1}{2}$% return on his or her capital contribution. Show their return on investment as a decimal and as a fraction. Reduce.

6–138. A machine that originally cost $2,400 was sold for $600 at the end of five years. What percent of the original cost is the selling price?

6–139. Joanne Byrne invested $75,000 in a candy shop and is making 12% per year on her investment. How much money per year is she making on her investment?

6–140. There was a fire in Bill Porper's store that caused 2,780 inventory items to be destroyed. Before the fire, 9,565 inventory items were in the store. What percent of inventory was destroyed? Round to nearest tenth percent.

6–141. Elyse's Dress Shoppe makes 25% of its sales for cash. If the cash receipts on January 21 were $799, what were the total sales for the day?

6–142. The YMCA is holding a fundraiser to collect money for a new gym floor. So far it has collected $7,875, which is 63% of the goal. What is the amount of the goal? How much more money must the YMCA collect?

6–143. Leslie Tracey purchased her home for $51,500. She sold it last year for $221,200. What percent profit did she make on the sale? Round to nearest tenth percent.

6–144. Maplewood Park Tool & Die had an annual production of 375,165 units this year. This is 140% of the annual production last year. What was last year's annual production?

CHALLENGE PROBLEMS

6–145. Excel On June 15, 2001, the *Herald-Journal* reported on the property taxes of Wellford, South Carolina. The city council took the first step toward approving next year's budget, which will more than double property taxes for Wellford residents. A 40-mill tax increase will be required, taking the rate from 29 mills to 69 mills. The assessment rate is 40%. The total proposed budget for Wellford is $739,000, about 18% more than last year. **(a)** What would the owner of a $50,000 home pay in property taxes? **(b)** How much did the $50,000 homeowner pay in property taxes the previous year? **(c)** What was the amount of last year's budget to nearest dollar? **(d)** What is the total assessed value of Wellford's property this year?

6–146. Art Neuner, an investor in real estate, bought an office condominium. The market value of the condo was $250,000 with a 70% assessment rate. Art feels that his return should be 1.2% per month on his investment after all expenses. The tax rate is $31.50 per $1,000. Art estimates it will cost $275 per month to cover general repairs, insurance, and so on. He pays a $140 condo fee per month. All utilities and heat are the responsibility of the tenant. Calculate the monthly rent for Art. Round your answer to the nearest dollar (at intermediate stages).

6–147. On October 11, 2000, the *Milwaukee Journal Sentinel* reported that the third-quarter earnings of a Milwaukee-based mortgage insurance firm were up 19% from $122.9 million. For the first nine months of 2000, net income totalled $409.7 million, up 23%. On October 10, 2000, the firm's shares closed up 50 cents, at $60. **(a)** How much were the earnings in 2000? Round to the nearest hundred thousands. **(b)** What was the third-quarter amount of the previous year's net income? Round to the nearest hundred thousands. **(c)** What was the percent increase in shares? Round to the nearest hundredth percent.

6–148. A local Coffee Time reported that its sales have increased exactly 22% per year for the last 2 years. This year's sales were $82,500. What were Coffee Time sales 2 years ago? Round each year's sales to the nearest dollar.

SUMMARY PRACTICE TEST

Convert the following decimals to percents. (p. 123)

1. .682 **2.** 8 **3.** 15.47 **4.** 8.00

Convert the following percents to decimals. (p. 124)

5. 42% **6.** 5.69% **7.** 600% **8.** $\frac{1}{4}\%$

Convert the following fractions to percents. Round to the nearest tenth percent. (p. 125)

9. $\frac{1}{6}$ **10.** $\frac{1}{8}$

Convert the following percents to fractions and reduce to lowest terms as needed. (p. 125)

11. $15\frac{3}{4}\%$ **12.** 7.2%

Solve the following problems for portion, base, or rate:

13. E-bus.ca has a net income before taxes of $900,000. The company's treasurer estimates that 40% of the company's net income will go to federal and provincial taxes. How much will E-bus.ca have left? (p. 128)

14. Papa Ginos projects a year-end net income of $650,000. The net income represents 30% of its projected annual sales. What are Papa Ginos's projected annual sales? Round to the nearest dollar. (p. 130)

15. Wal-Mart ordered 400 Sony Playstations. When Wal-Mart received the order, 20 Playstations were missing. What percent of the order did Wal-Mart receive? (p. 129)

16. Norma Maler, an employee at Putnam Investments, receives an annual salary of $80,000. Today, her boss informed her she would receive a $9,000 raise. What percent of her old salary is the $9,000 raise? Round to the nearest hundredth percent. (p. 129)

17. The price of an airline ticket from Toronto to Thunder Bay increased to $550. This is a 30% increase. What was the old fare? Round to the nearest cent. (p. 130)

18. Al Ring earns a gross pay of $600 per week at Staples. Al's payroll deductions are 29%. What is Al's take-home pay? (p. 128)

19. Tom Bruce is reviewing the total accounts receivable of Rich's Department Store. Credit customers paid $60,000 this month. This represents 30% of all receivables due. What is Tom's total accounts receivable? (p. 130)

20. Jay Brunner bought a new Gateway computer at Mega City for $1,700. The price included a 15% HST. What are the sales tax and the selling price before the tax? (p. 136)

21. Shelley Katz bought a ring for $5,000 from Long's. She must pay a 7% GST tax and an 8% PST. Since the jeweller is shipping the ring, Jane must also pay a $15 shipping charge. What is the total purchase price of Shelley's ring? (pp. 135, 136)

22. The market value of a home in Montreal, Quebec is $210,000. The assessment rate is 40%. What is the assessed value? (p. 137)

23. Richland County needs $980,000 from its property tax to meet the budget. The total value of assessed property in Richland is $184,000,000. What is Richland's tax rate? Round to the nearest ten thousandth. Express the rate in mills (to the nearest tenth). (pp. 129, 137, 138)

24. The home of Jamie Clair is assessed at $299,000. The tax rate is 8.15 mills. What is the tax on Jamie's home? (p. 138)

25. BJ's Warehouse has a market value of $800,000. The property in BJ's area is assessed at 40% of the market value. The tax rate is $58.50 per $1,000 of assessed value. What is BJ's property tax? (p. 138)

SOLUTIONS TO PRACTICE QUIZZES

LU 6–1

1. $.66.66 = 66.7\%$
2. $.83.2 = 83.2\%$
3. $.00.4 = .4\%$
4. $8.94.444 = 894.4\%$
5. $\frac{1}{4}\% = .25\% = .0025$
6. $6\frac{3}{4}\% = 6.75\% = .0675$
7. $87\% = .87. = .87$
8. $810.9\% = 8.10.9 = 8.109$
9. $\frac{1}{7} = .14.286 = 14.29\%$
10. $\frac{2}{9} = .22.2\overline{2} = 22.22\%$
11. $19\% = 19 \times \frac{1}{100} = \frac{19}{100}$
12. $71\frac{1}{2}\% = \frac{143}{2} \times \frac{1}{100} = \frac{143}{200}$
13. $130\% = 130 \times \frac{1}{100} = \frac{130}{100} = 1\frac{30}{100} = 1\frac{3}{10}$
14. $\frac{1}{2}\% = \frac{1}{2} \times \frac{1}{100} = \frac{1}{200}$
15. $19\frac{9}{10}\% = \frac{199}{10} \times \frac{1}{100} = \frac{199}{1{,}000}$

LU 6–2

1. $342 = 900 \times .38$
   $(P) = (B) \times (R)$
2. $\$5{,}400 = \$9{,}000 \times .60$
   $(P) = (B) \times (R)$
3. $\frac{(P)430}{(B)5{,}000} = .086 = 8.6\%\ (R)$
4. $\frac{(P)200}{(B)700} = .2857 = 28.6\%\ (R)$
5. $\frac{(P)55}{(R).40} = 137.5\ (B)$
6. $\frac{(P)900}{(R).045} = 20{,}000\ (B)$
7. Percent of Professor Ford's class that did not receive the "A" grade:

THE FACTS	SOLVING FOR?	STEPS TO TAKE	KEY POINTS
5 "A"s. 25 in class.	Percent that did not receive "A."	Identify key elements. *Base:* 25 *Rate:* ? *Portion:* 20(25 − 5) $\text{Rate} = \frac{\text{Portion}}{\text{Base}}$	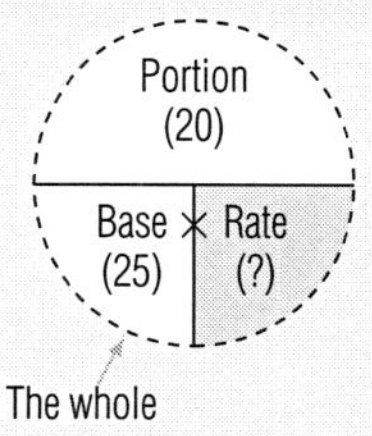 Portion and rate must relate to same piece of base.

Steps to solving problem

1. Set up the formula. $\text{Rate} = \frac{\text{Portion}}{\text{Base}}$

2. Calculate the rate. $R = \frac{20}{25}$

$R = 80\%$

8. Abby Biernet's original order:

THE FACTS	SOLVING FOR?	STEPS TO TAKE	KEY POINTS
60% of the order not in. 80 lobsters received.	Total order of lobsters.	Identify key elements. *Base:* ? *Rate:* 40 (100% − 60%) *Portion:* 80 $\text{Base} = \frac{\text{Portion}}{\text{Rate}}$	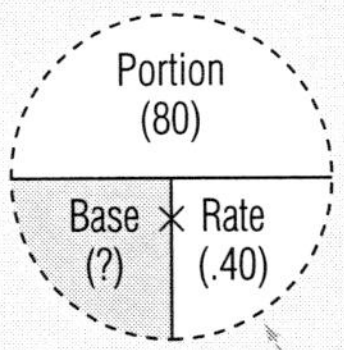 80 lobsters represent 40% of the order. Portion and rate must relate to same piece of base.

Steps to solving problem

1. Set up the formula. $\text{Base} = \frac{\text{Portion}}{\text{Rate}}$

2. Calculate the base. $B = \frac{80}{.40}$ ← 80 lobsters is 40% of base.

$B = 200$ lobsters

9. Amount of agent's fee as a portion of sales price:

THE FACTS	SOLVING FOR?	STEPS TO TAKE	KEY POINTS
B: Sales price: \$400,000 *R:* Fee rate: 2.5%	*P:* Amount of agent's fee $P = ?$	Identify key elements: $B = 400{,}000$ $R = 0.025$ $P = B \times R$ (6.4)	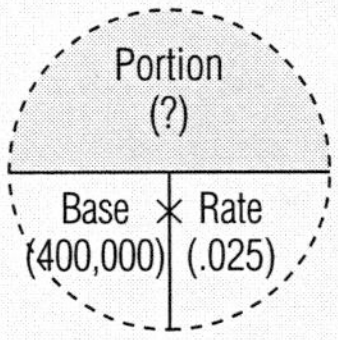 Portion is the product of base and rate.

Steps to solving problem

1. Set up the formula. Portion = Base × Rate $P = B \times R$ (6.4)
2. Calculate the portion. $P = 400{,}000 \times .025$

$P = 10{,}000$

10. Amount of agent's new suggested fee as a portion of sales price:

THE FACTS	SOLVING FOR?	STEPS TO TAKE	KEY POINTS
B: Sales price: \$400,000 R_1: Fee rate: 2.5%	*P:* Amount of suggested agent's fee $P = ?$	Identify key elements: $B = 400{,}000$ New rate $R = .0125$ $R = \frac{1}{2} \times R_1$ $= \frac{1}{2} \times .025$ $= .0125$ $P = B \times R$ (6.4)	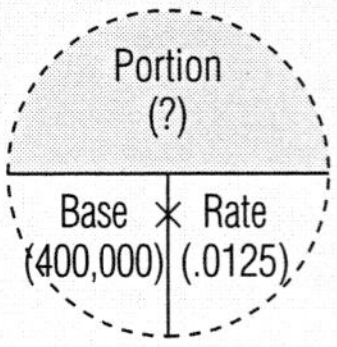 Portion is the product of base and rate.

Steps to solving problem

1. Set up a formula. Portion = Base × Rate $P = B \times R$ (6.4)
2. Calculate the portion: $P = 400{,}000 \times .0125$ ← .0125 is a new rate

$P = 5{,}000$

11. Percent of savings as a rate:

THE FACTS	SOLVING FOR?	STEPS TO TAKE	KEY POINTS
B: Initial fee: \$10,000 *P:* New fee: \$5,000	*R:* Percent saved $R = ?$	Identify key elements: $B = 10,000$ New fee $P = 5,000$ $R = \frac{P}{B}$ (6.2)	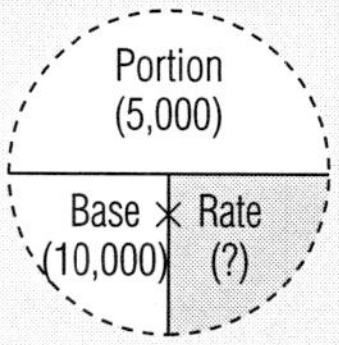 Rate is the fraction with base in denominator and portion in numerator.

Steps to solving problem

1. Set up the formula. Rate = Portion/Base $R = B/P$ (6.2)
2. Calculate the rate. $R = 5{,}000/10{,}000 = .5$ or 50%
   $R = 50\%$

LU 6–3

1. Tim Hortons sales for 2004:

THE FACTS	SOLVING FOR?	STEPS TO TAKE	KEY POINTS
V_o: *2003:* \$300,000 sales R_c: *2004:* Sales up 40% from 2003	Sales for 2004. $V_n = ?$	Identify key elements. *Base:* \$300,000 *Rate:* 1.40 $R_n =$ $(R_o + R_c) = ?$ Old year 100% New year + 40 140% *Portion:* ? V_n Portion = Base × Rate $V_n = V_o \times R_n$	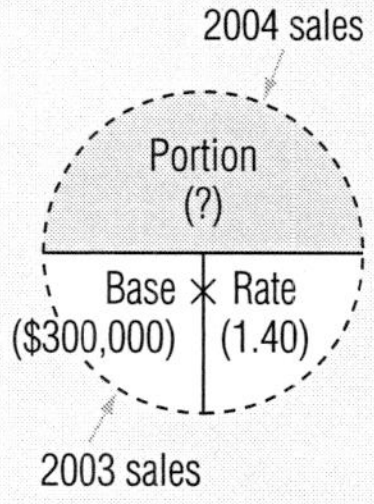 When rate is greater than 100%, portion will be larger than base.

Steps to solving problem

1. Set up the formula. Portion = Base × Rate $V_n = V_o \times R_n$
2. Calculate the portion. $P = \$300{,}000 \times 1.40$
   $P = \$420{,}000$

2. Percent decrease in Apple computer price:

THE FACTS	SOLVING FOR?	STEPS TO TAKE	KEY POINTS
Apple computer V_o: Was \$1,600 V_n: Now \$1,200	Percent decrease in price. $R_c = ?$	Identify key elements. *Base:* \$1,600 V_o *Rate:* ? R_c *Portion:* \$400 $(V_n - V_o)$ (\$1,600 − \$1,200) $\text{Rate} = \frac{\text{Portion}}{\text{Base}}$ $R_c = \frac{(V_n - V_o)}{V_o}$	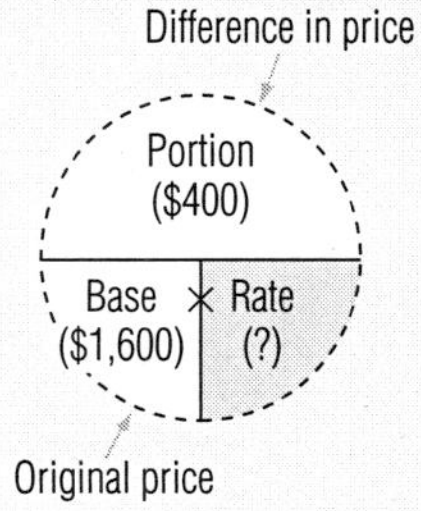

Steps to solving problem

1. Set up the formula. $\text{Rate} = \frac{\text{Portion}}{\text{Base}} \qquad R_c = \frac{(V_n - V_o)}{V_o}$

2. Calculate the rate. $R = \frac{-\$400}{\$1,600} = \frac{(1,200 - 1,600)}{1,600} = -.25$

$R = 25\%$ decrease

3. Percent increase in Kingston Celtics ticket:

THE FACTS	SOLVING FOR?	STEPS TO TAKE	KEY POINTS
V_o: $14 ticket (old) V_n: $50 ticket (new)	Percent increase in price. $R_c = ?$	Identify key elements. *Base:* $14 V_o *Rate:* ? R_c *Portion:* $36 ($V_n - V_o$) ($50 − $14) $\text{Rate} = \frac{\text{Portion}}{\text{Base}}$ $R_c = \frac{(V_n - V_o)}{V_o}$	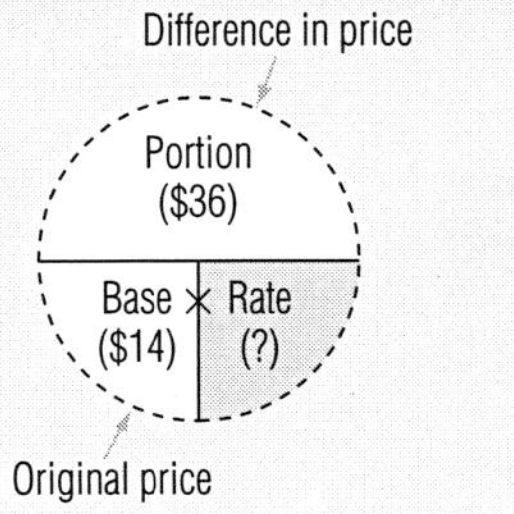 When portion is greater than base, rate will be greater than 100%.

Steps to solving problem

1. Set up the formula. $\text{Rate} = \frac{\text{Portion}}{\text{Base}} \qquad R_c = \frac{(V_n - V_o)}{V_o}$

2. Calculate the rate. $R = \frac{\$36}{\$14} = \frac{(50 - 14)}{14} = +2.5714$

$R = 2.5714 = 257.14\%$

4. Old price as a base:

THE FACTS	SOLVING FOR?	STEPS TO TAKE	KEY POINTS
P: New number: Price this week $0.699 R_c: 2% decrease in price (change of −2%)	*B*: Old number Price last week? $B = ?$	Old price $B = ?$ New rate $R_n = R_o - R_c$ $= 100\% - 2\% = 98\%$ Base = New number/R_n	When rate is smaller than 100%, the portion will be smaller than the base.

Steps to solving problem

1. Set up the formula. Base = New number/New rate

2. Calculate the base. $\text{Base} = \frac{.699}{.98} = .713$

The price last week was $0.713.

LU 6–4

1. Shampoo $4.10 + Laundry detergent $3.65 = $7.75. $7.75 × .08 = $0.62.

2.

(1) .40 × $210,000 = $84,000 (2) $\frac{\$176,000}{\$1,910,000}$ = .0922 per dollar

(3) **a.** .0922 = 9.22% **b.** .0922 × 100 = $9.22

c. .0922 × 1,000 = $92.20 **d.** $\frac{.0922}{.001}$ = 92.2 mills (or .0922 × 1,000)

(4) .0922 × $84,000 = $7,744.80

$9.22 × 840 = $7,744.80

$92.20 × 84 = $7,744.80

92.20 × .001 × $84,000 = $7,744.80

Business Math Scrapbook

WITH INTERNET APPLICATION

Putting Your Skills to Work

Used with permission of Future Shop.

PROJECT A

Your department at work needs a new fax machine. Go to www.futureshop.ca. Look under the pull-down Product Info menus for fax machines. Choose a fax machine you would like to purchase. Assume your organization is sales-tax-exempt in your province, but that your company's shipping and receiving department charges an 8% fee to handle all orders. How much will the fax machine cost before the surcharge? What is the amount of the surcharge?

PROJECT B

Calculate the amounts of change in population annual growth and workforce annual growth.

Discuss in groups what impact population growth will have on the workforce and the economic potential of Canada.

How Many Do We Need?

This year an estimated 256,000 immigrants and refugees will come to Canada. Some say the country is accepting too many people, others not enough. Since Ottawa will not release any projections, *Maclean's* asked Byron Spencer, a McMaster University economics professor, to calculate what would happen in future years to the population and the labour force if the annual immigration level remained unchanged, if it was halved to 128,000 or doubled to 512,000.

Year	**Canada's pop. (millions)**	**Pop. annual growth**	**Workforce annual growth**
2001	**31.1**	**+1.02%**	**+1.59%**
2011			
Halved	32.6	+0.33	+0.23
Unchanged	33.8	+0.75	+0.69
Doubled	36.3	+1.51	+1.52
2031			
Halved	33.4	−0.13	−0.58
Unchanged	37.7	+0.30	−0.04
Doubled	46.2	+0.93	+0.70

Source: Projections based on McMaster University MEDS model.

Source: *Maclean's,* December 16, 2002.

Ratios and Proportions

7

SMALL TOWNS, BIG VALUE

RURAL COMMUNITIES SHAPED PRESENT-DAY CANADA IN FACT, AND MUCH OF OUR FICTION

IN 1901, according to Canada's census, 63 per cent of Canadians lived in rural communities, 37 per cent in cities. Over a century later, 20 per cent of Canadians are country-dwellers, and 80 per cent live in cities. In short, the practices and traditions that carried us through our formative years as a nation are unknown or immaterial to most Canadians. And yet, our fascination with country life endures, in books and real life. As Senior Writer Brian Bethune noted recently in a review of new Canadian fiction: "To a remarkable extent, our stories are still rooted in that past, in smaller communities and dominant cultures."

Statistics Canada, 2001 census
www12statcan.ca/English/census01/home/index.ofm

LEARNING UNIT OBJECTIVES

LU 7–1: Ratios: Basic Concepts

- Set up ratios (p. 160).
- Perform operations with ratios (p. 160).
- Applications: Allocate values according to a ratio (p. 161).

LU 7–2: Proportions: Basic Concepts

- Use the cross-multiplication rule (p. 162).
- Applications: Solve problems involving proportions (p. 162).
- Applications: Allocate according to a ratio (p. 162).
- Applications: Use proportions in currency conversion (p. 163).

LEARNING UNIT 7–1
RATIOS: BASIC CONCEPTS

Be it reading newspapers, listening to the radio, or working on the Internet, we are often dealing with raw business data expressed in numbers. These numbers become more meaningful if we can make relevant comparisons and evaluate changes in time, contents, and value. To evaluate results, it is necessary to compare your data to a basis, average, or other related data.

If you are a Canadian female and you measure 170 centimetres in height, how will you know whether you are considered tall or short? You will be able to define this if you compare your height to the average height of Canadian females. According to a recent study, in 2002 this was 165 centimetres. Your height is related to the average height as 170 centimetres is to 165 centimetres and so you are considered tall in Canada.

Our decisions and estimates are based on comparisons. If you got 68 on your test, how will you know whether you did well or not? If you compare it to the maximum possible mark of 100 you probably did not do too well, but if you compare it to the class average of 60 you did do well. Your mark is related to the maximum mark as 68 is to 100 and to the class average as 68 is to 60.

In all these cases you used ratios. A **ratio** is a comparison performed by the division of two or more values.

Let's see how we can apply this. In the chapter opener we read that according to Canada's census in 1901, 63% of Canadians lived in rural communities and 37% in cities. The ratio of the rural to the urban population in 1901 was 63 to 37 or 63 : 37. This comparison becomes more meaningful if we compare it to the ratio of rural to urban population in 2001, which was 20 : 80.

The ratio of the rural population in 1901 to the rural population in 2001 is 63 : 20, and the ratio of the two urban populations is 37:80. These ratios can also be expressed as:

> This week, our cover story looks at disappearing rural Saskatchewan. In that province, the overall population is *decreasing*, from 990,237 residents in 1996 to 978,933 in the 2001 census.

- *A fraction.* $\frac{63}{20}$ for rural populations and $\frac{37}{80}$ for urban populations
- *A decimal equivalent of fraction.* 3.15 for rural populations and .4625 for urban populations
- *A percent.* 315% for rural populations and 46.25% for urban populations

From the *Maclean's* clipping here, taken from the same article, we see that the overall population of Saskatchewan has decreased from 990,237 residents in 1996 to 978,933 in 2001. This data can be expressed as a ratio of Saskatchewan's population in 1996 to 2001 in different forms:

- 990,237 to 978,933 using the word "to"
- 990,237 : 978,933 using the colon notation
- $\dfrac{990{,}237}{978{,}933}$ using fraction notation
- 1.0115 using the decimal equivalent of a fraction
- 101.15% using the percent equivalent of a decimal

FAMILY DINNERS

Dinner for 2 . . . . $15.95
2 Egg Rolls, Chicken Chow Mein, Sweet & Sour Spareribs, B.B.Q. Pork Fried Rice, Fortune Cookies

Dinner for 3 . . . . $23.50
3 Egg Rolls, Chicken Chow Mein, Sweet & Sour Chicken Balls, Beef with Vegetables, Pork Fried Rice, Fortune Cookies

Dinner for 5 . . . . $40.50
5 Egg Rolls, Honey Garlic Spareribs, Chicken Chow Mein, Sweet & Sour Chicken Balls, Beef with Broccoli, Breaded Shrimp, Chicken Fried Rice, Fortune Cookies

Darren Hick

Ratios can compare two or more values. For example, in this clipping of an advertisement for one of Edmonton's Chinese Buffets, the ratio of prices for dinners for two, for three, and for five people will be respectively \$15.95 : \$23.50 : \$40.50.

Ratios have properties similar to those of equations. Multiplication or division of all ratio members by the same number will not change the meaning of the ratio. Thus, ratios can be reduced to lowest terms by dividing all the members by a common factor:

$$12:6:3 = 4:2:1$$
$$18:9:3 = 6:3:1$$
$$100:50:25 = 4:2:1$$
$$63:36 = 7:4$$
$$27:13:44 = \frac{27}{31}:\frac{13}{31}:\frac{44}{31}$$

Ratios on the left side are said to be **equivalent ratios** to the ratios on the right side.

Comparisons and operations with ratios are much easier to do when all the terms of the ratio are whole numbers and when the ratio is reduced to its lowest terms. For example, the terms in the ratio $\frac{1}{2}:\frac{1}{4}$ are not easy to compare. When the terms of the ratio are fractions it is recommended that you multiply all of them by the lowest common denominator. In our example the lowest common denominator is 4. Multiplying both terms of the ratio $\frac{1}{2}:\frac{1}{4}$ by 4 results in a ratio of 2 : 1, and makes it much easier to read.

At this point you should have a clear understanding of ratios and their properties. Let's try to set up a ratio for a word problem and reduce it to lowest terms.

EXAMPLE

John, Mary, and Oksana share a three-room office. John's room is 160 square feet, Mary's is 180 square feet, and Oksana's is 250 square feet.

The ratio of office space is as follows:

J : M : O = 160 : 180 : 250

Please note that the order of presenting the ratio is very important. John is in the first position and his office is 160 square feet; Mary is second and her office space is 180 square feet; Oksana is third and her office space is 250 square feet.

Let's reduce it to lowest terms. The common factor is 10. Dividing all the terms by 10 we will get: 16 : 18 : 25

Ratios may be used for the allocation of different values as in the following example.

EXAMPLE

Office Management Inc. rents out office space of 550 square metres to three companies. Smart Printing rents 100 square metres, Convenience Store rents 150 square metres, and J.P. and Associates rents 300 square metres. How much rent does each company pay per month if Office Management Inc. collects $10,000? Assume that the ratio of the payments is the same as the ratio of the rented space.

Smart Printing (SP) → 100 m^2
Convenience Store (CS) → 150 m^2
J.P. & Associates (JPA) → 300 m^2

SP : CS : JPA = 100 : 150 : 300

Reducing this ratio to lowest terms, 2 : 3 : 6, we can see that SP rents 2 parts of the whole office space, CS rents 3 parts, and JPA rents 6 parts. Using these terms, the whole office space consists of 11 parts (2 + 3 + 6), of which SP's portion is $\frac{2}{11}$, CS's is $\frac{3}{11}$, and JPA's is $\frac{6}{11}$.

If the total monthly rent is $10,000, then:

SP pays $\frac{2}{11} \times \$10{,}000 = \$1{,}818.18$,

CS pays $\frac{3}{11} \times \$10{,}000 = \$2{,}727.27$, and

JPA pays $\frac{6}{11} \times \$10{,}000 = \$5{,}454.55$

Check: If you add up all the rents you should get $10,000:

$1,818.18 + $2,727.27 + $5,454.55 = $10,000

Now it's time for a Practice Quiz.

LU 7–1 PRACTICE QUIZ

1. Express ratios in the lowest terms:
   a. 52 : 65 : 91 **b.** 45 : 15 : 25
2. Express ratios in the lowest whole numbers:
   a. 0.96 : 0.02 : 0.1 **b.** $\frac{1}{3}:\frac{1}{8}$
3. Express ratios as an equivalent ratio with the smallest term 1, and round the terms to the nearest hundredth.
   a. 5 : 6 : 8 **b.** 11 : 17

Set up ratios for these word problems:

4. Sarah got 75%, Mike got 86%, and Kim got 98% on their math test. Express as a ratio how Sarah, Mike, and Kim performed on the test.
5. The prices per litre of gas in 1995, 1999, and 2003 were respectively $.52, $.62, and $.82. What is the ratio of gas prices in these years?

LEARNING UNIT 7–2
PROPORTIONS: BASIC CONCEPTS

In Learning Unit 7–1 we considered different ratios. Let's apply this knowledge to another clipping from *Maclean's*.

> **WANTED: MORE TV DRAMA**
>
> CBC president Robert Rabinovitch recently noted to us that if it costs \$3 million to produce an hour-long drama in the U.S., a Canadian broadcaster can buy it for about \$150,000. Producing a Canadian program might cost you about \$1 million for the same hour, and it will pull less ad revenue.

Here the CBC president notes that the production costs of an hour-long drama in the United States amount to \$3 million, and producing a similar program in Canada might cost about \$1 million for the same hour. So the ratio of producing an hour-long drama in the United States to producing one in Canada is 3 : 1. If we assign a variable X to represent the U.S. production costs and a variable Y to represent the Canadian production costs we may say that the ratio of X to Y is 3 : 1 or $X{:}Y = 3{:}1$. This equation is an example of a **proportion**—an equation of two ratios. In proportions, the ratio on the left side equals the ratio on the right side.

The standard form for proportions is a fraction notation of ratios on both sides of the equation.

$$\frac{X}{Y} = \frac{3}{1}$$

The above proportion contains four terms. If three terms are known, then it is easy to calculate the fourth one.

Proportions are often used for problem solving. Let's use proportions for solving a word problem.

EXAMPLE

Lisa and Sofia entered into a business partnership and agreed that their profits would be distributed in the ratio of their investments for startup of the business. As initial capital Lisa invested \$5,000 and Sofia \$2,500. At the end of the year Lisa received \$10,000. How much profit did Sofia make?

Let's assign the variable X to the unknown value of Sofia's profit. The problem states that the ratio of Lisa's investment to Sofia's investment was the same as Lisa's profit to Sofia's profit.

$$\$5{,}000 : \$2{,}500 = \$10{,}000 : X$$

Let's rewrite this in standard form.

$$\frac{\$5{,}000}{\$2{,}500} = \frac{\$10{,}000}{X}$$

To solve the proportion for the unknown X multiply both sides by the lowest common denominator 2,500X.

$$\frac{5{,}000}{2{,}500} \times 2{,}500X = \frac{\$10{,}000}{X} \times 2{,}500X$$

$$X = 25{,}000{,}000 \div 5{,}000 = 5{,}000$$

We can solve this proportion using the **cross-multiplication rule.** Both sides of proportion will remain equal if you multiply each numerator by the denominator from the other side of the equation.

$$5{,}000 \times X = 25{,}000{,}000$$

$$\frac{\$5{,}000}{\$2{,}500} = \frac{\$10{,}000}{X}$$

$$\frac{5{,}000}{2{,}500} = \frac{10{,}000}{X}$$

$$5{,}000X = 25{,}000{,}000 \longrightarrow X = 5{,}000$$

Sofia will get \$5,000 in profit for the year.

EXAMPLE

15 : 12 = Y : 4

Rewrite the proportion in standard form and use cross-multiplication.

$$\frac{15}{12} = \frac{Y}{4}$$

$60 = 12Y \rightarrow Y = 5$

It is possible to use only one of the two cross-multiplications. For example, in this case, solving for Y:

$$\frac{15}{12} = \frac{Y}{4}$$

$$Y = 4 \times \frac{15}{2}$$

$$Y = 5$$

To summarize the rules of solving proportions, let's express them as steps:

1. Express the proportion in standard form:

$$\frac{8}{5} = \frac{X}{14}$$

2. Cross-multiply.

$$\frac{8}{5} = \frac{X}{14}$$

$$112 = 5X$$

3. Divide both sides by the coefficient of the unknown variable X:

$$X = \frac{112}{5} = 22.4$$

It is possible to use proportions for solving problems with two or more unknowns.

EXAMPLE

4 : 6 : 9 = 100 : X : Y

In Learning Unit 7–1, we said that the order of terms is very important. Now we will show why.

The proportion 4 : 6 : 9 = 100 : X : Y may be split into two proportions, each with one unknown, but the ratios must be left the same. Thus:

4 : 6 = 100 : X and 4 : 9 = 100 : Y

Present these proportions in the standard fractional form and perform cross-multiplication:

$$\frac{4}{6} = \frac{100}{X} \quad \text{and} \quad \frac{4}{9} = \frac{100}{Y}$$

$$\frac{4}{6} = \frac{100}{X} \quad \text{and} \quad \frac{4}{9} = \frac{100}{Y}$$

$$4X = 600 \quad \text{and} \quad 4Y = 900$$

$$X = 150 \quad \text{and} \quad Y = 225$$

Properties of proportion may be used for currency conversion problems.

EXAMPLE

TRAFFIC London's great anti-traffic experiment may be working better than city fathers anticipated. Or not. About 60,000 drivers a day avoided the central London zone during the first two days—rather than pay the £5 ($12) daily charge. At that rate it will take longer than expected to recoup the cost of installing 950 traffic cameras and the system for same-day payment. There could also be less profit to invest in public transportation.

In this clipping the charge for entering central London by car is shown in U.K. pounds (£5) and translated into Canadian dollars ($12). What exchange rate did the author use?

Here we can say that £5 is to $12 as £1 is to $X:

£5 → $12

£1 → $X

Use the cross-multiplication rule.

$$\frac{£5}{£1} \times \frac{\$12}{\$X}$$

$5X = 12,\ X = 2.4$

The author used the exchange rate of £1 → $2.4 Canadian dollars.

Note: How you set up a proportion is very important in currency conversion. Remember to place the same currency in one column: pounds under pounds and dollars under dollars. Don't mix them up!

Now it's time for a Practice quiz.

LU 7–2 PRACTICE QUIZ

Solve these proportions for the unknowns:

1. $17:34 = X:150$
2. $1.5:4.5:6 = X:150:Y$

Solve these word problems:

3. Mr. Percival, a marketing manager, noticed that last year's costs for promotion were $120,000 and the company sales were $20,000,000. If the same proportionate costs of promotion and sales will remain for this year, how much funds should Mr. Percival assign for promotion to achieve $35,000,000 in sales?
4. The last time before travelling to Europe, Mr. Percival exchanged CDN$5,500 in his bank and received €3,395.06 (Euros). If the exchange rate remains the same, how many Canadian dollars will Mr. Percival get back from the exchange of €400, which were left after the trip?

CHAPTER ORGANIZER AND REFERENCE GUIDE

Topic	Key point, procedure, formula	Example(s) to illustrate situation
Ratio, p. 160	Ratio is a comparison, performed by division of two or more values. It can be: • Expressed using word "to" • Colon notation • Fraction notation • Decimal equivalent • Percent equivalent	In 2001 the ratio of rural to urban population in Saskatchewan was: • 20 to 80 • 20:80 • 20/80 • .25 • 25%
Properties of ratios, p. 160	Multiplication or division of all ratio members by the same number will not change the meaning of the ratio. Ratios can be reduced to lowest terms by dividing all the members by common factor.	20:80 is equivalent to 2:8 and to 1:4. 100:25 is equivalent to 4:1 (divided by 25).
Ratio allocation, p. 161	• Set up a ratio.	Mr. Banks indicated in his will that his inheritance must be split between his wife and son in the ratio 1:2. The total inheritance is $120,000. How much money will his wife and son inherit?

(continues)

CHAPTER ORGANIZER AND REFERENCE GUIDE (CONCLUDED)

Topic	Key point, procedure, formula	Example(s) to illustrate situation
	• Reduce it to lowest terms. • Add all the terms and find the sum—the total number of parts in the whole. • Identify each portion. • Add all portions to check your results.	• The ratio 1 : 2 is already in lowest terms. • Total number of parts is 3 = 1 + 2. • The wife gets $\frac{1}{3}$ and the son gets $\frac{2}{3}$ of \$120,000. Wife gets $\frac{1}{3} \times 120{,}000 = \$40{,}000$. Son gets $\frac{2}{3} \times 120{,}000 = \$80{,}000$. **Check:** \$40,000 + \$80,000 = \$120,000
Proportion, p. 162	Proportion is an equation of two ratios. To solve a proportion express it in fraction form and then use cross-multiplication. Proportions may be used to convert currencies. Remember to place the same currency in the same column. Don't mix them up!	$10:2 = X:4$ $\frac{10}{2} = \frac{X}{4}$ $20X = 40$ $X = 2$ $\frac{£250}{CDN\$575} = \frac{£1,200}{CDN\$X}$ $250X = 690{,}000$ $X = CDN\$2{,}760$
Key terms	Cross-multiplication rule, p. 162 Equivalent ratios, p. 160 Proportion, p. 162	Ratio, p. 160

CRITICAL THINKING DISCUSSION QUESTIONS

1. What is the difference between ratio and proportion?
2. What are the steps to solve a ratio-allocation problem?
3. What are the steps to solve a proportion with two unknowns?

END-OF-CHAPTER PROBLEMS

DRILL PROBLEMS

Express each of the ratios in the lowest terms:

7–1. **a.** 115 : 125 : 130 **b.** 25 : 225 : 1,225

7–2. **a.** 0.10 : 0.25 : 0.40 **b.** 0.36 : 0.66 : 0.72 : 0.42

7–3. **a.** 100 : 200 : 1,000 **b.** 300 : 30 : 900

Convert into ratios with the whole numbers and express ratios in the lowest terms:

7–4. **a.** $\frac{1}{3}:\frac{1}{6}:\frac{1}{12}$ **b.** $\frac{2}{3}:\frac{5}{6}:\frac{7}{8}$

7–5. **a.** $\frac{1}{17}:\frac{3}{85}$ **b.** $\frac{1}{65}:\frac{2}{39}$

Express these ratios as equivalent ratios with 1 as the smallest term:

7–6. $5\frac{1}{4}:20$ **7–7.** 14 : 28 : 19 **7–8.** $3\frac{1}{2}:5\frac{1}{4}:6$ **7–9.** 0.45 : 0.5 : 0.65 **7–10.** 0.14 : 0.0056

Solve the proportions for the unknown values. Round to two decimals:

7–11. $c:15 = 115:7$ **7–12.** $0.035:0.49 = 0.07:d$ **7–13.** $3:4:17 = x:y:8.5$

7–14. $1.84:x = 5.52:9.2$ **7–15.** $c:12:28 = 14:7:d$

WORD PROBLEMS

Set up a ratio for the following problems:

7–16. Peter, Oleg and Sunir entered into a partnership. Peter invested $2,000, Oleg $3,500, and Sounir $2,500. What was the ratio of their investments?

7–17. At a college athletic competition, John came first with a result of 13.5 seconds, Paul was next with a result of 13.8 seconds, Ying came third with a result of 13.85 seconds, and Bijan came forth with a result of 13.9 seconds. What is the ratio of the results?

7–18. During a certain period of time Salva solved 8 problems, Duka 9, and Kate 7. What is the ratio of problems solved during provided time?

7–19. Mr. Peef, Mr. Percival, and Mr. Sharky formed a partnership. According to the agreement their investments and profits should be calculated in the same ratio: 1 : 1.5 : 3 respectively.

(a) How much of initial capital did each partner invest, if the total investment was $700,000?

(b) How much profit did Mr. Percival receive in the first year, if the total profit was $120,000?

7–20. Mr. Chip decided to go on a healthy diet and every morning drinks freshly squeezed juices. His favourite juice is a mixture of apple, carrot, and celery in the ratio of 2 : 3 : 1.5 respectively. How much of each juice does Mr. Chip extract to get 1 litre of the juice mixture?

7–21. Blue Bay College employs 148 professors for 3,256 students. In the fall of 2003, with a "double cohort," the college expects to have 4,341 students. How many additional professors should the college hire to maintain the same professor-student ratio?

7–22. Mr. Peef received an offer from a U.S. company. His current payment is CDN$30 per hour. He was offered US$22 per hour. Should Mr. Peef accept the offer and move to the United States, assuming that the exchange rate is CDN$1 = US$0.64103?

7–23. On his business trip to the United States Mr. Sharky bought a laptop computer for US$2045. Was it a good deal, if a similar computer in Canada costs CDN$3500? Use exchange rate US$1 = CDN$1.50.

CHALLENGE PROBLEMS

7–24. This year Mr. Martin harvested 150 tonnes of pears, apples, and plums from his farm in the ratio 3 : 5 : 2. How many tonnes of each group of fruit did Mr. Martin get? How many tonnes of apples will he get next year if the ratio should happen to be the same and he plans to receive 180 tonnes of fruit?

7–25. Mr. Percival exchanged CDN$2,000 in U.S. funds before his flight to Florida. After three days in Florida he travelled to Italy. Mr. Percival exchanged the remaining US$1,200 for Euros and in a week returned to Canada with €300 in his wallet. How much American funds did Mr. Percival get for CDN$2,000? How much in Euros did he have flying to Italy? How much money will he get back in Canadian funds in Canada upon his return? Use the current exchange rates.

SUMMARY PRACTICE TEST

Express terms of the ratios as whole numbers and reduce ratios to the lowest terms: (p. 161)

1. 1.52 : 7

2. 3.45 : 2.85 : 9.005

3. $\frac{3}{7} : \frac{5}{63}$

4. 4.5 : 3.4 : 9

Solve the proportions for the unknown values. Round to two decimals: (p. 162)

5. $d : 150 = 430 : 180$

6. $380 : 75 : c = a : 120 : 48$

7. Jimmy has noticed that if he increases the time he spends studying at home, his marks go up in the same ratio. Last semester Jimmy spent 2 hours studying at home every workday, and his average was 3.6. How many hours per day must Jimmy study to get a 4.0 average? (p. 162)

8. Mr. and Mrs. Franek are planning to spend their summer holidays in Europe. They have calculated that they will need to have €4,000 for their trip. How much Canadian funds must they save during the year to afford the trip? Use €1 = CDN$1.65. (p. 162)

SOLUTIONS TO PRACTICE QUIZZES

LU 7–1

1. **a.** 52 : 65 : 91 has 13 as a common factor. Divide all terms by 13 and get the equivalent ratio:

   52 : 65 : 91 = 4 : 5 : 7

   b. 45 : 15 : 25 has 5 as a common factor. Divide all the terms by 5 and get an equivalent ratio:

   45 : 15 : 25 = 13 : 3 : 5

2. **a.** 0.96 : 0.02 : 0.1. This ratio is expressed in decimal notation. To convert its terms to whole numbers, multiply all of them by 100. The equivalent ratio will be 96 : 2 : 10. Then divide all terms by the common factor 2.

   96 : 2 : 10 = 48 : 1 : 5

   b. $\frac{1}{3}:\frac{1}{8}$. This ratio is expressed in fractional form. Multiply each term by the lowest common denominator, 24.

   $\frac{1}{3}:\frac{1}{8} = \frac{1}{3} \times 24 : \frac{1}{8} \times 24 = 8:3$

3. **a.** 5 : 6 : 8. Divide all terms by the smallest term, 5.

   $\frac{5}{5}:\frac{6}{5}:\frac{8}{5} = 1:1.20:0.16$

   b. 11 : 17. Divide both terms by the smallest, 11.

   $\frac{11}{11}:\frac{17}{11} = 1:1.55$

4. S : M : K is the ratio for the students.

   75 : 86 : 98 ratio for students' marks

   The order of the terms is very important. S (for Sarah) is in first place on the left side and is related to 75, which is also in first place on the right side; M (for Mike) is in second place and is related to 86, which is also in second place; K (for Kim) is in third place and is related to 98, which is also in third place on the right.

5. 1995 : 1999 : 2003 ratio for the years

   \$.52 : \$.62 : \$.82 ratio for the gas prices

LU 7–2

1. $\frac{17}{34} = \frac{X}{150}$

   $34X = 17 \times 150 = 2{,}550$

   $34X = 2{,}550$

   $X = 75$

2. $1.5:4.5:6 = X:150:Y$

   a. $\frac{1.5}{4.5} = \frac{X}{150}$

   $4.5X = 1.5 \times 150 = 225$

   $X = 50$

   b. $\frac{4.5}{6} = \frac{150}{Y}$

   $4.5Y = 900$

   $Y = 200$

3. Let's assign X for the unknown value of promotional costs for next year.

$X = ?$

$\$120{,}000 : \$20{,}000{,}000 = X : \$35{,}000{,}000$

$$\frac{120{,}000}{20{,}000{,}000} = \frac{X}{35{,}000{,}000}$$

$120{,}000 \times 35{,}000{,}000 = 20{,}000{,}000X$

$$X = \frac{120{,}000 \times 35{,}000{,}000}{20{,}000{,}000} = 210{,}000$$

$X = 210{,}000$

This year Mr. Percival should assign $210,000 for promotion of his products.

4. CDN$5,500 .... €3,395.06

CDN$X €400

Remember to place identical currencies in the same column: $ with $ and € with €.

Use cross-multiplication:

CDN$5,500 ↘↗ €3,395.06

CDN$X ↗↘ €400

$3{,}395.06X = 5{,}500 \times 400$

$3{,}395.06X = 2{,}200{,}000$

$X = 648$

Mr. Percival will get CDN$648 back in exchange for the remaining €400.

Business Math Scrapbook
WITH INTERNET APPLICATION
Putting Your Skills to Work

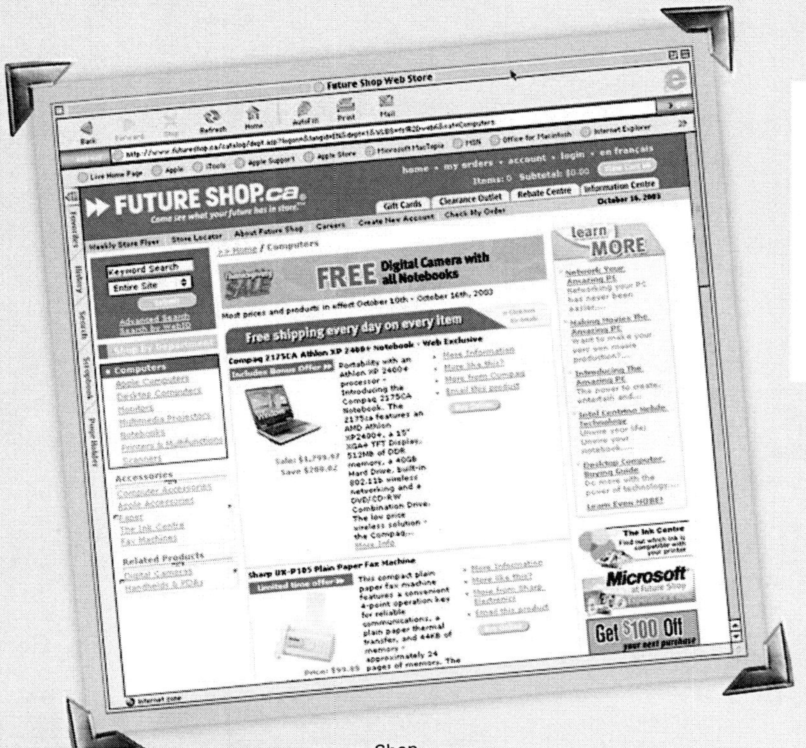

Used with permission of Future Shop.

PROJECT

Explore the Web sites www.futureshop.ca and www.bestbuy.com and find comparable products. Convert the prices of the Best Buy products to Canadian dollars and compare them to the prices at the local Future Shop.

Banking

8

TECHNOLOGY AND BANKING

A survey of consumer attitudes, conducted by the Strategic Counsel, found that 16 per cent of Canadians now use the Internet as their main means of banking, up from eight per cent when similar research was done in 2000. And it appears this trend will continue. When asked if they are likely to bank online in the next two to three years, 56 per cent of respondents now say yes compared with 46 per cent in 2000. Currently, about one-third of Canadians do at least some of their banking online.

The switch to online banking is offset by slight decreases among those who do most of their banking through automated banking machines (ABMs) and by telephone. The survey results show that 40 per cent of Canadians conduct the majority of their financial transactions at ABMs, down from 45 per cent in 2000, and eight per cent use telephone banking, a two per cent decrease from two years ago.

Source: *Canadian Banker* magazine, 2002.

LEARNING UNIT OBJECTIVES

LU 8–1: The Chequing Account; Credit Card Transactions

- Define and state the purpose of signature cards, cheques, deposit slips, cheque stubs, cheque registers, and endorsements (p. 172).
- Correctly prepare deposit slips and write cheques (p. 173).
- Explain how a merchant completes a credit card transaction for manual deposit or electronic deposit (p. 175).

LU 8–2: Bank Statement and Reconciliation Process; Trends in Online Banking

- Define and state the purpose of the bank statement (p. 178).
- Complete a cheque register and a bank reconciliation (p. 181).
- Explain the trends in online banking (p. 183).

Bachmann/PhotoEdit

An important fixture in today's banking is the **automatic teller machine (ATM)** or **automatic banking machine (ABM).** The ability to get instant cash is a convenience many bank customers enjoy. The effect of using an ATM card is the same as using a **debit card**—both transactions result in money being immediately deducted from your chequing account balance. As a result, debit cards have been called *enhanced ATM or ABM cards.* Often banks charge fees for these card transactions. However, usually banks offer their ATMs as a free service, if you use an ATM that is in the same network of banks as your bank.

Have you ever found it necessary to use an ABM when you are away from home, say on vacation? Be warned that this convenience could be costly. Independent ABMs or White Label ABMs have a surcharge of from $2 to $5 for use of the machine. A casino can charge from $3 to $5, and cruises can charge as much as $9. When you use an ABM card internationally through the CIRRUS or PLUS system, an additional processing fee will apply for each transaction. Plan ahead for the amount of vacation money you will need. Travellers' cheques can provide you with a money reserve at a lower cost—sometimes at no cost.

The use of debit cards also involves planning. You must be aware of your bank balance every time you use a debit card. Also, if you use a credit card instead of a debit card, you can only be held responsible for $50 of illegal charges, and during the time the credit card company investigates the illegal charges, they are removed from your account. However, with a debit card, this legal limit does not apply.

This chapter begins with a discussion of the chequing account and credit card transactions. You will follow Molly Kate as she opens a chequing account for Gracie's Natural Superstore and performs her banking and credit card transactions. Pay special attention to the procedure used by Gracie's to reconcile its chequing account and bank statement. This information will help you reconcile your chequebook records with the bank's record of your account. Finally, the chapter discusses how the trends in online banking may affect your banking procedures.

LEARNING UNIT 8–1
THE CHEQUING ACCOUNT; CREDIT CARD TRANSACTIONS

A **cheque** or **draft** is a written order instructing a bank, credit union, or savings and loan institution to pay a designated amount of your money on deposit to a person or an organization. Chequing accounts are offered to individuals and businesses. The business chequing account usually receives more services than the personal chequing account.

Most small businesses depend on a chequing account for efficient record keeping. In this chapter you will follow the chequing account procedures of a newly organized small business. You can use many of these procedures in your personal cheque writing.

ELEMENTS OF THE CHEQUING ACCOUNT

Molly Kate, treasurer of Gracie's Natural Superstore, went to First Canadian Bank to open a business chequing account. The bank manager gave Molly a **signature card.** The signature card contained space for the company's name and address, references, type of account, and the signature(s) of the person(s) authorized to sign cheques. If necessary, the bank will use the signature card to verify that Molly signed the cheques. Some companies authorize more than one person to sign cheques or require more than one signature on a cheque.

Molly then lists on a **deposit slip** the cheques and/or cash she is depositing in her company's business account. The bank gave Molly a temporary chequebook to use until the company's printed cheques arrived. Molly also will receive *preprinted* chequing account deposit slips like the one shown in Figure 8.1. Since the deposit slips are in duplicate, Molly can keep a record of her deposit.

Writing business cheques is similar to writing personal cheques. Before writing any cheques, however, you must understand the structure of a cheque and know how to write one. Carefully

FIGURE 8–1
Deposit slip

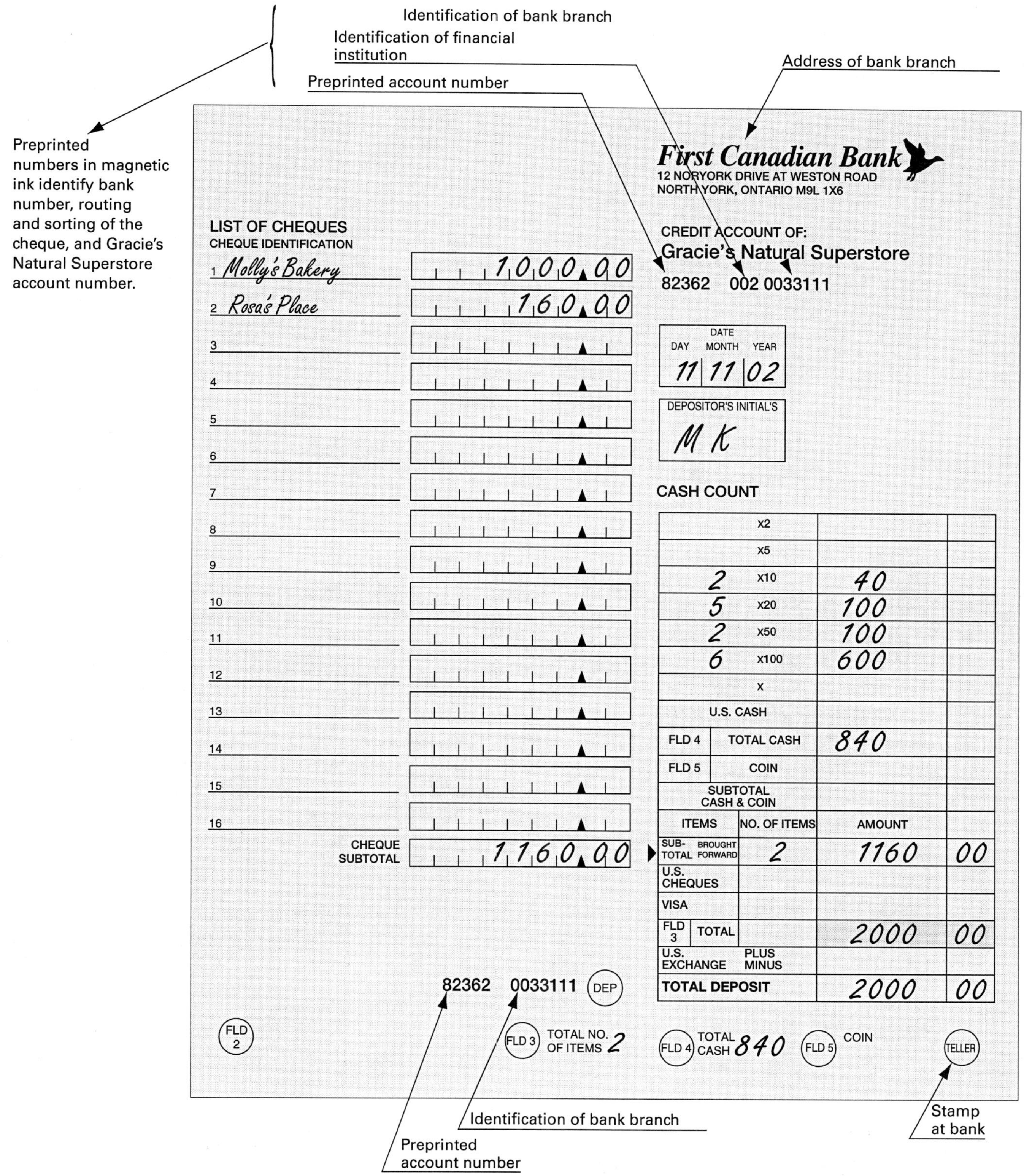

study Figure 8.2. Note that the verbal amount written in the cheque should match the figure amount. If these two amounts are different, by law the bank uses the verbal amount. Also, note the bank imprint on the bottom right section of the cheque. When processing the cheque, the bank imprints the cheque's amount. This makes it easy to detect bank errors.

FIGURE 8–2
The structure of a cheque

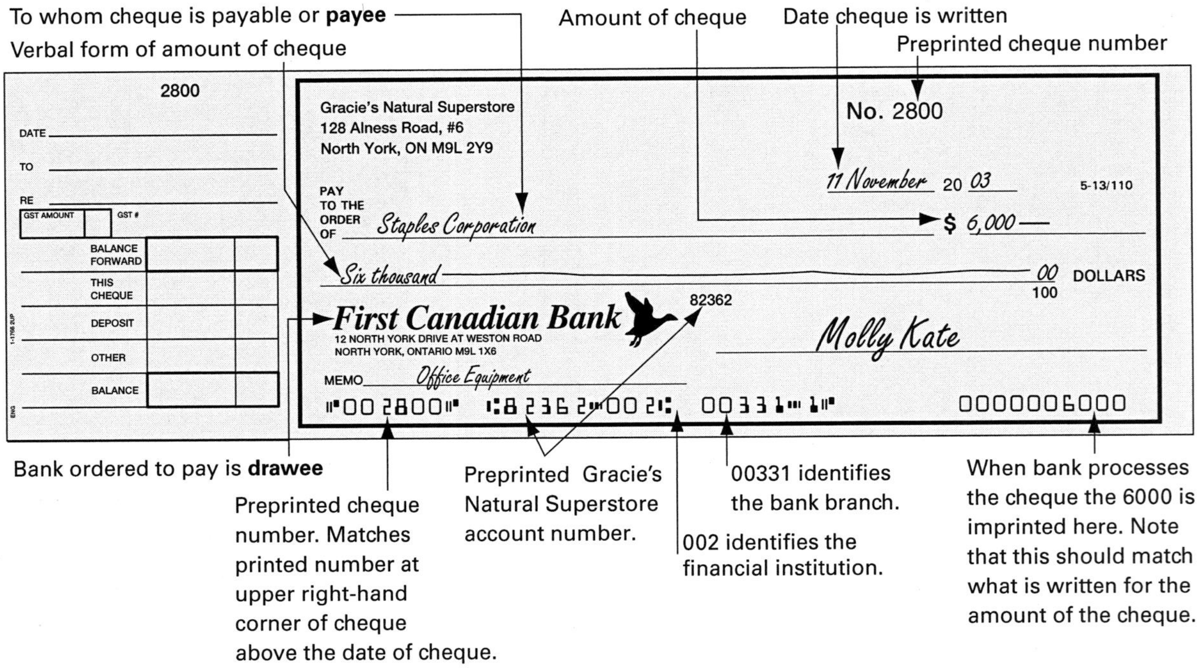

Cheque stub

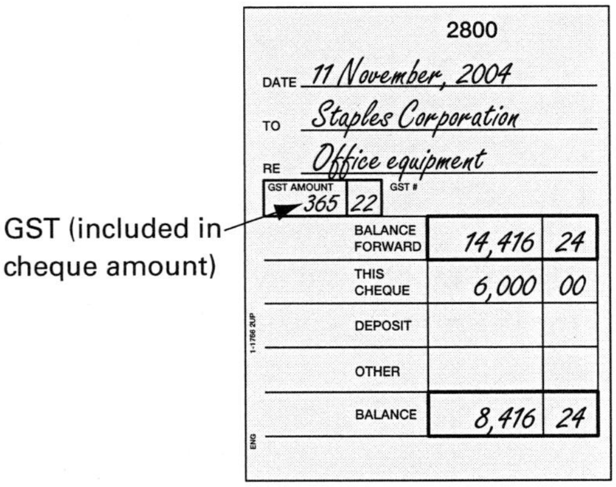

Once the cheque is written, the writer or **drawer** must keep a record of the cheque. Knowing the amount of your written cheques and the amount in the bank should help you avoid writing a bad cheque. Business chequebooks usually include attached **cheque stubs** to keep track of written cheques. The sample cheque stub in the margin shows the information that the cheque writer will want to record. Some companies use a **cheque register** to keep their cheque records instead of cheque stubs. Figure 8.10 later in the chapter shows a cheque register with a ✓ column that is often used in balancing the chequebook with the bank statement (Learning Unit 8–2).

Gracie's Natural Superstore has had a busy week, and Molly must deposit its cheques in the company's chequing account. However, before she can do this, Molly must **endorse,** or sign, the back top one-third of the cheques (see Figure 8.3). Figure 8.4 explains the three types of cheque endorsements: **blank endorsement, full endorsement,** and **restrictive endorsement.** These endorsements transfer Gracie's ownership to the bank, which collects the money from the person or company issuing the cheque.

FIGURE 8–3
Back side of cheque

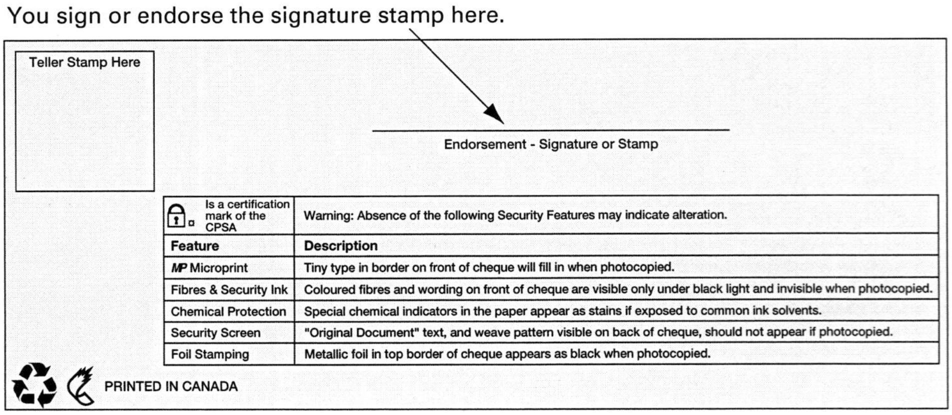

FIGURE 8–4
Types of common endorsements

A. Blank Endorsement

Gracie's Natural Superstore
82362

→ The company stamp or a signature alone on the back left side of a cheque legally makes the cheque payable to anyone holding the cheque. It can be *further* endorsed (signed). This is not a safe type of endorsement.

B. Full Endorsement

Pay to the order of
First Canadian Bank
Gracie's Natural Superstore
82362

→ Safer type of endorsement since Gracie's Natural Superstore indicates the name of the company or person to whom the cheque is to be payable to. Only the person or company named in the endorsement can transfer the cheque to someone else.

C. Restrictive Endorsement

Pay to the order of
First Canadian Bank
For deposit only
Gracie's Natural Superstore
82362

→ Safest endorsement for businesses. Gracie's stamps the back of the cheque so that this cheque must be deposited in the firm's bank account. This limits any further negotiation of the cheque.

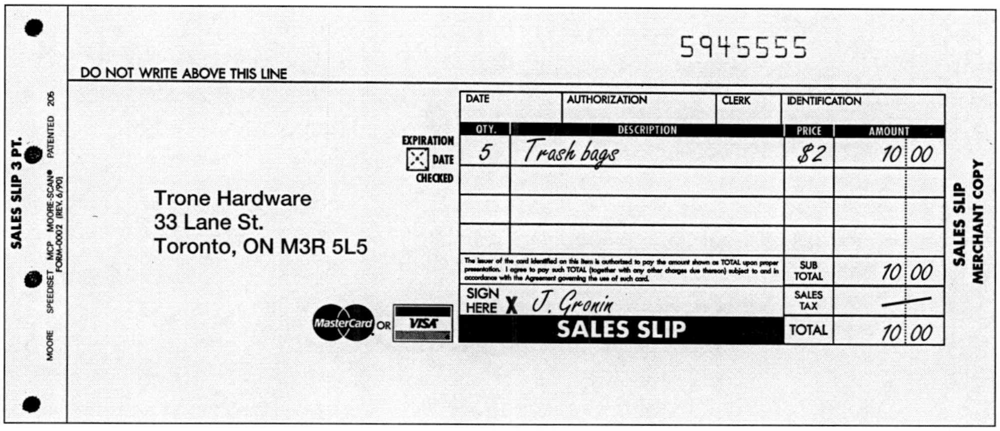

FIGURE 8–5
Charge slip

After the bank receives Molly's deposit slip, shown in Figure 8.1, it increases (or credits) Gracie's account by $2,000. Often Molly leaves the deposit in a locked bag in a night depository. Then the bank credits (increases) Gracie's account when it processes the deposit on the next working day.

Gracie's Natural Superstore handles many credit card transactions. Now let's see how the company records these transactions.

DEPOSITING CREDIT CARD TRANSACTIONS

On April 1, 2004, Gracie's Natural Superstore will begin using MasterCard and Visa. This should increase its sales and avoid the collection of past-due accounts.

First Canadian Bank has given Gracie's two options for depositing **credit card** transactions—option 1, manual deposits, and option 2, electronic deposits. Note that although some very small companies still use the manual deposit system, most companies favour the electronic system. Now let's study these two systems. By looking at the old manual system, you will appreciate the technology that is in place today.

Option 1: Manual Deposits

When Gracie's makes a charge sale with the **manual deposit** option, the salesperson fills out a MasterCard or Visa charge slip similar to the one in Figure 8.5, which is for another company. Charge slips give the specific details of the sale.

FIGURE 8–6
Merchant batch header slip

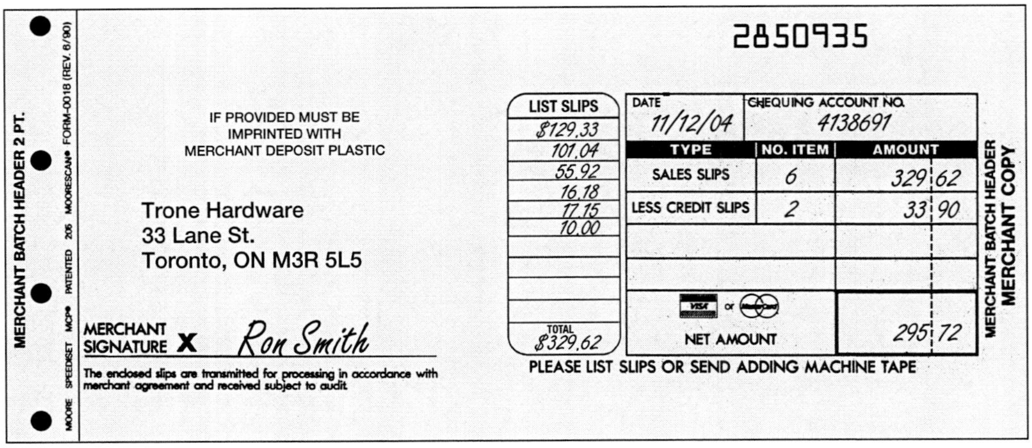
2850935

MERCHANT BATCH HEADER 2 PT.

MOORE SPEEDISET MCP• PATENTED 205 MOORESCAN• FORM-0018 (REV. 8/90)

IF PROVIDED MUST BE IMPRINTED WITH MERCHANT DEPOSIT PLASTIC

Trone Hardware
33 Lane St.
Toronto, ON M3R 5L5

MERCHANT SIGNATURE X Ron Smith

The enclosed slips are transmitted for processing in accordance with merchant agreement and received subject to audit.

LIST SLIPS
$129.33
101.04
55.92
16.18
17.15
10.00
TOTAL $329.62

DATE 11/12/04		CHEQUING ACCOUNT NO. 4138691
TYPE	NO. ITEM	AMOUNT
SALES SLIPS	6	329.62
LESS CREDIT SLIPS	2	33.90
VISA or MasterCard NET AMOUNT		295.72

PLEASE LIST SLIPS OR SEND ADDING MACHINE TAPE

MERCHANT BATCH HEADER MERCHANT COPY

At the end of *each business day,* Gracie's treasurer completes a **merchant batch header slip** and attaches copies of its charge slips. Figure 8.6 shows a sample batch header slip used by another company. Note that the company could list the slips on the form or provide an adding machine tape with the batch header slip. Also note that the total of the charge slips is shown less the total of the credit slips (refunds). The **net deposit** (net amount) is the difference between the total sales and the total credits. At the *end of the statement period,* First Canadian Bank charges $3\frac{1}{4}\%$ (this means $3\frac{1}{4}$ cents per dollar) of the net deposit and subtracts this from Gracie's chequing account.

Option 2: Electronic Deposits

Most retail stores use **electronic deposits.** If you use a MasterCard or Visa credit card, you have probably watched the salesperson run your card through an authorization terminal after you have made a purchase. You may also have noticed that some retail stores now use the cash register terminal as a credit card authorization terminal. These authorization terminals not only approve (or disapprove) the amount charged but also add this amount immediately to the store's bank balance—or in our example to Gracie's bank balance. Charge credits are also immediately subtracted from bank balances. The immediate authorizations and additions to a company's chequing account are important advantages of the electronic transaction. Now we go back to Gracie's to continue the electronic deposit procedure.

© PhotoDisc

Each day First Canadian Bank sends Gracie's a statement listing its MasterCard and Visa transactions. The bank charges Gracie's $2\frac{1}{2}\%$ ($2\frac{1}{2}$ cents per dollar) since it wants to encourage the use of electronic deposits. The statement Gracie's receives is similar to the statement in Figure 8.7 for another company. When we work with percents in Chapter 6, you will see how to calculate the amount Gracie's pays for using MasterCard and Visa. For now, focus on calculating net deposits.

FIGURE 8–7
Electronic deposit statement

DEPOSIT DETAILS:	CARDHOLDER	DATE	TRAN	AMOUNT	CST–TIME	CODE
	361060558	11/14/04	SALE	15.00	11:55 :36	431011
	336808479		SALE	28.60	12:08 :30	673011
	633615209		SALE	11.28	12:34 :31	934440
	484383		SALE	7.77	14:03 :38	482360
	611445		SALE	17.57	14:12 :48	371224
	343103551		SALE	24.15	15:13 :50	694492
	000115629		SALE	14.74	15:16 :33	378823
	380057254		SALE	16.38	15:33 :18	213011
	288121723		SALE	23.08	16:21 :29	682011
	503999		SALE	9.96	16:27 :41	714593
	309021229		SALE	38.82	16:32 :29	891816
	005291394		SALE	19.93	16:42 :43	731020
	387076		SALE	15.62	16:51 :09	700644
	199011544		SALE	21.00	19:39 :08	001640

	------- SALES -------		------- RETURNS -------		NET DEPOSIT
	14	263.90	0	.00	263.90
MASTERCARD	7	147.90	0	.00	147.90
VISA	7	116.00	0	.00	116.00

EXAMPLE

From the following credit card sales and returns, calculate the net deposit for the day.

Credit card sales:	$42.33, $16.88, $19.39, $47.66, $39.18.	
Returns:	$18.01, $13.04.	
Solution:	Total credit cards sales	$165.44
Less returns		− 31.05
Net deposit		$134.39

LU 8–1 PRACTICE QUIZ

1. Complete the following cheque and cheque stub for Long Company. Note the $9,500.60 balance brought forward on cheque stub No. 113. You must make a $690.60 deposit on June 5, 2004. Sign the cheque for Roland Small.

Date	Cheque no.	Amount	Payable to	For
June 5, 2004	113	$83.76	Angel Corporation	Rent

No. *113* $ ______
______ 20 ____
To ______
For ______

	DOLLARS	CENTS
BALANCE	*9,500*	*60*
AMT. DEPOSITED		
TOTAL		
AMT. THIS CHQ.		
BALANCE FORWARD		

Long Company
22 Aster Rd.
Scarborough, ON M1R 2Y3

No. 113

______ 20 ____ 5-13/110

PAY TO THE ORDER OF ______ $ ______

______ DOLLARS

First Canadian Bank

______

MEMO ______

⑆0110001381⑆ 14 0380 113

2. From the following information, complete Ryan Company's merchant batch header slip for August 19, 2004. Sign the slip for John Ryan, whose account number is 0139684.

Credit card sales	Credit card returns
$114.99	$14.07
21.15	15.19
72.80	
39.45	

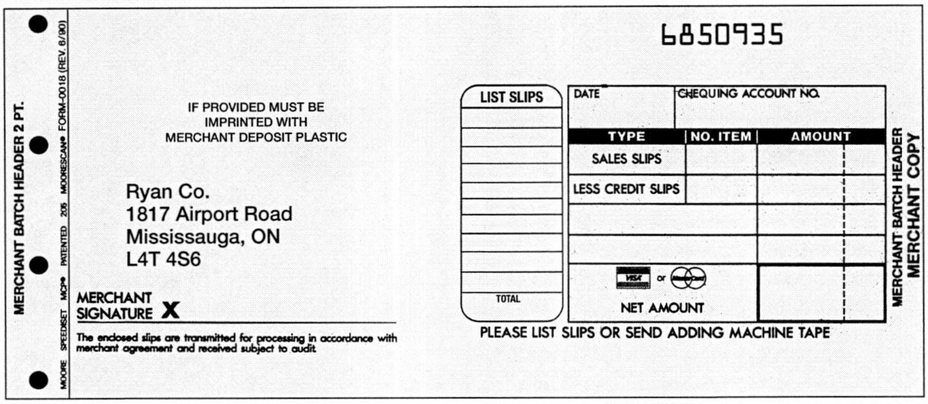

MERCHANT BATCH HEADER 2 PT.

MOORE SPEEDISET MCP® PATENTED 205 MOORESCAN® FORM-0018 (REV. 6/90)

6850935

IF PROVIDED MUST BE IMPRINTED WITH MERCHANT DEPOSIT PLASTIC

Ryan Co.
1817 Airport Road
Mississauga, ON
L4T 4S6

MERCHANT SIGNATURE **X**

The enclosed slips are transmitted for processing in accordance with merchant agreement and received subject to audit.

LIST SLIPS

TOTAL

DATE	CHEQUING ACCOUNT NO.	
TYPE	**NO. ITEM**	**AMOUNT**
SALES SLIPS		
LESS CREDIT SLIPS		
VISA or MasterCard NET AMOUNT		

PLEASE LIST SLIPS OR SEND ADDING MACHINE TAPE

MERCHANT BATCH HEADER MERCHANT COPY

LEARNING UNIT 8–2

BANK STATEMENT AND RECONCILIATION PROCESS; TRENDS IN ONLINE BANKING

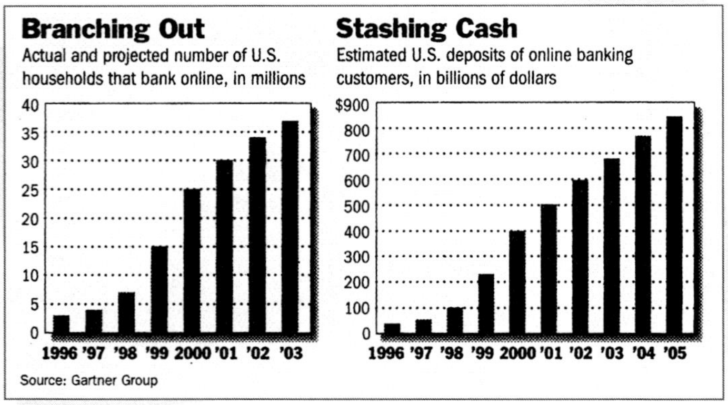

Source: © 2001 Dow Jones & Company, Inc.

This Learning Unit begins with a discussion of how Gracie's Natural Superstore reconciles its chequebook balance with the balance reported on its bank statement. You would use the same procedure in reconciling your personal chequing account.

Also discussed in this Unit is online banking. The *Wall Street Journal* clipping here presents these interesting facts: more than 35 million households in the United States will be branching out and banking online; by the year 2005, online banking customers will be depositing cash estimated to be more than $800 billion.

Each month First Canadian Bank sends Gracie's Natural Superstore a **bank statement** (Figure 8.8). The statement gives different types of information. We are interested in the following:

BANK STATEMENT

1. Beginning bank balance.
2. Total of all the account increases. Each time the bank increases the account amount, it *credits* the account.
3. Total of all account decreases. Each time the bank decreases the account amount, it *debits* the account.
4. Final ending balance.

Due to differences in timing, the bank balance on the bank statement frequently does not match the customer's chequebook balance. Also, the bank statement can show transactions that have not been entered in the customer's chequebook. Figure 8.9 tells you what to look for when comparing a chequebook balance with a bank balance.

FIGURE 8–8
Bank statement

First Canadian Bank
12 Noryork Drive at Weston Road
North York, ON M9L 1X6

Gracie's Natural Superstore
128 Alness Road, Unit #6
North York, ON M9L 2Y9

Account Number
82362 00331 11

STATEMENT OF BUSINESS ACCOUNT

FROM March 01 2004 TO March 31 2004

DESCRIPTION	WITHDRAWAL/ DEBITS	DEPOSITS/ CREDITS	DATE M D	BALANCE
Balance forward			02 29	13,112.24
Deposit		2,000.00	03 05	
Deposit		224.00	03 05	15,336.24
Cheque 301	200.00		03 07	15,136.24
Deposit		389.20	03 09	15,525.44
Cheque 635	200.00		03 11	15,325.44
Cheque 634	300.00		03 13	
Cheque 633	6,000.00		03 13	9,025.44
Cheque 636	200.00		03 18	
Direct deposit leasing: Bakery dept.		1,808.06	03 18	10,633.50
Direct payment health insurance	722.00		03 21	
NSF	104.00		03 21	9,807.50
Direct deposit leasing: Meat dept.		4,228.00	03 28	14,035.50
Cheque 637	2,200.00		03 31	
Service charge: Cheque printing	28.50		03 31	
Interest		56.02	03 31	11,863.02

No. of Debits	Total amount—Debits	No. of Credits	Total amount—Credits	No. of enclosures	More items on page
9	9,954.5	6	8,705.28	6	

FIGURE 8–9
Reconciling chequebook with bank statement

Chequebook balance		Bank balance
+ EFT (electronic funds transfer)	− NSF cheque	+ Deposits in transit
+ Interest earned	− Online fees	− Outstanding cheques
+ Notes collected	− Automatic payments*	± Bank errors
+ Direct deposits	− Overdrafts†	
− ATM withdrawals	− Service charges	
− Automatic withdrawals	− Stop payments‡	
− Cheque redeposits	± Book errors§	

*Preauthorized payments for utility bills, mortgage payments, insurance, etc.

†**Overdrafts** occur when the customer has no overdraft protection and a cheque bounces back to the company or person who received it because the customer has written it without enough money in the bank to pay its amount.

‡A stop payment is issued when the writer of cheque does not want the receiver to cash it.

§If a $60 cheque is recorded at $50, the chequebook balance must be decreased by $10.

Gracie's Natural Superstore is planning to offer to its employees the option of depositing their cheques directly into each employee's chequing account. This is accomplished through **electronic funds transfer (EFT),** which is used for either direct deposit into the account or direct payment from it. EFT is a computerized operation that electronically transfers funds between parties without the use of paper cheques. Gracie's, which sublets space in the store, receives rental payments by EFT as direct deposits. Gracie's also has the bank pay the store's health insurance premiums by EFT as direct payments.

To reconcile the difference between the amount on the bank statement and in the chequebook, the customer should complete a **bank reconciliation.** Today, many companies and home computer owners are using software such as QuickBooks and Quicken to complete their bank reconciliation. However, you should understand the following steps for manually reconciling a bank statement.

RECONCILING A BANK STATEMENT

Step 1. Identify the outstanding cheques (cheques written but not yet processed by the bank). You can use the ✓ column in the cheque register (Figure 8.10) to check the cancelled cheques listed in the bank statement against the ones you wrote in the cheque register. The unchecked cheques are the outstanding ones.

Step 2. Identify the deposits in transit (deposits made but not yet processed by the bank), using the same method as in Step 1.

Step 3. Analyze the bank statement for transactions not recorded in the cheque stubs or cheque registers (such as EFT direct payments deposits).

Step 4. Check for recording errors in cheques written, in deposits made, or in subtraction and addition.

Step 5. Compare the adjusted balances of the chequebook and the bank statement. If the balances are not the same, repeat Steps 1–4.

Molly uses a cheque register (Figure 8.10) to keep a record of Gracie's cheques and deposits. By looking at Gracie's cheque register, you can see how to complete Steps 1 and 2 above. The explanation that follows for the first four bank statement reconciliation steps will help you understand the procedure.

Step 1. Identify Outstanding Cheques

Outstanding cheques are cheques that Gracie's Natural Superstore has written but First Canadian Bank has not yet recorded for payment when it sends out the bank statement. Gracie's treasurer identifies the following cheques written on 3/31 as outstanding:

No. 638	$572.00
No. 639	638.94
No. 640	166.00
No. 641	406.28
No. 642	917.06

Step 2. Identify Deposits in Transit

Deposits in transit are deposits that did not reach First Canadian Bank by the time the bank prepared the bank statement. The March 30 deposit of $3,383.26 did not reach First Canadian Bank by the bank statement date. You can see this by comparing the company's bank statement with its cheque register.

Step 3. Analyze Bank Statement for Transactions Not Recorded in Cheque Stubs or Cheque Register

The bank statement of Gracie's Natural Superstore (Figure 8.8) begins with the deposits, or increases, made to Gracie's bank account. Increases to accounts are known as credits. These are the result of a **credit memo (CM).** Gracie's received the following increases or credits in March:

1. *EFT leasing* (direct deposit): $1,808.06 and $4,228.00. — Each month the bakery and meat departments pay for space they lease in the store.

2. *Interest credited:* $56.02. Gracie's has a chequing account that pays interest; the account has earned $56.02.

When Gracie's has charges against her bank account, the bank decreases, or debits, Gracie's account for these charges. Banks usually inform customers of a debit transaction by a **debit memo (DM).** The following items will result in debits to Gracie's account:

1. *Service charge:* $28.50. The bank charged $28.50 for printing Gracie's cheques.
2. *EFT payment:* $722. The bank made a health insurance payment for Gracie's.
3. *NSF check:* $104. One of Gracie's customers wrote Gracie's a cheque for $104. Gracie's deposited the cheque, but it bounced for **nonsufficient funds (NSF).** Thus, Gracie's has $104 less than it figured.

Step 4. Check for Recording Errors

The treasurer of Gracie's Natural Superstore, Molly Kate, recorded cheque No. 634 for the wrong amount—$1,020 (see the cheque register, Figure 8.10). The bank statement showed that cheque No. 634 cleared for $300. To reconcile Gracie's chequebook balance with the bank balance, Gracie's must add $720 to its chequebook balance. Neglecting to record a deposit also results in an error in the company's chequebook balance. As you can see, reconciling the bank's balance with a chequebook balance is a necessary part of business and personal finance.

FIGURE 8–10
Gracie's Natural Superstore cheque register

RECORD ALL CHARGES OR CREDITS THAT AFFECT YOUR ACCOUNT

NUMBER	DATE 2004	DESCRIPTION OF TRANSACTION	PAYMENT/DEBIT (−) $	√	FEE (IF ANY) (−) $	DEPOSIT/CREDIT (+) $	BALANCE $
							12,912 24
	3/04	Deposit		✓		2,000 00	+ 2,000 00
							14,912 24
	3/04	Deposit		✓		224 00	+ 224 00
							15,136 24
633	3/08	Staples Company	6,000 00	✓			− 6,000 00
							9,136 24
634	3/09	Health Foods Inc.	1,020 00	✓			− 1,020 00
							8,116 24
	3/09	Deposit				389 20	+ 389 20
							8,505 44
635	3/10	Liberty Insurance	200 00	✓			− 200 00
							8,305 44
636	3/18	Ryan Press	200 00	✓			− 200 00
							8,105 44
637	3/29	Logan Advertising	2,200 00	✓			− 2,200 00
							5,905 44
	3/30	Deposit				o/s 3,383 26	+ 3,383 26
							9,288 70
638	3/31	Sears Roebuck	572 00	o/s			− 572 00
							8,716 70
639	3/31	Flynn Company	638 94	o/s			− 638 94
							8,077 76
640	3/31	Lynn's Farm	166 00	o/s			− 166 00
							7,911 76
641	3/31	Ron's Wholesale	406 28	o/s			− 406 28
							7,505 48
642	3/31	Grocery Natural, Inc.	917 06	o/s*			− 917 06
							$6,588 42

REMEMBER TO RECORD AUTOMATIC PAYMENTS/DEPOSITS ON DATE AUTHORIZED.

*O/S: Outstanding.

Step 5. Completing the Bank Reconciliation

Now we can complete the bank reconciliation on the back side of the bank statement as shown in Figure 8.11. This form is usually on the back of a bank statement. If necessary, however, the person reconciling the bank statement can construct a bank reconciliation form similar to Figure 8.12.

FIGURE 8–11
Reconciliation process

CHEQUES OUTSTANDING
(NOT YET CHARGED TO ACCOUNT)

NUMBER OR DATE	DOLLARS	CENTS
638	$572	00
639	638	94
640	166	00
641	406	28
642	917	06
TOTAL	$2,700	28

CHEQUING ACCOUNT RECONCILEMENT

Enter the new balance shown on the other side of this statement.	$ 11,863.02
ADD	
Deposits not shown	3,383.26
ADD	
Advances and Transfers to Chequing not shown.	
SUBTOTAL	15,246.28
DEDUCT Cheques outstanding	2,700.28
SUBTOTAL	12,546.00
DEDUCT Transfers from Chequing not shown	
This amount should agree with the balance in your chequebook register.	$ 12,546.00

Chequebook balance		$6,588.42
+ EFT leasing	$6,036.06	
+ Interest	56.02	
+ Chequebook error	720.00	6,812.08
– Service charge	$ 28.50	
– EFT: health insurance	722.00	
– NSF	104.00	854.50
Ending chequebook balance		$12,546.00

FIGURE 8–12
Bank reconciliation

First Canadian Bank
12 Noryork Drive at Weston Road
North York, ON M9L 1X6

Gracie's Natural Superstore
128 Alness Road, Unit #6
North York, ON M9L 2Y9

Account Number
82362 00331 11

STATEMENT OF BUSINESS ACCOUNT FROM March 01 2004 TO March 31 2004

DESCRIPTION	WITHDRAWAL/ DEBITS	DEPOSITS/ CREDITS	DATE M D	BALANCE
Balance forward			02 29	13,112.24
Deposit		2,000.00	03 05	
Deposit		224.00	03 05	15,336.24
Cheque 301	200.00		03 07	15,136.24
Deposit		389.20	03 09	15,525.44
Cheque 635	200.00		03 11	15,325.44
Cheque 634	300.00		03 13	
Cheque 633	6,000.00		03 13	9,025.44
Cheque 636	200.00		03 18	
Direct deposit leasing: Bakery dept.		1,808.06	03 18	10,633.50
Direct payment health insurance	722.00		03 21	
NSF	104.00		03 21	9,807.50
Direct deposit leasing: Meat dept.		4,228.00	03 28	14,035.50
Cheque 637	2,200.00		03 31	
Service charge: Cheque printing	28.50		03 31	
Interest		56.02	03 31	11,863.02

No. of Debits	Total amount—Debits	No. of Credits	Total amount—Credits	No. of enclosures	More items on page
9	9,954.5	6	8,705.28	6	

RECORD ALL CHARGES OR CREDITS THAT AFFECT YOUR ACCOUNT

NUMBER	DATE 2004	DESCRIPTION OF TRANSACTION	PAYMENT/DEBIT (−)	√	FEE (IF ANY) (−)	DEPOSIT/CREDIT (+)	BALANCE
							$ 12,912 24
	3/04	Deposit		✓		$ 2,000 00	+ 2,000 00
							14,912 24
	3/04	Deposit		✓		224 00	+ 224 00
							15,136 24
633	3/08	Staples Company	6,000 00	✓			− 6,000 00
							9,136 24
634	3/09	Health Foods Inc.	1,020 00	✓			− 1,020 00
							8,116 24
	3/09	Deposit				389 20	+ 389 20
							8,505 44
635	3/10	Liberty Insurance	200 00	✓			− 200 00
							8,305 44
636	3/18	Ryan Press	200 00	✓			− 200 00
							8,105 44
637	3/29	Logan Advertising	2,200 00	✓			− 2,200 00
							5,905 44
	3/30	Deposit					+ 3,383 26
							9,288 70
638	3/31	Sears Roebuck					− 572 00
							8,716 70
639	3/31	Flynn Company					− 638 94
							8,077 76
640	3/31	Lynn's Farm					− 166 00
							7,911 76
641	3/31	Ron's Wholesale					− 406 28
							7,505 48
642	3/31	Grocery Natural, Inc.					− 917 06
							$6,588 42

REMEMBER TO RECORD AUTOMATIC PAYMENTS/DEPOSITS ON DATE AUTHORIZED.

GRACIE'S NATURAL SUPERSTORE
Bank Reconciliation as of March 31, 2004

Chequebook balance			Bank balance		
Gracie's chequebook balance		$ 6,588.42	Bank balance		$11,863.02
Add:			Add:		
EFT leasing: Bakery dept.	$ 1,808.06		Deposit in transit, 3/30		3,383.26
					$15,246.28
EFT leasing: Meat dept.	4,228.00				
Interest	56.02				
Error: Overstated cheque No. 634	720.00				
	$13,400.50				
Deduct:			Deduct:		
Service charge	$28.50		Outstanding cheques:		
NSF cheque	104.00				
EFT health insurance payment	722.00	854.50	No. 638	$572.00	
			No. 639	638.94	
			No. 640	166.00	
			No. 641	406.28	
			No. 642	917.06	2,700.28
Reconciled balance		$12,546.00	Reconciled balance		$12,546.00

Trends in Online Banking

Online banking is becoming more popular. Instead of receiving a refund cheque in the mail, more taxpayers are requesting the Canada Customs and Revenue Agency (CCRA) to directly deposit their refunds into their bank accounts. Direct deposits allow government to save on paper handling and postage, secure deposits in terms of safety and postal disruptions, and reduce the possibility of error.

Although banks are doing everything they can to get people to avoid writing cheques, many people do not want to give it up. To reduce the costs of paper cheques, some banks no longer return cancelled cheques. Instead, they use a **safekeeping** procedure that involves holding the cheques for a period of time, keeping microfilm copies of them for at least a year, and returning the cheque or a photocopy for a small fee. However, online banking will survive with the increased use of computers.

According to a nationwide survey commissioned by the Canadian Bankers Association, the percentage of Canadians who bank primarily through the Internet has doubled in the past two years. Young Canadians are more likely to bank online. According to the magazine *Canadian Banker,* 45% of 18-to-34-year-olds say they bank online and 71% expect to be doing so in the next two or three years.

For several years electronic bill paying has already been available to bank customers. This method of bill paying has several advantages. You do not have to write cheques, save the envelopes that come with bills, look for stamps, or be concerned that payments will not reach their destination in time to make a deadline. With the Internet, you can transfer money between accounts or chequing balances. If you want to make deposits or withdraw funds, however, you must do this by wire, mail, or ATM.

LU 8–2 PRACTICE QUIZ

Rosa Garcia has received her February 3, 2004, bank statement, which has a balance of $212.80. Rosa's chequebook shows a balance of $929.15. The bank statement showed an ATM fee of $12 and a deposited "cheque returned" fee of $20. Rosa earned interest of $1.05. She had three outstanding cheques: No. 300, $18.20; No. 302, $38.40; and No. 303, $68.12. A deposit for $810.12 was not on her bank statement. Prepare Rosa Garcia's bank reconciliation.

CHAPTER ORGANIZER AND REFERENCE GUIDE

Topic	Key point, procedure, formula	Example(s) to illustrate situation
Types of endorsements, p. 174	*Blank:* Not safe; can be further endorsed.	Jones Co. 21-333-9
	Full: Only person or company named in endorsement can transfer cheque to someone else.	Pay to the order of Regan Bank Jones Co. 21-333-9
	Restrictive: Cheque must be deposited. Limits any further negotiation of the cheque.	Pay to the order of Regan Bank. For deposit only. Jones Co. 21-333-9

(*continues*)

CHAPTER ORGANIZER AND REFERENCE GUIDE (CONCLUDED)

Topic	Key point, procedure, formula	Example(s) to illustrate situation
Credit card transactions, p. 175	*Manual deposit:* Need to calculate net deposit (credit card sales less returns). *Electronic deposit:* Eliminates deposit slips and summary batch header slip.	Calculate net deposit: Credit card sales $55.32 62.81 91.18 Credits − 10.16 − 8.15 $209.31 − 18.31 Net deposit = $191.00
Bank reconciliation, p. 180	**Chequebook balance** + EFT (electronic funds transfer) + Interest earned + Notes collected + Direct deposits − ATM withdrawals − Cheque redeposits − NSF cheque − Online fees − Automatic withdrawals − Overdrafts − Service charges − Stop payments ± Book errors* CM—adds to balance DM—deducts from balance **Bank balance** + Deposits in transit − Outstanding checks ± Bank errors *If a $60 cheque is recorded as $50, we must decrease chequebook balance by $10.	**Chequebook balance** Balance $800 −NSF 40 $760 −Service charge 4 $756 **Bank balance** Balance $ 632 + Deposits in transit 416 $1,048 − Outstanding cheques 292 $756
Key terms	Automatic banking machine (ABM), p. 172 Automatic teller machine (ATM), p. 172 Bank reconciliation, p. 180 Bank statement, p. 178 Blank endorsement, p. 174 Cheque, p. 172 Cheque register, p. 174 Cheque stub, p. 174 Credit card, p. 175 Credit memo (CM), p. 180 Debit card, p. 172 Debit memo (DM), p. 181 Deposit slip, p. 172 Deposits in transit, p. 180 Draft, p. 172 Drawee, p. 174 Drawer, p. 174 Electronic deposit, p. 176 Electronic funds transfer (EFT), p. 180 Endorse, p. 174 Full endorsement, p. 174 Manual deposit, p. 175 Merchant batch header slip, p. 176	Net deposit, p. 176 Nonsufficient funds (NSF), p. 181 Outstanding cheques, p. 180 Overdrafts, p. 179 Payee, p. 174 Restrictive endorsement, p. 174 Safekeeping, p. 183 Signature card, p. 172

CRITICAL THINKING DISCUSSION QUESTIONS

1. Explain the structure of a cheque. The trend in bank statements is not to return the cancelled cheques. Do you think this is fair?
2. List the three types of endorsements.
3. What is the difference between a manual and an electronic deposit of credit card transactions? Do you think credit cards should be used in supermarkets?
4. List the steps in reconciling a bank statement. Today, many banks charge a monthly fee for certain types of chequing accounts. Do you think all chequing accounts should be free? Please explain.
5. What are some of the trends in online banking? Will we become a cashless society in which all transactions are made with some type of credit card?

END-OF-CHAPTER PROBLEMS

DRILL PROBLEMS

8–1. Fill out the cheque register that follows with this information:

2004			
May 8	Cheque No. 611	Amazon.com	$ 81.96
15	Cheque No. 612	Dell Computer	33.10
19	Deposit		800.40
20	Cheque No. 613	Sprint	110.22
24	Cheque No. 614	Krispy Kreme	217.55
29	Deposit		198.10

RECORD ALL CHARGES OR CREDITS THAT AFFECT YOUR ACCOUNT

NUMBER	DATE 2004	DESCRIPTION OF TRANSACTION	PAYMENT/DEBIT (−)	√	FEE (IF ANY) (−)	DEPOSIT/CREDIT (+)	BALANCE
							$ 1,017 20
			$		$	$	

8–2. On December 1, 2004, Payroll.com, an Internet company, has a $9,482.10 chequebook balance. Record the following transactions for Payroll.com by completing the two cheques and cheque stubs provided. Sign the cheques Garth Scholten, controller.

a. November 8, 2004, deposited $595.10.

b. November 8, cheque No. 190 payable to Wal-Mart Corporation for office supplies—$750.10 (include GST).

c. November 15, cheque No. 191 payable to Compaq Corporation for computer equipment—$1,888.18 (include GST).

No. ________ $ ________
________ 20 ____
To ________
For ________

	DOLLARS	CENTS
BALANCE		
AMT. DEPOSITED		
GST Amount		
TOTAL		
AMT. THIS CHQ.		
BALANCE FORWARD		

PAYROLL.COM
1 LEDGER RD.
THUNDER BAY, ON
P7E 5M9

No. 190

________ 20 ____ 5-13/110

PAY TO THE ORDER OF ________ $ ________

________ DOLLARS

First Canadian Bank

MEMO________

⑆011000138⑆ 25 11103 190

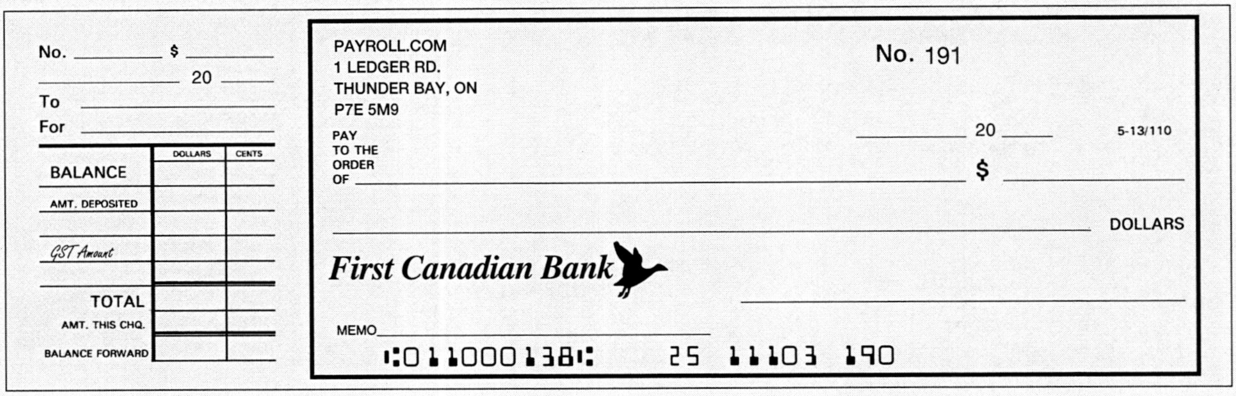

8–3. You are the bookkeeper of Reese Company and must complete a merchant batch header for November 10, 2004, from the following credit card transactions. The company lost the charge slips and doesn't include an adding machine tape. Reese's chequing account number is 3158062. The merchant's signature can be left blank. **Credit card sales** are $210.40, $178.99, $29.30, and $82.80. **Credit card returns** are $15.10 and $22.99.

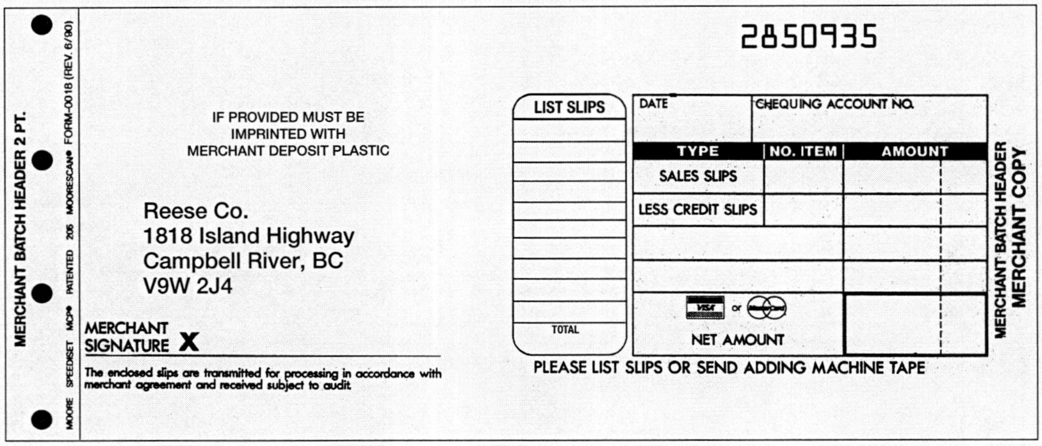

8–4. Using the cheque register in Problem 8–1 and the following bank statement, prepare a bank reconciliation for Lee.com.

Bank Statement

Date	Cheques	Deposits	Balance
5/1 balance			$1,017.20
5/18	$ 81.96		935.24
5/19		$ 800.40	1,735.64
5/26	217.55		1,518.09
5/30	15.00 SC		1,503.09

ADDITIONAL DRILL PROBLEMS

8–5. The following is a deposit slip made out by Fred Young of the F. W. Young Company.

a. How much cash did Young deposit? __________

b. How many cheques did Young deposit? __________

c. What was the total amount deposited? __________

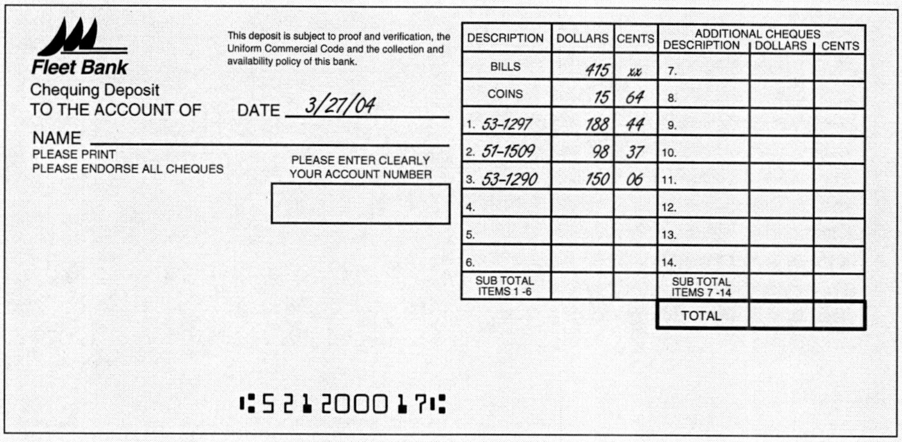
Fleet Bank
Chequing Deposit
TO THE ACCOUNT OF DATE 3/27/04
NAME
PLEASE PRINT
PLEASE ENDORSE ALL CHEQUES

This deposit is subject to proof and verification, the Uniform Commercial Code and the collection and availability policy of this bank.

PLEASE ENTER CLEARLY YOUR ACCOUNT NUMBER

DESCRIPTION	DOLLARS	CENTS	ADDITIONAL CHEQUES DESCRIPTION	DOLLARS	CENTS
BILLS	415	xx	7.		
COINS	15	64	8.		
1. 53-1297	188	44	9.		
2. 51-1509	98	37	10.		
3. 53-1290	150	06	11.		
4.			12.		
5.			13.		
6.			14.		
SUB TOTAL ITEMS 1-6			SUB TOTAL ITEMS 7-14		
			TOTAL		

⑆521200017⑆

8–6. Blackstone Company had a balance of $2,173.18 in its chequing account. Henry James, Blackstone's accountant, made a deposit that consisted of 2 fifty-dollar bills, 120 ten-dollar bills, 6 five-dollar bills, 14 one-dollar bills, $9.54 in change, and two cheques they had accepted, one for $16.38 and the other for $102.50. Find the amount of the deposit and the new balance in Blackstone's chequing account.

8–7. Answer the following questions using the illustration:

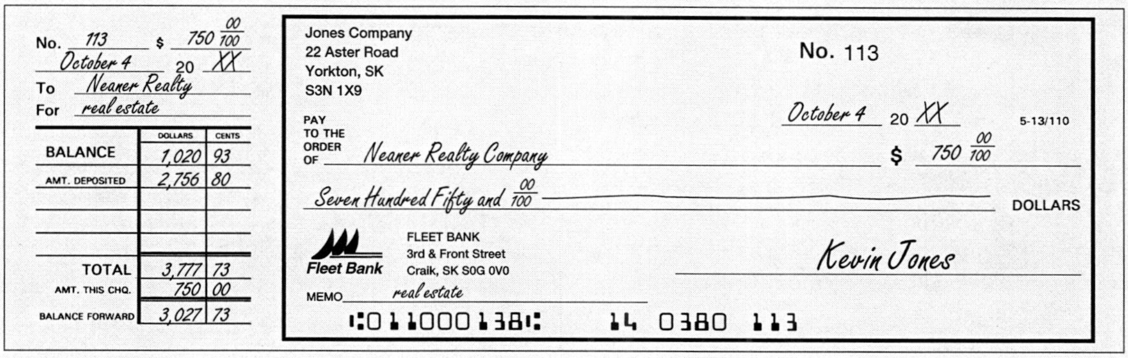
No. 113 $ 750 00/100
October 4 20 XX
To Neaner Realty
For real estate

	DOLLARS	CENTS
BALANCE	1,020	93
AMT. DEPOSITED	2,756	80
TOTAL	3,777	73
AMT. THIS CHQ.	750	00
BALANCE FORWARD	3,027	73

Jones Company
22 Aster Road
Yorkton, SK
S3N 1X9
No. 113
October 4 20 XX 5-13/110
PAY TO THE ORDER OF Neaner Realty Company $ 750 00/100
Seven Hundred Fifty and 00/100 DOLLARS
FLEET BANK
3rd & Front Street
Craik, SK S0G 0V0
Fleet Bank
MEMO real estate
Kevin Jones
⑆011000138⑆ 14 0380 113

a. Who is the payee?
b. Who is the drawer?
c. Who is the drawee?
d. What is the bank's identification number?
e. What is Jones Company's account number?
f. What was the balance in the account on September 30?
g. For how much did Jones write Cheque No. 113?
h. How much was deposited on October 1?
i. How much was left after Cheque No. 113 was written?

8–8. Write each of the following amounts in verbal form as you would on a cheque:
a. $25
b. $245.75
c. $3.98
d. $1,205.05
e. $3,013
f. $510.10

8–9. From the following credit card transactions, calculate the net deposit that would be recorded on the merchant batch summary slip for the day.

MasterCard sales	Returns
$22.95	$ 4.09
18.51	16.50
16.92	

WORD PROBLEMS

8–10. Some banks charge $20 or more a month, or $240 a year for chequing account services. Anna Carmen wants to balance her chequebook, which shows a balance of $1,018.25. The bank shows a balance of $210.20. The following cheques have not cleared the bank: No. 85, $20.50; No. 87, $145.50; and No. 88, $215.10. Anna has a $20 service fee and a $24 NSF fee. The bank pays her $110.15 electric bill through automatic withdrawal. She also made a stop payment order with a fee of $20. A $1,015.00 deposit does not appear on the bank statement. Prepare Anna's bank reconciliation.

8–11. In some banks a $2 fee kicks in after a certain number of teller visits. Jim Clinnin has an account in such a bank. This month Jim was charged for four extra visits to a teller—a total $8 cost to him. Jim's bank statement shows a balance of $35.56; his chequebook shows a $531.26 balance. He received $2.15 in interest. A $575.10 deposit was not recorded on his statement. The following cheques were outstanding: No. 50, $16.50; No. 52, $28.12; and No. 53, $40.63. Prepare Jim's bank reconciliation.

8–12. On June 8, 2004, Larson Company had the following MasterCard transactions (along with some returns). Sales were $28.96, $210.55, and $189.88. Returns were $11.10 and $29.85. As Larson's bookkeeper you must calculate the net deposit.

8–13. In his bank, Murray Mitchell pays $2.50 per transaction at an ATM. When he received his bank statement on March 15, 2002, he had a $12.50 ATM charge. The statement showed a balance of $205.15. Murray's chequebook showed a balance of $1,612.20. He belongs to the YMCA and has his monthly membership fee of $28 paid through his bank. The bank also pays his monthly Sun Life Insurance policy of $14.80. The following cheques did not clear: No. 512, $220.15; No. 514, $21.15; and No. 515, $123.60. On March 16 he made a $1,720.15 deposit that does not appear on his bank statement. Murray earned $3.50 in interest. Prepare Murray Mitchell's bank reconciliation.

8–14. Judy Smejek's bank charges a $2.50 monthly chequing fee, plus a 75-cent fee for each transaction over 10 per month. Judy has just received her April 3, 2002 bank statement. Included in the statement was a charge of 75 cents for 15 additional cheques written. She was also charged a $2.50 service fee. The statement shows a $1,768.01 balance. Judy's chequebook has a $1,085.81 balance. The following cheques have not cleared: No. 113, $312.50; No. 114, $50.40; and No. 115, $16.80. Judy made a $650.25 deposit that is not shown on the bank statement. She has her $540 monthly mortgage payment paid through the bank. Her $1,506.50 Canada Customs and Revenue Agency (CCRA) refund cheque was mailed to her bank. Prepare Judy Smejek's bank reconciliation.

8–15. In 2001, at some banks consumers who were unable to meet minimum balance requirements paid an average of $217 a year, or $18 a month, to maintain a chequing account. Kameron Gibson has a hard time maintaining the minimum balance. He was having difficulty balancing his chequebook because he did not notice this fee on his bank statement. His bank statement showed a balance of $717.72. Kameron's chequebook had a balance of $209.50. Cheque No. 104 for $110.07 and cheque No. 105 for $15.55 were outstanding. A $620.50 deposit was not on the statement. He has his payroll cheque electronically deposited to his chequing account—the payroll cheque was for $1,025.10. There was also a $4 teller fee and an $18 service charge. Prepare Kameron Gibson's bank reconciliation.

8–16. Excel Sue McVickers has received her bank statement with a $25 overdraft fee; she was also charged a $6.50 service fee. However, the good news is she had earned $5.15 interest. Her bank statement's balance was $315.65, but it did not show the $1,215.15 deposit she had made. Sue's chequebook balance shows $604.30. The following cheques have not cleared: No. 250, $603.15; No. 253, $218.90; and No. 254, $130.80. Prepare Sue's bank reconciliation.

8–17. Carol Stokke received her April 6, 2002 bank statement showing a balance of $859.75; her chequebook balance is $954.25. The bank statement shows an ATM charge of $25, NSF fee of $27, earned interest of $2.75, and Carol's $630.15 refund cheque, which was processed by the Canada

Customs and Revenue Agency (CCRA) and deposited to her account. Carol has two cheques that have not cleared—No. 115 for $521.15 and No. 116 for $205.50. There is also a deposit in transit for $1,402.05. Prepare Carol's bank reconciliation.

8–18. Lowell Bank reported the following chequing account fees: $2 to see a real-live teller, $20 to process a bounced cheque, and $1 to $3 if you need an original cheque to prove you paid a bill or made a charitable contribution. This past month you had to transact business through a teller six times—a total $12 cost to you. Your bank statement shows a $305.33 balance; your chequebook shows a $1,009.76 balance. You received $1.10 in interest. An $801.15 deposit was not recorded on your statement. The following cheques were outstanding: No. 413, $28.30; No. 414, $18.60; and No. 418, $60.72. Prepare your bank reconciliation.

ADDITIONAL WORD PROBLEMS

8–19. Find the bank balance on January 31.

Date	Cheques and payments (GST included)			Deposits	Balance
January 1					401.17
January 2	108.64				______
January 5	116.50			432.16	______
January 6	14.92	150.00	10.00		______
January 11	12.29			633.89	______
January 18	108.64	18.60			______
January 25	43.91	23.77		657.22	______
January 26	75.00				______
January 31	6.75 sc				______

8–20. Joe Madruga, of Madruga's Taxi Service, received a bank statement for the month of May showing a balance of $932.36. His records show that the bank had not yet recorded two of his deposits, one for $521.50 and the other for $98.46. There are outstanding cheques in the amounts of $41.67, $135.18, and $25.30. The statement also shows a service charge of $3.38. The balance in the cheque register is $1,353.55. Prepare a bank reconciliation for Madruga's as of May 31.

8–21. In reconciling the chequing account for Nasser Enterprises, Beth Accomando found that the bank had collected a $3,000 promissory note on the company's behalf and had charged a $15 collection fee. There was also a service charge of $7.25. What amount should be added/subtracted from the chequebook balance to bring it up to date?

Add: __________ Deduct: __________

8–22. In reconciling the chequing account for Colonial Cleaners, Steve Papa found that a cheque for $34.50 had been recorded in the cheque register as $43.50. The bank returned an NSF cheque in the amount of $62.55. Interest income of $8.25 was earned and a service charge of $10.32 was assessed. What amount should be added/subtracted from the chequebook balance to bring it up to date?

Add: __________ Deduct: __________

8–23. Matthew Stokes was completing the bank reconciliation for Parker's Tool and Die Company. The cheque register balance was $1,503.67. Matthew found that a $76.00 cheque had been recorded in the cheque register as $67.00; that a note for $1,500 had been collected by the bank for Parker's and the collection fee was $12.00; that $15.60 interest was earned on the account; and that an $8.35 service charge had been assessed. What should the cheque register balance be after Matthew updates it with the bank reconciliation information?

8–24. Long's Video Shop had the following MasterCard sales: $44.18, $66.10, $12.50, and $24.95. Returns for the day were $13.88 and $12.99. What will be the amount of the net deposit for Long's Video Shop on the merchant batch summary slip?

8–25. Consumers, community activists, and politicians are decrying the new line of accounts because several include a $3 service charge for some customers who use bank tellers for transactions that can be done through an automated teller machine. Bill Wade banks at a local bank that charges this fee. He was having difficulty balancing his chequebook because he did not notice this fee on his bank statement. His bank statement showed a balance of $822.18. Bill's chequebook had a balance of $206.48. Cheque No. 406 for $116.08 and Cheque No. 407 for $12.50 were outstanding. A $521 deposit was not on the statement. Bill has his payroll cheque electronically deposited to his chequing account—the payroll cheque was for $1,015.12 (Bill's payroll cheques vary each month). There are also a $1 service fee and a teller fee of $6. Complete Bill's bank reconciliation.

8–26. At First National Bank, some customers have to pay $25 each year as an ATM card fee. John Levi banks at First National and has just received his bank statement showing a balance of $829.25; his chequebook balance is $467.40. The bank statement shows an ATM card fee of $25, teller fee of $9, interest of $1.80, and John's $880 CCRA refund cheque, which was processed by the CCRA and deposited to his account. John has two cheques that have not cleared—No. 112 for $620.10 and No. 113 for $206.05. There is also a deposit in transit for $1,312.10. Prepare John's bank reconciliation.

CHALLENGE PROBLEMS

8–27. Margaret Luna received her January 5, 2002, bank statement, which shows a $782.19 balance. Her chequebook shows $748.20 balance. The following transactions occurred: $2.50 cheque processing fee (25 cheques at $.10), $159.36 automatic withdrawal to Nicor, $4 teller fee, NSF fee of $27, $8.50 ATM fee, $20 stop payment order, $6.50 earned interest, $1,350.20 Canada Customs and Revenue Agency (CCRA) refund cheque made to the bank, $7 service fee, $20 stop payment order, and $6.50 for cheque printing. A $1,430.50 deposit is not shown on the bank statement. The following cheques were outstanding: No. 202, $216.12; No. 203, $58.40; No. 205, $29.50; and No. 206, $58.63. Prepare Margaret Luna's bank reconciliation.

8–28. Excel Melissa Jackson, bookkeeper for Kinko Company, cannot prepare a bank reconciliation. From the following facts, can you help her complete the June 30, 2004 reconciliation?

The bank statement showed a $2,955.82 balance, while Melissa's chequebook showed a $3,301.82 balance. Melissa placed a $510.19 deposit in the bank's night depository on June 30. The deposit did not appear on the bank statement. The bank included two DMs and one CM with the returned cheques: $690.65 DM for a NSF cheque, $8.50 DM for service charges, and $400 CM (less a $10 collection fee) for collecting a $400 non-interest-bearing note. Cheque No. 811 for $110.94 and cheque No. 912 for $82.50, both written and recorded on June 28, were not with the returned cheques. The bookkeeper had correctly written cheque No. 884, $1,000, for a new cash register, but she recorded it as $1,069. The May bank reconciliation showed cheque No. 748 for $210.90 and cheque No. 710 for $195.80 outstanding on April 30. The June bank statement included cheque No. 710 but not cheque No. 748.

SUMMARY PRACTICE TEST

1. Colonial Cleaners had the following MasterCard sales for a day: $114.18, $15.10, $76.80, and $19.99. The company also issued two credits for returned merchandise: $11.20 and $14.99. What would be the amount of the net deposit for Colonial Cleaners on its merchant batch summary slip? (p. 176)

2. Walgreen has a $10,198.55 beginning chequebook balance. Record the following transactions in the cheque stubs provided. (GST is included in the amounts.) (p. 174)

   a. November 4, 2004, cheque No. 191 payable to Merck Corporation, $2,185.99 for drugs
   b. $1,500 deposit—November 24
   c. November 24, 2004, cheque No. 192 payable to Gillette Corporation, $895.22 for merchandise

No. ________ $ ________
________ 20____
To ________
For ________

	DOLLARS	CENTS
BALANCE		
AMT. DEPOSITED		
GST Amount		
TOTAL		
AMT. THIS CHQ.		
BALANCE FORWARD		

No. ________ $ ________
________ 20____
To ________
For ________

	DOLLARS	CENTS
BALANCE		
AMT. DEPOSITED		
GST Amount		
TOTAL		
AMT. THIS CHQ.		
BALANCE FORWARD		

3. On April 1, 2004, Gracemoll Company received a bank statement that showed a $9,200 balance. Gracemoll showed a $6,600 chequing account balance. The bank did not return cheque No. 115 for $870 or cheque No. 118 for $1,345. A $700 deposit made on March 31 was in transit. The bank charged Gracemoll $40 for printing and $175 for NSF cheques. The bank also collected a $1,400 note for Gracemoll. Gracemoll forgot to record a $100 withdrawal at the ATM. Prepare a bank reconciliation. (p. 180)

4. Hal Bean banks at Chris Federal Bank. Today he received his March 31, 2004, bank statement showing a $1,842.33 balance. Hal's chequebook shows a balance of $645.15. The following cheques have not cleared the bank: No. 140, $218.44; No. 149, $55.18; and No. 161, $88.51. Hal made a $615.35 deposit that is not shown on the bank statement. He has his $700 monthly mortgage payment paid through the bank. His $2,150.40 Canada Customs and Revenue Agency refund cheque was mailed to his bank. Prepare Hal Bean's bank reconciliation. (p. 180)

5. On June 30, 2004, Andy Company's bank statement showed a $7,182.11 bank balance. The bank statement also showed that it collected a $1,200.10 note for the company. A $1,200.50 June 30 deposit was in transit. Cheque No. 119 for $950.12 and cheque No. 130 for $455.79 are outstanding. Andy's bank charges 30 cents per processed cheque. This month, Andy wrote 80 cheques. Andy has a $5,800 chequebook balance. Prepare a reconciled statement. (p. 180)

SOLUTIONS TO PRACTICE QUIZZES

LU 8–1

1.

No. 113 $ 83.76
June 5 20 04
To Angel Corp.
For Rent

	DOLLARS	CENTS
BALANCE	9,500	60
AMT. DEPOSITED	690	60
TOTAL	10,191	20
AMT. THIS CHQ.	83	76
BALANCE FORWARD	10,107	44

Long Company
22 Aster Rd.
Scarborough, ON
M1R 2Y3

No. 113

June 5 20 04 5-13/110

PAY TO THE ORDER OF Angel Corporation $ 83 76/100

Eighty-three and 76/100 DOLLARS

First Canadian Bank

Roland Small

MEMO Rent

⑆01 1000 138⑆ 14 0380 113

2.

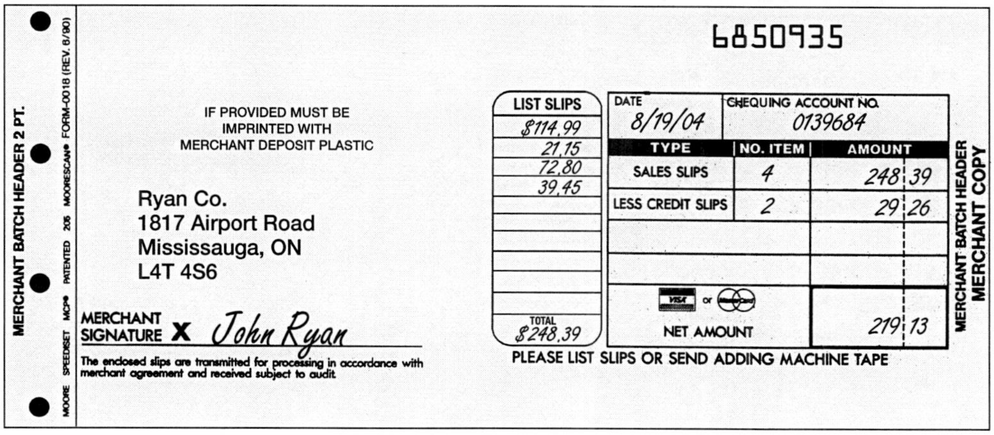
6850935

MERCHANT BATCH HEADER 2 PT.

MOORE SPEEDISET MCP® PATENTED 306 MOORESCAN® FORM-0018 (REV. 8/90)

IF PROVIDED MUST BE IMPRINTED WITH MERCHANT DEPOSIT PLASTIC

Ryan Co.
1817 Airport Road
Mississauga, ON
L4T 4S6

MERCHANT SIGNATURE X John Ryan

The enclosed slips are transmitted for processing in accordance with merchant agreement and received subject to audit.

LIST SLIPS
$114.99
21.15
72.80
39.45
TOTAL $248.39

DATE 8/19/04 CHEQUING ACCOUNT NO. 0139684

TYPE	NO. ITEM	AMOUNT
SALES SLIPS	4	248.39
LESS CREDIT SLIPS	2	29.26
NET AMOUNT		219.13

PLEASE LIST SLIPS OR SEND ADDING MACHINE TAPE

MERCHANT BATCH HEADER MERCHANT COPY

LU 8–2

ROSA GARCIA Bank Reconciliation as of February 3, 2004					
Chequebook balance			**Bank balance**		
Rosa's chequebook balance		$929.15	Bank balance		$ 212.80
Add:			Add:		
Interest		1.05	Deposit in transit		810.12
		$930.20			$1,022.92
			Deduct:		
Deduct:			Outstanding cheques:		
Deposited "cheque			No. 300	$18.20	
returned" fee	$20.00		No. 302	38.40	
ATM	12.00	32.00	No. 303	68.12	124.72
Reconciled balance		$898.20	Reconciled balance		$ 898.20

Business Math Scrapbook

WITH INTERNET APPLICATION

Putting Your Skills to Work

Online Banks Fail to Realize Cyber-Goals

By PETER EDMONSTON
WSJ.COM

In the beginning, online banks had a simple strategy: With the money they saved by not owning expensive, marble-clad branches, they could offer high-interest, low-fee bank accounts that would bring customers flocking to their virtual doors.

But things haven't worked out that way. Five years after the first Internet bank launched its Web site, online banks have failed to capture more than a sliver of the banking business. Meanwhile, their customers are demanding many of the conveniences associated with traditional banks—creating an added expense that Internet banks hadn't worked into their business plans.

These unexpected pressures have started to take a toll. Online banks are rolling back or abandoning the generous offers they once dangled in front of potential customers. BankDirect, a Dallas-based Internet bank, and WingspanBank.com, an online subsidiary of Chicago-based **Bank One** Corp., the nation's fourth-largest bank, are raising fees and cutting interest paid on deposits.

Meanwhile, other online banks have been bailing out of the business altogether. In November, a company called **X.com** Corp. decided to phase out its Internet-banking operations to focus on its person-to-person payment service, PayPal. Also last year, financial-services giant **Citigroup** Inc. pulled the plug on citi f/i, its Internet-only banking subsidiary.

Many other Web banks will soon be forced to become more tightfisted or even shut down, analysts and industry executives say. Battling to offer the highest rates and the lowest fees to online banking customers "is a strategy for failure," says Paul Van Dyke, senior analyst for Jupiter Research, a unit of New York-based Jupiter Media Metrix. "And I think online banks are beginning to see that now."

PROJECT A

Do you agree with this article?

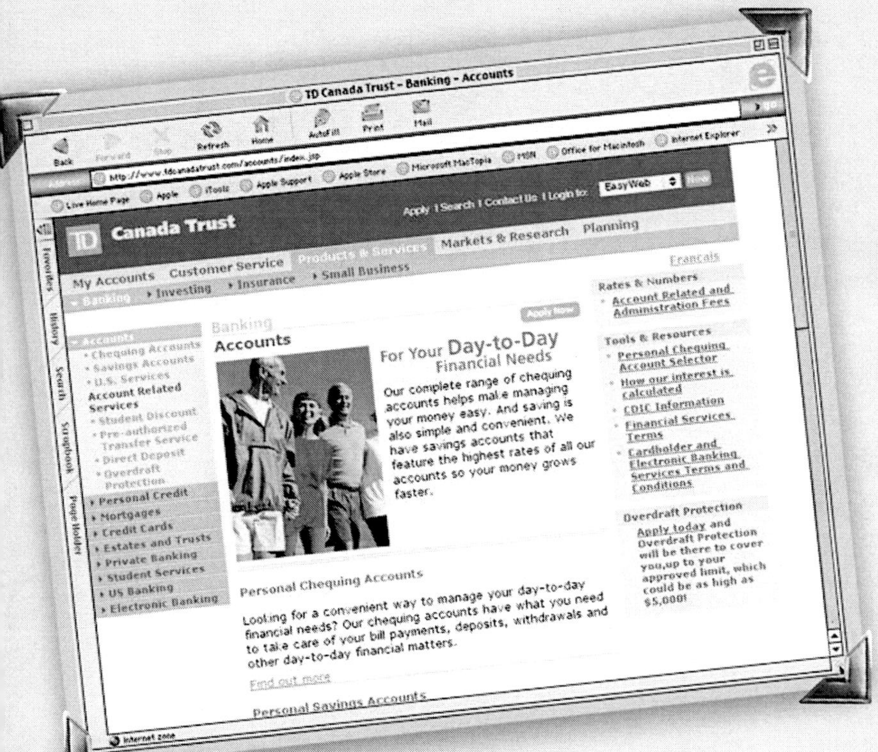

PROJECT B

Go to different Canadian banks' Web sites. Suppose you can only maintain a balance of $500 in your chequing account and that you write 25 cheques monthly. What is the most expensive and least expensive account for you to have?

Discounts: Trade and Cash

9

Stores Told To Lift Prices In Germany

Antitrust Office Says Wal-Mart and 2 Others Sold Food Below Cost

By Ernest Beck
Staff Reporter of The Wall Street Journal

Here's a new twist in consumer protection: forcing stores to raise prices.

German antitrust authorities ordered the German unit of **Wal-Mart Stores** Inc. of the U.S. and two German rivals to increase prices on certain products.

The authorities last week accused Wal-Mart of starting a retail price war on basic food items, such as milk, sugar and flour, forcing its competitors to lower prices. It said the companies exploited their size and market share to sell the products below cost on a continuing basis, which violates German trade laws. While this benefits consumers in the short term, the office said, it would hurt small and medium-size rivals that can't match the lower prices.

LEARNING UNIT OBJECTIVES

LU 9–1: Trade Discounts—Single and Chain (Includes Discussion of Freight)

- Calculate single trade discounts with formulas and complements (p. 197).
- Explain the freight terms *FOB shipping point* and *FOB destination* (p. 198).
- Find list price when net price and trade discount rate are known (p. 200).
- Calculate chain discounts with the net price equivalent rate and single equivalent discount rate (p. 200).

LU 9–2: Cash Discounts, Credit Terms, and Partial Payments

- List and explain typical discount periods and credit periods that a business may offer (p. 203).
- Calculate outstanding balance for partial payments (p. 211).

The word *discount* makes buyers stop and listen. Discounts in prices mean savings for buyers. In competition for customers, sellers give different discounts. As you can see from the above clipping, *Maclean's* offers 78% off the regular price if a customer subscribes to the magazine for a year and up to 80% off the retail price of $4.50 if a customer subscribes for two years.

Car rental companies sometimes offer 50% off the regular price when a customer rents a car from their company. *Maclean's* and Enterprise use discounts to encourage customers to have business with them and not with their competitors and to order products in bigger quantities. These are examples of trade discounts.

This chapter discusses two types of discounts taken by retailers—trade and cash. A **trade discount** is a reduction off the original selling price (list price) of an item and is not related to early payment. A **cash discount** is the result of an early payment based on the terms of the sale.

LEARNING UNIT 9–1
TRADE DISCOUNTS—SINGLE AND CHAIN (INCLUDES DISCUSSION OF FREIGHT)

The Distribution Chain

Manufacturer → Distributor → Wholesaler → Retailer → Final Customer

Why do Internet users often get lower prices? It costs less to sell services and products on the Internet. Many companies pass on some of these reduced costs to the Internet user. So before you buy a service or product, be sure to check the Internet for discount prices only available on the Internet.

Where do retailers such as the Internet get their merchandise? The merchandise sold by retailers is bought from manufacturers and wholesalers who sell only to retailers and not to customers. These manufacturers and wholesalers offer retailer discounts so they can resell the merchandise at a profit. The discounts are off the manufacturers' and wholesalers' **list price** (suggested retail price), and the amount of discount that retailers receive off the list price is the **trade discount amount.**

When you make a purchase, the seller gives you a purchase **invoice.** Invoices are important business documents that help sellers keep track of sales transactions and buyers keep track of purchase transactions. North Shore Community College Bookstore is a retail seller of textbooks to students. The bookstore usually purchases its textbooks directly from publishers.

Figure 9.1 shows a textbook invoice from McGraw-Hill Ryerson Ltd. to the North Shore Community College Bookstore. Note that the trade discount amount is given in percent. This is the **trade discount rate,** which is a percent off the list price that retailers can deduct. The following formula for calculating a trade discount amount gives the numbers from the Figure 9.1 invoice in parentheses:

TRADE DISCOUNT AMOUNT FORMULA

$$\text{Trade discount amount} = \text{List price} \times \text{Trade discount rate}$$
$$(\$896.53) \quad (\$3{,}586.10) \quad (25\%)$$
$$D_t = L \times d \qquad \textbf{(9.1)}$$

where D_t is the amount of trade discount, L the list price, and d the rate of discount.

FIGURE 9–1
Bookstore invoice showing a trade discount

Invoice No.: 5582

McGraw-Hill Ryerson Ltd.
300 Water Street
Whitby, ON LIN 9B6

Date: July 8, 2004
Ship: Two-day UPS
Terms: 2/10, n/30

Sold to: North Shore Community College Bookstore
11 Deerhurst Rd.
Deerhurst, ON D4N 3P0

Quantity	Description	Unit list price	Total amount
50	Managerial Accounting–Garrison/Noreen	$59.99	$2,999.50
10	Marketing–McCarthy	58.66	586.60
		Total List Price	$3,586.10
		Less: Trade Discount 25%	– 896.53
		Invoice Total	$2,689.57
		HST	403.44
		Shipping charges	75.50
		Total Amount Due	$3,168.51

The price that the retailer (bookstore) pays the manufacturer (publisher) or wholesaler is the **net price.** The following formula for calculating the net price gives the numbers from the Figure 9.1 invoice in parentheses:

NET PRICE FORMULA

$$\text{Net price} = \text{List price} - \text{Trade discount amount}$$
$$(\$2{,}689.57) \quad (\$3{,}586.10) \quad (\$896.53)$$
$$N = L - D_t \qquad \textbf{(9.2)}$$

where N is the net price.

Let's substitute instead of D_t its expression from formula 9.1, $N = L - L \times d$. Combining like terms and taking common factors out of the brackets, we can rearrange this formula into a well-known and frequently used one:

$$N = L(1 - d) \qquad \textbf{(9.3)}$$

Frequently, manufacturers and wholesalers issue catalogues to retailers containing list prices of the seller's merchandise and the available trade discounts. To reduce printing costs when prices change, these sellers usually update the catalogues with new *discount sheets.* The discount sheet also gives the seller the flexibility of offering different trade discounts to different classes of retailers. For example, some retailers buy in quantity and service the products. They may receive a larger discount than the retailer who wants the manufacturer to service the products. Sellers may also give discounts to meet a competitor's price, to attract new retailers, and to reward the retailers who buy product-line products. Sometimes the ability of the retailer to negotiate with the seller determines the trade discount amount.

Retailers cannot take trade discounts on freight, returned goods, sales tax, and so on. Trade discounts may be single discounts or a chain of discounts. Before we discuss single trade discounts, let's study freight terms.

FREIGHT TERMS

The most common **freight terms** are *FOB shipping point* and *FOB destination.* These terms determine how the freight will be paid. The key words in the terms are *shipping point* and *destination.*

FOB shipping point means free on board at shipping point; that is, the buyer pays the freight cost of getting the goods to the place of business.

For example, assume that IBM in San Diego bought goods from Argo Suppliers in Boston. Argo ships the goods "FOB Boston" by plane. IBM takes title to the goods when the aircraft in Boston receives the goods, so IBM pays the freight from Boston to San Diego. Frequently, the seller (Argo) prepays the freight and adds the amount to the buyer's (IBM) invoice. When paying the invoice, the buyer takes the cash discount off the net price and adds the freight cost. FOB shipping point can be illustrated as follows:

FOB shipping point (Boston)

FOB destination means the seller pays the freight cost until it reaches the buyer's place of business. If Argo ships its goods to IBM "FOB destination" or "FOB San Diego," the title to the goods remains with Argo. Then it is Argo's responsibility to pay the freight from Boston to IBM's place of business in San Diego. FOB destination can be illustrated as follows:

FOB destination (San Diego)

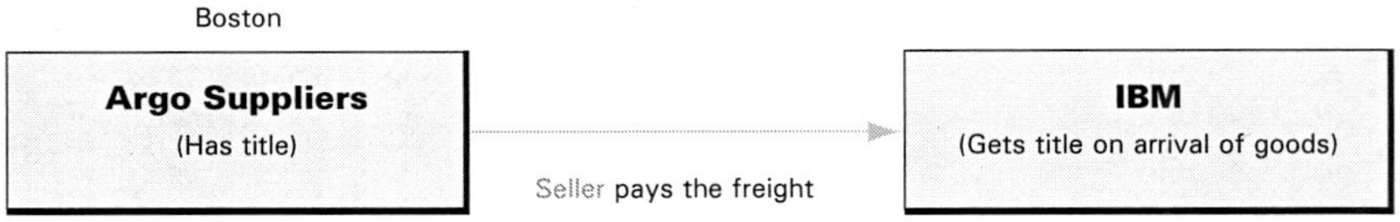

The *Wall Street Journal* clipping "Why Shoppers Are Wary" lists reasons why Internet users do not shop online. One of the leading reasons is that often the shipping charges are FOB shipping point—the buyer pays the freight. Another important reason is the difficulty in returning items. If you prefer to shop offline, is your reason for not shopping online listed in the clipping?

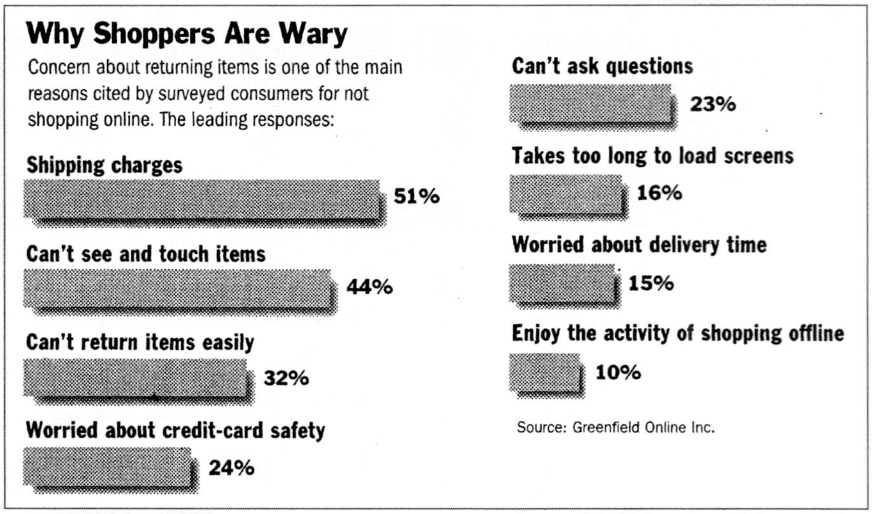

Source: © 2000 Dow Jones & Company, Inc.

Now you are ready for the discussion of single trade discounts.

Single Trade Discount

In the introduction to this Unit, we showed how to use the trade discount amount formula and the net price formula to calculate the McGraw-Hill Ryerson Ltd. textbook sale to the North Shore Community College Bookstore. Since McGraw-Hill Ryerson Ltd. gave the bookstore only one trade discount, it is a **single trade discount.** In the following word problem, we use the formulas to solve another example of a single trade discount. Again, we may also use a Blueprint Aid to help dissect and solve the word problem.

THE WORD PROBLEM The list price of a Macintosh computer is $2,700. The manufacturer offers dealers a 40% trade discount. What are the trade discount amount and the net price?

THE FACTS	SOLVING FOR?	STEPS TO TAKE	KEY POINTS
L: List price: $2,700. *d: Trade discount rate:* 40%.	*Trade discount amount.* $D_t = ?$ Net price. $N = ?$	Trade discount amount = List price × Trade discount rate. $D_t = L \times d$ (9.1) Net price = List price − Trade discount amount. $N = L - D_t$ (9.2) or $N = L(1 - d)$ (9.3)	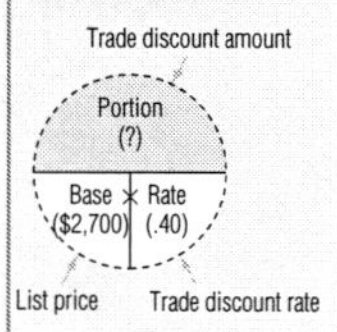

STEPS TO SOLVING PROBLEM

1. Calculate the trade discount amount. $2,700 × .40 = $1,080
2. Calculate the net price. $2,700 − $1,080 = **$1,620**

L = $2,700

d = 40%, transfer 40% into decimal form: $d = .4$

$D_t = ?$

$N = ?$

To find the amount of the trade discount, D_t, when the list price and the discount rate are given, use this formula:

$$D_t = L \times d \quad \textbf{(9.1)}$$

Substitute the known values and get the amount of D_t:

$D_t = 2{,}700 \times .4 = \$1{,}080$

To find the net price when the list price, amount of discount, and discount rate are given, use one of these two formulas:

$$N = L - D_t \quad \textbf{(9.2)}$$

or

$$N = L(1 - d) \quad \textbf{(9.3)}$$

Substitute the known values and get the amount of the net price.

$N = 2{,}700 - 1{,}080 = \$1{,}620$

or

$N = 2{,}700(1 - .4) = 2{,}700 \times .6 = \$1{,}620$

Formula 9.3 is a shortcut of the method of *calculation of net price, using the complement of trade discount rate* $(1 - d)$.

Now let's learn how to check the dealers' net price of $1,620 with an alternative procedure using a complement.

The **complement** of a trade discount rate is the difference between the discount rate and 100%. The following steps show you how to use the complement of a trade discount rate:

CALCULATING NET PRICE USING COMPLEMENT OF TRADE DISCOUNT RATE

Step 1. To find the complement, subtract the single discount rate from 100%.

Step 2. Multiply the list price times the complement (from Step 1).

Think of a complement of any given percent (decimal) as the result of subtracting the percent from 100%.

STEP 1.

100%
− 40 ← Trade discount rate
60% or .60
$(1 - d)$

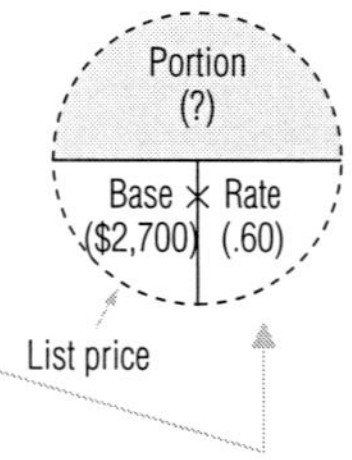

The complement means that we are spending 60 cents per dollar because we save 40 cents per dollar. Since we planned to spend \$2,700, we multiply .60 by \$2,700 to get a net price of \$1,620.

STEP 2. \$1,620 = \$2,700 × .60

Note how the portion (\$1,620) and rate (.60) relate to the same piece of the base (\$2,700). The portion (\$1,620) is smaller than the base, since the rate is less than 100%.

Be aware that some people prefer to use the trade discount amount formula and the net price formula to find the net price. Other people prefer to use the complement of the trade discount rate to find the net price. The result is always the same.

Finding List Price When You Know Net Price and Trade Discount Rate

The following formula has many useful applications:

CALCULATING LIST PRICE WHEN NET PRICE AND TRADE DISCOUNT RATE ARE KNOWN

$$\text{List price} = \frac{\text{Net price}}{\text{Complement of trade discount rate}} \qquad L = \frac{N}{(1-d)} \qquad \textbf{(9.4)}$$

This formula may be easily obtained rearranging formula 9.3.

Next, let's see how to dissect and solve a word problem calculating list price.

THE WORD PROBLEM A Macintosh computer has a \$1,620 net price and a 40% trade discount. What is its list price?

THE FACTS	SOLVING FOR?	STEPS TO TAKE	KEY POINTS
N: Net price: \$1,620. *d: Trade discount rate:* 40%.	List price. $L = ?$	List price = $\frac{\text{Net price}}{\text{Complement of trade discount rate}}$ $L = \frac{N}{(1-d)}$	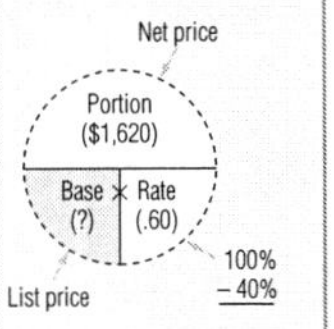

$N = \$1{,}620$

$d = 40\% \rightarrow d = .4$

To find the list price, when the net price and the rate of discount are given, use formula 9.4:

$$L = \frac{N}{(1-d)} = \frac{1{,}620}{(1-.4)} = \frac{1{,}620}{.6} = 2{,}700 \qquad \textbf{(9.4)}$$

$L = ?$

The list price was \$2,700.

STEPS TO SOLVING PROBLEM

1. Calculate the complement of the trade discount.
$$\begin{array}{r} 100\% \\ -\ 40 \\ \hline 60\% = .60 \end{array}$$
2. Calculate the list price. $\frac{\$1{,}620}{.60} = \$2{,}700$

Note that the portion (\$1,620) and rate (.60) relate to the same piece of the base.

Let's return to the McGraw-Hill Ryerson Ltd. invoice in Figure 9.1 and calculate the list price using the formula for finding list price when net price and trade discount rate are known. The net price of the textbooks is \$2,689.57. The complement of the trade discount rate $(1-d)$is 100% − 25% = 75% = .75. Dividing the net price \$2,689.57 by the complement .75 equals \$3,586.09,[1] the list price shown in the McGraw-Hill Ryerson Ltd. invoice. We can show this as follows:

$N = \$2{,}689.57$

$d = .25$

$L = ?$

$$L = \frac{N}{(1-d)} = \frac{\$2{,}689.57}{.75} = \$3{,}586.09$$

The list price is \$3,586.09.

CHAIN OR SERIES DISCOUNTS

Frequently, manufacturers want greater flexibility in setting trade discounts for different classes of customers, seasonal trends, promotional activities, and so on. To gain this flexibility, some

[1]Off by 1 cent due to rounding.

sellers give **chain** or **series discounts**—trade discounts in a series of two or more successive discounts. They are also known as *multiple discounts.*

Sellers list chain discounts as a group, for example, 20/15/10. Let's look at how Mick Company arrives at the net price of office equipment with a 20/15/10 chain discount.

EXAMPLE

The list price of the office equipment is $15,000. The chain discount is 20/15/10. The long way to calculate the net price is as follows:

STEP 1	STEP 2	STEP 3	STEP 4
$15,000	$15,000	$12,000	$10,200
× .20	− 3,000	− 1,800	− 1,020
$ 3,000	$12,000	$10,200	$ 9,180 net price
	× .15	× .10	
	$ 1,800	$ 1,020	

Note how we multiply the percent (in decimal) times the new balance after we subtract the previous trade discount amount. For example, in Step 3, we change the last discount, 10%, to decimal form and multiply times $10,200. Remember that each percent is multiplied by a successively *smaller* base. You could write the 20/15/10 discount rate in any order and still arrive at the same net price. Thus, you would get the $9,180 net price if the discount were 10/15/20 or 15/20/10. However, sellers usually give the larger discounts first. *Never try to shorten this step process by adding the discounts.* Your net price will be incorrect because, when done properly, each percent is calculated on a different base. There is a quicker way to calculate the net price after multiple discounts: we can use the following formula with a $(1 - d)$ factor for each of the discounts:

Never add the 20/15/10 together.

$$N = L(1 - d_1)(1 - d_2)(1 - d_3) \qquad (9.5)$$

If $L = \$15{,}000$, $d_1 = .2$, $d_2 = .15$ and $d_3 = .1$, then:

$$N = 15{,}000(1 - .2)(1 - .15)(1 - .1) = 15{,}000 \times .8 \times .85 \times .9 = \$9{,}180$$

Net Price Equivalent Rate

Formula 9.5 illustrates a shortcut method of finding the net price. Let's see how to use this rate to calculate net price in steps.

CALCULATING NET PRICE USING NET PRICE EQUIVALENT RATE

Step 1. Subtract each chain discount rate from 100% (find the complement) and convert each percent to a decimal.
Step 2. Multiply the decimals. Do not round off decimals, since this number is the **net price equivalent rate.**
Step 3. Multiply the list price times the net price equivalent rate (Step 2).

The following word problem, with its Blueprint Aid, illustrates how to use the net price equivalent rate method.

THE WORD PROBLEM The list price of office equipment is $15,000. The chain discount is 20/15/10. What is the net price?

THE FACTS	SOLVING FOR?	STEPS TO TAKE	KEY POINTS
L: List price: $15,000. *Chain discount:* 20/15/10 $d_1 = .2$ $d_2 = .15$ $d_3 = .1$	Net price. $N = ?$	Net price equivalent rate. Net price = List price × Net price equivalent rate. $N = L(1-d_1)(1-d_2)(1-d_3)$	Do not round net price equivalent rate.

STEPS TO SOLVING PROBLEM

1. Calculate the complement of each rate rate and convert each percent to a decimal.

100%	100%	100%
− 20	− 15	− 10
80%	85%	90%
↓	↓	↓
.8	.85	.9

2. Calculate the net price equivalent rate. (Do not round.)

$.8 \times .85 \times .9 = .612$ Net price equivalent rate. For each \$1, you are spending about 61 cents.

3. Calculate the net price (actual cost to buyer).

$\$15{,}000 \times .612 =$ **\$9,180**

Next we see how to calculate the trade discount amount with a simpler method. In the previous word problem, we could calculate the trade discount amount as follows:

\$15,000	←	List price
− 9,180	←	Net price
\$ 5,820	←	Trade discount amount

Single Equivalent Discount Rate

You can use another method to find the trade discount by using the **single equivalent discount rate.**

CALCULATING TRADE DISCOUNT AMOUNT USING SINGLE EQUIVALENT DISCOUNT RATE

Step 1. Subtract the net price equivalent rate from 1. This is the single equivalent discount rate.

Step 2. Multiply the list price times the single equivalent discount rate. This is the trade discount amount.

Let's now do the calculations.

STEP 1.

1.000 ← If you are using a calculator, just press 1.
− .612
.388 ← This is the single equivalent discount rate.

STEP 2. $\$15{,}000 \times .388 =$ **\$5,820** → This is the trade discount amount.

There is a shortcut way to find single equivalent discount rate, using the following formula:

$$d_e = 1 - (1 - d_1)(1 - d_2)(1 - d_3) \quad \textbf{(9.6)}$$

where d_e is a single equivalent to discount rate.

Using this formula for the example above, we will get a single equivalent discount rate of:

$$d_e = 1 - (1 - .2)(1 - .15)(1 - .1) = 1 - .8 \times .85 \times .1$$
$$= 1 - .612 = .388$$

This means that for each \$1 of the list price a customer will get a discount of \$.388. The customer pays only \$.612 and saves \$.388 on each \$1 of the list price. The .388 is the single equivalent discount rate for the 20/15/10 chain discount. Note how we use the .388 single equivalent discount rate as if it were the only discount.

To find the amount of the trade discount with series discounts we can use this formula:

$$D_t = L \times d_e \quad \textbf{(9.7)}$$
$$d_e = .388$$
$$D_t = 15{,}000 \times .388 = \$5{,}820$$

Have you noticed the display of magazines before you get to the supermarket cash register? Did you know that magazine companies pay for these valuable spaces that entice customers to buy their magazines? According to the *Wall Street Journal* clipping "Supermarkets Face Scrutiny over Fees," food retailers also collect so-called slotting fees on everything from soup cans to vegetables. This is why you see, for example, Coca-Cola displayed at a prominent place at the end slot of a grocery isle.

Supermarkets Face Scrutiny Over Fees

By JERRY GUIDERA
And SHELLY BRANCH
Staff Reporters of THE WALL STREET JOURNAL

WASHINGTON—Senators blasted food retailers for levying so-called slotting fees on everything from soup cans to vegetables, and put supermarkets on notice that they are determined to step up scrutiny of the industry.

The fees, which retailers routinely charge suppliers to guarantee shelf space, are "threatening the profitability and the future of the family produce farmer," said Missouri Republican Sen. Christopher "Kit" Bond, chairman of the Senate Small Business Committee, which held a hearing on the matter yesterday.

Federal antitrust regulators have also taken a renewed interest in the way retailers will accept discounts from large manufacturers, while demanding upfront payments from smaller ones, to secure prime shelf space.

The Federal Trade Commission is expected to issue a report examining slotting fees by the end of the year. Beginning next year, $900,000 will be earmarked for the agency to cover legal fees to force companies to cooperate with its probe.

It's time to try a Practice Quiz.[2]

LU 9–1 PRACTICE QUIZ

1. The list price of a dining room set with a 40% trade discount is $12,000. What are the trade discount amount and net price (use complement method for net price)?
2. The net price of a video system with a 30% trade discount is $1,400. What is the list price? Use formulas.
3. Lamps Outlet bought a shipment of lamps from a wholesaler. The total list price was $12,000 with a 5/10/25 chain discount. Calculate the net price and trade discount amount. Use formulas.

LEARNING UNIT 9–2
CASH DISCOUNTS, CREDIT TERMS, AND PARTIAL PAYMENTS

After a transaction, the seller prepares and sends the buyer an invoice. A sample invoice was introduced in Figure 9.1. The invoice presents information about the seller and the buyer, date, invoice number, terms of payment, credit terms, items purchased, unit list prices, applicable trade discounts, GST and PST or HST (Harmonized Sales Tax), shipping charges, and total invoice amount.

The credit period, cash discount, discount period, and freight terms are called *terms of sale.*

Buyers can often benefit from buying on credit. The time period that sellers give buyers to pay their invoices is called a **credit period.** Frequently, the buyers can sell the goods bought during this credit period. Then, at the end of the credit period, buyers can pay sellers with the funds obtained from their sale of the goods. When buyers can do this, they can use consumers' money to pay the invoice instead of their own money.

[2]For all three problems we will show Blueprint Aids. You might want to draw them on scrap paper.

A cash discount is for prompt payment. A trade discount is not.

Sellers can also offer a cash discount, or reduction from the invoice price, if buyers pay the invoice within a specific time. This time period is known as a **discount period,** which is part of the total credit period. Sellers offer this cash discount because they can use the dollars to better advantage sooner rather than later. Buyers who are not short of cash like cash discounts, because the goods will cost them less and, as a result, enable larger profits.

Trade discounts should be taken before cash discounts.

Remember that buyers take cash discounts, not on freight, returned goods, sales tax, and trade discounts, but on the net price of the invoice.

As you can see, the terms of the McGraw-Hill Ryerson Ltd. invoice shown in Figure 9.2 are 2/10, n/30. This is the information about the **terms of payment,** which includes the credit period, the cash discount, and the date on which the credit or discount period begins. (See Figure 9.4.)

FIGURE 9–2

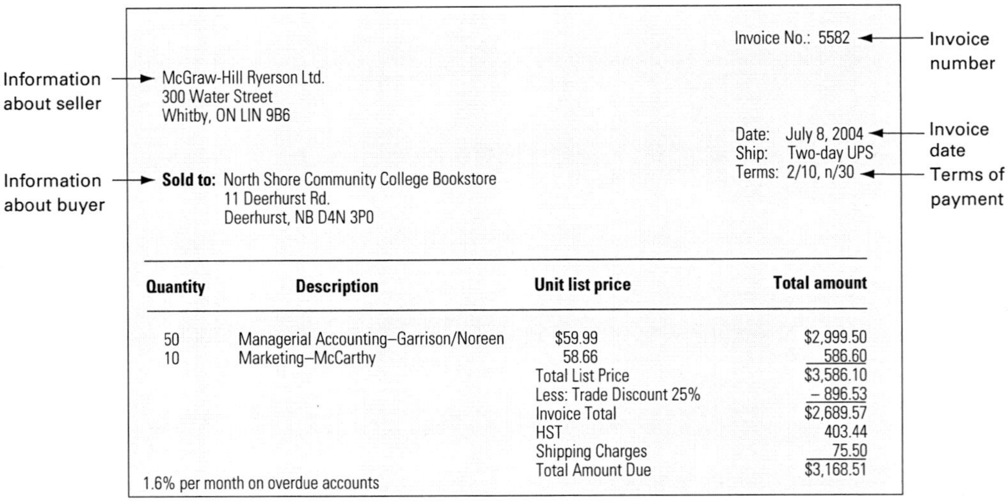
Information about seller → McGraw-Hill Ryerson Ltd.
300 Water Street
Whitby, ON LIN 9B6

Information about buyer → **Sold to:** North Shore Community College Bookstore
11 Deerhurst Rd.
Deerhurst, NB D4N 3P0

Invoice No.: 5582 ← Invoice number
Date: July 8, 2004 ← Invoice date
Ship: Two-day UPS
Terms: 2/10, n/30 ← Terms of payment

Quantity	Description	Unit list price	Total amount
50	Managerial Accounting–Garrison/Noreen	$59.99	$2,999.50
10	Marketing–McCarthy	58.66	586.60
		Total List Price	$3,586.10
		Less: Trade Discount 25%	– 896.53
		Invoice Total	$2,689.57
		HST	403.44
		Shipping Charges	75.50
		Total Amount Due	$3,168.51

1.6% per month on overdue accounts

FIGURE 9–3

NSCC Bookstore
11 Deerhurst Rd.
Deerhurst, NB D4N 3P0

4418
22-70/960

July 12 20 04

PAY TO THE ORDER OF McGraw-Hill Ryerson Ltd. $ 3,114.72
Three thousand one hundred fourteen 72/100 dollars

PARK BANK
183 Como Avenue
Deerhurst, NB D4N 2Z3

James Casley

"214" 35348 III 005 ⑆ 08493 "64

FIGURE 9–4
Explanation of Terms of Payment Abbreviations

Cash discount (2%) → 2/10, n/30 ← Credit period (30 days)

↑

Discount period (10 days)

The *credit period* or *net period* is the time for which the credit is given. No interest is charged for this period and at the end of it the invoice must be paid in full. After the due date on this invoice, as you see, a penalty of "1.6% per month" will be charged on the amounts that go overdue.

The term "2/10" contains information about the cash discount and the discount period. It means that a 2% discount is given for payments made in the first 10 days. In other words, "10 days" is the time within which payments will be qualified for cash discounts of 2%.

On this invoice, there is no additional code after the net period ("n/30"). This means that the invoice has **ordinary dating,** by which the credit period and the discount period start on the date of the invoice. There may be two other notations: ROG—receipt of goods; and EOM—end of month.

- If the terms of payment were stated as "2/10, n/30, ROG," it would mean that both the credit period and the discount period will start on the date when goods are received by buyer.
- If the terms of payment were stated as "2/10, n/30, EOM," it would mean that the credit period and the discount period will start at the end of the month (the last day of the month).

This means that if North Shore Community College Bookstore pays the invoice within 10 days, it may deduct 2% from the net price before adding the prepaid shipping charge (FOB shipping point). The cheque below the invoice (Figure 9.3) shows that the bookstore paid McGraw-Hill Ryerson Ltd. $3,114.72.

Invoice total (net)	$2,689.57	
Less cash discount	− 53.79	(.02 × 2,689.57)
Plus HST	+ 403.44	
Plus shipment	+ 75.50	
	$3,114.72	

Cash Discounts

In the McGraw-Hill Ryerson Ltd. invoice, the bookstore received a cash discount of $53.79. This amount is determined by the **terms of the sale,** which include the credit period, cash discount, discount period, and freight terms.

Please note that cash discounts apply to pre-GST amounts. GST calculated on the original invoice amount is the amount that must be remitted if the customer decides to take advantage of the cash discount.

In the province of Ontario, the PST is adjusted to reflect the amount of PST applicable on the discounted amount of the invoice.

Before we discuss how to calculate cash discounts, let's look at some aids that will help you calculate credit **due dates** and **end of credit periods.**

Aids in Calculating Credit Due Dates

Sellers usually give credit for 30, 60, or 90 days. Not all months of the year have 30 days. So you must count the credit days from the date of the invoice. The trick is to remember the number of days in each month. You can choose one of the following three options to help you do this.

Years divisible by 4 are leap years. Leap years occur in 2004 and 2008.

Option 1: Days-in-a-Month Rule You may already know this rule. Remember that every four years is a leap year.

> Thirty days has September, April, June, and November; all the rest have 31 except February has 28, and 29 in leap years.

Option 2: Knuckle Months Some people like to use the knuckles on their hands to remember which months have 30 or 31 days. Note in the following diagram that each knuckle represents a month with 31 days. The short months are in between the knuckles.

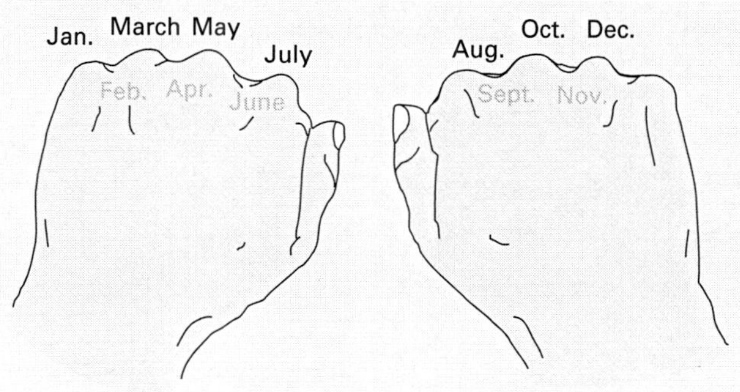

31 days: Jan., March, May, July, Aug., Oct., Dec.

Option 3: Days-in-a-Year Calendar The days-in-a-year calendar (excluding leap year) is another tool to help you calculate dates for discount and credit periods (Table 9.1). For example, let's use Table 9.1 to calculate 90 days from August 12.

EXAMPLE

By Table 9.1: August 12 = 224 days
+ 90
314 days

Search for day 314 in Table 9.1. You will find that day 314 is November 10. In this example, we stayed within the same year. Now let's try an example in which we overlap from year to year.

EXAMPLE

What date is 80 days after December 5?

Table 9.1 shows that December 5 is 339 days from the beginning of the year. Subtracting 339 from 365 (the end of the year) tells us that we have used up 26 days by the end of the year. This leaves 54 days in the new year. Go back in the table and start with the beginning of the year and search for 54 (80 − 26) days. The 54th day is February 23.

By table

365 days in year
− 339 days until December 5
26 days used in year

80 days from December 5
− 26 days used in year
54 days in new year or February 23

Without use of table

December 31
− December 5
26
+ 31 days in January
57
+ 23 due date (February 23)
80 total days

When you know how to calculate credit due dates, you can understand the common business terms sellers offer buyers involving discounts and credit periods. Remember that discount and credit terms vary from one seller to another.

Common Credit Terms Offered by Sellers

The common credit terms sellers offer buyers include *ordinary dating, receipt of goods (ROG),* and *end of month (EOM).* In this section we examine these credit terms. To determine the due dates, we used the days-in-a-year calendar (Table 9.1).

Ordinary Dating

Today, businesses frequently use the ordinary dating method. It gives the buyer a cash discount period that begins with the invoice date. The credit terms of two common ordinary dating methods are 2/10, n/30, and 2/10, 1/15, n/30.

2/10, n/30 Ordinary Dating Method The 2/10, n/30 is read "two ten, net thirty." Buyers can take a 2% cash discount off the gross amount of the invoice if they pay the bill within 10 days from the invoice date. If buyers miss the discount period, the net amount—without a discount—is due between day 11 and day 30. *Freight, returned goods, sales tax, and trade discounts must be subtracted from the gross before calculating a cash discount.*

EXAMPLE

$400 invoice dated July 5: terms 2/10, n/30; no freight; paid on July 11.

STEP 1. Calculate end of 2% discount period:

July 5 date of invoice
+ 10 days
July 15 end of 2% discount period

STEP 2. Calculate end of credit period:

July 5 by Table 9.1 → 186 days
+ 30
216 days

Search in Table 9.1 for 216 → August 4 → end of credit period

STEP 3. Calculate payment on July 11:

.02 × \$400 = \$8 cash discount
\$400 − \$8 = \$392 paid

> *Note:* A 2% cash discount means that you save 2 cents on the dollar and pay 98 cents on the dollar. Thus, \$.98 × \$400 = \$392.

TABLE 9–1
DAYS-IN-A-YEAR CALENDAR (EXCLUDING LEAP YEAR)

Day of month	31 Jan.	28 Feb.	31 Mar.	30 Apr.	31 May	30 June	31 July	31 Aug.	30 Sept.	31 Oct.	30 Nov.	31 Dec.
1	1	32	60	91	121	152	182	213	244	274	305	335
2	2	33	61	92	122	153	183	214	245	275	306	336
3	3	34	62	93	123	154	184	215	246	276	307	337
4	4	35	63	94	124	155	185	216	247	277	308	338
5	5	36	64	95	125	156	186	217	248	278	309	339
6	6	37	65	96	126	157	187	218	249	279	310	340
7	7	38	66	97	127	158	188	219	250	280	311	341
8	8	39	67	98	128	159	189	220	251	281	312	342
9	9	40	68	99	129	160	190	221	252	282	313	343
10	10	41	69	100	130	161	191	222	253	283	314	344
11	11	42	70	101	131	162	192	223	254	284	315	345
12	12	43	71	102	132	163	193	224	255	285	316	346
13	13	44	72	103	133	164	194	225	256	286	317	347
14	14	45	73	104	134	165	195	226	257	287	318	348
15	15	46	74	105	135	166	196	227	258	288	319	349
16	16	47	75	106	136	167	197	228	259	289	320	350
17	17	48	76	107	137	168	198	229	260	290	321	351
18	18	49	77	108	138	169	199	230	261	291	322	352
19	19	50	78	109	139	170	200	231	262	292	323	353
20	20	51	79	110	140	171	201	232	263	293	324	354
21	21	52	80	111	141	172	202	233	264	294	325	355
22	22	53	81	112	142	173	203	234	265	295	326	356
23	23	54	82	113	143	174	204	235	266	296	327	357
24	24	55	83	114	144	175	205	236	267	297	328	358
25	25	56	84	115	145	176	206	237	268	298	329	359
26	26	57	85	116	146	177	207	238	269	299	330	360
27	27	58	86	117	147	178	208	239	270	300	331	361
28	28	59	87	118	148	179	209	240	271	301	332	362
29	29	—	88	119	149	180	210	241	272	302	333	363
30	30	—	89	120	150	181	211	242	273	303	334	364
31	31	—	90	—	151	—	212	243	—	304	—	365

The following time line illustrates the 2/10, n/30, ordinary dating method beginning and ending dates of the above example:

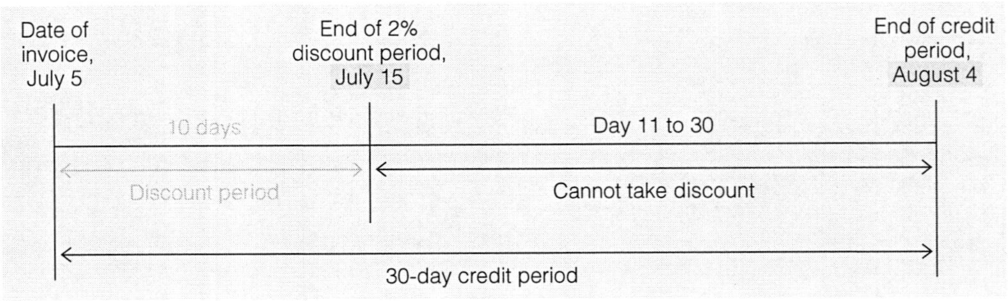

2/10, 1/15, n/30 Ordinary Dating Method The 2/10, 1/15, n/30 is read "two ten, one fifteen, net thirty." The seller will give buyers a 2% (2 cents on the dollar) cash discount if they pay within 10 days of the invoice date. If buyers pay between day 11 and day 15 from the date of the invoice, they can save 1 cent on the dollar. If buyers do not pay on day 15, the net or full amount is due 30 days from the invoice date.

EXAMPLE

$600 invoice dated May 8; $100 of freight included in invoice price; paid on May 22.

STEP 1. Calculate the end of the 2% discount period:

May 8 date of invoice
+ 10 days
May 18 end of 2% discount period

STEP 2. Calculate end of 1% discount period:

May 18 end of 2% discount period
+ 5 days
May 23 end of 1% discount period

STEP 3. Calculate end of credit period:

May 8 by Table 9.1 → 128 days
+ 30
158 days

Search in Table 9.1 for 158 → June 7 → end of credit period

STEP 4. Calculate payment on May 22 (14 days after date of invoice):

$600 invoice
− 100 freight
$500
× .01
$5.00
$500 − $5.00 + $100 freight = $595

A 1% discount means we pay $.99 on the dollar or
$500 × $.99 = $495 + $100 freight = $595.
Note: Freight is added back since no cash discount is taken on freight.

The following time line illustrates the 2/10, 1/15, n/30 ordinary dating method beginning and ending dates of the above example:

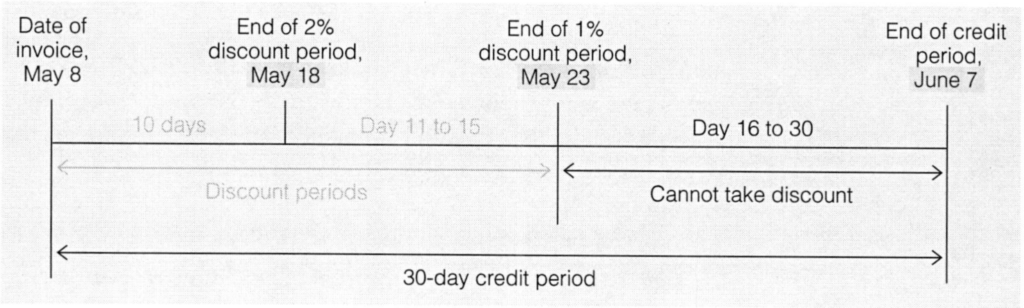

Receipt of Goods (ROG)

3/10, n/30 ROG With the **receipt of goods (ROG),** the cash discount period begins when buyer receives goods, *not* the invoice date. Industry often uses the ROG terms when buyers cannot expect delivery until a long time after they place the order. Buyers can take a 3% discount within 10 days *after* receipt of goods. Full amount is due between day 11 and day 30 if cash discount period is missed.

EXAMPLE

$900 invoice dated May 9; no freight or returned goods; the goods were received on July 8; terms 3/10, n/30 ROG; payment made on July 20.

STEP 1. Calculate the end of the 3% discount period:

July 8 date goods arrive
+ 10 days
July 18 end of 3% discount period

STEP 2. Calculate the end of the credit period:

July 8 by Table 9.1
+ 189 days
+ 30
219 days

Search in Table 9.1 for 219 → August 7 → end of credit period

STEP 3. Calculate payment on July 20:

Missed discount period and paid net or full amount of $900.

The following time line illustrates 3/10, n/30 ROG beginning and ending dates of the above example:

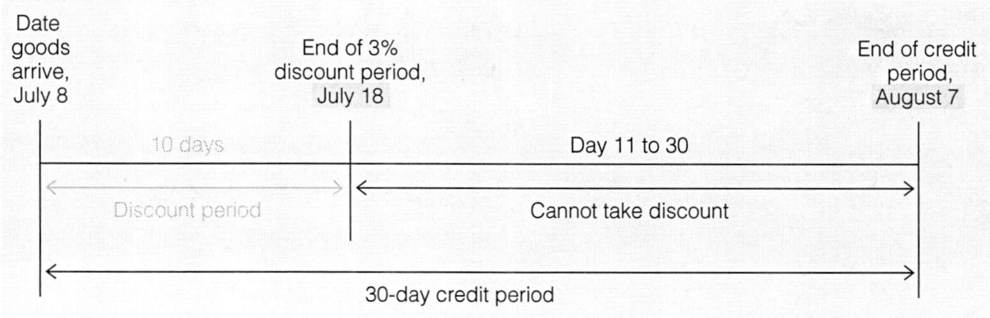

End of Month (EOM)

In this section we look at terms involving **end of month (EOM).**[3] If an invoice is dated the *25th or earlier* of a month, we follow one set of rules. If an invoice is dated after the 25th of the month, a new set of rules is followed. Let's look at each situation.

Invoice Dated 25th or Earlier in Month, 1/10 EOM If sellers date an invoice on the 25th or earlier in the month, buyers can take the cash discount if they pay the invoice by the first 10 days of the month following the sale (next month). If buyers miss the discount period, the full amount is due within 20 days after the end of the discount period.

EXAMPLE

$600 invoice dated July 6; no freight or returns; terms 1/10 EOM; paid on August 8.

STEP 1. Calculate the end of the 1% discount period:

August 10 ← First 10 days of month following sale

STEP 2. Calculate the end of the credit period:

August 10
+ 20 days
August 30 → Credit period is 20 days after discount period.

STEP 3. Calculate payment on August 8:

$.99 \times \$600 =$ $594

The following time line illustrates the beginning and ending dates of the EOM invoice of the above example:

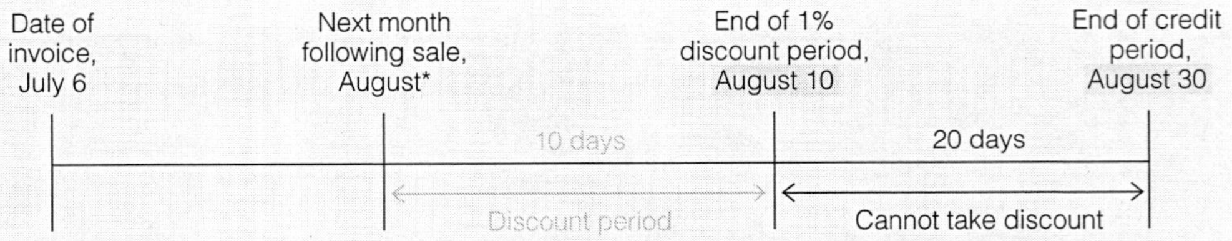

*Even though the discount period begins with the next month following the sale, if buyers wish, they can pay before the discount period (date of invoice until the discount period).

Invoice Dated After 25th of Month, 2/10 EOM When sellers sell goods *after* the 25th of the month, buyers gain an additional month. The cash discount period ends on the 10th day of the second month that follows the sale. Why? This occurs because the seller guarantees the 15 days' credit of the buyer. If a buyer bought goods on August 29, September 10 would be only 12 days. So the buyer gets the extra month.

EXAMPLE

$800 invoice dated April 29; no freight or returned goods; terms 2/10 EOM; payment made on June 18.

STEP 1. Calculate the end of the 2% discount period:

June 10 ← First 10 days of second month following sale

STEP 2. Calculate the end of the credit period:

June 10
+ 20 days
June 30 ← Credit period is 20 days after discount period.

STEP 3. Calculate the payment on June 18:

No discount; $800 paid.

[3]Sometimes the Latin term *proximo* is used. Other variations of EOM exist, but the key point is that the seller guarantees the buyer 15 days' credit. We assume a 30-day month.

The following time line illustrates the beginning and ending dates of the EOM invoice of the above example:

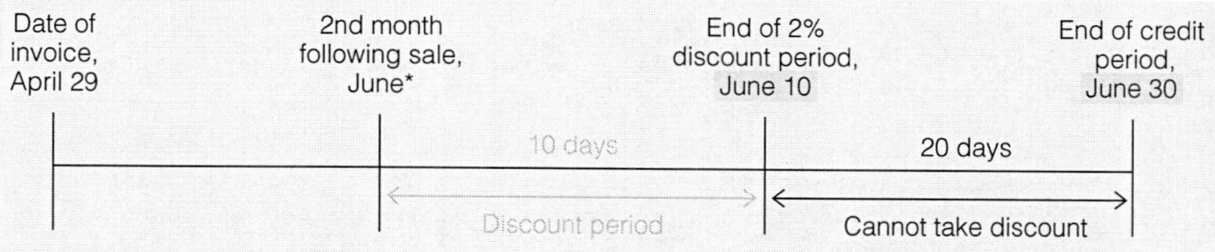

*Even though the discount period begins with the second month following the sale, if buyers wish, they can pay before the discount date (date of invoice until the discount period)

SOLVING A WORD PROBLEM WITH TRADE AND CASH DISCOUNT

Now that we have studied trade and cash discounts, let's look at a combination that involves both a trade and a cash discount.

THE WORD PROBLEM Hardy Company sent Regan Corporation an invoice for office equipment with a $10,000 list price. Hardy dated the invoice July 29 with terms of 2/10 EOM (end of month). Regan receives a 30% trade discount and paid the invoice on September 6. Since terms were FOB destination, Regan paid no freight charge. What was the cost of office equipent for Regan?

THE FACTS	SOLVING FOR?	STEPS TO TAKE	KEY POINTS
List price: $10,000. *Trade discount rate:* 30%. *Terms:* 2/10 EOM. *Invoice date:* 7/29. *Date paid:* 9/6.	Cost of office equipment.	Net price = List price × Complement of trade discount rate After 25th of month for EOM. Discount period is 1st 10 days of second month that follows sale.	Trade discounts are deducted before cash discounts are taken. Cash discounts are not taken on freight or returns.

STEPS TO SOLVING PROBLEM

1. Calculate the net price. $10,000 × .70 = $7,000 (100% − 30% (trade discount))

2. Calculate the discount period. Sale: 7/29 Month 1: Aug. Month 2: Sept. 10 Paid on Sept. 6—is entitled to 2% off.

3. Calculate the cost of office equipment. $7,000 × .98 = **$6,860** (100% − 2%) If you save 2 cents on a dollar, you are spending 98 cents.

PARTIAL PAYMENTS

Often buyers cannot pay the entire invoice before the end of the discount period. In this case they pay amounts available, which are smaller than the total amount due. Such payments are called *partial payments.* Partial payments are eligible for cash discounts, when they are paid within the discount period. Amounts credited to customer's account will be bigger than the amounts paid and may be calculated using this formula:

$$\text{Amount credited} = \frac{\text{Amount paid}}{(1 - d)}$$

$$\text{Cr} = \frac{P}{(1 - d)} \qquad \textbf{(9.8)}$$

Amounts paid within the discount period will be smaller than amounts credited to the customer's account and can be calculated using this formula:

$$P = \text{Cr} \times (1 - d) \quad (9.9)$$

The outstanding balance is the difference between the balance at the beginning of the transaction B_i and the amount credited:

$$B_o = B_i - \text{Cr} \quad (9.10)$$

Partial payments and outstanding balance may be also calculated by using the following steps:

CALCULATING PARTIAL PAYMENTS AND OUTSTANDING BALANCE

Step 1. Calculate the complement of a discount rate.
Step 2. Divide partial payments by the complement of a discount rate (Step 1). This gives the amount credited.
Step 3. Subtract Step 2 from the total owed. This is the outstanding balance.

EXAMPLE

Molly McGrady owed $400. Molly's terms were 2/10, n/30. Within 10 days, Molly sent a cheque for $80. The actual credit the buyer gave Molly is as follows:

STEP 1. 100% − 2% = 98% → .98

STEP 2. $\frac{\$80}{.98} = \$81.63$ $\qquad \frac{\$80}{1 - .02}$ ← Discount rate

STEP 3.
$400.00
− 81.63 partial payment—although sent in $80
$318.37 outstanding balance

Note: We do not multiply .02 × $80 because the seller did not base the original discount on $80. When Molly makes a payment within the 10-day discount period, 98 cents pays each $1 she owes. Before buyers take discounts on partial payments, they must have permission from the seller. Not all businesses allow partial payments.

To solve problems with several partial payments, the data may be arranged in a table like that shown in Figure 9.5. (Please note that the cash discount applies to pre-PST amounts.)

FIGURE 9–5

#	Invoice amount (amount due)	Cash discounts applicable	Amount paid $P = \text{Cr}(1-d)$	Amount credited $\text{Cr} = P/(1-d)$	Outstanding balance (2) − (5)
1	2	3	4	5	6

EXAMPLE

Tukmandu Supplies Inc. received an invoice from Johne Meer's Ltd. dated June 4, 2003 for $12,785 with the terms 3/10, 2/15, 1/20, n/30.

Tukmandu Supplies paid $4,000 on June 9, 2003 and $2,000 on June 19, 2003. How much is the outstanding balance after the third payment on June 24, 2003, for which Tukmandu Supplies were credited $1,500?

Start solving the problem by sorting the data and filling in the table (question marks stand for the final answer):

#	Invoice amount (amount due)	Terms and cash discounts applicable	Amount paid $P = \text{Cr}(1-d)$	Amount credited $\text{Cr} = P/(1-d)$	Outstanding balance (2) − (5)
1	2	3	4	5	6
1.	$12,785	3/10, 2/15, 1/20, n/30			$12,785
2.	$12,785		$4,000		
3.			$2,000		
4.				$1,500	?
5.	?				

In order to solve the problem and fill in the blanks in the table, it is necessary to ask yourself the following questions:

1. Were the first and second payments made in the discount periods?
2. If yes, what discounts were applicable?
3. What amounts were credited to the account after each of the first two payments?
4. What are the outstanding balances after the first two payments?
5. Was the third payment eligible for a discount?
6. What was the amount paid on June 24, 2003?
7. What is the outstanding balance after the last payment?

Here is how you might fill in the blanks in the table by answering those questions:

1. The first payment was made on June 9, 2003, within 5 days of the invoice date. The second payment was made within 15 days and is also eligible for a discount.
2. The first payment is eligible for a 3% discount and the second one for a 2% discount.
3. To define amounts credited, use formula 9.8:

   $Cr_1 = 4{,}000/(1 - .03) = \$4{,}123.71$

   $Cr_2 = \$2{,}000/(1 - .02) = \$2{,}040.82$
4. To define the outstanding balance after each payment, subtract the amount credited from the amount indicated in column 2:

   $B_1 = \$12{,}785 - \$4{,}123.71 = \$8{,}661.29$

   $B_2 = \$8{,}661.29 - \$2{,}040.82 = \$6{,}620.47$
5. The third payment was made on the 20th day from the date of invoice, so it was eligible for a 1% discount.
6. The amount credited was \$1,500, so to find the amount of payment use formula 9.9.

   $P = Cr(1 - d) = \$1{,}500\ (1 - .01) = \$1{,}485$
7. The outstanding balance after all three payments is:

   $\$6{,}620.47 - \$1{,}500 = \$5{,}120.47$

#	Invoice amount (amount due)	Terms and cash discounts applicable	Amount paid $P = Cr\ (1-d)$	Amount credited $Cr = P/(1-d)$	Outstanding balance (2)–(5)
1	2	3	4	5	6
1.	$12,785	3/10, 2/15, 1/20, n/30			$12,785
2.	$12,785	3%, $d_1 = .03$	$4,000	$4,123.71	$8,661.29
3.	$8,661.29	2%, $d_2 = .02$	$2,000	$2,040.82	$6,620.47
4.	$6,620.47	1%, $d_3 = .01$	$1,485	$1,500	$5,5120.47
5.	$5,120.47				

Tukmandu Supplies must pay \$5,120.47 to close the account.

How much money did Tukmandu Supplies save by paying within the discount periods?

Total amount paid: \$4,000 + \$2,000 + \$1,485 = \$7,485

Total amount credited: \$4,123.71 + \$2,040.82 + \$1,500 = \$7,664.53

Total savings = Total amount credited − Total amount paid

Tukmandu Supplies saved: \$179.53 (\$7,664.53 − \$7,485)

LU 9–2 PRACTICE QUIZ

Complete the following table:

	Date of invoice	Date goods received	Terms	Last day* of discount period	End of credit period
1.	July 6		2/10, n/30		
2.	February 19	June 9	3/10, n/30 ROG		
3.	May 9		4/10, 1/30, n/60		
4.	May 12		2/10 EOM		
5.	May 29		2/10 EOM		

*If more than one discount, assume date of last discount.

6. Metro Corporation sent Vasko Corporation an invoice for equipment with an $8,000 list price. Metro dated the invoice May 26. Terms were 2/10 EOM. Vasco receives a 20% trade discount and paid the invoice on June 3. What was the cost of equipment for Vasko?
7. Complete amount to be credited and balance outstanding:
   Amount of invoice: $600
   Terms: 2/10, 1/15, n/30
   Date of invoice: September 30
   Paid October 3: $400

CHAPTER ORGANIZER AND REFERENCE GUIDE

Topic	Key point, procedure, formula	Example(s) to illustrate situation
Trade discount amount, p. 196	Trade discount amount = List price × Trade discount rate $D_t = L \times d$ (9.1)	$600 list price 30% trade discount rate Trade discount amount = $600 × .30 = $180
Calculating net price, p. 197	Net price = List price − Trade discount amount $N = L - D_t$ (9.2) or List price × Complement of trade discount price $N = L \times (1 - d)$ (9.3)	$600 list price 30% trade discount rate Net price = $600 × .70 = $420 1.00 − .30 .70
Freight, p. 198	FOB shipping point—buyer pays freight. FOB destination—seller pays freight.	Moose Company of Calgary sells equipment to Agee Company of Manitoba. Terms of shipping are FOB Calgary. Agee pays cost of freight since terms are FOB shipping point.
Calculating list price when net price and trade discount rate are known, p. 200	List price = Net price / Complement of trade discount rate $L = \frac{N}{(1 - d)}$ (9.4)	40% trade discount rate Net price, $120 $\frac{\$120}{.60}$ = $200 list price .60 ← (1 − .40)
Chain discounts, p. 200	Successively lower base	d_1 = 5% and d_2 = 10% on a $100 list item: $ 100 × .05 = $ 5.00; $ 95 × .10 = $9.50 (running balance) $95.00 − 9.50 = $85.50 net price

(*continues*)

CHAPTER ORGANIZER AND REFERENCE GUIDE (CONTINUED)

TOPIC	KEY POINT, PROCEDURE, FORMULA	EXAMPLE(S) TO ILLUSTRATE SITUATION
Net price equivalent rate, p. 201	$\text{Actual cost to buyer} = \text{List price} \times \text{Net price equivalent rate}$ $N = L \times (1 - d_1)(1 - d_2)(1 - d_3)$ (9.5) Take complement of each chain discount and multiply—do not round. $\text{Trade discount amount} = \text{List price} - \text{Actual cost to buyer}$ $D_t = L - N$	Given: $d_1 = 5\%$ and $d_2 = 10\%$ on \$1,000 list price Take complement: $.95 \times .90 = .855$ (net price equivalent) $\$1,000 \times .855 =$ **\$855** (actual cost or net price) \$1,000 − 855 \$ 145 trade discount amount
Equivalent discount rate, p. 202	$d_e = 1 - (1 - d_1)(1 - d_2)(1 - d_3)$ (9.6)	$d_1 = 5\%, d_2 = 10\%, d_e = ?$ $d_e = 1 - .95 \times .9 = 1 - .145 = .855$
Single equivalent discount rate, p. 202	$\text{Trade discount amount} = \text{List price} \times \text{1 − Net price equivalent rate}$ $D_t = L \times d_e$	See preceding example for facts: $1 - .855 = .145$ $.145 \times \$1,000 =$ **\$145**
Cash discounts, p. 205	Cash discounts, due to prompt payment, are not taken on freight, returns, etc.	Gross \$1,000 (includes freight) Freight \$25 Terms, 2/10, n/30 Returns \$25 Purchased: Sept. 9; paid Sept. 15 Cash discount = $\$950 \times .02 =$ **\$19**
Calculating due dates, p. 205	*Option 1:* Thirty days has September, April, June, and November; all the rest have 31 except February has 28, and 29 in leap years. *Option 2:* Knuckles—31-day month; in between knuckles are short months. *Option 3:* Days-in-a-year table.	Invoice \$500 on March 5; terms 2/10, n/30. March 5 +10 *End of discount period:* → **March 15** *End of credit period by Table 9.1:* March 5 = 64 days + 30 → 94 days Search in Table 9.1 → **April 4**
Common terms of sale:		
a. Ordinary dating, p. 206	Discount period begins from date of invoice. Credit period ends 20 days from the end of the discount period unless otherwise stipulated; for example, 2/10, n/60—the credit period ends 50 days from end of discount period.	Invoice \$600 (freight of \$100 included in price) dated March 8; payment on March 16; 3/10, n/30. March 8 + 10 *End of discount period:* → **March 18** *End of credit period by Table 9.1:* March 8 = 67 days + 30 → 97 days Search in Table 9.1 → **April 7** *If paid on March 16:* $.97 \times \$500 = \$485$ + 100 freight \$585
b. Receipt of goods (ROG), p. 209	Discount period begins when goods are received. Credit period ends 20 days from end of discount period.	4/10, n/30, ROG. \$600 invoice; no freight; dated August 5; goods received October 2, payment made October 20. October 2 +10 *End of discount period:* → **October 12**

(*continues*)

CHAPTER ORGANIZER AND REFERENCE GUIDE (CONCLUDED)

Topic	Key point, procedure, formula	Example(s) to illustrate situation
		End of credit period by Table 9.1: October 2 = 275 + 30 = 305 Search in Table 9.1 → November 1 *Payment on October 20:* No discount, pay $600
c. End of month (EOM), p. 210	On or before 25th of the month, discount period is 10 days after month following sale. After 25th of the month, an additional month is gained. $Cr = \frac{P}{(1-d)}$ (9.10)	$1,000 invoice dated May 12; no freight or returns; terms 2/10 EOM. *End of discount period* → June 10 *End of credit period* → June 30
Partial payments, p. 211	$\text{Amount credited} = \frac{\text{Partial payment}}{1 - \text{Discount rate}}$ $P = Cr(1 - d)$ (9.9) To solve problems with several partial payments the data may be arranged in the following table:	$200 invoice, terms 2/10, n/30, dated March 2, paid $100 on March 5. $\frac{\$100}{1-.02} = \frac{\$100}{.98} = \$102.04$

#	Invoice amount (amount due)	Terms and cash discounts applicable	Amount paid $P = Cr(1-d)$	Amount credited $Cr = P/(1-d)$	Outstanding balance (2)−(5)
1	2	3	4	5	6

Key terms

Cash discount, p. 196
Chain discounts, p. 201
Complement, p. 199
Credit period, p. 203
Discount period, p. 204
Due dates, p. 205
End of credit period, p. 205
End of month (EOM), p. 210
FOB destination, p. 198
FOB shipping point, p. 198
Freight terms, p. 198
Invoice, p. 196
List price, p. 196
Net price, p. 197
Net price equivalent rate, p. 201
Ordinary dating, p. 204
Receipt of goods (ROG), p. 209
Series discounts, p. 201
Single equivalent discount rate, p. 202
Single trade discount, p. 199
Terms of payment, p. 204
Terms of the sale, p. 205
Trade discount, p. 196
Trade discount amount, p. 196
Trade discount rate, p. 197

CRITICAL THINKING DISCUSSION QUESTIONS

1. What is the net price? June Long bought a jacket from a catalogue company. She took her trade discount off the original price plus freight. What is wrong with June's approach? Who would benefit from June's approach—the buyer or the seller?
2. How do you calculate the list price when the net price and trade discount rate are known? A publisher tells the bookstore its net price of a book along with a suggested trade discount of 20%. The bookstore uses a 25%-of-list-price discount rate. Is this ethical when textbook prices are rising?
3. Explain FOB shipping point and FOB destination. Think back to your last major purchase. Was it FOB shipping point or FOB destination? Did you get a trade or a cash discount?
4. What are the steps to calculate the net price equivalent rate? Why is the net price equivalent rate *not* rounded?
5. What are the steps to calculate the single equivalent discount rate? Is this rate off the list or net price? Explain why this calculation of a single equivalent discount rate may not always be needed.
6. What is the difference between a discount and credit period? Are all cash discounts taken before trade discounts. Agree or disagree? Why?
7. Explain the following credit terms of sale:
   a. 2/10, n/30
   b. 3/10, n/30 ROG
   c. 1/10 EOM (on or before 25th of month)
   d. 1/10 EOM (after 25th of month)
8. Explain how to calculate a partial payment. Whom does a partial payment favour—the buyer or the seller?

END-OF-CHAPTER PROBLEMS

DRILL PROBLEMS

For all problems, round your final answer to the nearest cent. Do not round net price equivalent rates or single equivalent discount rates.

Complete the following:

	Item	List price	Chain discount	Net price equivalent rate (in decimals)	Single equivalent discount rate (in decimals)	Trade discount	Net price
9–1.	Sony Playstation	$399	7/2				
9–2.	DVD player	$349	20/10/10				
9–3.	IBM scanner	$269	7/3/1				

Complete the following:

	Item	List price	Chain discount	Net price	Trade discount
9–4.	Trotter treadmill	$3,000	9/4		
9–5.	Maytag dishwasher	$450	8/5/6		
9–6.	Hewlett-Packard scanner	$320	3/5/9		
9–7.	Land Rover roofrack	$1,850	12/9/6		

9–8. Which of the following companies, A or B, gives a higher discount? Use the single equivalent discount rate to make your choice (convert your equivalent rate to the nearest hundredth percent).
Excel

Company A	**Company B**
8/10/15/3	10/6/16/5

Complete the following:

	Invoice	Dates when goods received	Terms	Last day* of discount period	Final day bill is due (end of credit period)
9–9.	June 18		1/10, n/30		
9–10.	Nov. 27		2/10 EOM		
9–11.	May 15	June 5	3/10, n/30, ROG		
9–12.	April 10		2/10, 1/30, n/60		
9–13.	June 12		3/10 EOM		
9–14.	Jan. 10	Feb. 3 (no leap year)	4/10, n/30, ROG		

*If more than one discount, assume date of last discount.

Complete the following by calculating the cash discount and net amount paid:

	Gross amount of invoice (freight charge already included)	Freight charge	Date of invoice	Terms of invoice	Date of payment	Cash discount	Net amount paid
9–15.	$7,000	$100	4/8	2/10, n/60	4/15		
9–16.	$600	None	8/1	3/10, 2/15, n/30	8/13		
9–17.	$200	None	11/13	1/10 EOM	12/3		
9–18.	$500	$100	11/29	1/10 EOM	1/4		

Complete the following:

	Amount of invoice	Terms	Invoice date	Actual partial payment made	Date of partial payment	Amount of payment to be credited	Balance outstanding
9–19.	$700	2/10, n/60	5/6	$400	5/15		
9–20.	$600	4/10, n/60	7/5	$400	7/14		

ADDITIONAL DRILL PROBLEMS

9–21. Calculate the trade discount amount for each of the following items:

	Item	List price	Trade discount	Trade discount amount
a.	Gateway	$1,200	40%	
b.	Flat screen TV	$1,200	30%	
c.	Suit	$500	10%	
d.	Bicycle	$800	$12\frac{1}{2}\%$	
e.	David Yurman bracelet	$950	40%	

9–22. Calculate the net price for each of the following items:

	Item	List price	Trade discount amount	Net price
a.	Home Depot table	$600	$250	
b.	Bookcase	$525	$129	
c.	Rocking chair	$480	$95	

9–23. Fill in the missing amount for each of the following items:

	Item	List price	Trade discount amount	Net price
a.	Sears electric saw		$19	$56
b.	Electric drill	$90		$68.50
c.	Ladder	$56	$15.25	

9–24. For each of the following, find the percent paid (complement of trade discount) and the net price:

	List price	Trade discount	Percent paid	Net price
a.	$45	15%		
b.	$195	12.2%		
c.	$325	50%		
d.	$120	18%		

9–25. In each of the following examples, find the net price equivalent rate and the single equivalent discount rate:

	Chain discount	Net price equivalent rate	Single equivalent discount rate
a.	25/5		
b.	15/15		
c.	15/10/5		
d.	12/12/6		

9–26. In each of the following examples, find the net price and the trade discount:

	List price	Chain discount	Net price	Trade discount
a.	$5,000	10/10/5		
b.	$7,500	9/6/3		
c.	$898	20/7/2		
d.	$1,500	25/10		

In the following problems, all prices are quoted before taxes.

9–27. The list price of a handheld calculator is $19.50, and the trade discount is 18%. Find the trade discount amount.

9–28. The list price of a silver picture frame is $29.95, and the trade discount is 15%. Find the trade discount amount and the net price.

9–29. The net price of a set of pots and pans is $65, and the trade discount is 20%. What is the list price?

9–30. Jennie's Variety Store has the opportunity to purchase candy from three different wholesalers; each of the wholesalers offers a different chain discount. Company A offers 25/5/5, Company B offers 20/10/5, and Company C offers 15/20. Which company should Jennie deal with? *Hint:* Choose the company with the highest single equivalent discount rate.

9–31. The list price of a television set is $625. Find the net price after a series discount of 30/20/10.

9–32. Mandy's Accessories Shop purchased 12 purses with a total list price of $726. What was the net price of each purse if the wholesaler offered a chain discount of 25/20?

9–33. Kransberg Furniture Store purchased a bedroom set for $1,097.25 from Furniture Wholesalers. The list price of the set was $1,995. What trade discount rate did Kransberg receive?

9–34. Susan Monk teaches second grade and receives a discount at the local art supply store. Recently she paid $47.25 for art supplies after receiving a chain discount of 30/10. What was the regular price of the art supplies?

9–35. Complete the following table:

	Date of invoice	Date goods received	Terms	Last day of discount period	End of credit period
a.	February 8		2/10, n/30		
b.	August 26		2/10, n/30		
c.	October 17		3/10, n/60		
d.	March 11	May 10	3/10, n/30, ROG		
e.	September 14		2/10, EOM		
f.	May 31		2/10, EOM		

9–36. Calculate the cash discount and the net amount paid.

	Invoice amount	Cash discount rate	Discount amount	Net amount paid
a.	$75	3%		
b.	$1,559	2%		
c.	$546.25	2%		
d.	$9,788.75	1%		

9–37. Use the complement of the cash discount to calculate the net amount paid. Assume all invoices are paid within the discount period.

	Terms of invoice	Amount of invoice	Complement	Net amount paid
a.	2/10, n/30	$1,125		
b.	3/10, n/30 ROG	$4,500		
c.	2/10, EOM	$375.50		
d.	1/15, n/45	$3,998		

9–38. Calculate the amount of cash discount and the net amount paid.

	Date of invoice	Terms of invoice	Amount of invoice	Date paid	Cash discount	Amount paid
a.	January 12	2/10, n/30	$5,320	January 22		
b.	May 28	2/10, n/30	$975	June 7		
c.	August 15	2/10, n/30	$7,700	August 26		
d.	March 8	2/10, EOM	$480	April 10		
e.	January 24	3/10, n/60	$1,225	February 3		

9–39. Complete the following table:

	Total invoice	Freight charges included in invoice total	Date of invoice	Terms of invoice	Date of payment	Cash discount	Amount paid
a.	$852	$12.50	3/19	2/10, n/30	3/29		
b.	$669.57	$15.63	7/28	3/10, EOM	9/10		
c.	$500	$11.50	4/25	2/10, n/60	6/5		
d.	$188	$9.70	1/12	2/10, EOM	2/10		

9–40. In the following table, assume that all the partial payments were made within the discount period.

	Amount of invoice	Terms of invoice	Partial payment	Amount to be credited	Balance outstanding
a.	$481.90	2/10, n/30	$90		
b.	$1,000	2/10, EOM	$500		
c.	$782.88	3/10, n/30, ROG	$275		
d.	$318.80	2/15, n/60	$200		

WORD PROBLEMS (ROUND TO NEAREST CENT AS NEEDED)

9–41. The list price of a Fossil watch is $120.95. Jim O'Sullivan receives a trade discount of 40%. Find the trade discount amount and the net price.

9–42. A Radio Shack digital camera lists for $699 with a trade discount of 20%. What is the net price of the camera?

9–43. The November 2000 issue of *Business Horizons* featured an article titled "Discovering Hidden Pricing Power." Sharper Image Company asked for and received a discount from its suppliers. The discount was in the form of a $750 rebate. If Sharper Image Company placed an order of $7,650, what percent discount did they receive? Round to the nearest hundredth percent.

9–44. Levin Furniture buys a living room set with a $4,000 list price and a 55% trade discount. Freight (FOB shipping point) of $50 is not part of the list price. What is the delivered price (including freight) of the living room set, assuming a cash discount of 2/10, n/30, ROG? The invoice had an April 8 date. Levin received the goods on April 19 and paid the invoice on April 25.

9–45. A manufacturer of skateboards offered a 5/2/1 chain discount to many customers. Bob's Sporting Goods ordered 20 skateboards for a total $625 list price. What was the net price of the skateboards? What was the trade discount amount?

9–46. Home Depot wants to buy a new line of shortwave radios. Manufacturer A offers a 21/13 chain discount. Manufacturer B offers a 26/8 chain discount. Both manufacturers have the same list price. What manufacturer should Home Depot buy from?

9–47. Maplewood Supply received a $5,250 invoice dated 4/15/00. The $5,250 included $250 freight. Terms were 4/10, 3/30, n/60. **(a)** If Maplewood pays the invoice on April 27, what will it pay? **(b)** If Maplewood pays the invoice on May 21, what will it pay?

9–48. Sport Authority ordered 50 pairs of tennis shoes from Nike Corporation. The shoes were priced at $85 for each pair with the following terms: 4/10, 2/30, n/60. The invoice was dated October 15. Sports Authority sent in a payment on October 28. What should have been the amount of the cheque?

9–49. Macy of New York sold Marriott of Chicago office equipment with a $6,000 list price. Sale terms were 3/10, n/30 FOB New York. Macy agreed to prepay the $30 freight. Marriott pays the invoice within the discount period. What does Marriott pay Macy?

9–50. Royal Furniture bought a sofa for $800. The sofa had a $1,400 list price. What was the trade discount rate Royal received? Round to the nearest hundredth percent.

9–51. Amazon.com paid a $6,000 net price for textbooks. The publisher offered a 30% trade discount. What was the publisher's list price? Round to the nearest cent.

9–52. Bally Manufacturing sent Intel Corporation an invoice for machinery with a $14,000 list price. Bally dated the invoice July 23 with 2/10 EOM terms. Intel receives a 40% trade discount. Intel pays the invoice on August 5. What does Intel pay Bally?

9–53. On August 1, Intel Corporation (Problem 9–52) returns $100 of the machinery due to defects. What does Intel pay Bally on August 5? Round to nearest cent.

9–54. Stacy's Dress Shop received a $1,050 invoice dated July 8 with 2/10, 1/15, n/60 terms. On July 22, Stacy's sent a $242 partial payment. What credit should Stacy's receive? What is Stacy's outstanding balance?

9–55. On March 11, Jangles Corporation received a $20,000 invoice dated March 8. Cash discount terms were 4/10, n/30. On March 15, Jangles sent an $8,000 partial payment. What credit should Jangles receive? What is Jangles' outstanding balance?

ADDITIONAL WORD PROBLEMS

9–56. Prudential Life wants to buy a new line of high-speed computers. Manufacturer A offers a 10/5 chain discount. Manufacturer B offers a 9/6 chain discount. Both manufacturers have the same list price. Which manufacturer should Prudential buy from?

9–57. Borders.com paid a $79.99 net price for each calculus textbook. The publisher offered a 20% trade discount. What was the publisher's list price?

9–58. Home Office.com buys a computer from Compaq Corporation. The computers have a $1,200 list price with a 30% trade discount. What is the trade discount amount? What is the net price of the computer? Freight charges are FOB destination.

9–59. Whistler Ski Shop received a $1,201 invoice dated July 8 with 2/10, 1/15, n/60 terms. On July 22,

Whistler sent a $485 partial payment. What credit should Whistler receive? What is Whistler's outstanding balance?

9–60. True Value received an invoice dated 4/15/02. The invoice had a $5,500 balance that included $300 freight. Terms were 4/10, 3/30, n/60. True Value pays the invoice on April 29. What amount does True Value pay?

9–61. Staples purchased seven new computers for $850 each. It received a 15% discount because it purchased more than five and an additional 6% discount because it took immediate delivery. Terms of payment were 2/10, n/30. Staples pays the bill within the cash discount period. How much should the cheque be for? Round to the nearest cent.

9–62. On May 14, Roots sold Blue Mountain Sport Centre $7,000 of athletic sportswear. Terms were 2/10 EOM FOB Blue Mountain. Roots agreed to prepay the $80 freight. If Blue Mountain Centre pays the invoice on June 8, what will the Centre pay? If Blue Mountain Centre pays on June 20, what will it pay?

9–63. Sam's Ski Boards.com offers 5/4/1 chain discounts to many of its customers. The Ski Hut ordered 20 ski boards with a total list price of $1,200. What is the net price of the ski boards? What was the trade discount amount? Round to the nearest cent.

9–64. Majestic Manufacturing sold Jordans Furniture a living room set for an $8,500 list price with 35% trade discount. The $100 freight (FOB shipping point) was not part of the list price. Terms were 3/10, n/30 ROG. The invoice date was May 30. Jordans received the goods on July 18 and paid the invoice on July 20. What was the final price (include cost of freight) of the set?

9–65. Boeing Truck Company received an invoice showing 8 tires at $110 each, 12 tires at $160 each, and 15 tires at $180 each. Shipping terms are FOB shipping point. Freight is $400; trade discount is 10/5; and a cash discount of 2/10, n/30 is offered. Assuming Boeing paid within the discount period, what did Boeing pay?

9–66. The March 2000 issue of *Business Credit* discussed customers who pay less than the invoice amount to suppliers. A company received an invoice with terms 3/10, n/30. The bill was $13,450. The company is short of cash and sends in a partial payment of $6,400 within 10 days. **(a)** What credit should the company receive? **(b)** What is the outstanding balance? Round to the nearest cent.

9–67. Verizon offers to sell cellular phones listing for $99.99 with a chain discount of 15/10/5. Cellular Company offers to sell its cellular phones that list at $102.99 with a chain discount of 25/5. If Irene is to buy 6 phones, how much could she save if she buys from the lower-priced company?

9–68. Bryant Manufacture sells its furniture to wholesalers and retailers. It offers to wholesalers a chain discount of 15/10/5 and to retailers a chain discount of 15/10. If a sofa lists for $500, how much would the wholesaler and retailer pay?

Please note that, for easier learning, all invoice amounts are given before tax. In the real world, however, taxes are included in the invoice amount and they should be adjusted if the customer decides to take advantage of the cash discount.

9–69. Northwest Chemical Company received an invoice for $12,480, dated March 12, with terms of 2/10, n/30. If the invoice was paid March 22, what was the amount due?

9–70. On May 27, Trotter Hardware Store received an invoice for trash barrels purchased for $13,650 with terms of 3/10, EOM; the freight charge, which is included in the price, is $412. What are **(a)** the last day of the discount period and **(b)** the amount of the payment due on this date?

9–71. The Glass Sailboat received an invoice for $930.50 with terms 2/10, n/30 on April 19. On April 29, it sent a payment of $430.50. **(a)** How much credit will be given on the total due? **(b)** What is the new balance due?

9–72. Dallas Ductworks offers cash discounts of 2/10, 1/15, n/30 on all purchases. If an invoice for $544 dated July 18 is paid on August 2, what is the amount due?

9–73. The list price of a DVD player is $299.90 with trade discounts of 10/20 and terms of 3/10, n/30. If a retailer pays the invoice within the discount period, what amount must the retailer pay?

9–74. The invoice of a sneaker supplier totalled $2,488.50, was dated February 7, and offered terms 2/10, ROG. The shipment of sneakers was received on March 7. What are **(a)** the last date of the discount period and **(b)** the amount of the discount that will be lost if the invoice is paid after that date?

9–75. Toys R Us receives an invoice amounting to $1,152.30 with terms of 2/10, EOM and dated November 6. If a partial payment of $750 is made on December 8, what are **(a)** the credit given for the partial payment and **(b)** the balance due on the invoice?

9–76. Todd Sport Check received an invoice for soccer equipment dated July 26 with terms 3/10, 1/15, n/30 in the amount of $3,225.83, which included shipping charges of $375.50. If this bill is paid on August 5, what amount must be paid?

CHALLENGE PROBLEMS

9–77. In the October 9, 2000 issue of *Crain's New York Business,* a story appeared describing firms saving money by taking the plunge into online buying pools. Karen Curry was eager to find seven dozen soft-sided drink coolers for a company promotion. She found a good price, $24 each. However, through Mercata.com, a group purchasing Web site that offers volume discounts to smaller companies who electronically pool their orders, she found a lower price of $21. **(a)** What was Karen's final total net purchase price? **(b)** What was her total discount amount using the site? **(c)** What was the percent discount using the online buying pool? **(d)** If Karen meets the cash discount period of 2/10 net 30, what would be her final price?

9–78. On March 30, Century Television received an invoice dated March 28 from ACME Manufacturing for 50 televisions at a cost of $125 each. Century received a 10/4/2 chain discount. Shipping terms were FOB shipping point. ACME prepaid the $70 freight. Terms were 2/10 EOM. When Century received the goods, 3 sets were defective. Century returned these sets to ACME. On April 8, Century sent a $150 partial payment. Century will pay the balance on May 6. What is Century's final payment on May 6? Assume no taxes.

9–79. Smart Solutions Ltd. sent an invoice to Eager Beaver Inc. The invoice is dated January 20, 2004 and is for $23,987. Terms are 2/15, 1/25, n/45, EOM.

Eager Beaver made two payments. The first took place on February 1, 2004 and the account was credited for $6,400. The second payment of $8,478 was made on February 15, 2004. What was the outstanding balance after the second payment?

9–80. Tom is preparing for a math test. In the problem which he tries to solve, a company received an invoice for $6,000 with terms 3/10, 2/20, n/45. The invoice is dated December 1, 2003. The company made partial payments on December 10, December 20, and December 22 for $2,450, $1,340, and $580 respectively. What is the outstanding balance and its due date, which the company must pay to close the account?

SUMMARY PRACTICE TEST

Complete the following: (pp. 196, 197)

	Item	List price	Single trade discount	Net price
1.	Michelin tires	$300	30%	
2.	DVD player		30%	$210

Calculate the net price and trade discount (use net price equivalent rate and single equivalent discount rate) for the following: (pp. 196, 197)

	Item	List price	Chain discount	Net price	Trade discount
3.	Computer scanner	$299	3/2		

4. From the following, what is the last date for each discount period and credit period? (pp. 203, 204)

	Date of invoice	Terms	End of discount period	End of credit period
a.	Oct. 7	2/10, n/30		
b.	Nov. 12, 2004	3/10, n/30 ROG (Goods received Aug. 6, 2005)		
c.	May 8	2/10 EOM		
d.	March 28	2/10 EOM		

5. The Bay buys a television from a wholesaler with a $900 list price and a 30% trade discount. What is the trade discount amount? What is the net price of the television? (p. 197)

Excel

6. Ron Company of Vancouver sold Long Company of Montreal computer equipment with a $12,000 list price. Sale terms were 2/10, n/30 FOB Vancouver. Ron agreed to prepay the $200 freight. Long pays the invoice within the discount period. What does Long pay Ron? (p. 204)

7. Pat Manin wants to buy a new line of dolls for her shop. Manufacturer A offers a 16/10 chain discount. Manufacturer B offers a 20/9 chain discount. Both manufacturers have the same list price. Which manufacturer should Pat buy from? (p. 201)

8. Kurck Copy received a $6,000 invoice dated June 10. Terms were 3/10, 2/15, n/60. On June 23, Kurck Copy sent a $1,500 partial payment. What credit should Kurck Copy receive? What is Kurck Copy's outstanding balance? Round to the nearest cent. (p. 211)

9. Angel Company received from Woody Company an invoice dated September 28. Terms were 2/10 EOM. List price on the invoice was $8,000 (freight not included). Angel receives a 12/7 chain discount. Freight charges are Angel's responsibility, but Woody agreed to prepay the $150 freight. Angel pays the invoice on October 6. What does Angel Company pay Woody? (p. 201)

SOLUTIONS TO PRACTICE QUIZZES

LU 9–1

1. Dining room set trade discount amount and net price:

THE FACTS	SOLVING FOR?	STEPS TO TAKE	KEY POINTS
L: List price: $12,000. *d: Trade discount rate:* 40%.	Trade discount amount. D_t = ? Net price. N = ?	Trade discount amount = List price × Trade discount rate. $D_t = L \times d$ Net price = List price × Complement of trade discount rate. $N = L \times (1 - d)$	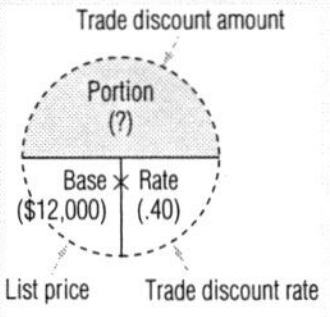

Steps to solving problem

1. Calculate the trade discount.

   $12,000 × .40 = **$4,800** Trade discount amount

2. Calculate the net price.

   $12,000 × .60 = **$7,200** (100% − 40% = 60%)

1. Given:

L = $12,000

d = 40% ⟶ d = .4

D_t = ?

N = ?

To find D_t when L and d are given, use formula 9.1:

$D_t = L \times d$

D_t = 12,000 × .4 = $4,800

The amount of trade discount is $4,800.

To find N when L, d, and D_t are given, use either formula 9.2 or formula 9.3:

$N = L - D_t$ or $N = L(1 - d)$

N = $12,000 − $4,800 = $7,200

or

N = $12,000 × (1 − .4) = $12,000 × .6
= $7,200

The net price is $7,200.

2. Video system list price:

THE FACTS	SOLVING FOR?	STEPS TO TAKE	KEY POINTS
N: Net price: \$1,400. *d: Trade discount rate:* 30%.	List price. $L = ?$	List price = $\frac{\text{Net price}}{\text{Complement of trade discount}}$ $L = \frac{N}{(1-d)}$	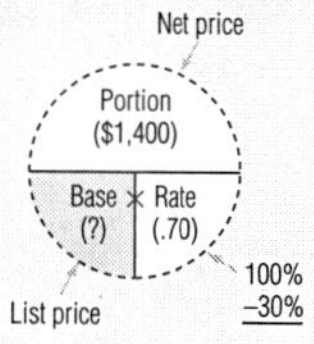

2. Given:

$N = \$1,400$

$d = 30\% \longrightarrow d = .3$

$L = ?$

To find L when N and d are given, use formula 9.4:

$$L = \frac{N}{(1-d)} = \frac{1,400}{(1-.3)} = \frac{1,400}{.7} = \$2,000$$

The list price is \$2,000.

Steps to solving problem

1. Calculate the complement of trade discount.

$$\begin{array}{r} 100\% \\ -\ 30 \\ \hline 70\% = .70 \end{array}$$

2. Calculate the list price.

$$\frac{\$1,400}{.70} = \$2,000$$

3. Lamps Outlet's net price and trade discount amount:

THE FACTS	SOLVING FOR?	STEPS TO TAKE	KEY POINTS
L: List price: \$12,000. *Chain discount:* 5/10/25. $d_1 = .05$ $d_2 = .1$ $d_3 = .25$	Net price. $N = ?$ Trade discount amount. $D_t = ?$	Net price = List price × Net price equivalent rate. $N = L(1 - d_e)$ Trade discount amount = List price × Single equivalent discount rate. $D_t = L \times d_e$	Do not round off net price equivalent rate or single equivalent discount rate.

3. Given:

$L = \$12,000$

$d_1 = .05;\ d_2 = .1;\ d_3 = .25$

$N = ?$

$D_t = ?$

To find N and D_t when the series discounts and list price are known, use formulas 9.6 and 9.7:

$$d_e = 1 - (1 - d_1)(1 - d_2)(1 - d_3) \quad (9.6)$$

$$D_t = L \times d_e \quad (9.7)$$

$$d_e = 1 - (1 - .05)(1 - .1)(1 - .25) = .35875$$

Do not round the intermediate result!

$D_t = \$12,000 \times .35875 = \$4,305$

The single equivalent rate of the trade discount is 35.875%. The amount of the trade discount is \$4,305.

Steps to solving problem

1. Calculate the complement of each chain discount.

$$\begin{array}{r} 100\% \\ -\ 5 \\ \hline 95\% \end{array} \qquad \begin{array}{r} 100\% \\ -\ 10 \\ \hline 90\% \end{array} \qquad \begin{array}{r} 100\% \\ -\ 25 \\ \hline 75\% \end{array}$$

2. Calculate the net price equivalent rate. $.95 \times .90 \times .75 = .64125$

3. Calculate the net price. $\$12,000 \times .64125 = \$7,695$

4. Calculate the single equivalent discount rate.

$$\begin{array}{r} 1.00000 \\ -\ .64125 \\ \hline .35875 \end{array}$$

5. Calculate the trade discount amount. $\$12,000 \times .35875 = \$4,305$

N.B.! A REMINDER:

To perform one-step calculation on your calculator do the following:

1 [−] [( ] 1 [−] .05 [ )] [×] [( ] 1 [−] .1 [ )] [×] [( ] 1 [−] .25 [ )] [=]

The result should be .35875.

LU 9–2

1. End of discount period: July 6 + 10 days = July 16

End of credit period: By Table 9.1, July 6 = 187 days
+ 30 days
217 → search → Aug. 5

2. End of discount period: June 9 + 10 days = June 19

End of credit period: By Table 9.1, June 9 = 160 days
+ 30 days
190 → search → July 9

3. End of discount period: By Table 9.1, May 9 = 129 days
+ 30 days
159 → search → June 8

End of credit period: By Table 9.1, May 9 = 129 days
+ 60 days
189 → search → July 8

4. End of discount period: June 10

End of credit period: June 10 + 20 = June 30

5. End of discount period: July 10

End of credit period: July 10 + 20 = July 30

6. Vasko Corporation's cost of equipment:

THE FACTS	SOLVING FOR?	STEPS TO TAKE	KEY POINTS
List price: \$8,000. *Trade discount rate:* 20%. *Terms:* 2/10 EOM. *Invoice date:* 5/26. *Date paid:* 7/3.	Cost of equipment.	Net price = List price × Complement of trade discount rate. *EOM before 25th:* Discount period is 1st 10 days of month that follows sale.	Trade discounts are deducted before cash discounts are taken. Cash discounts are not taken on freight or returns.

Steps to solving problem

1. Calculate the net price. \$8,000 × .80 = \$6,400 (100% − 20%)
2. Calculate the discount period. Until July 10
3. Calculate the cost of office equipment. \$6,400 × .98 = \$6,272 (100% − 2%)

You may also use the following table:

#	Invoice amount (amount due)	Terms and cash discounts applicable	Amount paid $P = Cr(1-d)$	Amount credited $Cr = P/(1-d)$	Outstanding balance (2) − (5)
1	2	3	4	5	6
	\$8,000 × (1 − .2) = \$6,400	2%, $d = .02$	P = \$6,400 × (1 − .02) = \$6,272	\$6,400	\$0

7. $\frac{\$400}{.98}$ = \$408.16, amount credited.

\$600 − \$408.16 = \$191.84 , balance outstanding.

Business Math Scrapbook

WITH INTERNET APPLICATION

Putting Your Skills to Work

Spanish Officials Raid Coca-Cola Office

By Betsy McKay

Staff Reporter of The Wall Street Journal

Spanish antitrust regulators raided the offices of **Coca-Cola Co.** and three of its bottlers, seeking evidence that the soft-drink giant has abused its strong market position to squelch competitors.

The unannounced visits were conducted in response to complaints filed last year by the Spanish division of **PepsiCo Inc.**, and a Spanish beverage company, **La Casera**. In a statement from its Spanish division, PepsiCo accused Coke of "illegal" marketing and sales practices "for the purpose of obtaining a monopolistic control of the sector." Such practices include discounts for large-volume purchases and exclusivity agreements between Coke, its bottlers, and retailers, which encourage retailers to cut back on Coke competitors' stocks, PepsiCo said.

Antitrust officials targeted Coke's regional corporate headquarters and one bottler in Madrid, as well as the offices of two other bottlers in Seville and Vizcaya. The bottlers are all independently owned.

The probe is the latest of several Coke is facing around the world, most of which were also prompted by complaints from PepsiCo. The European Union is already examining the practices of Coke and its bottlers in five European countries—the United Kingdom, Belgium, Germany, Austria and Denmark. Coke also recently began talks with Mexican antitrust officials with the hope of avoiding a legal tussle over the same issues there.

Coke Chairman Douglas Daft has said mending fences with regulators is a priority. He has made personal calls on several officials in Europe, and declared that Coke will play by the "house rules." The continued interest from regulators suggests that some have yet to be convinced.

A Coke executive said the company and its bottlers are cooperating. "The beverages market in Spain is very competitive," said Marcos de Quinto, president of Coke's Iberian division. "Coca-Cola is committed to operating in a very competitive environment. Coca-Cola Spain carries out its operations in compliance with Spanish and European law. We understand that the preference consumers and customers show for our brands is due to several decades of effort and investment by the company and its local bottlers, which are all local Spanish companies."

Spain is one of the most important soft-drink markets in the world because of its high per-capita consumption. It is Coke's second-largest market in Europe, and the company's Spanish unit has a reputation for posting consistent growth. Mr. Daft has singled out marketing programs drafted by Coke's executives in Spain as the kind of marketing he would like to see the rest of the company replicate.

Coke holds a 57% share of the carbonated soft-drinks market in Spain. Pepsi holds 16% and La Casera holds 10%, according to Beverage Digest, an industry publication.

Source: © 2000 Dow Jones & Company, Inc.

PROJECT A

Do think that the Spanish division of PepsiCo Inc. has a legitimate complaint? Check out PepsiCo Inc.'s Web site.

Young Mathmagician Magazine ORDER FORM

Affix FREE GIFT sticker here to renew **YMM**

YES! Please rush my FREE GIFT and extend my subsciption for an extra 4 issues FREE. I have completed my survey, affixed the appropriate stickers below, and would like to renew my **YMM** subscription at the Guaranteed Low Rate.

Choose one:

☐ 2 YRS (112 issues) @ $1.19 / issue + **4 FREE**= 116 issues ($113.25 total)

☐ 1 YR (56 issues) @ $1.29 / issue + **4 FREE** = 60 issues ($72.20 total)

☐ 6 MOS (28 issues) @ $1.39 / issue + **4 FREE** = 32 issues ($38.90 total)

CHARGE OPTION: Charge my credit card and enroll me in the **Preferred Subscriber's Automatic Renewal Plan** (see enclosed letter).

☐ Visa ☐ Mastercard ☐ Amex

Card Number ____ Exp Date __/__

CHEQUE OPTION: ☐ Payment enclosed. ☐ Bill me later in full. ☐ Bill me later in 4 equal monthly installments

☐ No, I do not want to renew at this time. I am returning the survey with the seals affixed. I understand that I will miss out on my FREE GIFT and 4 FREE extra issues of **YMM**.

Affix sticker here and receive 4 EXTRA ISSUES of **YMM** FREE with your renewal

IMPORTANT: **Return your completed Survey in the enclosed envelope today.**

PROJECT B

Discuss why magazines offer free issues. Can it be considered a trade discount? What other trade discounts are offered? What savings will a subscriber realize subscribing for six months? One year? Two years?

Markups and Markdowns:

INSIGHT INTO PERISHABLES; COST-PROFIT-VOLUME AND BREAKEVEN ANALYSIS

10

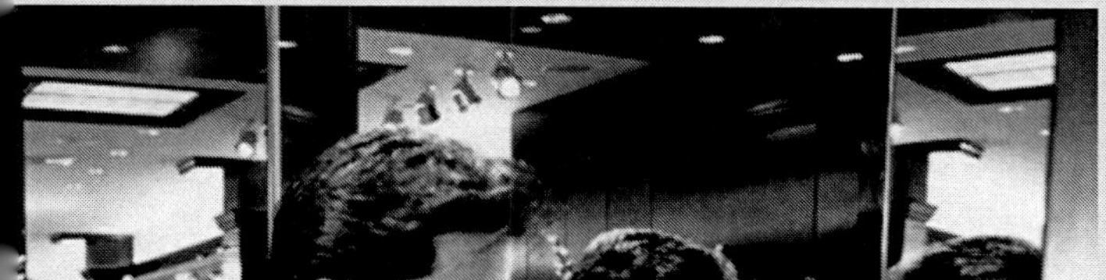

'N THE NEXT COUPLE of weeks, a nine-minute promotional videotape from **Univision Communications** will ar-'e in the office of August A. Busch III, esident of beer maker **Anheuser-Busch.** t the tape isn't a sample of the pro-ams showing on the Spanish-language network. Rather, it contains a clip m ABC's "Nightline" about the boom-growth of the Hispanic community de-led in the 2000 census.

"It's almost as if our industry hired the nsus Bureau to do our public relations," 's Tom McGarrity, Univision's presi-nt of network sales. "Companies can't erlook the Hispanic market now. They either consciously ignore it and justify ir decision to do so, or they must design lan to address it." Univision is sending "Nightline" tape to the CEOs of the 500 gest advertisers in the U.S. from Ace rdware to Zale.

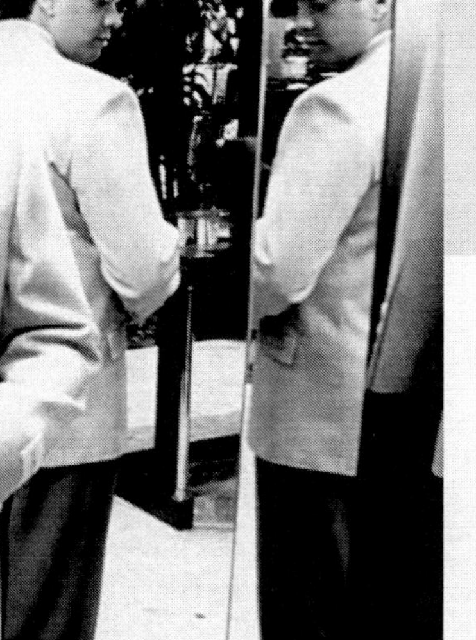

Source: © 2000 Dow Jones & Company, Inc.

LEARNING UNIT OBJECTIVES

LU 10–1: Markups[1] Based on Cost (100%)

- Calculate dollar markup and percent markup on cost (p. 232).
- Calculate selling price when you know the cost and percent markup on cost (p. 233).
- Calculate cost when dollar markup and percent markup on cost are known (p. 234).
- Calculate cost when you know the selling price and percent markup on cost (p. 234).

LU 10–2: Markups Based on Selling Price (100%)

- Calculate dollar markup and percent markup on selling price (p. 235).
- Calculate selling price when cost and percent markup on selling price are known (p. 236).
- Calculate cost when selling price and percent markup on selling price are known (p. 237).
- Convert from percent markup on cost to percent markup on selling price and vice versa (pp. 238, 239).

LU 10–3: Markdowns and Perishables

- Calculate markdowns; compare markdowns and markups (p. 240).
- Price perishable items to cover spoilage loss (p. 242).

LU 10–4: Cost-Profit-Volume and Breakeven Analysis

- Definitions and understanding of the terms (p. 243).
- Contribution margin approach (p. 243).

---

[1]Some texts use the term *markon* (selling price minus cost).

Nancy Ford is a retailer who owns a hardware store. One of the most important business decisions Nancy must make concerns the selling price of her goods. She knows that her selling price must include the cost of bringing the goods into her store, her operating expenses, and a profit. To remain in business, Nancy's selling price must also be competitive with that of other hardware retailers.

Before we study the two pricing methods available to Nancy (percent markup on cost and percent markup on selling price), we must know the following terms:

- **Selling price (*S*):** The price retailers charge consumers. The total selling price of all the retailer's goods represents the retailer's total sales.
- **Cost (*C*):** The price retailers pay to a manufacturer or supplier to bring the goods into the store.
- **Markup, margin, or gross profit (*M*):** These three terms refer to the difference between the cost of bringing the goods into the store and the selling price of the goods.
- **Operating expenses or overhead (*E*):** The regular expenses of doing business such as wages, rent, utilities, insurance, and advertising.
- **Net profit or net income (*P*):** The profit remaining after subtracting the cost of bringing the goods into the store and the operating expenses from the sale of the goods (including any returns or adjustments).

From these definitions, we can conclude that markup represents the amount that retailers must add to the cost of the goods to cover their operating expenses and make a profit.[2]

FIGURE 10–1

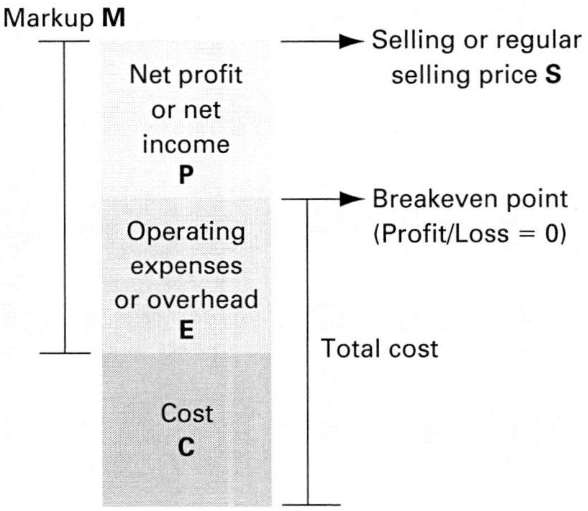

Figure 10.1 is a visualizing image of retail price components and will help you better understand the relationship between selling price, cost, markup, operating expenses, and net profit.

The figure allows us to illustrate these relationships with the help of the following formulas:

$$S = C + E + P \quad \textbf{(10.1)}$$
$$S = C + M \quad \textbf{(10.2)}$$
$$M = P + E \quad \textbf{(10.3)}$$
$$\text{Total cost} = C + E \quad \textbf{(10.4)}$$

where:

S = Selling price
C = Cost, or price paid to bring an item to a store
E = Operating expenses or overhead
P = Net profit or net income
M = Amount of markup in dollars to cover operating expenses and make a profit

To help you understand the basic selling price formula that follows, let's return to Nancy Ford and her True Value hardware store. Nancy has bought a Toro snowthrower from a supplier for $210. She plans to sell the snowthrower for $300.

Basic selling price formula

Selling price (S) =	Cost (C)	+	Markup (M)
↑	↑		↑
$300 (snowthrower) =	$210 (price paid to bring snowthrower into store)	+	$90 (amount in dollars to cover operating expenses and make a profit)

[2]In this chapter we concentrate on the markup of retailers. Manufacturers and suppliers also use markup to determine selling price.

> ## Bluefly's Goal: Raise Margins, But Keep Fans
>
> By REBECCA QUICK
> *Staff Reporter of* THE WALL STREET JOURNAL
>
> This was the plan: Sell designer-label clothing online for less than it goes for in stores, and make up the difference through the promised efficiencies of an Internet-only business.
>
> But a look at one key figure shows why **Bluefly** Inc. is struggling.
>
> For retailers, profit begins with "markup," the amount they charge above what goods cost them wholesale. To tempt shoppers Bluefly has kept its markup low, below that of many other retailers. For every $10 that Bluefly marks up the Prada pants and Gucci shoes it sells, for example, catalog retailer Lands' End marks up its own-label clothes by roughly $17, and department store Macy's marks up its wares by $14 on average.

Note that in this example, the markup is a dollar amount, or a **dollar markup.** Markup is also expressed in percent. When expressing markup in percent, retailers can choose a percent based on *cost* (Learning Unit 10–1) or a percent based on *selling price* (Learning Unit 10–2).

An example of a need for a change in markup strategy is reported by *The Wall Street Journal* in the clipping "Bluefly's Goal: Raise Margins, But Keep Fans." Bluefly's plan was to sell designer clothes online at a lower markup than Lands' End and Macy's. As "an outlet store in your home," shoppers received bargains when shopping at Bluefly.com. However, this low markup was a disaster for Bluefly's shareholders. After paying expenses, Bluefly has been running deep in red ink. The volume of Internet sales was not enough to make a profit for Bluefly. In other words, the price did not allow Bluefly to recover the **total cost** (Cost + Operating expenses). If a company can't recover total cost ($C + E$), it will suffer an **operating loss.** If the company's price does not allow it to even recover the cost of buying (C), this company will suffer an **absolute loss.** Now Bluefly will have to determine how to raise its markup margin and also keep its customers.

LEARNING UNIT 10–1
MARKUPS BASED ON COST (100%)

In Chapter 6 you were introduced to the portion formula, which we used to solve percent problems. We also used the portion formula in Chapter 9 to solve problems involving trade and cash discounts. In this unit you will see how we use the basic selling price formula and the portion formula to solve percent markup situations based on cost. You may also use Blueprint Aids to dissect and solve all word problems in this chapter.

Many manufacturers mark up goods on cost because manufacturers can get cost information more easily than sales information. Since retailers have the choice of using percent markup on cost or selling price, in this unit we assume Nancy Ford has chosen percent markup on cost for her True Value hardware store. In Learning Unit 10–2 we show how Nancy Ford would determine her markup if she decided to use percent markup on selling price.

Businesses that use **percent markup on cost** recognize that cost is 100%. This 100% represents the base of the portion formula. All situations in this unit use cost as 100%.

To calculate percent markup on cost, let's use Nancy Ford's Toro snowthrower purchase and begin with the basic selling price formula 10.2 given in the chapter introduction. When we know the dollar markup, we can use the portion formula to find the percent markup on cost.

Markup expressed in dollars: $S = C + M$

Selling price ($300) = Cost ($210) + Markup ($90)

Markup expressed as percent markup on cost is called **rate of markup.**[3]

Cost	100.00% →
+ Markup	+ 42.86
= Selling price	142.86%

> Cost is 100%—the base. Dollar markup is the portion, and percent markup on cost is the rate.

$$R_{M_c} = \frac{M}{C} \qquad \textbf{(10.5)}$$

[3]There is no consistent terminology used for rates of markup, based on cost and selling price. In this book we will use "rate of markup R_{M_c}" for the markup, based on cost, and "gross profit margin R_{M_s}" for rate of markup based on selling price.

In Situation 1 (see below) we show why Nancy has a 42.86% markup based on cost by presenting Nancy's snowthrower purchase as a word problem. We solve the problem in two ways with the Blueprint Aid used in earlier chapters and with the help of formulas. In the second column, however, you will see footnotes after two numbers. These refer to the steps we use below the Blueprint Aid to solve the problem. Throughout the chapter, the numbers that we are solving for are in red. Remember that cost is the base for this Unit.

Situation 1: Calculating Dollar Markup and Percent Markup on Cost

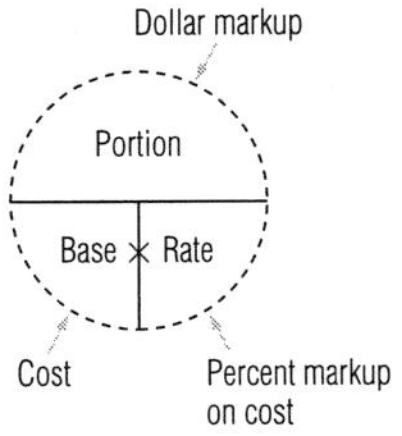

The dollar markup is calculated with the basic selling price formula $S = C + M$. When you know the cost and the selling price of the goods, you reverse the basic selling price formula to $M = S - C$. Subtract the cost from the selling price, and you have the dollar markup.

The percent markup on cost is calculated with the portion formula. For Situation 1 the *portion* (Por) is the dollar markup, which you know from the selling price formula. In this Unit the *rate* (R) is always the percent markup on cost and the *base* (B) is always the cost (100%). To find the percent markup on cost (R), use the portion formula $R = \frac{\text{Por}}{B}$ and divide the dollar markup (Por) by the cost (B). Convert your answer to a percent and round if necessary.

Now let's look at the Nancy Ford example to see how to calculate the 42.86% markup on cost.

REMINDER
Dealing with a word problem, first make note of what is known, organize material by listing components of the questions that are given, and identify what is unknown and yet to be determined.

THE WORD PROBLEM Nancy Ford bought a snowthrower that cost $210 for her True Value hardware store. She plans to sell the snowthrower for $300. What is Nancy's dollar markup? What is her rate of markup on cost R_{M_c} (round to the nearest hundredth percent)?

THE FACTS	SOLVING FOR?	STEPS TO TAKE	KEY POINTS
C: Snowthrower cost: $210. *S: Snowthrower selling price:* $300.	% | $ C 100.00% | $210 $+ M$ 42.86[2] | 90[1] $= S$ 142.86% | $300 [1]Dollar markup. [2]Percent markup on cost.	Dollar markup = Selling price − Cost. $M = S - C$ Percent markup on cost = $\frac{\text{Dollar markup}}{\text{Cost}}$ $R_{M_c} = \frac{M}{C}$	Dollar markup Portion ($90) Base × Rate ($210) (?) Cost

$S = \$300$
$C = \$210$

$$R_{M_c} = \frac{M}{C} \qquad (10.5)$$

$R_{M_c} = ?$

C is given. Ask yourself the question: Can we find M if S and C are given? Yes, if we use formula 10.2:

$S = C + M$
$\$300 = \$210 + M$
$M = \$300 - \$210$
$M = \$90$

With a simple rearrangement of formula 10.2 we can always find the markup:

$$M = S - C \qquad (10.2.1)$$

Now, we can substitute values of M and C into formula 10.5:

$$R_{M_c} = \frac{90}{210} = .4286 = 42.86\%$$

$R_{M_c} = 42.86\%$

The rate of markup is 42.86%. This means that markup M is 42.86% of the cost or $.4286 \times C$.

STEPS TO SOLVING PROBLEM

1. Calculate the dollar markup.
   Dollar markup = Selling price − Cost
   $90 = $300 − $210

2. Calculate the percent markup on cost.
   $$\text{Percent markup on cost} = \frac{\text{Dollar markup}}{\text{Cost}} = \frac{\$90}{\$210} = 42.86\%$$

$R = \frac{Por}{B}$ $S = C + M$ $M = S - C$

$C = \frac{M}{R}$

To check the percent markup on cost, you can use the basic selling price formula $S = C + M$. Convert the percent markup on cost found with the portion formula to a decimal and multiply it by the cost. This gives the dollar markup. Then add the cost and the dollar markup to get the selling price of the goods.

You could also check the cost (B) by dividing the dollar markup (P) by the percent markup on cost (R).

Check

$$\boxed{\text{Selling price} = \text{Cost} + \text{Markup}} \quad \textbf{or} \quad \boxed{\text{Cost } (B) = \frac{\text{Dollar markup } (P)}{\text{Percent markup on cost } (R)}}$$

$$\$300 = \$210 + .4286(\$210)$$
$$\$300 = \$210 + \$90^*$$
$$\$300 = \$300$$

$$= \frac{\$90}{.4286} = \$209.99^*$$

Parentheses mean that you multiply the percent markup on cost in decimal by the cost.

*Off 1 cent due to rounding of percent.

SITUATION 2: CALCULATING SELLING PRICE WHEN YOU KNOW COST AND RATE OF MARKUP ON COST

When you know the cost and the rate of markup, you calculate the selling price with the basic selling formula $S = C + M$. Remember that when goods are marked up on cost, the cost is the base (100%). So you can say that the selling price is the cost plus the markup in dollars (percent markup on cost times cost).

Now let's look at Mel's Furniture where we calculate Mel's dollar markup and selling price.

THE WORD PROBLEM Mel's Furniture bought a lamp that cost \$100. To make Mel's desired profit, he needs a 65% markup on cost. What is Mel's dollar markup? What is his selling price?

THE FACTS	SOLVING FOR?	STEPS TO TAKE	KEY POINTS
Lamp cost: \$100. *Markup on cost:* 65%.	% | \$ C 100% | \$100 $+ M$ 65 | 65[1] $= S$ 165% | \$165[2] [1]Dollar markup. [2]Selling price.	Dollar markup: $S = C + M$. or $S = \text{Cost} \times \left(1 + \begin{array}{c}\text{Percent}\\\text{markup}\\\text{on cost}\end{array}\right)$	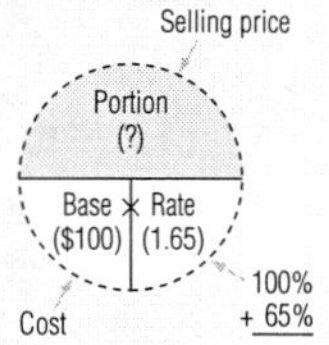

$C = \$100$
$R_{M_c} = .65$
$M = ?$
$S = ?$

The rate of markup is 65%. This means that markup M is 65% of C:
$M = .65C$
C is given: $C = \$100$. So we can find $M = .65 \times 100 = \$65$.
$M = \$65$

To find S, use formula 10.2: $S = \$100 + \$65 = \$165$.
$S = \$165$

STEPS TO SOLVING PROBLEM

1. Calculate the dollar markup. $S = C + M$

$S = \$100 + .65(\$100)$ ← Parentheses mean you multiply the percent markup in decimal by the cost.

$S = C + \%C$

$S = \$100 + \$65$ ← Dollar markup

2. Calculate the selling price. $S = \$165$

You can check the selling price with the portion formula Por $= B \times R$. You are solving for portion (Por)—the selling price. Rate (R_{M_c}) represents the 100% cost plus the 65% markup on cost. Since in this Unit the markup is on cost, the base is the cost. Convert 165% to a decimal and multiply the cost by 1.65 to get the selling price of \$165.

Check

Selling price = Cost × (1 + Percent markup on cost) (Por) (*B*) (R_{M_c})	= $100 × 1.65 =	$165

Situation 3: Calculating Cost When You Know Selling Price and Rate of Markup

When you know the selling price and the rate of markup, you calculate the cost with the basic selling formula $S = C + M$. Since goods are marked up on cost, the percent markup on cost is added to the cost.

Let's see how this is done in the following Jill Sport example.

THE WORD PROBLEM Jill Sport, owner of Sports, Inc., sells tennis rackets for $50. To make her desired profit, Jill needs a 40% markup on cost. What do the tennis rackets cost Jill? What is the dollar markup?

THE FACTS	SOLVING FOR?	STEPS TO TAKE	KEY POINTS
S: Selling price: $50. *M: Markup on cost:* 40%	% $ *C* 100% $36.71[1] + *M* 40 14.29[2] = *S* 140% $50.00 [1]Cost. [2]Dollar markup.	*S* = *C* + *M*. or Cost = Selling price / (1 + Percent markup on cost) *M* = *S* − *C*.	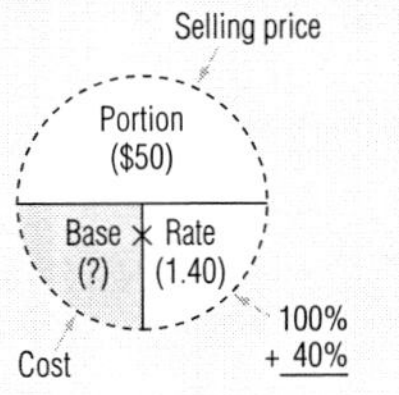

STEPS TO SOLVING PROBLEM

1. Calculate the cost.

$$S = C + M$$
$$\$50 = C + .40C$$

← This means 40% times cost. *C* is the same as 1*C*. Adding .40*C* to 1*C* gives the percent markup on cost of 1.40*C* in decimal.

$$\frac{\$50}{1.40} = \frac{1.40C}{1.40}$$
$$\$35.71 = C$$

2. Calculate the dollar markup.

$$M = S - C$$
$$M = \$50 - \$35.71$$
$$M = \$14.29$$

$S = \$50$

$M = 40\%$ of cost → $M = .4C$

$C = ?$

$M = ?$

Recall formula 10.2: $S = M + C$. S is given; M is expressed in terms of C. Let's substitute values of S and M:

$\$50 = .4C + C$

$S = M + C$

$\$50 = 1.4C$

$C = \$50$

$C = \$35.71$

When C is known, M can be found from the formula $M = .4C$:

$M = .4 \times \$35.71 = \$14.29$

$M = \$14.29$

M can also be defined by rearranging formula 10.2:

$S = C + M$

$M = S - C$

$M = \$50 - \$35.71 = \$14.29$

$M = \$14.29$

Either of the approaches is correct.

You can check your cost answer with the portion formula $B = \frac{\text{Por}}{R}$. Portion (Por) is the selling price. Rate (R) represents the 100% cost plus the 40% markup on cost. Convert the percents to decimals and divide the portion by the rate to find the base, or cost.

Check

$$\text{Cost } (B) = \frac{\text{Selling price } (P)}{1 + \text{Percent markup on cost } (R)} = \frac{\$50}{1.40} = \$35.71$$

$$C = \frac{S}{(1 + R_{M_c})}$$

Now try the following Practice Quiz to check your understanding of this Unit.

LU 10–1 PRACTICE QUIZ

Solve the following situations (markups based on cost):

1. Irene Westing bought a desk for $400 from an office supply house. She plans to sell the desk for $600. What is Irene's dollar markup? What is her percent markup on cost? Check your answer.
2. Sarah Komar bought dolls for her toy store that cost $12 each. To make her desired profit, Sarah must mark up each doll 35% on cost. What is the dollar markup? What is the selling price of each doll? Check your answer.
3. Jay Lyman sells calculators. His competitor sells a new calculator line for $14 each. Jay needs a 40% markup on cost to make his desired profit, and he must meet price competition. At what cost can Jay afford to bring these calculators into the store? What is the dollar markup? Check your answer.

LEARNING UNIT 10–2
MARKUPS BASED ON SELLING PRICE (100%)

Many retailers mark up their goods on the selling price since sales information is easier to get than cost information. These retailers use retail prices in their inventory and report their expenses as a percent of sales.

Businesses that mark up their goods on selling price recognize that selling price is 100%. We begin this Unit by assuming that Nancy Ford has decided to use percent markup based on selling price for her True Value hardware store. We repeat Nancy's selling price formula expressed in dollars.

Markup expressed in dollars:

$$S \quad = \quad C \quad + \quad M$$

Selling price ($300) = Cost ($210) + Markup ($90)

Gross profit margin is the markup based on selling price, $R_{M_S} = \frac{M}{S}$.

Markup expressed as **percent markup on selling price** is also known as **gross profit margin.**

Cost	70%
+ Markup	+ 30
= Selling price	100%

Selling price is 100%—the base. Dollar markup is the portion, and percent markup on selling price is the rate.

In Situation 1 (below) we show why Nancy has a 30% markup based on selling price ($M = .3S$). In the last Unit, markups were on cost. In this Unit, markups are on *selling price.*

SITUATION 1: CALCULATING DOLLAR MARKUP AND GROSS PROFIT MARGIN (PERCENT MARKUP ON SELLING PRICE)

The dollar markup is calculated with the selling price formula used in Situation 1, Learning Unit 10–1: $M = S - C$. To find the percent markup on selling price, use the portion formula $R = \frac{\text{Por}}{B}$, where rate (the percent markup on selling price) is found by dividing the portion (dollar markup) by the base (selling price). Note that when solving for percent markup on cost in Situation 1, Learning Unit 10–1, you divided the dollar markup by the cost.

$$R_{M_S} = \frac{M}{S} \qquad \textbf{(10.6)}$$

THE WORD PROBLEM Nancy Ford bought a snowthrower that cost $210 for her True Value hardware store. She plans to sell the snowthrower for $300. What is Nancy's dollar markup? What is her gross profit margin?

THE FACTS	SOLVING FOR?	STEPS TO TAKE	KEY POINTS
Snowthrower cost: $210. *Snowthrower selling price:* $300.	% $ C 70% $210 $+M$ 30%[2] 90[1] $=S$ 100% $300 [1]Dollar markup. [2]Percent markup on selling price.	Dollar markup = Selling price − Cost. Percent markup on selling price = Dollar markup / Selling price	Dollar markup Portion ($90) Base ($300) × Rate (?) Selling price

STEPS TO SOLVING PROBLEM

1. Calculate the dollar markup.

   Dollar markup = Selling price − Cost

   $90 = $300 − $210

2. Calculate the percent markup on selling price.

$$\text{Percent markup on selling price} = \frac{\text{Dollar markup}}{\text{Selling price}}$$

$$= \frac{\$90}{\$300} = 30\%$$

$C = \$210$

$S = \$300$

$M = ?$

$R_{M_S} = ?$

$M = S - C = \$300 - \$210 = \$90$

$M = \$90$

$$R_{M_S} = \frac{M}{S} = \frac{\$90}{\$300} = .30 = 30\%$$

$R_{M_S} = 30\%$

$R_{M_S} = 30\%$ means that markup M is 30% of selling price S or $M = .3S$.

Nancy's markup is $90 and her gross profit margin is 30%.

You can check the percent markup on selling price with the basic selling price formula $S = C + M$. You can also use the portion formula by dividing the dollar markup (Por) by the percent markup on selling price (R).

Check

Selling price = Cost + Markup

$\$300 = \$210 + .30(\$300)$

$\$300 = \$210 + \$90$

$\$300 = \$300$

or

$$\text{Selling price } (B) = \frac{\text{Dollar markup (Por)}}{\text{Percent markup on selling price } (R)}$$

$$= \frac{\$90}{.30} = \$300$$

Parentheses mean you multiply the percent markup on selling price in decimal by the selling price.

SITUATION 2: CALCULATING SELLING PRICE WHEN YOU KNOW COST AND GROSS PROFIT MARGIN (PERCENT MARKUP ON SELLING PRICE)

When you know the cost and percent gross profit margin, you calculate the selling price with the basic selling formula $S = C + M$. Remember that when goods are marked up on selling price, the selling price is the base (100%). Since you do not know the selling price, the percent of markup is based on the unknown selling price. To find the dollar markup after you find the selling price, use the selling price formula $M = S - C$.

THE WORD PROBLEM Mel's Furniture bought a lamp that cost $100. To make Mel's desired profit, he needs a 65% markup on selling price. What are Mel's selling price and his dollar markup?

THE FACTS	SOLVING FOR?	STEPS TO TAKE	KEY POINTS
Lamp cost: $100. *Markup on selling price:* 65%.	% / $ C: 35% / $100.00 $+M$: 65 / 185.71[2] $= S$: 100% / $285.71[1] [1]Selling price. [2]Dollar markup.	$S = C + M$. or $S = \frac{\text{Cost}}{1 - \text{Percent markup on selling price}}$	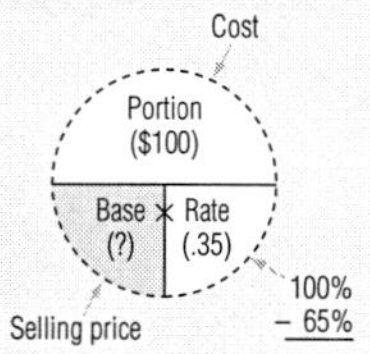

STEPS TO SOLVING PROBLEM

1. Calculate the selling price.

$$S = C + M$$
$$S = \$100 + .65S$$
$$-.65S \qquad -.65S$$
$$\frac{.35S}{.35} = \frac{\$100}{.35}$$
$$S = \$285.71$$

$1.00S - .65S = .35S$

Do not multiply the .65 times $100.00. The 65% is based on selling price, not cost.

2. Calculate the dollar markup.

$$M = S - C$$
$$\$185.71 = \$285.71 - \$100$$

$C = \$100$

$R_{M_S} = 65\%$. This means that markup M is 65% of selling price S: $M = .65S$.

$S = ?$

$M = ?$

$S = C + M$

Let's plug in the values for C and M:

$S = \$100 + .65S$

Rearrange the expression by combining the like terms:

$S - .65S = \$100$

$.35S = \$100$

$S = \frac{\$100}{.35} = \$285.71$

$S = \$285.71$

Don't be afraid of a situation in which you don't know the numerical value of a variable, and can only express it in terms of another variable. Go ahead and substitute this expression for the unknown variable and solve the equation.

$M = S - C = \$285.71 - \$100 = \$185.71$

$M = \$185.71$

Mel's selling price is $285.71 and his markup is $185.71.

Don't forget to write out your answer in full sentence form.

You can check your selling price with the portion formula $B = \frac{\text{Por}}{R}$. To find the selling price (B), divide the cost (Por) by the rate (100% − Percent markup on selling price).

Check

$$\text{Selling price } (B) = \frac{\text{Cost (Por)}}{1 - \text{Percent markup on selling price } (R)}$$

$$= \frac{\$100}{1 - .65} = \frac{\$100}{.35} = \$285.71$$

SITUATION 3: CALCULATING COST WHEN YOU KNOW SELLING PRICE AND GROSS PROFIT MARGIN (PERCENT MARKUP ON SELLING PRICE)

When you know the selling price and the percent markup on selling price, you calculate the cost with the basic formula $S = C + M$. To find the dollar markup, multiply the markup percent by the selling price. When you have the dollar markup, subtract it from the selling price to get the cost.

THE WORD PROBLEM Jill Sport, owner of Sports, Inc., sells tennis rackets for $50. To make her desired profit, Jill needs a 40% markup on the selling price. What is the dollar markup? What do the tennis rackets cost Jill?

THE FACTS	SOLVING FOR?	STEPS TO TAKE	KEY POINTS
S: Selling price: $50. R_{M_S}: Markup on selling price: 40%.	% $ C 60% $30[2] + M 40 20[1] = S 100% $50 [1]Dollar markup. [2]Cost.	$S = C + M$. or Cost = Selling price × (1 − Percent markup on selling price)	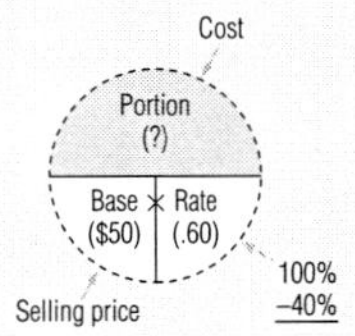

$S = \$50$

$R_{M_S} = 40\% \rightarrow R_{M_S} = .4 \rightarrow M = .4S$

$M = ?$

$C = ?$

$S = C + M$, substitute $.4S$ for M:

$S = C + .4S$

Combine the like terms:

$S - .4S = C$

$.6S = C$

Solve for C:

$C = .6 \times \$50 = \$30$

$C = \$30$

$M = .4 \times \$50 = \$20$

$M = \$20$

It is possible to find C from the formula $C = S - M$.

$C = \$50 - \$20 = \$30$

$C = \$30$

The cost of the tennis rackets was $30 and the markup was $20.

STEPS TO SOLVING PROBLEM

1. Calculate the dollar markup.
   $$S = C + M$$
   $$\$50 = C + .40(\$50)$$

2. Calculate the cost.
   $$\$50 = C + \$20$$
   $$-20 \qquad -20 \leftarrow \text{Dollar markup}$$
   $$\$30 = C$$

To check your cost, use the portion formula Cost (Por) = Selling price (*B*) × (100% selling price − Percent markup on selling price) (*R*).

Check

$$\text{Cost (Por)} = \text{Selling price } (B) \times \left(1 - \text{Percent markup on selling price } (R)\right) = \$50 \times .60 = \$30$$

(1.00 − .40)

In Table 10.1, we compare percent markup on cost with percent markup on retail (selling price). This table is a summary of the answers we calculated from the word problems in Learning Units 10–1 and 10–2. The word problems in the Units were the same, except in Learning Unit 10–1 we assumed markups were on cost, while in Learning Unit 10–2 markups were on selling price. Note that in Situation 1, the dollar markup is the same $90, but the percent markup is different.

Let's now look at how to convert from percent markup on cost to percent markup on selling price and vice versa. We will use Situation 1 from Table 10.1.

Formula for Converting Percent Markup on Cost to Percent Markup on Selling Price

To convert percent markup on cost ($R_{M_C} = .4286$) to percent markup on selling price:

$$\frac{\text{Percent markup on cost}}{1 + \text{Percent markup on cost}}$$

$$R_{M_S} = \frac{.4286}{1 + .4286} = 30\%$$

$$R_{M_S} = \frac{R_{M_C}}{(1 + R_{M_C})} \qquad \textbf{(10.7)}$$

TABLE 10–1
MARKUP ON COST VERSUS MARKUP ON SELLING PRICE

Markup based on cost–Learning Unit 10–1	**Markup based on selling price–Learning Unit 10–2**
Situation 1: Calculating dollar amount of markup and percent markup on cost. $M = ?$ $R_{M_c} = ?$ *C:* Snowthrower cost, \$210. *S:* Snowthrower selling price, \$300. $M = S - C$ $M = \$300 - \$210 = \$90$ markup (p. 196) $M \div C = \$90 \div \$210 = 42.86\%$	*Situation 1: Calculating dollar amount of markup and percent markup on selling price.* $M = ?$ $R_{M_S} = ?$ *C:* Snowthrower cost, \$210. *S:* Snowthrower selling price, \$300. $M = S - C$ $M = \$300 - \$210 = \$90$ markup (p. 200) $M \div S = \$90 \div \$300 = 30\%$ $R_{M_S} = \frac{M}{S} = \frac{\$90}{\$300} = 30\%$
Situation 2: Calculating selling price on cost. *C:* Lamp cost, \$100. 65% markup on cost $S = C \times (1 + \text{Percent markup on cost})\ R_{M_c}$ $S = \$100 \times 1.65 = \$165$ (p. 197) $(100\% + 65\% = 165\% = 1.65)$ or $S = C + R_{M_c} \times C$ $S = C + .65C$ $S = 1.65C$ $S = 1.65 \times \$100 = \$165$	*Situation 2: Calculating selling price on selling price.* *C:* Lamp cost, \$100. 65% markup on selling price R_{M_S}: $S = C \div (1 - \text{Percent markup on selling price})$ $S = \$100.00 \div .35$ $(100\% - 65\% = 35\% = .35)$ $S = \$285.71$ (p. 201) or $M = .65S$ $S = C + M$ $S = C + .65S$ $C = .35S$ $S = \frac{C}{.35} = \$285.71$
Situation 3: Calculating cost on cost. *S:* Tennis racket selling price, \$50. 40% markup on cost. R_{M_c} $C = S \div (1 + \text{Percent markup on cost})$ $C = \$50 \div 1.40$ $(100\% + 40\% = 140\% = 1.40)$ $C = \$35.71$ (p. 197) or $S = C + .4C$ $S = 1.4C$ $C = \frac{S}{1.4} = \frac{\$50}{1.4} = \$35.71$	*Situation 3: Calculating cost on selling price.* *S:* Tennis racket selling price, \$50. 40% markup on selling price $R_{M_S} = .4$ $C = S \times (1 - \text{Percent markup on selling price})$ $C = \$50 \times .60 = \$30$ (p. 201) $(100\% - 40\% = 60\% = .60)$ or $S = C + M$ $S = C + .4S$ $.6S = C$ $C = \$50 \times .6 = \$30$

Formula for Converting Percent Markup on Selling Price to Percent Markup on Cost

To convert percent markup on selling price ($R_{M_S} = 0.3$) to percent markup on cost:

$$\frac{\text{Percent markup on selling price}}{1 - \text{Percent markup on selling price}}$$

$$R_{M_c} = \frac{.30}{1 - .30} = \frac{.30}{.70} = 42.86\%$$

$$R_{M_c} = \frac{R_{M_S}}{(1 - R_{M_S})} \qquad \textbf{(10.8)}$$

Key point: A 30% markup on selling price or a 42.86% markup on cost results in same dollar markup of \$90.

TABLE 10–2
EQUIVALENT MARKUP

R_{M_s} Percent markup on selling price	R_{M_c} Percent markup on cost (round to nearest tenth percent)
20	25.0
25	33.3
30	42.9
33	49.3
35	53.8
40	66.7
50	100.0

Note: Rate of markup on selling price is always lower than on cost because the cost base is always lower than the selling price base.

Table 10.2 summarizes the calculations of these two formulas. As stated in the table, the rate of markup on selling price is always *lower* than the rate of markup on cost. Before you go on to the topic of markdowns and perishables, check your progress with the following Practice Quiz.

LU 10–2 PRACTICE QUIZ

Solve the following situations (markups based on selling price). Note numbers 1, 2, and 3 are parallel problems to those in Practice Quiz 10–1.

1. Irene Westing bought a desk for $400 from an office supply house. She plans to sell the desk for $600. What is Irene's dollar markup? What is her percent markup on selling price (round to the nearest tenth percent)? Check your answer. Selling price will be slightly off due to rounding.
2. Sarah Komar bought dolls for her toy store that cost $12 each. To make her desired profit, Sarah must mark up each doll 35% on the selling price. What is the selling price of each doll? What is the dollar markup? Check your answer.
3. Jay Lyman sells calculators. His competitor sells a new calculator line for $14 each. Jay needs a 40% markup on the selling price to make his desired profit, and he must meet price competition. What is Jay's dollar markup? At what cost can Jay afford to bring these calculators into the store? Check your answer.
4. Dan Flow sells wrenches for $10 that cost $6. What is Dan's percent markup at cost? Round to the nearest tenth percent. What is Dan's percent markup on selling price? Check your answer.

LEARNING UNIT 10–3
MARKDOWNS AND PERISHABLES

J.C. PENNEY CO.

Price-Error Suit Settlement Will Mean Fine of $100,000

J.C. **Penney** Co. agreed to pay a $100,000 fine and to correct pricing and scanning errors in its Michigan stores as part of a settlement of a lawsuit filed by the Michigan Attorney General's office. Michigan sued the Plano, Texas, retailer in Ingham County, Mich., circuit court after finding that 33% of items purchased at four Michigan Penney stores in December rang up incorrectly at the register. As part of the settlement, the retailer also agreed to reimburse Michigan $9,200 in legal expenses. J.C. Penney said it will also designate on-site "pricing associates" to monitor and immediately correct errors and report them to store management and the company's headquarters. Half the $100,000 penalty will be waived if Penney maintains a 96% scanner accuracy rate, the attorney general's office said.

Source: © 2000 Dow Jones & Company, Inc.

You know that when you shop at a supermarket, you should check cash register clerks for errors as they scan your groceries. From the *Wall Street Journal* clipping "Price-Error Suit Settlement Will Mean Fine of $100,000," you also learn that you should check all your purchases for scanning errors at the cash register. The clipping reports that J. C. Penney Co. agreed to pay a $100,000 fine for scanning errors at four stores in Michigan, and agreed to have "pricing associates" monitor for errors and report them to store management. It was interesting to note that half of the $100,000 penalty would be waived if Penney maintained a 96% scanner accuracy rate.

Now let's focus our attention on how to calculate markdowns. Then we'll learn how a business prices items that may spoil before customers buy them.

MARKDOWNS

Markdowns are reductions from the original selling price caused by seasonal changes, special promotions, style changes, and so on. They are basically a discount on selling price and are calculated as a percentage of selling price *S*.

FIGURE 10–2

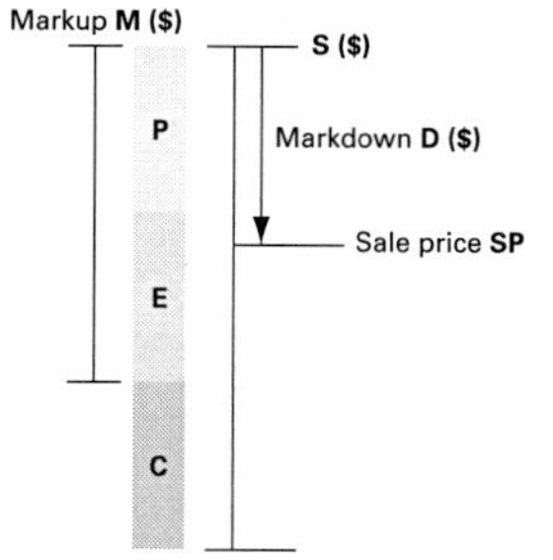

The dollar amount of markdown is labelled D. The markdown percent or **rate of markdown** is labelled R_D.

$$D = R_D \times S \qquad \textbf{(10.9)}$$

$$R_D = \frac{D}{S} \qquad \textbf{(10.10)}$$

$$\text{Markdown percent} = \frac{\text{Dollar markdown}}{\text{Selling price (original)}}$$

The price after markdown is labelled **sale price.**

$$\text{Sale price} = S - D \qquad \textbf{(10.11)}$$

By rearranging this formula we can find D when S and sale price are given:

$$D = S - \text{Sale price} \qquad \textbf{(10.11.1)}$$

Let's look at the following Kmart example.

EXAMPLE

Kmart marked down an $18 video to $10.80. Calculate the **dollar markdown** D and the markdown percent R_D. Use Figure 10.2 for better visualizing of the calculation.

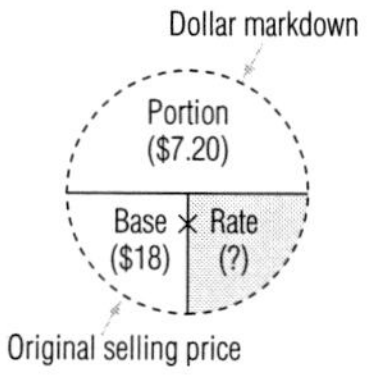

$18.00 Original selling price
− 10.80 Sale price
$ 7.20 Markdown

$$\frac{\text{Dollar markdown, \$7.20}}{\text{Selling price (original), \$18}} = 40\%$$

$$R_D = \frac{D}{S} \qquad \textbf{(10.10)}$$

$$D = S - \text{Sale price} \qquad \textbf{(10.11.1)}$$

Calculating a Series of Markdowns and Markups

Often the final selling price is the result of a series of markdowns (and possibly a markup in between markdowns). We calculate additional markdowns on the previous selling price. Note in the following example how we calculate markdown on selling price after we add a markup.

EXAMPLE

Jones Department Store paid its supplier $400 for a TV. On January 10, Jones marked the TV up 60% on selling price. As a special promotion, Jones marked the TV down 30% on February 8 and another 20% on February 28. No one purchased the TV, so Jones marked it up 10% on March 11. What was the selling price of the TV on March 11?

$C = \$400$
1. $M = 0.6S$
$S = 400 + 0.6S$
$0.4S = 400$
$S = \frac{400}{0.4} = \$1{,}000$
$M = \$600$
2. $\text{Sale price}_1 = S - 0.3S = 0.7S;\ S = \$700 = S_1$
3. $\text{Sale price}_2 = S_1 - 0.2S_1 = 0.8S_1 = \$560 = S_2$
4. $S_3 = S_2 + 0.1S_2 = 1.1S_2 = \$616$

January 10: Selling price = Cost + Markup

$$S = \$400 + .60S$$
$$S - .60S = \$400$$
$$\frac{.40S}{.40} = \frac{\$400}{.40}$$
$$S = \$1{,}000$$

Check

$$S = \frac{\text{Cost}}{1 - \text{Percent markup on selling price}}$$

$$S = \frac{\$400}{1 - .60} = \frac{\$400}{.40} = \$1{,}000$$

February 8 markdown:
100%
− 30
70% → .70 × $1,000 = $700 selling price

February 28 additional markdown:
100%
− 20
80% → .80 × $700 = $560

March 11 additional markup:
100%
+ 10
110% → 1.10 × $560 = $616

Pricing Perishable Items

The following formula can be used to determine the price of goods that have a short shelf life such as fruit, flowers, and pastry. (We limit this discussion to obviously **perishable** items.)

$$\text{Selling price of perishables} = \frac{\text{Total dollar sales}}{\text{Number of units produced} - \text{Spoilage}}$$

THE WORD PROBLEM Audrey's Bake Shop baked 20 dozen bagels. Audrey expects 10% of the bagels to become stale and not saleable. The bagels cost Audrey $1.20 per dozen. Audrey wants a 60% markup on cost. What should Audrey charge for each dozen bagels so she will make her profit? Round to the nearest cent.

THE FACTS	SOLVING FOR?	STEPS TO TAKE	KEY POINTS
Bagels cost: $1.20 per dozen. *Not saleable:* 10%. *Baked:* 20 dozen. *Markup on cost:* 60%.	Price of a dozen bagels.	Total cost of dozen. Total dollar markup. Total selling price. Bagel loss. TS = *C* + TM.	Markup is based on cost.

STEPS TO SOLVING PROBLEM

1. Calculate the total cost. TC = 20 dozen × $1.20 = $24
2. Calculate the total dollar markup.
   TS = *C* + TM
   TS = $24 + .60($24)
   TS = $24 + $14.40 ← Total dollar markup
3. Calculate the total selling price. TS = $38.40 ← Total selling price
4. Calculate the bagel loss. 20 dozen × .10 = 2 dozen
5. Calculate the selling price for a dozen bagels. $\frac{\$38.40}{18} = \$2.13$ per dozen (20 − 2 = 18)

It's time to try the Practice Quiz.

LU 10–3 PRACTICE QUIZ

1. Sunshine Music Shop bought a stereo for $600 and marked it up 40% on selling price. To promote customer interest, Sunshine marked the stereo down 10% for one week. Since business was slow, Sunshine marked the stereo down an additional 5%. After a week, Sunshine marked the stereo up 2%. What is the new selling price of the stereo to the nearest cent? What is the markdown percent based on the original selling price to the nearest hundredth percent?
2. Alvin Rose owns a fruit and vegetable stand. He knows that he cannot sell all his produce at full price. Some of his produce will be markdowns, and he will throw out some produce. Alvin must put a high enough price on the produce to cover markdowns and rotted produce and still make his desired profit. Alvin bought 300 pounds of tomatoes at 14 cents per pound. He expects a 5% spoilage and marks up tomatoes 60% on cost. What price per pound should Alvin charge for the tomatoes?

LEARNING UNIT 10–4
COST-PROFIT-VOLUME AND BREAKEVEN ANALYSIS

From Learning Units 10–1 through 10–3 you understand that all revenue that one gets from sales is distributed for three purposes: costs, operating expenses, and profit. Covering costs and expenses is a priority, and only when they are taken care of can profit be received.

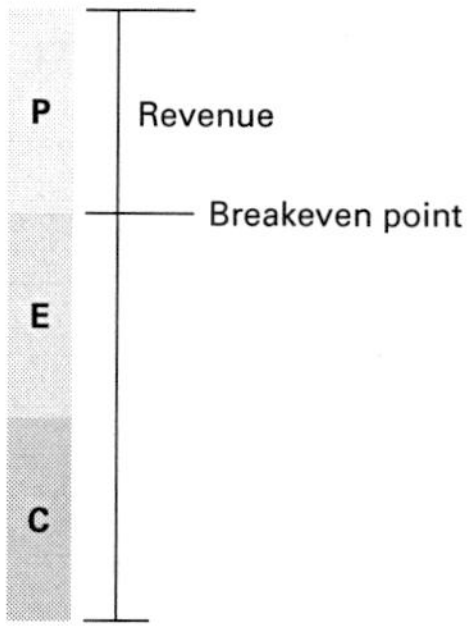

The point at which costs and expenses are paid is called the **breakeven point,** and at this point all expenses and costs are covered and the seller has not yet made any profit or suffered any loss. But every unit sold after the breakeven point will bring some profit or cause a loss.

Let's look at how this distribution of revenues works.

When you are in business you are dealing with two types of costs: **fixed costs (FC)** and **variable costs (VC).** Fixed costs don't change with increases or decreases in sales: they include such things as payments for insurance, a business licence, rent, a lease, utilities, return on investment, some labour, etc. Variable costs, on the other hand, do change in response to changes in the volume of sales: they include such things as payments for material, some labour, etc. The change is in direct proportion: if your unit sales increase by 15%, your variable costs will grow by 15% also.

FIGURE 10-3

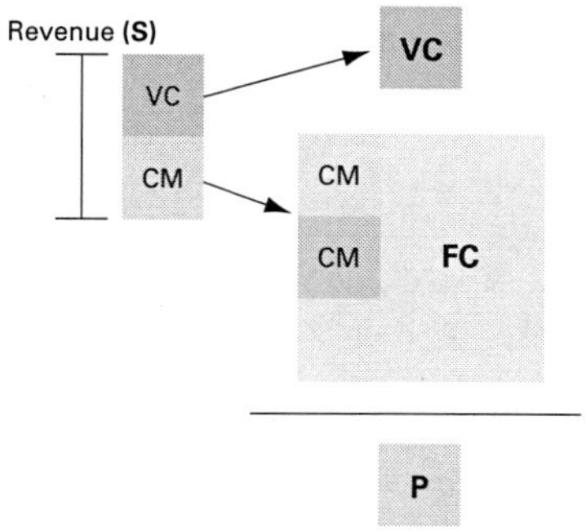

Revenue is received from selling goods or services. Think of revenue as the selling price per unit, consisting of two components, variable cost per unit and contribution margin. Variable cost per unit (VC) as a portion of revenue per unit will be used to cover variable costs in your business. The second part of revenue per unit (S), contribution margin (CM), is used to pay fixed costs of your business and to generate a profit.

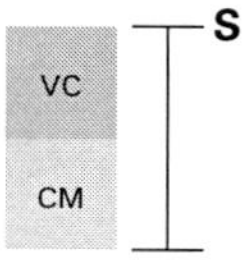

$$S = \text{VC} + \text{CM} \longrightarrow \text{CM} = S - \text{VC} \qquad \textbf{(10.12)}$$

FIGURE 10-3.1

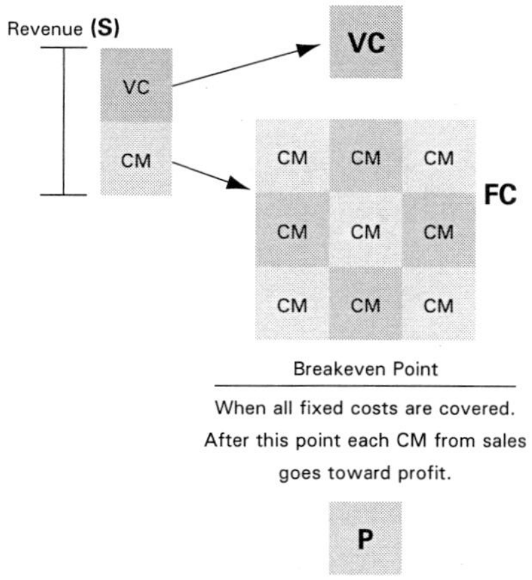

Contribution margin is the difference between revenue and variable costs. This difference goes first of all to pay off total fixed costs (FC), and, once they are covered, starts to accumulate in profit (Figure 10.3).

From Figure 10.3.1 you can see that, when all total fixed costs are paid off, the contribution margin from sales of each unit goes into profit. The more you sell after the breakeven point, the more profit you will make. $X_{b/e}$ is the number of units that it is necessary to sell to achieve the breakeven point—in other words, to cover total fixed costs.

To calculate $X_{b/e}$ we divide total fixed costs FC by contribution margin per unit CM.

FIGURE 10-3.2

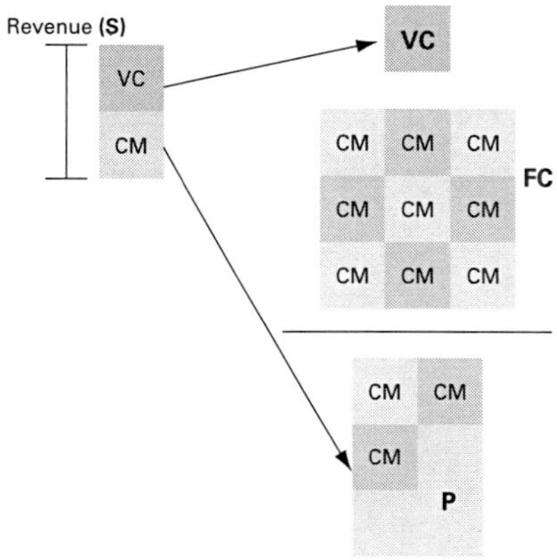

$$X_{b/e} = \frac{\text{FC}}{\text{CM}} \qquad \textbf{(10.13)}$$

To calculate net income or operating profit, we must find the difference between the total contribution margin collected from sales and the fixed costs.

Net income = Total contribution margin − Total fixed costs collected from sales

or

$$\text{NI} = (\text{CM}) \times X - \text{FC} \qquad \textbf{(10.14)}$$

where:

NI = Net income (operating profit) from the period
X = Total number of units sold for the period
FX = Total fixed costs

Contribution margin may be expressed as a rate or as a percentage of the unit selling price. In this case it is called the **contribution rate (CR)**:

$$CR = \frac{CM}{S} \times 100\% \tag{10.15}$$

Let's apply the material you have learned on some examples.

EXAMPLE

Peter, a college student, wants to open his own small business to earn some money for the next two years, while he is still in college. He considers opening a printing facility for students advertising services. Peter has acquired a used computer and monitor for $450, and a used colour printer and a scanner for $250. He has also bought used office furniture: one desk for $50, three chairs for $30, a filing cabinet for $30, and shelves for $25. He expects this furniture and equipment to serve for next two years after which he will donate it to an elementary school. He expects to get a 50% rate of return on his initial investment in the equipment and will pay himself a salary of $500 per month.

Peter will rent an office for $300 per month, including utilities.

One package of multipurpose paper (500 sheets) is $4.99 plus tax ($5.74), a black-and-white printing cartridge is $44.99 plus tax ($51.74), and a colour cartridge is $49.99 plus tax ($57.49). Peter has calculated that one coloured and one black-and-white cartridge will serve for 1,500 copies printed in econofast mode.

Peter has decided to accept a minimum order of 250 copies and will use his cellular phone, which costs him $58 per month, to maintain contact with clients. He will charge $50 per order for printing and distribution of the advertisement materials within the college.

1. Classify the costs into fixed and variable costs and calculate them.
2. Calculate FC—total fixed costs per month and VC—variable costs per order.
3. Identify contribution margin per order CM and interpret it.
4. Find a breakeven point in orders per month.
5. Calculate a breakeven revenue per month.
6. How much in salary and profit will Peter earn if he gets 100 orders per month?
7. If the average cartridge life were, not 1,500, but 1,000 copies, how many orders will be required to break even?

Solution

1. Fixed costs are the costs that don't change regardless of number of orders per month. Variable costs will change in direct proportion to the number of orders and will be calculated per order.
2. Fixed costs:

Rent of the office	$300.00 per month
Depreciation	$29.17 per month*
Furniture	$5.63 per month†
Salary	$500.00 per month
Return on investment	$350.00 per month
Cell phone	$58.00 per month
	Total FC = $1,242.80

*Equipment will be depreciated to $0 value over two years or 24 months. Initial cost of equipment was $700. So depreciation will be ($450 + $250) ÷ (2 × 12) = $700 ÷ 24 = $29.17 per month.

†Furniture will also depreciate completely to $0 within 24 months. Initial cost of furniture was $50 + $30 + $30 + $25 = $135, so depreciation will be $125 ÷ 24 = $5.63 per month.

Variable costs:

Paper packs	.5 per order	$2.87($5.74 × .5)
Cartridges	.17 per order (250 ÷ 1,500)	$18.57[($51.74 + $57.49) × .17]
		Total VC = $21.44

This means that each additional order will add $21.44 to Peter's costs.

3. The contribution margin per order will be:

   $CM = S - VC = \$50 - \$21.44 = \$28.56$

   This means that from each order, after paying $21.44 for variable costs per order $28.56 will be directed toward total fixed costs. Once total fixed costs are paid off, each next contribution margin of $28.56 will contribute to Peter's profit.

4. The breakeven point will be:

   $$X_{b/e} = \frac{FC}{CM} \qquad \textbf{(10.13)}$$

   $X_{b/e} = \$1{,}242.80 \div \$28.56 = 43.52$ orders ⟶ 44 orders per month

5. The breakeven revenue per month will be:

   $X_{b/e} \times S = 44 \times \$50 = \$2{,}200$

6. If Peter gets 100 orders per month he will get 56 orders above breakeven amount, so contribution margins from 56.48 orders (100 – 43.52) will go directly to his profit and will make:

   $56.48 \times \$28.56 = \$1{,}613.07$

   It is possible to calculate net income using formula 10.14:

   $$NI = (CM) \times X - FC \qquad \textbf{(10.14)}$$

   $NI = \$28.56 \times 100 - \$1{,}242.80 = \$2{,}856 - \$1.242.80 = \$1{,}613.20^*$

   *The 13-cent difference is due to rounding.

   Peter will also receive his $500 salary. So in total he will get $2,113.07:

   $\$1{,}613.07 + 500 = \$2{,}113.07$

7. VC = $21.44 was based on a cartridge life of 1,500 copies. If it were only 1,000 copies, VC = $30.18.

   Variable costs:

Paper packs	.5 per order	$2.87($5.74 × .5)
Cartridges	.25 per order (250 ÷ 1,000)	$27.31[($51.74 + $57.49) × .25]
		Total VC = $30.18

   $CM = \$50 - \$30.18 = \$19.82$

   $X_{b/e} = \$1{,}242.80 \div \$19.82 = 62.70$ orders ⟶ 63 orders per month

It's time to try the Practice Quiz.

LU 10–4 PRACTICE QUIZ

1. Blue Mountain store sells calculators for $19.99. Variable cost per calculator is $3.09.
   a. How many calculators must the bookstore sell just to break even, if the total fixed costs are $25,000 per month?
   b. How many calculators must be sold to receive $500 profit?
   c. What sales must be performed to receive $500 profit?
   d. What will the profit/loss be for a month in which 1,000 calculators were sold?*

   *Let's agree for this problem that the store sells calculators only.

CHAPTER ORGANIZER AND REFERENCE GUIDE

Topic	Key point, procedure, formula	Example(s) to illustrate situation
Selling price components, p. 230 Figure 10–1 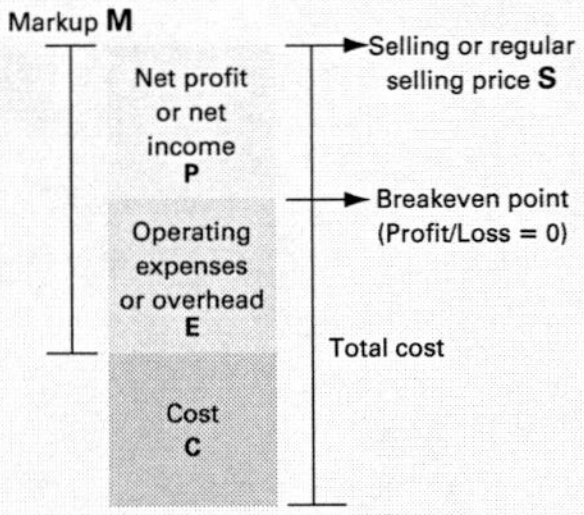 	$S = C + E + P$ **(10.1)** $S = C + M$ **(10.2)** $M = P + E$ **(10.3)** Total cost $= C + E$ **(10.4)** $R_{M_c} = \frac{M}{C}$ $R_{M_s} = \frac{M}{S}$ $R_{M_c} \rightarrow R_{M_s}$ $R_{M_s} \rightarrow R_{M_c}$ $D = R_D \times S$ **(10.9)** $R_D = \frac{D}{S}$ Sale price $= S - D$ **(10.11)**	\$12 P \$88 E \$300 C SP = \$400 E = \$88 P = \$12 C = \$300
Markups based on cost: cost is 100% (base), p. 231	Selling price (S) = Cost (C) + Markup (M) $S = C + M$	\$400 = \$300 + \$100 $S = C + M$
Percent markup on cost, p. 231	$\frac{\text{Dollar markup (portion)}\ M}{\text{Cost (base)}\ C}$ = Rate of markup R_{M_c}	$R_{M_c} = \frac{\$100}{\$300} = \frac{1}{3} = 33\frac{1}{3}\%$
Cost, p. 231	$R_{M_c} = \frac{M}{C}$ $C = \frac{M}{R_{M_c}}$	$\frac{\$100}{.33}$ = \$303 Off slightly due to rounding
Calculating selling price, p. 233	$S = C + M$ **Check** S = Cost × (1 + Percent markup on cost)	Cost, \$6; percent markup on cost, 20% $S = \$6 + .20(\$6)$ $S = \$6 + \$1.20$ $S = \$7.20$ **Check** \$6 × 1.20 = \$7.20
Calculating cost, p. 234	$S = C + M$ **Check** Cost $= \frac{\text{Selling price}}{1 + \text{Percent markup on cost}}$ $C = \frac{S}{(1 + R_{M_c})}$	$S = \$100$; M = 70% of cost $S = C + M$ $\$100 = C + .70C$ $\$100 = 1.7C$ (*Remember:* $C = 1.00C$) $\frac{\$100}{1.7} = C$ $\$58.82 = C$ **Check** $\frac{\$100}{1 + .70} = \$58.82$

(*continues*)

CHAPTER ORGANIZER AND REFERENCE GUIDE (CONTINUED)

Topic	Key point, procedure, formula	Example(s) to illustrate situation
Markups based on selling price: selling price is 100% (base), p. 235	Dollar markup = Selling price − Cost $M = S - C$	$M = S - C$ $\$600 = \$1{,}000 - \$400$
Percent markup on selling price, p. 235	$\frac{\text{Dollar markup (portion) } M}{\text{Selling price (base) } S} = \text{Gross profit margin } R_{M_s}$	$\frac{\$600}{\$1{,}000} = 60\%$
Selling price, p. 236	$S = \frac{\text{Dollar markup } M}{\text{Percent markup on selling price } R_{M_s}}$	$\frac{\$600}{.60} = \$1{,}000$
Calculating selling price, p. 236	$S = C + M$ **Check** $\text{Selling price} = \frac{\text{Cost}}{1 - \text{Percent markup on selling price (gross profit margin)}}$ $S = \frac{C}{(1 - R_{M_s})}$	Cost, \$400; percent markup on S, 60% $S = C + M$ $S = \$400 + .60S$ $S - .60S = \$400 + .60S - .60S$ $\frac{.40S}{.40} = \frac{\$400}{.40}$ $S = \$1{,}000$ **Check** → $\frac{\$400}{1 - .60} = \frac{\$400}{.40} = \$1{,}000$
Calculating cost, p. 237	$S = C + M$ **Check** $\text{Cost} = \text{Selling price} \times \left(1 - \text{Percent markup on selling price}\right)$ $C = S \times (1 - R_{M_s})$	$\$1{,}000 = C + 60\%(\$1{,}000)$ $\$1{,}000 = C + \$600$ $\$400 = C$ **Check** → $\$1{,}000 \times (1 - .60)$ $\$1{,}000 \times .40 = \$400$
Conversion of markup percent, p. 238	Percent markup on cost to Percent markup on selling price $R_{M_c} \rightarrow R_{M_s}$ $R_{M_s} = \frac{\text{Percent markup on cost}}{1 + \text{Percent markup on cost}}$ $R_{M_s} = \frac{R_{M_c}}{(1 + R_{M_c})}$ Percent markup on selling price to Percent markup on cost $R_{M_s} \rightarrow R_{M_c}$ $R_{M_c} = \frac{\text{Percent markup on selling price}}{1 - \text{Percent markup on selling price}}$ $R_{M_c} = \frac{R_{M_s}}{(1 - R_{M_s})}$	*Round to nearest percent:* 54% markup on cost → 35% markup on selling price $\frac{.54}{1 + .54} = \frac{.54}{1.54} = 35\%$ 35% markup on selling price → 54% markup on cost $\frac{.35}{1 - .35} = \frac{.35}{.65} = 54\%$
Markdowns, p. 240	$\text{Markdown percent} = \frac{\text{Dollar markdown}}{\text{Selling price (original)}}$	\$40 selling price 10% markdown $\$40 \times .10 = \$4$ markdown $\frac{\$4}{\$40} = 10\%$

(*continues*)

CHAPTER ORGANIZER AND REFERENCE GUIDE (CONCLUDED)

Topic	Key point, procedure, formula	Example(s) to illustrate situation
Pricing perishables, p. 242	1. Calculate total cost and total selling price. 2. Calculate selling price per unit by dividing total sales in Step 1 by units expected to be sold after taking perishables into account.	50 pastries cost 20 cents each; 10 will spoil before being sold. Markup is 60% on cost. 1. $TC = 50 \times \$.20 = \$10$ $TS = TC + TM$ $TS = \$10 + .60(\$10)$ $TS = \$10 + \$6$ $TS = \$16$ 2. $\dfrac{\$16}{40 \text{ pastries}} = \$.40$ per pastry
Key terms	Absolute loss, p. 231 Breakeven point, p. 243 Contribution margin, p. 243 Contribution rate (CR), p. 244 Cost, p. 230 Dollar markdown, p. 241 Dollar markup, p. 231 Fixed costs (FC), p. 243 Gross profit, p. 230 Gross profit margin, p. 235 Margin, p. 230 Markdowns, p. 240 Markup, p. 230 Net profit (net income), p. 230 Operating expenses (overhead), p. 230 Operating loss, p. 231 Percent markup on cost, p. 231	Percent markup on selling price, p. 235 Perishables, p. 242 Rate of markdown, p. 241 Rate of markup, p. 231 Sale price, p. 241 Selling price, p. 230 Total cost, p. 231 Variable costs (VC), p. 243

CRITICAL THINKING DISCUSSION QUESTIONS

1. Assuming markups are based on cost, explain how the formulas could be used to calculate cost, selling price, dollar markup, and rate of markup. Pick a company and explain why it would mark goods up on cost rather than on selling price. Use Figure 10.1.

2. Assuming markups are based on selling price, explain how the formulas could be used to calculate cost, selling price, dollar markup, and gross profit margin. Pick a company and explain why it would mark up goods on selling price rather than on cost. Use Figure 10.1.

3. What is the formula to convert percent markup on selling price to percent markup on cost? How could you explain that a 40% markup on selling price, which is a 66.7% markup on cost, would result in the same dollar markup?

4. Explain how to calculate markdowns. Do you think stores should run one-day-only markdown sales? Would it be better to offer the best price "all the time"?

5. Explain the five steps in calculating a selling price for perishable items. Recall a situation where you saw a store that did *not* follow the five steps. How did it sell its items?

END-OF-CHAPTER PROBLEMS

DRILL PROBLEMS

Assume markups in Problems 10–1 to 10–6 are based on cost. Find the dollar markup and selling price for the following problems. Round answers to the nearest cent.

	Item	Cost C	Markup percent R_{M_c}	Dollar markup M	Selling price S
10–1.	Sony DVD player	$100	40%	?	?
10–2.	Sharper Image Razor scooter	$65	40%	?	?
10–3.	Staples office furniture	?	40%	?	$6,000
10–4.	Home Depot lumber	?	30%	?	$4,000

Complete the following:

	Cost C	Selling price S	Dollar markup M	Percent markup on cost* R_{M_c}
10–5.	$15.10	$22	?	?
10–6.	?	?	$4.70	102.17%

*Round to the nearest hundredth percent.

Assume markups in Problems 10–7 to 10–12 are based on selling price.

Find the dollar markup and cost (round answers to the nearest cent):

	Item	Selling price S	Markup percent R_{M_S}	Dollar markup M	Cost C
10–7.	Kodak digital camera	$219	30%		
10–8.	IBM scanner	$80	30%		

Find the selling price (round to the nearest cent) of:

10–9. A complete set of pots and pans at Wal-Mart:
40% markup on selling price
Cost, actual, $66.50

10–10. Selling price of a dining room set at Brick's:
55% markup on selling price
Cost, actual, $800

Complete the following:

	Cost C	Selling price S	Dollar markup M	Gross profit margin (round to nearest tenth percent) R_{M_S}
10–11.	$14.80	$49	?	?
10–12.	?	?	$4	20%

By conversion of the markup formula, solve the following (round to the nearest whole percent as needed):

	Percent markup on cost, R_{M_c}	Percent markup on selling price, R_{M_S}
10–13.	12.4%	?
10–14.	?	13%

Complete the following:

10–15. Calculate the final selling price to the nearest cent and markdown percent to the nearest hundredth percent:

Original selling price	First markdown	Second markdown	Markup	Final markdown
$5,000	20%	10%	12%	5%

	Item	Total quantity bought	Unit cost	Total cost	Percent markup on cost	Total selling price	Percent that will spoil	Selling price per brownie
10–16.	Brownies	20	$.79	?	60%	?	10%	?

ADDITIONAL DRILL PROBLEMS

10–17. Fill in the missing numbers:

	Cost	Dollar markup	Selling price
a.	$9.20	$1.59	
b.	$8.32		$11.04
c.	$25.27		$29.62
d.		$75	$165
e.	$86.54	$29.77	

10–18. Calculate the markup based on cost (round to the nearest cent).

	Cost	Markup (percent of cost)	Dollar markup
a.	$425.00	30%	
b.	$1.52	20%	
c.	$9.90	$12\frac{1}{2}\%$	
d.	$298.10	50%	
e.	$74.25	38%	
f.	$552.25	100%	

10–19. Calculate the dollar markup and rate of the markup as a percent of cost (round percents to nearest tenth percent). Verify your result, which may be slightly off due to rounding.

	Cost	Selling price	Dollar markup	Markup (percent of cost)	Verify
a.	$2.50	$4.50			
b.	$12.50	$19			
c.	$.97	$1.25			
d.	$132.25	$175			
e.	$65	$89.99			

10–20. Calculate the dollar markup and the selling price.

	Cost	Markup (percent of cost)	Dollar markup	Selling price
a.	\$2.20	40%		
b.	\$2.80	16%		
c.	\$840	$12\frac{1}{2}$%		
d.	\$24.36	30%		

10–21. Calculate the cost (round to the nearest cent).

	Selling price	Rate of markup based on cost	Cost
a.	\$1.98	30%	
b.	\$360	60%	
c.	\$447.50	20%	
d.	\$1,250	100%	

10–22. Find the missing numbers. Round money to the nearest cent and percents to the nearest tenth percent.

	Cost	Dollar markup	Percent markup on cost	Selling price
a.	\$72		40%	
b.		\$7		\$35
c.	\$8.80	\$1.10		
d.			28%	\$19.84
e.	\$175			\$236.25

10–23. Calculate the markup based on the selling price.

	Selling price	Markup (percent of selling price)	Dollar markup
a.	\$12	40%	
b.	\$230	25%	
c.	\$81	42.5%	
d.	\$72.88	$37\frac{1}{2}$%	
e.	\$1.98	$7\frac{1}{2}$%	

10–24. Calculate the dollar markup and the markup as a percent of selling price (to the nearest tenth percent). Verify your answer, which may be slightly off due to rounding.

	Cost	Selling price	Dollar markup	Markup (percent of selling price)	Verify
a.	\$2.50	\$4.25			
b.	\$16	\$24			
c.	\$45.25	\$85			
d.	\$.19	\$.25			
e.	\$5.50	\$8.98			

10–25. Given the *cost* and the markup as a percent of *selling price,* calculate the selling price.

	Cost	Markup (percent of selling price)	Selling price
a.	$5.90	15%	
b.	$600	32%	
c.	$15	50%	
d.	$120	30%	
e.	$.29	20%	

10–26. Given the selling price and the percent markup on selling price, calculate the cost.

	Cost	Markup (percent of selling price)	Selling price
a.		40%	$6.25
b.		20%	$16.25
c.		19%	$63.89
d.		$62\frac{1}{2}$%	$44

10–27. Calculate the equivalent rate of markup (round to the nearest hundredth percent).

	Markup on cost	Markup on selling price
a.	40%	
b.	50%	
c.		50%
d.		35%
e.		40%

10–28. Find the dollar markdown and the sale price.

	Original selling price	Markdown percent	Dollar markdown	Sale price
a.	$80	20%		
b.	$2,099.98	25%		
c.	$729	30%		

10–29. Find the dollar markdown and the markdown percent on original selling price.

	Original selling price	Sale price	Dollar markdown	Markdown percent
a.	$19.50	$9.75		
b.	$250	$175		
c.	$39.95	$29.96		

10–30. Find the original selling price.

	Sale price	Markdown percent	Original selling price
a.	$328	20%	
b.	$15.85	15%	

10–31. Calculate the final selling price.

	Original selling price	First markdown	Second markdown	Final markup	Final selling price
a.	$4.96	25%	8%	5%	
b.	$130	30%	10%	20%	

10–32. Find the missing amounts.

	Number of units	Unit cost	Total cost	Estimated* spoilage	Desired markup (percent of cost)	Total selling price	Selling price per unit
a.	72	$3		12%	50%		
b.	50	$.90		16%	42%		

*Round to the nearest whole unit as needed.

WORD PROBLEMS

10–33. On an eBay auction, Mike Kaminsky bought an old Walter Lantz Woody Woodpecker oil painting for $4,000. He plans to resell it at a toy show for $7,000. What are the dollar markup and the percent markup on cost? Check the cost figure.

10–34. Chin Yov, store manager for Best Buy, does not know how to price a GE freezer that cost the store $600. Chin knows his boss wants a 45% markup on cost. Help Chin price the refrigerator.

10–35. Cecil Green sells golf hats. He knows that most people will not pay more than $20 for a golf hat. Cecil needs a 40% markup on cost. What should Cecil pay for his golf hats? Round to the nearest cent.

10–36. The results of after-Christmas sales in 2001 showed that Macy's was selling Calvin Klein jeans shirts that were originally priced at $58.00 for $8.70. **(a)** What was the amount of the markdown? **(b)** Based on selling price, what is the percent markdown?

10–37. On March 15, 2001, *The Seattle Times* reported that Boeing would increase its prices for Jetliners. With a selling price of $201.5 million and a cost of $190.1 million, what was the rate of markup? Round to the nearest percent.

10–38. The December 2000 issue of *Yahoo! Internet Life* reported that a 2001 Volkswagen New Beetle GLX with a dealer invoice price of $19,700 was retail priced at $23,000. **(a)** How much is the gross profit margin? Round to the nearest hundredth percent. **(b)** How much is the rate of markup (use the equivalent markup formula)? Round to the nearest hundredth percent.

10–39. Misu Sheet, owner of the Bedspread Shop, knows his customers will pay no more than $120 for a comforter. Misu wants a 30% markup on selling price. What is the most that Misu can pay for a comforter?

10–40. Assume Misu Sheet (Problem 10–39) wants a 30% markup on cost instead of on selling price. What is Misu's cost? Round to the nearest cent.

10–41. Misu Sheet (Problem 10–39) wants to advertise the comforter as "percent markup on cost." What is the equivalent rate of markup compared to the 30% of gross profit margin? Check your answer. Is this a wise marketing decision? Round to the nearest hundredth percent.

10–42. Excel DeWitt Company sells a kitchen set for $475. To promote July 1, DeWitt ran the following advertisement: "Beginning each hour up to 4 hours we will mark down the kitchen set 10%. At the end of each hour, we will mark up the set 1%."

Assume Ingrid Swenson buys the set 1 hour 50 minutes into the sale. What will Ingrid pay? Round each calculation to the nearest cent. What is the markdown percent? Round to the nearest hundredth percent.

10–43. Angie's Bake Shop makes birthday chocolate chip cookies that cost $2 each. Angie expects that 10% of the cookies will crack and be discarded. Angie wants a 60% markup on cost and produces 100 cookies. What should Angie price each cookie? Round to the nearest cent.

10–44. Assume that Angie (Problem 10–43) can sell the cracked cookies for $1.10 each. What should Angie price each cookie?

ADDITIONAL WORD PROBLEMS

10–45. Sears bought a treadmill for $510. Sears has a 60% markup on selling price. What is the selling price of the treadmill?

10–46. Sachi Wong, store manager for Hawk Appliance, does not know how to price a GE dishwasher that cost the store $399. Sachi knows her boss wants a 40% markup on cost. Can you help Sachi price the dishwasher?

10–47. On September 26, 2000, the *Amarillo Globe-News* reported on the concept of "Furniture Clubs" selling to the public at wholesale prices on a cash-only, no-frills basis. Working off an 18% margin, with markups based on cost, the clubs boast they have 5,000 members and a 200% increase in sales. The markup is 36% based on cost. What would be their percent markup if selling price were the base? Round to the nearest hundredth.

10–48. At a local Bed and Bath Superstore, the manager, Jill Roe, knows her customers will pay no more than $300 for a bedspread. Jill wants a 35% markup on selling price. What is the most that Jill can pay for a bedspread?

10–49. On September 3, 2003, *Music World News* reported the difference between the cost and selling price of CDs. A rock band can make a batch of CDs for around $4 each. The record companies charge $18 for new releases. **(a)** What would be the markup amount? **(b)** What would be the percent markup on cost? **(c)** What would be the percent markup on selling price? Round to nearest hundredth percent.

10–50. Circuit City sells a handheld personal planner for $199.99. Circuit City marked up the personal planner 35% on the selling price. What is the cost of the handheld personal planner?

10–51. Excel Arley's Bakery makes fat-free cookies that cost $1.50 each. Arley expects 15% of the cookies to fall apart and be discarded. Arley wants a 45% markup on cost and produces 200 cookies. What should Arley price each cookie? Round to the nearest cent.

10–52. Assume that Arley (Problem 10–51) can sell the broken cookies for $1.40 each. What should Arley price each cookie?

10–53. Ron's Computer Centre sells computers for $1,258.60. Assuming the computers cost $10,788 per dozen, find for each computer the **(a)** dollar markup, **(b)** rate of markup, and **(c)** gross profit margin (nearest hundredth percent). Prove **(b)** and **(c)** of the above problem using the equivalent formulas.

10–54. The cost of an office chair is $159 and the markup rate is 24% of the cost. What are **(a)** the dollar markup and **(b)** the selling price?

10–55. If Barry's Furniture Store purchased a floor lamp for $120 and plans to add a markup of $90, **(a)** what will the selling price be and **(b)** what is the markup as a percent of cost?

10–56. If Lesjardin's Jewellery Store is selling a gold bracelet for $349, which includes a markup of 35% on cost, what are **(a)** Lesjardin's cost and **(b)** the amount of the dollar markup?

10–57. Leeli's Variety Store sells an alarm clock for $14.75. The alarm clock cost Leeli's $9.90. What is the markup amount as a percent of cost? Round to the nearest whole percent.

10–58. Muskoka Audio Supply marks up its merchandise by 40% on cost. If the markup on a cassette player is $85, what are **(a)** the cost of the cassette player and **(b)** the selling price?

10–59. Brown's Department Store is selling a shirt for $55. If the markup is 70% on cost, what is Brown's cost (to the nearest cent)?

10–60. Ward's Greenhouse purchased tomato flats for $5.75 each. Ward's has decided to use a markup of 42% on cost. Find the selling price.

10–61. Fisher Equipment is selling a Wet/Dry Shop Vac for $49.97. If Fisher's markup is 40% of the selling price, what is the cost of the Shop Vac?

10–62. Alpa Lumber Company purchased a 10-inch table saw for $225 and will markup the price 35% on the selling price. What will the selling price be?

10–63. To realize a sufficient gross margin, City Paint and Supply Company marks up its paint 27% on the selling price. If a gallon of Latex Semi-Gloss Enamel has a markup of $4.02, find **(a)** the selling price and **(b)** the cost.

10–64. A Magnavox 20-inch colour TV cost $180 and sells for $297. What is the markup based on the selling price? Round to the nearest hundredth percent.

10–65. Bargain Furniture sells a five-piece country maple bedroom set for $1,299. The cost of this set is $700. What are **(a)** the markup on the bedroom set, **(b)** the markup percent on cost, and **(c)** the markup percent on the selling price? Round to the nearest hundredth percent.

10–66. Robert's Department Store marks up its sundries by 28% on the selling price. If a 6.4-ounce tube of toothpaste costs $1.65, what will the selling price be?

10–67. To be competitive, Terry's Toys must sell the Nintendo Control Deck for $89.99. To meet expenses and make a sufficient profit, Terry's Toys must add a markup on the selling price of 23%. What is the maximum amount that Terry's Toys can afford to pay a wholesaler for Nintendo?

10–68. Nicole's Restaurant charges $7.50 for a linguini dinner that costs $2.75 for the ingredients. What rate of markup is earned on the selling price? Round to the nearest hundredth percent.

10–69. Sleep Country is having a 30%-off sale on their box springs and mattresses. A queen-size, back-supporter mattress is priced at $325. What is the sale price of the mattress?

10–70. Murray and Sons sell a personal fax machine for $602.27. It is having a sale, and the fax machine is marked down to $499.88. What is the percent of the markdown?

10–71. Coleman's is having a clearance sale. A lamp with an original selling price of $249 is now selling for $198. Find the percent of the markdown. Round to the nearest hundredth percent.

10–72. Johnny's Sports Shop has advertised markdowns on certain items of 22%. A soccer ball is marked with a sale price of $16.50. What was the original price of the soccer ball?

10–73. Sam Grillo sells seasonal furnishings. Near the end of the summer a five-piece patio set that was priced $349.99 had not been sold, so he marked it down by 12%. As Labour Day approached, he still had not sold the patio set, so he marked it down an additional 18%. What was the final selling price of the patio set?

10–74. Calsey's Department Store sells their down comforters for a regular price of $325. During its white sale the comforters were marked down 22%. Then, at the end of the sale, Calsey's held a special promotion and gave a second markdown of 10%. When the sale was over, the remaining comforters were marked up 20%. What was the final selling price of the remaining comforters?

10–75. The New Howard Bakery wants to make a 60% profit on the cost of its pies. To calculate the price of the pies, it estimated that the usual amount of spoilage is 5 pies. Calculate the selling price for each pie if the number of pies baked each day is 24 and the cost of the ingredients for each pie is $1.80.

10–76. Sunshine Bakery bakes 660 loaves of bread each day and estimates that 10% of the bread will go stale before it is sold and will have to be discarded. The owner of the bakery wishes to realize a 55% markup on cost on the bread. If the cost to make a loaf of bread is $.46, what should the owner sell each loaf for?

CHALLENGE PROBLEMS

10–77. On October 27, 2000, *WWD (Woman's Wear Daily)* reported on tackling the newsstand challenge. *Woman's Day* had raised its price from $1.29 to $1.69. *Elle* magazine had raised its original price of $3 by 14.28%. *George* magazine had raised its price to $3.50, a 15.71% markup. Using markup based on selling price: **(a)** How much was *Woman's Day*'s percent markup? **(b)** What was *Elle*'s new selling price? **(c)** What was *George*'s original price? Round all answers to the nearest hundredth percent as needed.

10–78. On July 8, 2004, Leon's Kitchen Hut bought a set of pots with a $120 list price from Lambert Manufacturing. Leon's receives a 25% trade discount. Terms of the sale were 2/10, n/30. On July 14, Leon's sent a cheque to Lambert for the pots. Leon's expenses are 20% of the selling price. Leon's must also make a profit of 15% of the selling price. A competitor marked down the same set of pots 30%. Assume Leon's reduces its selling price by 30%.

a. What is the sale price at Kitchen Hut?
b. What was the operating profit or loss?

10–79. Kitchen Tools Ltd. produces juice extractors at a unit variable cost of $57. It sells them for $103 each. The company's production capacity is 2,500 juice extractors per month. Total annual fixed costs are $524,004.

a. What is the contribution margin per unit?
b. What is the amount of juice extractors produced for a breakeven?
c. What is the net income if the company works at full capacity?
d. What will the profit/loss be if the company operates at 75% of capacity?

10–80. Steven makes grocery deliveries to retirement homes and senior houses. His variable costs per delivery is $6.59, and his total fixed costs per month are $3,867. He charges a $30 flat rate for each delivery.

a. What is the contribution margin per delivery?

b. How many deliveries will make him break even?

c. What will Steven's net income be if he had 200 deliveries this month?

d. How many deliveries must Steven make for a profit of $2,500?

e. What changes in breakeven unit sales and breakeven revenue will occur if the flat rate and fixed costs remain the same, but variable costs per delivery increase by $1?

SUMMARY PRACTICE TEST

1. Bayside Appliance marks up merchandise 40% on cost. A television costs Bayside $320. What is Bayside's selling price? Round to the nearest cent. (p. 233)

2. The Levi Shop sells jeans for $49.99 that cost $30.25. What is the percent markup on cost? Round to the nearest hundredth percent. Check the cost. (p. 232)

3. Best Buy sells a flat-screen TV for $1,250. Best Buy marks up the TV 60% on cost. What is the cost and dollar markup of the TV? (p. 237)

4. The Fitness Shop marks up Nike sneakers $35 and sells them for $125. What are the cost and rate of markup to the nearest tenth percent? (p. 237)

5. The Boot Shop bought boots for $80 and marks up the boots 65% on the selling price. What is the selling price of the boots? Round to the nearest cent. (p. 236)

6. Office.com sells a desk for $599 and marks up the desk 30% on selling price. What did the desk cost Office.com? Round to the nearest cent. (p. 237)

7. Service Merchandise sells diamonds for $799 that cost $500. What is Service Merchandise's percent markup on selling price? Round to the nearest hundredth percent. Check the selling price. (p. 235)

8. Russell Amber, a customer of The Gap, will pay $200 for a new jacket. The Gap has a 60% markup on selling price. What is the most that The Gap can pay for this jacket? (p. 237)

9. Home Decorators marks up its merchandise 70% on cost. What is the company's equivalent markup on selling price? Round to the nearest tenth percent. (p. 238)

10. The Muffin Shop makes no-fat muffins that cost $.40 each. The Muffin Shop knows that 15% of the muffins will spoil. If Muffin wants 45% markup on cost and produces 600 muffins, what should Muffin Shop price each muffin? Round to the nearest cent. (p. 233)

SOLUTIONS TO PRACTICE QUIZZES

LU 10–1

Please keep in mind that these problems may be solved in different ways. We will discuss several possible approaches.

1. Irene's dollar markup and percent markup on cost:

THE FACTS	SOLVING FOR?	STEPS TO TAKE	KEY POINTS
C: Desk cost: $400. *S: Desk selling price:* $600.	| | % | $ | | C | 100% | $400 | | + M | 50[2] | 200[1] | | = S | 150% | $600 | [1]Dollar markup. [2]Percent markup on cost.	*M:* Dollar markup = Selling price − Cost. Percent markup on cost = $\frac{\text{Dollar markup}}{\text{Cost}}$ $R_{M_c} = \frac{M}{C}$	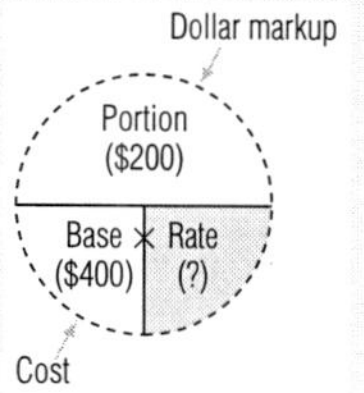

$C = \$400$
$S = \$600$
$M = ?$
$R_{M_S} = ?$

Recall Figure 10.1:

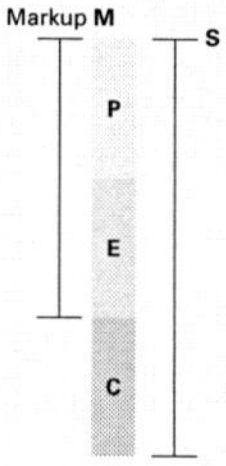

Steps to solving problem

1. Calculate the dollar markup.

Dollar markup = Selling price − Cost
$200 = $600 − $400

2. Calculate the percent markup on cost.

$$\text{Percent markup on cost} = \frac{\text{Dollar markup}}{\text{Cost}} = \frac{\$200}{\$400} = 50\%$$

$S = C + M$
$M = S - C$
$M = \$600 - \$400 = \$200$
$M = \$200$

$$R_{M_c} = \frac{M}{C} = \frac{\$200}{\$400} = .5 = 50\%$$

$R_{M_c} = 50\%$

Irene's markup was $200 and the rate of markup was 50%.

Check

Selling price = Cost + Markup
$600 = $400 + .50($400)
$600 = $400 + $200
$600 = $600

or

$$\text{Cost } (B) = \frac{\text{Dollar markup (Por)}}{\text{Percent markup on cost } (R)} = \frac{\$200}{.50} = \$400$$

2. Dollar markup and selling price of doll:

THE FACTS	SOLVING FOR?	STEPS TO TAKE	KEY POINTS
Doll cost: $12 each. *Markup on cost:* 35%.	| | % | $ | | C | 100% | $12.00 | | + M | 35 | 4.20[1] | | = S | 135% | $16.20[2] | [1]Dollar markup. [2]Selling price.	Dollar markup: $S = C + M$. or $S = \text{Cost} \times \left(1 + \text{Percent markup on cost}\right)$	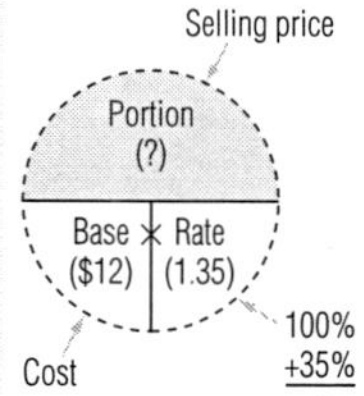

$C = \$12$
$R_{M_S} = .35C$
$M = ?$
$S = ?$

$R_{M_S} = .35C$ means that markup M is 35% of the cost C or $M = .35C$.

$M = .35 \times \$12 = \$4.20$
$M = \$4.20$
$S = C + M = \$12 + \$4.20 = \$16.20$
$S = \$16.20$

The selling price for a doll was $16.20 and the markup was $4.20.

Steps to solving problem

1. Calculate the dollar markup.

$S = C + M$
$S = \$12 + .35(\$12)$
$S = \$12 + \$4.20$ ← Dollar markup

2. Calculate the selling price.

$S = \$16.20$

Check

Selling price (Por) = Cost (*B*) × (1 + Percent markup on cost (*R*)) = $12 × 1.35 = $16.20

3. Cost and dollar markup:

THE FACTS	SOLVING FOR?	STEPS TO TAKE	KEY POINTS
S: Selling price: \$14. *M: Markup on cost:* 40%.	$\begin{array}{lrr} & \% & \$ \\ C & 100\% & \$10^{1} \\ +M & 40 & 4^{2} \\ =S & 140\% & \$14 \end{array}$ [1]Cost. [2]Dollar markup.	$S = C + M.$ or $\text{Cost} = \dfrac{\text{Selling price}}{\text{Percent } 1 + \text{markup on cost}}$ $M = S - C.$	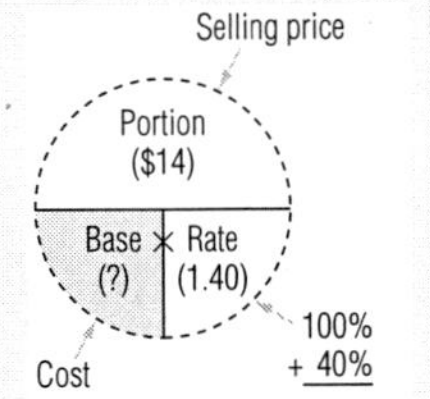

$S = \$14$
$R_{M_c} = .4$
$C = ?$
$M = ?$
$R_{M_c} = .4$ means that $M = .4C.$
$S = C + M$
$S = C + .4C = 1.4C$
$S = 1.4C$ and then $C = \dfrac{S}{1.4}$
$C = \dfrac{\$14}{1.4} = \$10$
$C = \$10$
$M = S - C$
$M = \$14 - \$10 = \$4$
$M = \$4$
or
$M = .4\ C = .4 \times \$10 = \$4$
$M = \$4$
The cost must be not more than \$10 and the markup is \$4.

Steps to solving problem

1. Calculate the cost.

$$S = C + M$$
$$\$14 = C + .40C$$
$$\frac{\$14}{1.40} = \frac{1.40C}{1.40}$$
$$\$10 = C$$

2. Calculate the dollar markup.

$$M = S - C$$
$$M = \$14 - \$10$$
$$M = \$4$$

Check

$$\text{Cost } (B) = \frac{\text{Selling price (Por)}}{1 + \text{Percent markup on cost } (R)} = \frac{\$14}{1.40} = \$10$$

LU 10–2

1. Irene's dollar markup and percent markup on selling price:

THE FACTS	SOLVING FOR?	STEPS TO TAKE	KEY POINTS
C: Desk cost: \$400. *S: Desk selling price:* \$600.	$\begin{array}{lrr} & \% & \$ \\ C & 66.7\% & \$400 \\ +M & 33.3^{2} & 200^{1} \\ =S & 100\% & \$600 \end{array}$ [1]Dollar markup. [2]Percent markup on selling price.	$\text{Dollar markup} = \text{Selling price} - \text{Cost}$ $M = S - C$ $\text{Percent markup on selling price} = \dfrac{\text{Dollar markup}}{\text{Selling price}}$ $R_{M_s} = \dfrac{M}{S}$	

$C = \$400$
$S = \$600$
$M = ?$
$R_{M_s} = ?$
$M = S - C = \$600 - \$400 = \$200$
$M = \$200$
$R_{M_s} = \dfrac{M}{S} = \dfrac{\$200}{\$600} = .3333 = 33.3\%$
$R_{M_s} = 33.3\%$
Irene's markup was \$200 and the gross profit margin was 33.3%.

Steps to solving problem

1. Calculate the dollar markup.

$$\text{Dollar markup} = \text{Selling price} - \text{Cost}$$
$$\$200 = \$600 - \$400$$

2. Calculate the percent markup on selling price.

$$\text{Percent markup on selling price} = \frac{\text{Dollar markup}}{\text{Selling price}}$$
$$= \frac{\$200}{\$600} = 33.3\%$$

Check

$$\begin{aligned} \text{Selling price} &= \text{Cost} + \text{Markup} \\ \$600 &= \$400 + .333(\$600) \\ \$600 &= \$400 + \$199.80 \\ \$600 &= \$599.80^{*} \end{aligned}$$

or

$$\text{Selling price } (B) = \frac{\text{Dollar markup (Por)}}{\text{Percent markup on selling price } (R)} = \frac{\$200}{.333} = \$600.60^{*}$$

*Off due to rounding.

2. Selling price of doll and dollar markup:

THE FACTS	SOLVING FOR?	STEPS TO TAKE	KEY POINTS
C: Doll cost: \$12 each. M_{R_s}: Markup on selling price: 35%.	% \$ *C* 65% \$12.00 + *M* 35 6.46[2] = *S* 100% \$18.46[1] [1]Selling price. [2]Dollar markup.	$S = C + M.$ or $S = \dfrac{\text{Cost}}{1 - \text{Percent markup on selling price}}$	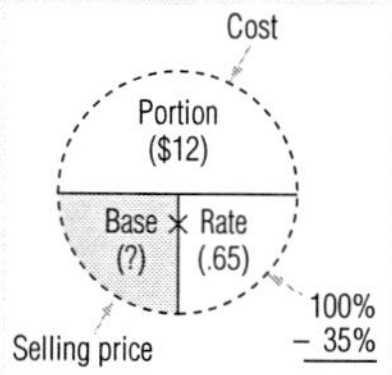

$C = \$12$
$R_{M_s} = 35\%$. This means that
$M = .35S.$
$S = ?$
$M = ?$
$S = C + M = C + .35S$
$.75S = C$
$S = \dfrac{C}{.65} = \dfrac{\$12}{.65} = \$18.46$
$S = \$18.46$
$M = S - C = \$18.46 - \$12 =$
$\$6.46$
$M = \$6.46$
The selling price of the doll was \$18.46 and the dollar markup was \$6.46.

Steps to solving problem

1. Calculate the selling price.

$$S = C + M$$
$$S = \$12 + .35S$$
$$-.35S \qquad -.35S$$
$$\frac{.65S}{.65} = \frac{\$12}{.65}$$
$$S = \$18.46$$

2. Calculate the dollar markup.

$$M = S - C$$
$$\$6.46 = \$18.46 - \$12$$

Check

$$\text{Selling price } (B) = \frac{\text{Cost (Por)}}{1 - \text{Percent markup on selling price } (R)} = \frac{\$12}{.65} = \$18.46$$

3. Dollar markup and cost:

THE FACTS	SOLVING FOR?	STEPS TO TAKE	KEY POINTS
S: Selling price: \$14. R_{M_s}: Markup on selling price: 40%.	% \$ *C* 60% \$ 8.40[2] + *M* 40 5.60[1] = *S* 100% \$14.00 [1]Dollar markup. [2]Cost.	$S = C + M.$ or Cost = Selling price × $\left(1 - \text{Percent markup on selling price}\right)$	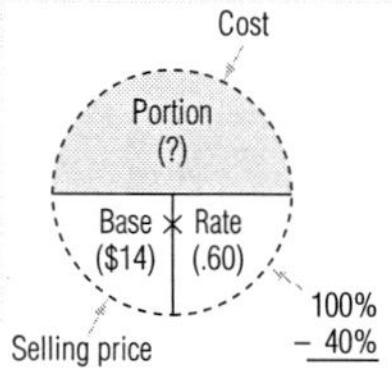

$S = \$14$
$R_{M_s} = .4 \longrightarrow M = .4S$
$M = ?$
$C = ?$
$S = C + M = C + .4S$
$C = S - .4S$
$C = .6S = .6 \times \$14 = \$8.40$
$C = \$8.40$
$M = S - C = \$14 - \$8.40 =$
$\$5.60$
$M = \$5.60$
Jay could afford to buy calculators at \$8.40 with a markup of \$5.60.

Steps to solving problem

1. Calculate the dollar markup.

2. Calculate the cost.

$$S = C + M$$
$$\$14.00 = C + .40(\$14)$$
$$\$14.00 = C + \$5.60 \longleftarrow \text{Dollar markup}$$
$$-5.60 \qquad -5.60$$
$$\$8.40 = C$$

Check

Cost = Selling price × (1 − Percent markup on selling price) = \$14 × .60 = \$8.40
(Por) (*B*) (*R*)

(1 − .40)

4. $R_{M_C} = \dfrac{\$4}{\$6} = 66.7\%$ $\qquad \dfrac{.40}{1 - .40} = \dfrac{.40}{.60} = \dfrac{2}{3} = 66.7\%\ R_{M_S}$

$R_{M_S} = \dfrac{\$4}{\$10} = 40\%$ $\qquad \dfrac{.667}{1 + .667} = \dfrac{.667}{1.667} = 40\%$ (due to rounding)

$S = \$10$
$C = \$6$
$R_{M_C} = ?$
$R_{M_S} = ?$
$M = S - C = \$10 - \$6 = \$4$
$M = \$4$

$R_{M_C} = \dfrac{\$4}{\$6} = .66666 = 66.7\%$

$R_{M_S} = \dfrac{\$4}{\$10} = .4 = 40\%$

$R_{M_S} = 40\%$
$R_{M_C} = 66.7\%$

Dan's rate of markup was 66.7% and the gross profit margin was 40%.

LU 10–3

1. $S = C + M$

$S = \$600 + .40S$

$-.40S \qquad -.40S$

$\dfrac{.60S}{.60} = \dfrac{\$600}{.60}$

$S = \$1{,}000$

First markdown: $.90 \times \$1{,}000 = \$900$ selling price
Second markdown: $.95 \times \$900 = \$855$ selling price
Markup: $1.02 \times \$855 = \$872.10$ final selling price

$\$1{,}000 - \$872.10 = \dfrac{\$127.90}{\$1{,}000} = 12.79\%$

$C = \$600;\ M = .4S_0;$
$R_{D_1} = .1S_0;\ R_{D_2} = .05S_1$
$M_2 = .02S_2;\ S_3 = ?$

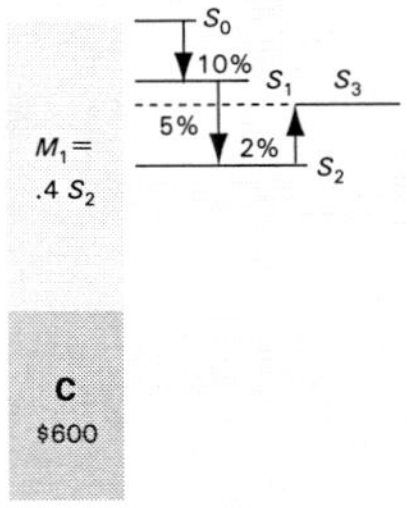

$S_0 = C + .4S_0 \rightarrow .6S_0 =$
$C \rightarrow S_0 = \dfrac{\$600}{.6} = \$1{,}000$
$S_1 = S_0 - .1S_0 = .9S_0 = \$900$
$S_2 = S_1 - .05S_1 = .95S_1 = .95 \times \$900 = \$855$
$S_3 = S_2 + .02S_2 = 1.02S_2 = \$872.10$
$D = S_0 - S_3 = \$1{,}000 = \$872.10 = \$127.90$
$R_D = \dfrac{D}{S_0} = \dfrac{\$127.90}{\$1{,}000} = 12.79\%$

2. Price of tomatoes per pound:

THE FACTS	SOLVING FOR?	STEPS TO TAKE	KEY POINTS
300 lb. tomatoes at \$.14 per pound. *Spoilage:* 5%. *Markup on cost:* 60%.	Price of tomatoes per pound.	Total cost. Total dollar markup. Total selling price. Spoilage amount. TS = *C* + TM.	Markup is based on cost.

Steps to solving problem

1. Calculate the total cost. $\qquad C = 300 \text{ lb.} \times \$.14 = \$42.00$
2. Calculate the total dollar markup. $\qquad TS = C + TM$

$TS = \$42.00 + .60(\$42)$

$TS = \$42.00 + \$25.20$ ← Total dollar markup

3. Calculate the total selling price. $\qquad TS = \$67.20$ ← Total selling price
4. Calculate the tomato loss. $\qquad 300 \text{ pounds} \times .05 = 15 \text{ pounds spoilage}$
5. Calculate the selling price per pound of tomatoes. $\qquad \dfrac{\$67.20}{285} = \$.24$ per pound (rounded to nearest hundredth)

(300 − 15)

LU 10–4

1. **a.** CM = S − VC = $19.99 − $3.09 = $16.90

   $X_{b/e}$ = $25,000 ÷ $16.90 = 1,479.29 orders ⟶ 1,480 calculators per month

   b. Rearranging formula 10.14:

   NI = (CM)X − FC

   We can find the formula for X:

   (CM)X = NI + FC

   X = (NI + FC)/CM

   NI = $500

   FC = $25,000

   CM = $16.90

   X = ($25,000 + $500)/$16.90 = 1,508.88 ⟶ 1,509 calculators per month

   Or—you might ask how many calculators above the breakeven amount must be sold to get $500 of profit:

   P/CM = $500/$16.90 = 29.60 calculators

   The breakeven amount is 1,479.3. All together it will be 1,479.3 + 29.6 = 1,508.9 ⟶ 1,509 calculators per month.

   c. The bookstore must produce $30,164.91 per month in sales to receive $500 of profit:

   $19.99 × 1,509 = $30,164.91 per month

   It looks like this business is too risky and not very profitable. It is recommended to add other products.

   d. X = 1,000

   The breakeven amount is 1,480 calculators. The store sold 480 calculators less. So it will face losses of $8,112 (since 480 × $16.90 = $8,112).

Business Math Scrapbook

WITH INTERNET APPLICATION

Putting Your Skills to Work

The Golden Arches: Burgers, Fries and 4-Star Rooms

McDonald's Plans to Open Two Hotels in Switzerland; Will Business Travelers Bite?

By MARGARET STUDER
And JENNIFER ORDONEZ
Staff Reporters of THE WALL STREET JOURNAL

ZURICH—The room prices at the four-star hotel will be listed on electronic signs strangely reminiscent of McDonald's menu boards. The color scheme will be a softer version of the fast-food chain's famous red and yellow. And guests will spend their nights on a 'Big Mac' bed.

After decades of serving up Happy Meals around the globe, **McDonald's** Corp. is cooking up something new: the Golden Arch Hotels. In March, the company will open two hotels in Switzerland, aimed at business travelers during the week and families on the weekend. The hotels will offer 24-hour service and room service—amenities necessary to qualify for four-star status in Switzerland.

If the venture is successful, more hotels could follow in other parts of the world.

"Innovation is always on the menu at McDonald's," Jack Greenberg, McDonald's chairman and chief executive officer, said in a video shown at a press conference last week announcing the hotels. "Our passion for making customers smile extends very naturally to the hotel sector."

Back at McDonald's headquarters in Oak Brook, Ill., spokesman Jack Daly says that hotels are a concept that may never expand beyond Switzerland. "This is definitely a Swiss project," he says, attributing its genesis to Urs Hammer, a hotelier before he became chairman and CEO in 1980 of McDonald's Swiss Holding AG, a joint venture.

Yet the hotel test fits into a larger pattern of McDonald's experiments in Europe. In Germany, the company is selling McDonald's brand ketchup in grocery stores. In countries including Portugal and Austria, it is operating McCafe, a coffee-bar concept that will be introduced in the U.S. next year.

A model of McDonald's Corp.'s Golden Arch Hotels opening in Switzerland next year.

The efforts represent the determination of Mr. Greenberg, chief executive since 1998, to leverage the McDonald's brand beyond hamburgers and french fries. In the U.S., where sales growth has been sluggish for years, that campaign has included the purchase of some or all of a Mexican restaurant chain, a pizza chain and Boston Chicken Inc.

Still, it is a bit of a leap to hotels. Mr. Greenberg said at the press conference that he believes clients will be attracted by the things they have come to expect from McDonald's: quality, service, cleanliness and value. A room will cost between 169 Swiss francs and 189 francs ($94.99 and $106.24), with 25 francs added for a second person.

"At a McDonald's, you have the security of knowing what you get," asserts Golden Arch Hotels Sales Director Mirjam von Zweden.

PROJECT A

Do you think this retailing strategy will work for McDonald's? Check out the McDonald's Web site to see if you can find any more updates on this strategy.

CUMULATIVE REVIEW

A WORD PROBLEM APPROACH—CHAPTERS 6–10

1. Assume Kellogg's produced 715,000 boxes of Corn Flakes this year. This was 110% of the annual production last year. What was last year's annual production? (p. 130)

2. A new Sony camcorder has a list price of $420. The trade discount is 10/20 with terms of 2/10, n/30. If a retailer pays the invoice within the discount period, what is the amount the retailer must pay? (p. 199)

3. The Bay sells loafers with a markup of $40. If the markup is 30% on cost, what did the loafers cost The Bay? Round to the nearest dollar. (p. 234)

4. Aster Computers received from Ring Manufacturers an invoice dated August 28 with terms 2/10 EOM. The list price of the invoice is $3,000 (freight not included). Ring offers Aster a 9/8/2 trade chain discount. Terms of freight are FOB shipping point, but Ring prepays the $150 freight. Assume Aster pays the invoice on October 9. How much will Ring receive? (p. 210)

5. Runners World marks up its Nike jogging shoes 25% on selling price. The Nike shoe sells for $65. How much did the store pay for them? (p. 237)

6. Ivan Rone sells antique sleds. He knows that the most he can get for a sled is $350. Ivan needs a 35% markup on cost. Since Ivan is going to an antiques show, he wants to know the maximum he can offer a dealer for an antique sled. (p. 234)

7. Bonnie's Bakery bakes 60 loaves of bread for $1.10 each. Bonnie's estimates that 10% of the bread will spoil. Assume a 60% markup on cost. What is the selling price of each loaf? If Bonnie's can sell the old bread for one-half the cost, what is the selling price of each loaf? (p. 233)

Payroll

11

Payroll Deductions Tables

Tables de retenues sur la paie

Ontario

Ontario

Effective January 1, 2003

En vigueur le 1er janvier 2003

he CPP and EI tables for 2003 are not part of this file. However, they are available on our Web site.

Les tables relatives au RPC et à l'AE pour 2003 ne font pas partie de ce fichier. Cependant, elles sont disponibles sur notre site Web.

The updated Form TD1ON is available at www.ccra.gc.ca/formspubs/forms/td1-e.html

Vous trouverez le formulaire TD1ON sur notre site Web à www.adrc.gc.ca/formspubs/forms/td1-f.html

must look up amounts in two tax deductions es – a federal table and a provincial table. more information, see the section called have to deduct both federal and provincial me tax".

Remarque
Vous devez consulter deux tables de retenues d'impôt pour déterminer les montants applicables – une table fédérale et une table provinciale. Pour obtenir plus de renseignements, consultez la section intitulée « Vous devez retenir de l'impôt fédéral et provincial sur le revenu ».

N-1

You Have to Deduct Both Federal and Provincial Income Tax

If you are using the income tax tables in this publication to determine your employees' and pensioners' total tax deductions, you have to look up the amounts in the federal tax table and the provincial tax table. ...

If not enough taxes have been deducted, employees and pensioners can ask to have more tax withheld at source to adjust any tax shortfall. To do so, employees and pensioners should complete a federal Form TDI and return it to you.

Source: Payroll Deductions Tables, January 2003 version, Canada Customs and Revenue Agency. Reproduced with permission of the Minister of Public Works and Government Services Canada, 2003.

LEARNING UNIT OBJECTIVES

LU 11–1: Calculating Various Types of Employees' Gross Pay

- Define, compare, and contrast weekly, biweekly, semimonthly, and monthly pay periods (p. 266).
- Calculate gross pay with overtime on the basis of time (p. 268).
- Calculate gross pay for piecework, differential pay schedule, straight commission with draw, variable commission scale, and salary plus commission (pp. 268–270).

LU 11–2: Computing Payroll Deductions for Employees' Pay; Employers' Responsibilities

- Explain and calculate federal and provincial income taxes, CPP, EI (pp. 270–273).

In this Statistics Canada clipping there is a reference to the report "Wages Rates, Salaries and Hours of Labour." This report, based on annual wage reports of the Department of Labour, contains information about index numbers of wages rates, wage rates, and salaries. The early data was received from trade unions, collective agreements, department field representatives, and the *Labour Gazette* field representatives in Canada.

The following summary of technical notes of the present survey is taken from *Wage Rates, Salaries and Hours of Labour*, Canada, October 1976.

The survey, covering all establishments in Canada with 20 or more employees, is conducted by means of a reporting form which is mailed to employers. The form includes, for each occupation surveyed, a short description of the work characteristically performed.

These occupational descriptions are based on the *Canadian Classification and Dictionary of Occupations*, commonly referred to as the CCDO, which was developed and published by the Canada Department of Manpower and Immigration in collaboration with Statistics Canada.

The subject of this report is different methods of employee remuneration: salary, hourly wage, straight piece rate pay, and straight and variable commission scale.

This chapter discusses (1) the type of pay people work for, (2) how employers calculate paycheques and deductions, and (3) what employers must report and pay in taxes.

LEARNING UNIT 11–1
CALCULATING VARIOUS TYPES OF EMPLOYEES' GROSS PAY

Logan Company manufactures dolls of all shapes and sizes. These dolls are sold worldwide. We study Logan Company in this Unit because of the variety of methods Logan uses to pay its employees.

Companies usually pay employees **weekly, biweekly, semimonthly,** or **monthly.** How often employers pay employees can affect how employees manage their money. Some employees prefer a weekly paycheque that spreads the inflow of money. Employees who have monthly bills may find the twice-a-month or monthly paycheque more convenient. All employees would like more money to manage.

Let's assume you earn $50,000 per year. The following table shows what you would earn each pay period. Remember that 13 weeks equals one quarter. Four quarters or 52 weeks equals a year.

Salary paid	Period (based on a year)	Earnings for period (dollars)	
Weekly	52 times (once a week)	$ 961.54	($50,000 ÷ 52)
Biweekly	26 times (every two weeks)	$1,923.08	($50,000 ÷ 26)
Semimonthly	24 times (twice a month)	$2,083.33	($50,000 ÷ 24)
Monthly	12 times (once a month)	$4,166.67	($50,000 ÷ 12)

Salaries are paid to employees if their workload is predictable and stable. Annual salary may be paid on a weekly, biweekly, monthly, or semimonthly basis. Such payments are calculated by dividing the annual salary by 12, 24, 52, and 26 respectively. However, every five or six years there will be 53 paydays on weekly payrolls. **Periodic payments** will be determined in the same way as usual, by dividing the annual salary by the number of paydays in the year:

$$\text{Periodic payment} = \frac{\text{Annual salary}}{\text{Number of paydays in the year}}$$

In a year with 53 paydays, weekly payments will usually be approximately 2% less than in a year with 52 paydays.

Paola Boiko earns $45,000 per year and is paid on weekly basis. In a regular year with 52 paydays she receives $865.39 gross pay every week.

$$\text{Gross pay} = \frac{\$45{,}000}{52} = \$865.39$$

In a year with 53 paydays her weekly gross earning will be:

$$\text{Gross pay} = \frac{\$45{,}000}{53} = \$849.06$$

Hourly wages are paid to employees who have a variable and unpredictable workload, when overtime is common. Typically, by agreement an employee should work $7\frac{1}{2}$ or 8 regular hours per day ($37\frac{1}{2}$ or 40 hours per week). Any excess of these hours is called **overtime,** which is paid at a different rate: "time-and-a-half" (1.5 times the regular rate).

If an employee works during a statutory holiday he/she is paid at least at time-and-a-half in addition to the regular payment. Hence, the statutory holiday rate will be 2.5 times the regular hourly rate.

Martin Kozak gets $25 per hour. He worked eight hours on New Year's Day. How much was he paid for this day?

Regular work hours × Regular hourly rate + Statutory holiday work hours × Statutory holiday rate

$= 8 \times \$25 + 8 \times (\$25 \times 1.5)$

$= 8 \times \$25 \times (1 + 1.5)$

$= 8 \times \$25 \times 2.5$

$= 200 + 300$

$= \$500$

SOME IMPORTANT FEATURES OF THE WAGE

1. The most common type of time rate for non-office employees is an hourly rate under which the employee is paid a fixed amount for each hour worked. Consequently, in cases where hourly rates are requested on survey forms but daily, weekly, or monthly rates are reported, the reported rates are converted to an hourly basis. However, daily, weekly or monthly rates are sometimes shown for occupations in industries in which such methods of wage payment are common. When monthly rates are converted to weekly rates, or vice versa, a conversion factor of four weeks per month is used. When weekly rates are converted to hourly rates, the weekly rate (exclusive of overtime or other premiums) is divided by the standard weekly hours of work as reported. All rates include cost-of-living bonus payments where applicable.
2. The most common types of straight-time earnings are those based on piecework or various production or incentive bonus systems; other types are based on commission or mileage/kilometrage.

Overtime premium rates are not included in the wage figures published. Also excluded are shift differentials, non-production bonuses (except cost-of-living allowance payments), shares in company profits, and the monetary value of fringe benefits such as group insurance, sick benefits, uniforms, etc. The rates are derived from the employee's wage before deductions are made for taxes, unemployment insurance contributions, pension payments, etc.

Now let's look at some pay schedule situations and examples of how Logan Company calculates its payroll for employees of different pay status.

SITUATION 1:
Hourly Rate of Pay: Calculation of Overtime

Logan Company is calculating the weekly pay of Ramon Valdez, who works in its manufacturing division. For the first 40 hours Ramon works, Logan calculates his **gross pay** (earnings before **deductions**) as follows:

Gross pay = Hours employee worked × Rate per hour

Ramon works more than 40 hours in a week. For every hour over his 40 hours, Ramon must be paid an overtime pay of at least 1.5 times his regular pay rate. The following formula is used to determine Ramon's overtime:

> Hourly overtime pay rate = Regular hourly pay rate × 1.5

Logan Company must include Ramon's overtime pay with his regular pay. To determine Ramon's gross pay, Logan uses the following formula:

> Gross pay = Earnings for 40 hours + Earnings at time-and-a-half rate (1.5)

Let's calculate Ramon's gross pay from the following data:

EXAMPLE

Employee	M	T	W	Th	F	S	Total hours	Rate per hour
Ramon Valdez	13	$8\frac{1}{2}$	10	8	$11\frac{1}{4}$	$10\frac{3}{4}$	$61\frac{1}{2}$	$9

$61\frac{1}{2}$ total hours
-40 regular hours
$21\frac{1}{2}$ hours overtime[1]   Time-and-a-half pay: $9 × 1.5 = $13.50

Gross pay = (40 hours × $9) + ($21\frac{1}{2}$ hours × $13.50)
= $360 + $290.25
= **$650.25**

Note that the $13.50 overtime rate came out even. However, throughout this text, *if an overtime rate is greater than two decimal places, do not round it. Round only the final answer. This gives greater accuracy.*

SITUATION 2:
Straight Piece Rate Pay (Piecework Rate)

Some companies, especially manufacturers, pay workers according to how much they produce. Logan Company pays Ryan Foss for the number of dolls he produces in a week. This gives Ryan an incentive to make more money by producing more dolls. Ryan receives $.96 per doll, less any defective units. The following formula determines Ryan's gross pay:

> Gross pay = Number of units produced × Rate per unit

Companies may also pay a guaranteed hourly wage and use a piece rate as a bonus. However, Logan uses straight piece rate as wages for some of its employees.

EXAMPLE

During the last week of April, Ryan Foss produced 900 dolls. Using the above formula, Logan Company paid Ryan $864.

Gross pay = 900 dolls × $.96
= **$864**

[1]Some companies pay overtime for time over 8 hours in one day; Logan Company pays overtime for time over 40 hours per week.

SITUATION 3:
Differential Pay Schedule

Some of Logan's employees can earn more than the $.96 straight piece rate for every doll they produce. Logan Company has set up a **differential pay schedule** for these employees. The company determines the rate these employees make by the amount of units the employees produce at different levels of production.

EXAMPLE

Logan Company pays Abby Rogers on the basis of the following schedule:

	Units produced	Amount per unit
First 50 →	1–50	$ .50
Next 100 →	51–150	.62
Next 50 →	151–200	.75
	Over 200	1.25

Last week Abby produced 300 dolls. What is Abby's gross pay?

Logan calculated Abby's gross pay as follows:

$(50 \times \$.50) + (100 \times \$.62) + (50 \times \$.75) + (100 \times \$1.25)$

$\$25 + \$62 + \$37.50 + \$125 = \$249.50$

We are now ready to study some of the other types of employee commission payment plans.

SITUATION 4:
Straight Commission with Draw

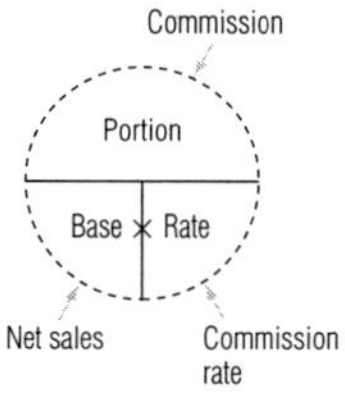

Companies frequently use **straight commission** to determine the pay of salespersons. This commission is usually a certain percentage of the amount the salesperson sells. Logan Company allows some of its salespersons to draw against this commission at the beginning of each month.

A **draw** is an advance on the salesperson's commission. Logan subtracts this advance later from the employee's commission earned based on sales. When the commission does not equal the draw, the salesperson owes Logan the difference between the draw and the commission.

EXAMPLE

Logan Company pays Jackie Okamoto a straight commission of 15% on her net sales (net sales are total sales less sales returns). In May, Jackie had net sales of $56,000. Logan gave Jackie a $600 draw in May. What is Jackie's gross pay?

Logan calculated Jackie's commission minus her draw as follows:

$\$56{,}000 \times .15 = \$8{,}400$
$- \quad 600$
$\$7{,}800$

Logan Company pays some people in the sales department on a variable commission scale. Let's look at this, assuming the employee had no draw.

SITUATION 5:
Variable Commission Scale (Graduated Commission)

A company with a **variable commission scale** uses different commission rates for different levels of net sales.

EXAMPLE

Last month, Jane Ring's net sales were $160,000. What is Jane's gross pay based on the following schedule?

Up to $35,000	4%
Excess of $35,000 to $45,000	6%
Over $45,000	8%

$\text{Gross pay} = (\$35{,}000 \times .04) + (\$10{,}000 \times .06) + (\$115{,}000 \times .08)$
$= \$1{,}400 + \$600 + \$9{,}200$
$= \$11{,}200$

SITUATION 6:
Salary Plus Commission

Logan Company pays Joe Roy a $3,000 monthly salary plus a 4% commission for sales over $20,000. Last month Joe's net sales were $50,000. Logan calculated Joe's gross monthly pay as follows:

$$\begin{aligned} \text{Gross pay} &= \text{Salary} + (\text{Commission} \times \text{Sales over } \$20{,}000) \\ &= \$3{,}000 + (\$.04 \times \$30{,}000) \\ &= \$3{,}000 + \$1{,}200 \\ &= \$4{,}200 \end{aligned}$$

Before you take the Practice Quiz, you should know that many managers today receive **overrides.** These managers receive a commission based on the net sales of the people they supervise.

LU 11–1 PRACTICE QUIZ

1. Jill Foster worked 52 hours in one week for Air Canada. Jill earns $10 per hour. What is Jill's gross pay, assuming overtime is at time-and-a-half after 40 hours?
2. Matt Long had $180,000 in sales for the month. Matt's commission rate is 9%, and he had a $3,500 draw. What was Matt's end-of-month commission?
3. Bob Meyers receives a $1,000 monthly salary. He also receives a variable commission on net sales based on the following schedule (commission doesn't begin until Bob earns $8,000 in net sales):

$8,000–$12,000	1%	Excess of $20,000 to $40,000	5%
Excess of $12,000 to $20,000	3%	More than $40,000	8%

Assume Bob earns $40,000 net sales for the month. What is his gross pay?

40×10 + 12×(10×1.5)

LEARNING UNIT 11–2

COMPUTING PAYROLL DEDUCTIONS FOR EMPLOYEES' PAY; EMPLOYERS' RESPONSIBILITIES

When you get your weekly pay slip, do you take time to check all the numbers? What amounts are deducted as federal and provincial taxes? Do you understand why at some point in the year you are not deducted for EI and CPP? How are tax deductions calculated? Did you know that the employers also make contributions to your Canada Pension Plan?

FIGURE 11–1
Example of pay slip

John Lee Employee #: **0000012345** Payday: **2003/04/01** **18212577**	Department #:12200 Employer #: **654-a**	Pay **08**	From **2003/03/30**	To **2003/04/12**	Sequence

Statement of Earnings					Employee Deductions and Employer Contributions					
TYPE	**HOURS**	**RATE**	**AMOUNT**	**Y.T.D.**	**TYPE**	**CURRENT**	**Y.T.D.**	**TYPE**	**CURRENT**	**Y.T.D.**
00Basic Pay			2,513.56	20,108.48	C.P.P.	118.13	944.67			
Insurance TB			7.59	52.95	E.I.	52.78	422.24			
					FED. TAX	487.75	3,887.89			
					Union Loc.	9.00	44.00			
					Comp P.P.	145.78	1,229.25			
					Insurance	68.59	480.77			
					Parking	18.00	144.00			
					Union Dues	39.59	316.72			

SUMMARY	**GROSS PAY**	**DEDUCTIONS**	**NET PAY**	**NET PAY ALLOCATION**
Current	2,513.56	939.62	1,573.94	1,573.94 DEPOSIT 0003 96304 0567892
Year-to-date	20,108.48	7,469.54	12,638.94	

Employer #: 654-a GLO COMPANY 185 MAIN STREET WEST YORK ONTARIO Z5H 3Y6

In this Unit we will consider the main positions on your pay slip: **federal and provincial tax deductions, Employment Insurance (EI) contributions,** and **Canada Pension Plan (CPP) contributions.** Other items may vary according to the terms of your employment agreement.

Computing Payroll Deductions for Employees

When you start a new job, you are asked to fill out the TD1 form, "2003 Personal Tax Credits Return" (for Ontario residents, the TD1ON form). According to the information in this form, your personal claim amount will determine the *Claim Code* you will use. (Note that the claim amounts corresponding to federal Claim Codes are not the same as those corresponding to provincial Claim Codes.) Codes are labelled from 0 to 10. Claim Code 0 means that no claim amount is allowed.

Many companies and organizations use computer programs for payroll deduction calculations. However, it is possible to calculate payroll deductions using income tax tables prepared by Canada Customs and Revenue Agency. As of January 1, 2003 some changes were introduced into the process, and the income thresholds and personal amounts were increased according to the Consumer Price Index.

In this Unit we will consider manual calculations based on the CCRA payroll deduction tables.

In Learning Unit 11–1 we learned that companies may pay employees on a weekly, biweekly, semimonthly, or monthly basis. Federal and provincial tax deductions are based on the same principles and are located on sections D and E of the tables respectively. They are organized by the number of payment periods per year or by the frequency of the payments.

Total Tax Deductions

Using the example from Learning Unit 11–1, let's consider how much of a total tax deduction will be made from your pay if: you are employed in Ontario, your Claim Code is 2, your salary is $50,000 per year, and you are paid $1,923.08 on a biweekly basis.

FIGURE 11–2

Chart 1 – Tableau 1
2003 Federal claim codes – Codes de demande fédéraux pour 2003

Total claim amount ($) Montant total de la demande ($)	Claim code Code de demande	Total claim amount ($) Montant total de la demande ($)	Claim code Code de demande
No claim amount – Nul	0	16,361.01 – 18,082.00	7
Minimum – 7,756.00	1	18,082.01 – 19,803.00	8
7,756.01 – 9,477.00	2	19,803.01 – 21,524.00	9
9,477.01 – 11,198.00	3	21,524.01 – 23,245.00	10
11,198.01 – 12,919.00	4	23,245.01 and over – et plus	X
12,919.01 – 14,640.00	5	A manual calculation is required by the employer. Un calcul manuel est requis par l'employeur.	
14,640.01 – 16,361.00	6	No withholding – Aucune retenue	E

Chart 2 – Tableau 2
2003 Ontario claim codes – Codes de demande de l'Ontario pour 2003

Total claim amount ($) Montant total de la demande ($)	Claim code Code de demande	Total claim amount ($) Montant total de la demande ($)	Claim code Code de demande
No claim amount – Nul	0	16,237.01 – 17,921.00	7
Minimum – 7,817.00	1	17,921.01 – 19,605.00	8
7,817.01 – 9,501.00	2	19,605.01 – 21,289.00	9
9,501.01 – 11,185.00	3	21,289.01 – 22,973.00	10
11,185.01 – 12,869.00	4	22,973.01 and over – et plus	X
12,869.01 – 14,553.00	5	A manual calculation is required by the employer. Un calcul manuel est requis par l'employeur.	
14,553.01 – 16,237.00	6	No withholding – Aucune retenue	E

Source: Income tax rates for payroll deductions used by employers in Ontario. Payroll Deductions Tables, January 2003 version, Canada Customs and Revenue Agency. Reproduced with permission of the Minister of Public Works and Government Services Canada, 2003.

FIGURE 11–3
Payroll deductions tables, Canada Customs and Revenue Agency

FEDERAL TAX for 2003		PROVINCIAL TAX for 2003	
Tax Rates and Income Thresholds		**Tax Rates and Income Thresholds**	
For 2003, as a result of federal indexing, the tax rates and income thresholds are a follows:		Ontario's tax rates and income thresholds for 2003 are revised as follows:	
Taxable Income	Tax Rate	Taxable Income	Tax Rate
0–$32,183	16%	0–$32,435	6.05%
>$32,183–$64,368	22%	>$32,435–$64,871	9.15%
>$64,368–$104,648	26%	Over $64,871	11.16%
Over $104,648	29%		

Source: Income tax rates for payroll deductions used by employers in Ontario. Payroll Deductions Tables, January 2003 version, Canada Customs and Revenue Agency. Reproduced with permission of the Minister of Public Works and Government Services Canada, 2003.

In the federal tax deduction table, federal deductions for $1,923.08 paid biweekly under Claim Code 2 are $282.30 (Figure 11.4). In the Ontario provincial tax deduction table, provincial deductions are $110.85 (Figure 11.5).

To find federal deductions in a case like this, follow Steps 1–3 (see Figure 11.4).

Step 1. You are paid on biweekly basis. Find in the section D (the "D" pages) the table that corresponds to this frequency of payments.

Step 2. In the first column of the table, called "Pay," find the line with your pay range (1923–1947). Note that this amount includes all taxable benefits.

Step 3. In the third column (Claim Code 2) find the line with your pay range. On the intercept you will find the amount of federal deductions: $282.30.

FIGURE 11–4

Federal tax deductions
Effective January 1, 2003
Biweekly (26 pay periods a year)
Also look up the tax deductions in the provincial table

Retenues d'impôt fédéral
En vigueur le 1er janvier 2003
Aux deux semaines (26 périodes de paie par année)
Cherchez aussi les retenues d'impôt dans la table provinciale

Pay / Rémunération		Federal claim codes/Codes de demande fédéraux										
From / De	Less than / Moins de	0	1	2	3	4	5	6	7	8	9	10
			Deduct from each pay / Retenez sur chaque paie									
1851.	1875	319.45	271.75	266.45	255.85	245.25	234.65	224.05	213.50	202.90	192.30	181.70
1875.	1899	324.75	277.00	271.70	261.15	250.55	239.95	229.35	218.75	208.15	197.60	187.00
1899.	1923	330.00	282.30	277.00	266.40	255.80	245.25	234.65	224.05	213.45	202.85	192.25
1923.	1947	335.30	287.55	282.30	271.70	261.10	250.50	239.90	229.30	218.75	208.15	197.55
1947.	1971	340.60	292.85	287.55	276.95	266.40	255.80	245.20	234.60	224.00	213.40	202.85
1971.	1995	345.85	298.15	292.85	282.25	271.65	261.05	250.45	239.90	229.30	218.70	208.10
1995.	2019	351.15	303.40	298.10	287.55	276.95	266.35	255.75	245.15	234.55	224.00	213.40
2019.	2043	356.40	308.70	303.40	292.80	282.20	271.65	261.05	250.45	239.85	229.25	218.65
2043.	2067	361.70	313.95	308.70	298.10	287.50	276.90	266.30	255.70	245.15	234.55	223.95
2067.	2091	367.00	319.25	313.95	303.35	292.80	282.20	271.60	261.00	250.40	239.80	229.25
2091.	2115	372.25	324.55	319.25	308.65	298.05	287.45	276.85	266.30	255.70	245.10	234.50
2115.	2139	377.55	329.80	324.50	313.95	303.35	292.75	282.15	271.55	260.95	250.40	239.80
2139.	2163	382.80	335.10	329.80	319.20	308.60	298.05	287.45	276.85	266.25	255.65	245.05
2163.	2187	388.10	340.35	335.10	324.50	313.90	303.30	292.70	282.10	271.55	260.95	250.35
2187.	2211	393.40	345.65	340.35	329.75	319.20	308.60	298.00	287.40	276.80	266.20	255.65
2211.	2235	398.65	350.95	345.65	335.05	324.45	313.85	303.25	292.70	282.10	271.50	260.90
2235.	2259	403.95	356.20	350.90	340.35	329.75	319.15	308.55	297.95	287.35	276.80	266.20
2259.	2283	409.20	361.50	356.20	345.60	335.00	324.45	313.85	303.25	292.65	282.05	271.45
2283.	2307	414.50	366.75	361.50	350.90	340.30	329.70	319.10	308.50	297.95	287.35	276.75
2307.	2331	419.80	372.05	366.75	356.15	345.60	335.00	324.40	313.80	303.20	292.60	282.05

Source: Federal Tax Deductions. Payroll Deductions Tables, January 2003 version, Canada Customs and Revenue Agency. Reproduced with permission of the Minister of Public Works and Government Services Canada, 2003.

FIGURE 11–5

Ontario
Provincial tax deductions effective January 1, 2003
Biweekly (26 pay periods a year)
Also look up the tax deductions in the federal table

Ontario
Retenues d'impôt provincial en vigueur le 1er janvier 2003
Aux deux semaines (26 périodes de paie par année)
Cherchez aussi les retenues d'impôt dans la table fédérale

Pay / Rémunération		Provincial claim codes/Codes de demande provinciaux										
From / De	Less than / Moins de	0	1	2	3	4	5	6	7	8	9	10
			Deduct from each pay / Retenez sur chaque paie									
1097.	1113	62.55	44.35	42.40	38.45	34.55	30.65	26.70	22.80	18.90	14.95	8.15
1113.	1129	63.45	45.25	43.30	39.35	35.45	31.55	27.60	23.70	19.80	15.85	9.95
1129.	1145	64.35	46.15	44.20	40.25	36.35	32.45	28.50	24.60	20.70	16.75	11.75
1145.	1161	65.25	47.05	45.10	41.15	37.25	33.35	29.40	25.50	21.60	17.65	13.55
1161.	1177	66.15	47.95	46.00	42.05	38.15	34.25	30.30	26.40	22.50	18.55	14.65
1817.	1833	122.25	104.05	102.10	98.15	94.25	90.35	86.40	82.50	78.60	74.65	70.75
1833.	1849	123.70	105.50	103.55	99.65	95.70	91.80	87.90	83.95	80.05	76.10	72.20
1849.	1865	125.15	106.95	105.00	101.10	97.20	93.25	89.35	85.40	81.50	77.60	73.65
1865.	1881	126.65	108.45	106.50	102.55	98.65	94.70	90.80	86.90	82.95	79.05	75.15
1881.	1897	128.10	109.90	107.95	104.00	100.10	96.20	92.25	88.35	84.45	80.50	76.60
1897.	1913	129.55	111.35	109.40	105.50	101.55	97.65	93.75	89.80	85.90	82.00	78.05
1913.	1929	131.00	112.85	110.85	106.95	103.05	99.10	95.20	91.30	87.35	83.45	79.50
1929.	1945	132.50	114.30	112.35	108.40	104.50	100.60	96.65	92.75	88.80	84.90	81.00
1945.	1961	133.95	115.75	113.80	109.90	105.95	102.05	98.10	94.20	90.30	86.35	82.45
1961.	1977	135.40	117.20	115.25	111.35	107.45	103.50	99.60	95.65	91.75	87.85	83.90

This table is available on diskette (TOD). **E-9** **Vous pouvez obtenir cette table sur disquette (TSD).**

Source: Provincial Tax deductions effective Jan. 1, 2003. Payroll Deductions Tables, January 2003 version, Canada Customs and Revenue Agency. Reproduced with permission of the Minister of Public Works and Government Services Canada, 2003.

To find **provincial deductions** follow the same three steps, but use section E. Your provincial deductions will be $110.85.

> Your total deductions are $393.15 per pay period. ($110.85 + $282.30)

The next position on your pay slip is the Canada Pension Plan—CPP (it may be labelled G.P.P.—Government Pension Plan).

CPP Contributions

From the information in Figure 11.6, note that the maximum amount of employee contributions is $1,801.80. Your employer must make contributions equal to yours, and this will be deducted from his remuneration.

When you reach the maximum CPP contribution per year, CPP deductions will stop and will not appear on your pay slip.

FIGURE 11–6
From payroll deduction tables, Canada Customs and Revenue Agency

CANADA PENSION PLAN (CPP) CONTRIBUTIONS FOR 2003

Maximum pensionable earnings	$39,000
Annual basic exemption	$3,500
Maximum contributory earnings	$36,400
Contribution rate (4.95%)	0.0495
Maximum employee premium	$1,801.80
Maximum employer contribution	$1,801.80

Source: Canada Pension Plan Contributions Biweekly. 2003 Personal Tax Credits Return. Canada Customs and Revenue Agency. Reproduced with permission of the Minister of Public Works and Government Services Canada, 2003.

To find your CPP deductions in this case, follow Steps 1–3 (see Figure 11.7).

Step 1. In section B find a page corresponding to your frequency of payments—biweekly.
Step 2. In the first column, "Pay," find your gross pay, including taxable benefits. Assume it is the same amount as before, $1,923.08.
Step 3. In the shaded column next to the one with your pay range, identify your CPP contributions. Your employer will contribute the same amount until it reaches the maximum.

In your case the CPP contributions will be $88.36.

FIGURE 11–7

Canada Pension Plan Contributions
Biweekly (26 pay periods a year)

Cotisations au Régime de pensions du Canada
Aux deux semaines (26 périodes de paie par année)

Pay Rémunération From - De	To - À		Pay Rémunération From - De	To - À		Pay Rémunération From - De	To - À		Pay Rémunération From - De	To - À	
1794.72	1804.71	82.42	2514.72	2524.71	118.06	3234.72	3244.71	153.70	3954.72	3964.71	189.34
1804.72	1814.71	82.92	2524.72	2534.71	118.56	3244.72	3254.71	154.20	3964.72	3974.71	189.84
1814.72	1824.71	83.41	2534.72	2544.71	119.05	3254.72	3264.71	154.69	3974.72	3984.71	190.33
1824.72	1834.71	83.91	2544.72	2554.71	119.55	3264.72	3274.71	155.19	3984.72	3994.71	190.83
1834.72	1844.71	84.40	2554.72	2564.71	120.04	3274.72	3284.71	155.68	3994.72	4004.71	191.32
1844.72	1854.71	84.90	2564.72	2574.71	120.54	3284.72	3294.71	156.18	4004.72	4014.71	191.82
1854.72	1864.71	85.39	2574.72	2584.71	121.03	3294.72	3304.71	156.67	4014.72	4024.71	192.31
1864.72	1874.71	85.89	2584.72	2594.71	121.53	3304.72	3314.71	157.17	4024.72	4034.71	193.81
1874.72	1884.71	86.38	2594.72	2604.71	122.02	3314.72	3324.71	157.66	4034.72	4044.71	193.30
1884.72	1894.71	86.88	2604.72	2614.71	122.52	3324.72	3334.71	158.16	4044.72	4054.71	193.80
1894.72	1904.71	87.37	2614.72	2624.71	123.01	3334.72	3344.71	158.65	4054.72	4064.71	194.29
1904.72	1914.71	87.87	2624.72	2634.71	123.51	3344.72	3354.71	159.15	4064.72	4074.71	194.79
1914.72	1924.71	88.36	2634.72	2644.71	124.00	3354.72	3364.71	159.64	4074.72	4084.71	195.28
1924.72	1934.71	88.86	2644.72	2654.71	124.50	3364.72	3374.71	160.14	4084.72	4094.71	195.78
1934.72	1944.71	89.35	2654.72	2664.71	124.99	3374.72	3384.71	160.63	4094.72	4104.71	196.27
1944.72	1954.71	89.85	2664.72	2674.71	125.49	3384.72	3394.71	161.13	4104.72	4114.71	196.77
1954.72	1964.71	90.34	2674.72	2684.71	125.98	3394.72	3404.71	161.62	4114.72	4124.71	197.26
1964.72	1974.71	90.84	2684.72	2694.71	126.48	3404.72	3414.71	162.12	4124.72	4134.71	197.76
1974.72	1984.71	91.33	2694.72	2704.71	126.97	3414.72	3424.71	162.61	4134.72	4144.71	198.25
1984.72	1994.71	91.83	2704.72	2714.71	127.47	3424.72	3434.71	163.11	4144.72	4154.71	198.75
1994.72	2004.71	92.32	2714.72	2724.71	127.96	3434.72	3444.71	163.60	4154.72	4164.71	199.24
2004.72	2014.71	92.82	2724.72	2734.71	128.46	3444.72	3454.71	164.10	4164.72	4174.71	199.74
2014.72	2024.71	93.31	2734.72	2744.71	128.95	3454.72	3464.71	164.59	4174.72	4184.71	200.23
2024.72	2034.71	93.81	2744.32	2754.71	129.45	3464.72	3474.71	165.09	4184.72	4194.71	200.73
2034.72	2044.71	94.30	2754.72	2764.71	129.94	3474.72	3484.71	165.58	4194.72	4204.71	201.22
2044.72	2054.71	94.80	2764.72	2774.71	130.44	3484.72	3494.71	166.08	4204.72	4214.71	201.72
2054.72	2064.71	95.29	2774.72	2784.71	130.93	3494.92	3504.71	166.57	4214.72	4224.71	202.21

Employee's maximum CPP contribution for 2003 is $1,801 80 B-39 La cotisation maximale de l'employé au RPC pour 2003 est de 1 801,80 $

Source: Canada Pension Plan Contributions Biweekly. 2003 Personal Tax Credits Return. Canada Customs and Revenue Agency. Reproduced with permission of the Minister of Public Works and Government Services Canada, 2003.

Employment Insurance (EI) Premiums

When you calculate EI premiums you base it on your insurable earnings, not on your gross remuneration. You start to pay EI premiums from the beginning of your payments and stop when you reach your maximum ($39,000).

FIGURE 11–8
From payroll deduction tables, Canada Customs and Revenue Agency

EMPLOYMENT INSURANCE (EI) PREMIUMS FOR 2003	
Maximum insurable earnings	$39,000
Premium rate (2.10%)	0.021
Maximum annual employee premium	$819.00

Source: Employment Insurance (EI) premiums for 2003. Personal Tax Credits Return. Canada Customs and Revenue Agency. Reproduced with permission of the Minister of Public Works and Government Services Canada, 2003.

The employer's premium is 1.4 times the employee's premium for the pay period, and its contributions stop with yours.

To define the amount of EI premiums per pay period follow Steps 1–3 (see Figure 11.9).

Step 1.	Find section C and the page that corresponds to your insurable earnings.
Step 2.	In the column "Insurable Earnings" look down until you find your range.
Step 3.	In the shaded column next to this one, identify the EI premium.

FIGURE 11–9

Employment Insurance Premiums **Cotisations à l'assurance-emploi**

Insurable Earnings Rémunération assurable			Insurable Earnings Rémunération assurable			Insurable Earnings Rémunération assurable			Insurable Earnings Rémunération assurable		
From - De	To - À		From - De	To - À		From - De	To - À		From - De	To - À	
1920.24 -	1920.71	40.33	1954.53 -	1954.99	41.05	1988.81 -	1989.28	41.77	2023.10 -	2023.57	42.49
1920.72 -	1921.19	40.34	1955.00 -	1955.47	41.06	1989.29 -	1989.76	41.78	2023.58 -	2024.04	42.50
1921.20 -	1921.66	40.35	1955.48 -	1955.95	41.07	1989.77 -	1990.23	41.79	2024.05 -	2024.52	42.51
1921.67 -	1922.14	40.36	1955.96 -	1956.42	41.08	1990.24 -	1990.71	41.80	2024.53 -	2024.99	42.52
1922.15 -	1922.61	40.37	1956.43 -	1956.90	41.09	1990.72 -	1991.19	41.81	2025.00 -	2025.47	42.53
1922.62 -	1923.09	40.38	1956.91 -	1957.38	41.10	1991.20 -	1991.66	41.82	2025.48 -	2025.95	42.54
1923.10 -	1923.57	40.39	1957.39 -	1957.85	41.11	1991.67 -	1992.14	41.83	2025.96 -	2026.42	42.55
1923.58 -	1924.04	40.40	1957.86 -	1958.33	41.12	1992.15 -	1992.61	41.84	2026.43 -	2026.90	42.56
1924.05 -	1924.52	40.41	1958.34 -	1958.80	41.13	1992.62 -	1993.09	41.85	2026.91 -	2027.38	42.57
1924.53 -	1924.99	40.42	1958.81 -	1959.28	41.14	1993.10 -	1993.57	41.86	2027.39 -	2027.85	42.58
1925.00 -	1925.47	40.43	1959.29 -	1959.76	41.15	1993.58 -	1994.04	41.87	2027.86 -	2028.33	42.59
1925.48 -	1925.95	40.44	1959.77 -	1960.23	41.16	1994.05 -	1994.52	41.88	2028.34 -	2028.80	42.60
1925.96 -	1926.42	40.45	1960.24 -	1960.71	41.17	1994.53 -	1994.99	41.89	2028.81 -	2029.28	42.61
1926.43 -	1926.90	40.46	1960.72 -	1961.19	41.18	1995.00 -	1995.47	41.90	2029.29 -	2029.76	42.62
1926.91 -	1927.38	40.47	1961.20 -	1961.66	41.19	1995.48 -	1995.95	41.91	2029.77 -	2030.23	42.63
1927.39 -	1927.85	40.48	1961.67 -	1962.14	41.20	1995.96 -	1996.42	41.92	2030.24 -	2030.71	42.64
1927.86 -	1928.33	40.49	1962.15 -	1962.61	41.21	1996.43 -	1996.90	41.93	2030.72 -	2031.19	42.65
1928.34 -	1928.80	40.50	1962.62 -	1963.09	41.22	1996.91 -	1997.38	41.94	2031.20 -	2031.66	42.66

Source: Employment Insurance Premiums. Personal Tax Credits Return. Canada Customs and Revenue Agency. Reproduced with permission of the Minister of Public Works and Government Services Canada, 2003.

In your case it will be \$40.38 per pay period. These deductions will stop after 21 payments, as soon as you reach the maximum of \$819.

Summary

On your pay slip your deductions will be as follows:

Total tax deduction: \$393.15 per pay period
CPP contribution: \$88.36 per pay period
EI premium: \$40.38 per pay period

The EI premium and CPP contributions will stop being deducted as soon as they reach their maximum amounts.

If you are paying union dues, local union dues, parking, or company pension plan contributions, these should be deducted from your taxable income. Some insurance contributions are also deducted, but some insurance benefits are added to it. Each case should be considered individually.

You receive your **net pay** after all deductions have been made.

Now it's time for a Practice Quiz

LU 11–2 PRACTICE QUIZ

1. Calculate total income tax deductions, Employment Insurance premiums, and CPP contributions for Joy Royce in the first quarter. Her monthly salary is \$8,500, Claim Code 3. Use the tables provided here for CPP, EI, and income tax deductions.
2. Jim Brewer, owner of the Arrow Company, has three employees who earn \$5,810, \$6,005, and \$6,500 a month. What will Jim pay for CPP contributions and EI premiums for December of this year?

Canada Customs and Revenue Agency | Agence des douanes et du revenu du Canada

2003 PERSONAL TAX CREDITS RETURN

TD1

Complete this TD1 form if you have a new employer or payer and you will receive salary, wages, commissions, pensions, Employment Insurance benefits, or any other remuneration. Be sure to sign and date it on the back page and give it to your employer or payer who will use it to determine the amount of your payroll tax deductions.

If you do not complete a TD1 form, your new employer or payer will deduct taxes after allowing the basic personal amount **only.**

You **do not** have to complete a new TD1 form every year unless there is a change in your entitlement to personal tax credits. Complete a new TD1 form no later than seven days after the change.

You can get the forms and publications mentioned on this form from our Internet site at **www.ccra.gc.ca/forms** or by calling 1-800-959-2221.

Last name	First name and initial(s)	Date of birth (YYYY/MM/DD)	Employee number
Address including postal code		**For non-residents only** – Country of permanent residence	Social insurance number

1. Basic personal amount – Every resident of Canada can claim this amount. If you will have more than one employer or payer at the same time in 2003, see the section called "Income from other employers or payers" on the back page. If you are a non-resident, see the section called "Non-residents" on the back page.	7,756
2. Age amount – If you will be 65 or older on December 31, 2003, and your net income for the year will be $28,193 or less, enter $3,787. If your net income will be between $28,193 and $53,440 and you want to calculate a partial claim, get the *Worksheet for the 2003 Personal Tax Credits Return* (TD1-WS) and complete the appropriate section.	
3. Pension Income amount – If you will receive regular pension payments from a pension plan or fund (excluding Canada or Quebec Pension Plans (CPP/QPP), Old Age Security, and guaranteed income supplements), enter $1,000 or your estimated annual pension income, whichever is less.	
4. Tuition and education amounts (full-time and part-time) – If you are a student enrolled at a university, college, or educational institution certified by Human Resources Development Canada, and you will pay more than $100 per institution in tuition fees, complete this section. If you are enrolled full-time, or if you have a mental or physical disability and are enrolled part-time, enter the total of the tuition fees you will pay, plus $400 for each month that you will be enrolled. If you are enrolled part-time and do not have a mental or physical disability, enter the total of the tuition fees you will pay plus $120 for each month that you will be enrolled part-time.	
5. Disability amount – If you will claim the disability amount on your income tax return by using Form T2201, *Disability Tax Credit Certificate,* enter $6,279.	
6. Spouse or common-law partner amount – If you are supporting your spouse or common-law partner who lives with you, and his or her net income for the year will be $659 or less, enter $6,586. If his or her net income for the year will be between $659 and $7,245 and you want to calculate a partial claim, get the *Worksheet for the 2003 Personal Tax Credits Return* (TD1-WS) and complete the appropriate section.	
7. Amount for an eligible dependant – If you do not have a spouse or common-law partner and you support a dependent relative who lives with you, and his or her net income for the year will be $659 or less, enter $6,586. If his or her net income for the year will be between $659 and $7,245 and you want to calculate a partial claim, get the *Worksheet for the 2003 Personal Tax Credits Return* (TD1-WS) and complete the appropriate section.	
8. Caregiver amount – If you are taking care of a dependant who lives with you, whose net income for the year will be $12,509 or less, and who is either your or your spouse's or common-law partner's: • parent or grandparent age 65 or older, **or** • relative age 18 or older who is dependent on you because of an infirmity, enter $3,663. If the dependant's net income for the year will be between $12,509 and $16,172 and you want to calculate a partial claim, get the *Worksheet for the 2003 Personal Tax Credits Return* (TD1-WS) and complete the appropriate section.	
9. Amount for infirm dependants age 18 or older – If you are supporting an infirm dependant age 18 or older who is your or your spouse's or common-law partner's relative, who lives in Canada, and his or her net income for the year will be $5,197 or less, enter $3,663. You cannot claim an amount for a dependant claimed on line 8. If the dependant's net income for the year will be between $5,197 and $8,860 and you want to calculate a partial claim, get the *Worksheet for the 2003 Personal Tax Credits Return* (TD1-WS) and complete the appropriate section.	
10. Amounts transferred from your spouse or common-law partner – If your spouse or common-law partner will not use all of his or her age amount, pension income amount, tuition and education amounts (maximum $5,000), or disability amount on his or her income tax return, enter the unused amount.	
11. Amounts transferred from a dependant – If your dependant will not use all of his or her tuition and education amounts (maximum $5,000) or disability amount on his or her income tax return, enter the unused amount.	
12. TOTAL CLAIM AMOUNT – Add lines 1 through line 11. Your employer or payer will use this amount to determine the amount of your payroll tax deductions.	

Form continues on the back →

2003 ONTARIO PERSONAL TAX CREDITS RETURN

TD1ON

Do I have to complete this form?

Complete this Ontario TD1 form if you have not previously provided an Ontario TD1 form to your employer or payer, or if there has been a change in your entitlement to personal tax credits, and you are:

- an employee working in Ontario; or
- a pensioner residing in Ontario.

If you complete this form, be sure to sign and date it on the back page and give it to your employer or payer. Your employer or payer will use both this form and your most recent federal TD1 form to determine the amount of your payroll tax deductions.

Last name	First name and initial(s)	Date of birth (YYYY/MM/DD)	Employee number
Address including postal code		**For non-residents only** – Country of permanent residence	Social insurance number

1. Basic personal amount – Every person employed in Ontario and every pensioner residing in Ontario can claim this amount. If you will have more than one employer or payer at the same time in 2003, see the section called "Income from other employers or payers" on the back page.	**7,817**
2. Age amount – If you will be 65 or older on December 31, 2003, and your net income from all sources will be $28,413 or less, enter $3,817. If your net income will be between $28,413 and $53,860 and you want to calculate a partial claim, get the *Worksheet for the 2003 Ontario Personal Tax Credits Return* (TD1ON-WS) and complete the appropriate section.	
3. Pension income amount – If you will receive regular pension payments from a pension plan or fund (excluding Canada or Quebec Pension Plans (CPP/QPP), Old Age Security, and guaranteed income supplements), enter $1,081 or your estimated annual pension income, whichever is less.	
4. Tuition and education amounts (full-time and part-time) – If you are a student enrolled at a university, college, or educational institution certified by Human Resources Development Canada, and you will pay more than $100 per institution in tuition fees, complete this section. If you are enrolled full-time, or if you have a mental or physical disability and are enrolled part-time, enter the total of the tuition fees you will pay, plus $421 for each month that you will be enrolled. If you are enrolled part-time and do not have a mental or physical disability, enter the total of the tuition fees you will pay, plus $126 for each month that you will be enrolled part-time.	
5. Disability amount – If you will claim the disability amount on your income tax return by using Form T2201, *Disability Tax Credit Certificate*, enter $6,316.	
6. Spouse or common-law partner amount – If you are supporting your spouse or common-law partner who lives with you, and his or her net income for the year will be $664 or less, enter $6,637. If his or her net income for the year will be between $664 and $7,301 and you want to calculate a partial claim, get the *Worksheet for the 2003 Ontario Personal Tax Credits Return* (TD1ON-WS) and complete the appropriate section.	
7. Amount for an eligible dependant – If you do not have a spouse or common-law partner and support a dependent relative who lives with you, and his or her net income for the year will be $664 or less, enter $6,637. If his or her net income for the year will be between $664 and $7,301 and you want to calculate a partial claim, get the *Worksheet for the 2003 Ontario Personal Tax Credits Return* (TD1ON-WS) and complete the appropriate section.	
8. Caregiver amount – If you are taking care of a dependant who lives with you, whose net income for the year will be $12,606 or less, and who is either your or your spouse's or common-law partner's: • parent or grandparent age 65 or older, or • relative age 18 or older who is dependent on you because of an infirmity, enter $3,684. If the dependant's net income for the year will be between $12,606 and $16,290 and you want to calculate a partial claim, get the *Worksheet for the 2003 Ontario Personal Tax Credits Return* (TD1ON-WS) and complete the appropriate section.	
9. Amount for infirm dependants age 18 or older – If you are supporting an infirm dependant age 18 or older who is your or your spouse's or common-law partner's relative, who lives in Canada, and his or her net income for the year will be $5,238 or less, enter $3,684. You cannot claim an amount for a dependant claimed on line 8. If the dependant's net income for the year will be between $5,238 and $8,922 and you want to calculate a partial claim, get the *Worksheet for the 2003 Ontario Personal Tax Credits Return* (TD1ON-WS) and complete the appropriate section.	
10. Amounts transferred from your spouse or common-law partner – If your spouse or common-law partner will not use all of his or her age amount, pension income amount, tuition and education amounts (maximum $5,405), or disability amount on his or her income tax return, enter the unused amount.	
11. Amounts transferred from a dependant – If your dependant will not use all of his or her tuition and education amounts maximum $5,405) or disability amount on his or her income tax return, enter the unused amount.	
12. TOTAL CLAIM AMOUNT – Add lines 1 through line 11. Your employer or payer will use your claim amount to determine the amount of your provincial payroll tax deductions.	

Form continues on the back ⟶

(Ce formulaire existe en français.)

Canada

Deduction for living in a prescribed zone

If you live in the Northwest Territories, Nunavut, Yukon, or another prescribed zone for more than six months in a row beginning or ending in 2003, you can claim:

- $7.50 for each day that you live in the prescribed zone; or
- $15 for each day that you live in the prescribed zone, if during that time you live in a dwelling that you maintain, and you are the only person living in that dwelling who is claiming this deduction. ____________

For more information, get Form T2222, *Northern Residents Deductions*, and the publication called *Northern Residents Deductions – PI in Prescribed Zones.*

Additional tax to be deducted

If you receive other income, including non-employment income such as CPP or QPP benefits, or Old Age Security pension, you may want to have more tax deducted. By doing this, you may not have to pay as much tax when you file your income tax return.

To choose this option, state the amount of additional tax you want to have deducted. To change this deduction later, you will have to complete a new *Personal Tax Credits Return.* ____________

Reduction in tax deductions

You can ask for a reduction in tax deductions if you are eligible for deductions or non-refundable tax credits that are not listed on this form (for example, periodic contributions to an RRSP, child care or employment expenses, and charitable donations). To make this request, complete Form T1213, *Request to Reduce Tax Deductions at Source*, to get a letter of authority from your tax services office.

Give the letter of authority to your employer or payer. You do not need a letter of authority if your employer deducts RRSP contributions from your salary.

Non-residents

If you are a non-resident of Canada, tick this box and answer the question below. If you are unsure of your residency status, call the International Tax Services Office at 1-800-267-5177. Non-resident

Will you include 90% or more of your world income when determining your taxable income earned in Canada in 2003? If yes, complete the front page. If no, enter "0" on line 12 on the front page and do not complete lines 2 to 11 as you are not entitled to the personal tax credits. Yes ☐ No ☐

Income from other employers or payers

Your earnings may not be subject to payroll tax deductions if your total income from all employers and payers for the year will be less than your total claim amount.

Will your total income for the year be less than your total claim amount on line 12 on the front page? Yes ☐ No ☐

If you have more than one employer or payer at the same time and you have already claimed personal tax credit amounts on another Form TD1 for 2003, you can choose not to claim them again. By doing this, you may not have to pay as much tax when you file your income tax return. To choose this option, enter "0" on line 12 on the front page and do not complete lines 2 to 11.

Certification

I certify that the information given in this return is, to the best of my knowledge, correct and complete.

Signature ______________________________ Date ______________

It is a serious offence to make a false return.

Provincial or Territorial Personal Tax Credits Return

In addition to this Form TD1, you may have to complete a *Provincial or Territorial Personal Tax Credits Return.*

If your claim amount on line 12 on the front page is more than $7,756, complete a provincial or territorial TD1 form in addition to this form. If you are an employee, use the TD1 form for your province or territory of employment. If you are a pensioner, use the TD1 form for your province or territory of residence. Your employer or payer will use both this form and your most recent provincial or territorial TD1 form to determine your tax deductions.

If you are claiming the basic personal amount **only** (your claim amount on line 12 on the front page is $7,756), do not complete a provincial or territorial TD1 form. Your employer or payer will deduct provincial or territorial taxes after allowing the provincial or territorial basic personal amount.

Note: If you are a Saskatchewan resident supporting children under 18 at any time during 2003, you may be entitled to claim the child amount on the *2003 Saskatchewan Personal Tax Credits Return* (TD1SK). Therefore, you may want to complete the TD1SK form ever if you are claiming the basic personal amount **only** on the front page of this form (your claim amount on line 12 is $7,756).

If you entered "0" on line 12 on the front page because you are a non-resident and you will not include 90% or more of your world income when determining your taxable income earned in Canada in 2003, do not complete a provincial or territorial TD1. You are not entitled to the provincial or territorial personal tax credits.

Printed in Canada

Canada Pension Plan Contributions
Weekly (52 pay periods a year)

Cotisations au Régime de pensions du Canada
Hebdomadaire (52 périodes de paie par année)

Pay Rémunération From - De	To - À		Pay Rémunération From - De	To - À		Pay Rémunération From - De	To - À		Pay Rémunération From - De	To - À	
765.39	765.58	34.56	1387.41	1397.40	65.59	2107.41	2117.40	101.23	2827.41	2837.40	136.87
765.59	765.78	34.57	1397.41	1407.40	66.09	2117.41	2127.40	101.73	2837.41	2847.40	137.37
765.79	765.98	34.58	1407.41	1417.40	66.58	2127.41	2137.40	102.22	2847.41	2857.40	137.86
765.99	766.18	34.59	1417.41	1427.40	67.08	2137.41	2147.40	102.72	2857.41	2867.40	138.36
766.19	766.39	34.60	1427.41	1437.40	67.57	2147.41	2157.40	103.21	2867.41	2877.40	138.85
766.40	766.59	34.61	1437.41	1447.40	68.07	2157.41	2167.40	103.71	2877.41	2887.40	139.35
766.60	766.78	34.62	1447.41	1457.40	68.56	2167.41	2177.40	104.20	2887.41	2897.40	139.84
766:79	766.99	34.63	1457.41	1467.40	69.06	2177.41	2187.40	104.70	2897.41	2907.40	140.34
767.00	767.19	34.64	1467.41	1477.40	69.55	2187.41	2197.40	105.19	2907.41	2917.40	140.83
767.20	767.40	34.65	1477.41	1487.40	70.05	2197.41	2207.40	105.69	2917.41	2927.40	141.33
767.41	777.40	34.90	1487.41	1497.40	70.54	2207.41	2217.40	106.18	2927.41	2937.40	141.82
777.41	787.40	35.40	1497.41	1507.40	71.04	2217.41	2227.40	106.68	2937.41	2947.40	142.32
787.41	797.40	35.89	1507.41	1517.40	71.53	2227.41	2237.40	107.17	2947.41	2957.40	142.81
797.41	807.40	36.39	1517.41	1527.40	72.03	2237.41	2247.40	107.67	2957.41	2967.40	143.31
807.41	817.40	36.88	1527.41	1537.40	72.52	2247.41	2257.40	108.16	2967.41	2977.40	143.80
817.41	827.40	37.38	1537.41	1547.40	73.02	2257.41	2267.40	108.66	2977.41	2987.40	144.30
827.41	837.40	37.87	1547.41	1557.40	73.51	2267.41	2277.40	109.15	2987.41	2997.40	144.79
837.41	847.40	38.37	1557.41	1567.40	74.01	2277.41	2287.40	109.65	2997.41	3007.40	145.29
847.41	857.40	38.86	1567.41	1577.40	74.50	2287.41	2297.40	110.14	3007.41	3017.40	145.78
857.41	867.40	39.36	1577.41	1587.40	75.00	2297.41	2307.40	110.64	3017.41	3027.40	146.28
867.41	877.40	39.85	1587.41	1597.40	75.49	2307.41	2317.40	111.13	3027.41	3037.40	146.77
877.41	887.40	40.35	1597.41	1607.40	75.99	2317.41	2327.40	111.63	3037.41	3047.40	147.27
887.41	897.40	40.84	1607.41	1617.40	76.48	2327.41	2337.40	112.12	3047.41	3057.40	147.76
897.41	907.40	41.34	1617.41	1627.40	76.98	2337.41	2347.40	112.62	3057.41	3067.40	148.26
907.41	917.40	41.83	1627.41	1637.40	77.47	2347.41	2357.40	113.11	3067.41	3077.40	148.75
917.41	927.40	42.33	1637.41	1647.40	77.97	2357.41	2367.40	113.61	3077.41	3087.40	149.25
927.41	937.40	42.82	1647.41	1657.40	78.46	2367.41	2377.40	114.10	3087.41	3097.40	149.74
937.41	947.40	43.32	1657.41	1667.40	78.96	2377.41	2387.40	114.60	3097.41	3107.40	150.24
947.41	957.40	43.81	1667.41	1677.40	79.45	2387.41	2397.40	115.09	3107.41	3117.40	150.73
957.41	967.40	44.31	1677.41	1687.40	79.95	2397.41	2407.40	115.59	3117.41	3127.40	151.23
967.41	977.40	44.80	1687.41	1697.40	80.44	2407.41	2417.40	116.08	3127.41	3137.40	151.72
977.41	987.40	45.30	1697.41	1707.40	80.94	2417.41	2427.40	116.58	3137.41	3147.40	152.22
987.41	997.40	45.79	1707.41	1717.40	81.43	2427.41	2437.40	117.07	3147.41	3157.40	152.71
997.41	1007.40	46.29	1717.41	1727.40	81.93	2437.41	2447.40	117.57	3157.41	3167.40	153.21
1007.41	1017.40	46.78	1727.41	1737.40	82.42	2447.41	2457.40	118.06	3167.41	3177.40	153.70
1017.41	1027.40	47.28	1737.41	1747.40	82.92	2457.41	2467.40	118.56	3177.41	3187.40	154.20
1027.41	1037.40	47.77	1747.41	1757.40	83.41	2467.41	2477.40	119.05	3187.41	3197.40	154.69
1037.41	1047.40	48.27	1757.41	1767.40	83.91	2477.41	2487.40	119.55	3197.41	3207.40	155.19
1047.41	1057.40	48.76	1767.41	1777.40	84.40	2487.41	2497.40	120.04	3207.41	3217.40	155.68
1057.41	1067.40	49.26	1777.41	1787.40	84.90	2497.41	2507.40	120.54	3217.41	3227.40	156.18
1067.41	1077.40	49.75	1787.41	1797.40	85.39	2507.41	2517.40	121.03	3227.41	3237.40	156.67
1077.41	1087.40	50.25	1797.41	1807.40	85.89	2517.41	2527.40	121.53	3237.41	3247.40	157.17
1087.41	1097.40	50.74	1807.41	1817.40	86.38	2527.41	2537.40	122.02	3247.41	3257.40	157.66
1097.41	1107.40	51.24	1817.41	1827.40	86.88	2537.41	2547.40	122.52	3257.41	3267.40	158.16
1107.41	1117.40	51.73	1827.41	1837.40	87.37	2547.41	2557.40	123.01	3267.41	3277.40	158.65
1117.41	1127.40	52.23	1837.41	1847.40	87.87	2557.41	2567.40	123.51	3277.41	3287.40	159.15
1127.41	1137.40	52.72	1847.41	1857.40	88.36	2567.41	2577.40	124.00	3287.41	3297.40	159.64
1137.41	1147.40	53.22	1857.41	1867.40	88.86	2577.41	2587.40	124.50	3297.41	3307.40	160.14
1147.41	1157.40	53.71	1867.41	1877.40	89.35	2587.41	2597.40	124.99	3307.41	3317.40	160.63
1157.41	1167.40	54.21	1877.41	1887.40	89.85	2597.41	2607.40	125.49	3317.41	3327.40	161.13
1167.41	1177.40	54.70	1887.41	1897.40	90.34	2607.41	2617.40	125.98	3327.41	3337.40	161.62
1177.41	1187.40	55.20	1897.41	1907.40	90.84	2617.41	2627.40	126.48	3337.41	3347.40	162.12
1187.41	1197.40	55.69	1907.41	1917.40	91.33	2627.41	2637.40	126.97	3347.41	3357.40	162.61
1197.41	1207.40	56.19	1917.41	1927.40	91.83	2637.41	2647.40	127.47	3357.41	3367.40	163.11
1207.41	1217.40	56.68	1927.41	1937.40	92.32	2647.41	2657.40	127.96	3367.41	3377.40	163.60
1217:41	1227.40	57.18	1937.41	1947.40	92.82	2657.41	2667.40	128.46	3377.41	3387.40	164.10
1227.41	1237.40	57.67	1947.41	1957.40	93.31	2667.41	2677.40	128.95	3387.41	3397.40	164.59
1237.41	1247.40	58.17	1957.41	1967.40	93.81	2677.41	2687.40	129.45	3397.41	3407.40	165.09
1247.41	1257.40	58.66	1967.41	1977.40	94.30	2687.41	2697.40	129.94	3407.41	3417.40	165.58
1257.41	1267.40	59.16	1977.41	1987.40	94.80	2697.41	2707.40	130.44	3417.41	3427.40	166.08
1267.41	1277.40	59.65	1987.41	1997.40	95.29	2707.41	2717.40	130.93	3427.41	3437.40	166.57
1277.41	1287.40	60.15	1997.41	2007.40	95.79	2717.41	2727.40	131.43	3437.41	3447.40	167.07
1287.41	1297.40	60.64	2007.41	2017.40	96.28	2727.41	2737.40	131.92	3447.41	3457.40	167.56
1297.41	1307.40	61.14	2017.41	2027.40	96.78	2737.41	2747.40	132.42	3457.41	3467.40	168.06
1307.41	1317.40	61.63	2027.41	2037.40	97.27	2747.41	2757.40	132.91	3467.41	3477.40	168.55
1317.41	1327.40	62.13	2037.41	2047.40	97.77	2757.41	2767.40	133.41	3477.41	3487.40	169.05
1327.41	1337.40	62.62	2047.41	2057.40	98.26	2767.41	2777.40	133.90	3487.41	3497.40	169.54
1337.41	1347.40	63.12	2057.41	2067.40	98.76	2777.41	2787.40	134.40	3497.41	3507.40	170.04
1347.41	1357.40	63.61	2067.41	2077.40	99.25	2787.41	2797.40	134.89	3507.41	3517.40	170.53
1357.41	1367.40	64.11	2077.41	2087.40	99.75	2797.41	2807.40	135.39	3517.41	3527.40	171.03
1367.41	1377.40	64.60	2087.41	2097.40	100.24	2807.41	2817.40	135.88	3527.41	3537.40	171.52
1377.41	1387.40	65.10	2097.41	2107.40	100.74	2817.41	2827.40	136.38	3537.41	3547.40	172.02

Employee's maximum CPP contribution for 2003 is $1,801.80 La cotisation maximale de l'employé au RPC pour 2003 est de 1 801,80 $

Canada Pension Plan Contributions / Cotisations au Régime de pensions du Canada
Biweekly (26 pay periods a year) / Aux deux semaines (26 périodes de paie par année)

Pay Rémunération From - De	To - À		Pay Rémunération From - De	To - À		Pay Rémunération From - De	To - À		Pay Rémunération From - De	To - À	
1530.88	1531.07	69.12	2064.72	2074.71	95.79	2784.72	2794.71	131.43	3504.72	3514.71	167.07
1531.08	1531.27	69.13	2074.72	2084.71	96.28	2794.72	2804.71	131.92	3514.72	3524.71	167.56
1531.28	1531.47	69.14	2084.72	2094.71	96.78	2804.72	2814.71	132.42	3524.72	3534.71	168.06
1531.48	1531.68	69.15	2094.72	2104.71	97.27	2814.72	2824.71	132.91	3534.72	3544.71	168.55
1531.69	1531.88	69.16	2104.72	2114.71	97.77	2824.72	2834.71	133.41	3544.72	3554.71	169.05
1531.89	1532.08	69.17	2114.72	2124.71	98.26	2834.72	2844.71	133.90	3554.72	3564.71	169.54
1532.09	1532.28	69.18	2124.72	2134.71	98.76	2844.72	2854.71	134.40	3564.72	3574.71	170.04
1532.29	1532.48	69.19	2134.72	2144.71	99.25	2854.72	2864.71	134.89	3574.72	3584.71	170.53
1532.49	1532.69	69.20	2144.72	2154.71	99.75	2864.72	2874.71	135.39	3584.72	3594.71	171.03
1532.70	1532.89	69.21	2154.72	2164.71	100.24	2874.72	2884.71	135.88	3594.72	3604.71	171.52
1532.90	1533.09	69.22	2164.72	2174.71	100.74	2884.72	2894.71	136.38	3604.72	3614.71	172.02
1533.10	1533.29	69.23	2174.72	2184.71	101.23	2894.72	2904.71	136.87	3614.72	3624.71	172.51
1533.30	1533.49	69.24	2184.72	2194.71	101.73	2904.72	2914.71	137.37	3624.72	3634.71	173.01
1533.50	1533.70	69.25	2194.72	2204.71	102.22	2914.72	2924.71	137.86	3634.72	3644.71	173.50
1533.71	1533.90	69.26	2204.72	2214.71	102.72	2924.72	2934.71	138.36	3644.72	3654.71	174.00
1533.91	1534.09	69.27	2214.72	2224.71	103.21	2934.72	2944.71	138.85	3654.72	3664.71	174.49
1534.10	1534.30	69.28	2224.72	2234.71	103.71	2944.72	2954.71	139.35	3664.72	3674.71	174.99
1534.31	1534.50	69.29	2234.72	2244.71	104.20	2954.72	2964.71	139.84	3674.72	3684.71	175.48
1534.51	1534.71	69.30	2244.72	2254.71	104.70	2964.72	2974.71	140.34	3684.72	3694.71	175.98
1534.72	1544.71	69.55	2254.72	2264.71	105.19	2974.72	2984.71	140.83	3694.72	3704.71	176.47
1544.72	1554.71	70.05	2264.72	2274.71	105.69	2984.72	2994.71	141.33	3704.72	3714.71	176.97
1554.72	1564.71	70.54	2274.72	2284.71	106.18	2994.72	3004.71	141.82	3714.72	3724.71	177.46
1564.72	1574.71	71.04	2284.72	2294.71	106.68	3004.72	3014.71	142.32	3724.72	3734.71	177.96
1574.72	1584.71	71.53	2294.72	2304.71	107.17	3014.72	3024.71	142.81	3734.72	3744.71	178.45
1584.72	1594.71	72.03	2304.72	2314.71	107.67	3024.72	3034.71	143.31	3744.72	3754.71	178.95
1594.72	1604.71	72.52	2314.72	2324.71	108.16	3034.72	3044.71	143.80	3754.72	3764.71	179.44
1604.72	1614.71	73.02	2324.72	2334.71	108.66	3044.72	3054.71	144.30	3764.72	3774.71	179.94
1614.72	1624.71	73.51	2334.72	2344.71	109.15	3054.72	3064.71	144.79	3774.72	3784.71	180.43
1624.72	1634.71	74.01	2344.72	2354.71	109.65	3064.72	3074.71	145.29	3784.72	3794.71	180.93
1634.72	1644.71	74.50	2354.72	2364.71	110.14	3074.72	3084.71	145.78	3794.72	3804.71	181.42
1644.72	1654.71	75.00	2364.72	2374.71	110.64	3084.72	3094.71	146.28	3804.72	3814.71	181.92
1654.72	1664.71	75.49	2374.72	2384.71	111.13	3094.72	3104.71	146.77	3814.72	3824.71	182.41
1664.72	1674.71	75.99	2384.72	2394.71	111.63	3104.72	3114.71	147.27	3824.72	3834.71	182.91
1674.72	1684.71	76.48	2394.72	2404.71	112.12	3114.72	3124.71	147.76	3834.72	3844.71	183.40
1684.72	1694.71	76.98	2404.72	2414.71	112.62	3124.72	3134.71	148.26	3844.72	3854.71	183.90
1694.72	1704.71	77.47	2414.72	2424.71	113.11	3134.72	3144.71	148.75	3854.72	3864.71	184.39
1704.72	1714.71	77.97	2424.72	2434.71	113.61	3144.72	3154.71	149.25	3864.72	3874.71	184.89
1714.72	1724.71	78.46	2434.72	2444.71	114.10	3154.72	3164.71	149.74	3874.72	3884.71	185.38
1724.72	1734.71	78.96	2444.72	2454.71	114.60	3164.72	3174.71	150.24	3884.72	3894.71	185.88
1734.72	1744.71	79.45	2454.72	2464.71	115.09	3174.72	3184.71	150.73	3894.72	3904.71	186.37
1744.72	1754.71	79.95	2464.72	2474.71	115.59	3184.72	3194.71	151.23	3904.72	3914.71	186.87
1754.72	1764.71	80.44	2474.72	2484.71	116.08	3194.72	3204.71	151.72	3914.72	3924.71	187.36
1764.72	1774.71	80.94	2484.72	2494.71	116.58	3204.72	3214.71	152.22	3924.72	3934.71	187.86
1774.72	1784.71	81.43	2494.72	2504.71	117.07	3214.72	3224.71	152.71	3934.72	3944.71	188.35
1784.72	1794.71	81.93	2504.72	2514.71	117.57	3224.72	3234.71	153.21	3944.72	3954.71	188.85
1794.72	1804.71	82.42	2514.72	2524.71	118.06	3234.72	3244.71	153.70	3954.72	3964.71	189.34
1804.72	1814.71	82.92	2524.72	2534.71	118.56	3244.72	3254.71	154.20	3964.72	3974.71	189.84
1814.72	1824.71	83.41	2534.72	2544.71	119.05	3254.72	3264.71	154.69	3974.72	3984.71	190.33
1824.72	1834.71	83.91	2544.72	2554.71	119.55	3264.72	3274.71	155.19	3984.72	3994.71	190.83
1834.72	1844.71	84.40	2554.72	2564.71	120.04	3274.72	3284.71	155.68	3994.72	4004.71	191.32
1844.72	1854.71	84.90	2564.72	2574.71	120.54	3284.72	3294.71	156.18	4004.72	4014.71	191.82
1854.72	1864.71	85.39	2574.72	2584.71	121.03	3294.72	3304.71	156.67	4014.72	4024.71	192.31
1864.72	1874.71	85.89	2584.72	2594.71	121.53	3304.72	3314.71	157.17	4024.72	4034.71	192.81
1874.72	1884.71	86.38	2594.72	2604.71	122.02	3314.72	3324.71	157.66	4034.72	4044.71	193.30
1884.72	1894.71	86.88	2604.72	2614.71	122.52	3324.72	3334.71	158.16	4044.72	4054.71	193.80
1894.72	1904.71	87.37	2614.72	2624.71	123.01	3334.72	3344.71	158.65	4054.72	4064.71	194.29
1904.72	1914.71	87.87	2624.72	2634.71	123.51	3344.72	3354.71	159.15	4064.72	4074.71	194.79
1914.72	1924.71	88.36	2634.72	2644.71	124.00	3354.72	3364.71	159.64	4074.72	4084.71	195.28
1924.72	1934.71	88.86	2644.72	2654.71	124.50	3364.72	3374.71	160.14	4084.72	4094.71	195.78
1934.72	1944.71	89.35	2654.72	2664.71	124.99	3374.72	3384.71	160.63	4094.72	4104.71	196.27
1944.72	1954.71	89.85	2664.72	2674.71	125.49	3384.72	3394.71	161.13	4104.72	4114.71	196.77
1954.72	1964.71	90.34	2674.72	2684.71	125.98	3394.72	3404.71	161.62	4114.72	4124.71	197.26
1964.72	1974.71	90.84	2684.72	2694.71	126.48	3404.72	3414.71	162.12	4124.72	4134.71	197.76
1974.72	1984.71	91.33	2694.72	2704.71	126.97	3414.72	3424.71	162.61	4134.72	4144.71	198.25
1984.72	1994.71	91.83	2704.72	2714.71	127.47	3424.72	3434.71	163.11	4144.72	4154.71	198.75
1994.72	2004.71	92.32	2714.72	2724.71	127.96	3434.72	3444.71	163.60	4154.72	4164.71	199.24
2004.72	2014.71	92.82	2724.72	2734.71	128.46	3444.72	3454.71	164.10	4164.72	4174.71	199.74
2014.72	2024.71	93.31	2734.72	2744.71	128.95	3454.72	3464.71	164.59	4174.72	4184.71	200.23
2024.72	2034.71	93.81	2744.72	2754.71	129.45	3464.72	3474.71	165.09	4184.72	4194.71	200.73
2034.72	2044.71	94.30	2754.72	2764.71	129.94	3474.72	3484.71	165.58	4194.72	4204.71	201.22
2044.72	2054.71	94.80	2764.72	2774.71	130.44	3484.72	3494.71	166.08	4204.72	4214.71	201.72
2054.72	2064.71	95.29	2774.72	2784.71	130.93	3494.72	3504.71	166.57	4214.72	4224.71	202.21

Employee's maximum CPP contribution for 2003 is $1,801 80

La cotisation maximale de l'employé au RPC pour 2003 est de 1 801,80 $

Canada Pension Plan Contributions
Monthly (12 pay periods a year)

Cotisations au Régime de pensions du Canada
Mensuel (12 périodes de paie par année)

Pay / Rémunération From - De	To - À		Pay / Rémunération From - De	To - À		Pay / Rémunération From - De	To - À		Pay / Rémunération From - De	To - À	
5805.10	5815.09	273.16	6525.10	6535.09	308.80	7245.10	7255.09	344.44	7965.10	7975.09	380.08
5815.10	5825.09	273.66	6535.10	6545.09	309.30	7255.10	7265.09	344.94	7975.10	7985.09	380.58
5825.10	5835.09	274.15	6545.10	6555.09	309.79	7265.10	7275.09	345.43	7985.10	7995.09	381.07
5835.10	5845.09	274.65	6555.10	6565.09	310.29	7275.10	7285.09	345.93	7995.10	8005.09	381.57
5845.10	5855.09	275.14	6565.10	6575.09	310.78	7285.10	7295.09	346.42	8005.10	8015.09	382.06
5855.10	5865.09	275.64	6575.10	6585.09	311.28	7295.10	7305.09	346.92	8015.10	8025.09	382.56
5865.10	5875.09	276.13	6585.10	6595.09	311.77	7305.10	7315.09	347.41	8025.10	8035.09	383.05
5875.10	5885.09	276.63	6595.10	6605.09	312.27	7315.10	7325.09	347.91	8035.10	8045.09	383.65
5885.10	5895.09	277.12	6605.10	6615.09	312.76	7325.10	7335.09	348.40	8045.10	8055.09	384.04
5895.10	5905.09	277.62	6615.10	6625.09	313.26	7335.10	7345.09	348.90	8055.10	8065.09	384.54
5905.10	5915.09	278.11	6625.10	6635.09	313.75	7345.10	7355.09	349.39	8065.10	8075.09	385.03
5915.10	5925.09	278.61	6635.10	6645.09	314.25	7355.10	7365.09	349.89	8075.10	8085.09	385.53
5925.10	5935.09	279.10	6645.10	6655.09	314.74	7365.10	7375.09	350.38	8085.10	8095.09	386.02
5935.10	5945.09	279.60	6655.10	6665.09	315.24	7375.10	7385.09	350.88	8095.10	8105.09	386.52
5945.10	5955.09	280.09	6665.10	6675.09	315.73	7385.10	7395.09	351.37	8105.10	8115.09	387.01
5955.10	5965.09	280.59	6675.10	6685.09	316.23	7395.10	7405.09	351.87	8115.10	8125.09	387.51
5965.10	5975.09	281.08	6685.10	6695.09	316.72	7405.10	7415.09	352.36	8125.10	8135.09	388.00
5975.10	5985.09	281.58	6695.10	6705.09	317.22	7415.10	7425.09	352.86	8135.10	8145.09	388.50
5985.10	5995.09	282.07	6705.10	6715.09	317.71	7425.10	7435.09	353.35	8145.10	8155.09	388.99
5995.10	6005.09	282.57	6715.10	6725.09	318.21	7435.10	7445.09	353.85	8155.10	8165.09	389.49
6005.10	6015.09	283.06	6725.10	6735.09	318.70	7445.10	7455.09	354.34	8165.10	8175.09	389.98
6015.10	6025.09	283.56	6735.10	6745.09	319.20	7455.10	7465.09	354.84	8175.10	8185.09	390.48
6025.10	6035.09	284.05	6745.10	6755.09	319.69	7465.10	7475.09	355.33	8185.10	8195:09	390.97
6035.10	6045.09	284.55	6755.10	6765.09	320.19	7475.10	7485.09	355.83	8195.10	8205.09	391.47
6045.10	6055.09	285.04	6765.10	6775.09	320.68	7485.10	7495.09	356.32	8205.10	8215.09	391.96
6055.10	6065.09	285.54	6775.10	6785.09	321.18	7495.10	7505.09	356.82	8215.10	8225.09	392.46
6065.10	6075.09	286.03	6785.10	6795.09	321.67	7505.10	7515.09	357.31	8225.10	8235.09	392.95
6075.10	6085.09	286.53	6795.10	6805.09	322.17	7515.10	7525.09	357.81	8235.10	8245.09	393.45
6085.10	6095.09	287.02	6805.10	6815.09	322.66	7525.10	7535.09	358.30	8245.10	8255.09	393.94
6095.10	6105.09	287.52	6815.10	6825.09	323.16	7535.10	7545.09	358.80	8255.10	8265.09	394.44
6105.10	6115.09	288.01	6825.10	6835.09	323.65	7545.10	7555.09	359.29	8265.10	8275.09	394.93
6115.10	6125.09	288.51	6835.10	6845.09	324.15	7555.10	7565.09	359.79	8275.10	8285.09	395.43
6125.10	6135.09	289.00	6845.10	6855.09	324.64	7565.10	7575.09	360.28	8285.10	8295.09	395.92
6135.10	6145.09	289.50	6855.10	6865.09	325.14	7575.10	7585.09	360.78	8295.10	8305.09	396.42
6145.10	6155.09	289.99	6865.10	6875.09	325.63	7585.10	7595.09	361.27	8305.10	8315.09	396.91
6155.10	6165.09	290.49	6875.10	6885.09	326.13	7595.10	7605.09	361.77	8315.10	8325.09	397.41
6165.10	6175.09	290.98	6885.10	6895.09	326.62	7605.10	7615.09	362.26	8325.10	8335.09	397.90
6175.10	6185.09	291.48	6895.10	6905.09	327.12	7615.10	7625.09	362.76	8335.10	8345.09	398.40
6185.10	6195.09	291.97	6905.10	6915.09	327.61	7625.10	7635.09	363.25	8345.10	8355.09	398.89
6195.10	6205.09	292.47	6915.10	6925.09	328.11	7635.10	7645.09	363.75	8355.10	8365.09	399.39
6205.10	6215.09	292.96	6925.10	6935.09	328.60	7645.10	7655.09	364.24	8365.10	8375.09	399.88
6215.10	6225.09	293.46	6935.10	6945.09	329.10	7655.10	7665.09	364.74	8375.10	8385.09	400.38
6225.10	6235.09	293.95	6945.10	6955.09	329.59	7665.10	7675.09	365.23	8385.10	8395.09	400.87
6235.10	6245.09	294.45	6955.10	6965.09	330.09	7675.10	7685.09	365.73	8395.10	8405.09	401.37
6245.10	6255.09	294.94	6965.10	6975.09	330.58	7685.10	7695.09	366.22	8405.10	8415.09	401.86
6255.10	6265.09	295.44	6975.10	6985.09	331.08	7695.10	7705.09	366.72	8415.10	8425.09	402.36
6265.10	6275.09	295.93	6985.10	6995.09	331.57	7705.10	7715.09	367.21	8425.10	8435.09	402.85
6275.10	6285.09	296.43	6995.10	7005.09	332.07	7715.10	7725.09	367.71	8435.10	8445.09	403.35
6285.10	6295.09	296.92	7005.10	7015.09	332.56	7725.10	7735.09	368.20	8445.10	8455.09	403.84
6295.10	6305.09	297.42	7015.10	7025.09	333.06	7735.10	7745.09	368.70	8455.10	8465.09	404.34
6305.10	6315.09	297.91	7025.10	7035.09	333.55	7745.10	7755.09	369.19	8465.10	8475.09	404.83
6315.10	6325.09	298.41	7035.10	7045.09	334.05	7755.10	7765.09	369.69	8475.10	8485.09	405.33
6325.10	6335.09	298.90	7045.10	7055.09	334.54	7765.10	7775.09	370.18	8485.10	8495.09	405.82
6335.10	6345.09	299.40	7055.10	7065.09	335.04	7775.10	7785.09	370.68	8495.10	8505.09	406.32
6345.10	6355.09	299.89	7065.10	7075.09	335.53	7785.10	7795.09	371.17	8505.10	8515.09	406.81
6355.10	6365.09	300.39	7075.10	7085.09	336.03	7795.10	7805.09	371.67	8515.10	8525.09	407.31
6365.10	6375.09	300.88	7085.10	7095.09	336.52	7805.10	7815.09	372.16	8525.10	8535.09	407.80
6375.10	6385.09	301.38	7095.10	7105.09	337.02	7815.10	7825.09	372.66	8535.10	8545.09	408.30
6385.10	6395.09	301.87	7105.10	7115.09	337.51	7825.10	7835.09	373.15	8545.10	8555.09	408.79
6395.10	6405.09	302.37	7115.10	7125.09	338.01	7835.10	7845.09	373.65	8555.10	8565.09	409.29
6405.10	6415.09	302.86	7125.10	7135.09	338.50	7845.10	7855.09	374.14	8565.10	8575.09	409.78
6415.10	6425.09	303.36	7135.10	7145.09	339.00	7855.10	7865.09	374.64	8575.10	8585.09	410.28
6425.10	6435.09	303.85	7145.10	7155.09	339.49	7865.10	7875.09	375.13	8585.10	8595.09	410.77
6435.10	6445.09	304.35	7155.10	7165.09	339.99	7875.10	7885.09	375.63	8595.10	8605.09	411.27
6445.10	6455.09	304.84	7165.10	7175.09	340.48	7885.10	7895.09	376.12	8605.10	8615.09	411.76
6455.10	6465.09	305.34	7175.10	7185.09	340.98	7895.10	7905.09	376.62	8615.10	8625.09	412.26
6465.10	6475.09	305.83	7185.10	7195.09	341.47	7905.10	7915.09	377.11	8625.10	8635.09	412.75
6475.10	6485.09	306.33	7195.10	7205.09	341.97	7915.10	7925.09	377.61	8635.10	8645.09	413.25
6485.10	6495.09	306.82	7205.10	7215.09	342.46	7925.10	7935.09	378.10	8645.10	8655.09	413.74
6495.10	6505.09	307.32	7215.10	7225.09	342.96	7935.10	7945.09	378.60	8655.10	8665.09	414.24
6505.10	6515.09	307.81	7225.10	7235.09	343.45	7945.10	7955.09	379.09	8665.10	8675.09	414.73
6515.10	6525.09	308.31	7235.10	7245.09	343.95	7955.10	7965.09	379.59	8675.10	8685.09*	415.23

Employee's maximum CPP contribution for 2003 is $1,801 80

*If the earnings are above this amount, follow the calculation method shown in publication T4001, *Payroll Deductions - Basic Information*

La cotisation maximale de l'employé au RPC pour 2003 est de

* Si la rémunération dépasse ce montant, consultez la méthode de calcul q dans la publication T4001, *Renseignements de base sur les retenues su*

Employment Insurance Premiums — Cotisations à l'assurance-emploi

Insurable Earnings Rémunération assurable From - De	To - À		Insurable Earnings Rémunération assurable From - De	To - À		Insurable Earnings Rémunération assurable From - De	To - À		Insurable Earnings Rémunération assurable From - De	To - À	
.00	.71	.01	34.53	34.99	.73	68.81	69.28	1.45	103.10	103.57	2.17
.72	1.19	.02	35.00	35.47	.74	69.29	69.76	1.46	103.58	104.04	2.18
1.20	1.66	.03	35.48	35.95	.75	69.77	70.23	1.47	104.05	104.52	2.19
1.67	2.14	.04	35.96	36.42	.76	70.24	70.71	1.48	104.53	104.99	2.20
2.15	2.61	.05	36.43	36.90	.77	70.72	71.19	1.49	105.00	105.47	2.21
2.62	3.09	.06	36.91	37.38	.78	71.20	71.66	1.50	105.48	105.95	2.22
3.10	3.57	.07	37.39	37.85	.79	71.67	72.14	1.51	105.96	106.42	2.23
3.58	4.04	.08	37.86	38.33	.80	72.15	72.61	1.52	106.43	106.90	2.24
4.05	4.52	.09	38.34	38.80	.81	72.62	73.09	1.53	106.91	107.38	2.25
4.53	4.99	.10	38.81	39.28	.82	73.10	73.57	1.54	107.39	107.85	2.26
5.00	5.47	.11	39.29	39.76	.83	73.58	74.04	1.55	107.86	108.33	2.27
5.48	5.95	.12	39.77	40.23	.84	74.05	74.52	1.56	108.34	108.80	2.28
5.96	6.42	.13	40.24	40.71	.85	74.53	74.99	1.57	108.81	109.28	2.29
6.43	6.90	.14	40.72	41.19	.86	75.00	75.47	1.58	109.29	109.76	2.30
6.91	7.38	.15	41.20	41.66	.87	75.48	75.95	1.59	109.77	110.23	2.31
7.39	7.85	.16	41.67	42.14	.88	75.96	76.42	1.60	110.24	110.71	2.32
7.86	8.33	.17	42.15	42.61	.89	76.43	76.90	1.61	110.72	111.19	2.33
8.34	8.80	.18	42.62	43.09	.90	76.91	77.38	1.62	111.20	111.66	2.34
8.81	9.28	.19	43.10	43.57	.91	77.39	77.85	1.63	111.67	112.14	2.35
9.29	9.76	.20	43.58	44.04	.92	77.86	78.33	1.64	112.15	112.61	2.36
9.77	10.23	.21	44.05	44.52	.93	78.34	78.80	1.65	112.62	113.09	2.37
10.24	10.71	.22	44.53	44.99	.94	78.81	79.28	1.66	113.10	113.57	2.38
10.72	11.19	.23	45.00	45.47	.95	79.29	79.76	1.67	113.58	114.04	2.39
11.20	11.66	.24	45.48	45.95	.96	79.77	80.23	1.68	114.05	114.52	2.40
11.67	12.14	.25	45.96	46.42	.97	80.24	80.71	1.69	114.53	114.99	2.41
12.15	12.61	.26	46.43	46.90	.98	80.72	81.19	1.70	115.00	115.47	2.42
12.62	13.09	.27	46.91	47.38	.99	81.20	81.66	1.71	115.48	115.95	2.43
13.10	13.57	.28	47.39	47.85	1.00	81.67	82.14	1.72	115.96	116.42	2.44
13.58	14.04	.29	47.86	48.33	1.01	82.15	82.61	1.73	116.43	116.90	2.45
14.05	14.52	.30	48.34	48.80	1.02	82.62	83.09	1.74	116.91	117.38	2.46
14.53	14.99	.31	48.81	49.28	1.03	83.10	83.57	1.75	117.39	117.85	2.47
15.00	15.47	.32	49.29	49.76	1.04	83.58	84.04	1.76	117.86	118.33	2.48
15.48	15.95	.33	49.77	50.23	1.05	84.05	84.52	1.77	118.34	118.80	2.49
15.96	16.42	.34	50.24	50.71	1.06	84.53	84.99	1.78	118.81	119.28	2.50
16.43	16.90	.35	50.72	51.19	1.07	85.00	85.47	1.79	119.29	119.76	2.51
16.91	17.38	.36	51.20	51.66	1.08	85.48	85.95	1.80	119.77	120.23	2.52
17.39	17.85	.37	51.67	52.14	1.09	85.96	86.42	1.81	120.24	120.71	2.53
17.86	18.33	.38	52.15	52.61	1.10	86.43	86.90	1.82	120.72	121.19	2.54
18.34	18.80	.39	52.62	53.09	1.11	86.91	87.38	1.83	121.20	121.66	2.55
18.81	19.28	.40	53.10	53.57	1.12	87.39	87.85	1.84	121.67	122.14	2.56
19.29	19.76	.41	53.58	54.04	1.13	87.86	88.33	1.85	122.15	122.61	2.57
19.77	20.23	.42	54.05	54.52	1.14	88.34	88.80	1.86	122.62	123.09	2.58
20.24	20.71	.43	54.53	54.99	1.15	88.81	89.28	1.87	123.10	123.57	2.59
20.72	21.19	.44	55.00	55.47	1.16	89.29	89.76	1.88	123.58	124.04	2.60
21.20	21.66	.45	55.48	55.95	1.17	89.77	90.23	1.89	124.05	124.52	2.61
21.67	22.14	.46	55.96	56.42	1.18	90.24	90.71	1.90	124.53	124.99	2.62
22.15	22.61	.47	56.43	56.90	1.19	90.72	91.19	1.91	125.00	125.47	2.63
22.62	23.09	.48	56.91	57.38	1.20	91.20	91.66	1.92	125.48	125.95	2.64
23.10	23.57	.49	57.39	57.85	1.21	91.67	92.14	1.93	125.96	126.42	2.65
23.58	24.04	.50	57.86	58.33	1.22	92.15	92.61	1.94	126.43	126.90	2.66
24.05	24.52	.51	58.34	58.80	1.23	92.62	93.09	1.95	126.91	127.38	2.67
24.53	24.99	.52	58.81	59.28	1.24	93.10	93.57	1.96	127.39	127.85	2.68
25.00	25.47	.53	59.29	59.76	1.25	93.58	94.04	1.97	127.86	128.33	2.69
25.48	25.95	.54	59.77	60.23	1.26	94.05	94.52	1.98	128.34	128.80	2.70
25.96	26.42	.55	60.24	60.71	1.27	94.53	94.99	1.99	128.81	129.28	2.71
26.43	26.90	.56	60.72	61.19	1.28	95.00	95.47	2.00	129.29	129.76	2.72
26.91	27.38	.57	61.20	61.66	1.29	95.48	95.95	2.01	129.77	130.23	2.73
27.39	27.85	.58	61.67	62.14	1.30	95.96	96.42	2.02	130.24	130.71	2.74
27.86	28.33	.59	62.15	62.61	1.31	96.43	96.90	2.03	130.72	131.19	2.75
28.34	28.80	.60	62.62	63.09	1.32	96.91	97.38	2.04	131.20	131.66	2.76
28.81	29.28	.61	63.10	63.57	1.33	97.39	97.85	2.05	131.67	132.14	2.77
29.29	29.76	.62	63.58	64.04	1.34	97.86	98.33	2.06	132.15	132.61	2.78
29.77	30.23	.63	64.05	64.52	1.35	98.34	98.80	2.07	132.62	133.09	2.79
30.24	30.71	.64	64.53	64.99	1.36	98.81	99.28	2.08	133.10	133.57	2.80
30.72	31.19	.65	65.00	65.47	1.37	99.29	99.76	2.09	133.58	134.04	2.81
31.20	31.66	.66	65.48	65.95	1.38	99.77	100.23	2.10	134.05	134.52	2.82
31.67	32.14	.67	65.96	66.42	1.39	100.24	100.71	2.11	134.53	134.99	2.83
32.15	32.61	.68	66.43	66.90	1.40	100.72	101.19	2.12	135.00	135.47	2.84
32.62	33.09	.69	66.91	67.38	1.41	101.20	101.66	2.13	135.48	135.95	2.85
33.10	33.57	.70	67.39	67.85	1.42	101.67	102.14	2.14	135.96	136.42	2.86
33.58	34.04	.71	67.86	68.33	1.43	102.15	102.61	2.15	136.43	136.90	2.87
34.05	34.52	.72	68.34	68.80	1.44	102.62	103.09	2.16	136.91	137.38	2.88

Yearly maximum insurable earnings are $39,000
Yearly maximum employee premiums are $819.00
The premium rate for 2003 is 2.10 %

Le maximum annuel de la rémunération assurable est de 39 000 $
La cotisation maximale annuelle de l'employé est de 819,00 $
La taux de cotisations pour 2003 est de 2,10 %

Employment Insurance Premiums — Cotisations à l'assurance-emploi

Insurable Earnings / Rémunération assurable From - De	To - À		Insurable Earnings / Rémunération assurable From - De	To - À		Insurable Earnings / Rémunération assurable From - De	To - À		Insurable Earnings / Rémunération assurable From - De	To - À	
685.96	686.42	14.41	720.24	720.71	15.13	754.53	754.99	15.85	788.81	789.28	16.57
686.43	686.90	14.42	720.72	721.19	15.14	755.00	755.47	15.86	789.29	789.76	16.58
686.91	687.38	14.43	721.20	721.66	15.15	755.48	755.95	15.87	789.77	790.23	16.59
687.39	687.85	14.44	721.67	722.14	15.16	755.96	756.42	15.88	790.24	790.71	16.60
687.86	688.33	14.45	722.15	722.61	15.17	756.43	756.90	15.89	790.72	791.19	16.61
688.34	688.80	14.46	722.62	723.09	15.18	756.91	757.38	15.90	791.20	791.66	16.62
688.81	689.28	14.47	723.10	723.57	15.19	757.39	757.85	15.91	791.67	792.14	16.63
689.29	689.76	14.48	723.58	724.04	15.20	757.86	758.33	15.92	792.15	792.61	16.64
689.77	690.23	14.49	724.05	724.52	15.21	758.34	758.80	15.93	792.62	793.09	16.65
690.24	690.71	14.50	724.53	724.99	15.22	758.81	759.28	15.94	793.10	793.57	16.66
690.72	691.19	14.51	725.00	725.47	15.23	759.29	759.76	15.95	793.58	794.04	16.67
691.20	691.66	14.52	725.48	725.95	15.24	759.77	760.23	15.96	794.05	794.52	16.68
691.67	692.14	14.53	725.96	726.42	15.25	760.24	760.71	15.97	794.53	794.99	16.69
692.15	692.61	14.54	726.43	726.90	15.26	760.72	761.19	15.98	795.00	795.47	16.70
692.62	693.09	14.55	726.91	727.38	15.27	761.20	761.66	15.99	795.48	795.95	16.71
693.10	693.57	14.56	727.39	727.85	15.28	761.67	762.14	16.00	795.96	796.42	16.72
693.58	694.04	14.57	727.86	728.33	15.29	762.15	762.61	16.01	796.43	796.90	16.73
694.05	694.52	14.58	728.34	728.80	15.30	762.62	763.09	16.02	796.91	797.38	16.74
694.53	694.99	14.59	728.81	729.28	15.31	763.10	763.57	16.03	797.39	797.85	16.75
695.00	695.47	14.60	729.29	729.76	15.32	763.58	764.04	16.04	797.86	798.33	16.76
695.48	695.95	14.61	729.77	730.23	15.33	764.05	764.52	16.05	798.34	798.80	16.77
695.96	696.42	14.62	730.24	730.71	15.34	764.53	764.99	16.06	798.81	799.28	16.78
696.43	696.90	14.63	730.72	731.19	15.35	765.00	765.47	16.07	799.29	799.76	16.79
696.91	697.38	14.64	731.20	731.66	15.36	765.48	765.95	16.08	799.77	800.23	16.80
697.39	697.85	14.65	731.67	732.14	15.37	765.96	766.42	16.09	800.24	800.71	16.81
697.86	698.33	14.66	732.15	732.61	15.38	766.43	766.90	16.10	800.72	801.19	16.82
698.34	698.80	14.67	732.62	733.09	15.39	766.91	767.38	16.11	801.20	801.66	16.83
698.81	699.28	14.68	733.10	733.57	15.40	767.39	767.85	16.12	801.67	802.14	16.84
699.29	699.76	14.69	733.58	734.04	15.41	767.86	768.33	16.13	802.15	802.61	16.85
699.77	700.23	14.70	734.05	734.52	15.42	768.34	768.80	16.14	802.62	803.09	16.86
700.24	700.71	14.71	734.53	734.99	15.43	768.81	769.28	16.15	803.10	803.57	16.87
700.72	701.19	14.72	735.00	735.47	15.44	769.29	769.76	16.16	803.58	804.04	16.88
701.20	701.66	14.73	735.48	735.95	15.45	769.77	770.23	16.17	804.05	804.52	16.89
701.67	702.14	14.74	735.96	736.42	15.46	770.24	770.71	16.18	804.53	804.99	16.90
702.15	702.61	14.75	736.43	736.90	15.47	770.72	771.19	16.19	805.00	805.47	16.91
702.62	703.09	14.76	736.91	737.38	15.48	771.20	771.66	16.20	805.48	805.95	16.92
703.10	703.57	14.77	737.39	737.85	15.49	771.67	772.14	16.21	805.96	806.42	16.93
703.58	704.04	14.78	737.86	738.33	15.50	772.15	772.61	16.22	806.43	806.90	16.94
704.05	704.52	14.79	738.34	738.80	15.51	772.62	773.09	16.23	806.91	807.38	16.95
704.53	704.99	14.80	738.81	739.28	15.52	773.10	773.57	16.24	807.39	807.85	16.96
705.00	705.47	14.81	739.29	739.76	15.53	773.58	774.04	16.25	807.86	808.33	16.97
705.48	705.95	14.82	739.77	740.23	15.54	774.05	774.52	16.26	808.34	808.80	16.98
705.96	706.42	14.83	740.24	740.71	15.55	774.53	774.99	16.27	808.81	809.28	16.99
706.43	706.90	14.84	740.72	741.19	15.56	775.00	775.47	16.28	809.29	809.76	17.00
706.91	707.38	14.85	741.20	741.66	15.57	775.48	775.95	16.29	809.77	810.23	17.01
707.39	707.85	14.86	741.67	742.14	15.58	775.96	776.42	16.30	810.24	810.71	17.02
707.86	708.33	14.87	742.15	742.61	15.59	776.43	776.90	16.31	810.72	811.19	17.03
708.34	708.80	14.88	742.62	743.09	15.60	776.91	777.38	16.32	811.20	811.66	17.04
708.81	709.28	14.89	743.10	743.57	15.61	777.39	777.85	16.33	811.67	812.14	17.05
709.29	709.76	14.90	743.58	744.04	15.62	777.86	778.33	16.34	812.15	812.61	17.06
709.77	710.23	14.91	744.05	744.52	15.63	778.34	778.80	16.35	812.62	813.09	17.07
710.24	710.71	14.92	744.53	744.99	15.64	778.81	779.28	16.36	813.10	813.57	17.08
710.72	711.19	14.93	745.00	745.47	15.65	779.29	779.76	16.37	813.58	814.04	17.09
711.20	711.66	14.94	745.48	745.95	15.66	779.77	780.23	16.38	814.05	814.52	17.10
711.67	712.14	14.95	745.96	746.42	15.67	780.24	780.71	16.39	814.53	814.99	17.11
712.15	712.61	14.96	746.43	746.90	15.68	780.72	781.19	16.40	815.00	815.47	17.12
712.62	713.09	14.97	746.91	747.38	15.69	781.20	781.66	16.41	815.48	815.95	17.13
713.10	713.57	14.98	747.39	747.85	15.70	781.67	782.14	16.42	815.96	816.42	17.14
713.58	714.04	14.99	747.86	748.33	15.71	782.15	782.61	16.43	816.43	816.90	17.15
714.05	714.52	15.00	748.34	748.80	15.72	782.62	783.09	16.44	816.91	817.38	17.16
714.53	714.99	15.01	748.81	749.28	15.73	783.10	783.57	16.45	817.39	817.85	17.17
715.00	715.47	15.02	749.29	749.76	15.74	783.58	784.04	16.46	817.86	818.33	17.18
715.48	715.95	15.03	749.77	750.23	15.75	784.05	784.52	16.47	818.34	818.80	17.19
715.96	716.42	15.04	750.24	750.71	15.76	784.53	784.99	16.48	818.81	819.28	17.20
716.43	716.90	15.05	750.72	751.19	15.77	785.00	785.47	16.49	819.29	819.76	17.21
716.91	717.38	15.06	751.20	751.66	15.78	785.48	785.95	16.50	819.77	820.23	17.22
717.39	717.85	15.07	751.67	752.14	15.79	785.96	786.42	16.51	820.24	820.71	17.23
717.86	718.33	15.08	752.15	752.61	15.80	786.43	786.90	16.52	820.72	821.19	17.24
718.34	718.80	15.09	752.62	753.09	15.81	786.91	787.38	16.53	821.20	821.66	17.25
718.81	719.28	15.10	753.10	753.57	15.82	787.39	787.85	16.54	821.67	822.14	17.26
719.29	719.76	15.11	753.58	754.04	15.83	787.86	788.33	16.55	822.15	822.61	17.27
719.77	720.23	15.12	754.05	754.52	15.84	788.34	788.80	16.56	822.62	823.09	17.28

Yearly maximum insurable earnings are $39,000
Yearly maximum employee premiums are $819.00
The premium rate for 2003 is 2.10 %

Le maximum annuel de la rémunération assurable est de 39 000 $
La cotisation maximale annuelle de l'employé est de 819,00 $
La taux de cotisations pour 2003 est de 2,10 %

Employment Insurance Premiums — Cotisations à l'assurance-emploi

Insurable Earnings / Rémunération assurable From - De	To - À		Insurable Earnings / Rémunération assurable From - De	To - À		Insurable Earnings / Rémunération assurable From - De	To - À		Insurable Earnings / Rémunération assurable From - De	To - À	
1234.53	1234.99	25.93	1268.81	1269.28	26.65	1303.10	1303.57	27.37	1337.39	1337.85	28.09
1235.00	1235.47	25.94	1269.29	1269.76	26.66	1303.58	1304.04	27.38	1337.86	1338.33	28.10
1235.48	1235.95	25.95	1269.77	1270.23	26.67	1304.05	1304.52	27.39	1338.34	1338.80	28.11
1235.96	1236.42	25.96	1270.24	1270.71	26.68	1304.53	1304.99	27.40	1338.81	1339.28	28.12
1236.43	1236.90	25.97	1270.72	1271.19	26.69	1305.00	1305.47	27.41	1339.29	1339.76	28.13
1236.91	1237.38	25.98	1271.20	1271.66	26.70	1305.48	1305.95	27.42	1339.77	1340.23	28.14
1237.39	1237.85	25.99	1271.67	1272.14	26.71	1305.96	1306.42	27.43	1340.24	1340.71	28.15
1237.86	1238.33	26.00	1272.15	1272.61	26.72	1306.43	1306.90	27.44	1340.72	1341.19	28.16
1238.34	1238.80	26.01	1272.62	1273.09	26.73	1306.91	1307.38	27.45	1341.20	1341.66	28.17
1238.81	1239.28	26.02	1273.10	1273.57	26.74	1307.39	1307.85	27.46	1341.67	1342.14	28.18
1239.29	1239.76	26.03	1273.58	1274.04	26.75	1307.86	1308.33	27.47	1342.15	1342.61	28.19
1239.77	1240.23	26.04	1274.05	1274.52	26.76	1308.34	1308.80	27.48	1342.62	1343.09	28.20
1240.24	1240.71	26.05	1274.53	1274.99	26.77	1308.81	1309.28	27.49	1343.10	1343.57	28.21
1240.72	1241.19	26.06	1275.00	1275.47	26.78	1309.29	1309.76	27.50	1343.58	1344.04	28.22
1241.20	1241.66	26.07	1275.48	1275.95	26.79	1309.77	1310.23	27.51	1344.05	1344.52	28.23
1241.67	1242.14	26.08	1275.96	1276.42	26.80	1310.24	1310.71	27.52	1344.53	1344.99	28.24
1242.15	1242.61	26.09	1276.43	1276.90	26.81	1310.72	1311.19	27.53	1345.00	1345.47	28.25
1242.62	1243.09	26.10	1276.91	1277.38	26.82	1311.20	1311.66	27.54	1345.48	1345.95	28.26
1243.10	1243.57	26.11	1277.39	1277.85	26.83	1311.67	1312.14	27.55	1345.96	1346.42	28.27
1243.58	1244.04	26.12	1277.86	1278.33	26.84	1312.15	1312.61	27.56	1346.43	1346.90	28.28
1244.05	1244.52	26.13	1278.34	1278.80	26.85	1312.62	1313.09	27.57	1346.91	1347.38	28.29
1244.53	1244.99	26.14	1278.81	1279.28	26.86	1313.10	1313.57	27.58	1347.39	1347.85	28.30
1245.00	1245.47	26.15	1279.29	1279.76	26.87	1313.58	1314.04	27.59	1347.86	1348.33	28.31
1245.48	1245.95	26.16	1279.77	1280.23	26.88	1314.05	1314.52	27.60	1348.34	1348.80	28.32
1245.96	1246.42	26.17	1280.24	1280.71	26.89	1314.53	1314.99	27.61	1348.81	1349.28	28.33
1246.43	1246.90	26.18	1280.72	1281.19	26.90	1315.00	1315.47	27.62	1349.29	1349.76	28.34
1246.91	1247.38	26.19	1281.20	1281.66	26.91	1315.48	1315.95	27.63	1349.77	1350.23	28.35
1247.39	1247.85	26.20	1281.67	1282.14	26.92	1315.96	1316.42	27.64	1350.24	1350.71	28.36
1247.86	1248.33	26.21	1282.15	1282.61	26.93	1316.43	1316.90	27.65	1350.72	1351.19	28.37
1248.34	1248.80	26.22	1282.62	1283.09	26.94	1316.91	1317.38	27.66	1351.20	1351.66	28.38
1248.81	1249.28	26.23	1283.10	1283.57	26.95	1317.39	1317.85	27.67	1351.67	1352.14	28.39
1249.29	1249.76	26.24	1283.58	1284.04	26.96	1317.86	1318.33	27.68	1352.15	1352.61	28.40
1249.77	1250.23	26.25	1284.05	1284.52	26.97	1318.34	1318.80	27.69	1352.62	1353.09	28.41
1250.24	1250.71	26.26	1284.53	1284.99	26.98	1318.81	1319.28	27.70	1353.10	1353.57	28.42
1250.72	1251.19	26.27	1285.00	1285.47	26.99	1319.29	1319.76	27.71	1353.58	1354.04	28.43
1251.20	1251.66	26.28	1285.48	1285.95	27.00	1319.77	1320.23	27.72	1354.05	1354.52	28.44
1251.67	1252.14	26.29	1285.96	1286.42	27.01	1320.24	1320.71	27.73	1354.53	1354.99	28.45
1252.15	1252.61	26.30	1286.43	1286.90	27.02	1320.72	1321.19	27.74	1355.00	1355.47	28.46
1252.62	1253.09	26.31	1286.91	1287.38	27.03	1321.20	1321.66	27.75	1355.48	1355.95	28.47
1253.10	1253.57	26.32	1287.39	1287.85	27.04	1321.67	1322.14	27.76	1355.96	1356.42	28.48
1253.58	1254.04	26.33	1287.86	1288.33	27.05	1322.15	1322.61	27.77	1356.43	1356.90	28.49
1254.05	1254.52	26.34	1288.34	1288.80	27.06	1322.62	1323.09	27.78	1356.91	1357.38	28.50
1254.53	1254.99	26.35	1288.81	1289.28	27.07	1323.10	1323.57	27.79	1357.39	1357.85	28.51
1255.00	1255.47	26.36	1289.29	1289.76	27.08	1323.58	1324.04	27.80	1357.86	1358.33	28.52
1255.48	1255.95	26.37	1289.77	1290.23	27.09	1324.05	1324.52	27.81	1358.34	1358.80	28.53
1255.96	1256.42	26.38	1290.24	1290.71	27.10	1324.53	1324.99	27.82	1358.81	1359.28	28.54
1256.43	1256.90	26.39	1290.72	1291.19	27.11	1325.00	1325.47	27.83	1359.29	1359.76	28.55
1256.91	1257.38	26.40	1291.20	1291.66	27.12	1325.48	1325.95	27.84	1359.77	1360.23	28.56
1257.39	1257.85	26.41	1291.67	1292.14	27.13	1325.96	1326.42	27.85	1360.24	1360.71	28.57
1257.86	1258.33	26.42	1292.15	1292.61	27.14	1326.43	1326.90	27.86	1360.72	1361.19	28.58
1258.34	1258.80	26.43	1292.62	1293.09	27.15	1326.91	1327.38	27.87	1361.20	1361.66	28.59
1258.81	1259.28	26.44	1293.10	1293.57	27.16	1327.39	1327.85	27.88	1361.67	1362.14	28.60
1259.29	1259.76	26.45	1293.58	1294.04	27.17	1327.86	1328.33	27.89	1362.15	1362.61	28.61
1259.77	1260.23	26.46	1294.05	1294.52	27.18	1328.34	1328.80	27.90	1362.62	1363.09	28.62
1260.24	1260.71	26.47	1294.53	1294.99	27.19	1328.81	1329.28	27.91	1363.10	1363.57	28.63
1260.72	1261.19	26.48	1295.00	1295.47	27.20	1329.29	1329.76	27.92	1363.58	1364.04	28.64
1261.20	1261.66	26.49	1295.48	1295.95	27.21	1329.77	1330.23	27.93	1364.05	1364.52	28.65
1261.67	1262.14	26.50	1295.96	1296.42	27.22	1330.24	1330.71	27.94	1364.53	1364.99	28.66
1262.15	1262.61	26.51	1296.43	1296.90	27.23	1330.72	1331.19	27.95	1365.00	1365.47	28.67
1262.62	1263.09	26.52	1296.91	1297.38	27.24	1331.20	1331.66	27.96	1365.48	1365.95	28.68
1263.10	1263.57	26.53	1297.39	1297.85	27.25	1331.67	1332.14	27.97	1365.96	1366.42	28.69
1263.58	1264.04	26.54	1297.86	1298.33	27.26	1332.15	1332.61	27.98	1366.43	1366.90	28.70
1264.05	1264.52	26.55	1298.34	1298.80	27.27	1332.62	1333.09	27.99	1366.91	1367.38	28.71
1264.53	1264.99	26.56	1298.81	1299.28	27.28	1333.10	1333.57	28.00	1367.39	1367.85	28.72
1265.00	1265.47	26.57	1299.29	1299.76	27.29	1333.58	1334.04	28.01	1367.86	1368.33	28.73
1265.48	1265.95	26.58	1299.77	1300.23	27.30	1334.05	1334.52	28.02	1368.34	1368.80	28.74
1265.96	1266.42	26.59	1300.24	1300.71	27.31	1334.53	1334.99	28.03	1368.81	1369.28	28.75
1266.43	1266.90	26.60	1300.72	1301.19	27.32	1335.00	1335.47	28.04	1369.29	1369.76	28.76
1266.91	1267.38	26.61	1301.20	1301.66	27.33	1335.48	1335.95	28.05	1369.77	1370.23	28.77
1267.39	1267.85	26.62	1301.67	1302.14	27.34	1335.96	1336.42	28.06	1370.24	1370.71	28.78
1267.86	1268.33	26.63	1302.15	1302.61	27.35	1336.43	1336.90	28.07	1370.72	1371.19	28.79
1268.34	1268.80	26.64	1302.62	1303.09	27.36	1336.91	1337.38	28.08	1371.20	1371.66	28.80

Yearly maximum insurable earnings are $39,000
Yearly maximum employee premiums are $819.00
The premium rate for 2003 is 2.10 %

Le maximum annuel de la rémunération assurable est de 39 000 $
La cotisation maximale annuelle de l'employé est de 819.00 $
La taux de cotisations pour 2003 est d 2,10 %

Employment Insurance Premiums — Cotisations à l'assurance-emploi

Insurable Earnings / Rémunération assurable			Insurable Earnings / Rémunération assurable			Insurable Earnings / Rémunération assurable			Insurable Earnings / Rémunération assurable		
From - De	To - À		From - De	To - À		From - De	To - À		From - De	To - À	
1783.10	1783.57	37.45	1817.39	1817.85	38.17	1851.67	1852.14	38.89	1885.96	1886.42	39.61
1783.58	1784.04	37.46	1817.86	1818.33	38.18	1852.15	1852.61	38.90	1886.43	1886.90	39.62
1784.05	1784.52	37.47	1818.34	1818.80	38.19	1852.62	1853.09	38.91	1886.91	1887.38	39.63
1784.53	1784.99	37.48	1818.81	1819.28	38.20	1853.10	1853.57	38.92	1887.39	1887.85	39.64
1785.00	1785.47	37.49	1819.29	1819.76	38.21	1853.58	1854.04	38.93	1887.86	1888.33	39.65
1785.48	1785.95	37.50	1819.77	1820.23	38.22	1854.05	1854.52	38.94	1888.34	1888.80	39.66
1785.96	1786.42	37.51	1820.24	1820.71	38.23	1854.53	1854.99	38.95	1888.81	1889.28	39.67
1786.43	1786.90	37.52	1820.72	1821.19	38.24	1855.00	1855.47	38.96	1889.29	1889.76	39.68
1786.91	1787.38	37.53	1821.20	1821.66	38.25	1855.48	1855.95	38.97	1889.77	1890.23	39.69
1787.39	1787.85	37.54	1821.67	1822.14	38.26	1855.96	1856.42	38.98	1890.24	1890.71	39.70
1787.86	1788.33	37.55	1822.15	1822.61	38.27	1856.43	1856.90	38.99	1890.72	1891.19	39.71
1788.34	1788.80	37.56	1822.62	1823.09	38.28	1856.91	1857.38	39.00	1891.20	1891.66	39.72
1788.81	1789.28	37.57	1823.10	1823.57	38.29	1857.39	1857.85	39.01	1891.67	1892.14	39.73
1789.29	1789.76	37.58	1823.58	1824.04	38.30	1857.86	1858.33	39.02	1892.15	1892.61	39.74
1789.77	1790.23	37.59	1824.05	1824.52	38.31	1858.34	1858.80	39.03	1892.62	1893.09	39.75
1790.24	1790.71	37.60	1824.53	1824.99	38.32	1858.81	1859.28	39.04	1893.10	1893.57	39.76
1790.72	1791.19	37.61	1825.00	1825.47	38.33	1859.29	1859.76	39.05	1893.58	1894.04	39.77
1791.20	1791.66	37.62	1825.48	1825.95	38.34	1859.77	1860.23	39.06	1894.05	1894.52	39.78
1791.67	1792.14	37.63	1825.96	1826.42	38.35	1860.24	1860.71	39.07	1894.53	1894.99	39.79
1792.15	1792.61	37.64	1826.43	1826.90	38.36	1860.72	1861.19	39.08	1895.00	1895.47	39.80
1792.62	1793.09	37.65	1826.91	1827.38	38.37	1861.20	1861.66	39.09	1895.48	1895.95	39.81
1793.10	1793.57	37.66	1827.39	1827.85	38.38	1861.67	1862.14	39.10	1895.96	1896.42	39.82
1793.58	1794.04	37.67	1827.86	1828.33	38.39	1862.15	1862.61	39.11	1896.43	1896.90	39.83
1794.05	1794.52	37.68	1828.34	1828.80	38.40	1862.62	1863.09	39.12	1896.91	1897.38	39.84
1794.53	1794.99	37.69	1828.81	1829.28	38.41	1863.10	1863.57	39.13	1897.39	1897.85	39.85
1795.00	1795.47	37.70	1829.29	1829.76	38.42	1863.58	1864.04	39.14	1897.86	1898.33	39.86
1795.48	1795.95	37.71	1829.77	1830.23	38.43	1864.05	1864.52	39.15	1898.34	1898.80	39.87
1795.96	1796.42	37.72	1830.24	1830.71	38.44	1864.53	1864.99	39.16	1898.81	1899.28	39.88
1796.43	1796.90	37.73	1830.72	1831.19	38.45	1865.00	1865.47	39.17	1899.29	1899.76	39.89
1796.91	1797.38	37.74	1831.20	1831.66	38.46	1865.48	1865.95	39.18	1899.77	1900.23	39.90
1797.39	1797.85	37.75	1831.67	1832.14	38.47	1865.96	1866.42	39.19	1900.24	1900.71	39.91
1797.86	1798.33	37.76	1832.15	1832.61	38.48	1866.43	1866.90	39.20	1900.72	1901.19	39.92
1798.34	1798.80	37.77	1832.62	1833.09	38.49	1866.91	1867.38	39.21	1901.20	1901.66	39.93
1798.81	1799.28	37.78	1833.10	1833.57	38.50	1867.39	1867.85	39.22	1901.67	1902.14	39.94
1799.29	1799.76	37.79	1833.58	1834.04	38.51	1867.86	1868.33	39.23	1902.15	1902.61	39.95
1799.77	1800.23	37.80	1834.05	1834.52	38.52	1868.34	1868.80	39.24	1902.62	1903.09	39.96
1800.24	1800.71	37.81	1834.53	1834.99	38.53	1868.81	1869.28	39.25	1903.10	1903.57	39.97
1800.72	1801.19	37.82	1835.00	1835.47	38.54	1869.29	1869.76	39.26	1903.58	1904.04	39.98
1801.20	1801.66	37.83	1835.48	1835.95	38.55	1869.77	1870.23	39.27	1904.05	1904.52	39.99
1801.67	1802.14	37.84	1835.96	1836.42	38.56	1870.24	1870.71	39.28	1904.53	1904.99	40.00
1802.15	1802.61	37.85	1836.43	1836.90	38.57	1870.72	1871.19	39.29	1905.00	1905.47	40.01
1802.62	1803.09	37.86	1836.91	1837.38	38.58	1871.20	1871.66	39.30	1905.48	1905.95	40.02
1803.10	1803.57	37.87	1837.39	1837.85	38.59	1871.67	1872.14	39.31	1905.96	1906.42	40.03
1803.58	1804.04	37.88	1837.86	1838.33	38.60	1872.15	1872.61	39.32	1906.43	1906.90	40.04
1804.05	1804.52	37.89	1838.34	1838.80	38.61	1872.62	1873.09	39.33	1906.91	1907.38	40.05
1804.53	1804.99	37.90	1838.81	1839.28	38.62	1873.10	1873.57	39.34	1907.39	1907.85	40.06
1805.00	1805.47	37.91	1839.29	1839.76	38.63	1873.58	1874.04	39.35	1907.86	1908.33	40.07
1805.48	1805.95	37.92	1839.77	1840.23	38.64	1874.05	1874.52	39.36	1908.34	1908.80	40.08
1805.96	1806.42	37.93	1840.24	1840.71	38.65	1874.53	1874.99	39.37	1908.81	1909.28	40.09
1806.43	1806.90	37.94	1840.72	1841.19	38.66	1875.00	1875.47	39.38	1909.29	1909.76	40.10
1806.91	1807.38	37.95	1841.20	1841.66	38.67	1875.48	1875.95	39.39	1909.77	1910.23	40.11
1807.39	1807.85	37.96	1841.67	1842.14	38.68	1875.96	1876.42	39.40	1910.24	1910.71	40.12
1807.86	1808.33	37.97	1842.15	1842.61	38.69	1876.43	1876.90	39.41	1910.72	1911.19	40.13
1808.34	1808.80	37.98	1842.62	1843.09	38.70	1876.91	1877.38	39.42	1911.20	1911.66	40.14
1808.81	1809.28	37.99	1843.10	1843.57	38.71	1877.39	1877.85	39.43	1911.67	1912.14	40.15
1809.29	1809.76	38.00	1843.58	1844.04	38.72	1877.86	1878.33	39.44	1912.15	1912.61	40.16
1809.77	1810.23	38.01	1844.05	1844.52	38.73	1878.34	1878.80	39.45	1912.62	1913.09	40.17
1810.24	1810.71	38.02	1844.53	1844.99	38.74	1878.81	1879.28	39.46	1913.10	1913.57	40.18
1810.72	1811.19	38.03	1845.00	1845.47	38.75	1879.29	1879.76	39.47	1913.58	1914.04	40.19
1811.20	1811.66	38.04	1845.48	1845.95	38.76	1879.77	1880.23	39.48	1914.05	1914.52	40.20
1811.67	1812.14	38.05	1845.96	1846.42	38.77	1880.24	1880.71	39.49	1914.53	1914.99	40.21
1812.15	1812.61	38.06	1846.43	1846.90	38.78	1880.72	1881.19	39.50	1915.00	1915.47	40.22
1812.62	1813.09	38.07	1846.91	1847.38	38.79	1881.20	1881.66	39.51	1915.48	1915.95	40.23
1813.10	1813.57	38.08	1847.39	1847.85	38.80	1881.67	1882.14	39.52	1915.96	1916.42	40.24
1813.58	1814.04	38.09	1847.86	1848.33	38.81	1882.15	1882.61	39.53	1916.43	1916.90	40.25
1814.05	1814.52	38.10	1848.34	1848.80	38.82	1882.62	1883.09	39.54	1916.91	1917.38	40.26
1814.53	1814.99	38.11	1848.81	1849.28	38.83	1883.10	1883.57	39.55	1917.39	1917.85	40.27
1815.00	1815.47	38.12	1849.29	1849.76	38.84	1883.58	1884.04	39.56	1917.86	1918.33	40.28
1815.48	1815.95	38.13	1849.77	1850.23	38.85	1884.05	1884.52	39.57	1918.34	1918.80	40.29
1815.96	1816.42	38.14	1850.24	1850.71	38.86	1884.53	1884.99	39.58	1918.81	1919.28	40.30
1816.43	1816.90	38.15	1850.72	1851.19	38.87	1885.00	1885.47	39.59	1919.29	1919.76	40.31
1816.91	1817.38	38.16	1851.20	1851.66	38.88	1885.48	1885.95	39.60	1919.77	1920.23	40.32

Yearly maximum insurable earnings are $39,000
Yearly maximum employee premiums are $819.00
The premium rate for 2003 is 2.10 %

Le maximum annuel de la rémunération assurable est de 39 000 $
La cotisation maximale annuelle de l'employé est de 819,00 $
La taux de cotisations pour 2003 est de 2,10 %

Employment Insurance Premiums — Cotisations à l'assurance-emploi

Insurable Earnings / Rémunération assurable From - De	To - À		Insurable Earnings / Rémunération assurable From - De	To - À		Insurable Earnings / Rémunération assurable From - De	To - À		Insurable Earnings / Rémunération assurable From - De	To - À	
1920.24	1920.71	40.33	1954.53	1954.99	41.05	1988.81	1989.28	41.77	2023.10	2023.57	42.49
1920.72	1921.19	40.34	1955.00	1955.47	41.06	1989.29	1989.76	41.78	2023.58	2024.04	42.50
1921.20	1921.66	40.35	1955.48	1955.95	41.07	1989.77	1990.23	41.79	2024.05	2024.52	42.51
1921.67	1922.14	40.36	1955.96	1956.42	41.08	1990.24	1990.71	41.80	2024.53	2024.99	42.52
1922.15	1922.61	40.37	1956.43	1956.90	41.09	1990.72	1991.19	41.81	2025.00	2025.47	42.53
1922.62	1923.09	40.38	1956.91	1957.38	41.10	1991.20	1991.66	41.82	2025.48	2025.95	42.54
1923.10	1923.57	40.39	1957.39	1957.85	41.11	1991.67	1992.14	41.83	2025.96	2026.42	42.55
1923.58	1924.04	40.40	1957.86	1958.33	41.12	1992.15	1992.61	41.84	2026.43	2026.90	42.56
1924.05	1924.52	40.41	1958.34	1958.80	41.13	1992.62	1993.09	41.85	2026.91	2027.38	42.57
1924.53	1924.99	40.42	1958.81	1959.28	41.14	1993.10	1993.57	41.86	2027.39	2027.85	42.58
1925.00	1925.47	40.43	1959.29	1959.76	41.15	1993.58	1994.04	41.87	2027.86	2028.33	42.59
1925.48	1925.95	40.44	1959.77	1960.23	41.16	1994.05	1994.52	41.88	2028.34	2028.80	42.60
1925.96	1926.42	40.45	1960.24	1960.71	41.17	1994.53	1994.99	41.89	2028.81	2029.28	42.61
1926.43	1926.90	40.46	1960.72	1961.19	41.18	1995.00	1995.47	41.90	2029.29	2029.76	42.62
1926.91	1927.38	40.47	1961.20	1961.66	41.19	1995.48	1995.95	41.91	2029.77	2030.23	42.63
1927.39	1927.85	40.48	1961.67	1962.14	41.20	1995.96	1996.42	41.92	2030.24	2030.71	42.64
1927.86	1928.33	40.49	1962.15	1962.61	41.21	1996.43	1996.90	41.93	2030.72	2031.19	42.65
1928.34	1928.80	40.50	1962.62	1963.09	41.22	1996.91	1997.38	41.94	2031.20	2031.66	42.66
1928.81	1929.28	40.51	1963.10	1963.57	41.23	1997.39	1997.85	41.95	2031.67	2032.14	42.67
1929.29	1929.76	40.52	1963.58	1964.04	41.24	1997.86	1998.33	41.96	2032.15	2032.61	42.68
1929.77	1930.23	40.53	1964.05	1964.52	41.25	1998.34	1998.80	41.97	2032.62	2033.09	42.69
1930.24	1930.71	40.54	1964.53	1964.99	41.26	1998.81	1999.28	41.98	2033.10	2033.57	42.70
1930.72	1931.19	40.55	1965.00	1965.47	41.27	1999.29	1999.76	41.99	2033.58	2034.04	42.71
1931.20	1931.66	40.56	1965.48	1965.95	41.28	1999.77	2000.23	42.00	2034.05	2034.52	42.72
1931.67	1932.14	40.57	1965.96	1966.42	41.29	2000.24	2000.71	42.01	2034.53	2034.99	42.73
1932.15	1932.61	40.58	1966.43	1966.90	41.30	2000.72	2001.19	42.02	2035.00	2035.47	42.74
1932.62	1933.09	40.59	1966.91	1967.38	41.31	2001.20	2001.66	42.03	2035.48	2035.95	42.75
1933.10	1933.57	40.60	1967.39	1967.85	41.32	2001.67	2002.14	42.04	2035.96	2036.46	42.76
1933.58	1934.04	40.61	1967.86	1968.33	41.33	2002.15	2002.61	42.05	2036.43	2036.90	42.77
1934.05	1934.52	40.62	1968.34	1968.80	41.34	2002.62	2003.09	42.06	2036.91	2037.38	42.78
1934.53	1934.99	40.63	1968.81	1969.28	41.35	2003.10	2003.57	42.07	2037.39	2037.85	42.79
1935.00	1935.47	40.64	1969.29	1969.76	41.36	2003.58	2004.04	42.08	2037.86	2038.33	42.80
1935.48	1935.95	40.65	1969.77	1970.23	41.37	2004.05	2004.52	42.09	2038.34	2038.80	42.81
1935.96	1936.42	40.66	1970.24	1970.71	41.38	2004.53	2004.99	42.10	2038.81	2039.28	42.82
1936.43	1936.90	40.67	1970.72	1971.19	41.39	2005.00	2005.47	42.11	2039.29	2039.76	42.83
1936.91	1937.38	40.68	1971.20	1971.66	41.40	2005.48	2005.95	42.12	2039.77	2040.23	42.84
1937.39	1937.85	40.69	1971.67	1972.14	41.41	2005.96	2006.42	42.13	2040.24	2040.71	42.85
1937.86	1938.33	40.70	1972.15	1972.61	41.42	2006.43	2006.90	42.14	2040.72	2041.19	42.86
1938.34	1938.80	40.71	1972.62	1973.09	41.43	2006.91	2007.38	42.15	2041.20	2041.66	42.87
1938.81	1939.28	40.72	1973.10	1973.57	41.44	2007.39	2007.85	42.16	2041.67	2042.14	42.88
1939.29	1939.76	40.73	1973.58	1974.04	41.45	2007.86	2008.33	42.17	2042.15	2042.61	42.89
1939.77	1940.23	40.74	1974.05	1974.52	41.46	2008.34	2008.80	42.18	2042.62	2043.09	42.90
1940.24	1940.71	40.75	1974.53	1974.99	41.47	2008.81	2009.28	42.19	2043.10	2043.57	42.91
1940.72	1941.19	40.76	1975.00	1975.47	41.48	2009.29	2009.76	42.20	2043.58	2044.04	42.92
1941.20	1941.66	40.77	1975.48	1975.95	41.49	2009.77	2010.23	42.21	2044.05	2044.52	42.93
1941.67	1942.14	40.78	1975.96	1976.42	41.50	2010.24	2010.71	42.22	2044.53	2044.99	42.94
1942.15	1942.61	40.79	1976.43	1976.90	41.51	2010.72	2011.19	42.23	2045.00	2045.47	42.95
1942.62	1943.09	40.80	1976.91	1977.38	41.52	2011.20	2011.66	42.24	2045.48	2045.95	42.96
1943.10	1943.57	40.81	1977.39	1977.85	41.53	2011.67	2012.14	42.25	2045.96	2046.42	42.97
1943.58	1944.04	40.82	1977.86	1978.33	41.54	2012.15	2012.61	42.26	2046.43	2046.90	42.98
1944.05	1944.52	40.83	1978.34	1978.80	41.55	2012.62	2013.09	42.27	2046.91	2047.38	42.99
1944.53	1944.99	40.84	1978.81	1979.28	41.56	2013.10	2013.57	42.28	2047.39	2047.85	43.00
1945.00	1945.47	40.85	1979.29	1979.76	41.57	2013.58	2014.04	42.29	2047.86	2048.33	43.01
1945.48	1945.95	40.86	1979.77	1980.23	41.58	2014.05	2014.52	42.30	2048.34	2048.80	43.02
1945.96	1946.42	40.87	1980.24	1980.71	41.59	2014.53	2014.99	42.31	2048.81	2049.28	43.03
1946.43	1946.90	40.88	1980.72	1981.19	41.60	2015.00	2015.47	42.32	2049.29	2049.76	43.04
1946.91	1947.38	40.89	1981.20	1981.66	41.61	2015.48	2015.95	42.33	2049.77	2050.23	43.05
1947.39	1947.85	40.90	1981.67	1982.14	41.62	2015.96	2016.42	42.34	2050.24	2050.71	43.06
1947.86	1948.33	40.91	1982.15	1982.61	41.63	2016.43	2016.90	42.35	2050.72	2051.19	43.07
1948.34	1948.80	40.92	1982.62	1983.09	41.64	2016.91	2017.38	42.36	2051.20	2051.66	43.08
1948.81	1949.28	40.93	1983.10	1983.57	41.65	2017.39	2017.85	42.37	2051.67	2052.14	43.09
1949.29	1949.76	40.94	1983.58	1984.04	41.66	2017.86	2018.33	42.38	2052.15	2052.61	43.10
1949.77	1950.23	40.95	1984.05	1984.52	41.67	2018.34	2018.80	42.39	2052.62	2053.09	43.11
1950.24	1950.71	40.96	1984.53	1984.99	41.68	2018.81	2019.28	42.40	2053.10	2053.57	43.12
1950.72	1951.19	40.97	1985.00	1985.47	41.69	2019.29	2019.76	42.41	2053.58	2054.04	43.13
1951.20	1951.66	40.98	1985.48	1985.95	41.70	2019.77	2020.23	42.42	2054.05	2054.52	43.14
1951.67	1952.14	40.99	1985.96	1986.42	41.71	2020.24	2020.71	42.43	2054.53	2054.99	43.15
1952.15	1952.61	41.00	1986.43	1986.90	41.72	2020.72	2021.19	42.44	2055.00	2055.47	43.16
1952.62	1953.09	41.01	1986.91	1987.38	41.73	2021.20	2021.66	42.45	2055.48	2055.95	43.17
1953.10	1953.57	41.02	1987.39	1987.85	41.74	2021.67	2022.14	42.46	2055.96	2056.42	43.18
1953.58	1954.04	41.03	1987.86	1988.33	41.75	2022.15	2022.61	42.47	2056.43	2056.90	43.19
1954.05	1954.52	41.04	1988.34	1988.80	41.76	2022.62	2023.09	42.48	2056.91	2057.38	43.20

Yearly maximum insurable earnings are $39,000
maximum employee premiums are $819.00
The premium rate for 2003 is 2.10 %

Le maximum annuel de la rémunération assurable est de 39 000 $
La cotisation maximale annuelle de l'employé est de 819,00 $
La taux de cotisations pour 2003 est de 2,10 %

C-15

Federal tax deductions
Effective January 1, 2003
Monthly (12 pay periods a year)
Also look up the tax deductions in the provincial table

Retenues d'impôt fédéral
En vigueur le 1er janvier 2003
Mensuelle (12 périodes de paie par année)
Cherchez aussi les retenues d'impôt dans la table provinciale

Pay / Rémunération		Federal claim codes/Codes de demande fédéraux										
		0	1	2	3	4	5	6	7	8	9	10
From / De	Less than / Moins de	Deduct from each pay / Retenez sur chaque paie										
6833.	6903	1375.25	1271.80	1260.35	1237.40	1214.45	1191.50	1168.55	1145.60	1122.65	1099.70	1076.80
6903.	6973	1393.45	1290.00	1278.55	1255.60	1232.65	1209.70	1186.75	1163.80	1140.85	1117.90	1095.00
6973.	7043	1411.65	1308.20	1296.75	1273.80	1250.85	1227.90	1204.95	1182.00	1159.05	1136.10	1113.20
7043.	7113	1429.85	1326.40	1314.95	1292.00	1269.05	1246.10	1223.15	1200.20	1177.25	1154.30	1131.40
7113.	7183	1448.05	1344.60	1333.15	1310.20	1287.25	1264.30	1241.35	1218.40	1195.45	1172.50	1149.60
7183.	7253	1466.25	1362.80	1351.35	1328.40	1305.45	1282.50	1259.55	1236.60	1213.65	1190.70	1167.80
7253.	7323	1484.45	1381.00	1369.55	1346.60	1323.65	1300.70	1277.75	1254.80	1231.85	1208.90	1186.00
7323.	7393	1502.65	1399.20	1387.75	1364.80	1341.85	1318.90	1295.95	1273.00	1250.05	1227.10	1204.20
7393.	7463	1520.85	1417.40	1405.95	1383.00	1360.05	1337.10	1314.15	1291.20	1268.25	1245.30	1222.40
7463.	7533	1539.05	1435.60	1424.15	1401.20	1378.25	1355.30	1332.35	1309.40	1286.45	1263.50	1240.60
7533.	7603	1557.25	1453.80	1442.35	1419.40	1396.45	1373.50	1350.55	1327.60	1304.65	1281.70	1258.80
7603.	7673	1575.45	1472.00	1460.55	1437.60	1414.65	1391.70	1368.75	1345.80	1322.85	1299.90	1277.00
7673.	7743	1593.65	1490.20	1478.75	1455.80	1432.85	1409.90	1386.95	1364.00	1341.05	1318.10	1295.20
7743.	7813	1611.85	1508.40	1496.95	1474.00	1451.05	1428.10	1405.15	1382.20	1359.25	1336.30	1313.40
7813.	7883	1630.05	1526.60	1515.15	1492.20	1469.25	1446.30	1423.35	1400.40	1377.45	1354.50	1331.60
7883.	7953	1648.25	1544.80	1533.35	1510.40	1487.45	1464.50	1441.55	1418.60	1395.65	1372.70	1349.80
7953.	8023	1666.45	1563.00	1551.55	1528.60	1505.65	1482.70	1459.75	1436.80	1413.85	1390.90	1368.00
8023.	8093	1684.65	1581.20	1569.75	1546.80	1523.85	1500.90	1477.95	1455.00	1432.05	1409.10	1386.20
8093.	8163	1702.85	1599.40	1587.95	1565.00	1542.05	1519.10	1496.15	1473.20	1450.25	1427.30	1404.40
8163.	8233	1721.05	1617.60	1606.15	1583.20	1560.25	1537.30	1514.35	1491.40	1468.45	1445.50	1422.60
8233.	8303	1739.25	1635.80	1624.35	1601.40	1578.45	1555.50	1532.55	1509.60	1486.65	1463.70	1440.80
8303.	8373	1757.45	1654.00	1642.55	1619.60	1596.65	1573.70	1550.75	1527.80	1504.85	1481.90	1459.00
8373.	8443	1775.65	1672.20	1660.75	1637.80	1614.85	1591.90	1568.95	1546.00	1523.05	1500.10	1477.20
8443.	8513	1793.85	1690.40	1678.95	1656.00	1633.05	1610.10	1587.15	1564.20	1541.25	1518.30	1495.40
8513.	8583	1812.05	1708.60	1697.15	1674.20	1651.25	1628.30	1605.35	1582.40	1559.45	1536.50	1513.60
8583.	8653	1830.25	1726.80	1715.35	1692.40	1669.45	1646.50	1623.55	1600.60	1577.65	1554.70	1531.80
8653.	8723	1848.45	1745.00	1733.55	1710.60	1687.65	1664.70	1641.75	1618.80	1595.85	1572.90	1550.00
8723.	8793	1867.80	1764.40	1752.90	1729.95	1707.00	1684.05	1661.10	1638.15	1615.25	1592.30	1569.35
8793.	8863	1888.10	1784.70	1773.20	1750.25	1727.30	1704.35	1681.40	1658.45	1635.55	1612.60	1589.65
8863.	8933	1908.40	1805.00	1793.50	1770.55	1747.60	1724.65	1701.70	1678.75	1655.85	1632.90	1609.95
8933.	9003	1928.70	1825.30	1813.80	1790.85	1767.90	1744.95	1722.00	1699.05	1676.15	1653.20	1630.25
9003.	9073	1949.00	1845.60	1834.10	1811.15	1788.20	1765.25	1742.30	1719.35	1696.45	1673.50	1650.55
9073.	9143	1969.30	1865.90	1854.40	1831.45	1808.50	1785.55	1762.60	1739.65	1716.75	1693.80	1670.85
9143.	9213	1989.60	1886.20	1874.70	1851.75	1828.80	1805.85	1782.90	1759.95	1737.05	1714.10	1691.15
9213.	9283	2009.90	1906.50	1895.00	1872.05	1849.10	1826.15	1803.20	1780.25	1757.35	1734.40	1711.45
9283.	9353	2030.20	1926.80	1915.30	1892.35	1869.40	1846.45	1823.50	1800.55	1777.65	1754.70	1731.75
9353.	9423	2050.50	1947.10	1935.60	1912.65	1889.70	1866.75	1843.80	1820.85	1797.95	1775.00	1752.05
9423.	9493	2070.80	1967.40	1955.90	1932.95	1910.00	1887.05	1864.10	1841.15	1818.25	1795.30	1772.35
9493.	9563	2091.10	1987.70	1976.20	1953.25	1930.30	1907.35	1884.40	1861.45	1838.55	1815.60	1792.65
9563.	9633	2111.40	2008.00	1996.50	1973.55	1950.60	1927.65	1904.70	1881.75	1858.85	1835.90	1812.95
9633.	9703	2131.70	2028.30	2016.80	1993.85	1970.90	1947.95	1925.00	1902.05	1879.15	1856.20	1833.25
9703.	9773	2152.00	2048.60	2037.10	2014.15	1991.20	1968.25	1945.30	1922.35	1899.45	1876.50	1853.55
9773.	9843	2172.30	2068.90	2057.40	2034.45	2011.50	1988.55	1965.60	1942.65	1919.75	1896.80	1873.85
9843.	9913	2192.60	2089.20	2077.70	2054.75	2031.80	2008.85	1985.90	1962.95	1940.05	1917.10	1894.15
9913.	9983	2212.90	2109.50	2098.00	2075.05	2052.10	2029.15	2006.20	1983.25	1960.35	1937.40	1914.45
9983.	10053	2233.20	2129.80	2118.30	2095.35	2072.40	2049.45	2026.50	2003.55	1980.65	1957.70	1934.75
10053.	10123	2253.50	2150.10	2138.60	2115.65	2092.70	2069.75	2046.80	2023.85	2000.95	1978.00	1955.05
10123.	10193	2273.80	2170.40	2158.90	2135.95	2113.00	2090.05	2067.10	2044.15	2021.25	1998.30	1975.35
10193.	10263	2294.10	2190.70	2179.20	2156.25	2133.30	2110.35	2087.40	2064.45	2041.55	2018.60	1995.65
10263.	10333	2314.40	2211.00	2199.50	2176.55	2153.60	2130.65	2107.70	2084.75	2061.85	2038.90	2015.95
10333.	10403	2334.70	2231.30	2219.80	2196.85	2173.90	2150.95	2128.00	2105.05	2082.15	2059.20	2036.25
10403.	10473	2355.00	2251.60	2240.10	2217.15	2194.20	2171.25	2148.30	2125.35	2102.45	2079.50	2056.55
10473.	10543	2375.30	2271.90	2260.40	2237.45	2214.50	2191.55	2168.60	2145.65	2122.75	2099.80	2076.85
10543.	10613	2395.60	2292.20	2280.70	2257.75	2234.80	2211.85	2188.90	2165.95	2143.05	2120.10	2097.15
10613.	10683	2415.90	2312.50	2301.00	2278.05	2255.10	2232.15	2209.20	2186.25	2163.35	2140.40	2117.45

Ontario
Provincial tax deductions effective January 1, 2003
Monthly (12 pay periods a year)
Also look up the tax deductions in the federal table

Ontario
Retenues d'impôt provincial en vigueur le 1er janvier 2003
Mensuelle (12 périodes de paie par année)
Cherchez aussi les retenues d'impôt dans la table fédérale

Pay / Rémunération		Provincial claim codes/Codes de demande provinciaux										
		0	1	2	3	4	5	6	7	8	9	10
From / De	Less than / Moins de	Deduct from each pay / Retenez sur chaque paie										
7106.	7176	718.20	656.70	650.05	636.85	623.60	610.35	597.10	583.85	570.60	557.35	544.10
7176.	7246	730.35	668.90	662.25	649.00	635.75	622.55	609.30	596.05	582.80	569.55	556.30
7246.	7316	742.55	681.05	674.45	661.20	647.95	634.70	621.45	608.20	595.00	581.75	568.50
7316.	7386	754.75	693.25	686.65	673.40	660.15	646.90	633.65	620.40	607.15	593.90	580.70
7386.	7456	766.90	705.45	698.80	685.60	672.35	659.10	645.85	632.60	619.35	606.10	592.85
7456.	7526	779.10	717.65	711.00	697.75	684.50	671.25	658.05	644.80	631.55	618.30	605.05
7526.	7596	791.30	729.80	723.20	709.95	696.70	683.45	670.20	656.95	643.75	630.50	617.25
7596.	7666	803.50	742.00	735.40	722.15	708.90	695.65	682.40	669.15	655.90	642.65	629.40
7666.	7736	815.65	754.20	747.55	734.30	721.10	707.85	694.60	681.35	668.10	654.85	641.60
7736.	7806	827.85	766.40	759.75	746.50	733.25	720.00	706.75	693.55	680.30	667.05	653.80
7806.	7876	840.05	778.55	771.95	758.70	745.45	732.20	718.95	705.70	692.45	679.25	666.00
7876.	7946	852.25	790.75	784.15	770.90	757.65	744.40	731.15	717.90	704.65	691.40	678.15
7946.	8016	864.40	802.95	796.30	783.05	769.85	756.60	743.35	730.10	716.85	703.60	690.35
8016.	8086	876.60	815.10	808.50	795.25	782.00	768.75	755.50	742.30	729.05	715.80	702.55
8086.	8156	888.80	827.30	820.70	807.45	794.20	780.95	767.70	754.45	741.20	727.95	714.75
8156.	8226	901.00	839.50	832.85	819.65	806.40	793.15	779.90	766.65	753.40	740.15	726.90
8226.	8296	913.15	851.70	845.05	831.80	818.55	805.35	792.10	778.85	765.60	752.35	739.10
8296.	8366	925.35	863.85	857.25	844.00	830.75	817.50	804.25	791.00	777.80	764.55	751.30
8366.	8436	937.55	876.05	869.45	856.20	842.95	829.70	816.45	803.20	789.95	776.70	763.50
8436.	8506	949.70	888.25	881.60	868.40	855.15	841.90	828.65	815.40	802.15	788.90	775.65
8506.	8576	961.90	900.45	893.80	880.55	867.30	854.05	840.85	827.60	814.35	801.10	787.85
8576.	8646	974.10	912.60	906.00	892.75	879.50	866.25	853.00	839.75	826.55	813.30	800.05
8646.	8716	986.30	924.80	918.20	904.95	891.70	878.45	865.20	851.95	838.70	825.45	812.20
8716.	8786	998.45	937.00	930.35	917.10	903.90	890.65	877.40	864.15	850.90	837.65	824.40
8786.	8856	1010.65	949.20	942.55	929.30	916.05	902.80	889.60	876.35	863.10	849.85	836.60
8856.	8926	1022.85	961.35	954.75	941.50	928.25	915.00	901.75	888.50	875.25	862.05	848.80
8926.	8996	1035.05	973.55	966.95	953.70	940.45	927.20	913.95	900.70	887.45	874.20	860.95
8996.	9066	1047.20	985.75	979.10	965.85	952.65	939.40	926.15	912.90	899.65	886.40	873.15
9066.	9136	1059.40	997.90	991.30	978.05	964.80	951.55	938.30	925.10	911.85	898.60	885.35
9136.	9206	1071.60	1010.10	1003.50	990.25	977.00	963.75	950.50	937.25	924.00	910.80	897.55
9206.	9276	1083.80	1022.30	1015.70	1002.45	989.20	975.95	962.70	949.45	936.20	922.95	909.70
9276.	9346	1095.95	1034.50	1027.85	1014.60	1001.35	988.15	974.90	961.65	948.40	935.15	921.90
9346.	9416	1108.15	1046.65	1040.05	1026.80	1013.55	1000.30	987.05	973.85	960.60	947.35	934.10
9416.	9486	1120.35	1058.85	1052.25	1039.00	1025.75	1012.50	999.25	986.00	972.75	959.50	946.30
9486.	9556	1132.50	1071.05	1064.40	1051.20	1037.95	1024.70	1011.45	998.20	984.95	971.70	958.45
9556.	9626	1144.70	1083.25	1076.60	1063.35	1050.10	1036.85	1023.65	1010.40	997.15	983.90	970.65
9626.	9696	1156.90	1095.40	1088.80	1075.55	1062.30	1049.05	1035.80	1022.55	1009.35	996.10	982.85
9696.	9766	1169.10	1107.60	1101.00	1087.75	1074.50	1061.25	1048.00	1034.75	1021.50	1008.25	995.00
9766.	9836	1181.25	1119.80	1113.15	1099.90	1086.70	1073.45	1060.20	1046.95	1033.70	1020.45	1007.20
9836.	9906	1193.45	1132.00	1125.35	1112.10	1098.85	1085.60	1072.40	1059.15	1045.90	1032.65	1019.40
9906.	9976	1205.65	1144.15	1137.55	1124.30	1111.05	1097.80	1084.55	1071.30	1058.05	1044.85	1031.60
9976.	10046	1217.85	1156.35	1149.75	1136.50	1123.25	1110.00	1096.75	1083.50	1070.25	1057.00	1043.75
10046.	10116	1230.00	1168.55	1161.90	1148.65	1135.45	1122.20	1108.95	1095.70	1082.45	1069.20	1055.95
10116.	10186	1242.20	1180.75	1174.10	1160.85	1147.60	1134.35	1121.10	1107.90	1094.65	1081.40	1068.15
10186.	10256	1254.40	1192.90	1186.30	1173.05	1159.80	1146.55	1133.30	1120.05	1106.80	1093.60	1080.35
10256.	10326	1266.60	1205.10	1198.50	1185.25	1172.00	1158.75	1145.50	1132.25	1119.00	1105.75	1092.50
10326.	10396	1278.75	1217.30	1210.65	1197.40	1184.15	1170.95	1157.70	1144.45	1131.20	1117.95	1104.70
10396.	10466	1290.95	1229.45	1222.85	1209.60	1196.35	1183.10	1169.85	1156.65	1143.40	1130.15	1116.90
10466.	10536	1303.15	1241.65	1235.05	1221.80	1208.55	1195.30	1182.05	1168.80	1155.55	1142.30	1129.10
10536.	10606	1315.35	1253.85	1247.20	1234.00	1220.75	1207.50	1194.25	1181.00	1167.75	1154.50	1141.25
10606.	10676	1327.50	1266.05	1259.40	1246.15	1232.90	1219.70	1206.45	1193.20	1179.95	1166.70	1153.45
10676.	10746	1339.70	1278.20	1271.60	1258.35	1245.10	1231.85	1218.60	1205.35	1192.15	1178.90	1165.65
10746.	10816	1351.90	1290.40	1283.80	1270.55	1257.30	1244.05	1230.80	1217.55	1204.30	1191.05	1177.85
10816.	10886	1364.05	1302.60	1295.95	1282.75	1269.50	1256.25	1243.00	1229.75	1216.50	1203.25	1190.00
10886.	10956	1376.25	1314.80	1308.15	1294.90	1281.65	1268.40	1255.20	1241.95	1228.70	1215.45	1202.20

This table is available on diskette (TOD).

Vous pouvez obtenir cette table sur disquette (TSD).

CHAPTER ORGANIZER AND REFERENCE GUIDE

Topic	Key point, procedure, formula	Example(s) to illustrate situation
Gross pay, p. 267	Hours employee worked × Rate per hour	\$6.50 per hour at 36 hours Gross pay = 36 × \$6.50 = **\$234**
Overtime, p. 267	Gross earnings (pay) = Regular pay + Earnings at overtime rate ($1\frac{1}{2}$)	\$6 per hour; 42 hours Gross pay = (40 × \$6) + (2 × \$9) = \$240 + \$18 = **\$258**
Straight piece rate, p. 268	Gross pay = Number of units produced × Rate per unit	1,185 units; rate per unit, \$.89 Gross pay = 1,185 × \$.89 = **\$1,054.65**
Differential pay schedule, p. 269	Rate on each item is related to the number of items produced.	1–500 at \$.84; 501–1,000 at \$.96; 900 units produced. Gross pay = (500 × \$.84) + (400 × \$.96) = \$420 + \$384 = **\$804**
Straight commission, p. 269	Total sales × Commission rate Any draw (advance on commission) would be subtracted from earnings.	\$155,000 sales; 6% commission \$155,000 × .06 = **\$9,300**
Variable commission scale, p. 269	Sales at different levels pay different rates of commission.	Up to \$5,000, 5%; \$5,001 to \$10,000, 8%; over \$10,000, 10% Sold: \$6,500 Solution: (\$5,000 × .05) + (\$1,500 × .08) = \$250 + \$120 = **\$370**
Salary plus commission, p. 269	Regular wages (fixed) + Commissions earned	Base \$400 per week + 2% on sales over \$14,000 Actual sales: \$16,000 \$400 (base) + (.02 × \$2,000) = **\$440**
Federal income taxes, p. 272	To find federal deductions, follow Steps 1–3. **Step 1.** You are paid on biweekly basis. Find in section D ("D" pages) a table that corresponds to this frequency of payments. **Step 2.** In the first column of the table, "Pay," find the line with your pay range. Note that this amount includes all taxable benefits. **Step 3.** In the column with the correct Claim Code, find the row with your pay range, and on the intercept you will find the amount of federal deductions.	Federal income taxes for \$1,923.08 paid biweekly under Claim Code 2: **Step 1.** Page D-9. **Step 2.** Under "Pay" find the pay range 1923–1947. **Step 3.** In the column with Claim Code 2, on the intercept with your pay range you will find the amount of federal deductions: \$282.30.
Provincial income taxes, p. 273	To find provincial deductions, follow the same three steps, but use section E (example for Ontario).	To find provincial deductions, follow the same three steps, but use section E, page E-9. Your provincial deductions will be \$110.85.
Total income tax deductions, p. 273		Total income tax deduction: \$282.30 + \$110.85 = \$393.15
CPP (Canada Pension Plan) contributions, p. 273	To find your CPP deductions, follow Steps 1–3. **Step 1.** In section B, find the page corresponding to your frequency of payments—biweekly.	**Step 1.** In section B, find page B-39.

(continues)

CHAPTER ORGANIZER AND REFERENCE GUIDE (CONCLUDED)

Topic	Key point, procedure, formula	Example(s) to illustrate situation
	Step 2. In the first column, "Pay," find your gross pay, including taxable benefits. Assume in your case the same amount as before, $1,923.08. **Step 3.** In the shaded column next to the one with your pay range, identify your CPP contributions. Your employer will contribute the same amount until it reaches the maximum.	**Step 2.** Under "Pay," find your gross pay, including taxable benefits: $1,923.08. **Step 3.** In the shaded column next to the one with your pay range, identify your CPP contributions: $88.36 per pay period. Your employer will contribute the same amount until it reaches the maximum.
Employment Insurance (EI) premiums, p. 274	To define the amount of EI premiums per pay period, follow Steps 1–3. **Step 1.** Find section C and the page that corresponds to your insurable earnings. **Step 2.** In the column "Insurable Earnings," find your range. **Step 3.** In the shaded column next to this one, identify the EI premium.	To define the amount of EI premiums per pay period, follow Steps 1–3. **Step 1.** Find page C-15. **Step 2.** Under "Insurable Earnings" find your range, 1922.62–1923.09. **Step 3.** In the shaded column next to this one, identify the EI premium: $40.38. You start to pay EI premiums from the beginning of your payments, and stop when you reach the maximum of $39,000. The employer's premium is 1.4 times the employee's premium for the pay period, and his/her contributions stop with yours.
Key terms	Biweekly, p. 266 Canada Pension Plan (CPP) contributions, p. 271 Deductions, p. 267 Differential pay schedule, p. 269 Draw, p. 269 Employment Insurance (EI) contributions, p. 271 Federal and provincial tax deductions, p. 271 Gross pay, p. 267 Monthly, p. 266 Net pay, p. 275 Overrides, p. 269 Overtime, p. 267 Periodic payment, p. 266 Provincial tax deductions, p. 273 Salary, p. 266 Semimonthly, p. 266	Straight commission, p. 269 Variable commission scale, p. 269 Weekly, p. 266

END-OF-CHAPTER PROBLEMS

DRILL PROBLEMS

Complete the following table:

	Employee	M	T	W	Th	F	Hours	Rate per hour	Gross pay
11–1.	Jane Reese	9	7	6	8	5	?	$6.60	?
11–2.	Pete Joll	7	9	8	8	8	?	$7.25	?

Complete the following table (assume the overtime for each employee is a time-and-a-half rate after 40 hours):

	Employee	M	T	W	Th	F	Sa	Total regular hours	Total overtime hours	Regular rate	Overtime rate	Gross earnings
11–3.	Blue	12	9	9	9	9	3	?	?	$8	?	?
11–4.	Tagney	14	8	9	9	5	1	?	?	$7.60	?	?

Calculate gross earnings:

	Worker	Number of units produced	Rate per unit	Gross earnings
11–5.	Lang	510	$2.10	?
11–6.	Swan	846	$.58	?

Calculate the gross earnings for each apple picker based on the following differential pay scale:

1–1,000: $.03 each   1,001–1,600: $.05 each   over 1,600: $.07 each

	Apple picker	Number of apples picked	Gross earnings
11–7.	Ryan	1,600	?
11–8.	Rice	1,925	?

Find Reese's end-of-month commission:

	Employee	Total sales	Commission rate	Draw	End-of-month commission received
11–9.	Reese	$300,000	7%	$8,000	?

Ron Company has the following commission schedule:

Commission rate	Sales
2%	Up to $80,000
3.5%	Excess of $80,000 to $100,000
4%	More than $100,000

Calculate the gross earnings of Ron Company's two employees:

	Employee	Total sales	Gross earnings
11–10.	Bill Moore	$70,000	?
11–11.	Ron Ear	$155,000	?

Complete the following table, given that A Publishing Company pays its salespeople a weekly salary plus a 2% commission on all net sales over $5,000 (no commission on returned goods):

	Employee	Gross sales	Return	Net sales	Given quota	Commission sales	Commission rates	Total commission	Regular wage	Total wage
11–12.	Ring	$8,000	$25	?	$5,000	?	2%	?	$250	?
11–13.	Porter	$12,000	$100	?	$5,000	?	2%	?	$250	?

Complete the table. For CPP and EI use formulas and compare with tables where possible.

Based on 2003	Employee	Gross annual income, 2003	Payment frequency	Pays per year	Gross pay amount this period	Federal tax deductions	Ontario provincial tax deductions	Employee EI premiums	Employer's EI contributions first quarter	CPP contributions (See Note 1)	Employer's CPP contributions in first quarter	Claim Code
								Factor × periodic pay	= 3 × 1.4 × Employee's contribution	Factor × periodic day	= 3 × Employee's contribution	
								f = .021	?	f = .0495		
11–14.	Clancey	$48,984	Biweekly	26	?	?	?	?	?	?	?	2
11–15.	Sklar	$94,620	Monthly	12	?	?	?	?	?	?	?	3
11–16.	Sanchez	?	Monthly	12	$7,120	?	?	?	?	?	?	4
11–17.	Liung	$33,800	Weekly	52	?	$56.65	$21.55	?	?	?	?	5
11–18.	Ali	?	Weekly	52	$1,400	$221.60	$95.15	?	?	?	?	6
11–19.	Zubko	?	Biweekly	26	$1,971	$229.30	$91.75	?	?	?	?	8

Note 1: For CPP contributions, each periodic pay must be reduced by an amount calculated $3,500/Number of pay periods per year. The resultant amount is multiplied by .0495 to obtain the correct contribution, subject to maximum for the year.

Note 2: Use 2003 tables from this chapter or the CCRA site at www.ccra-adrc.gc.ca/tax/business/payroll to find the necessary information for the current year.

ADDITIONAL DRILL PROBLEMS

11–20. Fill in the missing amounts for each of the following employees. Do not round the overtime rate in your calculations and round your final answers to the nearest cent. Assume overtime occurs after 40 hours.

	Employee	Total hours	Rate per hour	Regular pay	Overtime pay	Gross pay
a.	Ben Badger	40	$6.85	?	?	?
b.	Casey Guitare	43	$9.22	?	?	?
c.	Norma Harris	37	$18.76	?	?	?
d.	Ed Jackson	45	$14.35	?	?	?

11–21. Calculate each employee's gross from the following data. Do not round the overtime rate in your calculation but round your final answers to the nearest cent. Assume overtime occurs after 40 hours.

	Employee	S	M	Tu	W	Th	F	S	Total hours	Rate per hour	Regular pay	Overtime pay	Gross pay
a.	L. Adams	0	8	8	8	8	8	0	?	$8.10	?	?	?
b.	M. Card	0	9	8	9	8	8	4	?	$11.35	?	?	?
c.	P. Kline	2	$7\frac{1}{2}$	$8\frac{1}{4}$	8	$10\frac{3}{4}$	9	2	?	$10.60	?	?	?
d.	J. Mack	0	$9\frac{1}{2}$	$9\frac{3}{4}$	$9\frac{1}{2}$	10	10	4	?	$9.95	?	?	?

11–22. Calculate the gross wages of the following production workers.

	Employee	Rate per unit	No. of units produced	Gross pay
a.	A. Bossie	$.67	655	?
b.	J. Carson	$.87$\frac{1}{2}$	703	?

11–23. Using the given differential scale, calculate the gross wages of the following production workers.

Units Produced	Amount per unit
1–50	$.55
51–100	.65
101–200	.72
More than 200	.95

	Employee	Units produced	Gross pay
a.	F. Burns	190	?
b.	B. English	210	?
c.	E. Jackson	200	?

11–24. Calculate the following salespersons' gross wages.

a. Straight commission:

Employee	Net sales	Commission	Gross pay
M. Salley	$40,000	13%	?

b. Straight commission with draw:

Employee	Net sales	Commission	Draw	Commission minus draw
G. Gorsbeck	$38,000	12%	$600	?

c. Variable commission scale:

Up to $25,000	8%
Excess of $25,000 to $40,000	10%
More than $40,000	12%

Employee	Net sales	Gross pay
H. Lloyd	$42,000	?

d. Salary plus commission:

Employee	Salary	Commission	Quota	Net sales	Gross pay
P. Floyd	$2,500	3%	$400,000	$475,000	?

Use the tables given on the CCRA Web site for 2004 or current year.

	Employee	Claim Code	Cumulative gross earnings	Salary per week	CPP	EI	Income Taxes	
							Fed.	*Ont.*
11–25.	Pete Small	3	$79,000	$2,300	**a.** ?	**b.** ?	**g.** ?	**h.** ?
11–26.	Alice Hall	1	$57,200	$1,100	**c.** ?	**d.** ?	**i.** ?	**j.** ?
11–27.	Jean Rose	2	$51,480	$990	**e.** ?	**f.** ?	**k.** ?	**l.** ?

WORD PROBLEMS

11–28. On November 7, 2004, the *Bay-Creek Times* reported on the hourly wages for building equipment operators. The top wage for union members will be $20.95, an increase of $1.25 or 6.3%. This week N. W. Ourban worked 48 hours and is entitled to time-and-a-half overtime. How much did N. W. earn?

11–29. The March 13, 2003 issue of the *Moonside Tribune* reported that stagehands would be paid $22.40 per hour. Bill Craw, a stagehand, worked 33 hours. **(a)** How much will be deducted from Bill's pay for EI? **(b)** CPP?

11–30. On December 10, 2003, the *James Bay Post* reported that retailers were attempting to entice workers to James Bay area stores with higher wages. Alex Healey is employed by Pilier 1 and earns $6.25 per hour plus a 3% commission on sales. This week Alex worked 36 hours and sold $2,340 in merchandise. How much did Alex earn?

11–31. Dennis Toby is a sales clerk at Northwest Department Store. Dennis receives $8 per hour plus a commission of 3% on all sales. Assume Dennis works 30 hours and has sales of $1,900. What is his gross pay?

11–32. Excel Blinn Corporation pays its employees on a graduated commission scale: 3% on first $40,000 sales, 4% on sales from $40,001 to $85,000, and 6% on sales greater than $85,000. Bill Burns had $87,000 sales. What commission did Bill earn?

11–33. Robin Hartman earns $600 per week plus 3% of sales over $6,500. Robin's sales are $14,000. How much does Robin earn?

11–34. Pat Maninen earns a gross salary of $2,100 each week. What are Pat's first week's deductions for EI and CPP? Will any of Pat's wages be exempt from EI and CPP for the calendar year? Assume a rate of 2.1% and refer to the tables from the CCRA site at www.ccra-adrc.gc.ca/tax/business/payroll.

11–35. Richard Gaziano is a manager for Health Care Inc. The company deducts EI, CPP, and income taxes from his earnings. Assume the same EI and CPP rate as in Problem 11–36. Before this payroll, Richard is $1,000 below the maximum level for CPP earnings. Richard's Claim Code is 4. He is paid weekly. What is Richard's net pay for the week if he earns $1,300? Use the Web site from the previous problem.

ADDITIONAL WORD PROBLEMS

For all problems with overtime, be sure to round only the final answer.

11–36. In the first week of December, Dana Robinson worked 52 hours. His regular rate of pay is $11.25 per hour. What was Dana's gross pay for the week?

11–37. Davis Fisheries pays its workers for each box of fish they pack. Sunny Melanson receives $.30 per box. During the third week of July, Sunny packed 2,410 boxes of fish. What is Sunny's gross pay?

11–38. Maye George is a real estate broker who receives a straight commission of 6%. What would her commission be for a house that sold for $197,500?

11–39. Devon Company pays Eileen Haskins a straight commission of $12\frac{1}{2}$% on net sales. In January, Devon gave Eileen a draw of $600. She had net sales that month of $35,570. What was Eileen's commission minus draw?

11–40. Parker and Company pays Selma Stokes on a variable commission scale. In a month when Selma had net sales of $155,000, what was her gross pay based on the following schedule?

Net sales	Commission rate
Up to $40,000	5%
Excess of $40,000 to $75,000	5.5%
Excess of $75,000 to $100,000	6%
More than $100,000	7%

11–41. Marsh Furniture Company pays Joshua Charles a monthly salary of $1,900 plus a commission of $2\frac{1}{2}$% on sales over $12,500. Last month, Joshua had net sales of $17,799. What was Joshua's gross pay for the month?

11–42. Amy McWha works at Lamplighter Bookstore where she earns $7.75 per hour plus a commission of 2% on her weekly sales in excess of $1,500. Last week, Amy worked 39 hours and had total sales of $2,250. What was Amy's gross pay for the week?

11–43. Cynthia Pratt has earned $79,200 thus far this year. This week she earned $3,500. Find her total tax deduction Claim Code 2. (Use CCRA Web site.)

11–44. If Cynthia (Problem 11–45) earns $1,050 the following week, what will be her new total tax deduction? (Use CCRA Web site.)

CHALLENGE PROBLEM

11–45. A school psychologist earns $50,000 a year in the Earl-Dade public school. Her Claim Code is 1. **(a)** What would be taken out of her cheque each month for CPP? **(b)** What would be taken out each week for EI? **(c)** What would be taken out for income taxes in Ontario? Use the tables given in this chapter or at the CCRA site at www.ccra-adrc.gc.ca/tax/business/payroll.

SUMMARY PRACTICE TEST

1. Calculate Jeff's gross pay (he is entitled to time-and-a-half). (p. 223)

M	T	W	Th	F	Total hours	Rate per hour	Gross pay
$9\frac{1}{2}$	$8\frac{1}{4}$	$10\frac{1}{2}$	$7\frac{1}{4}$	$11\frac{1}{2}$	?	$9	?

2. Lee Winn sells shoes for The Bay. The Bay pays Lee $8 per hour plus a 3% commission on all sales. Assume Lee works 37 hours for the week and has $7,000 sales. What is Lee's gross pay? (p. 267)
3. Long Company pays its employees on a graduated commission scale: 4% on the first $30,000 sales; 6% on sales from $30,001 to $80,000; and 10% on sales of more than $80,000. Larry Felt, an employee of Long, has $180,000 in sales. What commission did Larry earn? (p. 269)
4. Maggie Kate earns $900 per week. Her Claim Code is 3. What is Maggie's income tax? Refer to the tables given in this chapter or at the CCRA site at www.ccra-adrc.gc.ca/tax/business/payroll. Use CCRA Web site for current values. Answer key has 2003 values. (p. 272)
5. John Jones pays his two employees $690 and $900 per week. What provincial and federal income taxes will John pay at the end of quarter 1? Assume the Claim Codes are 2. Use CCRA Web site for current values. Answer key has 2003 values. (pp. 272, 273)

SOLUTIONS TO PRACTICE QUIZZES

LU 11–1

1. 40 hours × $10 = $400
   12 hours × $15 = 180 ($10 × 1.5 = $15)
   $580
2. $180,000 × .09 = $16,200
   − 3,500
   $12,700
3. Gross pay = $1,000 + ($4,000 × .01) + ($8,000 × .03) + ($20,000 × .05)
   = $1,000 + $40 + $240 + $1,000
   = **$2,280**

LU 11–2

1. **a.** Joy's federal deductions per month: $1,656.00
   b. Joy's provincial deductions per month: $868.40
   c. Joy's total deductions per month: $2,524.44
   d. Joy's total deductions per quarter: 3 × $2,524.44 = $7,573.20
   e. Joy's EI premium per month: $8,500 × .0210 = $178.50
   f. Joy's EI premiums for the first quarter: 3 × $178.5 = $535.50. In the first quarter her EI premium will not reach its maximum ($819), so she will pay EI premiums all three months.
   g. Joy's CPP contributions per month: $406.32
   h. During three months of the first quarter she will contribute $406.32 × 3 = $1,218.96. She will not reach the maximum amount of $1,801.80, so she will pay CPP contributions every month of the first quarter.
2. Jim must pay the amount matching his employees' contributions to CPP. The employees' contributions should be $273.16, $282.57, and $307.32 respectively. They will pay CPP contributions until they reach the maximum of $1,801.80. So in December, neither Jim nor his employees will have to pay these deductions.

   The employees' EI premiums are $5,810 × .0210 = $122.01; $6,005 × .0210 = $126.11; and $6,500 × .0210 = $136.50 respectively. None of them will pay EI premiums in December, so Jim will not pay them either.

Business Math Scrapbook

Putting Your Skills to Work

PROJECT A

Investigate the concept of work for hire. Does the artist have a case? Check out the Universal Pictures Web site.

ART & MONEY

By Robert J. Hughes

Veteran Comics Artist Fired Over Suit

DANIEL S. DECARLO, the principal cartoonist on "Betty and Veronica" for Archie Comics for the past 40 years, has been fired after filing a breach-of-contract lawsuit against the comic-book publisher.

The artist seeks $250,000 in damages because a coming Universal Pictures film, "Josie and the Pussycats," is based on characters Mr. DeCarlo created.

The groovy, fictional all-girl band may be familiar from the popular comic books and television cartoons. Mr. DeCarlo's suit, filed in New York State Supreme Court, alleges that Archie Comic Publications Inc. is using his characters, Josie, Melody and Pepper, for "purposes other than newsstand comic strips and comic books." A movie based on the comic begins filming in August, starring newcomer Rachel Leigh Cook (star of "She's All That") as Josie and Parker Posey as her nemesis, Alexandra.

The case goes to the heart of "work-for-hire" disputes that have shaken the comic-book industry in recent years.

The creator of **Josie** *(above) has sued Archie Comics.*

Archie Comic Publications, Inc.

Many artists signed away rights to characters they created only to see the characters become the center of lucrative film franchises such as "Superman" and "Batman."

Mr. DeCarlo, 80, says he invented Josie in 1957, basing her on his wife of the same name. His wife's spotted-cat outfit for a costume party inspired the group's outfits.

Archie Comics acknowledges that Mr. DeCarlo is the creator of Josie. But a prepared statement from the company notes that Archie Comics is the copyright owner and terms his claims "baseless."

Archie Comics informed Mr. DeCarlo earlier this month that his services were no longer needed. The company disputes the suit's contention that it is using the characters beyond what Mr. DeCarlo agreed to.

"He is making certain claims relating to ownership that we believe fail to actively portray the role that others had," says Charles Grimes, the company's legal counsel, who says that some characters were a collaboration with other cartoonists. Archie will be happy to "embrace" Mr. DeCarlo after the lawsuit is settled, he adds, but "it was hard on a day-to-day basis to interact with him, when he was allowing his attorney to pursue such an aggressive posture."

Universal Pictures Inc., which is producing the movie, said the company doesn't comment on pending lawsuits.

Simple Interest

12

LEARNING UNIT OBJECTIVES

LU 12–1: Time Value of Money

- Compare money values at different points in time (p. 298).

LU 12–2: Calculation of Simple Interest and Maturity Value

- Calculate simple interest and maturity value for months and years (p. 299).
- Calculate simple interest and maturity value by **(a)** exact interest and **(b)** ordinary interest (pp. 300–301).

LU 12–3: Finding an Unknown in the Simple Interest Formula

- Use the interest formula, calculate the unknown when the other two (principal, rate, or time) are given (p. 301).

LU 12–4: Present Value of Simple Interest and Equivalent Payments

- Calculate the timing and amount of payments using a time line diagram (p. 304).
- Compute the equivalent value of a single payment or serial payments on any date (p. 304).

We live in a credit society. For various reasons many people and businesses use credit. An article in *The Wall Street Journal* titled "Loan Totaling $25 Billion Is Arranged to Repay Debt" reports on a $25 billion business loan of AT&T Corp. When you need a personal loan, you can get your loan from a single bank. There are three banks arranging the loan for AT&T; they are asking five banks to share in making the loan.

The price people and businesses must pay to get credit is *interest,* which is a rental charge for money. Can you imagine the interest that must be paid on a loan of $25 billion?

This chapter is about simple interest. The principles discussed apply whether you are paying interest or receiving interest. Let's begin by learning about the time value of money.

LEARNING UNIT 12–1
TIME VALUE OF MONEY

Interest is a charge that borrowers pay to lenders for the privilege of use of their money. If you borrowed $100 today for one year at 10% interest, in one year you will return the principal of $100 plus $10 interest (10% of $100), or in other words $110.

To illustrate this process we will introduce a diagram called a **time line**—a line that reflects time flow (from left to right).

FIGURE 12–1

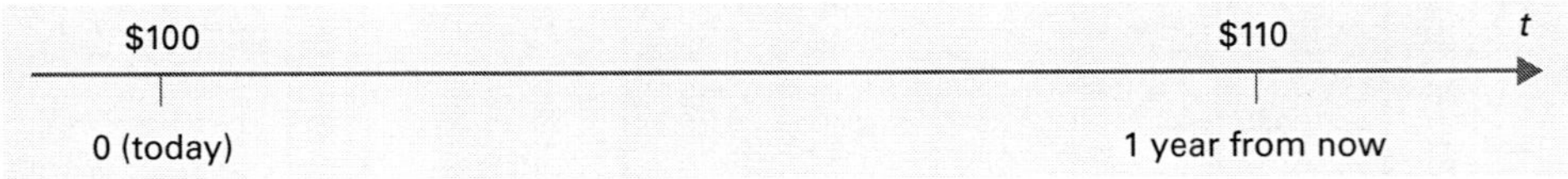

From Figure 12.1 you can see that $100 today would be equivalent to $110 in one year's time. Every day the value of money is growing in proportion to the interest rate. This tendency of money to change its value over time is called the **time value of money.**

One dollar today and one dollar 20 years ago do not have the same value. Ten years ago you could buy 2.5 litres of gas for $1. Today, for the same amount, you can get only 1.2 litres. If you borrowed money from the bank today, you would have to return a bigger amount at the end of term of the loan.

If you move along the time line from left to right, the money value increases; if you move from right to left, it decreases.

FIGURE 12–2

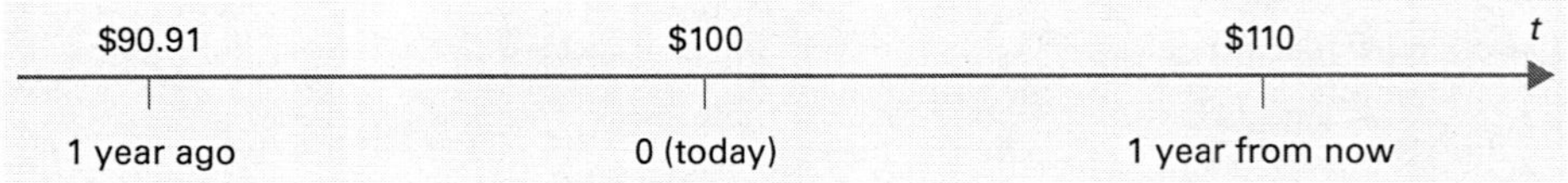

To compare money values at different points in time you must bring them to the same point in time.

It is interest that determines the value of money. Interest can be measured in percent, which is called an **interest rate** (r), and in dollars, which is called **dollar value of interest** or interest (I).

The initial amount borrowed is called the **principal** (P) and the amount due on return is called **future value** (FV) or **maturity value** (MV). Term of the loan or deposit is labelled t. It is always expressed in years. If, in a problem, the time is given in days or months, it will be necessary for you to express it in terms of a year.

It's time for a Practice Quiz.

LU 12–1 PRACTICE QUIZ

Draw time diagrams for the following:

1. Shirley needs $200 ten months from now. How much money does she need to deposit today at a 12% interest rate?
2. Tom had to repay $400 two months ago. He will pay his debt in three months.

LEARNING UNIT 12–2

CALCULATION OF SIMPLE INTEREST AND MATURITY VALUE

Jan Carley, a young attorney, rented an office in a professional building. Since Jan recently graduated from law school, she was short of cash. To purchase office furniture for her new office, Jan went to her bank and borrowed $30,000 for six months at an 8% annual interest rate.

The original amount Jan borrowed ($30,000) is the principal (face value) of the loan. Jan's price for using the $30,000 is the interest rate (8%) the bank charges on a yearly basis. Since Jan is borrowing the $30,000 for six months, Jan's loan will have a future value (FV) of $31,200—the principal plus the interest on the loan. Thus, Jan's price for using the furniture before she can pay for it is $1,200 interest, which is a percent of the principal for a specific time period. To make this calculation, we use the following formula:

| Future value (FV) = Principal (P) + Interest (I) |

$$\text{FV} = P + I \qquad \textbf{(12.1)}$$

$$\$31{,}200 = \$30{,}000 + \$1{,}200$$

Jan's furniture purchase introduces **simple interest**—the cost of a loan, usually for 1 year or less. Simple interest is only on the original principal or amount borrowed. Let's examine how the bank calculated Jan's $1,200 interest.

SIMPLE INTEREST FORMULA

To calculate simple interest, we use the following **simple interest formula:**

| Simple Interest (I) = Principal (P) × Rate (r) × Time (t) |

$$I = P \times r \times t \qquad \textbf{(12.2)}$$

In this formula, rate is expressed as a decimal, fraction, or percent; and time is expressed in years or a fraction of a year.

By simply rearranging formula 12.2 it is possible to find each variable, P, r, t, when the other values are given (we will discuss this in more detail in Learning Unit 12–3):

$I = Prt$

Formulas Interest on top:

$$t = \frac{I}{Pr} \qquad \textbf{(12.2.1)}$$

$$P = \frac{I}{rt} \qquad \textbf{(12.2.2)}$$

$$r = \frac{I}{Pt} \qquad \textbf{(12.2.3)}$$

EXAMPLE

Jan Carley borrowed $30,000 for office furniture. The loan was for six months at an annual interest rate of 8%. What are Jan's interest and maturity value?

Using the simple interest formula, the bank determined Jan's interest as follows:

In your calculator, multiply $30,000 times .08 times 6. Divide your answer by 12. You could also use the % key—multiply $30,000 times 8% times 6 and then divide your answer by 12.

Given: $P = \$30{,}000$; $r = .08$; $t = \frac{6}{12} = .5$ years; $I = ?$

STEP 1. Calculate the interest. $I = Prt$

$$I = \underset{(P)}{\$30{,}000} \times \underset{(r)}{.08} \times \underset{(t)}{\frac{6}{12}} = \$1{,}200$$

STEP 2. Calculate the maturity value.

$$\text{FV} = \underset{(P)}{\$30{,}000} + \underset{(I)}{\$1{,}200} = \$31{,}200$$

Now let's use the same example and assume Jan borrowed \$30,000 for 1 year. The bank would calculate Jan's interest and maturity value as follows:

Given: $P =$ \$3,000; $t = 1$; $r = .08$; $I = ?$

STEP 1. Calculate the interest. $I = \$30{,}000 \times .08 \times 1$ year
(P) (r) (t)

$I = Prt$ $= \$2{,}400$

STEP 2. Calculate the maturity value. $FV = \$30{,}000 + \$2{,}400$
(P) (I)

$FV = P + I$ $= \$32{,}400$

Let's consider a one-step solution to the problem of finding a future (maturity) value of a loan. We'll substitute into formula 12.1 an expression from formula 12.2 replacing I with its value.

$$I = Prt$$
$$FV = P + I = P + Prt$$

Take the common factor P out of the brackets and rewrite the formula:

$$FV = P + Prt = P(1 + rt)$$
$$FV = P(1 + rt) \qquad \textbf{(12.3)}$$

Now consider the same example again by using formula 12.3 and assume Jan borrowed \$30,000 for 18 months.[1] Jan's interest and maturity value would be calculated as follows:

Given: $P = \$30{,}000$; $r = .08$; $t = \frac{18}{12} = 1.5$ years; $FV = ?$

$$FV = \$30{,}000(1 + .08 \times 1.5) = \$33{,}600$$

Next we'll turn our attention to two common methods we can use to calculate simple interest when a loan specifies its beginning and ending dates.

From the exact-days-in-a-year calendar:

July 6	187th day
March 4	− 63rd day
	124 days (exact time of loan)
March	31
	− 4
	27
April	30
May	31
June	30
July	+ 6
	124 days

Two Methods for Calculating Simple Interest and Maturity Value

Method 1: Exact Interest (365 Days) Banks in Canada, and the government, use the **exact interest** method. The *exact interest* is calculated by using a 365-day year. For **time,** we count the exact number of days in the month that the borrower has the loan. The day the loan is made is not counted, but the day the money is returned is counted as a full day. This method calculates interest by using the following fraction to represent time in the formula:

$$\text{Time} = \frac{\text{Exact number of days}}{365}$$ ← Exact interest

For this calculation, we use the exact-days-in-a-year calendar.

EXAMPLE

On March 4, Peg Carry borrowed \$40,000 at 8% interest. Interest and principal are due on July 6. What is the interest cost and the maturity value?

STEP 1. Calculate the interest.
$I = P \times R \times T$
$= \$40{,}000 \times .08 \times \frac{124}{365}$
$= \$1{,}087.12$ (rounded to nearest cent)

STEP 2. Calculate the maturity value.
$MV = P + I$
$= \$40{,}000 + \$1{,}087.12$
$= \$41{,}087.12$

$P = \$40{,}000$
$r = .08$
$t = \frac{124}{365}$ (years)
$FV = ?$; $I = ?$

$I = Prt = \$40{,}000 \times .08 \times \frac{124}{365}$

$FV = P(1 + rt)$

$FV = \$40{,}000\left(1 + .08 \times \frac{124}{365}\right) = \$41{,}087.12$

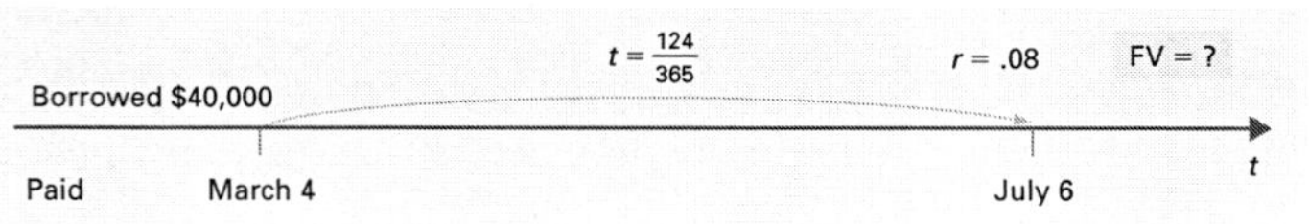

[1] This is the same as 1.5 years.

Method 2: Ordinary Interest (360 Days) In the **ordinary interest** method, often used in the United States, time in the formula $I = P \times r \times t$ is equal to the following:

$$\text{Time} = \frac{\text{Exact number of days}}{360} \leftarrow \text{Ordinary interest}$$

Since U.S. banks commonly use the ordinary interest method, it is known there as the **Banker's Rule.** American banks charge a slightly higher rate of interest because they use 360 days instead of 365 in the denominator. By using 360 instead of 365, the calculation is supposedly simplified. Consumer groups, however, are questioning why banks can use 360 days, since this benefits the bank and not the customer. The use of computers and calculators no longer makes the simplified calculation necessary. For example, after a court case in Oregon, banks began calculating interest on 365 days except in mortgages.

Now let's replay the Peg Carry example we used to illustrate Method 1 to see the difference in bank interest when we use Method 2.

EXAMPLE

On March 4, Peg Carry borrowed $40,000 at 8% interest. Interest and principal are due on July 6. What are the interest cost and the maturity value?

STEP 1. Calculate the interest.

$$I = \$40{,}000 \times .08 \times \frac{124}{360}$$
$$= \$1{,}102.22$$

STEP 2. Calculate the maturity value.

$$MV = P + I$$
$$= \$40{,}000 + \$1{,}102.22$$
$$= \$41{,}102.22$$

Note: By using Method 2, the bank increases its interest by $15.10.

$1,102.22	← Method 2
− 1,087.12	
$ 15.10	← Method 1

LU 12–2 PRACTICE QUIZ

Calculate simple interest (round to the nearest cent):

1. $14,000 at 4% for 9 months
2. $25,000 at 7% for 5 years
3. $40,000 at $10\frac{1}{2}$% for 19 months
4. On May 4, Dawn Kristal borrowed $15,000 at 8%. Dawn must pay the principal and interest on August 10. What are Dawn's simple interest and maturity value if you use the exact interest method?
5. What are Dawn Kristal's simple interest and maturity value if you use the ordinary interest method?

LEARNING UNIT 12–3
FINDING AN UNKNOWN IN THE SIMPLE INTEREST FORMULA

John Lei/Stock Boston

The *Wall Street Journal* clipping "Size of Loan Problem Is Debated in Japan" reports on the seriousness of Japan's loan problem. Many Japanese companies are having trouble paying the interest or the principal on their loans. For some of these companies, their loan problems are related to the amount of principal they borrowed. Think of the loan principal as its face value.

This Unit begins with the formula used to calculate the principal of a loan. Then it discusses how to calculate the rate of interest and the time. In all the calculations, we use 365 days and round only final answers.

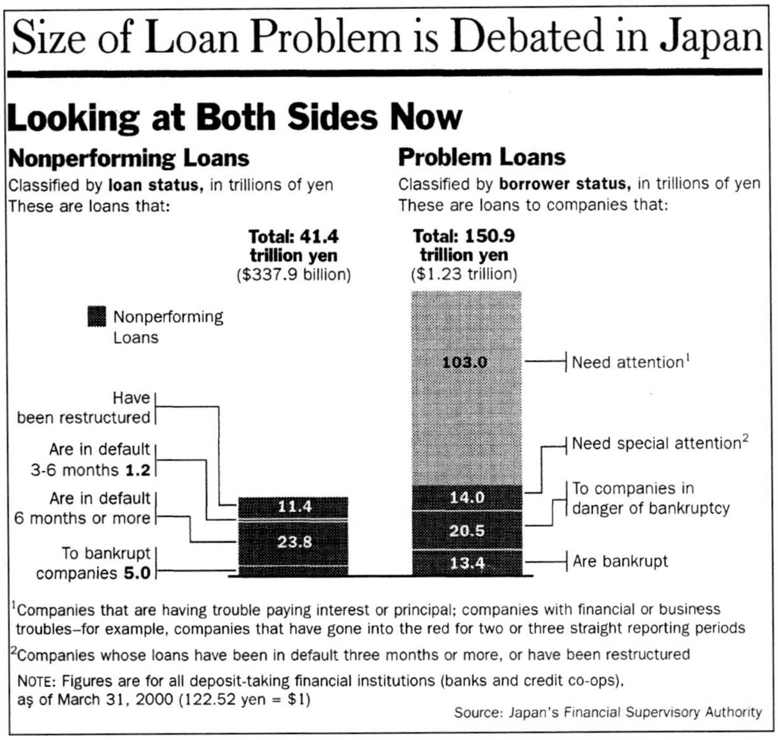

Source: © 2001 Dow Jones & Company, Inc.

Finding the Principal

Example

Tim Jarvis paid the bank $19.48 interest at 9.5% for 90 days. How much did Tim borrow?

The following formula is used to calculate the principal of a loan:

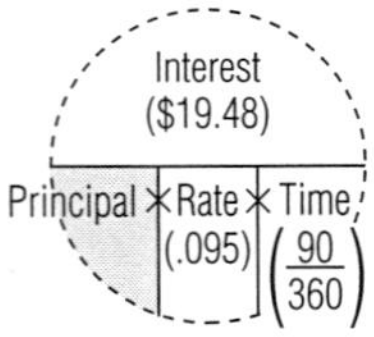

$$\text{Principal} = \frac{\text{Interest}}{\text{Rate} \times \text{Time}} \qquad P = \frac{I}{rt} \tag{12.4}$$

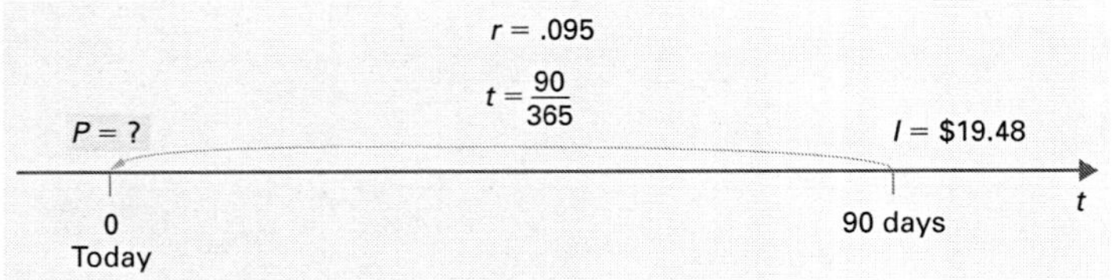

Note how we illustrate this in the margin. The shaded area is what we are solving for. When solving for principal, rate, or time, you are dividing. Interest will be in the numerator, and the denominator will be the other two elements multiplied by each other.

STEP 1. Set up the formula.

$$P = \frac{\$19.48}{.095 \times \frac{90}{365}}$$

STEP 2. Multiply the denominator.

.095 times 90 divided by 365 (do not round)

$$P = \frac{\$19.48}{.02375} = 831.60$$

Step 2. When using a calculator, press

.095 [×] 90 [÷] 365 [M+] [STO] [X].

STEP 3. Divide the numerator by the result of Step 2. 831.60

Step 3. When using a calculator, press

19.48 [÷] [MR] [=] [RCL] [X].

STEP 4. Check your answer.

$$\underset{(I)}{\$19.48} = \underset{(P)}{\$831.60} \times \underset{(r)}{.095} \times \underset{(t)}{\frac{90}{365}}$$

Finding the Rate

Example

Tim Jarvis borrowed $831.60 from a bank. Tim's interest is $19.48 for 90 days. What rate of interest did Tim pay?

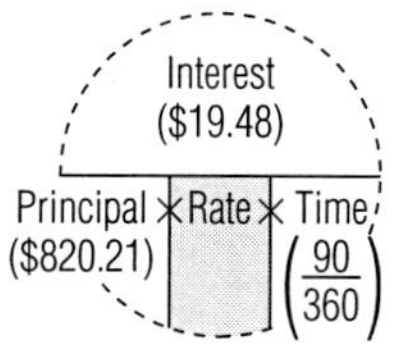

The following formula is used to calculate the rate of interest:

$$\text{Rate} = \frac{\text{Interest}}{\text{Principal} \times \text{Time}} \qquad r = \frac{I}{Pt} \qquad \textbf{(12.5)}$$

STEP 1. Set up the formula. $r = \dfrac{\$19.48}{\$831.60 \times \frac{90}{365}}$

STEP 2. Multiply the denominator. Do not round the answer. $r = \dfrac{\$19.48}{\$205.0520548}$ Don't round!

STEP 3. Divide the numerator by the result of Step 2. $r = 9.5\%$

STEP 4. Check your answer. $\underset{(I)}{\$19.48} = \underset{(P)}{\$831.60} \times \underset{(r)}{.095} \times \underset{(t)}{\frac{90}{365}}$

Finding the Time

EXAMPLE

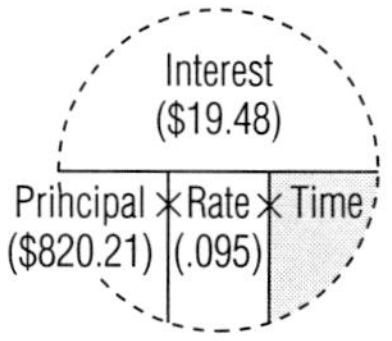

Tim Jarvis borrowed $831.60 from a bank. Tim's interest is $19.48 at 9.5%. How much time does Tim have to repay the loan?

The following formula is used to calculate time:

$$\text{Time (in years)} = \frac{\text{Interest}}{\text{Principal} \times \text{Rate}} \qquad t = \frac{I}{Pr} \qquad \textbf{(12.6)}$$

STEP 1. Set up the formula. $t = \dfrac{\$19.48}{\$831.60 \times .095}$

STEP 2. Multiply the denominator. Do not round the answer. $t = \dfrac{\$19.48}{\$79.002}$ Don't round

STEP 3. Divide the numerator by the result of Step 2. $T = .246576036$ years

STEP 4. Convert years to days (assume 365 days). $.246576036 \times 365 = 90$ days

STEP 5. Check your answer. $\underset{(I)}{\$19.48} = \underset{(P)}{\$831.60} \times \underset{(r)}{.095} \times \underset{(t)}{\frac{90}{365}}$

Step 2. When using a calculator, press
20.21 [×] .095 [M+] [STO] [Y].

Step 3. When using a calculator, press
19.48 [÷] [MR] [=] [RCL] [Y].

Before we go on to Learning Unit 12–4, let's check your understanding of this Unit.

LU 12–3 PRACTICE QUIZ

Complete the following (assume 365 days):

	Principal *P*	Interest rate *r*	Time (days) *t*	Simple interest *I*
1.	?	5%	90 days	$8,000
2.	$7,000	?	220 days	$350
3.	$1,000	8%	?	$300

LEARNING UNIT 12–4
PRESENT VALUE OF SIMPLE INTEREST AND EQUIVALENT PAYMENTS

It is also possible to calculate the principal or the present value by rearranging formula 12.3.
We use this formula when future value, interest rate, and time are given.

$$FV = P(1 + rt)$$

$$P = \frac{FV}{(1 + rt)} \qquad \textbf{(12.7)}$$

Let's use formula 12.3 for the following example.

EXAMPLE

Mr. Jones repaid $15,879 in principal and interest for his loan. The term of the loan was 180 days and the interest rate was 10%. How much money did Mr. Jones borrow? (In other words, what was the principal?)

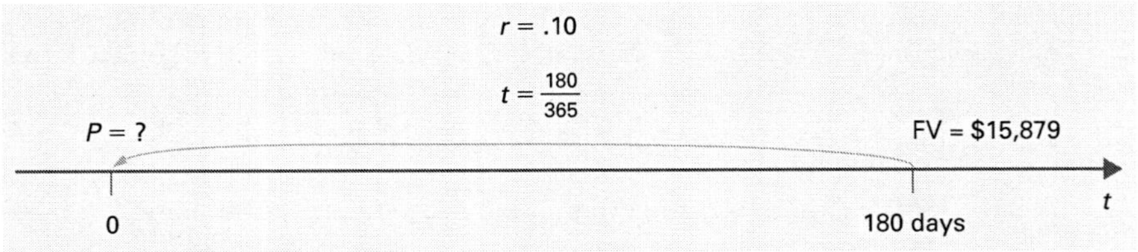

$FV = \$15{,}879;\ t = \frac{180}{365}$ years; $r = .10;\ P = ?$

$$P = \frac{FV}{(1 + rt)} = \frac{\$15{,}879}{\left(1 + .1 \times \frac{180}{365}\right)} = \$15{,}132.73$$

Mr. Jones borrowed $15,132.73.

Let's consider another example.

EXAMPLE

Mr. and Mrs. Chan plan to spend their vacation in Australia. They will fly to Sydney in 11 months from now. How much money must they deposit in the bank account today to have $10,000 ready on the day of their flight? The interest rate is 12%.

$r = .12;\ t = \frac{180}{365}$ years

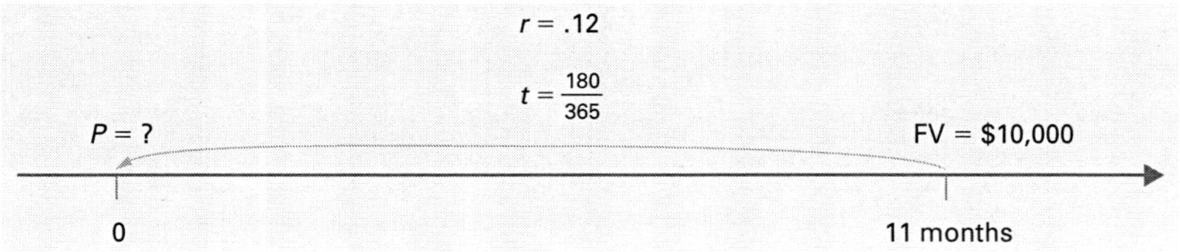

$$P = \frac{\$10{,}000}{\left(1 + .12 \times \frac{180}{365}\right)} = \$9{,}441.28$$

Mr. and Mrs. Chan must deposit $9,441.28 today in order to receive $10,000 eleven months from now.

These values are called *equivalent values.* With an interest rate of 12%, $9,441.28 today is equal to $10,000 in 11 months.

This time value of money may be used for calculations of **equivalent payments.**

EXAMPLE

Mr. Sharky is selling his boat for $6,870. He has received two offers: one buyer agrees to pay the asking price today and the other will pay $7,200 in a year's time. Which offer is better for Mr. Sharky if the current interest rate is 4%?

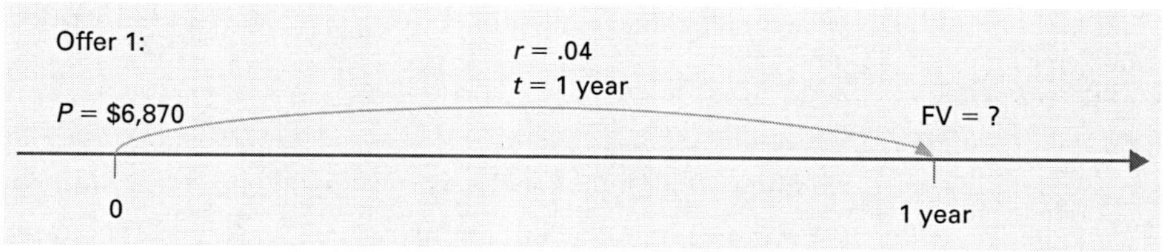

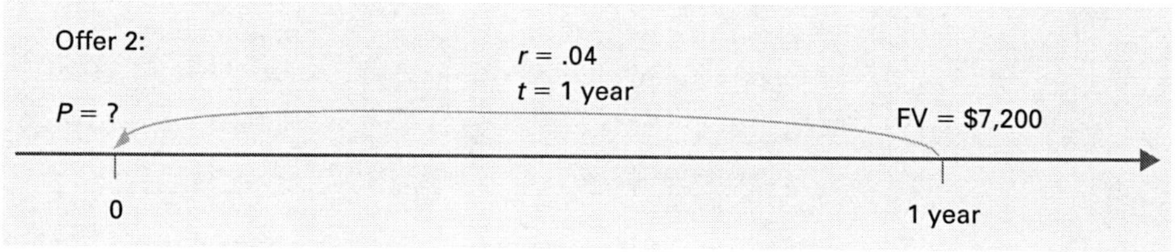

To compare these two offers we must bring money values to the same point in time: either to today's day or to the point of one year from now. So there are two ways to solve the problem:

1. To calculate the future value of \$6,870 in one year's time and compare the two offers
2. To calculate the present value of \$7,200 and compare the two offers

The solutions using each method are:

1. $P = \$6{,}870;\ r = .04;\ t = 1$

$$\text{FV} = \$6{,}870 \times (1 + .04 \times 1) = \$7{,}144.80$$

The value of \$6,870 in one year will be \$7,144.80. The second buyer is offering to pay \$7,200 in one year's time. So the second offer is better.

2. $\text{FV} = \$7{,}200;\ r = .04;\ t = 1$

$$P = \frac{\$7{,}200}{(1 + .04 \times 1)} = \$6{,}923.08$$

The present value of the second offer is \$6,923.08. If we compare the first offer of \$6,870 and the second one with the equivalent value of \$6,923.08 we can see that Mr. Sharky should accept the second offer.

The idea of the time value of money has many different applications. Let's consider how it can be used in determining the final payment after several **partial payments** that have been made before the due date.

Mr. Tom Banks borrowed \$9,000 dollars for a year to buy new dining room furniture. In three months he repaid \$3,000 and at the seven-month point he repaid another \$4,000. What is the final balance due if the money value (interest rate) is 4%?

Let's start from the time diagram. Remember to make it clear and well organized: everything that was borrowed we place above the time line, and everything that was paid, or is due to be paid, we place below it.

Amount borrowed = Amount paid

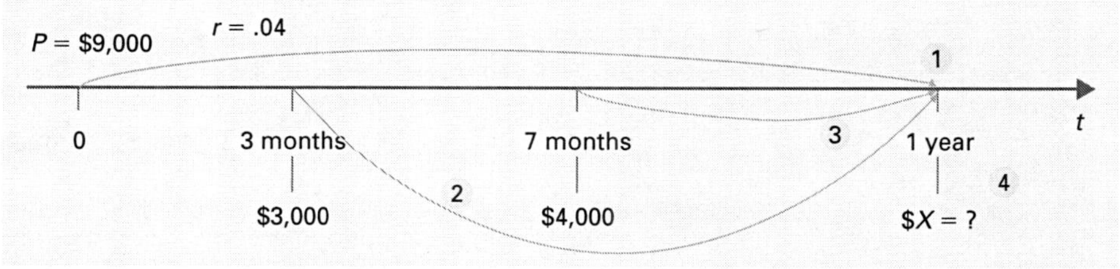

First of all, we need to bring all money values to the same point in time—the due date. In other words, we need to calculate future values of the amount borrowed or the maturity value of the loan FV = ? ①, and the future values of the amounts paid at the three-month ② and the seven-month point ③. Only then will we be able to define the amount of the final payment ④.

Remember the statement of the equation: amount borrowed is equal to amount paid.

① = ② + ③ + ④

① $FV = \$9{,}000\ (1 + .04 \times 1) = \$9{,}360$; Mr. Banks must pay $9,360 back.

② $FV_{\text{payment 1}} = \$3{,}000\ (1 + .04 \times \frac{9}{12}) = \$3{,}090$.

The value of this payment on the due date will be $3,090. Please note that in this case we moved $3,000 along the time line to the one-year point, or for (12 months minus 3 months) 9 months, which is $\frac{9}{12}$ of a year.

③ $FV_{\text{payment 2}} = \$4{,}000\ (1 + .04 \times \frac{5}{12}) = \$4{,}066.67$.

The value of the second payment on the due date will be $4,066.67. We moved the value of payment five months along the time line to the one-year point (12 months minus 7 months equals 5 months or $\frac{5}{12}$ of a year).

④ $\$X$ is a value of a final payment.

Let's substitute values of ① through ④ in the highlighted equation:

$$\$9{,}360 = \$3{,}090 + \$4{,}066.67 + \$X$$

From this equation we can define X.

$$X = \$9{,}360 - \$3{,}090 - \$4{,}066.67$$

$$X = \$2{,}203.33$$

Mr. Banks must pay $2,203.33 on the due date to repay the loan.

Now it's time for a Practice Quiz.

LU 12-4 PRACTICE QUIZ

Olga Russ is supposed to pay Stella Lee $4,348 on August 31. **(a)** How much money did she borrow on March 15, if the interest rate is 3.5%? **(b)** If Olga can't pay on the due date, how much money should satisfy Stella on October 1?

CHAPTER ORGANIZER AND REFERENCE GUIDE

Topic	Key point, procedure, formula	Example(s) to illustrate situation
Simple interest for months, p. 299	Interest = Principal × Rate × Time (*I*) (*P*) (*r*) (*t*)	$2,000 at 9% for 17 months $I = \$2{,}000 \times .09 \times \frac{17}{12}$ $I = \$255$

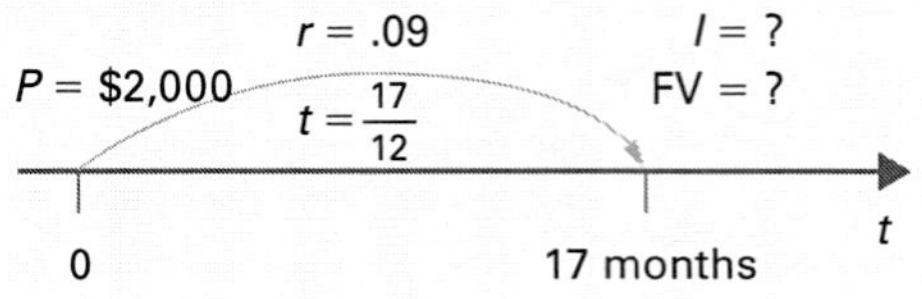

(*continues*)

CHAPTER ORGANIZER AND REFERENCE GUIDE (CONTINUED)

Topic	Key point, procedure, formula		Example(s) to illustrate situation
Exact interest, p. 300	$t = \frac{\text{Exact number of days}}{365}$ $I = P \times r \times t$	(12.2)	\$1,000 at 10% from January 5 to February 20 $I = \$1,000 \times .10 \times \frac{46}{365}$ Feb. 20: 51 days Jan. 5: − 5 46 days $I =$ \$12.60 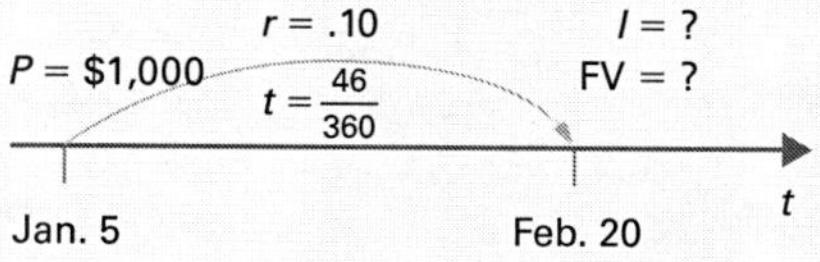
Ordinary interest (Banker's Rule), p. 301	$t = \frac{\text{Exact number of days}}{360}$ $I = P \times r \times t$ Higher interest costs		$I = \$1,000 \times .10 \times \frac{46}{360}$ ← (51 − 5) $I =$ \$12.78
Finding unknown in simple interest formula (use 360 days), p. 301	$I = P \times r \times t$		Use this example for illustrations of simple interest formula parts: \$1,013.89 loan at 9%, 60 days $I = \$1,013.89 \times .09 \times \frac{60}{365} =$ \$15
Finding the principal, p. 302	$P = \frac{I}{r \times t}$ 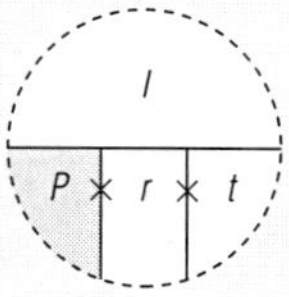	(12.4)	$P = \frac{\$15}{.09 \times \frac{60}{365}} = \frac{\$15}{.01479452} =$ \$1,013.89 Don't round the intermediate result.
Finding the rate, p. 302	$r = \frac{I}{P \times t}$ 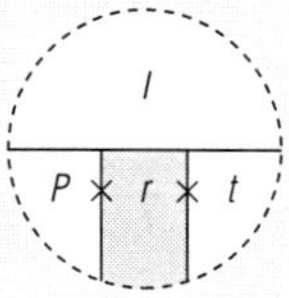	(12.5)	$R = \frac{\$15}{\$1,013.89 \times \frac{60}{365}} = \frac{\$15}{166.66666} = .09$ = 9% *Note:* We did not round the denominator.
Finding the time, p. 303	$t = \frac{I}{P \times r}$ (in years) 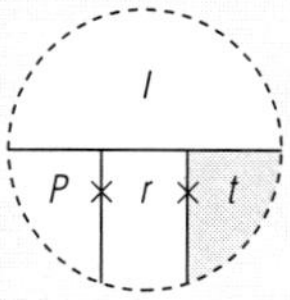 Multiply answer by 365 days to convert answer to days for exact interest.	(12.6)	$t = \frac{\$15}{\$1,013.89 \times .09} = \frac{\$15}{\$91.25} = .164383561$ Don't round the intermediate result. $.164383561 \times 365 =$ 60 days
Finding the principal when future value, time, and rate are given, p. 304	$P = \frac{FV}{(1 + rt)}$	(12.7)	Vlad repaid to Olena \$500. Term of the loan was 9 months, interest rate—5%. How much money did Vlad borrow from Olena? $FV = \$500;\ r = .05;\ t = \frac{9}{12};\ P = ?$ $P = \frac{\$500}{\left(1 + .05 \times \frac{9}{12}\right)} = \$481.93$ $P =$ \$481.93

(*continues*)

CHAPTER ORGANIZER AND REFERENCE GUIDE (CONCLUDED)

TOPIC	KEY POINT, PROCEDURE, FORMULA	EXAMPLE(S) TO ILLUSTRATE SITUATION	
Calculating equivalent values, p. 305	**Amount borrowed = Amount paid** To calculate equivalent values, use the time value of money property. To compare money values, bring them to the same point in time.	Nikita borrowed \$10,000 from Michael. Term of the loan is 11 months and the interest rate is 10%. In 6 month from the starting date she returned \$7,000. How much money should Nikita repay to Michael on the due date? 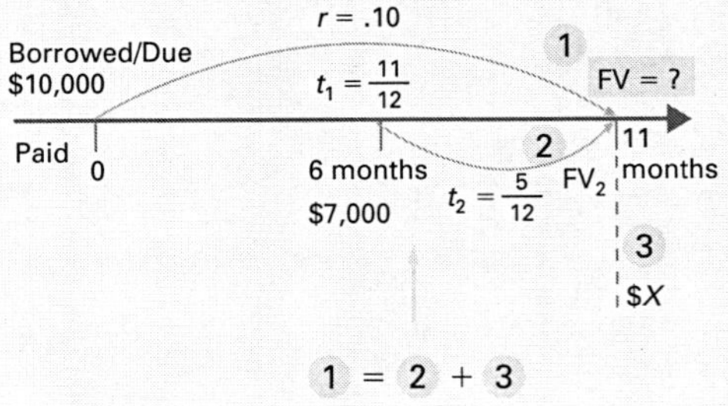 ① $FV = \$10{,}000\left(1 + .10 \times \frac{11}{12}\right)$ $= \$10{,}916.67$ ② $FV_2 = \$7{,}000\left(1 + .10 \times \frac{5}{12}\right)$ $= \$7{,}291.67$ ① = ② + ③ $\$10{,}916.67 = \$7{,}291.67 + \$X$ $X = \$10{,}916.67 - \$7{,}291.67 = \$3{,}625$ Nikita should pay \$3,625 on the due date.	
Key terms	Banker's Rule, p. 301 Dollar value of interest, p. 298 Equivalent payments, p. 304 Exact interest, p. 300 Future value, p. 298 Interest, p. 298	Interest rate, p. 298 Maturity value, p. 298 Ordinary interest, p. 301 Partial payments, p. 305 Principal, p. 298 Simple interest, p. 299	Simple interest formula, p. 299 Time, p. 300 Time line, p. 298 Time value of money, p. 298

CRITICAL THINKING DISCUSSION QUESTIONS

1. What is the difference between exact interest and ordinary interest? With the increase of computers in banking, do you think that the ordinary interest method is a dinosaur in business today?
2. Explain how to use the portion formula to solve the unknowns in the simple interest formula. Why would rounding the answer of the denominator result in an inaccurate final answer?
3. Explain why we need to bring money values to the same point in time to compare them.

END-OF-CHAPTER PROBLEMS

DRILL PROBLEMS

Calculate the simple interest and maturity value for the following problems. Round to the nearest cent as needed.

	Principal P	Interest rate r	Time t	Simple interest I	Maturity value FV
12–1.	$9,000	4%	13 mo.	?	?
12–2.	$12,000	5%	$1\frac{3}{4}$ yr.	?	?
12–3.	$7,000	$8\frac{1}{4}$%	7 mo.	?	?

Complete the following, using ordinary interest:

	Principal P	Interest rate r	Date borrowed	Date repaid	Exact time t	Interest I	Maturity value FV
12–4.	$1,000	8%	Mar. 8	June 9	?	?	?
12–5.	$585	9%	June 5	Dec. 15	?	?	?
12–6.	$1,200	12%	July 7	Jan. 10	?	?	?

Complete the following, using exact interest:

	Principal P	Interest rate r	Date borrowed	Date repaid	Exact time t	Interest I	Maturity value FV
12–7.	$1,000	8%	Mar. 8	June 9	?	?	?
12–8.	$585	9%	June 5	Dec. 15	?	?	?
12–9.	$1,200	12%	July 7	Jan. 10	?	?	?

Solve for the missing item in the following (round to the nearest hundredth as needed):

	Principal P	Interest rate r	Time (months years) t	Simple interest I
12–10.	$400	5%	?	$100
12–11.	?	7%	$1\frac{1}{2}$ years	$200
12–12.	$5,000	?	6 months	$300

12–13. Mr. Martin borrowed $10,000 for 240 days at 8%. On the 100th day of the term he paid $4,000 back, and on the 180th day another $2,000. How much will Mr. Martin need to pay on the last day of the term of the loan to close the account? (Use a time line diagram.)

ADDITIONAL DRILL PROBLEMS

12–14. Find the simple interest for each of the following loans:

	Principal	Rate	Time	Interest
a.	$2,000	9%	1 year	?
b.	$3,000	12%	3 years	?
c.	$18,000	$8\frac{1}{2}$%	10 months	?

12–15. Find the simple interest for each of the following loans; use the exact interest method. Use the days-in-a-year calendar when needed.

	Principal	Rate	Time	Interest
a.	$700	14%	30 days	?
b.	$4,290	8%	250 days	?
c.	$1,500	8%	Made March 11 Due July 11	?

12–16. Find the simple interest for each of the following loans using the ordinary interest method used in the United States (the Banker's Rule).

	Principal	Rate	Time	Interest
a.	$5,250	$7\frac{1}{2}$%	120 days	?
b.	$700	12%	70 days	?
c.	$2,600	11%	Made on June 15 Due October 17	?

12–17. Find the principal in each of the following. Round to the nearest cent. Assume 365 days. *Calculator hint:* Do the denominator calculation first, and do not round; when the answer is displayed, save it in memory by pressing M+ . Now key in the numerator (interest amount), ÷ , MR , = for the answer. Be sure to clear memory after each problem by pressing MR again so that the "M" is no longer in the display.

	Rate	Time	Interest	Principal
a.	8%	70 days	$68	?
b.	11%	90 days	$125	?
c.	9%	120 days	$103	?
d.	$8\frac{1}{2}$%	60 days	$150	?

12–18. Find the rate in each of the following. Round to the nearest tenth of a percent. Assume 365 days.

	Principal	Time	Interest	Rate
a.	$7,500	120 days	$350	?
b.	$975	60 days	$25	?
c.	$20,800	220 days	$910	?
d.	$150	30 days	$2.10	?

12–19. Complete the table.

FV	*t*	*I*	*r*	PV
$1,200	1	?	.1	?
$600	1.5	100	.08	?
$11,200	3	?	.04	?

WORD PROBLEMS

12–20. The May 2001 issue of *Credit Union Magazine* stated that federal credit unions are limited to charging interest rates of no more than 18% per annum on any loan. A $2,500 loan is given to a member at 18%, and the interest is $225. When will the loan be due (assume 365 days)?

12–21. Rebecca Shore borrowed $80,000 to pay for her child's education at Centennial College. Rebecca must repay the loan at the end of eight months in one payment with $7\frac{1}{2}\%$ interest. How much interest must Rebecca pay? What is the maturity value?

12–22. Excel On September 12, Jody Jansen went to Sunshine Bank to borrow $2,300 at 9% interest. Jody plans to repay the loan on January 27. Assume the loan is on ordinary interest. What interest will Jody owe on January 27? What is the total amount Jody must repay at maturity?

12–23. Excel Kelly O'Brien met Jody Jansen (Problem 12–22) at Sunshine Bank and suggested she consider the loan on exact interest. Recalculate the loan for Jody under this assumption.

12–24. On May 3, 2003, Excellon Resources Inc. negotiated a short-term loan of $685,000. On May 28, 2003, *Market News Publishing* reported that the loan is due October 1, 2003, and carries a 6.86% interest rate. Use exact interest to calculate the interest. What is the total amount Excellon would pay on the maturity date?

12–25. Gordon Rosel went to his bank to find out how long it will take for $1,200 to amount to $1,650 at 8% simple interest. Solve Gordon's problem. Round time in years to the nearest tenth.

12–26. Bill Moore is buying a van. His April monthly interest at 12% was $125. What was Bill's principal balance at the beginning of April? Use 365 days.

12–27. On April 5, 2004, Janeen Camoct took out an $8\frac{1}{2}\%$ loan for $20,000. The loan is due March 9, 2005. Use ordinary interest to calculate the interest. What total amount will Janeen pay on March 9, 2005?

12–28. Sabrina Bowers took out the same loan as Janeen (Problem 12–27). Sabrina's terms, however, are exact-interest. What is Sabrina's difference in interest? What will she pay on March 9, 2005?

12–29. Max Wholesaler borrowed $2,000 on a 10%, 120-day note. After 45 days, Max paid $700 on the note. Thirty days later, Max paid an additional $630. What is the final balance due? Determine the total interest and ending balance due.

ADDITIONAL WORD PROBLEMS

12–30. On April 30, 2001, PR Newswire reported on a company that received a short-term loan. The loan was dated April 12, 2001, due April 30, 2001. The rate of interest was 6.5%. The interest earned was $162.50. Using exact interest, what was the original amount of the loan?

12–31. The January 2001 issue of *Consumer Reports* gave a report on interest charges. The article mentioned that with a good payment history you could be paying only 9% to 12% on credit cards. With a $560 charge, what would be the interest amount at 9% and at 12% for one month?

12–32. On September 14, Jennifer Rick went to Park Bank to borrow $2,500 at $11\frac{3}{4}\%$ interest. Jennifer plans to repay the loan on January 27. Assume the loan is on ordinary interest. What interest will Jennifer owe on January 27? What is the total amount Jennifer must repay at maturity?

12–33. Steven Linden met Jennifer Rick (Problem 12–32) at Park Bank and suggested she consider the loan on exact interest. Recalculate the loan for Jennifer under this assumption.

12–34. Excel Lance Lopes went to his bank to find out how long it will take for $1,000 to amount to $1,700 at 12% simple interest. Can you solve Lance's problem? Round time in years to the nearest tenth.

12–35. Margie Pagano is buying a car. Her June monthly interest at $12\frac{1}{2}\%$ was $195. What was Margie's principal balance at the beginning of June? Use 365 days. Do not round the denominator before dividing.

12–36. Shawn Bixby borrowed $17,000 on a 120-day, 12% note. After 65 days, Shawn paid $2,000 on the note. On day 89, Shawn paid an additional $4,000. What is the final balance due? Determine total interest and ending balance due.

12–37. Carol Miller went to Europe and forgot to pay her $740 mortgage payment on her Whistler ski house. For her 59 days overdue on her payment, the bank charged her a penalty of $15. What was the rate of interest charged by the bank? Round to the nearest hundredth percent (assume 365 days).

12–38. Abe Wolf bought a new kitchen set at Sears. Abe paid off the loan after 60 days with an interest charge of $9. If Sears charges 10% interest, what did Abe pay for the kitchen set (assume 365 days)?

12–39. Joy Kirby made a $300 loan to Robinson Landscaping at 11%. Robinson paid back the loan with interest of $6.60. How long in days was the loan outstanding (assume 365 days)? Check your answer.

12–40. Molly Ellen, bookkeeper for Keystone Company, forgot to send in the payroll taxes due on April 15. She sent the payment November 8. She was charged a penalty of 8% simple interest on the unpaid taxes of $4,100. Calculate the penalty.

12–41. Oakwood Plowing Company purchased two new plows for the upcoming winter. In 200 days, Oakwood must make a single payment of $23,200 to pay for the plows. As of today, Oakwood has $22,500. If Oakwood puts the money in a bank today, what rate of interest will it need to pay off the plows in 200 days (assume 365 days)?

12–42. On October 17, Nina Verga borrowed $3,136 at a rate of 12%. She promised to repay the loan in 10 months. What are **(a)** the amount of the simple interest and **(b)** the total amount owed upon maturity?

12–43. Marjorie Folsom borrowed $5,500 to purchase a computer. The loan was for 9 months at an annual interest rate of $12\frac{1}{2}$%. What are **(a)** the amount of interest Marjorie must pay and **(b)** the maturity value of the loan?

12–44. Roger Lee borrowed $5,280 at $13\frac{1}{2}$% on May 24 and agreed to repay the loan on August 24. The lender calculates interest using the exact interest method. How much will Roger be required to pay on August 24?

12–45. Dianne Smith's real estate taxes of $641.49 were due on November 1, 2004. Due to financial difficulties, Dianne was unable to pay her tax bill until January 15, 2005. The penalty for late payment is $13\frac{3}{8}$% exact interest. What is the penalty Dianne will have to pay, and what is Dianne's total payment on January 15?

12–46. On August 8, Rex Eason had a credit card balance of $550, but he was unable to pay his bill. The credit card company charges interest of $18\frac{1}{2}$% annually on late payments. What amount will Rex have to pay if he pays his bill one month late?

12–47. An issue of *Your Money* discussed average consumers who carry a balance of $2,000 on one credit card. If the yearly rate of interest is 18%, how much are consumers paying in interest per year?

12–48. A credit union charges a credit card interest rate of 11% per year. If you had a credit card debt of $1,500, what would your interest amount be after 3 months?

Use 365 days for the following problems.

12–49. In June, Becky opened a $20,000 bank CD paying 6% interest, but she had to withdraw the money in a few days to cover one child's college tuition. The bank charged her $600 in penalties for the withdrawal. What percent of the $20,000 was she charged?

12–50. Dr. Vaccarro invested his money at $12\frac{1}{2}$% for 175 days and earned interest of $760. How much money did Dr. Vaccarro invest?

12–51. If you invested $10,000 at 5% interest in a 6-month CD compounding interest daily, you would earn $252.43 in interest. How much would the same $10,000 invested in a bank paying simple interest earn?

12–52. Thomas Kyrouz opened a savings account and deposited $750 in a bank that was paying 7.2% simple interest. How much were his savings worth in 200 days?

12–53. Mary Millitello paid the bank $53.90 in interest on a 66-day loan at 9.8%. How much money did Mary borrow? Round to the nearest dollar.

12–54. John Joseph borrowed $10,800 for 1 year at 14%. After 60 days, he paid $2,500 on the note. On the 200th day, he paid an additional $5,000. Find the final balance due.

CHALLENGE PROBLEMS

12–55. Debbie McAdams paid 8% interest on a $12,500 loan balance. Jan Burke paid $5,000 interest on a $62,500 loan. Based on 1 year: **(a)** What was the amount of interest paid by Debbie? **(b)** What was the interest rate paid by Jan? **(c)** Debbie and Jan are both in the 28% tax bracket. Since the interest is deductible, how much would Debbie and Jan each save in taxes?

12–56. Janet Foster bought a computer and printer at Future Store. The printer had a $600 list price with a $100 trade discount and 2/10, n/30 terms. The computer had a $1,600 list price with a 25% trade discount but no cash discount. On the computer, Future Store offered Janet the choice of (1) paying $50 per month for 17 months with the 18th payment paying the remainder of the balance or (2) paying 8% interest for 18 months in equal payments.

a. Assume Janet could borrow the money for the printer at 8% to take advantage of the cash discount. How much would Janet save (assume 365 days)?

b. On the computer, what is the difference in the final payment between choices 1 and 2?

SUMMARY PRACTICE TEST

1. Gracie Sullivan's real estate tax of \$1,820.50 was due on December 10, 2004. Gracie lost her job and could not pay her tax bill until February 16, 2005. The penalty for late payment is $9\frac{1}{2}$% interest. (p. 299)
   a. What is the penalty Gracie must pay?
   b. What is the total amount Gracie must pay on February 16?
2. Damien Spaine borrowed \$140,000 to pay for his child's education. He must repay the loan at the end of 8 years in one payment with $8\frac{1}{2}$% interest. What is the maturity value Damien must repay? (p. 299)
3. On May 11, Frank Soy borrowed \$8,000 from Briar Bank at $9\frac{1}{2}$% interest. Frank plans to repay the loan on February 15. Assume the loan is on ordinary interest. How much will Frank repay on February 15? (p. 301)
4. Joy Blass met Frank Soy (Problem 3) at Briar Bank. After talking with Frank, Joy decided she would like to consider the same loan on exact interest. Can you recalculate the loan for Joy under this assumption? (p. 300)
5. Hing Hon is buying a car. Her September monthly interest was \$180 at $9\frac{1}{4}$% interest. What is Hing's principal balance (to the nearest dollar) at the beginning of September? Use 365 days. Do not round the denominator in your calculation. (p. 300)
6. Baffour Silva borrowed \$12,000 on an 8%, 60-day note. After 10 days, Baffour paid \$4,000 on the note. On day 45, Baffour paid \$3,000 on the note. What are the total interest and ending balance due? (p. 300)

SOLUTIONS TO PRACTICE QUIZZES

LU 12–1

1.

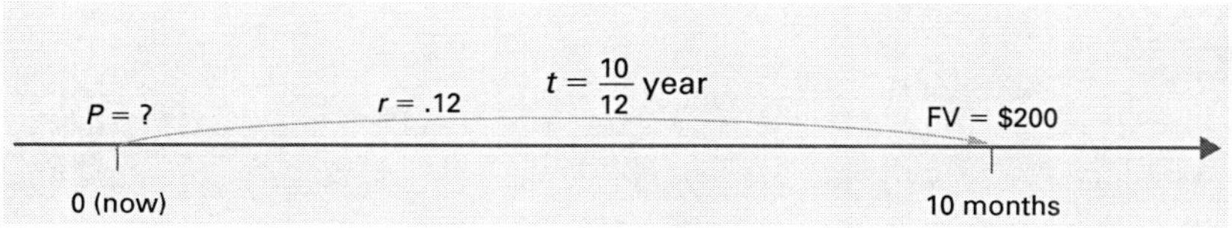

2.

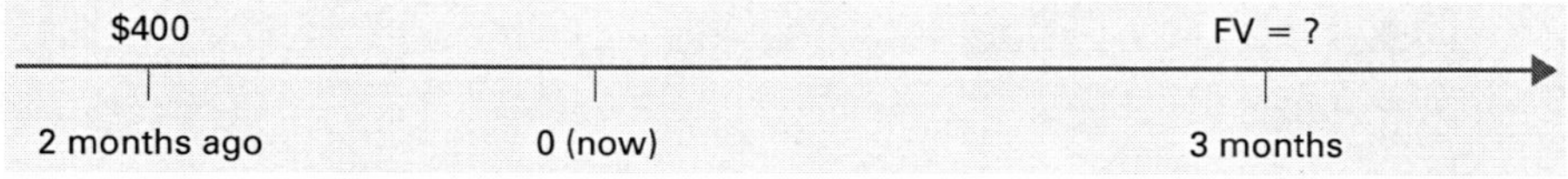

LU 12–2

1. $\$14{,}000 \times .04 \times \frac{9}{12} = \$420$

2. $\$25{,}000 \times .07 \times 5 = \$8{,}750$

3. $\$40{,}000 \times .105 \times \frac{19}{12} = \$6{,}650$

4. August 10 → 222 $\quad \$15{,}000 \times .08 \times \frac{98}{365} = \$322.19$
   May 4 → − 124
   98 $\quad MV = \$15{,}000 + \$322.19 = \$15{,}322.19$

5. $\$15{,}000 \times .08 \times \frac{98}{360} = \$326.67 \qquad MV = \$15{,}000 + \$326.67 = \$15{,}326.67$

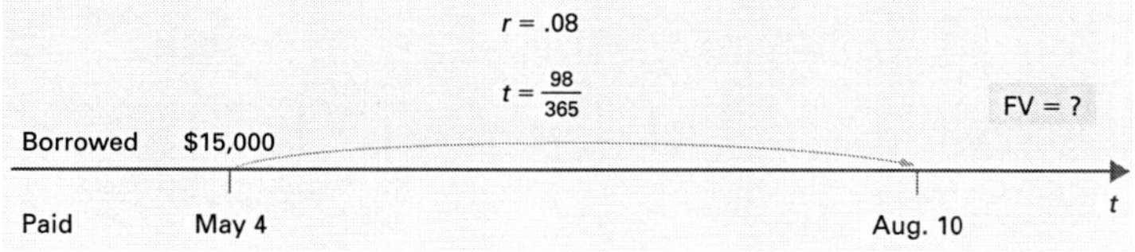

LU 12–3

1. $\dfrac{\$8{,}000}{.05 \times \dfrac{90}{365}} = \dfrac{\$8{,}000}{.012328767} = \$648{,}888.90$ $\quad P = \dfrac{I}{r \times t}$

2. $\dfrac{\$350}{\$7{,}000 \times \dfrac{220}{365}} = \dfrac{\$350}{\$4{,}219.178082} = 8.30\%$ $\quad r = \dfrac{I}{P \times t}$

   (Do not round)

3. $\dfrac{\$300}{\$1{,}000 \times .08} = \dfrac{\$300}{\$80} = 3.75 \times 365 = 1{,}369 \text{ days}$ $\quad t = \dfrac{I}{P \times r}$

LU 12–4

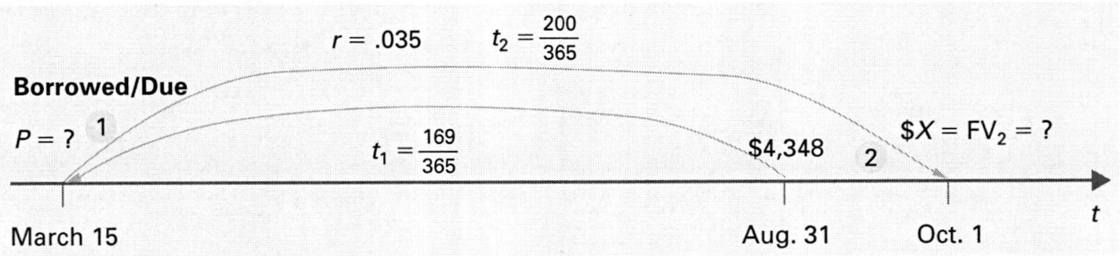

a. t_1—is the term of the loan from March 15 until August 31.

March	16 days
April	30 days
May	31 days
June	30 days
July	31 days
August	31 days

$$169 \text{ days} = \frac{169}{365} \text{ years}$$

b. t_2—is the new term of the loan from March 31 until October 1.

We calculated that from March 31 until August 31 we have 169 days, and:

September	30 days
October	1 day
	31 days

$$t_2 = 169 + 31 = 200 \text{ days} = \frac{200}{365} \text{ years}$$

① $P = \dfrac{\$4{,}348}{\left(1 + .035 \times \dfrac{169}{365}\right)} = \$4{,}278.66$

② $FV_2 = \$4{,}278.66\left(1 + .035 \times \dfrac{200}{365}\right) = \$4{,}360.72$

Business Math Scrapbook
WITH INTERNET APPLICATION

Putting Your Skills to Work

PROJECT A

Suppose you have taken advantage of this great sale on the perfect sofa, love seat, and coffee table set that costs $3,000—and you have one year to pay! If you have a savings account that pays 5% (annual rate) simple interest for 12 months, how much would you have to invest today in order to pay for the furniture next year?

Promissory Notes, Simple Discount Notes, and the Discount Process

13

As part of the offering, Oplink converted a $50 million promissory note to **Cisco Systems Inc.** into roughly 3.3 million common shares. Under terms of the agreement, the conversion was set at 85% of the offering price.

LEARNING UNIT OBJECTIVES

LU 13–1: Structure of Promissory Notes; the Simple Discount Note

- Differentiate between interest-bearing and non-interest-bearing notes (p. 319).
- Calculate bank discount and proceeds for simple discount notes (p. 319).
- Calculate and compare the interest, maturity value, proceeds, and effective rate of a simple interest note with a simple discount note (p. 319).

LU 13–2: Discounting an Interest-Bearing Note Before Maturity

- Calculate the maturity value, bank discount, and proceeds of discounting an interest-bearing note before maturity (p. 321).
- Identify and complete the four steps of the discounting process (p. 322).

Table 376-0018 - International transactions in securities, portfolio transactions, net and gross sales and purchases, by type and sector, annual (Dollars × 1M)

Survey or program details:
Canada's Balance of International Payments - **1534**
Canada's International Transactions in Securities - **1535**

Geography=Canada

Canadian portfolio securities[1]	2001
Loans under repurchase agreements, government of Canada Treasury bills, liabilities, net	–170
Loans under repurchase agreements, government of Canada Treasury bills, liabilities, purchases	14,745
Loans under repurchase agreements, government of Canada Treasury bills, liabilities, sales	–14,915

Source: Statistics Canada

Footnotes:
1. In the capital and financial account, a minus sign denotes an outflow of capital resulting from an increase in claims on non-residents or a decrease in liabilities to non-residents.

In this chapter we begin with a discussion of promissory notes and simple discount notes. We also look at the application of discounting with Treasury bills. The chapter concludes with an explanation of how to calculate the discounting of promissory notes.

LEARNING UNIT 13–1
STRUCTURE OF PROMISSORY NOTES; THE SIMPLE DISCOUNT NOTE

Although businesses frequently sign promissory notes, customers also sign promissory notes. For example, some student loans may require the signing of promissory notes. Appliance stores often ask customers to sign a promissory note when they buy large appliances on credit. As you will see in this Unit, promissory notes usually involve the payment of interest.

STRUCTURE OF PROMISSORY NOTES

To borrow money, you must find a lender (a bank or a company selling goods on credit). You must also be willing to pay for the use of the money. In Chapter 12 you learned that interest is the cost of borrowing money for periods of time.

Money lenders usually require that borrowers sign a **promissory note.** This note states that the borrower will repay a certain sum at a fixed time in the future. The note often includes the charge for the use of the money, or the rate of interest. Figure 13.1 shows a sample promissory note with its terms identified and defined. Take a moment to look at each term.

FIGURE 13–1
Interest-bearing promissory note

$10,000 a. OAKVILLE, ONTARIO *October 2, 2005* c.

Sixty days b. AFTER DATE *we* PROMISE TO PAY

TO THE ORDER OF *G. J. Equipment Company* d.

Ten thousand and 00/100--------------------DOLLARS.

PAYABLE AT *Soyuz Credit Union Limited*

VALUE RECEIVED WITH INTEREST AT 9% PER ANNUM e. REGAL CORPORATION f.

NO. *114* DUE *December 1, 2005* g.

J. M. Moore
TREASURER

a. **Face value:** Amount of money borrowed—$10,000. The face value is also the principal of the note.
b. **Term:** Length of time that the money is borrowed—60 days.
c. **Date:** The date that the note is issued—October 2, 2005.
d. **Payee:** The company extending the credit—G. J. Equipment Company.
e. **Rate:** The annual rate for the cost of borrowing the money—9% per annum.
f. **Maker:** The company issuing the note and borrowing the money—Regal Corporation.
g. **Maturity date:** The date the principal and interest rate are due—December 1, 2005.

In this section you will learn the difference between interest-bearing notes and non-interest-bearing notes.

Interest-Bearing Versus Non-Interest-Bearing Notes

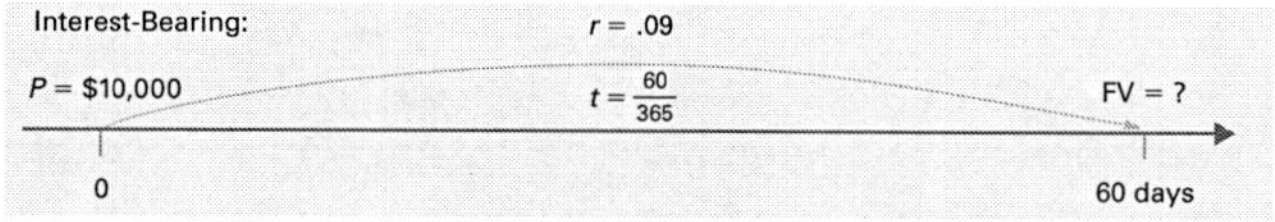

Interest = Face value (principal) × Rate × Time
Maturity value = Face value (principal) + Interest

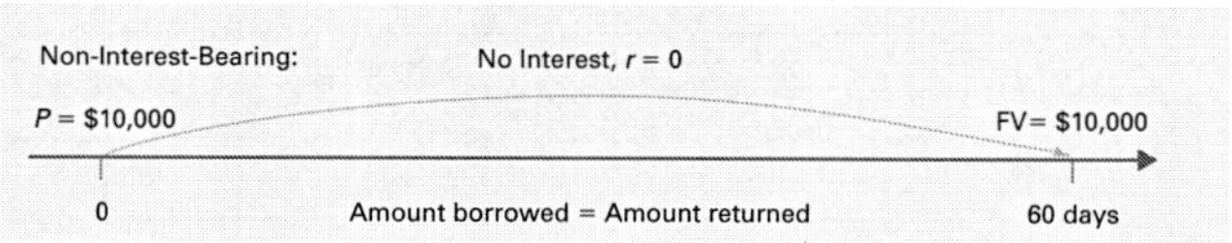

A promissory note can be interest-bearing or non-interest-bearing. To be **interest-bearing,** the note must state the rate of interest. Since the promissory note in Figure 13.1 states that its interest is 9%, it is an interest-bearing note. When the note matures, Regal Corporation will pay back the original amount (**face value**) borrowed plus interest. The simple interest formula (also known as the interest formula) and the maturity value formula from Chapter 12 are used for this transaction.

FV = $P(1 + rt)$, where P is the face value of a promissory note.

If you sign a **non-interest-bearing** promissory note for $10,000, you pay back $10,000 at maturity. The maturity value of a non-interest-bearing note is the same as its face value. Usually, non-interest-bearing notes occur for short time periods under special conditions. For example, money borrowed from a relative could be secured by a non-interest-bearing promissory note.

SIMPLE DISCOUNT NOTE

The total amount due at the end of the loan, the **maturity value** or future value of the loan (FV) is the sum of the face value (principal) and the interest. Let's study the example, and then you can review Table 13.1.

TABLE 13–1
SIMPLE INTEREST NOTE (CALCULATIONS FROM THE PETE RUNNELS EXAMPLE)

Simple interest note (Chapter 12)

1. A promissory note for a loan with a term of usually less than 1 year. *Example:* 60 days.
2. Paid back by one payment at maturity. Face value equals actual amount (or principal) of loan (this is not maturity value).
3. Interest computed on face value or what is actually borrowed. *Example:* $186.67
4. Maturity value = Face value + Interest. *Example:* $14,186.67.
5. Borrower receives the face value. *Example:* $14,000.
6. Effective rate (true rate is same as rate stated on note). *Example:* 8%.
7. Used frequently instead of the simple discount note. *Example:* 8%.

EXAMPLE

Pete Runnels has signed a note that has a face value (principal) of $14,000 for 60 days. The note has a simple interest rate of 8%. Calculate (a) interest owed, (b) maturity value, (c) proceeds, and (d) effective rate.

Simple interest note—Chapter 12

Interest

a. I = Face value (principal) × r × t

$$I = \$14{,}000 \times .08 \times \frac{60}{360}$$

$$I = \$186.67$$

Proceeds

c. Proceeds = Face value = $14,000

Maturity value

b. FV = Face value + Interest

FV = $14,000 + $186.67

FV = $14,186.67

Effective rate

d. $$\text{Rate} = \frac{\text{Interest}}{\text{Proceeds} \times \text{Time}} = \frac{\$186.67}{\$14{,}000 \times \frac{60}{360}} = 8\%$$

Treasury bills are sold biweekly by public tender on a discount basis to primary distributors of Government of Canada securities with terms to maturity of 12 months or less.

Source: Statistics Canada, 2003.

Application of Discounting—Treasury Bills

When the government needs money, it sells Treasury bills. A **Treasury bill** (or T-bill) is a short-term loan to the federal or provincial government (for a term less than 1 year).

The borrowing government sells its Treasury bills to lenders through auctions. The initial lenders who buy the T-bills are usually banks, investment dealers, and large financial institutions. The Bank of Canada acts as an agent for the government of Canada and manages T-bill auctions, which happen every second Tuesday. Individual investors can purchase Treasury bills from these financial institutions in amounts that are multiples of $1,000.

The Bank of Canada clipping here shows T-bill auctions, average **yields** (or **rates of return**) for one month, three months, six months, and one year. On March, 25, 2003, the rate of return per year (abbreviated *p.a.* for *per annum,* which means "per year") on the 6-month T-bills

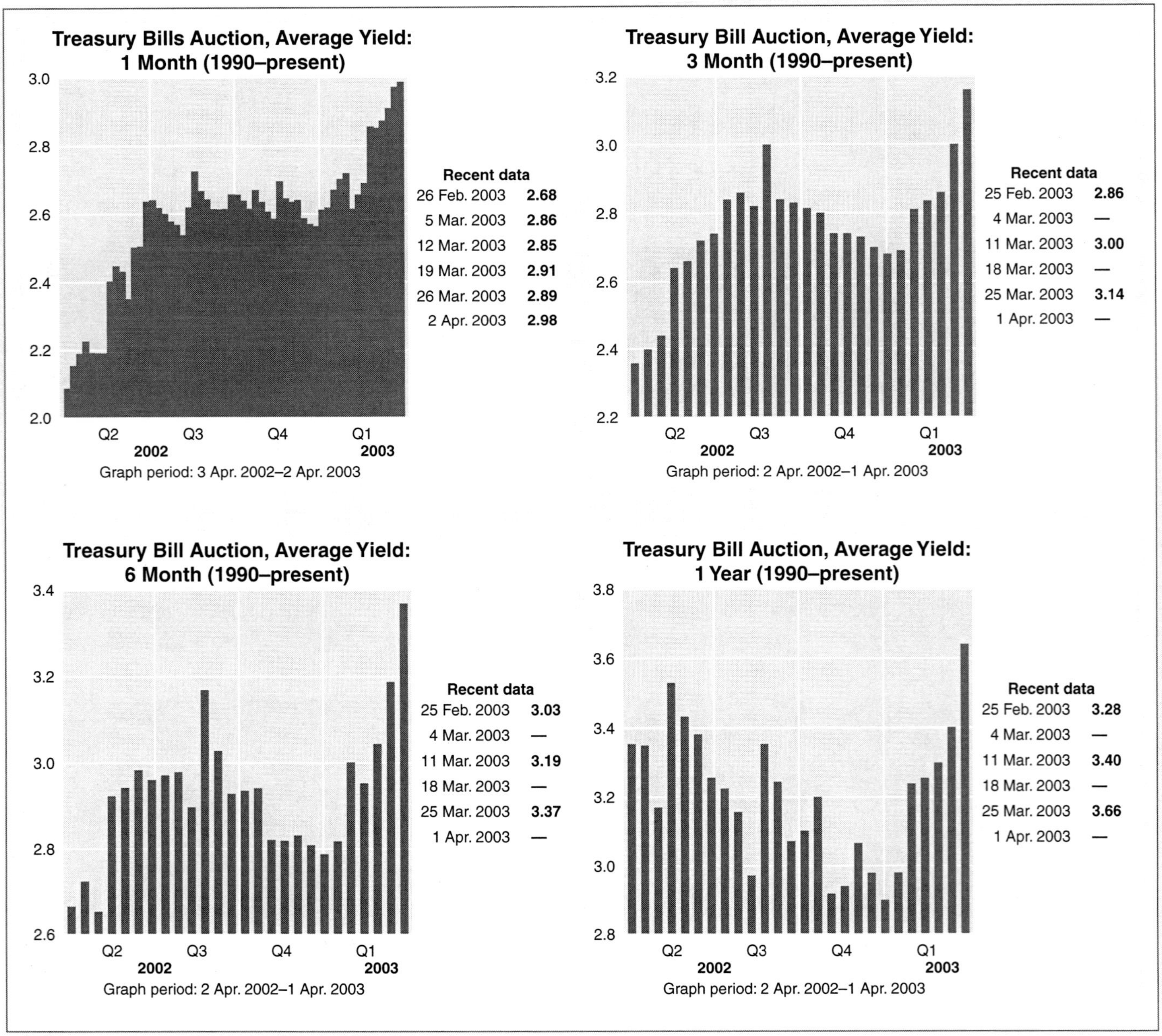

Source: 2003 Bank of Canada.

TABLE 13–2
RATES OF RETURN (YIELD) OF TREASURY BILLS ON MARCH 25, 2003

Term (time remaining until maturity)	Yield (rate of return) p.a.
1 month	2.89%
3 months	3.14%
6 months	3.37%
1 year	3.66%

was 3.37%, on the 3-month bills it was 3.14%, and on the one-month bills it was 2.89%. This data is presented in Table 13.2.

"Three months," "six months," and "one year" indicate the time remaining until maturity. These time periods are actually calculated in days: for three-month T-bills the time remaining until maturity is 98 days; for six-month T-bills it is 182 days.

Because a new issue **(tranche)** of six-month T-bills may be sold at the second biweekly auction, the remaining time until maturity may be only 168 days (182 − 14 = 168). Remember that when we discuss six-month T-bills the term may be either 182 or 168 days.

It is very important to understand that the **face value** of a Treasury bill is the amount redeemable at maturity. In other words, if you purchased a $10,000 182-day T-bill today, you would get $10,000 back on the maturity date, 182 days from now. To buy this T-bill you paid a present value of $10,000 today. To calculate the **market price** or **market value of a T-bill** you must *discount* the face value at its rate of return. The price of a T-bill is a present value of its face value.

For example, the price for a $10,000 six-month (182-day) Treasury bill will be $9,834.74:

$$\text{Price} = \text{Present value of } \$10{,}000 \text{ discounted at } 3.37\% \text{ for } 182 \text{ days}$$

$$\text{Price} = \frac{\$10{,}000}{\left(1 + .0337 \times \dfrac{182}{365}\right)} = \$9{,}834.74$$

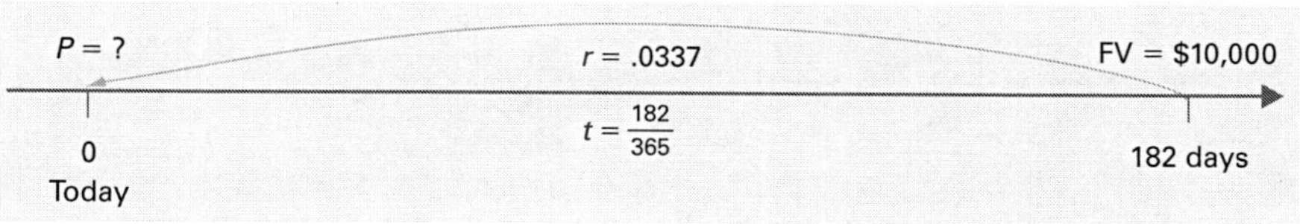

Now it's time to try the Practice Quiz and check your progress.

LU 13–1 PRACTICE QUIZ

1. Warren Ford borrowed $12,000 on a non-interest-bearing, $9\frac{1}{2}\%$, 60-day note. Assume exact interest. What are **(a)** the maturity value, **(b)** the bank's discount, and **(c)** Warren's proceeds?
2. Jane Long buys a $10,000, 3-month Treasury bill. How much does she pay for it? Use rates from Table 13.2.

LEARNING UNIT 13–2
DISCOUNTING AN INTEREST-BEARING NOTE BEFORE MATURITY

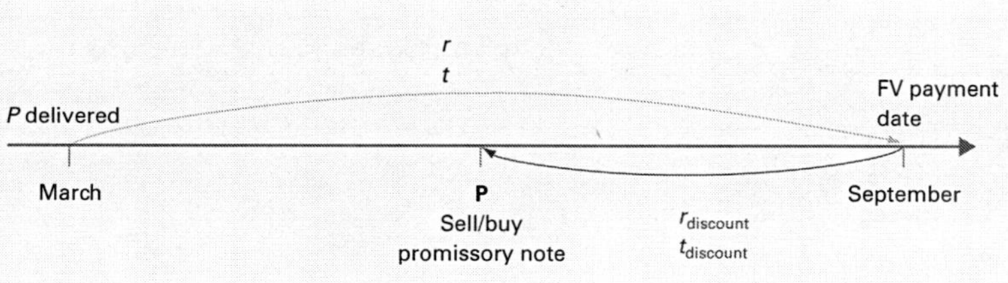

Manufacturers frequently deliver merchandise to retail companies and do not request payment for several months. For example, Roger Company manufactures outdoor furniture that it delivers to Sears in March. Payment for the furniture is not due until September. Roger will have its money tied up in this furniture until September. So Roger requests that Sears sign promissory notes.

If Roger Company needs cash sooner than September, what can it do? Roger Company can take one of its promissory notes to the bank, assuming the company that signed the note is reliable. The bank will buy the note from Roger. Now Roger has discounted the note and has cash instead of waiting until September when Sears would have paid Roger.

Remember that when Roger Company discounts the promissory note to the bank, the company agrees to pay the note at maturity if the maker of the promissory note fails to pay the bank. The potential liability that may or may not result from discounting a note is called a **contingent liability.**

Think of **discounting a note** as a three-party arrangement. Roger Company realizes that the bank will charge for this service. The bank's charge is a **bank discount.** The actual amount Roger receives is the **proceeds** of the note, **P.** The four steps below and the formulas in the example that follows will help you understand this discounting process.

DISCOUNTING A NOTE

Step 1. Calculate the maturity value of the promissory note (Amount borrowed *or* Present value + Interest).
Step 2. Calculate the **discount period** (time the bank holds note).
Step 3. Calculate the proceeds (value of the promissory note on the specific date of sale to the bank).
Step 4. Calculate the bank discount.

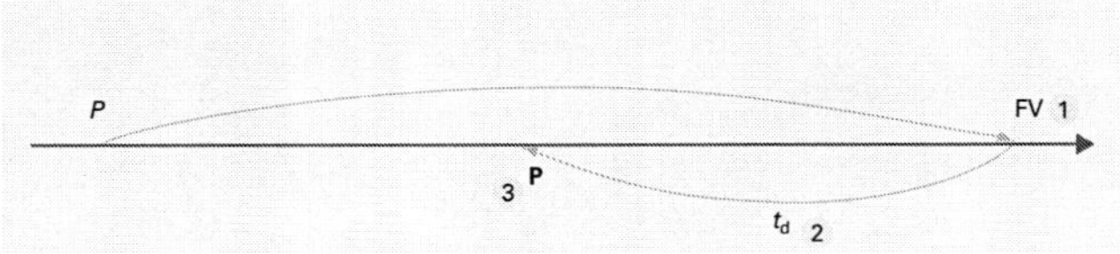

EXAMPLE

Roger Company sold the following promissory note to the bank:

Date of note	Face value of note	Length of note	Interest rate	Bank discount rate	Date of discount
March 8	$2,000	185 days	10%	9%	August 9

What are Roger's (1) interest and maturity or face value (FV)? (2) What is the discount period? (3) What are the proceeds? (4) What is the bank discount?

1. *Calculate Roger's interest and maturity value (FV):*

FV = Face value (principal) + Interest

$$\text{Interest} = \$2{,}000 \times .10 \times \frac{185}{365} \quad \leftarrow \text{Exact number of days over 365}$$

$$= \$101.37$$

$$\text{FV} = \$2{,}000 + \$101.37 \quad \text{or} \quad \text{FV} = P(1 + rt)$$
$$= \$2{,}101.37$$

2. *Calculate discount period:* Determine the number of days that the bank will have to wait for the note to come due (discount period).

August 9	221 days
March 8	− 67
	154 days passed before note is discounted
	185 days
	−154
	31 days bank waits for note to come due

Calculating days without table:

March	31
	− 8
	23
April	30
May	31
June	30
July	31
August	9
	154

185 days—length of note
−154 days Roger held note
31 days bank waits

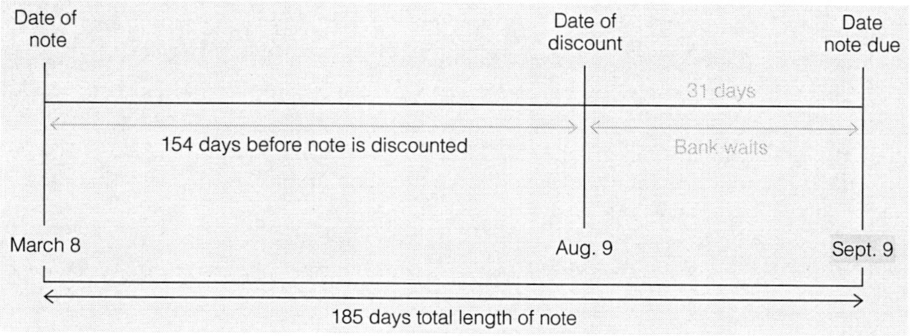

3. *Calculate proceeds:*

$$\text{Proceeds} = \frac{FV}{(1 + rt)} = \frac{\$2{,}101.37}{\left(1 + .09 \times \frac{31}{365}\right)} = \$2{,}085.43$$

If Roger had waited until September 9, it would have received $2,101.37. Now, in August 9, Roger receives $2,000 plus $85.43 interest.

4. *Calculate bank discount (charge):*

Bank discount (charge) = FV − Proceeds

Xerox Taps $7 Billion Line of Bank Credit

Firm Denies Cash Crunch, As It Responds to Surge In Its Trading Volume

By JOHN HECHINGER
And JOSEPH PEREIRA
Staff Reporters of THE WALL STREET JOURNAL

Xerox Corp. tapped a $7 billion line of bank credit for the first time after its borrowing was constrained in the commercial paper market.

The No. 1 copying-machine maker also issued a statement denying it was in a cash crunch and said that it had plenty of borrowing room. Xerox was responding to a surge in trading Friday that hurt its already struggling stock. The activity was touched off by speculation that it was headed toward a court filing to seek protection from creditors.

Source: © 2000 Dow Jones & Company, Inc.

Now let's assume Roger Company received a non-interest-bearing note. Then we follow the four steps for discounting a note except the maturity value is the amount of the loan. No interest accumulates on a non-interest-bearing note. Today, many banks use simple interest instead of discounting. Also, instead of discounting notes, many companies set up *lines of credit* so that additional financing is immediately available.

The *Wall Street Journal* clipping "Xerox Taps $7 Billion Line of Bank Credit" reports that for the first time, Xerox tapped a $7 billion line of credit. (The company denies that tapping this line of credit was necessary because of a cash crunch.)

It is time to test your understanding of this Unit with the following Practice Quiz.

LU 13–2 PRACTICE QUIZ

Date of note	Face value (principal) of note	Length of note	Interest rate	Bank discount rate	Date of discount
April 8	$35,000	160 days	11%	9%	June 8

From the above, calculate **(a)** interest and maturity value, **(b)** discount period, **(c)** proceeds, and **(d)** bank discount. Assume exact interest.

CHAPTER ORGANIZER AND REFERENCE GUIDE

Topic	Key point, procedure, formula	Example(s) to illustrate situation
Bank discount, p. 319	Bank discount (interest) = FV × Bank discount rate × Time or FV − **P** Interest based on amount paid back and not what received. FV = $P(1 + rt)$	$\$6{,}000 \times .09 \times \frac{60}{360} = \$90$ or $6,000 − $5,910 = $90 Borrower receives $5,910 (the proceeds) and pays back $6,000 at maturity after 60 days. A Treasury bill is a good example of a simple discount note.
Effective rate, p. 319	$\text{Rate} = \frac{\text{Interest}}{\text{Proceeds} \times \text{Time}}$	
Proceeds, p. 319	What borrower receives (Face value − Discount) $\mathbf{P} = \frac{FV}{(1 + r_d t_d)}$	*Example:* $10,000 note, discount rate 12% for 60 days. Amount borrower received, $\mathbf{P} = \frac{\$10{,}000}{\left(1 + .12 \times \frac{60}{365}\right)} = \$9{,}806.56$
Discounting an interest-bearing note, p. 319	1. Calculate interest and maturity value. I = Face value × Rate × Time FV = Face value + Interest 2. Calculate number of days bank will wait for note to come due (discount period). 3. Calculate proceeds. $\mathbf{P} = \frac{FV}{(1 + r_d t_d)}$ 4. Calculate bank discount (bank charge). Bank discount = FV − **P**	*Example:* $1,000 note, 6%, 60-day, dated November 1 and discounted on December 1 at 8%. 1. $I = \$1{,}000 \times .06 \times \frac{60}{365} = \$9.86$ FV = $1,000 + $9.86 = $1,009.86 2. 30 days 3. $\mathbf{P} = \frac{\$1{,}009.86}{\left(1 + .08 \times \frac{30}{365}\right)} = \$1{,}003.26$ 4. Bank discount = FV − **P** $1,009.86 − $1,003.26 = $6.60
Key terms	Contingent liability, p. 322 Date, p. 318 Discounting a note, p. 322 Discount period, p. 322 Effective rate, p. 319 Face value, p. 321 Interest-bearing note, p. 319 Maker, p. 318 Market price/value of T-bill, p. 321 Maturity date, p. 318 Maturity value (FV), p. 319 Non-interest-bearing note, p. 319 Payee, p. 318 Proceeds (**P**), p. 322	Promissory note, p. 318 Rate of return, p. 320 Term, p. 318 Treasury bill, p. 320 Tranche, p. 321 Yield, p. 320

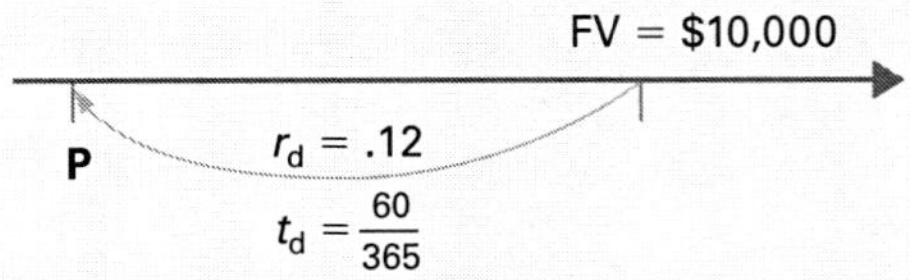

CRITICAL THINKING DISCUSSION QUESTIONS

1. What are the differences between an interest-bearing note and a non-interest-bearing note? Which type of note would you prefer to sign? Why?
2. What are the four steps of the discounting process? Could the proceeds of a discounted note be less than the face value of the note?
3. What is a line of credit? What could be a disadvantage of having a large credit line?

END-OF-CHAPTER PROBLEMS

DRILL PROBLEMS

Complete the following table for these simple discount notes. Use the exact interest method.

	Amount due at maturity	Discount rate	Time	Bank discount	Proceeds
13–1.	$18,000	$4\frac{3}{4}$%	190 days	?	?
13–2.	$6,000	$7\frac{1}{4}$%	240 days	?	?

Calculate the discount period for the bank to wait to receive its money:

	Date of note	Length of note	Date note discounted	Discount period
13–3.	April 12	45 days	May 2	?
13–4.	March 7	120 days	June 8	?

Solve for maturity value, discount period, bank discount, and proceeds (assume for Problems 13–5 and 13–6 a bank discount rate of 9%).

	P Face value (principal)	*r* Rate of interest	*t* Length of note	FV Maturity value	Date of note	Date note discounted	t_d Discount period	Bank discount	P Proceeds
13–5.	$50,000	11%	95 days	?	June 10	July 18	?	?	?
13–6.	$25,000	9%	60 days	?	June 8	July 10	?	?	?

13–7. Calculate the present price of a $10,000 Treasury bill, 6% for 3 months.

ADDITIONAL DRILL PROBLEMS

13–8. Identify each of the following characteristics of promissory notes with an **I** for simple interest note, a **D** for simple discount note, or a **B** if it is true for both.

__ Interest is computed on face value, or what is actually borrowed.
__ A promissory note for a loan usually less than 1 year.
__ Borrower receives proceeds = Face value − Bank discount.
__ Maturity value = Face value + Interest.
__ Maturity value = Face value.
__ Borrower receives the face value.
__ Paid back by one payment at maturity.
__ Interest computed on maturity value, or what will be repaid, and not on actual amount borrowed.

13–9. Find the bank discount and the proceeds for the following (assume 365 days):

	Maturity value	Discount rate	Time (days)	Bank discount	Proceeds
a.	$7,000	9%	60	?	?
b.	$4,550	8.1%	110	?	?
c.	$19,350	12.7%	55	?	?
d.	$63,400	10%	90	?	?
e.	$13,490	7.9%	200	?	?
f.	$780	$12\frac{1}{2}$%	65	?	?

13–10. Calculate the maturity value for each of the following promissory notes (use 365 days):

	Date of note	Principal of note	Length of note (days)	Interest rate	Maturity value
a.	April 12	$4,800	135	10%	?
b.	August 23	$15,990	85	13%	?
c.	December 10	$985	30	11.5%	?

13–11. Find the maturity date and the discount period for the following; assume no leap years.

	Date of note	Length of note (days)	Date of discount	Maturity date	Discount period
a.	March 11	200	June 28	?	?
b.	January 22	60	March 2	?	?
c.	April 19	85	June 6	?	?
d.	November 17	120	February 15	?	?

WORD PROBLEMS

Use future and present value formulas and show time line diagrams for each of the following problems.

13–12. Excel Matt French borrowed $9,000 for 150 days from Lee Bank. The bank discounted the note at 7%. What proceeds does Matt receive?

13–13. Jack Tripper signed a $9,000 note at Fleet Bank. Fleet charges a $9\frac{1}{4}$% discount rate. If the loan is for 200 days, find the proceeds.

13–14. On June 19, 2003, a financial source reported on short-term Bank of Canada securities. The 3-month interest rate was the lowest in the past 7 years. The Bank of Canada sold $14 billion in 3-month bills at a discount rate of 3.435%. An additional $12 billion were sold in 6-month bills at a rate of 3.38%. **(a)** What amount did the Bank receive for the 3-month bills? **(b)** What amount did the Bank receive for the 6-month bills? (Use a 182-day term.)

13–15. On September 5, Sheffield Company discounted at Sunshine Bank a $9,000 (maturity value), 120-day note dated June 5. Sunshine's discount rate was 9%. What proceeds did Sheffield Company receive?

13–16. On May 16, 2001, the *Columbus Ledger-Enquirer* reported that Sun Trust Bank lowered interest from 7.5% to 7%. Joe Carter, a manufacturer of electric generators, sold $9,880 of goods to Browns Electronics. Browns signed a 90-day promissory note with a maturity value of $10,015.85. Browns decided to discount the note at Sun Trust. The loan has 40 days left to maturity. **(a)** What proceeds will Joe receive with the new rate? **(b)** What proceeds would Joe have received if Sun Trust hadn't lowered its interest rate?

13–17. Annika Scholten bought a $10,000, 3-month Treasury bill at 4%. How much did she pay for it? Round to the nearest cent. Use 98 days.

13–18. Ron Prentice bought goods from Shelly Katz. On May 8, Shelly gave Ron a time extension on his bill by accepting a $3,000, 8%, 180-day note. On August 16, Shelly discounted the note at Roseville Bank at 9%. What proceeds does Shelly Katz receive?

13–19. Excel Rex Corporation accepted a $5,000, 8%, 120-day note dated August 8 from Regis Company in settlement of a past bill. On October 11, Rex discounted the note at Park Bank at 9%. What are the note's maturity value, discount period, and bank discount? What proceeds does Rex receive?

13–20. On May 12, Scott Rinse accepted an $8,000, 12%, 90-day note for a time extension of a bill for goods bought by Ron Prentice. On June 12, Scott discounted the note at Able Bank at 10%. What proceeds does Scott receive?

13–21. Hafers, an electrical supply company, sold $4,800 of equipment to Jim Coates Wiring, Inc. Coates signed a promissory note May 12 with 4.5% interest. The due date was August 10. Short of funds, Hafers contacted Charter One Bank on July 20; the bank agreed to take over the note at a 6.2% discount. What proceeds will Hafers receive?

ADDITIONAL WORD PROBLEMS

Assume 365 days.

13–22. Mary Smith signed a $7,500 note for 135 days at a discount rate of 13%. Find the discount and the proceeds Mary received.

13–23. The Salem Cooperative Bank charges an $8\frac{3}{4}\%$ discount rate. What are the discount and the proceeds for a $16,200 note for 60 days?

13–24. Bill Jackson is planning to buy a used car. He went to City Credit Union to take out a loan for $6,400 for 300 days. If the credit union charges a discount rate of $11\frac{1}{2}\%$, what will the proceeds of this loan be?

13–25. Mike Drislane goes to the bank and signs a note for $9,700. The bank charges a 15% discount rate. Find the discount and the proceeds if the loan is for 210 days.

13–26. Connors Company received a $4,000, 90-day, 10% note dated April 6 from one of its customers. Connors Company held the note until May 16, when the company discounted it at a bank at a discount rate of 12%. What were the proceeds that Connors Company received?

13–27. Souza & Sons accepted a 9%, $22,000, 120-day note from one of its customers on July 22. On October 2, the company discounted the note at TD Bank. The discount rate was 12%. What were **(a)** the bank discount and **(b)** the proceeds?

13–28. The Fargate Store accepted an $8,250, 75-day, 9% note from one of its customers on March 18. Fargate's discounted the note at Royal Bank at $9\frac{1}{2}\%$ on March 29. What proceeds did Fargate receive?

13–29. On June 4, Johnson Company received from Marty Russo a 30-day, 11% note for $720 to settle Russo's debt. On June 17, Johnson discounted the note at Royal Bank whose discount rate was 15%. What proceeds did Johnson receive?

13–30. On December 15, Lawlers Company went to the bank and discounted a 10%, 90-day, $14,000 note dated October 21. The bank charged a discount rate of 12%. What were the proceeds of the note?

CHALLENGE PROBLEMS

13–31. Three-month Treasury bills totalling $12 billion were sold in $10,000 denominations at a discount rate of 3.605%. In addition, the Bank of Canada sold 6-month bills totalling $10 billion at a discount rate of 3.55%. **(a)** What is the discount amount for 3-month bills? **(b)** What is the discount amount for 6-month bills? **(c)** What is the effective rate for 3-month bills? Use 98 days. **(d)** What is the effective rate for 6-month bills? Round to nearest hundredth percent.

13–32. Tina Mier must pay a $2,000 furniture bill. A finance company will loan Tina $2,000 for 8 months at a 9% discount rate. The finance company told Tina that if she wants to receive exactly $2,000, she must borrow more than $2,000. The company gave Tina the following formula:

$$\text{What to ask for} = \frac{\text{Amount in cash to be received}}{1 - (\text{Discount rate} \times \text{Time of loan})}$$

Calculate Tina's loan request.

SUMMARY PRACTICE TEST

1. On July 10, Sapient Corporation accepted a $130,000, 90-day, non-interest-bearing note from Link.com. What is the maturity value of the note? (p. 319)
2. The face value of a simple discount note is $7,000. The discount is 6% for 95 days. Calculate the following. (p. 319)
   a. Amount of interest charged for each note.
   b. Amount borrower would receive.
   c. Amount payee would receive at maturity.
3. On August 5, Jeff Jones accepted a $30,000, 8%, 160-day note from Dick Hercher. On October 5, Bill Flynn discounted the note at Roger Bank at 9%. What proceeds did Jeff receive? (p. 319)
4. Angle.com accepted a $40,000, $9\frac{1}{4}$%, 120-day note on August 18. Angle discounts the note on September 25 at Rio Bank at 9%. What proceeds did Angle receive? (p. 319)
5. The owner of Pete.com signed a $20,000 note at See Bank. See charges a $7\frac{1}{2}$% discount rate. If the loan is for 160 days, find the proceeds. (p. 319)
6. John Tobey buys a $10,000, 3-month Treasury bill at a discount of $5\frac{1}{2}$%. What is the effective rate? How much does he pay for the bill? Use 98 days. (p. 320)

SOLUTIONS TO PRACTICE QUIZZES

LU 13–1

1. a. Maturity value = Face value = $12,000
   b. Bank discount = FV × Bank discount rate × Time

$$= \$12{,}000 \times .095 \times \frac{60}{365}$$

$$= \$187.40$$

   c. Proceeds = FV − Bank discount
   = $12,000 − $187.40
   = $11,812.60

2. $$\text{Price} = \frac{\$10{,}000}{\left(1 + .0314 \times \frac{98}{365}\right)} = \$9{,}916.40$$

LU 13–2

a. $$\left.\begin{aligned} I &= \$35{,}000 \times .11 \times \frac{160}{365} = \$1{,}687.67 \\ FV &= \$35{,}000 + 1{,}687.67 = \$36{,}687.67 \end{aligned}\right\} \text{ or } \$35{,}000\left(1 + .11 \times \frac{160}{365}\right) = \$36{,}687.67$$

b. Discount period = 160 − 61 = 99 days.

April	30
	− 8
	22
May	+ 31
	53
June	+ 8
	61

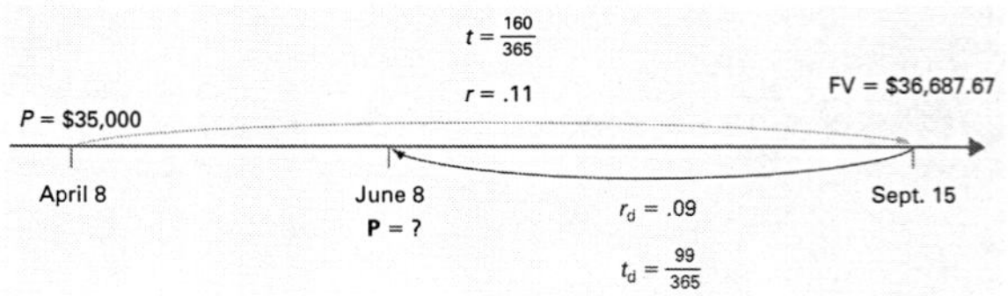

c. $$P = \frac{\$36{,}687.67}{\left(1 + .09 \times \frac{99}{365}\right)} = \$35{,}813.43$$

d. Bank discount (charge) = $36,687.67 − $35,813.43 = $874.24

Putting Your Skills to Work

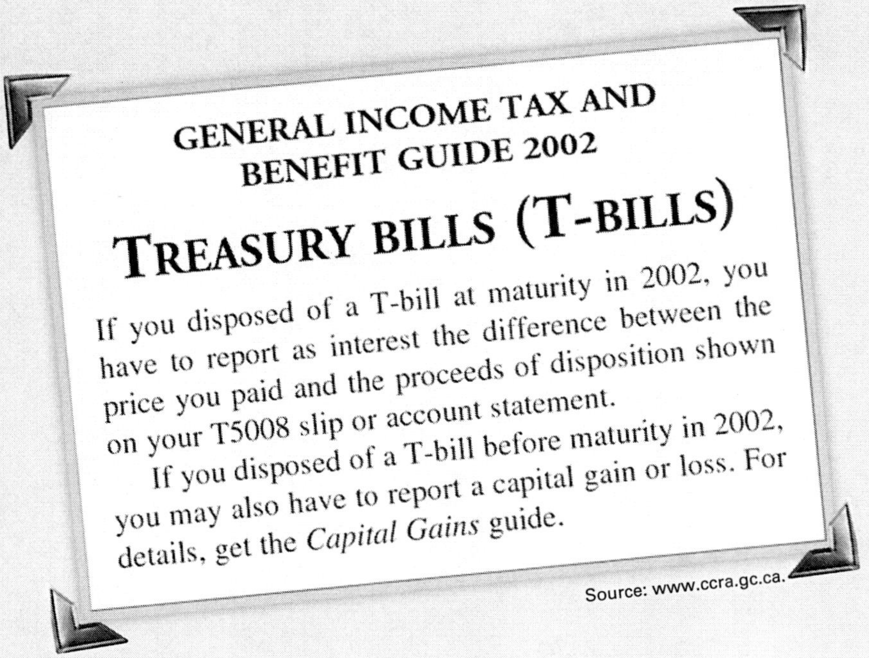

GENERAL INCOME TAX AND BENEFIT GUIDE 2002

TREASURY BILLS (T-BILLS)

If you disposed of a T-bill at maturity in 2002, you have to report as interest the difference between the price you paid and the proceeds of disposition shown on your T5008 slip or account statement.

If you disposed of a T-bill before maturity in 2002, you may also have to report a capital gain or loss. For details, get the *Capital Gains* guide.

Source: www.ccra.gc.ca.

PROJECT A

Discuss what is said in the statement. How will you calculate and report the interest?

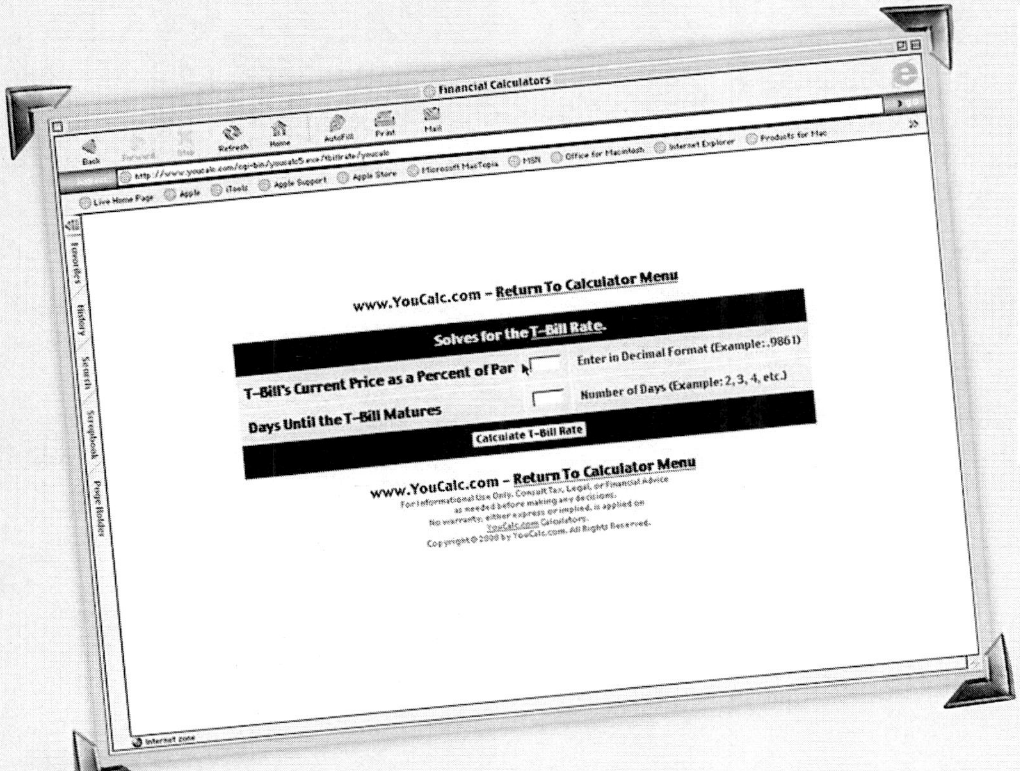

PROJECT B

Go to www.youcalc.com/cgi-bin/youcalc5.exe/tbillrate/youcalc. Assume that you paid $9,875 for a 91-day Treasury bill with a $10,000 face value. Use the T-bill rate calculator to find the effective yield rounded to the nearest hundredth percent. You should calculate the ratio of the price paid to the face value in decimal format.

Compound Interest:

Present Value; Future Value; Equivalent Payments; Effective, Nominal, and Equivalent Interest Rates

14

Conseco Removes Two Directors Who Failed to Pay Back Loans

By Joseph T. Hallinan
Staff Reporter of The Wall Street Journal

Conseco Inc. said it removed two of its directors after they failed to repay more than $130 million of company-backed loans used to buy Conseco stock.

The removals suggest new Conseco Chief Executive Gary C. Wendt is taking a tough stance in handling the effects of a disastrous stock-purchase program initiated under his predecessor, Stephen C. Hilbert. The program called for Conseco to guarantee $557.6 million of bank loans to 170 current and former directors, officers and employees to buy 19 million company shares. In addition, the Carmel, Ind., finance and insurance company provided $79.2 million of loans to participants to cover interest payments on the bank loans.

But a subsequent misguided acquisition and other bad moves sent Conseco ...

... cism from outsiders that board members found it difficult to function.

"It became a dysfunctional board when you had this kind of issue on the table," Mr. Mutz said. "We took the position that it was difficult for a director to be totally independent and still owe the company large sums of money." He said all directors who borrowed money under the program—including himself—were asked to repay their loans or leave the board.

Mr. Mutz, who paid his debt, said Dr. Decatur and Mr. Murray declined to do either. After a resolution was proposed by Mr. Wendt, the board voted to remove Dr. Decatur and Mr. Murray.

Asked if Dr. Decatur and Mr. Murray didn't pay off their loans because they couldn't afford to do so, Mr. Mutz said, "I think that's fair to say."

"Some of the people invol...

Source: © 2000 Dow Jones & Company, Inc.

LEARNING UNIT OBJECTIVES

LU 14–1: Basic Concepts, Terminology, and Time Line Diagrams

- Present the timing and amount of payments using a time line diagram (p. 332).

LU 14–2: Compound Interest (Future Value)—The Big Picture

- Compare simple interest with compound interest (p. 335).
- Calculate compound amount and interest manually (p. 335).

LU 14–3: Present Value—The Big Picture

- Compare present value (PV) with compound interest (FV) (p. 338).
- Compute present value (p. 339).

LU 14–4: Equivalent Payments

- Compute the equivalent value of a single payment or serial payments on any date (p. 340).

LU 14–5: Effective Interest Rate

- Explain and compute the effective rate (p. 342).
- Define an effective interest rate when a nominal interest rate is given (p. 342).

LU 14–6: Equivalent Interest Rates

- Compute the equivalent interest rate when a nominal interest rate is given (p. 344).

Confused by Investing?" asks the following *Wall Street Journal* clipping. Read it carefully. It explains how money increases when you invest. The important word is *compounding*. See also Figure 14.1.

CONFUSED BY INVESTING?

If there's something about your investment portfolio that doesn't seem to add up, maybe you should check your math.

Lots of folks are perplexed by the mathematics of investing, so I thought a refresher course might help. Here's a look at some key concepts:

■ 10 Plus 10 is 21

Imagine you invest \$100, which earns 10% this year and 10% next. How much have you made? If you answered 21%, go to the head of the class.

Here's how the math works. This year's 10% gain turns your \$100 into \$110. Next year, you also earn 10%, but you start the year with \$110. Result? You earn \$11, boosting your wealth to \$121.

Thus, your portfolio has earned a *cumulative* 21% return over two years, but the *annualized* return is just 10%. The fact that 21% is more than double 10% can be attributed to the effect of investment compounding, the way that you earn money each year not only on your original investment, but also on earnings from prior years that you've reinvested.

■ The Rule of 72

To get a feel for compounding, try the rule of 72. What's that? If you divide a particular annual return into 72, you'll find out how many years it will take to double your money. Thus, at 10% a year, an investment will double in value in a tad over seven years.

Source: © 1996 Dow Jones & Company, Inc.

FIGURE 14–1

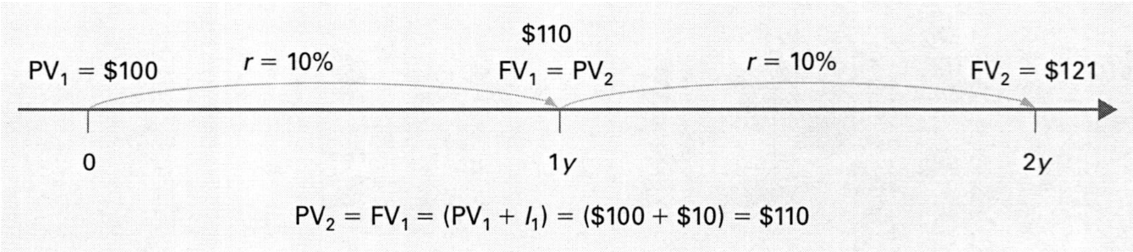

$$\text{Doubling time (years)} \approx \frac{72}{\text{Annual rate of return (\%)}} \qquad \textbf{(14.1)}$$

$$\text{Doubling time} \approx \frac{72}{10\%} \approx 7 \text{ years}$$

LEARNING UNIT 14–1

BASIC CONCEPTS, TERMINOLOGY, AND TIME LINE DIAGRAMS

Sometimes we want to quickly find out how long it would take to double an investment at a certain annual interest rate. For an estimate of this time period, we may use the "Rule of 72," as shown in the following example.

EXAMPLE

Mrs. Percival intends to invest \$12,000 at 8% a year. How long will it take for her money to double?

To answer a question like this, simply find out how many times the interest rate goes into 72. In this case:

$$T_{\text{doubled}} = \frac{72}{8} = 9 \text{ years} \qquad \textbf{(14.1)}$$

At an annual rate of 8% per year it will take nine years for Mrs. Percival to double her initial investment amount.

In this chapter you will also be introduced to a compound interest method and learn new terms, such as *compounding period; periodic, nominal, effective,* and *equivalent interest rate;* and *compounding frequency.*

Upon completion of this chapter you will be able to calculate present and future values of an investment or of a debt; define timing and amount of payments; determine nominal, periodic, equivalent, and effective interest rates to compare different nominal rates and compare investment opportunities; determine values at different points in time; and compute equivalent payments using formulas and calculators. You will be able to use time line diagrams to illustrate the compounding process, and also for solutions of word problems and practice exercises.

LU 14–1 PRACTICE QUIZ

Assess quickly how long it will take to double a principal of $5,000 at these different investment options:

1. 4% annually
2. 6% annually
3. 1.5% annually

LEARNING UNIT 14–2
COMPOUND INTEREST (FUTURE VALUE)—THE BIG PICTURE

So far we have discussed only simple interest, which is interest on the principal alone. Simple interest is either paid at the end of the loan period or deducted in advance. From the chapter introduction, you know that interest can also be compounded.

Compounding involves the calculation of interest periodically over the life of the loan (or investment). After each calculation, the interest is added to the principal. Future calculations are on the adjusted principal (old principal plus interest [$FV_1 + I$]). **Compound interest,** then, is the interest on the principal plus the interest of prior periods. **Future value (FV),** or the **compound amount,** is the final amount of the loan or investment at the end of the last period. Now, at the beginning of this Unit, do not be concerned with how to calculate compounding but try to understand the meaning of compounding.

Figure 14.2 shows how $1 will grow if it is calculated for 4 years at 8% annually. This means that the interest is calculated on the balance once a year. In Figure 14.2, we start with $1, which is the **present value (PV).** After year 1, the dollar with interest is worth $1.08. At the end of year 2, the dollar is worth $1.17. By the end of year 4, the dollar is worth $1.36. (See also Figure 14.3.) Note how we start with the present and look to see what the dollar will be worth in the future. *Compounding goes from present value to future value.*

FIGURE 14–2
Future value of $1 at 8% for four periods

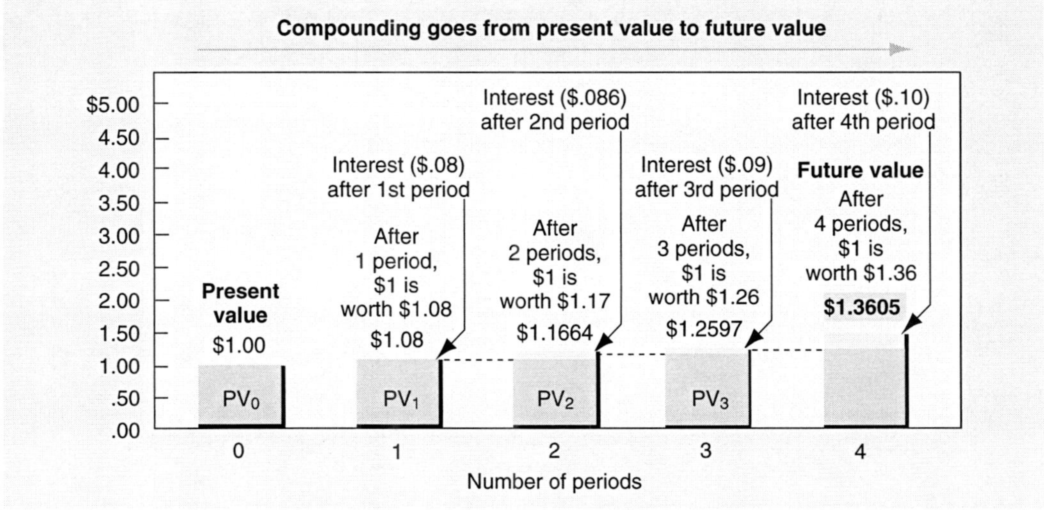

FIGURE 14–3

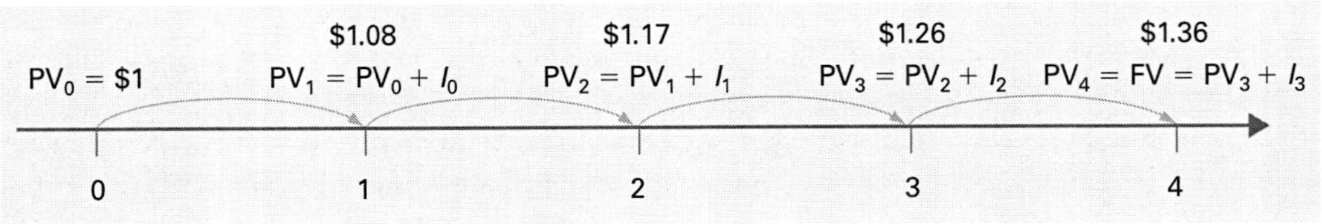

Before you learn how to calculate compound interest and compare it to simple interest, you must understand the terms that follow. These terms are also used in Chapter 15.

The term m is used for the compounding frequency per year or number of compounding periods per 1 year:

- **Compounded annually:** Interest calculated on the balance once a year. $m = 1$
- **Compounded semiannually:** Interest calculated on the balance every 6 months or every $\frac{1}{2}$ year. $m = 2$
- **Compounded quarterly:** Interest calculated on the balance every 3 months or every $\frac{1}{4}$ year. $m = 4$
- **Compounded monthly:** Interest calculated on the balance each month. $m = 12$
- **Compounded daily:** Interest calculated on the balance each day. $m = 365$
- ***n*: Number of periods** per term of investment/loan, equal to the number of years multiplied by the number of times the interest is compounded per year:

$$\boxed{n = m \times t} \qquad \textbf{(14.2)}$$

where m = Compounding frequency per year
n = Number of compounding periods per term of investment/loan
t = Term of investment/loan, in years

For example, if you compound $1 for 4 years at 8% annually, semiannually, or quarterly, the following compounding periods per term will result:

	$t \times m =$	n
Annually:	4 years × 1 =	4 periods
Semiannually:	4 years × 2 =	8 periods
Quarterly:	4 years × 4 =	16 periods

Simple interest is quoted as a certain percent per year ("9%"); compound interest, on the other hand, is quoted with two parts: an **annual interest rate,** also called the **nominal interest rate** (j), and a **compounding frequency** (m). For example:

"8% compounded quarterly" means $j = 8\%$ and $m = 4$
"10% compounded weekly" means $j = 10\%$ and $m = 52$

A nominal rate of 12% compounded monthly means, in effect, that 1% of interest is earned on the investment or loan every month. This effective interest rate per compounding period is called the **periodic interest rate** (i). It is calculated as:

$$i = \frac{j}{m} \qquad \textbf{(14.3)}$$

To calculate the nominal interest rate when the periodic interest rate and compounding frequency are given, multiply these values. Thus:

$$j = i \times m \qquad \textbf{(14.4)}$$

Using these formulas we can calculate periodic and nominal interest rates.

The following example will illustrate how compounding changes the interest rate for annual, semiannual, and quarterly periods:

Annually:	8% ÷ 1 = 8%
Semiannually:	8% ÷ 2 = 4%
Quarterly:	8% ÷ 4 = 2%

Note that both the number of periods (4) and the rate (8%) for the annual example did not change. You will see later that rate and periods (not years) will always change unless interest is compounded yearly.

Now you are ready to learn more about the difference between simple interest and compound interest.

Simple Versus Compound Interest

The following three situations of Bill Smith will clarify the difference between simple interest and compound interest.

Situation 1: Calculating Simple Interest and Maturity Value

Example

Bill Smith deposited $80 in a savings account for 4 years at an annual interest rate of 8%. What is Bill's simple interest?

To calculate simple interest, we use the following simple interest formula:

Interest (I) = Principal (P) × Rate (r) × Time (t)

$25.60 = $80 × .08 × 4

In 4 years Bill receives a total of $105.60 ($80 + $25.60)—principal plus simple interest.

Now let's look at the interest Bill would earn if the bank compounded Bill's interest on his savings.

Situation 2: Calculating Compound Amount and Interest without Tables[1]

You can use the following steps to calculate the compound amount and the interest manually:

CALCULATING COMPOUND AMOUNT AND INTEREST MANUALLY

Step 1. Calculate the simple interest and add it to the principal. Use this total to figure next year's interest.

Step 2. Repeat for the total number of periods.

Step 3. Compound amount − Principal = Compound interest.

Example

Bill Smith deposited $80 in a savings account for 4 years at an annual compounded rate of 8%. What are Bill's compound amount and interest?

The following shows how the compounded rate affects Bill's interest:

	Year 1	Year 2	Year 3	Year 4
	$80.00	$86.40	$ 93.31	$100.77
	× .08	× .08	× .08	× .08
Interest	$ 6.40	$ 6.91	$ 7.46	$ 8.06
Beginning balance	+ 80.00	+ 86.40	+ 93.31	+ 100.77
Amount at year-end	$86.40	$93.31	$100.77	$108.83

Note that the beginning year 2 principal is the result of the interest of year 1 added to the principal. At the end of each interest period, we add on the period's interest. This interest becomes part of the principal we use for the calculation of the next period's interest.

Compound amount	$108.83	
Principal	− 80.00	*Note:* In Situation 1 the interest was $25.60.
Compound interest	$ 28.83	

[1]For simplicity of presentation, round each calculation to nearest cent before continuing the compounding process. The compound amount will be off by 1 cent.

We could have used the following simplified process to calculate the compound amount and interest:

Year 1	Year 2	Year 3	Year 4	
\$80.00	\$86.40	\$ 93.31	\$100.77	
× 1.08	× 1.08	× 1.08	× 1.08	
\$86.40	\$93.31	\$100.77	\$108.83	← Future value

When using this simplification, you do not have to add the new interest to the previous balance. Remember that compounding results in higher interest than simple interest. Compounding is the *sum* of principal and interest multiplied by the interest rate we use to calculate interest for the next period. So 1.08 above is 108%, with 100% as the base and 8% as the interest.

However, there is a shortcut formula for calculating the future value at compound interest:

$$FV = PV(1 + i)^n \qquad \textbf{(14.5)}$$

where:

FV = Maturity value at end of term of an investment or a loan
PV = Present (initial) value or principal of an investment or a loan
i = Periodic interest
n = Number of compounding periods during the term of the investment or loan

Let's calculate the future value of Bill Smith's deposit.

PV = \$80
t = 4 years
m = 1 (annual compounding)
j = 8%

STEP 1. First of all determine i:

$$i = \frac{j}{m}$$

$$i = \frac{.08}{1} = .08$$

STEP 2. Calculate n:

$$n = m \times t$$

$$n = 1 \times 4 = 4$$

STEP 3. Substitute values into formula 14.5:

$$FV = \$80(1 + .08)^4 = 108.84$$

Bill Smith will receive \$108.84 at the end of term of his investment.[2]

The calculator sequence for this example will be as follows:

\$80 [×] [(] 1 [+] .08 [)] [y^x] 4 [=]
or
[^]

FIGURE 14–4

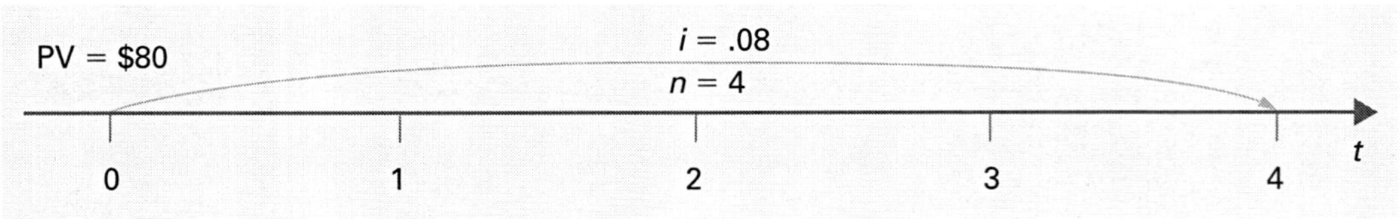

Now let's look at two examples that illustrate compounding more than once a year.

[2]Off 1 cent due to rounding.

EXAMPLE

Find the interest on \$6,000 at 10% compounded semiannually for 5 years. We calculate the interest as follows:

$$I = \text{FV} - \text{PV} \qquad \textbf{(14.6)}$$

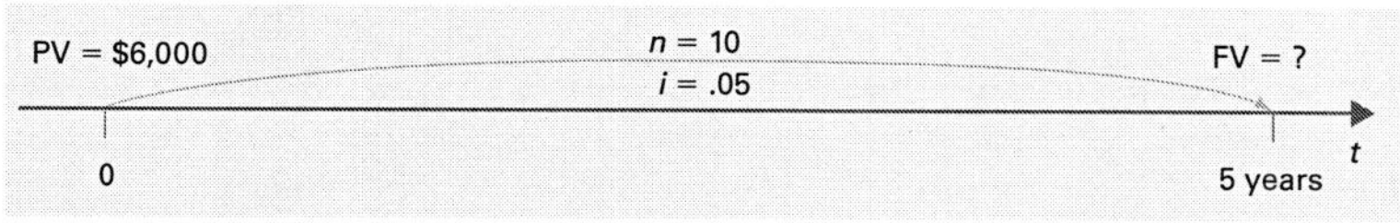

$n = m \times t$

$n = 2 \times 5 \text{ years} = 10$

$i = j \div m$

$i = .10 \div 2 = .05$

$\text{FV} = \$6{,}000(1 + .05)^{10} = \$9{,}773.40$

$I = \$9{,}773.40 - \$6{,}000 = \$3{,}773.40$

EXAMPLE

Pam Donahue deposits \$8,000 in her savings account that pays 6% interest compounded quarterly. What will be the balance of her account at the end of 5 years?

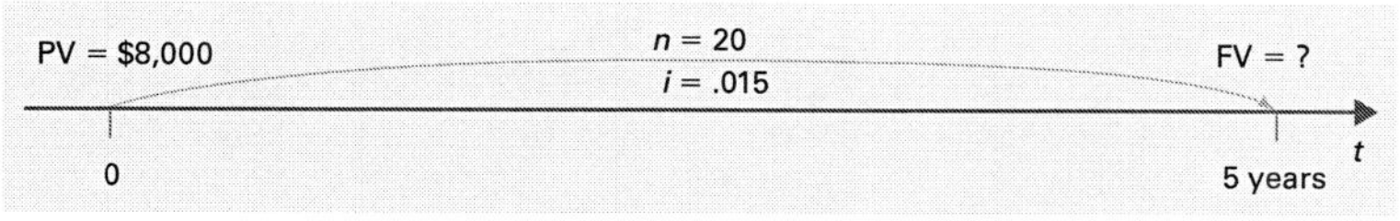

$n = 4 \times 5 \text{ years} = 20$

$i = .06 \div 4 = .015$

$\text{FV} = \$8{,}000(1 + .015)^{20} = \$10{,}775$

LU 14–2 PRACTICE QUIZ

1. Complete the following (round each calculation to the nearest cent as needed). Use formulas.

Principal, PV	Time, *t*	Rate of compound interest, *j*	Compounded, *m*	Number of periods to be compounded, *n*	Total amount, FV	Total interest, *I*
\$200	1 year	8%	Quarterly	**a. ?**	**b. ?**	**c. ?**

2. Lionel Rodgers deposits \$6,000 in Victory Bank, which pays 3% interest compounded semiannually. How much will Lionel have in his account at the end of 8 years?

LEARNING UNIT 14–3
PRESENT VALUE—THE BIG PICTURE

CP/Paul Chiasson

Figure 14.2 in Learning Unit 14–2 showed how by compounding, the *future value* of \$1 became \$1.36. This Unit discusses *present value.* Before we look at specific calculations involving present value, let's look at the concept of present value.

Figure 14.5 shows that if we invested 74 cents today, compounding would cause the 74 cents to grow to \$1 in the future. For example, let's assume you ask this question: "If I need \$1 in 4 years in the future, how much must I put in the bank *today* (assume an 8% annual interest)?" To answer this question, you must know the present value of that \$1 today. From Figure 14.5, you can see that the present value of \$1 is .7350. Remember that the \$1 is only worth 74 cents if you wait 4 periods to receive it. This is one reason why so many athletes get such big contracts—much of the money is paid in later years when it is not worth as much.

FIGURE 14–5
Present value of $1 at 8% for four periods

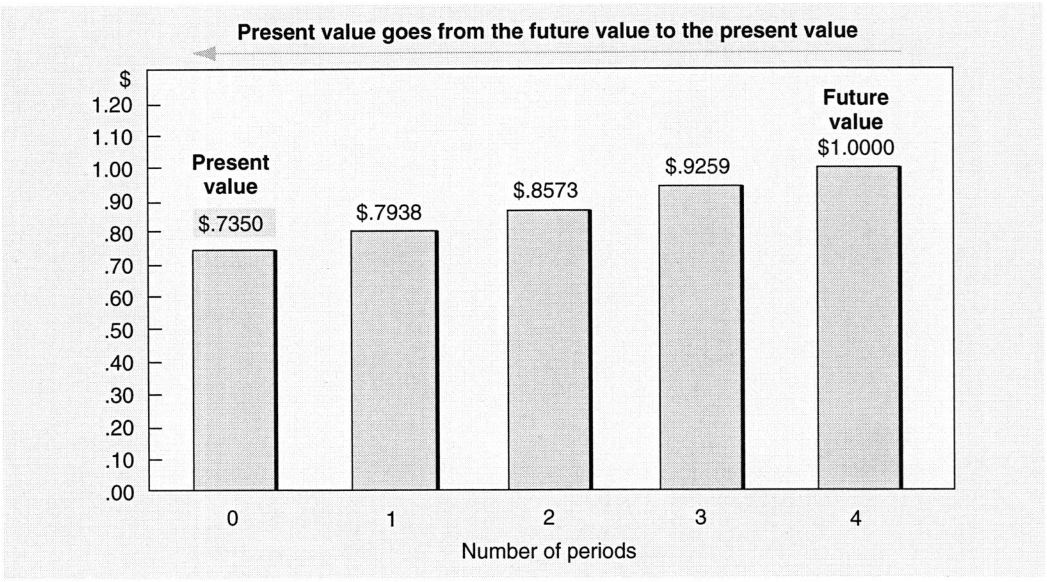

FIGURE 14–6
Present value

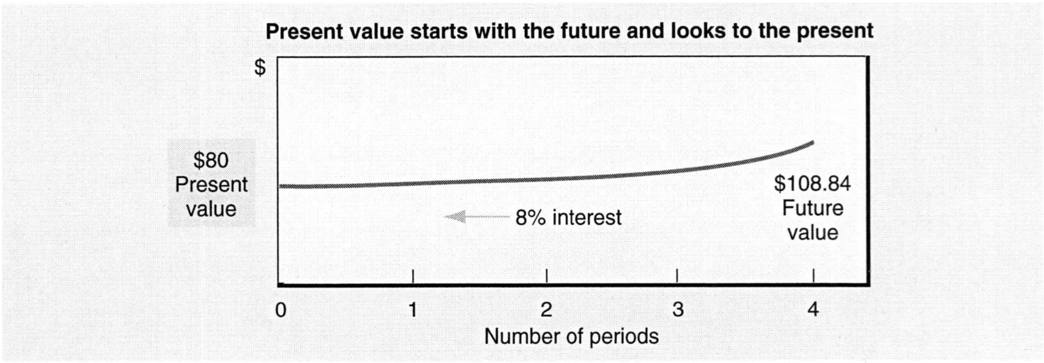

FIGURE 14–7

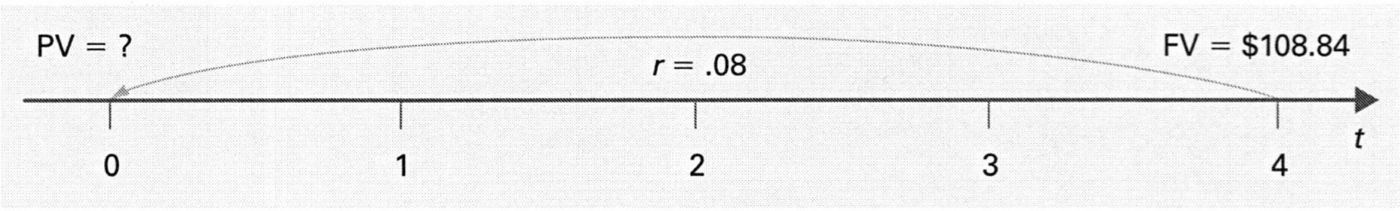

RELATIONSHIP OF COMPOUNDING (FV) TO PRESENT VALUE (PV)—THE BILL SMITH EXAMPLE CONTINUED

In Learning Unit 14–2, our consideration of compounding started in the *present* ($80) and looked to find the *future* amount of $108.84. Present value (PV) starts with the *future* and tries to calculate its worth in the *present* ($80). For example, in Figure 14.6, we assume Bill Smith knew that in 4 years he wanted to buy a bike that cost $108.84 (future). Bill's bank pays 8% interest compounded annually. How much money must Bill put in the bank *today* (present) to have $108.84 in 4 years? To work from the future to the present, we can use a present value (PV) table. In the next section you will learn how to use this table.

HOW TO USE PRESENT VALUE (PV)

You will recall that money has a special property: a time value. With time, the value of money changes—under normal economic conditions, it increases.

Notice that in Figure 14.7 we are moving backward in time, so the value of money is decreasing. In other words, we are discounting the *future value* to a *present value.* There is a shortcut formula that allows calculating money's present value when its future value, interest rate, and time period are given. For future value (FV) we use formula 14.5:

$$\text{FV} = \text{PV}(1 + i)^n$$

You can find the formula for PV by rearrangement of that formula:

$$\text{PV} = \frac{\text{FV}}{(1 + i)^n} \qquad \textbf{(14.7)}$$

The more common form of this formula may be obtained by using the following property of powers:

$$a^{-n} = \frac{1}{a^n} = a^{-n}$$

Then:

$$\text{PV} = \text{FV}(1 + i)^{-n} \qquad \textbf{(14.8)}$$

where:

PV = Present value
FV = Future value
n = Number of compounding periods in the term
i = Periodic interest rate

To continue our Bill Smith example, let's summarize what is given:

$$\text{FV} = \$108.84$$

$$i = \frac{.08}{1} = .08$$

$$n = 4 \times 1 = 4$$

The calculator sequence would be as follows:

108.84 [×] [(] 1 [+] .08 [)] [y^x] [(] 4 [+/−] [)] [=]
or
[∧]

Substituting these values into formula 14.8:

$$\text{PV} = \$108.84(1 + .08)^{-4} = \$80$$

This means that, four years from now, \$108.84 will be worth \$80 in today's dollars.

Let's look at another example before trying the Practice Quiz.

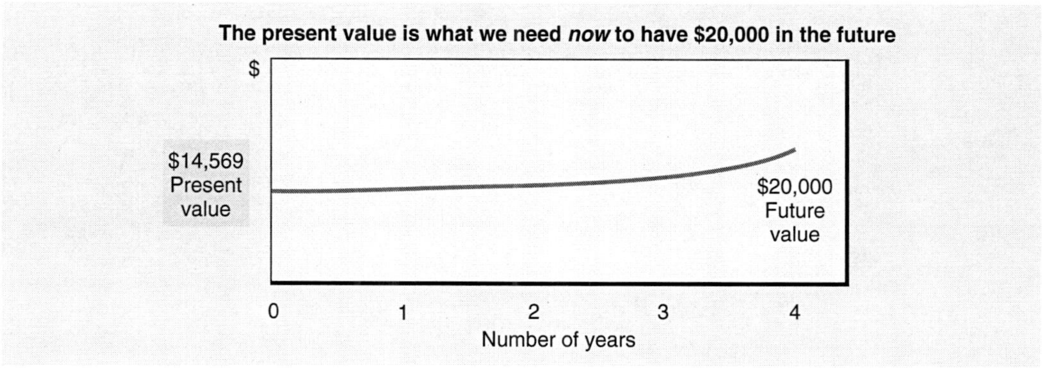

FIGURE 14–8
Present value

EXAMPLE

Rene Weaver needs \$20,000 for college in 4 years. She can earn 8% compounded quarterly at her bank. How much must Rene deposit at the beginning of the year to have \$20,000 in 4 years?

Remember that in this example the bank compounds the interest *quarterly*. Let's first determine the period and rate on a quarterly basis:

$$\text{FV} = \$20{,}000,\ m = 4,\ t = 4,\ j = .08$$

$$n = m \times t$$

$$i = \frac{j}{m}$$

Periods = 4 × 4 years = 16 periods $\qquad i = \frac{8\%}{4} = 2\% = .02$

FIGURE 14–9

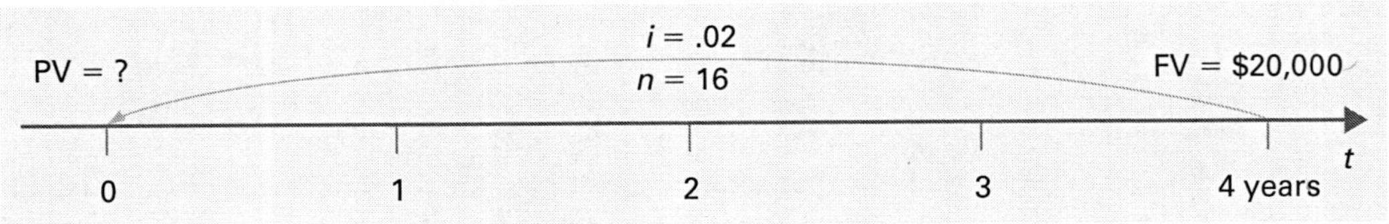

The calculator sequence will be as follows:

20,000 [×] [(] 1 [+] .02 [)] [y^x] [(] 16 [+/−] [)] [=]

Substitute the known values into formula 14.8:

$PV = \$20{,}000(1 + .02)^{-16} = \$14{,}568.92$

Now Rene must deposit $14,568.92 at 8% compounded quarterly in order to receive $20,000 in four years.

Let's test your understanding of this Unit with the Practice Quiz.

LU 14–3 PRACTICE QUIZ

Use the present-value formula to complete:

	Future amount desired	Length of time	Rate compounded	Compounding frequency, m	Periodic rate, i	n	PV amount
1.	$7,000	6 years	6% semiannually	?	?	?	?
2.	$15,000	20 years	10% annually	?	?	?	?

3. Bill Plum needs $20,000 six years from today to attend V.P.R. Tech. How much must Bill put in the bank today (12% quarterly) to reach his goal?
4. Bob Fry wants to buy his grandson a Ford Taurus in four years. The cost of a car will be $24,000. Assuming a bank rate of 8% compounded quarterly, how much must Bob put in the bank today?

LEARNING UNIT 14–4
EQUIVALENT PAYMENTS

As we learned from Chapter 12, money has a "time value." This property of money is used in amortization schedules, assessments of investment opportunities, rescheduling of payment streams, etc. We already know how to work with equivalent payments at simple interest. In this Unit we will learn how to calculate **equivalent payments** at compound interest.

The approach is a very similar: it is a two-step procedure:

Step 1. Bring all the values of payments to the same point in time and calculate their equivalent values, using formulas 14.5 and 14.8.
Step 2. Add them up and calculate the unknown replacement value.

Let's consider an example.

EXAMPLE

Vera Kaplun must pay $3,000 for her bedroom furniture three months from now and $8,000 for the family car in a year. She has won the lottery and wants to pay all her debts today. How much must she pay in order to satisfy her creditors if the money value is 5.5% compounded monthly?

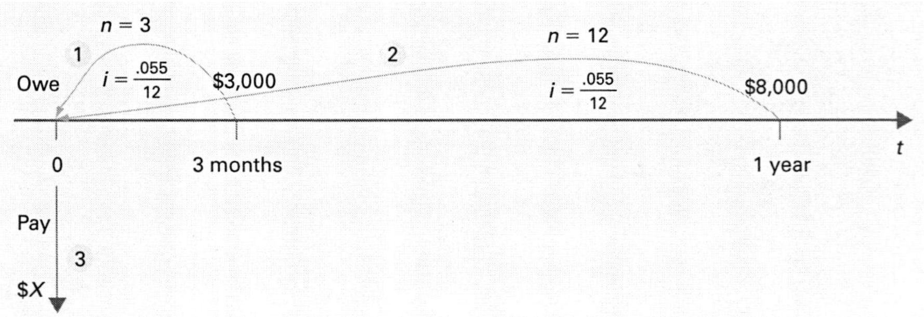

Remember: amount owed must equal amount paid:

① + ② = ③

In this problem we must ① find today's equivalent value of payment for furniture; ② find today's equivalent value of payment for the family car; and ③ add these values to find today's equivalent value for both debts.

In all such cases we are looking for present values and discounting the debts. From the time diagram it is clear that we are moving these values backward in time—to the left along the time line.

> *A useful tip.* If you are moving money values to the left along the time line, use the present value formula, formula 14.8, to find the equivalent value. In this case n must be negative. If you are moving values to the right along the time line, use formula 14.5 to calculate the equivalent future values. In this case n is positive.

Let's perform the calculations.

① $FV = \$3{,}000$, $t = \frac{3}{12}$ years, $j = .055$, $i_1 = \frac{.055}{12} = .004583333$ (don't round)

$m = 12$, n is negative, $n = \frac{3}{12} \times 12 = 3$; calculate PV

$PV_1 = \$3{,}000(1 + .004583333)^{-3} = \$2{,}959.13$

② $FV = \$8{,}000$, $t = 1$ year, $j = .055$, $i_1 = \frac{.055}{12} = .004583333$ (don't round)

$m = 12$, n is negative, $n = \frac{12}{12} \times 12 = 12$; calculate PV_2

$PV_2 = \$8{,}000(1 + .004583333)^{-12} = \$7{,}572.83$

① + ② = ③ = \$2,959.13 + \$7,572.83 = \$10,531.96

If Vera wants to cover her debts today she will have to pay \$10,531.96.

Now it's time for a Practice Quiz.

LU 14–4 PRACTICE QUIZ

Calculate the equivalent payments:

	Scheduled payments	Equivalent payments and total payment	Nominal interest rate	Compounding frequency
1.	**a.** \$500 one month ago **b.** \$1,000 in three months	\$? in six months	10%	Semiannually
2.	**a.** \$450 six months ago **b.** \$200 today	\$? in one month	5%	Annually

LEARNING UNIT 14–5
EFFECTIVE INTEREST RATE

BANK RATES—NOMINAL VERSUS EFFECTIVE RATES (ANNUAL PERCENTAGE YIELD, OR APY)

Banks often advertise their annual (nominal) interest rates and *not* their true or effective rate (annual percentage yield, or APY). This has made it difficult for investors and depositors to determine the actual rates of interest they were receiving. The Annual Percentage Yield (APY) is defined in the U.S.' Truth in Savings law as the percentage rate expressing the total amount of

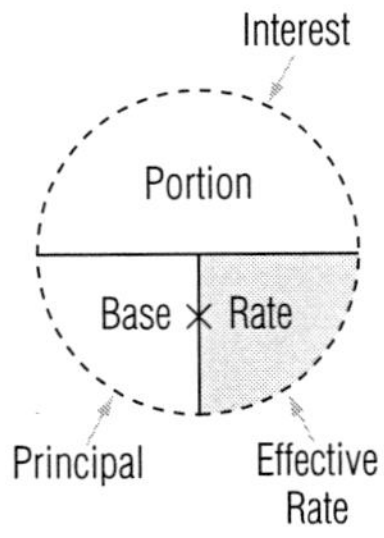

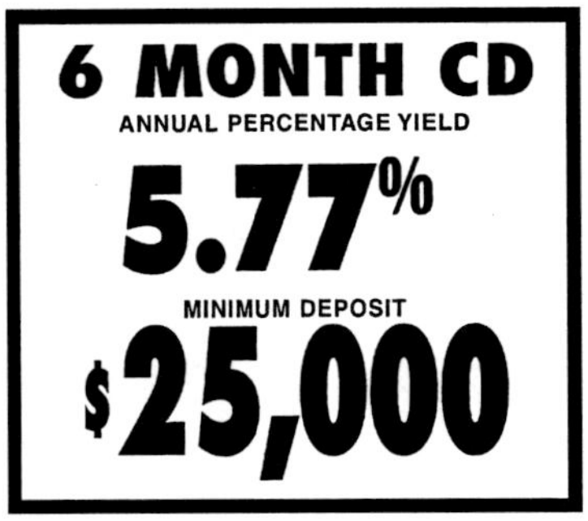

interest that would be received on a $100 deposit based on the annual rate and frequency of compounding for a 365-day period. As you can see from the following advertisement, banks now refer to the effective rate of interest as the *annual percentage yield.*

Let's study the rates of two banks to see which bank has the better return for the investor. Blue Bank pays 8% interest compounded quarterly on $8,000. Sun Bank offers 8% interest compounded semiannually on $8,000. The 8% rate is the nominal rate, or stated rate, on which the bank calculates the interest. To calculate the **effective rate (annual percentage yield,** or **APY),** however, we can use the following formula:[3]

$$\text{Effective rate (APY)} = \frac{\text{Interest for 1 year}}{\text{Principal}} = \frac{I}{PV}$$

Now let's calculate the effective rate (APY) for Blue Bank and Sun Bank.

BLUE, 8% COMPOUNDED QUARTERLY	**SUN, 8% COMPOUNDED SEMIANNUALLY**
$n = 4(4 \times 1)$	$n_2 = 2(2 \times 1)$
$i = \frac{8\%}{4} = 2\%$	$i_2 = \frac{8\%}{2} = 4\%$
$PV_1 = \$8{,}000$	$PV_2 = \$8{,}000$
$FV = 8{,}000(1 + .02)^4$	$FV = 8{,}000(1 + .04)^2$
$= \$8{,}659.46$	$= \$8{,}652.80$
Less principal $- 8{,}000.00$	$- 8{,}000.00$
$I_1 = \$\ 659.46$	$I_2 = \$\ 652.80$
Effective rate (APY) $= \frac{\$659.46}{\$8{,}000} = .0824$	$\frac{\$652.80}{\$8{,}000} = .0816$
$= 8.24\%$	$= 8.16\%$

FIGURE 14–10

Nominal and effective rates (APY) of interest compared

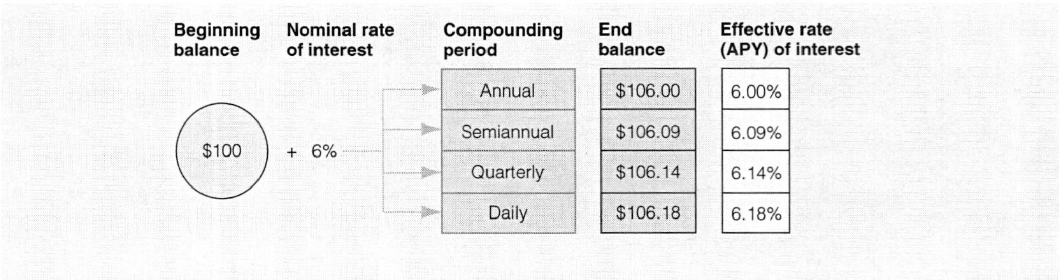

Figure 14.10 illustrates a comparison of nominal and effective rates (APY) of interest. In the example, the amount of interest earned in the first year ($6) is equal to the effective interest rate of 6%. It is possible to use this approach for comparison of two or more nominal interest rates in order to find the best opportunity for an investment or a loan.

Suppose two banks—Blue Bank and Sun Bank—offer you 4% semiannually and 3.85% compounded monthly respectively. Which bank offers the best rate for your investment?

To compare these rates, find the interest which you will receive at each bank at the end of one year on an imaginary investment of $100.

BLUE BANK	SUN BANK
$PV = \$100;\ j = .04;\ m = 2;\ t = 1$	$PV = \$100;\ j = .0385;\ m = 12;\ t = 1$
$n = m \times t = 2 \times 1 = 2$	$n = m \times t = 12$
$i = \frac{j}{m} = \frac{.04}{2} = .02$	$i = \frac{j}{m} = \frac{.0385}{12} = .003208333$ (don't round)
$FV = \$100(1 + .01)^2 = 104.04$	$FV = \$100(1 + .003208333)^{12} = \$103.92$
Interest is $4.04.	Interest is $3.92.
Effective interest rate will be equal to the amount of interest, 4.04%.	Effective interest rate will be equal to the amount of interest, 3.92%.

[3]Round to the nearest hundredth percent as needed. (In practice, the rate is often rounded to the nearest thousandth.)

As you see, the Blue Bank offers better opportunities for an investment.

There is a shortcut formula for calculation of an effective interest rate:

$$f = (1 + i)^m - 1 \qquad \textbf{(14.9)}$$

where f is the effective interest rate, m is the compounding frequency, and i is the periodic interest rate. Let's use this shortcut to compare rates offered by the two banks from the previous example:

BLUE BANK	SUN BANK
$m = 2$	$m = 12$
$i = \frac{j}{m} = \frac{.04}{2} = .02$	$i = \frac{j}{m} = \frac{.0385}{12} = .003208333$ (don't round)
$f = (1 + .02)^2 - 1 = .0404$	$f = (1 + .003208333)^{12} - 1 = .03918679$
Effective interest rate is 4.04%.	Effective interest rate is 3.92%.

This comparison should make you question any advertisement of interest rates before depositing your money.

Before concluding this Unit, we briefly discuss compounding interest daily.

Compounding Interest Daily

Although many banks add interest to each account quarterly, some banks pay interest that is *compounded daily*, and other banks use *continuous compounding*. Continuous compounding may sound great, but in fact it yields only a fraction of a percent more interest over a year than daily compounding. Today, computers perform these calculations.

Now it's time to check your progress with a Practice Quiz.

LU 14–5 PRACTICE QUIZ

1. Find the effective rate (APY) for the year: principal, $7,000; interest rate, 12%; and compounded quarterly.

2. Which rate is better for borrowing: 7% compounded daily or 7.15% compounded semiannually?

LEARNING UNIT 14–6
EQUIVALENT INTEREST RATES

Equivalent interest rates result in the same future value (FV) on an investment or loan in one year's time. For example, 4% compounded quarterly and 4.02% compounded semiannually are equivalent.

Let's check this out. If you invest an imaginary amount of $100 at each of these interest rates for one year you will get the same future values of your investment.

Option I

$j_1 = .04,\ m_1 = 4,\ i_1 = .01,\ n_1 = 4,\ PV_1 = \$100$

$FV_1 = \$100(1 + .01)^4 = \$104.060401$

Option II

$j_2 = .0402,\ m_2 = 2,\ i_2 = .0201,\ n_2 = 2,\ PV_2 = \$100$

$FV_2 = \$100(1 + .0201)^2 = \$104.060401$

$FV_1 = \$104.06 = FV_2$

Note that equivalent nominal interest rates have equivalent periodic interest rates: if j_1 is equivalent to j_2, then i_1 is equivalent to i_2 ($i_1 = \frac{.04}{4} = .01$). One percent per quarter is equivalent to 2.01% per half-year ($i_1 = \frac{.0402}{2} = .0201$).

Calculations of equivalent interest rates are usually performed either by the substitution method or by a shortcut formula.

EXAMPLE

What rate compounded semiannually will be equivalent to 12% compounded monthly?

To calculate the nominal interest rate, you must use a two-step approach:

Step 1. Calculate the periodic interest rate.
Step 2. Calculate the nominal interest rate $j = i \times m$.

First let's use the substitution method. The equivalent interest rate will produce equivalent future values at the end of one year.

$$FV_1 = FV_2$$

$$PV_1(1 + i_1)^{n_1} = PV_2(1 + i_2)^{n_2}$$

For the variables, substitute known values, and for the present value substitute an imaginary \$100. (Note that given values below are coded "1": i_1, m_1. Equivalent values are coded "2": i_2, m_2.)

$$PV_{1 \text{ and } 2} = \$100,\ j_1 = .12,\ m_1 = 12,\ i_1 = .01,\ n_1 = 12,\ m_2 = 2,\ n_2 = 2$$

$$\$100(1 + .01)^{12} = \$100(1 + i_2)^2$$

$$\$112.682503 = \$100(1 + i_2)^2$$

Divide both parts of the equation by \$100:

$$1.12682503 = (1 + i_2)^2$$

Undo the power:

$$\sqrt{1.12682503} = 1 + i_2$$

$$i_2 = \sqrt{1.12682503} - 1 = 1.061520151 - 1 = .061520151$$

$$i_2 = 6.15\%$$

To find nominal interest j multiply periodic interest rate by compounding frequency:

$$\boxed{j = i \times m}$$

$$j_2 = 6.15\% \times 2 = 12.30\%$$

Answer: 12.30% compounded semiannually is equivalent to 12% compounded monthly.

Now, let's use a shortcut formula for calculating equivalent interest rates. To use this formula you have to remember the following two things:

1. To calculate the nominal interest rate you should first calculate the periodic interest rate. This is a two-step approach.
2. Using shortcut formula assign variables with code "1" to the given values and variables with code "2" to the values to be defined.

$$i_2 = (1 + i_1)^{m_1/m_2} - 1 \qquad \textbf{(14.10)}$$

Let's use the previous example.

$$j_1 = .12,\ m_1 = 12,\ i_1 = .01,\ m_2 = 2$$

STEP 1. Define i_2:

$$i_2 = (1 + .01)^{12/2} - 1 = 1.01^6 - 1 = .06152015$$

$$i_2 = 6.15\%$$

STEP 2. Define j_2:

$$j_2 = 6.15\% \times 2 = 12.30\%$$

Answer: 12.30% compounded semiannually is equivalent to 12% compounded monthly.

Now it's time for a Practice Quiz.

LU 14–6 PRACTICE QUIZ

1. What quarterly compounded interest rate is equivalent to 10% compounded weekly?
2. A trust offers a rate of 1.2% compounded monthly on its two-year GIC. What annual rate should it quote in order to get the same rate of return?

CHAPTER ORGANIZER AND REFERENCE GUIDE

Topic	Key point, procedure, formula	Example(s) to illustrate situation
Calculating compound amount without formulas (future value),* p. 335	Determine new amount by multiplying rate times new balance (that includes interest added on). Start in present and look to future. $\text{Compound interest} = \text{Compound amount} - \text{Principal}$ PV —Compounding→ FV	\$100 in savings account, compounded annually for 2 years at 8%: \$100 × 1.08 = \$108 \$108 × 1.08 = \$116.64 (future value)
Calculating compound amount (future value) by formulas, p. 336	$\text{Periods } (n) = \text{Number of times compounded per year } (m) \times \text{Years of loan } (t)$ $\text{Periodic rate } (i) = \dfrac{\text{Annual rate } (j)}{\text{Number of times compounded per year } (m)}$ $FV = PV(1 + i)^n$	*Example:* \$2,000 @ 12% 5 years compounded quarterly: $n = \text{Periods} = 4 \times 5 \text{ years} = 20$ $i = \text{Periodic rate} = \dfrac{12\%}{4} = 3\% = .03$ PV = \$2,000 $n = 20$ periods, 3%; $FV = \$2{,}000 \times (1 + .03)^{20} = \$3{,}612.22$
Calculating present value (PV),† p. 339	Start with future and calculate worth in the present. Periods and rate computed like in compound interest. PV ←Present value— FV $PV = FV(1 + i)^{-n}$	*Example:* Want \$3,612.20 after 5 years with rate of 12% compounded quarterly: $FV = \$3{,}612.20;\ i = \dfrac{.12}{4} = .03$ $n = \text{Periods} = 4 \times 5 = 20;\ \% = 3\%$ $PV = \$3{,}612.20(1 + .03)^{-20} = \$2{,}000.08$ Invested today will yield desired amount in future.
Effective rate (APY), p. 342	$\text{Effective rate (APY)} = \dfrac{\text{Interest for 1 year}}{\text{Principal}} = \dfrac{I}{PV}$ or by shortcut formula: $f = (1 + i)^m - 1$ **(14.9)**	\$1,000 at 10% compounded semiannually for 1 year: $j = .10;\ i = .05;\ n = 1.2 \approx 2$ $FV = \$1{,}000(1 + .05)^2 \approx 1{,}102.50$ \$1,000 × 1.1025 = \$1,102.50 − 1,000.00 \$ 102.50 $\dfrac{\$102.50}{\$1{,}000} = 10.25\%$ effective rate (APY) $f = (1 + .05)^2 - 1 = .1025 \rightarrow f = 10.25\%$
Equivalent payments, p. 340	**Step 2.** Calculate equivalent nominal interest rate j_2: $j_2 = i_2 \times m_2$	**Step 2.** $j_2 = 1.51\% \times 4 = 6.03\%$ 6% compounded monthly is equivalent to 6.03% compounded quarterly.

$^*P(1 + i)^N$. †$\dfrac{FV}{(1 + i)^N}$ if table not used.

(continues)

CHAPTER ORGANIZER AND REFERENCE GUIDE (CONCLUDED)

Topic	Key point, procedure, formula	Example(s) to illustrate situation
	The approach is a two-step procedure. **Step 1.** Bring all the payment values to the same point in time and calculate their equivalent values, using formulas 14.5 and 14.8. **Step 2.** Add them up and calculate the unknown replacement value. *A useful tip.* If moving money values to the left along the time line, use the present value formula (14.8) to find the equivalent value. In this case n must be negative. If moving values to the right along the time line, use formula 14.5 to calculate the equivalent future values. In this case n is positive.	How much should you pay today for the two debts of $1,000 and $2,000 that are due in 3 months and 1 year respectively? Rate of return is 3% compounded monthly. 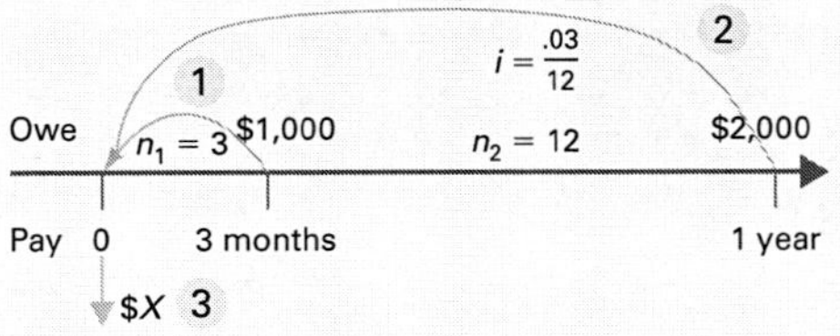 $i = \frac{.03}{12}$; $t_1 = \frac{3}{12}$; $t_2 = 1$; $n_1 = 12 \times \frac{3}{12} = 3$; $n_2 = 12$; ① + ② = ③ ① $\$1{,}000\left(1 + \frac{.03}{12}\right)^{-3} = \$992.54$ ② $\$2{,}000\left(1 + \frac{.03}{12}\right)^{-12} = \$1{,}940.96$ $992.54 + $1,940.96 = $2,933.50
Equivalent interest rate, p. 343	*Equivalent interest rates* result in the same future value (FV) on investment or loan in one year's time. **Step 1.** Calculate equivalent periodic rate i_2: $i_2 = (1 + i_1)^{m_1/m_2} - 1$	What rate compounded quarterly will be equivalent to 6% compounded monthly? **Step 1.** $j_1 = .06$, $m_1 = 12$, $m_2 = 4$, $i_1 = \frac{.06}{12} = .005$ $i_2 = (1 + .005)^{12/4} - 1 = .015075124 \rightarrow 1.51\%$

Key terms

Annual interest rate, p. 334
Annual percentage yield (APY), p. 342
Compound amount, p. 333
Compounded annually, p. 334
Compounded daily, p. 334
Compounded monthly, p. 334
Compounded quarterly, p. 334
Compounded semiannually, p. 334
Compounding, p. 333
Compounding frequency, p. 334
Compound interest, p. 333
Effective rate, p. 342
Equivalent interest rates, p. 343
Equivalent payments, p. 340
Future value (FV), p. 333
Nominal interest rate, p. 334
Number of periods (n), p. 334
Periodic interest rate, p. 334
Present value (PV), p. 333

CRITICAL THINKING DISCUSSION QUESTIONS

1. Explain how periods and rates are calculated in compounding problems. Compare simple interest to compound interest.
2. What are the steps to calculate the compound amount by formula?

END-OF-CHAPTER PROBLEMS

DRILL PROBLEMS

Complete the following table using formulas (round to the nearest cent for each calculation).

	Principal	Time (years)	Rate of compound interest	Compounded	Periods	Rate	Total amount	Total interest
14–1.	$700	2	6%	Semiannually	?	?	?	?

Complete the following using compound future value formulas:

	Time, t	Principal, PV	Rate, j	Compounded, m	Amount, FV	Interest, I
14–2.	7 years	$8,000	4%	Semiannually	?	?
14–3.	6 months	$10,000	8%	Quarterly	?	?
14–4.	3 years	$2,000	12%	Semiannually	?	?

Calculate the effective rate (APY) of interest for 1 year.

14–5. Principal: $15,500
Interest rate: 12%
Compounded quarterly
Effective rate (APY): ________

14–6. Calculate what $700 would grow to at $6\frac{1}{2}$% per year compounded daily for 7 years.

Complete the following:

	Amount desired at end of period	Length of time	Rate	Compounded	Period used, n	Rate used, i	PV of amount desired at end of period
14–7.	$2,600	6 years	4%	Semiannually	?	?	?
14–8.	$7,650	2 years	12%	Monthly	?	?	?
14–9.	$17,600	7 years	12%	Quarterly	?	?	?
14–10.	$20,000	20 years	8%	Annually	?	?	?

14–11. Check your answer in Problem 14–9 by formulas using the step approach. Is the answer different? If so, why?

ADDITIONAL DRILL PROBLEMS

14–12. In the following examples, calculate manually the amount at year-end for each of the deposits, assuming that interest is compounded annually. Round to the nearest cent each year.

	Principal	Rate	Number of years	Year 1	Year 2	Year 3	Year 4
a.	$530	8%	2	?	?	?	?
b.	$1,980	12%	4	?	?	?	?

14–13. In the following examples, calculate the simple interest, the compound interest, and the difference between the two. Round to the nearest cent; do not use tables.

	Principal	Rate	Number of years	Simple interest	Compound interest	Difference
a.	$4,600	10%	2	?	?	?
b.	$18,400	9%	4	?	?	?
c.	$855	$7\frac{1}{5}$%	3	?	?	?

14–14. Find the future value and the compound interest using the future value formulas. Round to the nearest cent.

	Principal	Investment terms	Future value	Compound interest
a.	$10,000	6 years at 8% compounded annually	?	?
b.	$10,000	6 years at 8% compounded quarterly	?	?
c.	$8,400	7 years at 12% compounded semiannually	?	?
d.	$2,500	15 years at 10% compounded daily	?	?
e.	$9,600	5 years at 6% compounded quarterly	?	?
f.	$20,000	2 years at 6% compounded monthly	?	?

14–15. Use formulas to find the present value for each of the following:

	Future value	Rate	Number of years	Compounded	Present value
a.	$1	10%	5	Annually	?
b.	$1	12%	8	Semiannually	?
c.	$1	6%	10	Quarterly	?
d.	$1	12%	2	Monthly	?
e.	$1	8%	15	Semiannually	?

14–16. Find the present value and the interest earned for the following:

	Future value	Number of years	Rate	Compounded	Present value	Interest earned
a.	$2,500	6	8%	Annually	?	?
b.	$4,600	10	6%	Semiannually	?	?
c.	$12,800	8	10%	Semiannually	?	?
d.	$28,400	7	8%	Quarterly	?	?
e.	$53,050	1	12%	Monthly	?	?

14–17. Find the missing amount (present value or future value) for each of the following:

	Present value	Investment terms	Future value
a.	$3,500	5 years at 8% compounded annually	?
b.	?	6 years at 12% compounded semiannually	$9,000
c.	$4,700	9 years at 14% compounded semiannually	?

WORD PROBLEMS

14–18. On March 25, 2004, *The Neverland Times* reported on certificate of deposit rates. A savings account in the Emigrant Savings Bank in Neverland now earns 2.25% simple interest a year. Bank One pays 6% interest compounded semiannually on a certificate of deposit. Robert Wier wants to deposit $1,500 in his savings account, how much additional interest will he earn by placing the money in a GIC?

14–19. Jean Rich, owner of a local Tim Hortons, loaned $14,000 to Mel Lyon to help him open an Internet business. Mel plans to repay Jean at the end of 6 years with 6% interest compounded semiannually. How much will Jean receive at the end of 6 years?

14–20. Molly Slate deposited $35,000 at Quazi Bank at 6% interest compounded quarterly. What is the effective rate (APY) to the nearest hundredth percent?

14–21. Excel Melvin Indecision has difficulty deciding whether to put his savings in Mystic Bank or Four Rivers Bank. Mystic offers 10% interest compounded semiannually. Four Rivers offers 8% interest compounded quarterly. Melvin has $10,000 to invest. He expects to withdraw the money at the end of 4 years. Which bank gives Melvin the better deal? Check your answer.

14–22. Brian Costa deposited $20,000 in a new savings account at 12% interest compounded semiannually. At the beginning of year 4, Brian deposits an additional $30,000 at 12% interest compounded semiannually. At the end of 6 years, what is the balance in Brian's account?

14–23. Lee Wills loaned Audrey Chin $16,000 to open a hair salon. After 6 years, Audrey will repay Lee with 8% interest compounded quarterly. How much will Lee receive at the end of 6 years?

14–24. Financial planning for retirement was a topic in the July 31, 2000, issue of *Business Week*. Jim Fortunate received a large insurance settlement of $200,000. When Jim retires in 25 years, he would like to have at least $80,000 yearly income for 10 years. A local bank pays 6% interest compounded semiannually on a certificate of deposit. **(a)** How much of the settlement must Jim place in the bank to meet his retirement goal? **(b)** What amount would he receive if he invested the entire $200,000 in the bank?

14–25. John Roe, an employee of The Gap, loans $3,000 to another employee at the store. He will be repaid at the end of 4 years with interest at 6% compounded quarterly. How much will John be repaid?

14–26. An article in the June 21, 2001, *Sun Publications* mentioned the increasing cost of attending college. A child entering college 11 years from now can expect to pay more than $20,000 a year to attend a public institution and almost $60,000 a year for an Ivy League school. Assume you are planning your child's education and have received an inheritance that will cover the child's costs. You place the inheritance in a bank paying 6% interest compounded quarterly. **(a)** How much money should you put away to send your child to a public institution for 4 years? **(b)** How much money should you put away to send your child to a private institution? Use formulas.

14–27. St. Paul Federal Bank is quoting 1-year GICs at an interest rate of 5% compounded semiannually. Joe Saver purchased a $5,000 GIC. What is the GIC's effective rate (APY) to the nearest hundredth percent? Use formulas.

14–28. Jim Jones, an owner of a Burger King restaurant, assumes that his restaurant will need a new roof in 7 years. He estimates the roof will cost him $9,000 at that time. What amount should Jim invest today at 6% compounded quarterly to be able to pay for the roof? Check your answer.

14–29. Tony Ring wants to attend Northeast College. He will need $60,000 four years from today.

Assume Tony's bank pays 12% interest compounded semiannually. What must Tony deposit today so he will have $60,000 in four years?

14–30. Check your answer (to the nearest dollar) in Problem 14–29 by using the step approach. (The answer will be slightly off due to rounding.)

14–31. Pete Air wants to buy a used Jeep in 5 years. He estimates the Jeep will cost $15,000. Assume Pete invests $10,000 now at 12% interest compounded semiannually. Will Pete have enough money to buy his Jeep at the end of 5 years?

14–32. Lance Jackson deposited $5,000 at Basil Bank at 9% interest compounded daily. What is Lance's investment at the end of 4 years?

14–33. Paul Havlik promised his grandson Jamie that he would give him $6,000 eight years from today for graduating from high school. Assume money is worth 6% interest compounded semiannually. What is the present value of this $6,000?

14–34. Earl Ezekiel wants to retire in Victoria when he is 65 years old. Earl is now 50. He believes he will need $300,000 to retire comfortably. To date, Earl has set aside no retirement money. Assume Earl gets 6% interest compounded semiannually. How much must Earl invest today to meet his $300,000 goal?

14–35. Lorna Evenson would like to buy a $19,000 car in 4 years. Lorna wants to put the money aside now. Lorna's bank offers 8% interest compounded semiannually. How much must Lorna invest today?

14–36. John Smith invests $15,000 at 4% compounded monthly for 9 months. How much will he receive at the end of the term of his deposit? Explain how you obtained the value of *t* in years.

Calculate equivalent interest rates both by the substitution method and by formula 4.10.

	Given interest rate j_1	Equivalent interest rate j_2
14–37.	4% compounded annually	? compounded weekly
14–38.	4% compounded semiannually	? compounded annually
14–39.	4% compounded monthly	? compounded semimonthly
14–40.	4% compounded weekly	? compounded quarterly
14–41.	4% compounded daily	? compounded annually

Calculate the equivalent payments.

	Scheduled payments	Equivalent payments	Nominal interest rate	Compounding frequency
14–42.	$450 six months ago	$200 today and $? in a month	5%	Compounded annually
14–43.	$3,000 a year ago; $2,000 in 1.5 years	$? in 2 years	8%	Compounded monthly

14–44. Ihor Shub has to pay two debts, $4,000 and $3,000. One is due in eight months and the other in three years. How much must he pay today in order to cover his debts, if the money value is 4% compounded quarterly?

14–45. Use the data from the previous problem. How much money would Ihor save if he covered his debts today?

14–46. Julia needs to pay $300 in a month, $1,000 in a year, and $1,500 in two years. She wants to consolidate her debts and pay them all in two years. How much will she pay at that point in time, if the money value is 3% compounded annually?

ADDITIONAL WORD PROBLEMS

14–47. John Mackey deposited $5,000 in his savings account at TD Bank. If the bank pays 6% interest compounded quarterly, what will be the balance of his account at the end of 3 years?

14–48. Jack Billings loaned $6,000 to his brother-in-law Dan, who was opening a new business. Dan promised to repay the loan at the end of 5 years, with interest of 8% compounded semiannually. How much will Dan pay Jack at the end of 5 years?

14–49. Eileen Hogarty deposits $5,630 at Royal Bank, which pays 12% interest, compounded quarterly. How much money will Eileen have in her account at the end of 7 years?

14–50. Burlington Trust pays 6% compounded semiannually. How much interest would be earned on $7,200 for 1 year?

14–51. A credit union pays 9% compounded quarterly. Find the amount and the interest on $3,000 after three quarters. Do not use a table.

14–52. David Siderski bought a $7,500 bank certificate paying 16% compounded semiannually. How much money did he obtain upon cashing in the certificate 3 years later?

Solve for future value or present value.

14–53. Paul Palumbo assumes that he will need to have a new roof put on his house in 4 years. He estimates that the roof will cost him $18,000 at that time. What amount of money should Paul invest today at 8%, compounded semiannually, to be able to pay for the roof?

14–54. Tilton, a pharmacist, rents his store and has signed a lease that will expire in 3 years. When the lease expires, Tilton wants to buy his own store. He wants to have a down payment of $35,000 at that time. How much money should Tilton invest today at 6% compounded quarterly to yield $35,000?

14–55. Brad Morrissey loans $8,200 to his brother-in-law. He will be repaid at the end of 5 years, with interest at 10% compounded semiannually. Find out how much he will be repaid.

14–56. Mary Wilson wants to buy a new set of golf clubs in 2 years. They will cost $775. How much money should she invest today at 9% compounded annually so that she will have enough money to buy the new clubs?

14–57. Jack Beggs plans to invest $30,000 at 10% compounded semiannually for 5 years. What is the future value of the investment?

CHALLENGE PROBLEMS

14–58. The U.S. government has ended 20 years of litigation by agreeing to pay $18 million to the estate of Richard M. Nixon. On June 14, 2000, the *Los Angeles Times* reported that the estate had demanded $35 million plus $8\frac{1}{2}$% interest compounded annually for items confiscated after Nixon resigned the presidency. **(a)** How much interest did the estate want? **(b)** What was the total amount the estate wanted? **(c)** How much did the government save by settling for $18 million?

14–59. You are the financial planner for Johnson Controls. Last year's profits were $700,000. The board of directors decided to forgo dividends to stockholders and retire high-interest outstanding bonds that were issued 5 years ago at a face value of $1,250,000. You have been asked to invest the profits in a bank. The board must know how much money you will need from the profits earned to retire the bonds in 10 years. Bank A pays 6% compounded quarterly, and Bank B pays $6\frac{1}{2}$% compounded annually. Which bank would you recommend, and how much of the company's profit should be placed in the bank? If you recommended that the remaining money not be distributed to stockholders but be placed in Bank B, how much would the remaining money be worth in 10 years? Use formulas. Round final answer to nearest dollar.

SUMMARY PRACTICE TEST

1. Joy Bayo, owner of Travel.com, loaned $13,000 to Jeff Line to help him open a flower shop online. Jeff plans to repay Joe at the end of 8 years with 6% interest compounded semiannually. How much will Joe receive at the end of 8 years? (p. 335)

2. Roy Hunter wants to attend Conestoga College. Six years from today he will need $28,000. If Roy's bank pays 4% interest compounded semiannually, what must Roy deposit today to have $28,000 in 6 years? (p. 339)

3. Warren Ford deposited $18,000 in a savings account at 6% interest compounded semiannually. At the beginning of year 4, Warren deposits an additional $80,000 at 6% interest compounded semiannually. At the end of 6 years, what is the balance in Warren's account? (p. 335)

4. Joe Jones, owner of a Taco Bell, wants to buy a new delivery truck in 4 years. He estimates the truck will cost $17,000. If Joe invests $11,000 now at 10% interest compounded semiannually, will Joe have enough money to buy his delivery truck at the end of 4 years? (p. 335)

5. Abby Ellen deposited $12,000 in Street Bank at 9% interest compounded semiannually. What was the effective rate (APY)? Round to the nearest hundredth percent. (p. 342)

6. Paul Mahar, owner of Jeff's Lube, estimates that he will need $40,000 for new equipment in 8 years. Paul decided to put aside the money today so it will be available in 8 years. Lester Bank offers Paul 10% interest compounded semiannually. How much must Paul invest to have $40,000 in 8 years? (p. 339)

7. Gracie Lantz wants to retire to British Columbia when she is 65 years of age. Gracie is now 45. She believes that she Excel will need $500,000 to retire comfortably. To date, Gracie has set aside no retirement money. If Gracie gets 8% compounded semiannually, how much must Gracie invest today to meet her $500,000 goal? (p. 339)

8. Bernie Sullivan deposited $12,000 in a savings account at 6% interest compounded daily. At the end of 20 years, what is the balance in Bernie's account? (p. 335)

SOLUTIONS TO PRACTICE QUIZZES

LU 14–1

1. $t = \frac{72}{4\%} = 18$ years
2. $t = \frac{72}{6\%} = 12$ years
3. $t = \frac{72}{1.5\%} = 48$ years

LU 14–2

1. **a.** 4 (4 × 1) **b.** $216.48 **c.** $16.48 ($216.48 − $200)

   $\text{FV} = \$200(1+.02)^4 = \$216.48$

2. 16 periods, $1\frac{1}{2}\%$, $6,000 × 1.2690 = $7,614

LU 14–3

1. $m = 2$	$i = 3\%$ (6% ÷ 2)	$n = 12$ periods (6 years × 2)	$\text{PV} = \$7{,}000 \times 1.03^{-12} = \$4{,}909.66$
2. $m = 1$	$i = 10\%$ (10% ÷ 1)	$n = 20$ periods (20 years × 1)	$\text{PV} = \$15{,}000 \times 1.10^{-20} = \$2{,}229.65$
3. $n = 6$ years × 4 = 24 periods		$i = \frac{12\%}{4} = 3\%$	$\$20{,}000 \times 1.03^{-24} = \$9{,}838.67$
4. $n = 4 \times 4$ years = 16 periods		$i = \frac{8\%}{4} = 2\%$	$\$24{,}000 \times 1.02^{-16} = \$17{,}482.70$

LU 14–4

1.

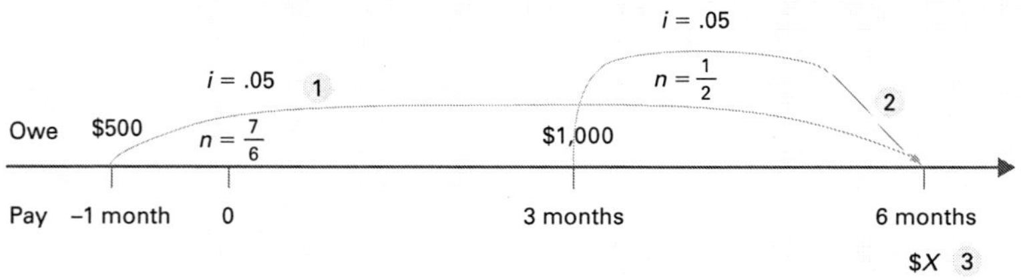

① $\text{FV} = \$500(1 + .05)^{7/6} = \$529.29$

$I = \frac{.1}{2} = .05;\ t = \frac{7}{12}$ years; $n = \frac{7}{12} \times 2$

② $\text{FV} = \$1{,}000(1 + .05)^{1/2} = \$1{,}024.70$

$I = .05;\ t = \frac{3}{12}$ years; $n = \frac{3}{12} \times 2 = \frac{3}{6} = \frac{1}{2}$

③ $529.27 + $1,024.70 = $1,553.97

2.

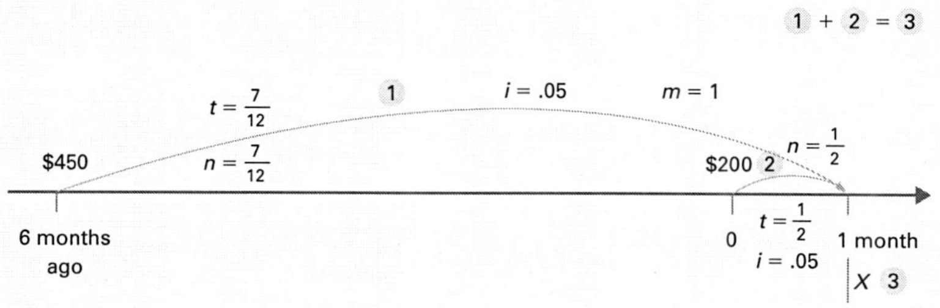

① $\$450 \times (1 + .05)^{7/12} = \$462.99$

$n = t \times m$

$i = \frac{.05}{1} = .05$

$t_1 = \frac{7}{12}$

$t_2 = \frac{1}{12}$

② $\$200 \times (1 + .05)^{1/12} = \$200.81$

③ = ① + ②

$x = \$462.99 + \$200.81$

$= \$663.80$

LU 14–5

1. $j = .12,\ m = 4$

$i = \frac{.12}{4} = .03$

$f = (1 + .03)^4 - 1 = .1255$

$f = 12.55\%$

2.

Option I:	**Option II:**
	$f = 7.25\%$
$j = .07,\ m = 365$	$j = .0715,\ m = 2$
$i = \frac{.07}{365} = .00019178$	$i = \frac{.0715}{2} = .03575$
$f = (1 + .00019178)^{365} - 1 = .0725$	$f = (1 + .03575)^2 - 1 = .07278$
	$f = 7.28\%$

Of course, when you are borrowing money you are interested in the smallest interest rate possible. So the first option is better.

LU 14–6

1. $i_2 = \left(1 + \frac{.10}{52}\right)^{52/4} - 1 = 1.025290505 - 1 = .025290505$; 2.53% per quarter

$j_2 = 2.53\% \times 4 = 10.12\%$; 10.12% compounded quarterly

2. $i_2 = \left(1 + \frac{.012}{12}\right)^{12/1} - 1 = 1.01206622 - 1 = .01206622$; 1.21% p.a.

$j_2 = i_2$ (as the interest is compounded annually)

Business Math Scrapbook

WITH INTERNET APPLICATION

Putting Your Skills to Work

	When you deposit	30-month C.D. interest rate	30-month interest at maturity	If 12% interest at maturity	Interest difference
A.	$100,000	12.28% Annual percentage yield 11.75% Interest rate	$33,578		
B.	$80,001	12.28% Annual percentage yield 11.75% Interest rate	$26,863		
C.	$60,001	12.28% Annual percentage yield 11.75% Interest rate	$20,147		
D.	$40,001	12.28% Annual percentage yield 11.75% Interest rate	$13,431		
E.	$20,001	12.28% Annual percentage yield 11.75% Interest rate	$6,716		
F.	$15,001	12.28% Annual percentage yield 11.75% Interest rate	$5,037		
G.	$10,001	12.28% Annual percentage yield 11.75% Interest rate	$3,358		

This yield assumes that principal and interest remain on deposit for a full year interest compounded quarterly

PROJECT A

Bill Smith saw this bank advertisement. He feels the interest rate may rise to 12% next month. If you use the formulas explained in the text, what would the interest be at maturity for each amount? By waiting until next month, how much interest could Bill gain over depositing now? Assume that Bill wants to work out the interest rate for each deposit shown. What would be the annual effective yield (APY) with an interest rate of 12%? Visit the rbc.com site (www.royalbank.com). What are the current rates?

Annuities and Sinking Funds

15

Year	Amount invested: Early investor	Amount invested: Late investor
1	$2,000	$0
2	$2,000	$0
3	$2,000	$0
4	$2,000	$0
5	$2,000	$0
6	$2,000	$0
7	$2,000	$0
8	$2,000	$0
9–40	$0 every year	$2,000 every year

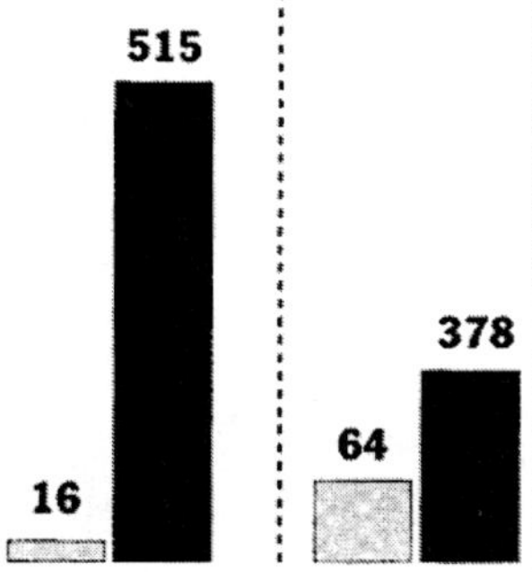

Total invested over 40 years (In thousands of dollars)

Total earnings after 40 years (In thousands of dollars)

Source: www.financialfinesse.com; www.netxclient.com; S&P's *The Outlook*

Source: © 2001 Dow Jones & Company, Inc.

LEARNING UNIT OBJECTIVES

LU 15–1: Annuities: Basic Concepts and Types

- Learn main terms and definitions (p. 356).
- Distinguish simple, general, ordinary, and deferred annuities, and annuities due (p. 357).

LU 15–2: Simple Ordinary Annuities and Simple Annuities Due; Calculating Maturity Value of an Annuity Manually and Using Table Lookup

- Calculate the maturity value of an annuity manually (p. 359).
- Calculate the maturity value of an annuity using table lookup (p. 360).

LU 15–3: Simple Ordinary Annuities and Simple Annuities Due; Calculating Present Values and Periodic Payments (Sinking Funds)

- Calculate the present value of an annuity using formulas and table lookup (p. 364).
- Calculate periodic payments (p. 366).
- Compare calculation of the present value of one lump sum and the present value of an ordinary annuity (p. 368).

LU 15–4: General Ordinary Annuities; Calculating Present Values, Maturity Values, and Periodic Payments Using Formulas

- Calculate the present value of an annuity using formulas (p. 369).
- Calculate the future value of an annuity using formulas (p. 369).
- Calculate periodic payments of an annuity (p. 370).

As you can see from the *Wall Street Journal* clipping "Building a Nest Egg" shown here, many workers are not planning or saving for their retirement. A footnote to the clipping said that workers were asked to include savings in defined contribution plans, profit sharing plans, and other investments. Expected payments from pensions or other defined benefit plans weren't included.

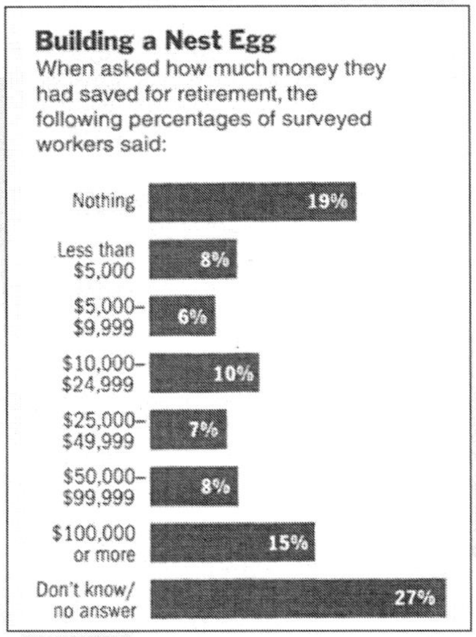

Source: © 2000 Dow Jones & Company, Inc.

This chapter shows how to compute compound interest that results from a *stream* of payments, or an annuity. Chapter 14 showed how to calculate compound interest on a lump-sum payment deposited at the beginning of a particular time. Knowing how to calculate interest compounding on a lump sum will make the calculation of interest compounding on annuities easier to understand.

We begin the chapter by explaining different terms and definitions, as well as the difference between simple and general annuities, ordinary and deferred annuities, and annuities due. Then you learn how to find the future value, present value, and periodic payment of a simple and general annuity, manually and using formulas. The chapter ends with a discussion of sinking funds.

LEARNING UNIT 15–1
ANNUITIES: BASIC CONCEPTS AND TYPES

Many parents of small children are concerned about being able to afford to pay for their children's college educations. Some parents deposit a lump sum in a financial institution when the child is in diapers. The interest on this sum is compounded until the child is 18, when the parents withdraw the money for college expenses. Parents could also fund their children's educations with annuities by depositing a series of payments for a certain time. The concept of annuities is the first topic in this Learning Unit.

CONCEPT OF AN ANNUITY—THE BIG PICTURE

All of us would probably like to win $1 million in a lottery. What happens when you have the winning ticket? You take it to the lottery headquarters. When you turn in the ticket, do you immediately receive a cheque for $1 million? Not always.

Annuity: a series of equal payments over equal intervals of time.

Some lottery winners receive a series of payments over a period of time—usually years. This *stream* of payments is an **annuity.** By paying the winners an annuity, lotteries do not actually spend $1 million. The lottery deposits a sum of money in a financial institution. The continual growth of this sum through compound interest provides the lottery winner with a series of payments.

FIGURE 15–1
Future value of an annuity of $1 at 8%

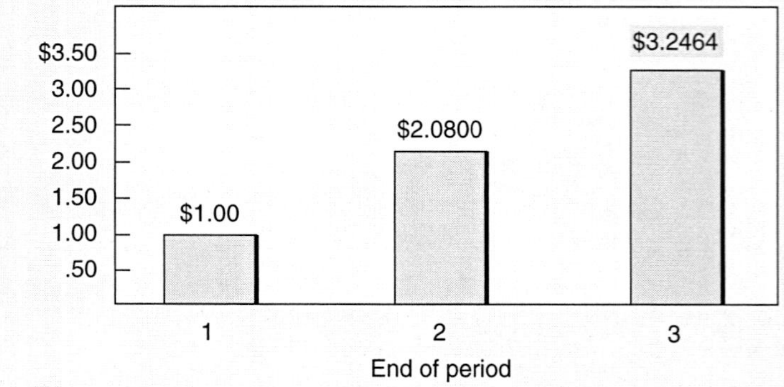

When we calculated the maturity value of a lump-sum payment in Chapter 14, the maturity value was the principal and its interest. Now we are looking not at lump-sum payments but at a series of **periodic payments** (usually of equal amounts over regular **payment periods**) plus the interest that accumulates. So the **future value of an annuity** is the future *dollar amount* of a series of payments plus interest.

In considering the example with a lottery, we learned several important terms:

- Annuity—a series of equal payments over regular and equal intervals in time
- Payment interval—time between two consecutive payments
- Amount of an annuity—its future value
- Term of an annuity—the time from the beginning of the first payment period to the end of the last payment period

Typical examples of an annuity are mortgages, RRSPs, and regular investments.

We will use the time line diagram to illustrate the **terms** of annuities.

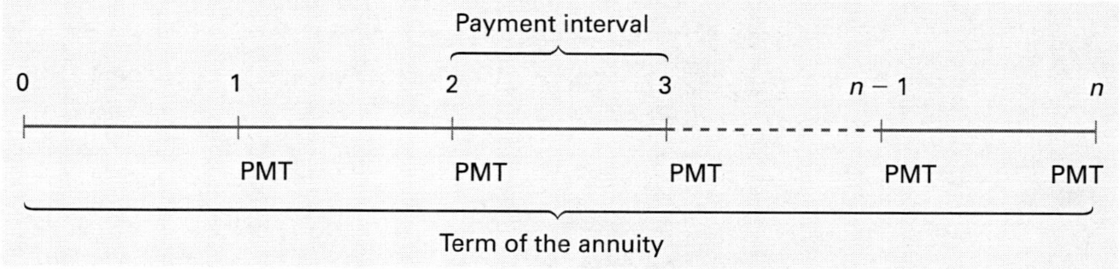

> This diagram illustrates an annuity with payments at the end of each payment period. Such an annuity is called an **ordinary annuity.**

In an ordinary annuity you should recognize the difference between the beginning of the annuity and the date of the first payment. The beginning of the annuity is the beginning of its term, at point 0. The beginning of the payments starts at the end of the first payment period interval.

The end of an ordinary annuity is at the end of its term or at the end of its last payment interval.

> An annuity in which the payment is made at the beginning of each payment period is called an **annuity due.**

One must be sure to distinguish terms *end of the annuity* and *end of the payments.* The end of an annuity is the end of its term or the end of its last payment interval; the end of the payments is the last date of the payments, which is at the beginning of the last payment interval.

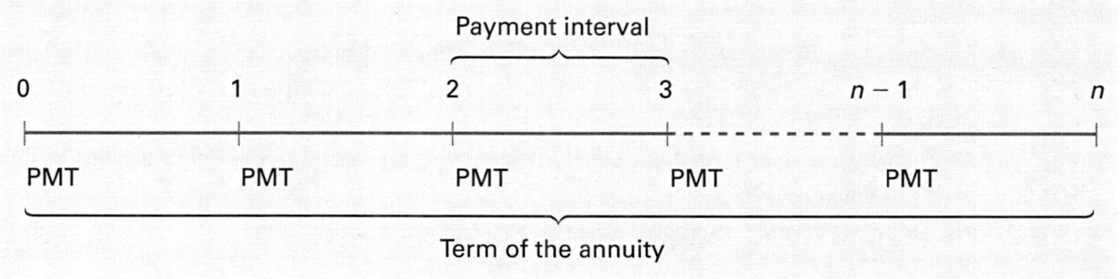

In some cases an annuity does not begin until after a certain time interval, called the *deferred period.* Such an annuity is called a **deferred annuity.** The equivalent number of payment intervals during the period of deferral is designated d in the following diagram.

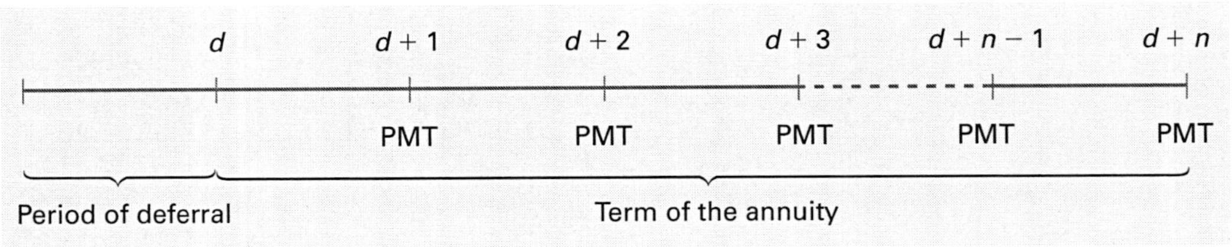

Ordinary annuities and annuities due are classified as *simple* and *general* annuities.

In **simple annuities,** the compounding period coincides with the payment period. For example, a loan of $12,000 at 4% compounded monthly must be repaid by 12 equal monthly payments. In this case, interest is compounded monthly and payments are to be made monthly. The compounding frequency is equal to the annual payment frequency.

In a loan of $12,000 at 4% compounded annually, which is to be repaid in 12 equal monthly payments, the compounding frequency ($m = 1$) is not equal to the payment frequency (12).

A **general annuity** is one in which the compounding frequency and the frequency of payments are not equal.

Let's summarize what we have learned in this Unit in a table:

Categories of annuity	Payment in each payment interval	Compounding frequency vs. payment frequency per year
Simple ordinary annuity	At the end of the period	Equal
General ordinary annuity	At the end of the period	Not equal
Simple annuity due	At the beginning of the period	Equal
General annuity due	At the beginning of the period	Not equal

EXAMPLE

Mr. Sharky has been contributing $50 to his savings plan at the end of each month for two years. The interest is 3% compounded monthly.

In this example Mr. Sharky contributes equal amounts of $50 over equal and regular time intervals—each month—so this is an annuity. He makes his contributions every month and the interest is also compounded monthly, so this is a simple annuity. He pays $50 at the end of each month, so this is an ordinary annuity.

In this chapter we will consider only ordinary annuities and annuities due, but we will work with both simple and general annuities.

Now it's time for a Practice Quiz.

LU 15–1 PRACTICE QUIZ

Define the type and category of annuity. Explain your answers.

1. Tom borrowed $15,000 at 6% compounded annually. He must repay it in 16 quarterly payments at the end of each quarter.
2. Mrs. Percival invests $1,000 at the beginning of every month into her RRSP account. The money value is 3% compounded semiannually.
3. Mr. and Mrs. Pif are setting up a fund for their grandson's education. They have established the fund on the following terms:
   - Their grandson will be able to withdraw $500 at the end of each month for three years.
   - The first withdrawal should be at the beginning of his education in four years.
   - The fund can earn 5.5% compounded monthly.

LEARNING UNIT 15–2

SIMPLE ORDINARY ANNUITIES AND SIMPLE ANNUITIES DUE; CALCULATING MATURITY VALUE OF AN ANNUITY MANUALLY AND USING TABLE LOOKUP

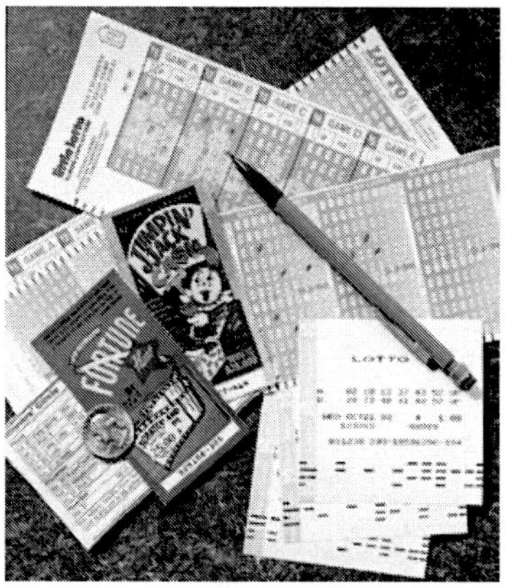

Sharon Hoogstraten

The amount of an annuity or the future value of an annuity, as well as maturity value of an annuity, is the sum of the future values of all payments or withdrawals evaluated at the end of the last payment interval.

The concept of the future value of an annuity is illustrated in Figure 15.1. Do not be concerned about the calculations (we will do them soon). Let's first focus on the big picture of annuities. In the figure, we see the following:

At end of period 1: The $1 is still worth $1 because it was invested at the *end* of the period.

At end of period 2: An additional $1 is invested. The $2 is now worth $2.08. Note the $1 from period 1 earns interest but not the $1 invested at the end of period 2.

At end of period 3: An additional $1 is invested. The $3 is now worth $3.25. Remember that the last dollar invested earns no interest.

ORDINARY ANNUITIES: MONEY INVESTED AT END OF PERIOD (FIND FUTURE VALUE)

Before we explain how to use a table that simplifies calculating ordinary annuities, let's first determine how to calculate the future value of an ordinary annuity manually.

Calculating Future Value of Ordinary Annuities Manually

Remember that an ordinary annuity invests money at the *end* of each year (period). After we calculate ordinary annuities manually, you will see that the total value of the investment comes from the *stream* of yearly investments and the buildup of interest on the current balance.

CALCULATING FUTURE VALUE OF AN ORDINARY ANNUITY MANUALLY

Step 1. For period 1, no interest calculation is necessary, since money is invested at the end of the period.
Step 2. For period 2, calculate interest on the balance and add the interest to the previous balance.
Step 3. Add the additional investment at the end of period 2 to the new balance.
Step 4. Repeat Steps 2 and 3 until the end of the desired period is reached.

EXAMPLE

Find the value of an investment after 3 years for a $3,000 ordinary annuity at 8%.
We calculate this manually as follows:

STEP 1.	End of year 1:	$3,000.00	No interest, since this is put in at end of year 1. (Remember, payment is made at end of period.)
	Year 2:	$3,000.00	Value of investment before investment at end of year 2.
STEP 2.		+ 240.00	Interest (.08 × $3,000) for year 2.
		$3,240.00	Value of investment at end of year 2 before second investment.
STEP 3.	End of year 2:	+ 3,000.00	Second investment at end of year 2.
	Year 3:	$6,240.00	Investment balance going into year 3.
		+ 499.20	Interest for year 3 (.08 × $6,240).
STEP 4.		$6,739.20	Value before investment at end of year 3.
		+ 3,000.00	Investment at end of year 3.
	End of year 3:	$9,739.20	Total value of investment after investment at end of year 3.

Note: In total, we invested $9,000 over three different periods. It is now worth $9,739.20.

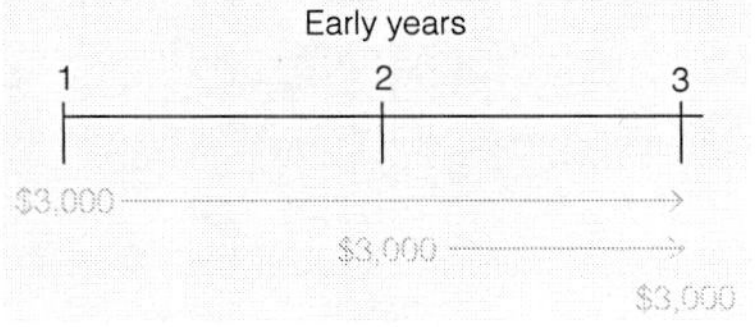

When you deposit \$3,000 at the end of each year at an annual rate of 8%, the total value of the annuity is \$9,739.20. What we called *maturity value* in compounding is now called the *future value of the annuity.* Remember that Interest = Principal × Rate × Time, with the principal changing because of the interest payments and the additional deposits. We can make this calculation easier by using Table 15.1.

There is a shortcut formula for calculating future value of an ordinary annuity:

$$FV = PMT\left[\frac{(1+i)^n - 1}{i}\right] \tag{15.1}$$

where:

FV = Future or the maturity value of an annuity
PMT = Amount of each periodic payment in an annuity
i = Periodic interest per period of compounding
n = Number of payments in an annuity
$n = m_2 \times t$, where m_2 is the payment frequency per year
$i = j \div m_1$, where m_1 is the compounding frequency per year

> *Note:* If $m_1 = m_2$ it's a simple annuity. If $m_1 \neq m_2$ it's a general annuity.

The calculator sequence for this example is:

3000 × ((1 + .08) ^ 3 − 1) ÷ .08 = 9739.20

For the example above:

$t = 3$; PMT = \$3,000; $j = .08$; $m_1 = 1$; $m_2 = 1$

So $i = .08$; $n = 3$

$$FV = \$3,000\left[\frac{(1+.08)^3 - 1}{.08}\right] = \$9,739.20$$

Calculating Future Value of Ordinary Annuities by Table Lookup

Use the following steps to calculate the future value of an ordinary annuity by table lookup.

TABLE 15-1
ORDINARY ANNUITY TABLE: COMPOUND SUM OF AN ANNUITY OF \$1

Period	2%	3%	4%	5%	6%	7%	8%	9%	10%	11%	12%	13%
1	1.0000	1.0000	1.0000	1.0000	1.0000	1.0000	1.0000	1.0000	1.0000	1.0000	1.0000	1.0000
2	2.0200	2.0300	2.0400	2.0500	2.0600	2.0700	2.0800	2.0900	2.1000	2.1100	2.1200	2.1300
3	3.0604	3.0909	3.1216	3.1525	3.1836	3.2149	3.2464	3.2781	3.3100	3.3421	3.3744	3.4069
4	4.1216	4.1836	4.2465	4.3101	4.3746	4.4399	4.5061	4.5731	4.6410	4.7097	4.7793	4.8498
5	5.2040	5.3091	5.4163	5.5256	5.6371	5.7507	5.8666	5.9847	6.1051	6.2278	6.3528	6.4803
6	6.3081	6.4684	6.6330	6.8019	6.9753	7.1533	7.3359	7.5233	7.7156	7.9129	8.1152	8.3227
7	7.4343	7.6625	7.8983	8.1420	8.3938	8.6540	8.9228	9.2004	9.4872	9.7833	10.0890	10.4047
8	8.5829	8.8923	9.2142	9.5491	9.8975	10.2598	10.6366	11.0285	11.4359	11.8594	12.2997	12.7573
9	9.7546	10.1591	10.5828	11.0265	11.4913	11.9780	12.4876	13.0210	13.5795	14.1640	14.7757	15.4157
10	10.9497	11.4639	12.0061	12.5779	13.1808	13.8164	14.4866	15.1929	15.9374	16.7220	17.5487	18.4197
11	12.1687	12.8078	13.4863	14.2068	14.9716	15.7836	16.6455	17.5603	18.5312	19.5614	20.6546	21.8143
12	13.4120	14.1920	15.0258	15.9171	16.8699	17.8884	18.9771	20.1407	21.3843	22.7132	24.1331	25.6502
13	14.6803	15.6178	16.6268	17.7129	18.8821	20.1406	21.4953	22.9534	24.5227	26.2116	28.0291	29.9847
14	15.9739	17.0863	18.2919	19.5986	21.0150	22.5505	24.2149	26.0192	27.9750	30.0949	32.3926	34.8827
15	17.2934	18.5989	20.0236	21.5785	23.2759	25.1290	27.1521	29.3609	31.7725	34.4054	37.2797	40.4174
16	18.6392	20.1569	21.8245	23.6574	25.6725	27.8880	30.3243	33.0034	35.9497	39.1899	42.7533	46.6717
17	20.0120	21.7616	23.6975	25.8403	28.2128	30.8402	33.7503	36.9737	40.5447	44.5008	48.8837	53.7390
18	21.4122	23.4144	25.6454	28.1323	30.9056	33.9990	37.4503	41.3014	45.5992	50.3959	55.7497	61.7251
19	22.8405	25.1169	27.6712	30.5389	33.7599	37.3789	41.4463	46.0185	51.1591	56.9395	63.4397	70.7494
20	24.2973	26.8704	29.7781	33.0659	36.7855	40.9954	45.7620	51.1602	57.2750	64.2028	72.0524	80.9468
25	32.0302	36.4593	41.6459	47.7270	54.8644	63.2489	73.1060	84.7010	98.3471	114.4133	133.3338	155.6194
30	40.5679	47.5754	56.0849	66.4386	79.0580	94.4606	113.2833	136.3077	164.4941	199.0209	241.3327	293.1989
40	60.4017	75.4012	95.0254	120.7993	154.7616	199.6346	259.0569	337.8831	442.5928	581.8260	767.0913	1013.7030
50	84.5790	112.7968	152.6669	209.3470	290.3351	406.5277	573.7711	815.0853	1163.9090	1668.7710	2400.0180	3459.5010

Note: This is only a sampling of tables available.

CALCULATING FUTURE VALUE OF AN ORDINARY ANNUITY BY TABLE LOOKUP

Step 1. Calculate the number of periods and rate per period.

Step 2. Look up the periods and rate in an ordinary annuity table. The intersection gives the table factor for the future value of $1.

Step 3. Multiply the payment each period by the table factor. This gives the future value of the annuity.

$$\text{Future value of ordinary annuity} = \text{Annuity payment each period} \times \text{Ordinary annuity table factor}$$

EXAMPLE

Find the value of an investment after 3 years for a $3,000 ordinary annuity at 8%.

STEP 1. $n = 3 \text{ years} \times 1 = 3$ $\qquad i = \frac{8\%}{\text{Annually}} = 8\%$

STEP 2. Go to Table 15.1, an ordinary annuity table. Look for 3 under the Period column. Go across to 8%. At the intersection is the entry 3.2464. (This was the example we showed in Figure 15.1.)

STEP 3. Multiply $3,000 × 3.2464 = $9,739.20 (the same figure we calculated manually).

ANNUITIES DUE: MONEY INVESTED AT BEGINNING OF PERIOD (FIND FUTURE VALUE)

In this section we look at what the difference in the total investment would be for an annuity due. As in the previous section, we will first make the calculation manually and then use table lookup.

Calculating Future Value of Annuities Due Manually

Use the steps that follow to calculate the future value of an annuity due manually.

CALCULATING FUTURE VALUE OF AN ANNUITY DUE MANUALLY

Step 1. Calculate the interest on the balance for the period and add it to the previous balance.

Step 2. Add additional investment at the *beginning* of the period to the new balance.

Step 3. Repeat Steps 1 and 2 until the end of the desired period is reached.

Remember that in an annuity due, we deposit the money at the *beginning* of the year and gain more interest. Common sense should tell us that the *annuity due* will give a higher final value. We will use the same example that we used before.

EXAMPLE

Find the value of an investment after 3 years for a $3,000 annuity due at 8%.

We calculate this manually as follows:

	Beginning year 1:	$3,000.00	→ First investment (will earn interest for 3 years).
STEP 1. →		+ 240.00	→ Interest (.08 × $3,000).
		$3,240.00	→ Value of investment at end of year 1.
STEP 2. →	Year 2:	+ 3,000.00	→ Second investment (will earn interest for 2 years).
		$6,240.00	
STEP 3. →		+ 499.20	→ Interest for year 2 (.08 × $6,240).
		$6,739.20	→ Value of investment at the end of year 2.
	Year 3:	+ 3,000.00	
		$9,739.20	→ Third investment (will earn interest for 1 year).
		+ 779.14	→ Interest (.08 × $9,739.20).
	End of year 3:	$10,518.34	→ At the end of year 3, final value.

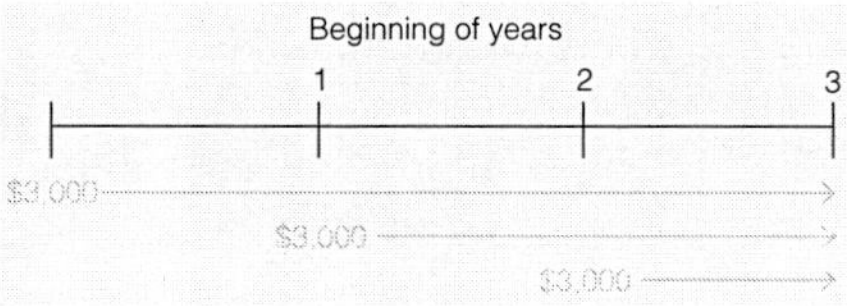

Note: Our total investment of $9,000 is worth $10,518.34. For an ordinary annuity, our total investment was only worth $9,739.20.

There is a shortcut formula for calculating future/maturity value of an annuity due:

$$FV_{due} = FV \times (1 + i) = PMT\left[\frac{(1 + i)^n - 1}{i}\right](1 + i) \qquad \textbf{(15.2)}$$

where:

FV_{due} = Future value of an annuity due
i = Periodic interest per period of compounding
n = Number of payments in an annuity
$n = m_2 \times t$, where m_2 is the payment frequency per year
$i = j \div m_1$, where m_1 is the compounding frequency per year

Let's calculate the future value of an annuity due, which was considered in the example above.

The calculator sequence would be as follows:

3000 [×] [(] [(] 1 [+] .08 [)]
[^] 3 [−] 1 [)] [÷] .08 [×]
[(] 1 [+] .08 [)] [=]

PMT = \$3,000; $i = .08$; $n = 3$

$m_1 = m_2$, so this is a simple annuity due.

$$FV_{due} = \$3{,}000\left[\frac{(1 + .08)^3 - 1}{.08}\right] \times (1 + .08) = \$10{,}518.34$$

> *Note:* The future value of an annuity due is higher than the future value of an ordinary annuity with the same terms, because the investments were made at the beginning of each payment period and the last installment also produced an interest.

Calculating Future Value of Annuities Due by Table Lookup

To calculate the future value of an annuity due with a table lookup, use the steps that follow.

CALCULATING FUTURE VALUE OF AN ANNUITY DUE BY TABLE LOOKUP

Step 1. Calculate the number of periods and the rate per period. Add one extra period.
Step 2. Look up in an ordinary annuity table the periods and rate. The intersection gives the table *factor* for future value of \$1.
Step 3. Multiply payment each period by the table factor.
Step 4. Subtract 1 payment from Step 3.

$$\text{Future value of an annuity due} = \left(\begin{matrix}\text{Annuity} \\ \text{payment} \\ \text{each period}\end{matrix} \times \begin{matrix}\text{Ordinary*} \\ \text{annuity} \\ \text{table factor}\end{matrix}\right) - 1\text{ payment}$$

*Add 1 period.

Let's check the \$10,518.34 by table lookup.

STEP 1. n = 3 years × 1 = 3
+ 1 extra
4

$i = \dfrac{8\%}{\text{Annually}} = 8\%$

STEP 2. Table factor, 4.5061

STEP 3. \$3,000 × 4.5061 = \$13,518.30

STEP 4. − 3,000.00 ← Be sure to subtract 1 payment.
= \$10,518.34 (off 4 cents due to rounding)

Note that the annuity due shows an ending value of \$10,518.30, while the ending value of ordinary annuity was \$9,739.20. We had a higher ending value with the annuity due because the investment took place at the beginning of each period.

Annuity payments do not have to be made yearly. They could be made semiannually, monthly, quarterly, and so on. Let's look at one more example with a different number of periods and rate.

Different Number of Periods and Rates

By using a different number of periods and rates, we will contrast an ordinary annuity with an annuity due in the following example.

EXAMPLE

Using Table 15.1, find the value of a $3,000 investment after 3 years made quarterly at 8%.

In the annuity due calculation, be sure to add one period and subtract one payment from the total value.

	Ordinary annuity	Annuity due	
STEP 1.	Periods = 3 years × 4 = 12	Periods = 3 years × 4 = 12	**STEP 1**
	Rate = 8% ÷ 4 = 2%	Rate = 8% ÷ 4 = 2%	
STEP 2.	Table 15.1:	Table 15.1:	**STEP 2**
	12 periods, 2% = 13.4120	13 periods, 2%= 14.6803	
STEP 3.	$3,000 × 13.4120 = $40,236	$3,000 × 14.6803 = $44,040.90	**STEP 3**
		− 3,000.00	**STEP 4**
		$41,040.90	

Again, note that with annuity due, the total value is greater since you invest the money at the beginning of each period.

Now check your progress with the Practice Quiz.

LU 15–2 PRACTICE QUIZ

1. Using Table 15.1 and formulas 15.2 and 15.1, **(a)** find the value of an investment after 4 years on an ordinary annuity of $4,000 made semiannually at 10%; and **(b)** recalculate, assuming an annuity due.
2. Wally Beaver won a lottery and will receive a cheque for $4,000 at the beginning of each 6 months for the next 5 years. If Wally deposits each cheque into an account that pays 6%, compounded semiannually, how much will he have at the end of the 5 years?

LEARNING UNIT 15–3

SIMPLE ORDINARY ANNUITIES AND SIMPLE ANNUITIES DUE; CALCULATING PRESENT VALUES AND PERIODIC PAYMENTS (SINKING FUNDS)

This Unit begins with the concept of present value of an ordinary annuity. Then you will learn how to use a table to calculate the present value of an ordinary annuity.

CONCEPT OF PRESENT VALUE OF AN ORDINARY ANNUITY—THE BIG PICTURE

Let's assume that we want to know how much money we need to invest *today* to receive a stream of payments for a given number of years in the future. This is called the **present value of an ordinary annuity.**

In Figure 15.2 you can see that if you wanted to withdraw $1 at the end of one period, you would have to invest 93 cents *today.* If at the end of each period for three periods, you wanted to withdraw $1, you would have to put $2.58 in the bank *today* at 8% interest. (Note that we go from the future back to the present.)

Now let's look at how we could use tables to calculate the present value of annuities and then check our answer.

FIGURE 15–2
Present value of an annuity of $1 at 8%

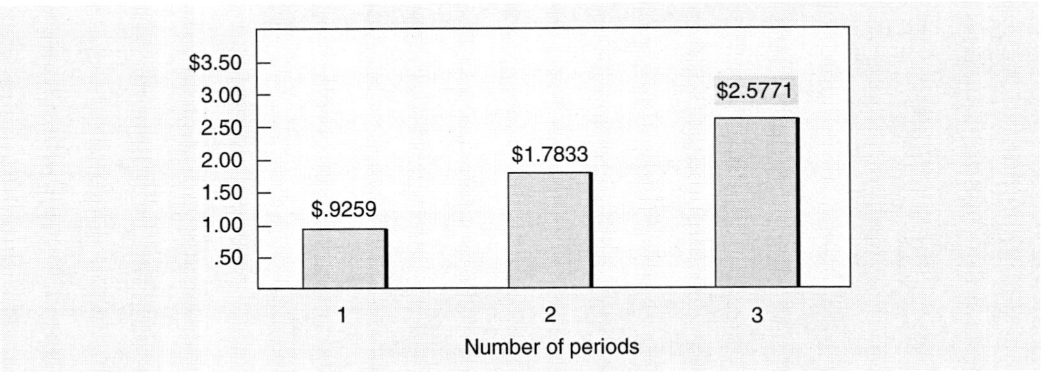

CALCULATING PRESENT VALUE OF AN ORDINARY ANNUITY BY FORMULA AND TABLE LOOKUP

Use the following steps to calculate by table lookup the present value of an ordinary annuity.

CALCULATING PRESENT VALUE OF AN ORDINARY ANNUITY BY TABLE LOOKUP

Step 1. Calculate the number of periods and rate per period (n and i).

Step 2. Look up the periods and rate in the present value of an annuity table. The intersection gives the table factor for the present value of $1.

Step 3. Multiply the withdrawal for each period by the table factor. This gives the present value of an ordinary annuity.

$$\text{Present value of ordinary annuity payment} = \text{Annuity payment} \times \text{Present value of ordinary annuity table}$$

EXAMPLE

John Fitch wants to receive an $8,000 annuity for 3 years. Interest on the annuity is 8% annually. John will make withdrawals at the end of each year. How much must John invest today to receive a stream of payments for 3 years? Use Table 15.2. Remember that interest could be earned semiannually, quarterly, and so on, as shown in the previous unit.

STEP 1. $n = 3 \text{ years} \times 1 = 3 \text{ periods}$ $\quad i = \frac{8\%}{\text{Annually}} = 8\%$

STEP 2. Table factor, 2.5771 (we saw this in Figure 15.2)

STEP 3. $8,000 × 2.5771 = $20,616.80

If John wants to withdraw $8,000 at the end of each period for 3 years, he will have to deposit $20,616.80 in the bank *today*.

$20,616.80	
+ 1,649.34	→ Interest at end of year 1 (.08 × $20,616.80)
$22,266.14	
− 8,000.00	→ First payment to John
$14,266.14	
+ 1,141.29	→ Interest at end of year 2 (.08 × $14,266.14)
$15,407.43	
− 8,000.00	→ Second payment to John
$ 7,407.43	
+ 592.59	→ Interest at end of year 3 (.08 × $7,407.43)
$ 8,000.02	
− 8,000.00	→ After end of year 3 John receives his last $8,000
.02[1]	

[1]Off due to rounding.

TABLE 15–2
PRESENT VALUE OF AN ANNUITY OF $1

Period	2%	3%	4%	5%	6%	7%	8%	9%	10%	11%	12%	13%
1	0.9804	0.9709	0.9615	0.9524	0.9434	0.9346	0.9259	0.9174	0.9091	0.9009	0.8929	0.8850
2	1.9416	1.9135	1.8861	1.8594	1.8334	1.8080	1.7833	1.7591	1.7355	1.7125	1.6901	1.6681
3	2.8839	2.8286	2.7751	2.7232	2.6730	2.6243	2.5771	2.5313	2.4869	2.4437	2.4018	2.3612
4	3.8077	3.7171	3.6299	3.5459	3.4651	3.3872	3.3121	3.2397	3.1699	3.1024	3.0373	2.9745
5	4.7134	4.5797	4.4518	4.3295	4.2124	4.1002	3.9927	3.8897	3.7908	3.6959	3.6048	3.5172
6	5.6014	5.4172	5.2421	5.0757	4.9173	4.7665	4.6229	4.4859	4.3553	4.2305	4.1114	3.9975
7	6.4720	6.2303	6.0021	5.7864	5.5824	5.3893	5.2064	5.0330	4.8684	4.7122	4.5638	4.4226
8	7.3255	7.0197	6.7327	6.4632	6.2098	5.9713	5.7466	5.5348	5.3349	5.1461	4.9676	4.7988
9	8.1622	7.7861	7.4353	7.1078	6.8017	6.5152	6.2469	5.9952	5.7590	5.5370	5.3282	5.1317
10	8.9826	8.5302	8.1109	7.7217	7.3601	7.0236	6.7101	6.4177	6.1446	5.8892	5.6502	5.4262
11	9.7868	9.2526	8.7605	8.3064	7.8869	7.4987	7.1390	6.8052	6.4951	6.2065	5.9377	5.6869
12	10.5753	9.9540	9.3851	8.8632	8.3838	7.9427	7.5361	7.1607	6.8137	6.4924	6.1944	5.9176
13	11.3483	10.6350	9.9856	9.3936	8.8527	8.3576	7.9038	7.4869	7.1034	6.7499	6.4235	6.1218
14	12.1062	11.2961	10.5631	9.8986	9.2950	8.7455	8.2442	7.7862	7.3667	6.9819	6.6282	6.3025
15	12.8492	11.9379	11.1184	10.3796	9.7122	9.1079	8.5595	8.0607	7.6061	7.1909	6.8109	6.4624
16	13.5777	12.5611	11.6523	10.8378	10.1059	9.4466	8.8514	8.3126	7.8237	7.3792	6.9740	6.6039
17	14.2918	13.1661	12.1657	11.2741	10.4773	9.7632	9.1216	8.5436	8.0216	7.5488	7.1196	6.7291
18	14.9920	13.7535	12.6593	11.6896	10.8276	10.0591	9.3719	8.7556	8.2014	7.7016	7.2497	6.8399
19	15.6784	14.3238	13.1339	12.0853	11.1581	10.3356	9.6036	8.9501	8.3649	7.8393	7.3658	6.9380
20	16.3514	14.8775	13.5903	12.4622	11.4699	10.5940	9.8181	9.1285	8.5136	7.9633	7.4694	7.0248
25	19.5234	17.4131	15.6221	14.0939	12.7834	11.6536	10.6748	9.8226	9.0770	8.4217	7.8431	7.3300
30	22.3964	19.6004	17.2920	15.3724	13.7648	12.4090	11.2578	10.2737	9.4269	8.6938	8.0552	7.4957
40	27.3554	23.1148	19.7928	17.1591	15.0463	13.3317	11.9246	10.7574	9.7790	8.9511	8.2438	7.6344
50	31.4236	25.7298	21.4822	18.2559	15.7619	13.8007	12.2335	10.9617	9.9148	9.0417	8.3045	7.6752

There are shortcuts for calculating present value of an ordinary simple annuity and simple annuity due.

To define a present value of a simple ordinary annuity, use this formula:

$$PV = PMT\left[\frac{1-(1+i)^{-n}}{i}\right] \qquad \textbf{(15.3)}$$

where:

PV = Present value of an annuity
PMT = Amount of each periodic payment in an annuity
i = Periodic interest per period of compounding
n = Number of payments in an annuity
$n = m_2 \times t$, where m_2 is the payment frequency per year
$i = j \div m_1$, where m_1 is the compounding frequency per year

To calculate a present value of an annuity due, use this formula:

$$PV_{due} = PV(1+i) = PMT\left[\frac{1-(1+i)^{-n}}{i}\right] \times (1+i) \qquad \textbf{(15.4)}$$

where:

PV = Present value of an annuity due
PMT = Amount of each periodic payment in an annuity

i = Periodic interest per period of compounding
n = Number of payments in an annuity
$n = m_2 \times t$, where m_2 is the payment frequency per year
$i = j \div m_1$, where m_1 is the compounding frequency per year

To illustrate these formulas, consider the example with John Fitch. In the left corner of our page let's write down the given values:

$t = 3$ years; PMT = \$8,000; $j = .08$; $m_2 = 1$; $m_1 = 1$; $m_1 = m_2$, so it's a simple annuity

Withdrawals are made at the end of each year—so this is an ordinary annuity.

PV = ?

We should use formula 15.3:

$$i = \frac{.08}{1} = .08;\ n = 1 \times 3 = 3$$

$$\text{PV} = \$8{,}000\left[\frac{1-(1+.08)^{-3}}{.08}\right] = \$20{,}616.78$$

The calculator sequence would be as follows:

8000 [×] [(] 1 [−] [(] 1 [+] .08 [)] [^] [(] 3 [+/−] [)] [)] [÷] .08 [=]

This is different from the manual calculation results due to rounding in the manual approach.

Now, let's assume that John Fitch wants to receive \$8,000 at the beginning of each year. In this case we will have to deal with an annuity due and use formula 15.4:

$$\text{PV}_{\text{due}} = \text{PV}(1+i) = \text{PMT}\left[\frac{1-(1+i)^{-n}}{i}\right] \times (1+i)$$

In the left corner of our page let's write down the given values:

$t = 3$ years; PMT = \$8,000; $j = .08$; $m_2 = 1$; $m_1 = 1$; $m_1 = m_2$, so it's a simple annuity

PV = ?

The calculator sequence would be as follows:

8000 [×] [(] 1 [−] [(] 1 [+] .08 [)] [^] [(] 3 [+/−] [)] [)] [÷] .08 [×] [(] 1 [+] .08 [)] [=]

$$i = \frac{.08}{1} = .08;\ n = 1 \times 3 = 3$$

$$\text{PV}_{\text{due}} = \$8{,}000\left[\frac{1-(1+.08)^{-3}}{.08}\right] \times (1+.08) = \$22{,}266.12$$

To be able to withdraw his money at the beginning of each year John Fitch must invest \$22,266.12.

Calculating Size of Periodic Payment or Withdrawal (Sinking Funds)

A **sinking fund** is a financial arrangement that sets aside regular periodic payments of a particular amount of money. Compound interest accumulates on these payments up to a specific sum at a predetermined future date. Corporations use sinking funds to discharge bonded indebtedness, to replace worn-out equipment, to finance plant expansion, and so on.

A sinking fund is just a different type of annuity. In a sinking fund, you determine the amount of periodic payments you need to achieve a given financial goal. In these and other cases, when it is necessary to calculate amount of PMT:

a. The periodic payments of a loan or a mortgage
b. The amount to be paid periodically to reach a saving objective
c. The size of withdrawals from an annuity

we use the same formulas, 15.1, 15.2, 15.3 and 15.4.

First of all you must determine whether you are dealing with a simple or a general annuity and whether you know the future or the present value.

For a simple annuity you will need to undertake only one of the steps; for a general annuity, you will follow four steps.

STEP 1. Omit this step and move directly onto Step 2.

STEP 2. Let's consider it using the example of an ordinary annuity. You will use the same procedure for annuities due.

If you know FV of an annuity, substitute the values of FV, *i*, and *n* into formula 15.1.	**If you know PV of an annuity, substitute the values of PV, *n*, and *i* into formula 15.3.**
$FV = PMT\left[\frac{(1+i)^n - 1}{i}\right]$	$PV = PMT\left[\frac{1-(1+i)^{-n}}{i}\right]$

STEP 3. Calculate the value in the square brackets.

STEP 4. Substitute the value from Step 3 into the formula and find the unknown value of PMT.

Useful tip. To determine which formula to use, *future value* or *present value*, look for key words:

- *Future value.* Future value, maturity value, amount of an annuity
- *Present value.* Amount of a loan, amount borrowed, purchase price, mortgage, present value, amount of an investment

Let's use the same example with John Fitch. Fitch can invest $20,616.78 to start an ordinary annuity at 8% compounded annually for three years. He wants to make regular withdrawals at the end of each year. How much will he be able to withdraw at the end of each year?

In this problem, we have an amount of investment, so this is a *present value* and we will use formula 15.3:

$PV = \$20{,}616.78;\ i = .08;\ n = 3;\ PMT = ?$

$$\$20{,}616.78 = PMT\left[\frac{1-(1+.08)^{-3}}{.08}\right]$$

$\$20{,}616.78 = PMT \times 2.577096987$ *Note:* Do not round the intermediate result. Keep all the decimals.

$$PMT = \frac{\$20{,}616.78}{2.577096987}$$

$$PMT = \$8{,}000.001599$$

$$PMT = \$8{,}000$$

John will be able to withdraw $8,000 at the end of each of three years.

The calculator sequence would be as follows:

Step 1. [(] 1 [−] [(] 1 [+] .08 [)] [^] [(] 3 [+/−] [)] [)] [÷] .08 [=] 2.577096987

Step 2. Put this result into the calculator's memory: [STO] [A]. This will save you a few seconds in the following calculations. If you don't have a memory feature on your calculator, write down precisely all the numbers of the result. Don't round—otherwise the final answer will not be precise and correct for annuities due.

Step 3. 20616.78 [÷] [RCL] [A] [=] 8000.001599 or 20616.78 [÷] 2.577096987 [=] 8000.001599

Before we leave this Unit, let's work out two examples that show the relationship of Chapter 15 to Chapter 14.

LUMP SUM VERSUS ANNUITIES

EXAMPLE

John Sands made deposits of \$200 semiannually to Floor Bank, which pays 8% interest compounded semiannually. After 5 years, John makes no more deposits. What will be the balance in the account 6 years after the last deposit?

STEP 1. Calculate amount of annuity: Table 15.1

10 periods, 4% $\$200 \times 12.0061 = \$2{,}401.22$

or $FV = \$200\left(\frac{(1+.04)^{10} \times 1}{.04}\right) = \$2{,}401.22$

STEP 2. Calculate how much the final value of the annuity will grow by the compound interest table.

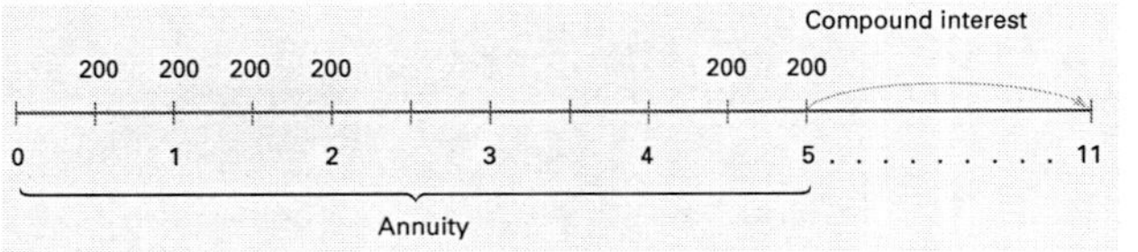

12 periods, 4%

$n = 12$; $i = .04$

$FV = P(1 + i)^n = \$2{,}401.22 \times 1.04^{12} = \$3{,}844.43$

For John, the stream of payments grows to \$2,401.22. Then this *lump sum* grows for 6 years to \$3,844.35. Now let's look at a present value example.

EXAMPLE

Mel Rich decided to retire in 8 years to New Mexico. What amount should Mel invest today so he will be able to withdraw \$40,000 at the end of each year for 25 years *after* he retires? Assume Mel can invest money at 5% interest (compounded annually).

STEP 1. Calculate the present value of the annuity: Table 13.2

$n = 25$ periods, $5\% = i = .05$ $\$40{,}000 \times 14.0939 = \$563{,}756$ or

$PV_{ann} = \$40{,}000\left(\frac{1-(1+.05)^{-25}}{.05}\right) = \$563{,}757.78$

(difference is present because of the roundings in the table)

STEP 2. Find the present value of \$563,756 since Mel will not retire for 8 years:

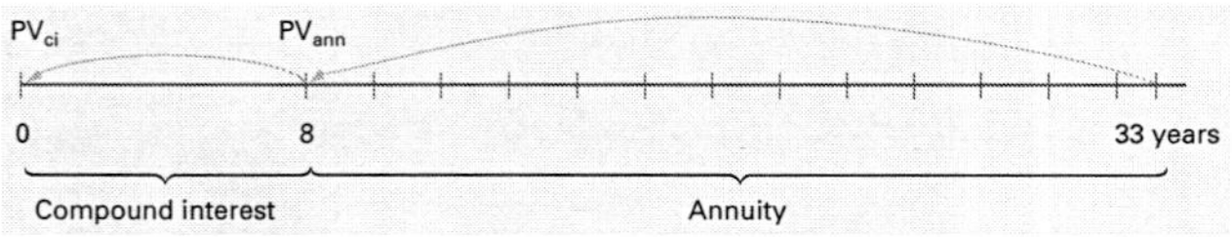

$n = 8$ periods, 5% (PV table)

$PV = FV(1 + i)^{-n} = \$563{,}757.78(1 + .05)^{-8} = \$381{,}573.46$

If Mel deposits \$381,573.46 in year 1, it will grow to \$563,756 after 8 years.

It's time to try the Practice Quiz and check your understanding of this Unit.

LU 15–3 PRACTICE QUIZ

1. What must you invest today to receive an \$18,000 annuity for 5 years semiannually at 10% compounded semiannually? All withdrawals will be made at the end of each period.
2. Rase High School wants to set up a scholarship fund to provide five \$2,000 scholarships for the next 10 years. If money can be invested at an annual rate of 9%, how much should the scholarship committee invest today?
3. Joe Wood decided to retire in 5 years in Arizona. What amount should Joe invest today so he can withdraw \$60,000 at the end of each year for 30 years after he retires? Assume Joe can invest money at 6% compounded annually.

LEARNING UNIT 15–4

GENERAL ORDINARY ANNUITIES; CALCULATING PRESENT VALUES, MATURITY VALUES, AND PERIODIC PAYMENTS USING FORMULAS

In the previous Learning Units we dealt only with simple annuities, where compounding frequency was equal to the frequency of payments per year: $m_1 = m_2$. In real life this does not happen all the time. For example, in Canada mortgage interest is usually compounded on semiannually and payments are made on monthly or biweekly basis, so m_1 (2) $\neq$ m_2 (12 or 26).

Recall that an annuity in which the compounding frequency is different from the payment frequency is called a *general annuity*. In this Unit, we will deal with ordinary annuities. To calculate future values, present values, and the size of periodic payments/withdrawals we need to adjust formulas 15.1 and 15.3, which we used for simple annuities. These adjustments will be related to finding the periodic rate for the payment interval equivalent to the periodic rate for the period of compounding frequency. In other words, in our example we must find a periodic rate i_2 for payment frequency 12 or 26 equivalent to the periodic rate i_1 for compounding frequency 2.

Let's use this formula, which we learned in Chapter 14:

$$i_2 = (1 + i_1)^{m_1/m_2} - 1$$

where:

i_1 = Given periodic rate
m_1 = Number of compoundings per year
m_2 = Number of compoundings per year at the equivalent rate (number of payments per year)
i_2 = Equivalent periodic interest rate for a payment interval

Let's consider the following example. Mr. Percival pays \$470 biweekly for his mortgage at 5.4% compounded semiannually. What mortgage does he have, if it must be repaid in 25 years?

$m_1 = 2$; $m_2 = 26$; $m_1 \neq m_2$; PMT = \$470; $j = .054$; $i_1 = .027$; $n = 25 \times 26 = 650$; i_2 = ?; PV = ?

This is a general annuity. To find PV and to use formula 15.3 first we need to find i_2.

$$i_2 = (1 + .027)^{2/26} - 1 = .00205148$$

Note: Don't round the intermediate result!

$$\text{PV} = \text{PMT}\left[\frac{1 - (1 + i_2)^{-n}}{i_2}\right] = \$470\left[\frac{1 - (1 + .00205148)^{-650}}{.00205148}\right] = \$168{,}637.26$$

Mr. Percival's mortgage is \$168,637.26.

To find the future value of a general annuity use formula 15.1:

$$\text{FV} = \text{PMT}\left[\frac{(1 + i_2)^n - 1}{i_2}\right]$$

$$i_2 = (1 + i_1)^{m_1/m_2} - 1$$

Let's consider an example. Mr. Pif deposits \$1,000 at the end of each month into his savings account. How much money will he have in five years if the interest in his saving account is 4% compounded quarterly?

$m_1 = 4$; $m_2 = 12$; $m_1 \neq m_2$, so it's a general annuity

PMT = \$1,000; $t = 5$; $n = 12 \times 5 = 60$; FV = ?

$$i_2 = (1 + .01)^{4/12} - 1 = .003322284$$

$$\text{FV} = 1{,}000\left[\frac{(1 + .003322284)^{60} - 1}{.003322284}\right] = 66{,}276.72$$

Mr. Pif will have $66,276.72 in his account in five years.

To find the periodic payment or withdrawal, use the same approach as for simple annuities.

EXAMPLE

Julia needs to have $5,000 in her account in five years. How much must she deposit at the end of each month to save this amount if the interest rate is 3% compounded semiannually?

FV = $5,000; $t = 5$; $m_1 = 2$; $m_2 = 12$; $m_1 \neq m_2$; $n = 60$; $j = .03$; $i_1 = .03 \div 2 = .015$; $i_2 = ?$; PMT = ?

$i_2 = (1 + .015)^{2/12} - 1 = .002484516$

$$5{,}000 = \text{PMT}\left[\frac{(1 + .002484516)^{60} - 1}{.002484516}\right]$$

$$5{,}000 = \text{PMT} \times 64.61651874$$

PMT = $77.38

Julia must deposit $77.38 at the end of each month in order to get $5,000 in five years.

Now, time for a Practice Quiz.

LU 15-4 PRACTICE QUIZ

1. Today, Arrow Company issued bonds that will mature to a value of $90,000 in 10 years. Arrow's controller is planning to set up a sinking fund. Interest rates are 12% compounded semiannually. How much will Arrow have to set aside on a quarterly basis to meet its obligation in 10 years?
2. Fill in the table.

	PMT	Term (years), t	Nominal interest rate, j (%)	Compounding frequency, m_1	Payment interval	Calculate FV or PV
a.	$200	10	8%	Semiannually	One quarter	FV = ?
b.	$1,000	5	4%	Monthly	Semiannually	PV = ?

CHAPTER ORGANIZER AND REFERENCE GUIDE

TOPIC	KEY POINT, PROCEDURE, FORMULA	EXAMPLE(S) TO ILLUSTRATE SITUATION
Annuity due, p. 357	Payments or investments are made at the beginning of the payment period.	
Ordinary annuity, p. 357	Payments or investments are made at the end of the payment period.	
Simple annuity, p. 358	Compounding frequency is equal to payment frequency: $m_1 = m_2$	Loan is paid semiannually and interest is compounded semiannually: $m_1 = m_2 = 2$
Simple ordinary annuity (find future value), p. 360	Invest money at end of each period. Find future value at maturity. Answers question of how much money accumulates.	Use Table 15.1: 2 years, $4,000 ordinary annuity at 8% annually. Value = $4,000 × 2.0800 = $8,320 (2 periods, 8%)

(*continues*)

CHAPTER ORGANIZER AND REFERENCE GUIDE (CONTINUED)

Topic	Key point, procedure, formula	Example(s) to illustrate situation
	Future value of ordinary annuity = Annuity payment each period × Ordinary annuity table factor $FV = PMT\left[\frac{(1+i)^n - 1}{i}\right]$	$FV = 4{,}000\left[\frac{(1+.08)^2 - 1}{.08}\right] = 8{,}320$
Annuities due (find future value), p. 360	Invest money at beginning of each period. Find future value at maturity. Should be higher than ordinary annuity since it is invested at beginning of each period. Use Table 15.1, but add one period and subtract one payment from answer. Future value of an ordinary due = (Annuity payment each period × Ordinary* annuity table factor) − 1 payment *Add 1 period. $FV_{due} = PMT\left[\frac{(1+i)^n - 1}{i}\right](1+i)$	Same example as above but invest money at beginning of period. $4,000 × 3.2464 = $12,985.60 − 4,000.00 $ 8,985.60 (3 periods, 8%) $FV_{due} = 4{,}000\left(\frac{(1+.08)^2 - 1}{.08}\right)(1+.08)$ = $8,985.60
Present value of a simple ordinary annuity (find present value), p. 362	Calculate number of periods and rate per period. Use Table 15.2 to find table factor for present value of $1. Multiply withdrawal for each period by table factor to get present value of an ordinary annuity. Present value of an ordinary annuity payment = Annuity payment × Present value of ordinary annuity table $PV = PMT\left[\frac{1-(1+i)^{-n}}{i}\right]$	Receive $10,000 for 5 years. Interest is 10% compounded annually. Table 15.2: 5 periods, 10% 3.7908 × $10,000 What you put in today = $37,908 ↑ Not precise due to the rounding. $PV = 10{,}000\left[\frac{1-(1+.1)^{-5}}{.1}\right] = \$37{,}907.88$
Sinking funds (find periodic payment: PMT = ?), p. 366	Paying a particular amount of money for a set number of periodic payments to accumulate a specific sum. We know the future value and must calculate the periodic payments needed. Answer can be proved by ordinary annuity table. Sinking fund payment = Future value × Sinking fund table factor	$200,000 bond to retire 15 years from now. Interest is 6% compounded annually. By Table 15.3: $200,000 × .0430 = $8,600 ← Result is not precise because of rounding. Check by Table 15.1: $8,600 × 23.2759 = $200,172.74 $200{,}000 = PMT\left[\frac{(1+.06)^{15} - 1}{.06}\right]$ $PMT = \frac{200{,}000}{23.27596988} = \$8{,}592.55$ Don't round!

(continues)

CHAPTER ORGANIZER AND REFERENCE GUIDE (CONCLUDED)

TOPIC	KEY POINT, PROCEDURE, FORMULA	EXAMPLE(S) TO ILLUSTRATE SITUATION
General annuity, p. 369	Compounding frequency is different from payment frequency: $m_1 \neq m_2$ $i_2 = (1 + i_1)^{m_1/m_2} - 1$ where: i_1 is given periodic rate m_1 is the number of compoundings per year m_2 is the number of compoundings per year at the equivalent rate (number of payments per year) i_2 is the equivalent periodic interest rate for a payment interval For a simple annuity you need to undertake only one step; for a general annuity, you need four: **Step 1.** Calculate periodic interest: $i_2 = (1 + i_1)^{m_1/m_2} - 1$ **Step 2.** Consider it using the example of an ordinary annuity. Use the same procedure for annuities due. **If you know FV of an annuity, substitute the values of FV, *i*, and *n* into formula 15.1:** $FV = PMT\left[\frac{(1+i)^n - 1}{i}\right]$ **If you know PV of an annuity, substitute the values of PV, *n*, and *i* into formula 15.3:** $PV = PMT\left[\frac{1-(1+i)^{-n}}{i}\right]$ **Step 3.** Calculate the value in the square brackets. **Step 4.** Substitute the value from Step 3 into the formula and find the unknown value of PMT.	Mortgage at 4% compounded semiannually is paid by monthly payments: $m_1 = 2;\ m_2 = 12$ $i_2 = (1 + .02)^{2/12} - 1 = .00330589$
Key terms	Annuity, p. 356 Annuity due, p. 357 Deferred annuity, p. 357 Future value of an annuity, p. 357 General annuity, p. 358 Ordinary annuity, p. 357 Payment periods, p. 357 Periodic payment, p. 357 Present value of an ordinary annuity, p. 363 Simple annuity, p. 358	Sinking fund, p. 366 Term of an annuity, p. 357

CRITICAL THINKING DISCUSSION QUESTIONS

1. What is the difference between an ordinary annuity and an annuity due? If you were to save money in an annuity, which would you choose and why?
2. Explain how you would calculate ordinary annuities and annuities due by table lookup. Create an example to explain the meaning of a table factor from an ordinary annuity. Why do calculations using tables differ from calculations using formulas?
3. What is a present value of an ordinary annuity? Create an example showing how one of your relatives might plan for retirement by using the present value of an ordinary annuity. Would you ever have to use lump-sum payments in your calculation from Chapter 14?
4. What is a sinking fund? Why could an ordinary annuity table be used to check the sinking fund payment?

END-OF-CHAPTER PROBLEMS

DRILL PROBLEMS

Complete the ordinary annuities for the following using tables or formulas (at the instructor's discretion):

	Amount of payment	Payment payable	Years	Interest rate	Value of annuity
15–1.	$5,000	Quarterly	5	4%	?
15–2.	$3,000	Semiannually	10	10%	?

15–3. Redo Problem 15–1 as an annuity due.

Calculate the value of the following annuity using formulas.

	Amount of payment	Payment payable	Years	Interest rate	Value of annuity
15–4.	$2,000	Annually	3	6%	

Complete the following, using Table 15–2 or formulas, for the present value of an ordinary annuity:

	Amount of annuity expected	Payment	Time	Interest rate	Present value (amount needed now to invest to receive annuity)
15–5.	$900	Annually	4 years	6%	?
15–6.	$12,000	Quarterly	4 years	12%	?

15–7. Check Problem 15–5 using Table 15–2.

Complete the following:

	Required amount	Frequency of payment	Length of time	Interest rate	Payment amount end of each period
15–8.	$25,000	Quarterly	6 years	8%	?
15–9.	$15,000	Annually	8 years	8%	?

15–10. Check the answer in Problem 15–9 using Table 15–1.

ADDITIONAL DRILL PROBLEMS

15–11. Find the value of the following ordinary annuities (calculate using formulas):

	Amount of each annual deposit	Interest rate	Value at end of year 1	Value at end of year 2	Value at end of year 3
a.	$1,000	8%	?	?	?
b.	$2,500	12%	?	?	?
c.	$7,200	10%	?	?	?

15–12. Use Table 15–1 to find the value of the following ordinary annuities:

	Annuity payment	Payment period	Term of annuity	Interest rate	Value of annuity
a.	$650	Semiannually	5 years	6%	?
b.	$3,790	Annually	13 years	12%	?
c.	$500	Quarterly	1 year	8%	?

15–13. Find the annuity due (deposits are made at beginning of period) for each of the following using the Table 15–1:

	Amount of payment	Payment period	Interest rate	Time (years)	Amount of annuity
a.	$900	Annually	7%	6	?
b.	$1,200	Annually	11%	4	?
c.	$550	Semiannually	10%	9	?

15–14. Find the amount of each annuity:

	Amount of payment	Payment period	Interest rate	Time (years)	Type of annuity	Amount of annuity
a.	$600	Semiannually	12%	8	Ordinary	?
b.	$600	Semiannually	12%	8	Due	?
c.	$1,100	Annually	9%	7	Ordinary	?

15–15. Use Table 15–2 to find the amount to be invested today to receive a stream of payments for a given number of years in the future. Use formulas to check your answer. (The check may be a few pennies off due to rounding.)

	Amount of expected payments	Payment period	Interest rate	Term of annuity	Present value of annuity
a.	$1,500	Yearly	9%	2 years	?
b.	$2,700	Yearly	13%	3 years	?
c.	$2,700	Yearly	6%	3 years	?

15–16. Find the present value of the following annuities. Use Table 15–2. Use formulas to check your answer.

	Amount of each payment	Payment period	Interest rate	Time (years)	Compounded	Present value of annuity
a.	$2,000	Year	7%	25	Annually	?
b.	$7,000	Year	11%	12	Annually	?
c.	$850	6 months	12%	5	Semiannually	?
d.	$1,950	6 months	14%	9	Semiannually	?
e.	$500	Quarter	12%	10	Quarterly	?

15–17. Given the number of years and the interest rate, use formulas to calculate the amount of the periodic payment.

	Frequency of payment	Length of time	Interest rate	Future amount	Periodic payment
a.	Annually	19 years	5%	$125,000	?
b.	Annually	7 years	10%	$205,000	?
c.	Semiannually	10 years	6%	$37,500	?
d.	Quarterly	9 years	12%	$12,750	?

WORD PROBLEMS

15–18. Ellen Sullivan, an employee at Wal-Mart, made deposits of $900 at the end of each year for 7 years. Interest is 7% compounded annually. What is the value of Sullivan's annuity at the end of 7 years?

15–19. Pete King promised to pay his son $300 semiannually for 9 years. Assume Pete can invest his money at 8% in an ordinary annuity. How much must Pete invest today to pay his son $300 semiannually for 9 years?

15–20. Excel Assuming the stock market earns the historical market average return of 10.5%, you will have a nice retirement nest egg if you save $5,000 a year for 31 years. What is the value of this ordinary annuity?

15–21. Alice Cooper begins saving at age 35 and wants to withdraw $25,000 at the end of each year for 10 years after she retires at age 65. At 8% interest compounded annually, how much should Alice invest today?

15–22. If you were able to invest only $1,200 at the end of each quarter and placed it in a vehicle that produced an average annual return of 6% compounded quarterly, how much would you receive in 10 years?

15–23. Patricia and Joe Payne are divorced. The divorce settlement stipulated that Joe pay $525 at the end of each month for their daughter Suzanne until she turns 18 in 4 years. How much must Joe set aside today to meet the settlement? Interest is 6% a year compounded monthly.

15–24. Josef Company borrowed money that must be repaid in 20 years. The company wants to make sure the loan will be repaid at the end of year 20. So it invests $12,500 at the end of each year at 12% interest compounded annually. What was the amount of the original loan?

15–25. Jane Frost wants to receive yearly payments of $15,000 at year's end for 10 years. How much must she deposit at her bank today at 11% interest compounded annually?

15–26. Toby Martin invests $2,000 at the end of each year for 10 years in an ordinary annuity at 11% interest compounded annually. What is the final value of Toby's investment at the end of year 10?

15–27. Excel Alice Longtree has decided to invest $400 quarterly for 4 years in an ordinary annuity at 8%. As her financial advisor, calculate for Alice the total cash value of the annuity at the end of year 4.

15–28. At the beginning of each period for 10 years, Merl Agnes invests $500 semiannually at 6%. What is the cash value of this annuity due at the end of year 10?

15–29. Jeff Associates borrowed $30,000. The company plans to set up a sinking fund that will repay the loan at the end of 8 years. Assume a 12% interest rate compounded semiannually. What must Jeff pay into the fund each period of time? Check your answer by Table 15.1. Why are the answers a little bit different?

15–30. On Joe's graduation from college, Joe Martin's uncle promised him a gift of $12,000 in cash or $900 every quarter for the next 4 years after graduation. If money could be invested at 8% compounded quarterly, which offer is better for Joe?

15–31. An article appearing in the *Modesto Bee* on March 21, 2000, stated that the Institute of Certified Financial Planners recommends putting a minimum of 10% of your gross income toward retirement and as much as 20% if you are getting close to retiring. You are earning an average of $46,500 and will retire in 10 years. If you put 20% of your gross average income in an ordinary annuity compounded at 7% annually, what will be the value of the annuity when you retire?

15–32. Maple Leaf Syrup Corporation must buy a new piece of equipment in 5 years that will cost $88,000. The company is setting up a sinking fund to finance the purchase. What will the quarterly deposit be if the fund earns 8% interest?

15–33. Mike Macaro is selling a piece of land. Two offers are on the table. Morton Company offered a $40,000 down payment and $35,000 a year for the next 5 years. Flynn Company offered $25,000 down and $38,000 a year for the next 5 years. If money can be invested at 8% compounded annually, which offer is better for Mike?

15–34. Al Vincent has decided to retire to Huntsville in 10 years. What amount should Al invest today so that he will be able to withdraw $28,000 at the end of each year for 15 years *after* he retires? Assume he can invest the money at 8% interest compounded annually.

15–35. Victor French made deposits of $5,000 at the end of each quarter to First Canadian Bank, which pays 8% interest compounded quarterly. After 3 years, Victor made no more deposits. What will be the balance in the account 2 years after the last deposit?

15–36. Janet Woo decided to retire to Victoria Island in 6 years. What amount should Janet invest today so she can withdraw $50,000 at the end of each year for 20 years after she retires? Assume Janet can invest money at 6% compounded annually.

ADDITIONAL WORD PROBLEMS

15–37. At the end of each year for the next 9 years, D'Aldo Company will deposit $25,000 in an ordinary annuity account paying 9% interest compounded annually. Find the value of the annuity at the end of the 9 years. Use formulas.

15–38. David McCarthy is a professional baseball player who expects to play in the major leagues for 10 years. To save for the future, he will deposit $50,000 at the beginning of each year into an account that pays 11% interest compounded annually. How much will he have in this account at the end of 10 years?

15–39. Tom and Sue plan to get married soon. Because they hope to have a large wedding, they are going to deposit $1,000 at the end of each month into an account that pays 24% compounded monthly. How much will they have in this account at the end of 1 year?

15–40. Chris Dennen deposits $15,000 at the end of each year for 13 years into an account paying 7% interest compounded annually. What is the value of her annuity at the end of 13 years? How much interest will she have earned? Use formulas.

15–41. Tom Hanson would like to receive $200 each quarter for the 4 years he is in college. If his bank account pays 8% compounded quarterly, how much must he have in his account when he begins college?

15–42. Jean Reith has just retired and will receive a $12,500 retirement cheque every 6 months for the next 20 years. If her employer can invest money at 12% compounded semiannually, what amount must be invested today to make the semiannual payments to Jean? Use formulas.

15–43. Tom Herrick will pay $4,500 at the end of each year for the next 7 years to pay the balance of his college loans. If Tom can invest his money at 7% compounded annually, how much must he invest today to make the annual payments?

15–44. Helen Grahan is planning an extended sabbatical for the next 3 years. She would like to invest a lump sum of money at 10% interest so that she can withdraw $6,000 every 6 months while on sabbatical. What is the amount of the lump sum that Helen must invest? Use formulas.

15–45. Linda Rudd has signed a rental contract for office equipment, agreeing to pay $3,200 at the end of each quarter for the next 5 years. If Linda can invest money at 12% compounded quarterly, find the lump sum she can deposit today to make the payments for the length of the contract.

15–46. Sam Adams is considering lending his brother John $6,000. John said that he would repay Sam $775 every 6 months for 4 years. If money can be invested at 8%, calculate the equivalent cash value of the offer today. Should Sam go ahead with the loan? Use formulas.

15–47. Thomas Martin's uncle has promised him upon graduation a gift of $20,000 in cash or $2,000 every quarter for the next 3 years. If money can be invested at 8%, which offer will Thomas accept? (Thomas is a business major.)

15–48. Paul Sasso is selling a piece of land. He has received two solid offers. Jason Smith has offered a $60,000 down payment and $50,000 a year for the next 5 years. Kevin Bassage offered $35,000 down and $55,000 a year for the next 5 years. If money can be invested at 7% compounded annually, which offer should Paul accept? (To make the comparison, find the equivalent cash price of each offer.)

15–49. Abe Hoster decided to retire to Spain in 10 years. What amount should Abe invest today so that he will be able to withdraw $30,000 at the end of each year for 20 years after he retires? Assume he can invest money at 8% interest compounded annually. Use formulas. *Note:* Answers can differ due to rounding.

15–50. To finance a new police station, the town of Georgian Bay issued bonds totalling $600,000. The town treasurer set up a sinking fund at 8% compounded quarterly in order to redeem the bonds in 7 years. What is the quarterly payment that must be deposited into the fund?

15–51. Calgary Oil Corporation plans to build a new garage in 6 years. To finance the project, the financial manager established a $250,000 sinking fund at 6% compounded semiannually. Find the semiannual payment required for the fund.

15–52. The City Fisheries Corporation sold $300,000 worth of bonds that must be redeemed in 9 years. The corporation agreed to set up a sinking fund to accumulate the $300,000. Find the amount of the periodic payments made into the fund if payments are made annually and the fund earns 8% compounded annually.

15–53. The Best Corporation must buy a new piece of machinery in $4\frac{1}{2}$ years that will cost $350,000. If the firm sets up a sinking fund to finance this new machine, what will the quarterly deposits be assuming the fund earns 8% interest compounded quarterly?

CHALLENGE PROBLEMS

15–54. A research organization reported in May 2004 that in 11 years it would cost approximately $80,000 for 4 years at a public university and $240,000 to send your child to a private university. Bank A quoted 6% interest compounded annually. Bank B quoted 7% interest compounded annually. **(a)** How much would you have to deposit in Bank A each year to pay for the public university? **(b)** How much would you have to deposit in Bank A each year to pay for the private university? **(c)** How much would you have to deposit in Bank B each year to pay for the public university? **(d)** How much would you have to deposit in Bank B each year to pay for the private university?

15–55. Ajax Corporation has hired Brad O'Brien as its new president. Terms included the company's agreeing to pay retirement benefits of $18,000 at the end of each semiannual period for 10 years. This will begin in 3,285 days. If the money can be invested at 8% compounded semiannually, what must the company deposit today to fulfill its obligation to Brad?

15–56. Mr. Shoihet would like to provide each of his sons extra support of $5,000 for each of four years at college 10 years from now. **(a)** How much will he need at the start of four years for each son? For both sons? **(b)** How much should he invest at the end of each month at 4% compounded semiannually to cover both sons? The fund providing for his sons is also at 4% compounded semiannually.

SUMMARY PRACTICE TEST

1. Rio Sung plans to deposit $1,400 at the end of every 6 months for the next 15 years at 8% interest compounded semiannually. What is the value of Rio's annuity at the end of 15 years? (p. 359)
2. On Ray Long's graduation from law school, Ray's uncle, Paul Brown, promised him a gift of $24,000 or $2,400 every quarter for the next 4 years after graduating from law school. If the money could be invested at 6% compounded quarterly, which offer should Ray choose? (p. 359)
3. Ginny Kadu wants to receive $6,000 each year for 19 years. How much must Ginny invest today at 4% interest compounded annually? (p. 364)
4. In 7 years, Age.com will have to repay an $80,000 loan. Assume a 6% interest rate compounded quarterly. How much must Age.com pay each period to have $80,000 at the end of 7 years? (p. 366)
5. Ron Enterprise borrowed $70,000. The company plans to set up a sinking fund that will repay the loan at the end of 10 years. Assume a 6% interest rate compounded semiannually. What amount must Ron Enterprise pay into the fund each period? Check your answer against Table 15–1. (p. 366)
6. Sachi Lee wants to receive $12,000 each year for the next 30 years. Assume a 7% interest rate compounded annually. How much must Sachi invest today? (p. 364)
7. Twice a year for 10 years, Wayne Burton invested $1,400 compounded semiannually at 6% interest. What is the value of this annuity due? (p. 359)

8. Scupper Rurse invested \$1,200 semiannually for 20 years at 8% interest compounded semiannually. What is the value of this annuity due? (p. 359)

9. Morris Katz decided to retire to Mexico in 8 years. What amount should Morris deposit so that he will be able to withdraw \$80,000 at the end of each year for 30 years after he retires? Assume Morris can invest money at 8% interest compounded annually. (p. 364)

10. Terri Swanson made deposits of \$8,000 at the end of each quarter to Rio Bank, which pays 4% interest compounded quarterly. After 9 years, Terri made no more deposits. What will be the account's balance 4 years after the last deposit? (p. 360)

Complete the table: (p. 369)

	PMT (\$)	t (years)	j (%)	m_1	m_2	i_1	i_2	n	PV/FV
11.	500	10	4	Semiannually	Monthly	?	?	?	FV = ?
12.	2,000	25	6	Annually	Quarterly	?	?	?	PV = ?
13.	?	6	5	Annually	Semiannually	?	?	?	FV = \$100,000

SOLUTIONS TO PRACTICE QUIZZES

LU 15–1

1. Tom will make 16 equal and regular payments every quarter, so this is an annuity. These payments are to be made at the end of each quarter, so this is an ordinary annuity. The frequency of payments (quarterly) is different from the compounding frequency, so this is a general annuity.
2. Mrs. Percival regularly invests equal amounts of money every month, so this is an annuity. She makes her investments at the beginning of every month, so this is an annuity due. The investment frequency (monthly) is different from the compounding frequency (semiannually), so this is a general annuity.
3. Mr. and Mrs. Pif's money will stay in the account for four years, before the first withdrawal, so this is a period of deferral.
   - Their grandson will regularly withdraw an equal amount of \$500 over equal intervals of time—every month—so this is an annuity. Because it starts after the deferral period, this is a deferred annuity.
   - The withdrawals will be at the end of each month, so this is an ordinary annuity.
   - The compounding frequency (monthly) coincides with the withdrawal frequency (monthly), so this is a simple annuity.

LU 15–2

1. *Manual Calculations*

a. **Step 1.** $n = 4$ years $\times 2 = 8$

$i = 10\% \div 2 = 5\%$

Step 2. Factor = 9.5491

Step 3. \$4,000 × 9.5491
= \$38,196.40

b. $n = 4$ years $\times 2$ **Step 1**
$= 8 + 1 = 9$
$i = 10\% \div 2 = 5\%$

Factor = 11.0265 **Step 2**

\$4,000 × 11.0265 = \$44,106 **Step 3**
− 1 payment − 4,000 **Step 4**
\$40,106

Using Formulas

a. Ordinary annuity:

$t = 4$ years; PMT $= \$4{,}000$; $m_2 = 2$; $j = 10\%$; $m_1 = 2$; $m_1 = m_2$; FV = ?

$n = 2 \times 4 = 8$; $i = \frac{.1}{2} = .05$

$$\text{FV} = \$4{,}000\left[\frac{(1 + .05)^8 - 1}{.05}\right] = \$38{,}196.44$$

The calculator sequence would be as follows:

4000 [×] [(] [(] 1 [+] .05 [)] [^] 8 [−] 1 [)] [÷] .05 [=]

This is different from the manual calculation results due to rounding in the manual approach.

b. Annuity due:

$t = 4$ years; PMT $= \$4{,}000$; $m_2 = 2$; $j = 10\%$; $m_1 = 2$; $m_1 = m_2$; FV = ?

$n = 2 \times 4 = 8$; $i = \frac{.1}{2} = .05$

$$FV = \$4{,}000\left[\frac{(1+.05)^8 - 1}{.05}\right] \times (1+.05) = \$40{,}106.26$$

The calculator sequence would be as follows:

4000 [×] [(] [(] 1 [+] .05 [)] [^] 8 [−] 1 [)] [÷] .05 [×] [(] 1 [+] .05 [)] [=]

This is different from the manual calculation results due to rounding in the manual approach.

2. *Manual Calculations*

Step 1. $n = 5$ years $\times 2 = 10$ $i = \frac{6\%}{2} = 3\%$

$+ 1$

11 periods

Step 2. Table factor, 12.8078

Step 3. $4,000 × 12.8078 = $51,231.20

Step 4. − 4,000.00

$47,231.20

Using Formulas

Annuity due (at the beginning of each period):

$t = 5$ years; PMT $= \$4{,}000$; $m_2 = 2$; $j = 6\%$; $m_1 = 2$; $m_1 = m_2$; FV = ?

$n = 2 \times 5 = 10$; $i = \frac{.1}{2} = .03$

$$FV = \$4{,}000\left[\frac{(1+.03)^{10} - 1}{.03}\right] \times (1+.03) = \$47{,}231.18$$

The calculator sequence would be as follows:

4000 [×] [(] [(] 1 [+] .03 [)] [^] 10 [−] 1 [)] [÷] .03 [×] [(] 1 [+] .03 [)] [=]

This is different from the manual calculation results due to rounding in the manual approach.

LU 15–3

1. PMT $= \$18{,}000$ at the end of each period; $t = 5$; $m_1 = m_2 = 2$; $j = .10$; $i = .10 \div 2 = .05$; $n = 10$; PV = ?

   Simple ordinary annuity:

$$PV = 18{,}000\left[\frac{(1-(1+.05)^{-10})}{.05}\right] = \$138{,}991.23$$

   $138,991.23 must be invested today to receive $18,000 annuity for five years semiannually at 10% compounded semiannually.

2. PMT $= \$2{,}000 \times 5 = \$10{,}000$ at the end of each period; $t = 10$; $m_1 = m_2 = 1$; $j = .09$; $i = .09$; $n = 10$; PV = ?

$$PV = 10{,}000\left[\frac{(1-(1+.09)^{-10})}{.09}\right] = \$64{,}176.58$$

   The high school must raise $64,176.58 to set up five scholarships of $2,000.

3.

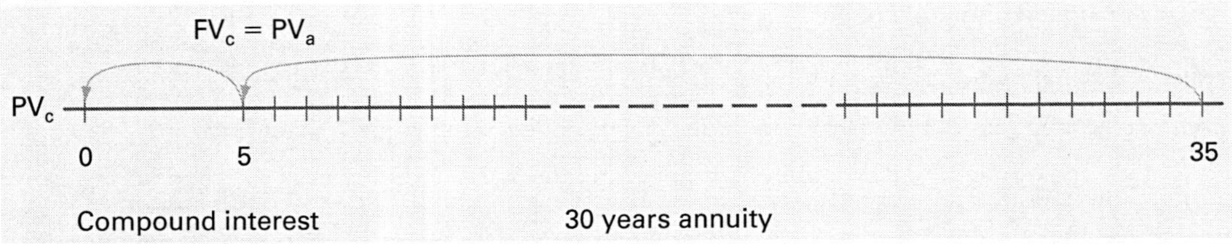

Step 1. PMT = \$60,000 at the end of each year; $t = 30$; $m_1 = m_2 = 1$; $j = .06$; $i = .06$; $n = 30$; $PV_a = ?$

Step 2. $PV_c = ?$

Step 1. Simple ordinary annuity:

$$PV_a = 60{,}000\left[\frac{1-(1+.06)^{-30}}{.06}\right] = \$825{,}889.87$$

Step 2. PV_a becomes FV of a compound interest problem.

$$PV_a = FV_c = \$825{,}889.87$$

$$n = 5$$

$$PV_c = FV_c(1+i)^n = \$825{,}889.97(1+.06)^{-5} = \$617{,}153.03$$

Joe Wood should invest \$617,153.03 today.

LU 15–4

1. FV = \$90,000; $t = 10$ years; $j = 12\%$; $m_1 = 2$; $i_1 = .06$; $m_2 = 4$; $n = 40$

$i_2 = (1+.06)^{2/4} - 1 = .029563014$

$$90{,}000 = PMT\left[\frac{(1+.029563014)^{40}-1}{.029563014}\right]$$

$$90{,}000 = PMT \times 74.65867519$$

PMT = \$1,205.49

2. a. PMT = \$200; $t = 10$; $j = .08$; $m_1 = 2$; $m_2 = 4$; $i_1 = .04$; $n = 40$; FV = ?

$i_2 = (1+.04)^{2/4} - 1 = .019803902$

$$FV = 200\left[\frac{(1+.019803902)^{40}-1}{.019803902}\right] = 12{,}029.18$$

b. PMT = \$1,000; $t = 5$; $j = .04$; $m_1 = 12$; $m_2 = 2$; $n = 10$; $i_1 = \frac{.04}{12} = .003333333$; PV = ?

$i_2 = (1+.003333333)^{12/2} - 1 = .020167407$

$$PV = \$1{,}000\left[\frac{1-(1+.020167407)^{-10}}{.020167407}\right] = 8{,}974.72$$

Business Math Scrapbook

WITH INTERNET APPLICATION

Putting Your Skills to Work

SMALL CHANGE IS BIG MONEY

How much does it cost for one large pizza a week? If you said $250,000, you obviously know a thing or two about investing. Financial planner Allyson Lewis, author of *The Million Dollar Car and $250,000 Pizza* (Dearborn Trade, 2000), says that if $20 spent on pizza were invested weekly in a mutual fund with a 9 percent annual return, it'd be worth a quarter of a million dollars in 30 years.

ITEM	COST	ANNUAL COST	YOU COULD'VE USED IT FOR . . .	IF YOU INVESTED IT IN A 401(K), IN 2020 IT'D BE WORTH . . .
ATM FEES	$2.50 per week (didn't use your own bank)	$130	Session with a financial planner	$7,280
SODA	$.75 per can, five times per week	$195	Limousine tour of Napa wineries	$10,192
PEDICURE	$35 per session, four times per year	$210	Donation to Habitat for Humanity	$11,595
LOTTERY TICKETS	$1 per ticket, five times per week	$260	Springsteen tickets (four)	$13,302
FROZEN YOGURT	$3 for a large (with sprinkles), two times per week	$312	Spring ski weekend at Vail	$15,962
CIGARS	$5 per stogie (box of 25), four boxes per year	$500	Autographed photo of Humphrey Bogart	$25,580

Source: *Modern Maturity*, July/August 2000.

PROJECT A

Can you add a new example to this table from your own experience? Go to the Internet and find a consumer Web site to add an additional example.

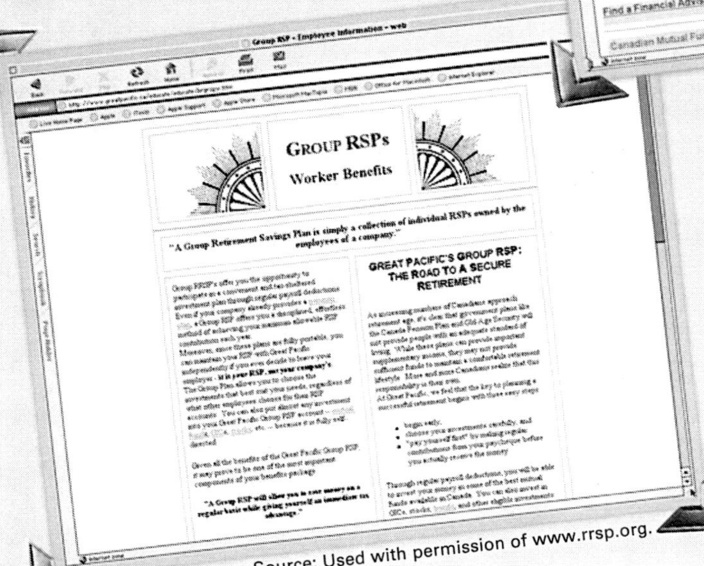

Source: Used with permission of www.rrsp.org.

PROJECT B

a. Go to the Web site www.rrsp.org and take the RRSP quiz to test your RRSP knowledge.

b. Go to www.gptc.com/educate and click to the "Education" section. Explore "Group RSPs—Worker Benefits" and find out what benefits a group RSP brings to a customer.

The Cost of Home Ownership

16

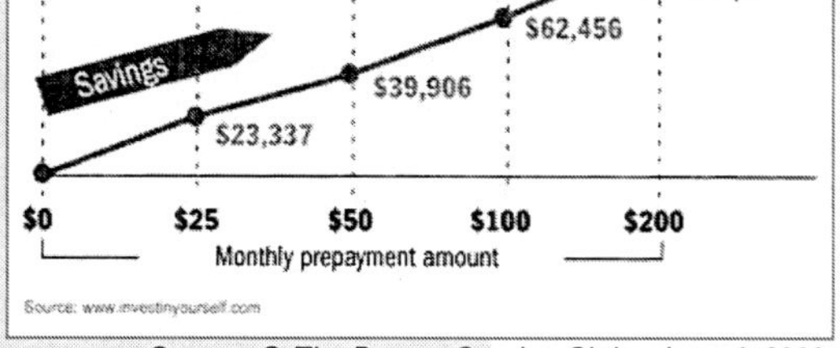

Source: © *The Boston Sunday Globe*, June 4, 2000.

LEARNING UNIT OBJECTIVES

LU 16–1: Types of Mortgages and the Monthly Mortgage Payment

- List the types of mortgages available (p. 384).
- Utilize an amortization chart to compute monthly mortgage payments (p. 385).
- Calculate the total cost of interest over the life of a mortgage (p. 386).

LU 16–2: Amortization Schedule—Breaking Down the Monthly Payment

- Calculate and identify the interest and principal portion of each monthly payment (p. 387).
- Prepare an amortization schedule (p. 387).

A mortgage is a loan guaranteed by some physical property. The value of the initial amount of the principal borrowed is called **face value** of a mortgage.

The terms and conditions of a mortgage are indicated in a mortgage contract. Usually mortgages have an amortization period of 15, 20, or 25 years. The borrower and the lender make an agreement for a fixed interest rate for a shorter period of time, which is known as the **term of a mortgage.** Many financial institutions offer terms of from six months up to seven years. When one term expires, the mortgage is usually renewed for another term.

Under the federal Interest Act, the interest rate of mortgages must be disclosed as an equivalent to semiannual or annual interest rates. Most financial institutions in Canada show interest rates as compounded semiannually. Mortgage payments are made on a monthly or biweekly basis. That's why they form a general annuity.

Chapter 16 could save you thousands of dollars! In Units 16–1 and 16–2 you will learn how to calculate periodic payments, why a mortgage may be paid seven years earlier if you are paying biweekly instead of monthly, how to prepare an amortization schedule, and many other useful applications.

LEARNING UNIT 16–1
TYPES OF MORTGAGES AND THE MONTHLY MORTGAGE PAYMENT

In the past several years, interest rates have been low, which has caused an increase in home sales. Today, more people are buying homes than are renting homes. The question facing prospective buyers concerns which type of **mortgage** will be best for them. Table 16.1 lists the types of mortgages available to home buyers. Depending on how interest rates are moving when you purchase a home, you may find one type of mortgage to be the most advantageous for you.

Have you heard that elderly people who are house-rich and cash-poor can use their home to get cash or monthly income? It is possible for older homeowners to take out a **reverse mortgage** on their homes. Under reverse mortgages, senior homeowners borrow against the equity in their property, often getting fixed monthly cheques. The debt is repaid only when the homeowners or their estate sells the home.

Now let's learn how to calculate a monthly mortgage payment and the total cost of loan interest over the life of a mortgage. We will use the following example in our discussion.

EXAMPLE

Gary bought a home for \$200,000. He made a 20% down payment. The 9% mortgage is for 30 years ($30 \times 12 = 360$ payments). What are Gary's monthly payment and total cost of interest?

TABLE 16–1
TYPES OF MORTGAGES AVAILABLE TO HOME BUYERS

Loan types	Advantages	Disadvantages
30-year **fixed rate mortgage**	A predictable monthly payment.	If interest rates fall, you are locked in to higher rate unless you refinance. (Application and appraisal fees along with other closing costs will result.)
15-year **fixed rate mortgage**	Interest rate lower than 30-year fixed (usually $\frac{1}{4}$ to $\frac{1}{2}$ of a percent). Your equity builds up faster while interest costs are cut by more than one-half.	A larger down payment is needed. Monthly payment will be higher.
Biweekly mortgage	Shortens term loan; saves substantial amount of interest; 26 biweekly payments per year. Builds equity twice as fast.	Not good for those not seeking an early loan payoff.
Variable rate mortgage	Lower rate than fixed. If rates fall, could be adjusted down without refinancing. Caps available that limit how high rate could go for each adjustment period over term of loan.	Monthly payment could rise if interest rates rise. Riskier than fixed rate mortgage in which monthly payment is stable.
Home equity loan	Cheap and reliable accessible lines of credit backed by equity in your home. Rates can be locked in. Reverse mortgages may be available to those 62 or older.	Could lose home if not paid. No annual or interest caps.

COMPUTING THE MONTHLY PAYMENT FOR PRINCIPAL AND INTEREST

You can calculate the principal and interest of Gary's monthly payment using the **amortization table** shown in Table 16.2 and the following steps.

COMPUTING MONTHLY PAYMENT BY USING AN AMORTIZATION TABLE

Step 1. Divide the amount of the mortgage by $1,000.

Step 2. Look up the rate and term in the amortization table. At the intersection is the table factor.

Step 3. Multiply the results of Step 1 by the results of Step 2.

For Gary, we calculate the following:

$$\frac{\$160{,}000 \text{ (amount of mortgage)}}{\$1{,}000} = 160 \times 7.9283 \text{ (table rate)} = \$1{,}268.528$$

So $160,000 is the amount of the mortgage ($200,000 less 20%). The $7.9283 is the table factor of 9% for 30 years per $1,000. Since Gary is mortgaging 160 units of $1,000, the factor of 7.9283 is multiplied by 160. Remember that the $1,268.53 payment does not include taxes, insurance, and so on.

TABLE 16–2
MONTHLY PAYMENT NECESSARY TO AMORTIZE A LOAN OF $1,000

Rate (%)	5 Years	10 Years	15 Years	20 Years	25 Years	30 Years
4	18.4017	10.1089	7.3804	6.0425	5.2602	4.7552
4.25	18.5127	10.2260	7.5040	6.1725	5.3966	4.8977
4.5	18.6241	10.3438	7.6287	6.3041	5.5347	5.0422
4.75	18.7358	10.4623	7.7544	6.4370	5.6746	5.1886
5	18.8477	10.5815	7.8812	6.5713	5.8160	5.3369
5.25	18.9600	10.7014	8.0091	6.7069	5.9592	5.4871
5.5	19.0726	10.8219	8.1380	6.8439	6.1039	5.6391
5.75	19.1854	10.9432	8.2679	6.9822	6.2502	5.7928
6	19.2986	11.0651	8.3988	7.1219	6.3981	5.9482
6.25	19.4120	11.1877	8.5308	7.2628	6.5474	6.1053
6.5	19.5257	11.3109	8.6637	7.4050	6.6982	6.2640
6.75	19.6398	11.4348	8.7976	7.5484	6.8505	6.4243
7	19.7541	11.5594	8.9325	7.6931	7.0042	6.5860
7.25	19.8687	11.6846	9.0683	7.8390	7.1592	6.7492
7.5	19.9835	11.8105	9.2051	7.9860	7.3155	6.9139
7.75	20.0987	11.9370	9.3429	8.1342	7.4732	7.0798
8	20.2142	12.0641	9.4815	8.2836	7.6321	7.2471
8.25	20.3299	12.1918	9.6211	8.4340	7.7923	7.4156
8.5	20.4459	12.3202	9.7616	8.5856	7.9536	7.5854
8.75	20.5622	12.4492	9.9029	8.7382	8.1161	7.7563
9	20.6787	12.5789	10.0452	8.8919	8.2798	7.9283
9.25	20.7956	12.7091	10.1883	9.0466	8.4445	8.1014
9.5	20.9127	12.8399	10.3323	9.2023	8.6103	8.2755
9.75	21.0300	12.9713	10.4771	9.3590	8.7771	8.4506
10	21.1477	13.1034	10.6227	9.5166	8.9449	8.6267
10.25	21.2656	13.2360	10.7691	9.6752	9.1136	8.8036
10.5	21.3838	13.3692	10.9164	9.8347	9.2833	8.9814
10.75	21.5023	13.5029	11.0644	9.9951	9.4539	9.1600
11	21.6210	13.6373	11.2133	10.1564	9.6253	9.3394
11.25	21.7400	13.7722	11.3629	10.3185	9.7975	9.5195
11.5	21.8592	13.9077	11.5132	10.4815	9.9706	9.7003
11.75	21.9787	14.0437	11.6643	10.6452	10.1444	9.8818
12	22.0985	14.1803	11.8161	10.8097	10.3190	10.0639
12.25	22.2185	14.3174	11.9686	10.9750	10.4943	10.2466
12.5	22.3387	14.4550	12.1219	11.1411	10.6702	10.4298
12.75	22.4593	14.5932	12.2758	11.3078	10.8468	10.6136
13	22.5801	14.7320	12.4304	11.4753	11.0241	10.7979
13.25	22.7011	14.8712	12.5856	11.6434	11.2019	10.9826
13.5	22.8224	15.0110	12.7416	11.8123	11.3803	11.1678
13.75	22.9439	15.1512	12.8981	11.9817	11.5593	11.3534
14	23.0657	15.2920	13.0553	12.1518	11.7388	11.5394
14.25	23.1877	15.4333	13.2131	12.3224	11.9187	11.7257
14.5	23.3100	15.5750	13.3715	12.4937	12.0992	11.9124
14.75	23.4325	15.7173	13.5305	12.6655	12.2801	12.0994
15	23.5552	15.8600	13.6901	12.8378	12.4615	12.2867
15.25	23.6782	16.0033	13.8502	13.0107	12.6432	12.4742
15.5	23.8015	16.1469	14.0109	13.1841	12.8253	12.6620
15.75	23.9249	16.2911	14.1722	13.3580	13.0078	12.8500
16	24.0486	16.4357	14.3339	13.5324	13.1907	13.0382
16.25	24.1726	16.5808	14.4962	13.7072	13.3739	13.2266
16.5	24.2967	16.7263	14.6590	13.8824	13.5574	13.4152
16.75	24.4211	16.8722	14.8223	14.0581	13.7411	13.6039
17	24.5457	17.0186	14.9861	14.2342	13.9252	13.7928
17.25	24.6706	17.1655	15.1503	14.4107	14.1095	13.9817
17.5	24.7957	17.3127	15.3151	14.5875	14.2940	14.1708
17.75	24.9210	17.4604	15.4802	14.7648	14.4788	14.3600
18	25.0465	17.6085	15.6458	14.9423	14.6638	14.5492
18.25	25.1723	17.7570	15.8119	15.1202	14.8490	14.7386
18.5	25.2982	17.9059	15.9783	15.2984	15.0343	14.9279
18.75	25.4244	18.0552	16.1452	15.4769	15.2198	15.1173

What Is the Total Cost of Interest?

We can use the following formula to calculate Gary's total interest cost over the life of the mortgage:

$$\text{Total cost of interest} = \text{Total of all monthly payments} - \text{Amount of mortgage}$$

$$\$296{,}670.80 = \$456{,}670.80 - \$160{,}000$$

$$= (\$1{,}268.53 \times 360)$$

Effects of Interest Rates on Monthly Payment and Total Interest Cost

Table 16.3 shows the effect that an increase in interest rates would have on Gary's monthly payment and his total cost of interest. Note that if Gary's interest rate rises to 11%, the 2% increase will result in Gary paying an additional $81,277.20 in total interest.

TABLE 16–3
EFFECT OF INTEREST RATES ON MONTHLY PAYMENTS

	9%	11%	Difference
Monthly payment	$1,268.53 (160 × $7.9283)	$1,494.30 (160 × $9.3394)	$225.77 per month
Total cost of interest	$296,670.80 ($1,268.53 × 360) − $160,000	$377,948 ($1,494.30 × 360) − $160,000	$81,277.20 ($225.77 × 360)

For most people, purchasing a home is a major lifetime decision. Many factors must be considered before this decision is made. One of these factors is how to pay for the home. The purpose of this Unit is to tell you that being informed about the types of available mortgages can save you thousands of dollars.

In addition to the mortgage payment, buying a home can include the following costs:

- **Closing costs.** When property passes from seller to buyer, closing costs may include fees for credit reports, recording costs, lawyer's fees, title search, and so on.
- **Land transfer tax.**
- **Mortgage insurance.**
- *Repairs and maintenance.* This includes paint, wallpaper, landscaping, plumbing, electrical expenses, and so on.

As you can see, the cost of owning a home can be high.

LU 16–1 PRACTICE QUIZ

Given: Price of home, $225,000; 20% down payment; 9% interest rate; 25-year mortgage.

Solve for:

1. Monthly payment and total cost of interest over 25 years.
2. If rate fell to 8%, what would be the total decrease in interest cost over the life of the mortgage?

LEARNING UNIT 16–2
AMORTIZATION SCHEDULE—BREAKING DOWN THE MONTHLY PAYMENT

In Learning Unit 16–1, we saw that over the life of Gary's $160,000 loan, he would pay $296,670.80 in interest. Now let's use the following steps to determine what portion of Gary's first monthly payment reduces the principal and what portion is interest. Table 16.1 is based on a general annuity with annual rate compounded semiannually and the payment monthly.

CALCULATING INTEREST, PRINCIPAL, AND NEW BALANCE OF MONTHLY PAYMENT

Step 1. Calculate the interest for a month (use current principal) where monthly rate = i_2 $= \left(1+\frac{i}{2}\right)^{2/12} - 1 = \left(1+\frac{.09}{2}\right)^{2/12} - 1 = .0073631230$; Interest = Principal × i_2.

Step 2. Calculate the amount used to reduce the principal: Principal reduction = Monthly payment − Interest (Step 1).

Step 3. Calculate the new principal: Current principal − Reduction of principal (Step 2) = New principal.

Step 1. Interest (I) = Principal (P) × Monthly rate (i_2)

$1,178.10 = $160,000 × .0073631230

Step 2. The reduction of the $160,000 principal each month is equal to the payment less interest, so we can calculate Gary's new principal balance at the end of month 1 as follows:

Monthly payment at 9% (from Table 16.1)	$1,268.53	= (160 × $7.9283)
− Interest for first month	− 1,178.10	
= Principal reduction	$ 90.43	

Step 3. As the years go by, the interest portion of the payment decreases and the principal portion increases:

Principal balance	$160,000.00
Principal reduction	− 90.43
Balance of principal	$159,909.57

Let's do month 2:

Step 1. Interest (I) = Principal (P) × Monthly rate (i_2)

$1,177.43 = $159,909.57 × .0073631230

Step 2.

Monthly payment	$1,268.53
− Interest for month 2	− 1,177.43
= Principal reduction	$ 91.10

Step 3.

Principal balance	$159,909.57
Principal reduction	− 91.10
Balance of principal	$159,818.47

Note that in month 2, interest costs drop by 67 cents ($1,178.10 − $1,177.43). So in two months, Gary has reduced his mortgage balance by $181.43 ($90.43 + $91.10). After two months, Gary has paid a total interest of $2,355.53 ($1,178.53 + $1,177.10).

EXAMPLE OF AN AMORTIZATION SCHEDULE

The partial **amortization schedule** given in Table 16.4 shows the breakdown of Gary's monthly payment. Note the amount that goes toward reducing the principal and toward payment of actual interest. Also note how the outstanding balance of the loan is reduced. After 7 months, Gary still owes $159,352.82. Often when you take out a mortgage loan, you will receive an amortization schedule from the company that holds your mortgage.

TABLE 16–4
MONTHLY PAYMENT $1,268.53
Monthly rate = .0073631230 = .73631%; opening balance = $160,000.00

Payment number	Payment	Interest	Principal reduction	Balance of principal
1	$1,268.53	$1,178.10	$90.43	$159,909.57
2	$1,268.53	$1,177.43	$91.10	$159,818.47
3	$1,268.53	$1,176.76	$91.77	$159,726.70
4	$1,268.53	$1,176.09	$92.44	$159,634.26
5	$1,268.53	$1,175.41	$93.13	$159,541.13
6	$1,268.53	$1,174.72	$93.81	$159,447.32
7	$1,268.53	$1,174.03	$94.50	$159,352.82

LU 16–2 PRACTICE QUIZ

Prepare an amortization schedule for first three periods for the following: mortgage, $100,000; 11%; 30 years.

CHAPTER ORGANIZER AND REFERENCE GUIDE

Topic	Key point, procedure, formula	Example(s) to illustrate situation
Computing monthly mortgage payment, p. 385	Based on per $1,000 Table 16.1: $\frac{\text{Amount of mortgage}}{\$1{,}000} \times \text{Table rate}$	Use Table 16.1: 12% on $60,000 mortgage for 30 years. $\frac{\$60{,}000}{\$1{,}000} = 60 \times \$10.0639$ $= \$603.83$
Calculating total interest cost, p. 386	Total of all monthly payments − Amount of mortgage	Using example above: 30 years = 360 (payments) × $603.83 $217,378.80 − 60,000.00 $157,378.80 (mortgage interest over life of mortgage)
Amortization schedule, p. 387	$I = P \times i_2$ Interest (I) = Principal (P) × Monthly rate (i_2) where $i_2 = \left(1 + \frac{j}{2}\right)^{2/12} - 1$; j = annual rate Principal reduction = Monthly payment − Interest New principal = Current principal − Reduction of principal	Using same example: Portion To: Payment number / Interest / Principal reduction / Balance of principal 1 — Interest $585.53 — Principal reduction $18.30 — Balance $59,981.70 ($60,000 × .0097587942) ($603.83 − $585.53) ($60,000.00 − $18.38) 2 — Interest $585.35 — Principal reduction $18.48 — Balance $59,963.22 ($59,981.70 × .0097587942) ($603.83 − $585.35) ($59,981.70 − $18.48)
Key terms	Amortization schedule, p. 387 Amortization table, p. 385 Biweekly mortgage, p. 384 Closing costs, p. 386 Face value, p. 384 Fixed rate mortgage, p. 384 Home equity loan, p. 384 Land transfer tax, p. 386 Mortgage, p. 384 Mortgage insurance, p. 386	Reverse mortgage, p. 384 Term of mortgage, p. 384 Variable rate mortgage, p. 384

CRITICAL THINKING DISCUSSION QUESTIONS

1. Explain the advantages and disadvantages of the following loan types: 30-year fixed rate, 15-year fixed rate, biweekly mortgage, variable rate mortgage, and home equity loan.
2. How is an amortization schedule calculated? Is there a best time to refinance a mortgage?

END-OF-CHAPTER PROBLEMS

DRILL PROBLEMS

Complete the following amortization chart by using Table 16.1.

	Selling price of home	Down payment	Principal (loan)	Rate of interest	Years	Payment per $1,000	Monthly mortgage payment
16–1.	$159,000	$10,000	?	$6\frac{1}{2}\%$	25	?	?
16–2.	$70,000	$12,000	?	11%	30	?	?
16–3.	$275,000	$50,000	?	9%	30	?	?

16–4. What is total cost of interest in Problem 16–2?

16–5. If the interest rate rises to 13% in Problem 16–2, what is the total cost of interest?

Complete the following:

	Selling price	Down payment	Amount mortgage	Rate	Years	Monthly payment	First payment broken down into:		Balance at end of month
							Interest	Principal	
16–6.	$125,000	$5,000	?	7%	30	?	?	?	?
16–7.	$199,000	$40,000	?	$7\frac{1}{2}\%$	15	?	?	?	?

16–8. Bob Jones bought a new log cabin for $70,000 at 11% interest for 25 years. Please prepare an amortization schedule for first two periods.

Payment number	Portion to:		Balance of loan outstanding
	Interest	Principal	
?	?	?	?
?	?	?	?

ADDITIONAL DRILL PROBLEMS

16–9. Use Table 16.1 to calculate the monthly payment for principal and interest for the following mortgages:

	Price of home	Down payment	Interest rate	Term in years	Monthly payment
a.	$200,000	15%	$6\frac{1}{2}\%$	25	?
b.	$200,000	15%	$10\frac{1}{2}\%$	30	?
c.	$450,000	10%	$11\frac{3}{4}\%$	30	?
d.	$450,000	10%	11%	30	?

16–10. For each of the mortgages in Problem 16–9, calculate the amount of interest that will be paid over the life of the loan.

	Price of home	Down payment	Interest rate	Term in years	Total interest paid
a.	\$200,000	15%	$6\frac{1}{2}$%	25	?
b.	\$200,000	15%	$10\frac{1}{2}$%	30	?
c.	\$450,000	10%	$11\frac{3}{4}$%	30	?
d.	\$450,000	10%	11%	30	?

16–11. In the following, calculate the monthly payment for each mortgage, the portion of the first monthly payment that goes to interest, and the portion of the payment that goes toward the principal.

	Amount of mortgage	Interest rate	Term in years	Monthly payment	Portion to interest	Portion to principal
a.	\$170,000	8%	20	?	?	?
b.	\$222,000	$11\frac{3}{4}$%	30	?	?	?
c.	\$167,000	$10\frac{1}{2}$%	25	?	?	?

WORD PROBLEMS

16–12. A local financial source reported on 15-year versus 30-year fixed rate mortgages. The total interest for 15 years would be \$72,000 and \$164,000 for 30 years; this is based on a \$100,000 loan at 8%. Doug Tweeten wants to take advantage of this savings. **(a)** How much would his monthly payments be on a 15-year loan? **(b)** How much would his monthly payments be on a 30-year loan? **(c)** How much more would he pay each month on a 15-year loan?

16–13. On January 5, 2001, *USA Today* reported that million-dollar homes sold at a record pace during the year 2000. For example, Oprah Winfrey has closed on a 17-hectare estate near Santa Barbara, California, for \$50,000,000. If Oprah puts 20% down and finances at 7% for 30 years, what would her monthly payment be?

16–14. Excel Bill Allen bought a home in London, Ontario for \$108,000. He put down 25% and obtained a mortgage for 30 years at 11%. What is Bill's monthly payment? What is the total interest cost of the loan?

16–15. If in Problem 16–14 the rate of interest is 14%, what is the difference in interest cost?

16–16. Mike Jones bought a new split-level home for \$150,000 with 20% down. He decided to use TD Bank for his mortgage. They were offering $13\frac{3}{4}$% for 25-year mortgages. Provide Mike with an amortization schedule for the first three periods.

Payment number	Portion to: Interest	Portion to: Principal	Balance of loan outstanding
?	?	?	?
?	?	?	?
?	?	?	?

16–17. Harriet Marcus is concerned about the financing of a home. She saw a small cottage that sells for \$50,000. If she puts 20% down, what will her monthly payment be at **(a)** 25 years, $11\frac{1}{2}$%; **(b)** 25 years, $12\frac{1}{2}$%; **(c)** 25 years, $13\frac{1}{2}$%; **(d)** 25 years, 15%? What is the total cost of interest over the cost of the loan for each assumption? **(e)** What is the savings in interest cost between $11\frac{1}{2}$% and 15%? **(f)** If Harriet uses 30 years instead of 25 for both $11\frac{1}{2}$% and 15%, what is the difference in interest?

16–18. Jesse Garza wants to avoid paying mortgage insurance and has to put 25% down. The most Jesse has for a down payment is \$43,000. His bank is offering 15-year fixed loans at $6\frac{1}{2}$%.

(a) What is the most Jesse can pay for a home? **(b)** Based on what he can afford, what would be Jesse's monthly payments?

ADDITIONAL WORD PROBLEMS

16–19. The Counties are planning to purchase a new home that costs \$329,000. The bank is charging them $10\frac{1}{2}\%$ interest and requires a 20% down payment. The Counties are planning to take a 25-year mortgage. How much will their monthly payment be for principal and interest?

16–20. The MacEacherns wish to buy a new house that costs \$299,000. The bank requires a 15% down payment and charges $11\frac{1}{2}\%$ interest. If the MacEacherns take out a 15-year mortgage, what will their monthly payment for principal and interest be?

16–21. Because the monthly payments are so high, the MacEacherns (Problem 16–20) want to know what the monthly payments would be for **(a)** a 25-year mortgage and **(b)** a 30-year mortgage. Calculate these two payments.

16–22. If the MacEacherns choose a 30-year mortgage instead of a 15-year mortgage, **(a)** how much money will they "save" monthly?

16–23. Complete the 2002 year.

	1980	2002
Cost of median-priced new home	\$44,200	\$136,600
10% down payment	\$4,420	
Fixed-rate, 30-year mortgage		
Interest rate	8.9%	$7\frac{1}{2}\%$
Total monthly principal and interest	\$316	

CHALLENGE PROBLEMS

16–24. Local Trust Company provided a chart to enable readers to figure out how refinancing would affect their mortgage payments. To use this chart, drop the last three zeros from your current mortgage amount and multiply that by the multiplier that most closely corresponds to your new interest rate and loan term. Subtract that number from your current loan payment, and that's your monthly savings.

Loan rate	Multipliers	
	30-year loan	**15-year loan**
8.0%	7.2471	9.4815
7.75%	7.0798	9.3429
7.5%	6.9139	9.2051
7.4%	6.5860	8.9325

Consider a \$200,000 loan at 8% with a monthly payment of \$1,467.53. Calculate refinancing at 7.5% for 30 years. **(a)** What would be the savings per month? **(b)** If the loan costs were \$2,000, how many months would it take for refinancing to pay off?

SUMMARY PRACTICE TEST

1. Patty Cole bought a home for \$120,000 with a down payment of \$5,000. Her rate of interest is $6\frac{1}{2}\%$ for 25 years. Calculate her **(a)** monthly payment; **(b)** first payment, broken down into interest and principal; and **(c)** balance of mortgage at the end of the month. (pp. 385, 387)

2. Jay Miller bought a home in New Brunswick for \$90,000. He put down 20% and obtained a mortgage for 25 years at 7%. What are Jay's monthly payment and the total interest cost of the loan? (pp. 385, 386)

3. Katie Hercher bought a home for \$125,000 with a down payment of \$5,000. Her rate of interest is 9% for 25 years. Calculate Katie's payment per \$1,000 and her monthly mortgage payment. (p. 385)

4. Using Problem 3, calculate the total cost of interest for Katie Hercher. (p. 386)

SOLUTIONS TO PRACTICE QUIZZES

LU 16–1

1. $225,000 − $45,000 = $180,000

$\frac{\$180{,}000}{\$1{,}000} = 180 \times \$8.2798 = \$1{,}490.36$

$267,108 = $447,108 − $180,000
($1,490.36 × 300) 25 years × 12 payments per year

2. 8% = $1,373.78 monthly payment
(180 × $7.6321)

Total interest cost $232,134 = ($1,373.78 × 300) − $180,000 = $412,134 − $180,000 = $232,134
Savings $34,974 = ($267,108 − $232,134)

LU 16–2

Monthly rate = .0089633939 = .89634%
Opening balance = $100,000

Payment number	Payment	Interest	Principal reduction	Balance of principal
1	$933.94	$896.34	$37.60	$99,962.40
2	$933.94	$896.00	$37.94	$99,924.47
3	$933.94	$895.66	$38.28	$99,886.19

Business Math Scrapbook

WITH INTERNET APPLICATION

Putting Your Skills to Work

Their Presence Is Growing...

Although it's still relatively small, the market for online mortgages is growing. Meanwhile, thanks to improvements in the sites, customer satisfaction has improved significantly.

Total value of mortgage loans made each year	approximately $1 trillion
Loans closed through online providers in 2000	about $20 billion
Loans closed through online providers in 1999	about $10 billion
Loans closed through online providers in 1998	less than $5 billion
Estimated mortgage Web sites	more than 100
Borrowers satisfied with service at a major online lender, Q4 2000	92%
Borrowers satisfied with service at a major online lender, Q4 1999	50%

...But Many Are Still Struggling to Survive

Even though some sites are making profits, many others have closed or are struggling. Some of the most high-profile sites:

■ **E-LOAN.COM** One of the most widely recognized names in the business, E-Loan provides auto and other consumer loans in addition to mortgages. But it reported a $20.7 million loss in the fourth quarter of 2000*

■ **LENDINGTREE.COM** A popular marketplace for home loans through which loan requests are farmed out to other lenders, LendingTree nevertheless reported a $15 million loss in the third quarter of 2000.

■ **INDYMAC.COM** An online lender that receives high marks in consumer surveys for good service. The company is profitable, but much of its revenue comes from a second business that buys loans and sells them to other lenders or investors.

■ **COUNTRYWIDE.COM** One of the most popular "bricks-and-clicks" sites, serving as the online site for Countrywide Home Loans, a profitable traditional lender.

■ **HOMESPACE.COM** The online provider of mortgages and other real-estate services received lots of hype, but wound up selling its mortgage business to LendingTree last August.

■ **MORTGAGE.COM** A high-profile flameout. Originally designed to provide loans directly to consumers, the company switched to offer business-to-business services to banks and others. Announced plans to wind down its operations in October.

■ **IOWN.COM** Previously an online mortgage provider, the company stopped accepting new loan applications in August and laid off 140 people. It now operates as a referral service to help consumers find other lenders, compare rates and shop for houses.

■ **ONLOAN.COM** Once an online mortgage provider, the company exited the mortgage business last fall and shut down its Web site.

■ **LOANSDIRECT.COM** An online loan provider, recently acquired by E*Trade Group Inc., that gets high marks for service. Does not publicly disclose revenue or profits.

■ **KEYSTROKE.COM** Ranked as the cheapest online mortgage provider by Gomez Advisors this summer, the company soon after ended its consumer mortgage business and turned to developing software for the mortgage industry.

*E-Loan reported a pro-forma net loss of $6.5 million, which excludes compensation charges related to the company's stock-option plan, amortization of goodwill on the acquisition of CarFinance.com, and amortization of marketing costs related to warrants issued to purchase the company's common stock.

Source: Gomez Advisors, the companies

Source: © 2001 Dow Jones & Company, Inc.

PROJECT A

Visit some of these Web sites to see how they are doing today.

PROJECT B

a. Visit gemortgage.ca/content/Homebuyer/MortgageInsurance. Find out what mortgage insurance is, who must pay it, and what the premium rates are.

b. Visit lowrate.ca/land_transfer_tax.htm and find out how much land transfer tax you should pay for homes of $160,000 and $290,000.

Business Statistics

17

Source: Statistics Canada, "Your Guide to the Consumer Price Index," www.statcan.ca/english/IPS/Data/62-557-XPB.htm.

Most commodities are priced once a month. Some items, such as haircuts and dry-cleaning services, are priced each quarter. Property taxes and tuition fees are monitored once a year. Generally, the more often prices change, the more often they are collected. In cases where goods appear on the market seasonally, prices are collected during the season when they are available. Also, when prices change outside the scheduled time of collection, a special price collection may be carried out to ensure that such changes are reported in the CPI in a timely fashion.

The pricing cycle starts in the first week of each reference month and extends to the third week of the month. The indexes that result from this price collection activity represent the entire month. Some users ask for the index for a particular day of the month, like April 1, June 15 or December 31. This information is not available, and users have to decide which month's index best meets their particular requirements.

1992 CPI Weights by Major Component, for Canada, Expressed in Percentages

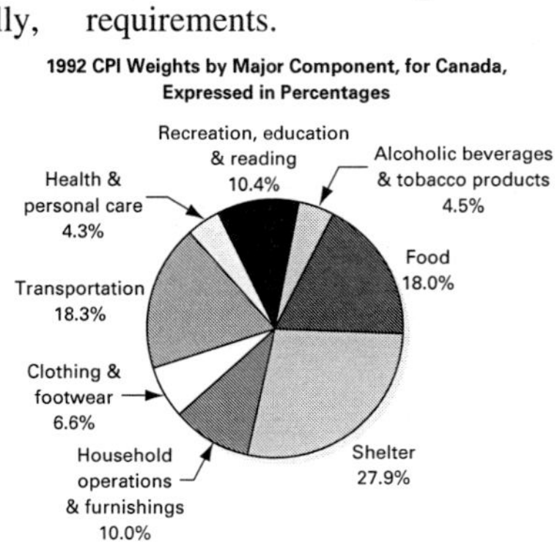

Source: Statistics Canada, Catalogue No. 62-557-XPB.

LEARNING UNIT OBJECTIVES

LU 17–1: Central Measurements: Mean, Median, and Mode

- Define and calculate the mean (p. 396).
- Explain and calculate a weighted mean (p. 397).
- Define and calculate the median (p. 398).
- Define and identify the mode (p. 399).

LU 17–2: Frequency Distributions and Graphs

- Prepare a frequency distribution (p. 400).
- Prepare bar, line, and circle graphs (p. 401).
- Calculate price relatives and cost comparisons (p. 403).

LU 17–3: Measures of Dispersion (Optional Section)

- Explain and calculate the range (p. 405).
- Define and calculate the standard deviation (p. 405).
- Estimate percentage of data by using standard deviations (p. 405).

Business statistics can be important in predicting future sales. Note how the graph "Bigger But Thinner" predicts the increased sales of plasma-based flat TVs in the future. TV dealers could use this prediction to guide them in determining the amount of such TVs they should stock for future customers.

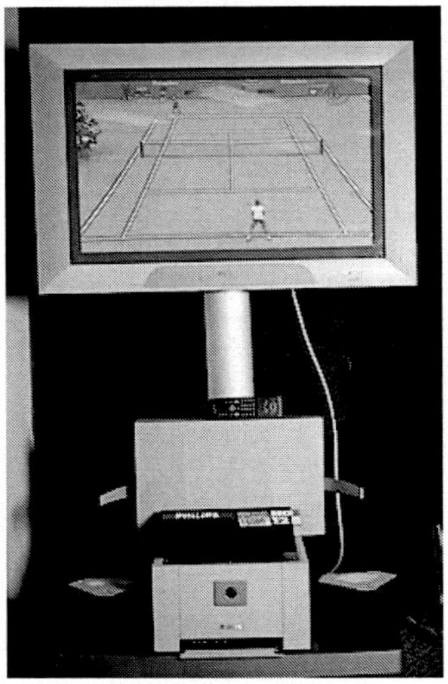

Michael Newman/PhotoEdit

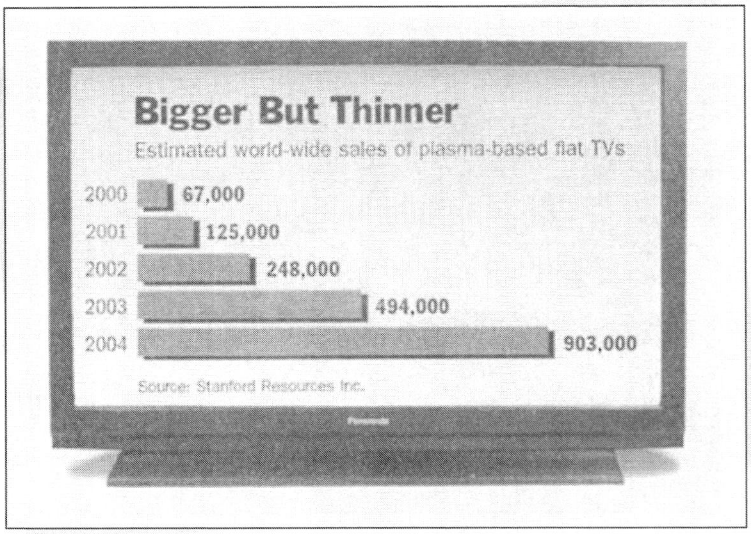

Source: © 2000 Dow Jones & Company, Inc.

In this chapter we look at various techniques that analyze and graphically represent business statistics. Learning Unit 17–1 discusses the mean, median, and mode. Learning Unit 17–2 explains how to gather data by using frequency distributions and to express these data visually in graphs. Emphasis is put on whether graphs are indeed giving accurate information. The chapter concludes with an introduction to index numbers—an application of statistics—and an optional Learning Unit on measures of dispersion.

LEARNING UNIT 17–1

CENTRAL MEASUREMENTS: MEAN, MEDIAN, AND MODE

Companies frequently use averages and measurements to guide their business decisions. The *mean* and *median* are the two most common averages used to indicate a single value that represents an entire group of numbers. The *mode* can also be used to describe a set of data. Such values are known collectively as **central measurements.**

MEAN: THE ARITHMETIC AVERAGE OF VALUES IN A DATA SET

$\mu = \text{Mean} = \frac{\sum X_N}{N}$ (17.1)

where N is the number of values in a set. We use N for the number of values in a population and n for the number of values in a sample.

The accountant of Bill's Sport Shop told Bill, the owner, that the average daily sales for the week were $150.14. The accountant stressed that $150.14 was an average and did not represent specific daily sales. Bill wanted to know how the accountant arrived at $150.14.

The accountant went on to explain that he used an arithmetic average, or **mean** (a measurement), to arrive at $150.14 (rounded to the nearest hundredth). He showed Bill the following formula:

$$\text{Mean} = \frac{\text{Sum of all values}}{\text{Number of values}} \quad \textbf{(17.1)}$$

The accountant used the following data:

	DAYS Sun.	Mon.	Tues.	Wed.	Thur.	Fri.	Sat.
Sport Shop sales	$400	$100	$68	$115	$120	$68	$180

To compute the mean, the accountant used these data:

$$\mu = \text{Mean} = \frac{\$400 + \$100 + \$68 + \$115 + \$120 + \$68 + \$180}{7} = \$150.14$$

When values appear more than once, businesses often look for a **weighted mean.** The format for the weighted mean is slightly different from that for the mean. The concept, however, is the same except that you weight each value by how often it occurs (its frequency). Thus, considering the frequency of the occurrence of each value allows a weighting of each day's sales in proper importance. To calculate the weighted mean, use the following formula:

$$\text{Weighted mean} = \frac{\text{Sum of products}}{\text{Sum of frequencies}} = \frac{\Sigma f \times X_n}{n} \qquad \textbf{(17.2)}$$

where n = Sum of frequencies or the number of observations in a set of data.

Let's change the sales data for Bill's Sport Shop and see how to calculate a weighted mean:

	DAYS Sun.	Mon.	Tues.	Wed.	Thur.	Fri.	Sat.
Sport Shop sales	$400	$100	$100	$80	$80	$100	$400

Rearrange this data into a table with indicated frequencies.

Value, X_n	Frequency, f	Product, $f \times X_n$
$400	2	$800
100	3	300
80	2	160
	$\Sigma f = n = 7$	$\Sigma fX_n = \$1,260$

$$\text{The weighted mean is } \frac{\$1,260}{7} = \$180 \quad \begin{cases} \Sigma fX_n = \$1,260 \\ n = \Sigma f = 7 \end{cases} \qquad \textbf{(17.3)}$$

Note how we multiply each value by its frequency of occurrence to arrive at the product. Then we divide the sum of the products by the sum of the frequencies.

When you calculate your grade point average (GPA), you are using a weighted average. The following formula is used to calculate GPA:

$$\text{GPA} = \frac{\text{Total points}}{\text{Total credits}}$$

Now let's show how Jill Rivers calculated her GPA to the nearest tenth.

Given A = 4; B = 3; C = 2; D = 1; F = 0

Courses	Credits attempted	Grade received	Points (Credits × Grade)
Introduction to Computers	4	A	16 (4 × 4)
Psychology	3	B	9 (3 × 3)
English Composition	3	B	9 (3 × 3)
Business Law	3	C	6 (2 × 3)
Business Math	3	B	9 (3 × 3)
	16		49 $\qquad \frac{49}{16} = 3.1$

In market research and analysis, the mean is used to estimate a market size or potential for a product or service. For example, if, on average, cellular phones are used 250 minutes per month by 3 million users in the region, the market potential is 750,000 air minutes per month.

When high or low numbers do not significantly affect a list of numbers, the mean is a good indicator of the centre of the data. If high or low numbers do have an effect—in other words there are extreme values in a set—the median may be a better indicator to use.

MEDIAN

The *Wall Street Journal* clipping "Who the Buyers Are" gives the statistics of median entry-level buyers of Mercedeses and BMWs for the model year 2000. The **median** is another measurement that indicates the centre of the data. One or more extreme values will not distort the median. For example, let's look at the yearly salaries of the employees of Rusty's Clothing Shop:

Who the Buyers Are

Demographics of buyers of entry-level Mercedeses and BMWs*

CATEGORY	MERCEDES	BMW
Median Age	**51**	40
Median Household Income	**$98,900**	$98,200
Percent Male	**49%**	61%
Percent Married	**71%**	59%
Use the Internet	**77%**	92%

*Figures are for buyers of model-year 2000 Mercedes C-Class and BMW 3-Series cars. Source: Strategic Vision

Source: © 2000 Dow Jones & Company, Inc.

Employee	Salary	Employee	Salary
Alice Knight	$95,000	Jane Wang	$67,000
Jane Hess	27,000	Bill Joy	40,000
Joel Floyd	32,000		

Note how Alice's salary of $95,000 will distort an average calculated by the mean:

$$\mu = \frac{\$95,000 + \$27,000 + \$32,000 + \$67,000 + \$40,000}{5} = \$52,200$$

The $52,200 average salary is considerably more than the salary of three of the employees. So it is not a good representation of the store's average salary. Let's use the following three steps to find the median. Note that you should not omit any of the steps.

FINDING THE MEDIAN OF A GROUP OF VALUES

Step 1. Rearrange the data set in ascending or descending order (arrange the set into an array) either from the smallest to the largest value or from the largest to the smallest.

Step 2. Find the location of the median–the middle value–using this formula:

$$\text{Location} = (n + 1) \div 2 \qquad \textbf{(17.4)}$$

where n is the number of observations or values in the data set.

a. If you have an odd number of observations in your array, find the exact location of the median. (For example, if there are five values in your set of data, $n = 5$. Using the above formula: $(5 + 1) \div 2 = 6 \div 2 = 3$. Our median will therefore be in the third position of the array.)

b. If you have an even number of observations, you will have two middle values. (For example, if there are six values in your set of data, $n = 6$. Using the above formula: $(6 + 1) \div 2 = 7 \div 2 = 3.5$. Your median will be located between the third and the fourth value. More precisely, the position of the median will be 3.5.)

Step 3. Now that we know the location of the median, we can define its value:

a. Find the value in the defined position (in a set with an odd number of values), or

b. Find the average of the two middle values (in a set with an even number of values).

Medians are used when there are extremes in a set of data.

For Rusty's Clothing Shop, we would find the median as follows:

1. Arrange values from smallest to largest:

   $27,000; $32,000; $40,000; $67,000; $95,000

2. $n = 5$; Location $= \frac{(5 + 1)}{2} = 3$

3. Since the middle position is an odd number, $40,000 is the median. Note that half of the salaries fall below the median and half fall above.

If Jane Hess ($27,000) were not on the payroll, we would find the median as follows:

1. Arrange values from smallest to largest:
   $32,000; $40,000; $67,000; $95,000

2. $n = 4$; Location $= \frac{(4 + 1)}{2} = 2.5$

Median

$32,000; $40,000; $67,000; $95,000
① ② ③ ④

3. Average the two middle values:

$$\text{Median} = \frac{\$40{,}000 + \$67{,}000}{2} = \$53{,}500$$

Note that the median results in two salaries below and two salaries above the average.

Now we'll look at another central measurement tool, the mode.

MODE: THE MOST FREQUENTLY APPEARING VALUE IN A SET

In a series of numbers, the value that occurs most often is called the **mode.** If all the values are different, there is no mode. If two or more numbers appear most often, you may have two or more modes. Note that we do not have to arrange the numbers in lowest-to-highest order, although this could make it easier to find the mode.

EXAMPLE

3, 4, 5, 6, 3, 8, 9, 3, 5, 3

3 is the mode, since it is listed 4 times and none of the others appears as frequently.

Now let's check your progress with a Practice Quiz.

LU 17–1 PRACTICE QUIZ

Barton Company's sales reps sold the following last month:

Sales rep	Sales volume
A	$16,500
B	$15,000

Sales rep	Sales volume
C	$12,000
D	$48,900

n	Mean	Median	Mode
?	?	?	?

Calculate the mean and the median. Which is the better indicator of the centre of the data? Is there a mode?

LEARNING UNIT 17–2
FREQUENCY DISTRIBUTIONS AND GRAPHS

In this Unit you will learn how to gather data and illustrate them. Today, computer software programs can make beautiful colour graphics. But how accurate are they? This *Wall Street Journal* clipping gives an example of misleading graphics. All readers should check the actual numbers illustrated by graphics.

What's Wrong With this Picture? Utility's Glasses Are Never Empty

By Kathleen Deveny
Staff Reporter of The Wall Street Journal

When Les Waas, an investor in Philadelphia Suburban Corp., paged through the company's 1994 annual report, he was impressed by what he saw.

The water utility had used a series of charts to represent its revenues, net income and book value per share, among other results. Each figure was represented by the level of water in a glass. Each chart showed strong growth.

Then Mr. Waas looked a little more carefully. The bars in the chart seemed to indicate far more impressive growth than the numbers beneath them. A chart showing the growth in the number of Philadelphia Suburban's water customers, for example, seemed to indicate the company's customer base had more than tripled since 1990. But the numbers actually increased only 6.4%.

The reason for the disparity: The charts don't begin at zero. Even an empty glass in the accompanying chart would represent a customer base of 230,000.

Source: © 1995 Dow Jones & Company, Inc.

Collecting raw data and organizing them is a prerequisite to presenting statistics graphically. Let's illustrate this by an example.

A computer industry consultant wants to know how much college freshmen are willing to spend to set up a computer in their dormitory rooms. After visiting a local college dorm, the consultant gathered the following data on the amount of money 20 students spent on computers:

\$1,000	\$2,000	\$6,000	\$ 5,000	\$8,000
5,000	6,000	1,000	3,000	1,000
3,000	4,000	3,000	10,000	3,000
7,000	3,000	1,000	1,000	9,000

Note that these raw data are not arranged in any order. To make the data more meaningful, the consultant made the **frequency distribution** table shown here.

Price of computer X_n	Tally	Frequency f	Relative frequency $f_{rel} = \frac{f}{n}$	Cumulative frequency f_{cum}	Relative cumulative frequency $f_{relcum} = \frac{f_{cum}}{n}$
\$1,000	|||||	5	$\frac{5}{20} = \frac{1}{4} = .25 = 25\%$	5	$\frac{5}{20} = \frac{1}{4} = .25 = 25\%$
\$2,000	|	1	$\frac{1}{20} = .05 = 5\%$	6	$\frac{6}{20} = .30 = 30\%$
\$3,000	|||||	5	$\frac{5}{20} = .25 = 25\%$	11	$\frac{11}{20} = .55 = 55\%$
\$4,000	|	1	.05 = 5%	12	$\frac{12}{20} = .60 = 60\%$
\$5,000	||	2	.10 = 10%	14	$\frac{14}{20} = .70 = 70\%$
\$6,000	||	2	.10 = 10%	16	$\frac{16}{20} = .80 = 80\%$
\$7,000	|	1	.05 = 5%	17	$\frac{17}{20} = .85 = 85\%$
\$8,000	|	1	.05 = 5%	18	$\frac{18}{20} = .90 = 90\%$
\$9,000	|	1	.05 = 5%	19	$\frac{19}{20} = .95 = 95\%$
\$10,000	|	1	.05 = 5%	$n = 20$	$\frac{20}{20} = 1.00 = 100\%$
Total		$\Sigma f = n = 20$	$\Sigma f_{rel} = 1.00 = 100\%$		

In the first column of this table, we arranged data into a number (10) of equal groups or categories, called *classes*. The size or width of each class in this example is \$1,000, and the data is arranged in ascending order from \$1,000 to \$10,000. In the second column the consultant used "tallies" to check each value, and then by counting tallies he obtained frequencies (f) of appearance for each of the values.

Think of this distribution table as a way to organize a list of numbers to show the patterns that may exist.

In the fourth column you can see **relative frequency,** which shows what percentage of students spent the amounts indicated in the first column. As you see, 25% $(= \frac{5}{20} = \frac{1}{4} = 25\%)$ of the students spent $1,000 and another 25% spent $3,000.

Cumulative frequency, which is indicated in the fifth column, shows how many students spent up to the amount of dollars indicated in the respective class. For example, 16 students spent *up to* $6,000 and 11 spent up to $3,000. Values in this column ("Cumulative frequency") are also used to determine the median in frequency distributions (you can learn more about this in a statistics course).

Relative cumulative frequency indicates what percentage of students spent up to a certain amount of money. For example, you can see that 55% of students spent up to $3,000 and 80% spent up to $6,000.

Important Tips to Remember

- The sum of frequencies should be equal to the number of values, *n*.

$$\Sigma f = n \tag{17.3}$$

- The sum of relative frequencies must be always equal to 1 or 100%.

$$\Sigma f_{rel} = 1.00 = 100\%$$

- The cumulative frequency for the last class (category) must be equal to the number of values, *n*.
- The relative cumulative frequency for the last class must be equal to 1 or 100%.

This way of arranging data allows a researcher to work with huge quantities of data in condensed form and to quickly estimate the results of a survey. For example, the researcher can note in our case that only four students spent $7,000 or more. Most of the students spent either $1,000 for a cheaper set or $3,000 for a more advanced one.

Now let's see how we can use bar graphs.

BAR GRAPHS

Bar graphs help readers visualize the results of surveys or changes that have occurred over a period of time. This is especially true when the same type of data is repeatedly studied. A **histogram** is a type of bar graph in which each bar represents part of a *range* of data, with no gaps.

Let's return to our computer consultant example and make a bar graph of the computer purchases data collected by the consultant. Note that the height of the bar represents the frequency of each purchase. Bar graphs can be vertical or horizontal.

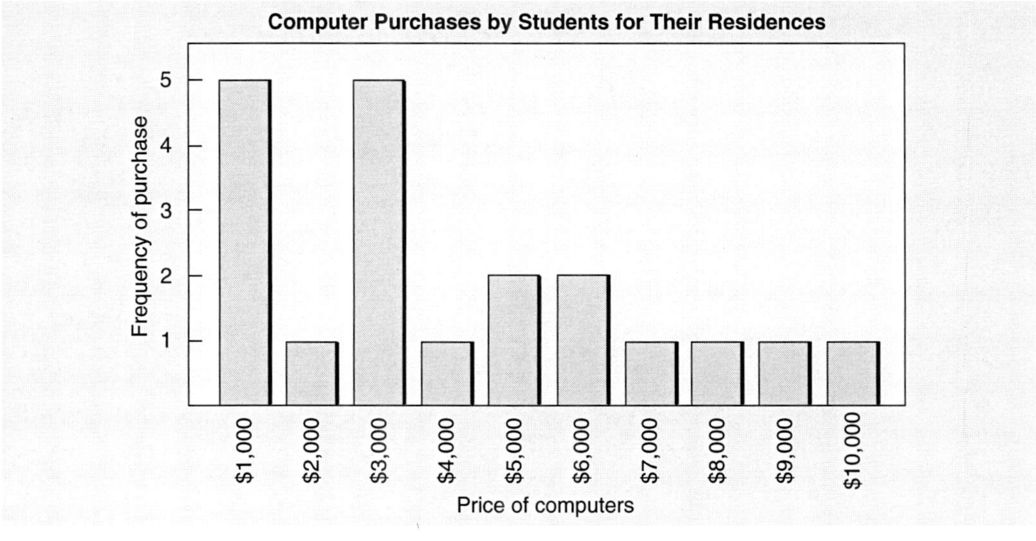

We can simplify this bar graph by grouping the prices of the computers. The grouping, or *intervals,* should be of equal sizes.

Class	Frequency
$1,000–$ 3,000.99	11
3,001– 5,000.99	3
5,001– 7,000.99	3
7,001– 9,000.99	2
9,001– 11,000.99	1

A bar graph for the grouped data follows.

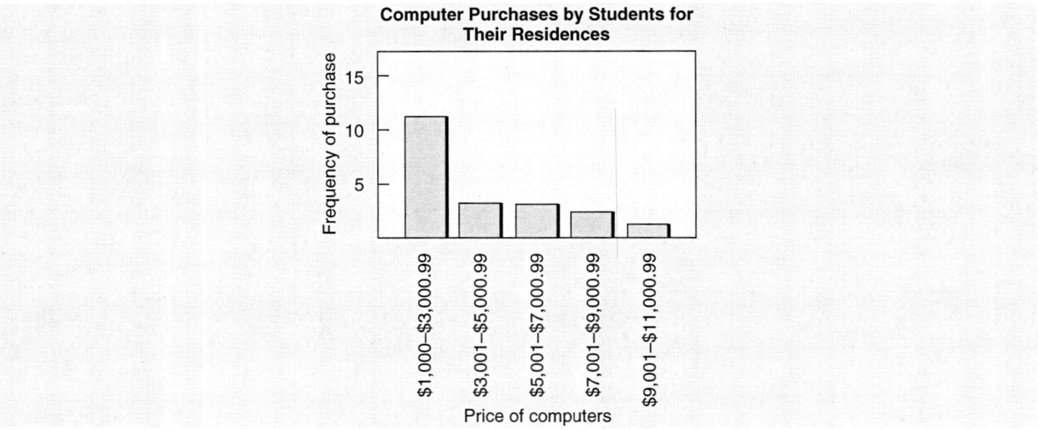

Useful Tips for Preparing Graphs

- Always put a title for the graph. The title will explain what is shown on the graph and the relevant information *in brief form:* for example, in what units, for what period of time, for what company, etc.
- The graph must be prepared on a suitable scale and be easy to understand.
- Numbers and explanations should not interfere with bars, lines, points, and other elements of the graph.
- Each of the axes must be labelled as to the type of data it indicates. For example, the Y-axis in the example shows the frequency of purchases; the X-axis shows computer prices.
- Colour should not be used in the graph to influence the reader. The reader must make his or her own judgments and conclusions.

Next, let's see how we can use line graphs.

LINE GRAPHS

A **line graph** shows trends over a period of time. Often separate lines are drawn to show the comparison between two or more trends. Note that time is always shown on the X-axis.

The *Wall Street Journal* clipping "Ford Builds a Car to Suit India's Tastes" uses a line graph to show the projected number of cars and commercial vehicles sold (in thousands of units). Note the "Even Faster Than Elsewhere" table showing India with the greatest projected compound annual growth.

We conclude our discussion of graphics with the use of the circle graph.

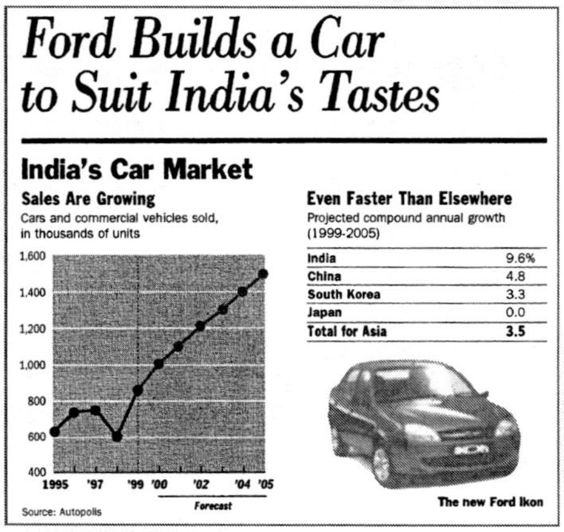

Source: © 2000 Dow Jones & Company, Inc.

CIRCLE GRAPHS

Circle graphs, often called *pie charts,* are especially helpful for showing the relationship of parts to a whole. The entire circle represents 100%, or 360°; the pie-shaped pieces represent the subcategories. Note how the circle graph in the next clipping, "Age and Activity," shows Web users by age.

Age and Activity

Web Users by Age

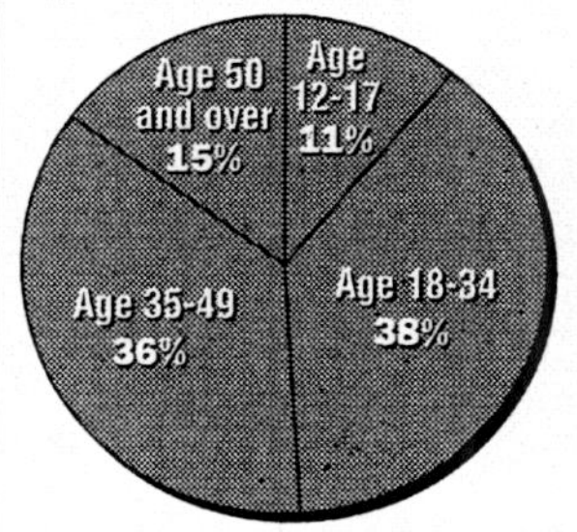

NOTE: *Age data were compiled by RelevantKnowledge Inc. from a sample of 1,990 Web users selected using random-digit telephone dialing. Internet usage data were compiled by IntelliQuest Information Group Inc. based on a survey of 764 on-line users selected using random-digit methodology.*

What They're Doing

Percentage of users attempting each of these on-line activities in the past month

Access the World Wide Web	95%
Send or receive e-mail	89
Obtain information about a hobby or personal interest	87
Obtain information about a product or service	83
Obtain general news	71
Obtain information for business/work	66
Download and save pictures/images	64
Obtain information for school	56
Check current weather or forecast	55
Participate in chat rooms/forums	48

Source: © 1998 Dow Jones & Company, Inc.

$15 \times 360° =$	54.0
$11 \times 360° =$	39.6
$36 \times 360° =$	129.6
$38 \times 360° =$	136.8
	360.0

To draw a circle graph (or pie chart), begin by drawing a circle. Then take the percentages and convert each percentage to a decimal. Next multiply each decimal by 360° to get the degrees represented by the percentage. Circle graphs must total 360°.

We conclude this Unit with a brief discussion of index numbers.

AN APPLICATION OF STATISTICS: INDEX NUMBERS

The financial section of a newspaper often presents lists of different numbers describing the changes in business. These **index numbers** express the relative changes in a variable compared with some base, which is taken as 100. The changes may be measured from time to time or from place to place. Index numbers function as percents and are calculated like percents.

Frequently, a business will use index numbers to make comparisons of a current price relative to a given year. For example, a calculator may cost \$9 today relative to a cost of \$75 some 30 years ago. The **price relative** of the calculator is $\frac{\$9}{\$75} \times 100 = 12\%$. The calculator now costs 12% of what it cost some 30 years ago. A price relative, then, is the current price divided by some previous year's price—the base year—multiplied by 100.

$$\boxed{\text{Price relative} = \frac{\text{Current price}}{\text{Base year's price}} \times 100} \qquad \textbf{(17.5)}$$

Index numbers can also be used to estimate current prices at various geographical locations. The frequently quoted Consumer Price Index (CPI), calculated and published monthly the Prices Division of Statistics Canada, records the price relative percentage cost of many goods and services nationwide compared to a base period. Table 17.1 gives the CPI and its major components in Canada for selected months with 1986 as a base period. CPI data reflect changes in the general price level, and are also used for assessments of changes in the purchasing power of the Canadian dollar.

TABLE 17–1
THE CONSUMER PRICE INDEX AND MAJOR COMPONENTS, (NOT SEASONALLY ADJUSTED), CANADA, 1986=100

	Indexes			Percentage change May 1996 From:	
	May 1996	April 1996	May 1995	April 1996	May 1995
All items	135.7	135.3	133.7	0.3	1.5
Food	127.8	128.3	126.8	−0.4	0.8
Shelter	134.2	134.1	133.9	0.1	0.2
Household operations and furnishings	124.0	123.9	121.6	0.1	2.0
Clothing and footwear	131.5	132.0	131.7	−0.4	−0.2
Transportation	144.9	143.1	138.8	1.3	4.4
Health and personal care	136.7	136.7	135.9	0.0	0.6
Recreation, education, and reading	145.7	144.0	142.5	1.2	2.2
Alcoholic beverages and tobacco products	146.3	145.5	143.6	0.5	1.9
Goods	129.4	128.9	127.4	0.4	1.6
Services	143.6	143.2	141.4	0.3	1.6
All items excluding food and energy	137.8	137.6	135.8	0.1	1.5
Energy	135.0	130.8	130.2	3.2	3.7
Purchasing power of the consumer dollar expressed in cents, compared to 1986	73.7	73.9	74.8		
All items (1981=100)	179.7				

Source: Adapted from Statistics Canada publication "Your Guide to the CPI,"1996, Catalogue No. 62-557-XPB, December 1996, Table 1, p. 12.

You can see that the base period, 1986, is taken to represent 100. In May 1996, the all-items CPI was 135.7, meaning that consumer prices increased by 35.7% over the period of 1986 and May 1996. In other words, to buy what you could buy for $1 in 1986 you must pay $1.36 ($1.357) in May 1996.

If, for example, "Household operations and furnishings" costs (see table) amounting to $1,000 in 1986 amounted to $1,357 in May 1996, a house built for $90,000 in 1986 would cost $122,130 in May 1996.

As is indicated in the table, the purchasing power of $1 in May 1996 compared to 1986 was 73.7 cents:

$$\left(\frac{100.0}{135.7}\right) \times \$1 = \$.737 \text{ or } 73.7 \text{ cents}$$

That is, $1 in May 1996 had the same value as 73.7 cents in 1986.

Now for a Practice Quiz.

LU 17–2 PRACTICE QUIZ

1. The following is the number of sales made by 20 salespeople on a given day. Prepare a frequency distribution and a bar graph. Do not use intervals for this example.

5	8	9	1	4	4	0	3	2	8
8	9	5	1	9	6	7	5	9	10

2. Assuming the following market shares for diapers 5 years ago, prepare a circle graph:

Pampers	32%	Huggies	24%
Luvs	20%	Others	24%

3. Today a new Explorer costs $30,000. In 1991 the Explorer cost $19,000. What is the price relative? Round to the nearest tenth percent.

LEARNING UNIT 17–3
MEASURES OF DISPERSION (OPTIONAL SECTION)

In Learning Unit 17–1 you learned how companies use the mean, median, and mode to indicate a single value, or number, that represents an entire group of numbers, or data. Often it is valuable to know how the information is scattered (spread or dispersed) within a data set. A **dispersion** is a number that expresses this.

This Learning Unit discusses three measures of dispersion—range, standard deviation, and normal distribution.

The simplest **measure of dispersion** is the *range.*

RANGE

Range, which is the difference between the two extreme values (highest and lowest) in a group of values or a set of data. For example, often the actual extreme values of hourly temperature readings during the past 24 hours are given but not the range or difference between the high and low readings. To find the range in a group of data, subtract the lowest value from the highest value.

$$\text{Range} = \text{Highest value} - \text{Lowest value} \qquad \textbf{(17.6)}$$

Thus, if the high temperature reading during the past 24 hours was 30° and the low temperature reading was 10°, the range is 30° − 10°, or 20°.

The difficulty in using the range is that it depends only on the values of the extremes and does not consider any other values in the data set. The range gives only a general idea of the spread of the values in a set of data.

EXAMPLE

Find the range of the following values: 83.6, 77.3, 69.2, 93.1, 85.4, 71.6.

Range = 93.1 − 69.2 = 23.9

STANDARD DEVIATION

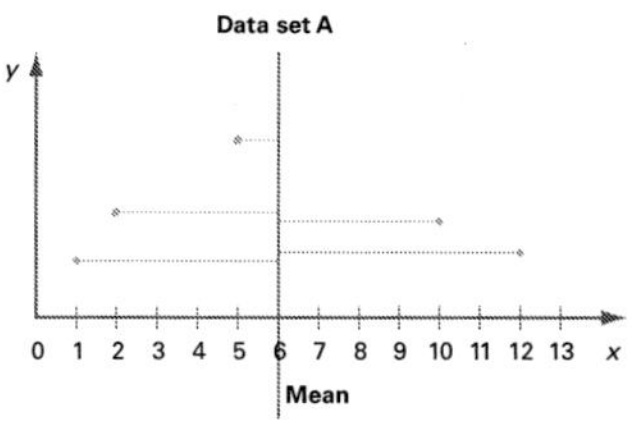

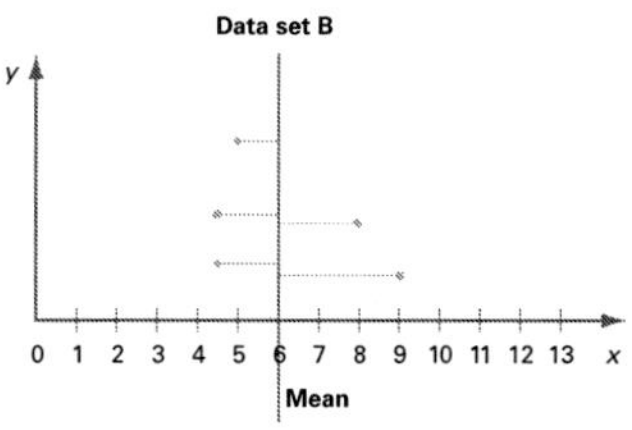

Since the **standard deviation** is intended to measure the spread of data around the mean, the first step in finding the standard deviation of a set of data is to determine its mean. The following diagram shows two sets of data—A and B. Note that, as shown in the diagram, the means of these two data are equal. Now look at how the data in both sets are spread or dispersed.

Data set A	Data set B
	X
X X X X X	X X X X
0 1 2 3 4 5 6 7 8 9 10 11 12 13	0 1 2 3 4 5 6 7 8 9 10 11 12 13
Mean = (1 + 2 + 5 + 10 + 12) ÷ 5 = 6	Mean = (4 + 4 + 5 + 8 + 9) ÷ 5 = 6

You can see that although the means of data sets A and B are equal, data set A is clearly more widely dispersed; therefore, the data in set B will have a smaller standard deviation than the data in set A.

To find the standard deviation of an ungrouped set of data, use the following steps:

FINDING THE STANDARD DEVIATION

Step 1. Find the mean of the set of data.
Step 2. Subtract the mean from each piece of data to find each deviation. Take its absolute value.
Step 3. Square each deviation (multiply the deviation by itself).
Step 4. Sum all squared deviations.
Step 5. Divide the sum of the squared deviations by $n - 1$, where n equals the number of pieces of data.
Step 6. Find the square root ($\sqrt{\ }$) of the number obtained in Step 5 (use a calculator). This is the standard deviation. (The square root is a number that when multiplied by itself equals the amount shown inside the square root symbol.)

To arrange the data for step calculations, use the following table format:

Data, X	Mean, μ Step 1	$\lvert X - \mu \rvert$ Step 2 (absolute value)	$\lvert X - \mu \rvert^2$ Step 3

Two additional points should be made. First, Step 2 sometimes results in negative numbers. Since the sum of the deviations obtained in Step 2 should always be zero, we would not be able to find the average deviation. This is why we square each deviation—to generate positive quantities only. Second, the standard deviation we refer to is used with *sample* sets of data, that is, a collection of data from a population. The population is the *entire* collection of data. When the standard deviation for a population is calculated, the sum of the squared deviations is divided by n instead of by $n - 1$. In all problems that follow, sample sets of data are being examined.

There are shortcut formulas for calculating standard deviation S of a sample or a population. For standard deviation of a sample, use the following formula:

$$S = \sqrt{\frac{n\sum x^2 - (\sum x)^2}{n(n-1)}} \qquad \textbf{(17.7)}$$

where n is the size of the sample.

For standard deviation of a population (entire data set) use this shortcut formula:

$$G = \sqrt{\frac{N\sum x^2 - (\sum x)^2}{N^2}} \qquad \textbf{(17.8)}$$

where N is the size of the population.

Using this formula you must perform only three steps:

STEP 1. Prepare a table and insert the values of X in the first column.

STEP 2. Square these values and insert the results into the second column.

STEP 3. Calculate the sums of the first and second columns and substitute them into the relevant formula (either 17.7 or 17.8).

Data, X	X^2
$\Sigma X =$	$\Sigma X^2 =$

Note that, most likely, the bigger the standard deviation that S indicates, the higher the risk of your enterprise.

EXAMPLE

Calculate the standard deviations for the sample data sets A and B given in the table earlier. Round the final answer to the nearest tenth. Note that Step 1—find the mean—is given in the table.

$S = \sqrt{\frac{\sum (x - \bar{x})^2}{n - 1}}$ where $\bar{x}$ = mean; x = individual values.

STANDARD DEVIATION OF DATA SETS A AND B: The first of the two tables that follow uses Steps 2 through 6 to find the standard deviation of data set A, and the other table uses Steps 2 through 6 to find the standard deviation of data set B.

Data	Step 2 Data − Mean	Step 3 (Data − Mean)^2
1	1 − 6 = −5	25
2	2 − 6 = −4	16
5	5 − 6 = −1	1
10	10 − 6 = 4	16
12	12 − 6 = 6	36
	Total 0	94 **(Step 4)**

Step 5: Divide by $n - 1$: $\frac{94}{5-1} = \frac{94}{4} = 23.5$

Step 6: The square root of $\sqrt{23.5}$ is 4.8 (rounded).
The standard deviation of data set A is 4.8.

Data	Step 2 Data − Mean	Step 3 (Data − Mean)^2
4	4 − 6 = −2	4
4	4 − 6 = −2	4
5	5 − 6 = −1	1
8	8 − 6 = 2	4
9	9 − 6 = 3	9
	Total 0	22 **(Step 4)**

Step 5: Divide by $n - 1$: $\frac{22}{5-1} = \frac{22}{4} = 5.5$

Step 6: The square root of $\sqrt{5.5}$ is 2.3.
The standard deviation of data set B is 2.3.

As suspected, the standard deviation of data set B is less than that of set A. The standard deviation value reinforces what we see in the diagram.

Let's do these calculations using the shortcut formula. Prepare the data in table format (see the sample below).

Set A, $n = 5$ Data X (Step 1)	X^2 (Step 2)
1	1
2	4
5	25
10	100
12	144
$\Sigma X = 30$ **(Step 3)**	$\Sigma X^2 = 274$ **(Step 3)**

Set B, $n = 5$ Data X (Step 1)	X^2 (Step 2)
4	16
4	16
5	25
8	64
9	81
$\Sigma X = 30$ **(Step 3)**	$\Sigma X^2 = 202$ **(Step 3)**

To calculate the standard deviation, substitute the values from the last line of the tables into formula 17.7.

$$S = \sqrt{\frac{n\Sigma x^2 - (\Sigma x)^2}{n(n-1)}} = \sqrt{\frac{5 \times 274 - 900}{5 \times 4}} = \sqrt{\frac{470}{20}} = \sqrt{23.5} = 4.8$$

Standard deviation of set A is 4.8.

$$S = \sqrt{\frac{n\Sigma x^2 - (\Sigma x)^2}{n(n-1)}} = \sqrt{\frac{5 \times 202 - 900}{5 \times 4}} = \sqrt{\frac{110}{20}} = \sqrt{5.5} = 2.3$$

Standard deviation of set B is 2.3.

If we were talking about risks, set B would be less risky than set A.

Normal Distribution

One of the most important distributions of data is the **normal distribution.** In a normal distribution, data are spread *symmetrically* about the mean. A graph of such a distribution looks like the bell-shaped curve in Figure 17.1. Many data sets are normally distributed. Examples are the life span of automobile engines, women's heights, and intelligence quotients.

In a normal distribution, the data are spread out symmetrically—50% of the data lie above the mean, and 50% of the data lie below the mean (to the left or right of mean). Additionally, if the data are normally distributed, 68% of the data should be found within one standard deviation above and below the mean. About 95% of the data should be found within two standard deviations above and below the mean. Figure 17.1 illustrates these facts. 99.7% of the data should be within 3 standard deviations from the mean.

FIGURE 17–1

Standard deviation and the normal distribution

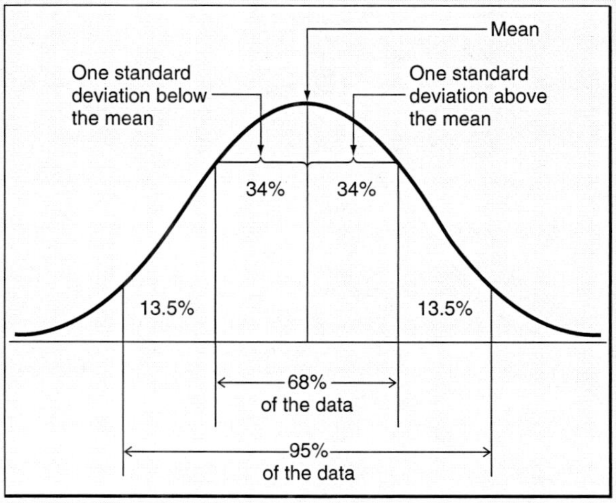

EXAMPLE

Assume that the mean useful life of a particular lightbulb is 2,000 hours and is normally distributed with a standard deviation of 300 hours. Calculate the life of the lightbulb within **(a)** one standard deviation of the mean and **(b)** two standard deviations of the mean; also **(c)** calculate the percent of lightbulbs that will last 2,300 hours or longer.

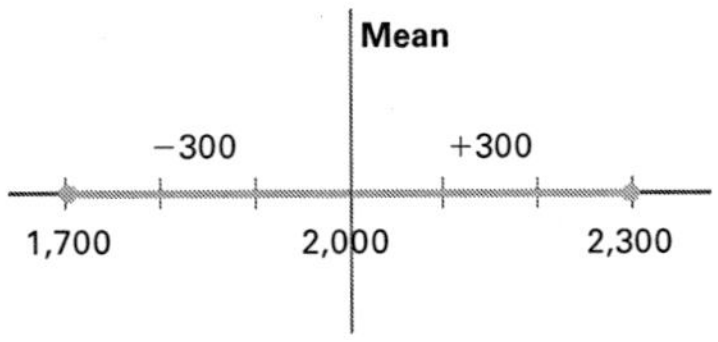

a. 68% of this type of lightbulb will last from 1,700 to 2,300 hours.

$2{,}000 \pm 300 = 1{,}700$ and 2,300 hours—in statistics this is called the **interval estimate.**

b. 95% of this type of lightbulb will last from 1,400 to 2,600 hours.

$2{,}000 \pm 2(300) = 1{,}400$ and 2,600 hours

c. Since 50% of the data in a normal distribution lie below the mean and 34% represent the amount of data one standard deviation above the mean, we must calculate the percent of data that lies beyond one standard deviation above the mean.

$100\% - (50\% + 34\%) = 16\%$

So 16% of the bulbs should last 2,300 hours or longer.

It's time for another Practice Quiz.

LU 17–3 PRACTICE QUIZ

1. Calculate the range for the following data: 58, 13, 17, 26, 5, 41.
2. Calculate the standard deviation for the following sample set of data: 113, 92, 77, 125, 110, 93, 111. Round answers to the nearest tenth.

CHAPTER ORGANIZER AND REFERENCE GUIDE

<table>
<tr><th>TOPIC</th><th>KEY POINT, PROCEDURE, FORMULA</th><th>EXAMPLE(S) TO ILLUSTRATE SITUATION</th></tr>
<tr><td>Mean, p. 396</td><td>Population mean:
$\frac{\text{Sum of all values}}{\text{Number of values}} \quad \mu = \frac{\Sigma X_N}{N} \quad (17.1)$
N = Number of values in a set.
Example: Mean $\bar{X} = \frac{\Sigma X_n}{n}$ for a sample</td><td>Age of basketball team: 22, 28, 31, 19, 15
$\text{Mean} = \frac{(22 + 28 + 31 + 19 + 15)}{5}$
$= 23$</td></tr>
<tr><td>Weighted mean, p. 397</td><td>$\frac{\text{Sum of products}}{\text{Sum of frequencies}} \quad \mu = \frac{\Sigma fX_N}{N} \quad (17.2)$
$N = \Sigma f \quad (17.3)$

For sample:
$\bar{X} = \frac{\Sigma fX_n}{n} \quad \Sigma f = n$</td><td>
<table>
<tr><th></th><th colspan="7">Days</th></tr>
<tr><th></th><th>S.</th><th>M.</th><th>T.</th><th>W.</th><th>Th.</th><th>F.</th><th>S.</th></tr>
<tr><td>Sales</td><td>$90</td><td>$75</td><td>$80</td><td>$75</td><td>$80</td><td>$90</td><td>$90</td></tr>
</table>
<table>
<tr><th>Value, X</th><th>Frequency, f</th><th>Product, $f \times X$</th></tr>
<tr><td>$90</td><td>3</td><td>$270</td></tr>
<tr><td>75</td><td>2</td><td>150</td></tr>
<tr><td>80</td><td>2</td><td>160</td></tr>
<tr><td></td><td>$\Sigma f = 7 = n$</td><td>$580 $= \Sigma fX$</td></tr>
</table>
$\mu = \text{Mean} = \frac{\$580}{7} = \$82.86$</td></tr>
<tr><td>Median, p. 398</td><td>Step 1. Rearrange the data set in ascending or descending order (arrange the set into an array) either from the smallest to the largest value or from the largest to the smallest value.</td><td>12, 15, 8, 6, 3
<table>
<tr><th></th><th>1</th><th>2</th><th>3</th><th>4</th><th>5</th></tr>
<tr><td>Step 1.</td><td>3</td><td>6</td><td>8</td><td>12</td><td>15</td></tr>
</table></td></tr>
</table>

(continues)

CHAPTER ORGANIZER AND REFERENCE GUIDE (CONTINUED)

Topic	Key point, procedure, formula	Example(s) to illustrate situation
	Step 2. Find the location of median—the middle value: Location = $(n + 1) \div 2$ (17.4) where n is the number of observations/values in the data set. a. If you have an odd number of observations in your array, you will find the exact location of the median. For example, there are 5 values in your set of data: $n = 5$. Using the above formula find the location of the median, $(5 + 1) \div 2 = 6 \div 2 = 3$. Our median will be in the third position in the array. b. If you have an even number of observations, you will have two middle values. For example, there are 6 values in your set of data: $n = 6$. Using the above formula find the location of the median, $(6 + 1) \div 2 = 7 \div 2 = 3.5$. Your median will be located between the third and the fourth values, in position 3.5. **Step 3.** Knowing the location of your median, define its value. a. Find the value in the defined position (in a set with an odd number of values). b. Find the average of the two middle values (in a set with an even number of values).	**Step 2.** Location $\frac{(5 + 1)}{2} = 3$. **Step 3.** Median is the third number: 8.
Frequency distribution, p. 400	Method of listing numbers or amounts not arranged in any particular way by columns for numbers (amounts), tally, and frequency	Number of sodas consumed in one day: 1, 5, 4, 3, 4, 2, 2, 3, 2, 0 (see table below)
Bar graphs, p. 401	Height of bar represents frequency. Bar graph used for grouped data. Bar graphs can be vertical or horizontal.	From soda example above: 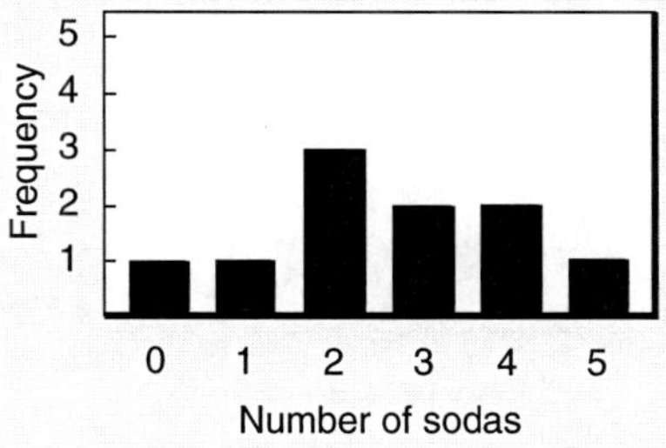

Number of sodas	Tally	Frequency
0	|	1
1	|	1
2	|||	3
3	||	2
4	||	2
5	|	1

(continues)

CHAPTER ORGANIZER AND REFERENCE GUIDE (CONTINUED)

TOPIC	KEY POINT, PROCEDURE, FORMULA	EXAMPLE(S) TO ILLUSTRATE SITUATION
Line graphs, p. 402	Shows trend. Helps to put numbers in order.	**Sales** 2003 $1,000 2004 2,000 2005 3,000 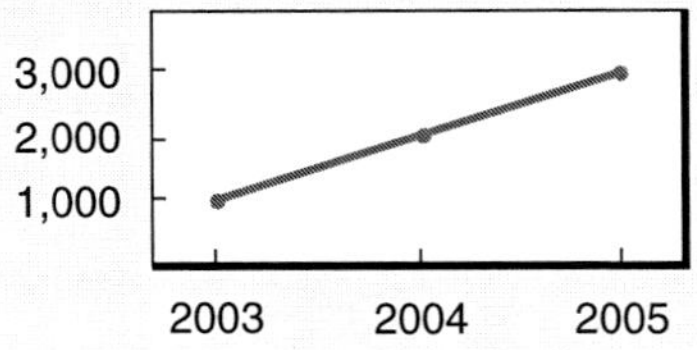
Circle graphs, p. 403	Circle = 360° % × 360° = Degrees of pie to represent percent Total should = 360°	60% favour diet soda 40% favour sugared soda 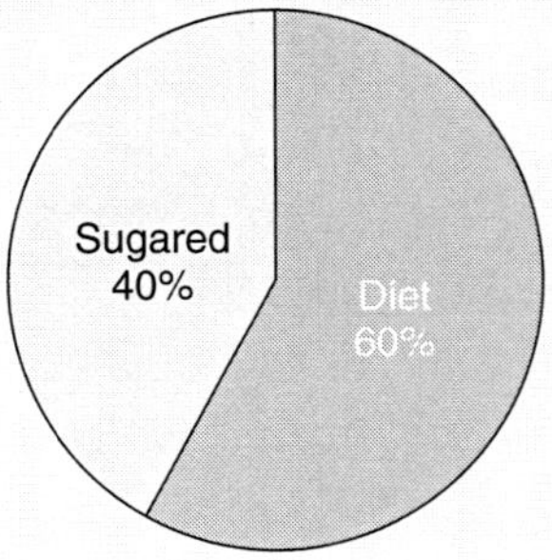 $.60 \times 360° = 216°$ $.40 \times 360° = \underline{144°}$ 360°
Index numbers, p. 403	$\text{Price relative} = \left(\frac{\text{Current Price}}{} \div \frac{\text{Base year's price}}{}\right) \times 100$ (17.5)	
Price relative, p. 403	$\text{Price relative} = \frac{\text{Current price}}{\text{Base year's price}} \times 100$ (17.5)	A station wagon's sticker price was $8,799 in 1982. Today it is $14,900. $\text{Price relative} = \frac{\$14,900}{\$8,799} \times 100 = 169.3\%$ (rounded to nearest tenth percent)
Range, p. 405	Range = Highest value − Lowest value (17.6)	Prices for different watches in a store were $23, $125, $48, $2,435, $10. Price range is $2,435 − $10 = $2,425.
Standard deviation (optional), p. 405	**1.** Calculate mean. **2.** Subtract mean from each piece of data. **3.** Square each deviation. **4.** Sum squares. **5.** Divide sum of squares by $n - 1$, where n = number of pieces of data. **6.** Take square root of number obtained in Step 5, to find the standard deviation.	Calculate the standard deviation of this set of data: 7, 2, 5, 3, 3. **1.** $\mu = \text{Mean} = \frac{20}{5} = 4$ **2.** $7 - 4 = 3$ $2 - 4 = -2$ $5 - 4 = 1$ $3 - 4 = -1$ $3 - 4 = -1$

(*continues*)

CHAPTER ORGANIZER AND REFERENCE GUIDE (CONCLUDED)

Topic	Key point, procedure, formula	Example(s) to illustrate situation
		3. $(3)^2 = 9$ $(-2)^2 = 4$ $(1)^2 = 1$ $(-1)^2 = 1$ $(-1)^2 = 1$ 4. 16 5. $16 \div 4 = 4$ 6. Standard deviation = 2
Standard deviation (shortcut formula), for a sample (optional), p. 406	$S = \sqrt{\frac{n\sum x^2 - (\sum x)^2}{n(n-1)}}$ (17.7) Using this formula you must perform only three steps: **Step 1.** Prepare a table and insert the values of X in the first column. **Step 2.** Square these values and insert the results into the second column. **Step 3.** Calculate the sums of the first and second columns and substitute them into the relevant formula (either 17.7 or 17.8). Data X | X^2 $\Sigma X =$ | $\Sigma X^2 =$	Data X | X^2 7 | 49 2 | 4 5 | 25 3 | 9 3 | 9 $\Sigma X = 20$ | $\Sigma X^2 = 240$ $S = \sqrt{\frac{5 \times 96 - 400}{5 \times 4}} = \sqrt{4} = 2$ Standard deviation is 2. Data X | X^2 $\Sigma X =$ | $\Sigma X^2 =$
Standard deviation for a population (optional), p. 406	$G = \sqrt{\frac{N\sum x^2 - (\sum x)^2}{N^2}}$ where N = Size of population	
Key terms	Bar graph, p. 401 Central measurements, p. 396 Circle graph, p. 403 Cumulative frequency, p. 401 Dispersion, p. 405 Frequency distribution, p. 400 Histogram, p. 401 Index numbers, p. 403 Interval estimate, p. 408 Line graph, p. 402 Mean, p. 396 Measure of dispersion, p. 405 Median, p. 398 Mode, p. 399 Normal distribution, p. 407	Price relative, p. 403 Range, p. 405 Relative cumulative frequency, p. 401 Relative frequency, p. 401 Standard deviation, p. 405 Weighted mean, p. 397

CRITICAL THINKING DISCUSSION QUESTIONS

1. Explain the mean, median, and mode. Give an example that shows you must be careful when you read statistics in an article.
2. Explain frequency distributions and the types of graphs. Locate a company annual report and explain how the company shows graphs to highlight its performance. Does the company need more or fewer of these visuals? Could price relatives be used?

END-OF-CHAPTER PROBLEMS

DRILL PROBLEMS (*Note:* Problems for optional Learning Unit 17–3 follow the Challenge Problems)

Calculate the mean (to the nearest hundredth):

17–1. 6, 9, 7, 4

17–2. 8, 11, 19, 17, 15

17–3. \$55.83, \$66.92, \$108.93

17–4. \$1,001, \$68.50, \$33.82, \$581.95

17–5. Calculate the grade-point average: A = 4, B = 3, C = 2, D = 1, F = 0 (to nearest tenth).

Excel

Courses	Credits	Grade
Computer Principles	3	B
Business Law	3	C
Logic	3	D
Biology	4	A
Marketing	3	B

17–6. Find the weighted mean (to the nearest tenth):

Value	Frequency	Product
4	7	
8	3	
2	9	
4	2	

Find the median:

17–7. 55, 10, 19, 38, 100, 25

17–8. 95, 103, 98, 62, 31, 15, 82

Find the mode:

17–9. 8, 9, 3, 4, 12, 8, 8, 9

17–10. 22, 19, 15, 16, 18, 18, 5, 18

17–11. Given:

Truck cost	2004	\$30,000
Truck cost	2001	\$21,000

Calculate the price relative (round to the nearest tenth percent).

17–12. Given the following sales of Lowe Corporation, prepare a line graph (run sales from \$5,000 to \$20,000).

2003	\$ 8,000
2004	11,000
2005	13,000
2006	18,000

17–13. Prepare a frequency distribution from the following weekly salaries of teachers at Moore Community College. Use the following intervals:

\$200–\$299.99
300– 399.99
400– 499.99
500– 599.99

\$210	\$505	\$310	\$380	\$275
290	480	550	490	200
286	410	305	444	368

17–14. Prepare a histogram from the frequency distribution in Problem 17–13.

17–15. How many degrees on a pie chart would each be given from the following?

Wear digital watch	42%
Wear traditional watch	51%
Wear no watch	7%

ADDITIONAL DRILL PROBLEMS

17–16. Find the mean for the following lists of numbers. Round to the nearest hundredth.

a. 12, 16, 20, 25, 29 Mean ________

b. 80, 91, 98, 82, 68, 82, 79, 90 Mean ________

c. 9.5, 12.3, 10.5, 7.5, 10.1, 18.4, 9.8, 6.2, 11.1, 4.8, 10.6 Mean ________

17–17. Find the weighted mean for the following. Round to the nearest hundredth.

a. 4, 4, 6, 8, 8, 13, 4, 6, 8 Weighted mean ________

b. 82, 85, 87, 82, 82, 90, 87, 63, 100, 85, 87 Weighted mean________

17–18. Find the median for the following:

a. 56, 89, 47, 36, 90, 63, 55, 82, 46, 81 Median ________

b. 59, 22, 39, 47, 33, 98, 50, 73, 54, 46, 99 Median ________

17–19. Find the mode for the following:

24, 35, 49, 35, 52, 35, 52 Mode ________

17–20. Find the mean, median, and mode for each of the following:

a. 72, 48, 62, 54, 73, 62, 75, 57, 62, 58, 78
Mean ________ Median ________ Mode ________

b. \$0.50, \$1.19, \$0.58, \$1.19, \$2.83, \$1.71, \$2.21, \$0.58, \$1.29, \$0.58
Mean ________ Median ________ Mode ________

c. \$92, \$113, \$99, \$117, \$99, \$105, \$119, \$112, \$95, \$116, \$102, \$120
Mean ________ Median ________ Mode ________

d. 88, 105, 120, 119, 105, 128, 160, 151, 90, 153, 107, 119, 105
Mean ________ Median ________ Mode ________

17–21. A local dairy distributor wants to know how many containers of yogurt health club members consume in a month. The distributor gathered the following data:

17	17	22	14	26	23	23	15	18	16
18	15	23	18	29	20	24	17	12	15
18	19	18	20	28	21	25	21	26	14
16	18	15	19	27	15	22	19	19	13
20	17	13	24	28	18	28	20	17	16

Construct a frequency distribution table to organize this data.

17–22. Construct a bar graph for the Problem 17–21 data. The height of each bar should represent the frequency of each amount consumed.

17–23. To simplify the amount of data concerning yogurt consumption, construct a relative frequency distribution table. The range will be from 1 to 30 with five class intervals: 1–6, 7–12, 13–18, 19–24, and 25–30.

17–24. Construct a bar graph for the grouped data.

17–25. Prepare a pie chart to represent the above data.

WORD PROBLEMS

17–26. The June 18, 2004 issue of *Advertising Age* reported on the April 2004 top 10 multichannel Internet retailers ranked by visitors. From the following information, find the mean and median visits:

1. ticketmaster.com	4,824,000
2. barnesandnoble.com	4,509,000
3. dell.com	4,050,000
4. hallmark.com	3,683,000
5. apple.com	3,588,000
6. hp.com	3,347,000
7. mcafee.com	3,331,000
8. intuit.com	2,993,000
9. sears.com	2,959,000
10. bluelight.com	2,823,000

17–27. The March 20, 2003 issue of *Industry Week/IW* reported on the latest interest yields. United States interest rates were compared to European Union rates. From the following information, prepare a line graph comparing the United States and European Union:

	Latest	**3 months (ago)**	**6 months (ago)**	**12 months (ago)**
U.S.A.	6.59%	6.75%	6.50%	6.20%
European Union	5.56	5.30	5.40	5.50

17–28. The latest weekly market shares of record companies are based on current albums sold. This is an indicator of music-company performance. Market shares were: Universal, 31.4%; WEA, 18.2%; Sony, 15.0%; BMG, 12.0%; EMD, 8.2%; and others, 15.2%. From this information, construct a circle graph of these market shares.

17–29. Bill Small, a travel agent, provided Alice Hall with the following information regarding the cost of her upcoming vacation:

Transportation	35%
Hotel	28%
Food and entertainment	20%
Miscellaneous	17%

Construct a circle graph for Alice.

17–30. Jim Smith, a marketing student, observed how much each customer spent in a local convenience store. Using the following results, prepare **(a)** a frequency distribution and **(b)** a histogram. Use intervals of $0–$5.99, $6–$11.99, $12–$17.99, and $18–$23.99.

$18.50	$18.24	$ 6.88	$9.95
16.10	3.55	14.10	6.80
12.11	3.82	2.10	
15.88	3.95	5.50	

17–31. Angie's Bakery bakes bagels. Find the weighted mean (to the nearest whole bagel) given the following daily production for June:

200	150	200	150	200
150	190	360	360	150
190	190	190	200	150
360	400	400	150	200
400	360	150	400	360
400	400	200	150	150

17–32. Melvin Company reported sales in 2005 of $300,000. Sales were $150,000 in 2004 and $100,000 in 2003. Construct a line graph for Melvin Company.

ADDITIONAL WORD PROBLEMS

17–33. The sales for the year at the 8 Bed and Linen Stores were $1,442,897, $1,556,793, $1,703,767, $1,093,320, $1,443,984, $1,665,308, $1,197,692, and $1,880,443. Find the mean earnings for a Bed and Linen Store for the year.

17–34. To avoid having an extreme number affect the average, the manager of Bed and Linen Stores (Problem 6) would like you to find the median earnings for the 8 stores.

17–35. The Bed and Linen Store in Salem sells many different towels. Following are the prices of all the towels that were sold on Wednesday: $7.98, $9.98, $9.98, $11.49, $11.98, $7.98, $12.49, $12.49, $11.49, $9.98, $9.98, $16, and $7.98. Find the mean price of a towel.

17–36. Looking at the towel prices, the Salem manager (Problem 17–35) decided that he should have calculated a weighted mean. Find the weighted mean price of a towel.

17–37. The manager of the Salem Bed and Linen Store above would like to find another measure of the central tendency called the *median.* Find the median price for the towels sold.

17–38. The manager at the Salem Bed and Linen Store would like to know the most popular towel among the group of towels sold on Wednesday. Find the mode for the towel prices for Wednesday.

17–39. The women's department of a local department store lists its total sales for the year: January,

$39,800; February, $22,400; March, $32,500; April, $33,000; May, $30,000; June, $29,200; July, $26,400; August, $24,800; September, $34,000; October, $34,200; November, $38,400; December, $41,100. Draw a line graph to represent the monthly sales of the women's department for the year. The vertical axis should represent the dollar amount of the sales.

17–40. The following list shows the number of television sets sold in a year by the sales associates at Souza's TV and Appliance Store.

115	125	139	127	142	153	169	126	141
130	137	150	169	157	146	173	168	156
140	146	134	123	142	129	141	122	141

Construct a relative frequency distribution table to represent the data. The range will be from 115 to 174 with intervals of 10.

17–41. Use the data in the distribution table for Problem 17–40 to construct a bar graph for the grouped data.

17–42. Expenses for Flora Foley Real Estate Agency for the month of June were as follows: salaries expense, $2,790; utilities expense, $280; rent expense, $2,000; commissions expense, $4,800; and other expenses, $340. Present these data in a circle graph. (First calculate the percent relationship between each item and the total, then determine the number of degrees that represents each item.)

17–43. Today a new Jeep costs $25,000. In 1970, the Jeep cost $4,500. What is the price relative? (Round to nearest tenth percent.)

CHALLENGE PROBLEMS

17–44. On June 15, 2004, a research company reported on the annual revenue of the largest travel agencies in the Bay Area. The results are as follows:

AAA Travel Agency	$86,700,000
Riser Group	63,200,000
Casto Travel	62,900,000
Balboa Travel	36,200,000
Hunter Travel Managers	36,000,000

(a) What would be the mean and the median? **(b)** What is the total revenue percent of each agency? **(c)** Prepare a circle graph depicting the percents.

17–45. The following circle graph is a suggested budget for Ron Rye and his family for a month:

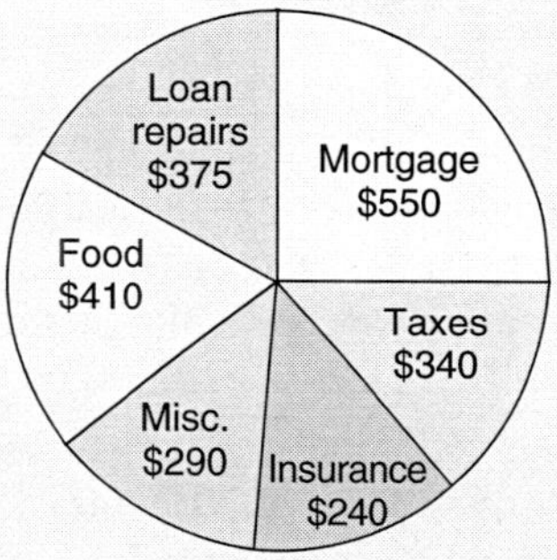

Ron would like you to calculate the percent (to the hundredth) for each part of the circle graph along with the appropriate number of degrees.

LEARNING UNIT 17–3 OPTIONAL ASSIGNMENTS

DRILL PROBLEMS

17–46. Calculate the range for the following set of data: 117, 98, 133, 52, 114, 35.

Calculate the standard deviation for the following sample sets of data. Round the final answers to the nearest tenth.

17–47. 83.6, 92.3, 56.5, 43.8, 77.1, 66.7

17–48. 7, 3, 12, 17, 5, 8, 9, 9, 13, 15, 6, 6, 4, 5

17–49. 41, 41, 38, 27, 53, 56, 28, 45, 47, 49, 55, 60

WORD PROBLEMS

17–50. The mean useful life of car batteries is 48 months. They have a standard deviation of 3. If the useful life of batteries is normally distributed, calculate **(a)** the percent of batteries with a useful life of less than 45 months and **(b)** the percent of batteries that will last longer than 54 months.

17–51. The average weight of a particular box of crackers is 24.5 ounces with a standard deviation of .8 ounce. The weights of the boxes are normally distributed. What percent of the boxes **(a)** weigh more than 22.9 ounces and **(b)** weigh less than 23.7 ounces?

17–52. The results of an examination are normally distributed with a mean score of 77 and a standard deviation of 6. Find the percent of individuals scoring as indicated below.

a. Between 71 and 83
b. Between 83 and 65
c. Above 89
d. Less than 65
e. Between 77 and 65

17–53. Listed below are the sales figures in thousands of dollars for a group of insurance salespeople. Calculate the mean sales figure and the standard deviation.

$117	$350	$400	$245	$420
223	275	516	265	135
486	320	285	374	190

17–54. The time in seconds it takes for 20 individual sewing machines to stitch a border onto a particular garment is listed below. Calculate the mean stitching time and the standard deviation to the nearest hundredth.

67	69	64	71	73
58	71	64	62	67
62	57	67	60	65
60	63	72	56	64

SUMMARY PRACTICE TEST

1. In June, Logan Realty sold 10 homes at the following prices: $135,000; $170,000; $90,000; $98,000; $185,000; $150,000; $108,000; $114,000; $142,000; and $250,000. Calculate the mean and median. (pp. 482, 483)

Excel

2. Sears Hardware Store counted the number of customers entering the store for a week. The results were 1,300; 950; 1,300; 1,700; 880; 920; and 1,210. What is the mode? (p. 484)

3. This semester Lee Win took four 3-credit courses at Middlesex Community College. She received an A in accounting and Bs in history, psychology, and algebra. What is her cumulative grade-point average (assume A = 4 and B = 3) to the nearest hundredth? (p. 483)

4. Ron's Sub Shop reported the following sales for the first 20 days of June. (p. 485)

$200	$100	$600	$300	$400	$700	$200
300	400	600	200	500	600	700
200	600	600	100	500	700	

Prepare a frequency distribution for Ron.

5. Star Company produced the following number of maps during the first 5 weeks of last year. Prepare a bar graph. (p. 486)

Week	Maps
1	800
2	700
3	300
4	750
5	400

6. Leser Corporation reported record profits of 10%. It stated in the report that the cost of sales was 40% with expenses of 50%. Prepare a circle graph for Leser. (p. 488)

7. Today a new Land Rover costs $39,000. In 1990, the Rover cost $22,000. What is the price relative to the nearest tenth percent? (p. 488)

***8.** Calculate the standard deviation for the following set of data: 20, 32, 45, 26, 35, 42, 40. Round final answer to nearest tenth. (p. 490)

---

*Optional problem.

SOLUTIONS TO PRACTICE QUIZZES

LU 17–1

$$\text{Mean} = \frac{\$16{,}500 + \$15{,}000 + \$12{,}000 + \$48{,}900}{4} = \$23{,}100$$

① ② ③ ④

Step 1. \$12,000 | \$15,000, \$16,500, | \$48,900

Note how we arrange numbers from smallest to highest to calculate median.

Step 2. $n = 4$; Location $= \dfrac{4+1}{2} = 2.5$

Step 3. Median $= \dfrac{\$15{,}000 + \$16{,}500}{2} = \$15{,}750$

The median is the better indicator, since in calculating the mean the \$48,900 puts the average of \$23,100 much too high. There is no mode.

LU 17–2

1.

Number of sales	Tally	Frequency
0	I	1
1	II	2
2	I	1
3	I	1
4	II	2
5	III	3
6	I	1
7	I	1
8	III	3
9	IIII	4
10	I	1

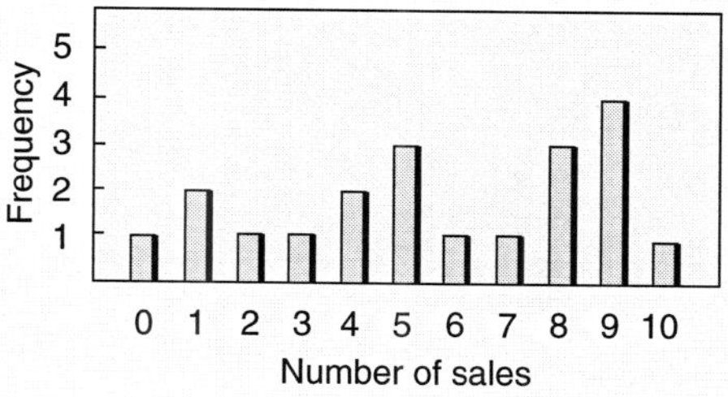

2.

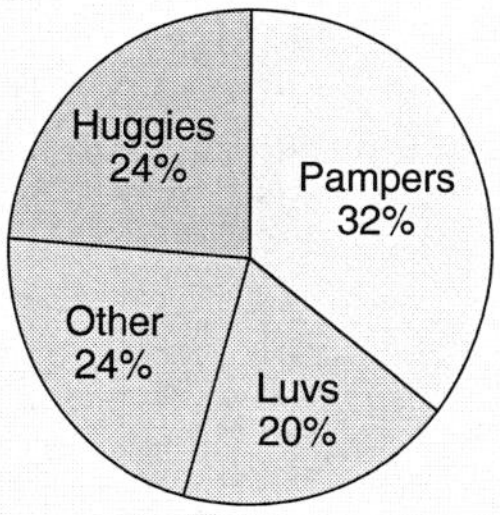

$.32 \times 360° = 115.20°$
$.20 \times 360° = 72.00°$
$.24 \times 360° = 86.40°$
$.24 \times 360° = 86.40°$

3. $\dfrac{\$30{,}000}{\$19{,}000} \times 100 = 157.9\%$

LU 17–3

1. $58 - 5 = 53$ range

2.

Data	Data − Mean	(Data − Mean)^2
113	113 − 103 = 10	100
92	92 − 103 = −11	121
77	77 − 103 = −26	676
125	125 − 103 = 22	484
110	110 − 103 = 7	49
93	93 − 103 = −10	100
111	111 − 103 = 8	64
		Total 1,594

$1{,}594 \div (7 - 1) = 265.6666667$

$\sqrt{265.6666667} = 16.3$ standard deviation

Business Math Scrapbook

WITH INTERNET APPLICATION

Putting Your Skills to Work

TABLE 17-2
Consumer Price Index for Canada, All Items (Not Seasonally Adjusted), 1972–1996, 1986 = 100

	Jan.	Feb.	March	April	May	June	July	Aug.	Sept.	Oct.	Nov.	Dec.	Annual average[1]
Indexes													
1972	32.7	32.8	32.9	33.0	33.1	33.1	33.5	33.8	33.9	33.9	34.0	34.2	33.4
1973	34.5	34.7	34.8	35.2	35.4	35.8	36.1	36.6	36.8	36.9	37.2	37.4	36.0
1974	37.7	38.1	38.4	38.7	39.4	39.9	40.1	40.6	40.8	41.2	41.6	42.0	39.9
1975	42.2	42.5	42.7	43.0	43.4	44.0	44.6	45.0	45.1	45.5	45.9	46.0	44.2
1976	46.2	46.5	46.6	46.8	47.2	47.4	47.6	47.8	48.0	48.3	48.5	48.7	47.5
1977	49.1	49.5	50.1	50.4	50.8	51.1	51.6	51.8	52.1	52.6	52.9	53.3	51.3
1978	53.5	53.9	54.5	54.6	55.4	55.8	56.6	56.7	56.6	57.2	57.6	57.8	55.9
1979	58.2	58.8	59.5	59.9	60.5	60.8	61.3	61.5	62.0	62.5	63.1	63.4	61.0
1980	63.8	64.4	65.0	65.4	66.2	66.9	67.4	68.1	68.7	69.3	70.2	70.5	67.2
1981	71.5	72.2	73.1	73.7	74.3	75.5	76.1	76.7	77.3	78.0	78.7	79.1	75.5
1982	79.6	80.6	81.6	82.0	83.2	84.0	84.4	84.8	85.3	85.8	86.4	86.4	83.7
1983	86.2	86.6	87.5	87.5	87.7	88.7	89.0	89.5	89.5	90.0	90.0	90.3	88.5
1984	90.8	91.3	91.5	91.8	91.9	92.3	92.8	92.8	92.9	93.1	93.7	93.7	92.4
1985	94.1	94.7	94.9	95.3	95.5	96.1	96.4	96.5	96.7	97.0	97.4	97.8	96.0
1986	98.3	98.6	98.9	99.0	99.5	99.6	100.4	100.7	100.7	101.2	101.7	101.9	100.0
1987	102.1	102.6	103.0	103.5	104.1	104.4	105.1	105.2	105.2	105.6	106.0	106.1	104.4
1988	106.3	106.7	107.3	107.6	108.3	108.5	109.1	109.4	109.5	110.0	110.3	110.3	108.6
1989	110.9	111.6	112.2	112.5	113.7	114.3	115.0	115.1	115.3	115.7	116.1	116.0	114.0
1990	117.0	117.7	118.1	118.1	118.7	119.2	119.8	119.9	120.2	121.2	121.9	121.8	119.5
1991	125.0	125.0	125.5	125.5	126.1	126.7	126.8	126.9	126.7	126.5	127.0	126.4	126.2
1992	127.0	127.1	127.5	127.6	127.8	128.1	128.4	128.4	128.3	128.5	129.1	129.1	128.1
1993	129.6	130.0	129.9	129.9	130.1	130.2	130.5	130.6	130.7	130.9	131.5	131.3	130.4
1994	131.3	130.3	130.1	130.2	129.9	130.2	130.7	130.8	130.9	130.7	131.4	131.6	130.7
1995	132.1	132.7	133.0	133.4	133.7	133.7	134.0	133.8	133.9	133.8	134.1	133.9	133.5
1996	134.2	134.4	134.9	135.3	135.7	135.6	135.6	135.7	135.9	136.2			
Monthly percentage changes													
1982	0.6	1.3	1.2	0.5	1.5	1.0	0.5	0.5	0.6	0.6	0.7	0.0	
1983	−0.2	0.5	1.0	0.0	0.2	1.1	0.3	0.6	0.0	0.6	0.0	0.3	
1984	0.6	0.6	0.2	0.3	0.1	0.4	0.5	0.0	0.1	0.2	0.6	0.0	
1985	0.4	0.6	0.2	0.4	0.2	0.6	0.3	0.1	0.2	0.3	0.4	0.4	
1986	0.5	0.3	0.3	0.1	0.5	0.1	0.8	0.3	0.0	0.5	0.5	0.2	
1987	0.2	0.5	0.4	0.5	0.6	0.3	0.7	0.1	0.0	0.4	0.4	0.1	
1988	0.2	0.4	0.6	0.3	0.7	0.2	0.6	0.3	0.1	0.5	0.3	0.0	
1989	0.5	0.6	0.5	0.3	1.1	0.5	0.6	0.1	0.2	0.3	0.3	−0.1	
1990	0.9	0.6	0.3	0.0	0.5	0.4	0.5	0.1	0.3	0.8	0.6	−0.1	
1991	2.6	0.0	0.4	0.0	0.5	0.5	0.1	0.1	−0.2	−0.2	0.4	−0.5	
1992	0.5	0.1	0.3	0.1	0.2	0.2	0.2	0.0	−0.1	0.2	0.5	0.0	
1993	0.4	0.3	−0.1	0.0	0.2	0.1	0.2	0.1	0.1	0.2	0.5	−0.2	
1994	0.0	−0.8	−0.2	0.1	−0.2	0.2	0.4	0.1	0.1	−0.2	0.5	0.2	
1995	0.4	0.5	0.2	0.3	0.2	0.0	0.2	−0.1	0.1	−0.1	0.2	−0.1	
1996	0.2	0.1	0.4	0.3	0.3	−0.1	0.0	0.1	0.1	0.2			
Annual percentage changes													
1982	11.3	11.6	11.6	11.3	12.0	11.3	10.9	10.6	10.3	10.0	9.8	9.2	10.9
1983	8.3	7.4	7.2	6.7	5.4	5.6	5.5	5.5	4.9	4.9	4.2	4.5	5.7
1984	5.3	5.4	4.6	4.9	4.8	4.1	4.3	3.7	3.8	3.4	4.1	3.8	4.4
1985	3.6	3.7	3.7	3.8	3.9	4.1	3.9	4.0	4.1	4.2	3.9	4.4	3.9
1986	4.5	4.1	4.2	3.9	4.2	3.6	4.1	4.4	4.1	4.3	4.4	4.2	4.2
1987	3.9	4.1	4.1	4.5	4.6	4.8	4.7	4.5	4.5	4.3	4.2	4.1	4.4
1988	4.1	4.0	4.2	4.0	4.0	3.9	3.8	4.0	4.1	4.2	4.1	4.0	4.0
1989	4.3	4.6	4.6	4.6	5.0	5.3	5.4	5.2	5.3	5.2	5.3	5.2	5.0
1990	5.5	5.5	5.3	5.0	4.4	4.3	4.2	4.2	4.2	4.8	5.0	5.0	4.8
1991	6.8	6.2	6.3	6.3	6.2	6.3	5.8	5.8	5.4	4.4	4.2	3.8	5.6
1992	1.6	1.7	1.6	1.7	1.3	1.1	1.3	1.2	1.3	1.6	1.7	2.1	1.5
1993	2.0	2.3	1.9	1.8	1.8	1.6	1.6	1.7	1.9	1.9	1.9	1.7	1.8
1994	1.3	0.2	0.2	0.2	−0.2	0.0	0.2	0.2	0.2	−0.2	−0.1	0.2	0.2
1995	0.6	1.8	2.2	2.5	2.9	2.7	2.5	2.3	2.3	2.4	2.1	1.7	2.1
1996	1.6	1.3	1.4	1.4	1.5	1.4	1.2	1.4	1.5	1.8			

[1]The annual index level is the average of the 12 individual monthly indexes. The percentage change for a given calendar year is calculated using the annual average indexes.

Source: Adapted from Statistics Canada, "Your Guide to the CPI," 1996, Catalogue No. 62-557-XPB, December 1996, Table 2.

PROJECT A

Examine Table 17.2 and calculate the equivalent prices of a house that cost $255,000 in 1986 for May 1972, June 1978, September 1984, May 1990, and July 1996. Explain the meaning of monthly and annual percentage changes in Table 17.2.

APPENDIX A

ANSWERS TO DRILL AND WORD PROBLEMS (ODDS), CHALLENGE PROBLEMS, SUMMARY PRACTICE TESTS, AND CUMULATIVE REVIEWS

CHAPTER 1

Drill Problems

1–1. 112
1–3. 198
1–5. 13,580
1–7. 113,690
1–9. 38
1–11. 1,700
1–13. 1,074
1–15. 31,110
1–17. 340,531
1–19. 126,000
1–21. 90
1–23. 86 R4
1–25. 187
1–27. 1,616
1–29. 24,876
1–31. 17,989; 18,000
1–33. 80
1–35. 104
1–37. 216
1–39. 19 R21
1–41. 2,227
1–43. 15,589
1–45. 2,162,000
1–47. 850
1–49. 12 R600; 12 R610

Additional Drill (LU 1–1)

1–51. a. 80,181 c. 280,005 e. 67,760
1–53. a. 4,750; 4,800; 5,000; 5,000
c. 9,390; 9,400; 9,000; 9,000
e. 408,120; 408,100; 408,000; 400,000

(LU 1–2)

1–55. a. 741 c. 1,319 e. 2,188
g. 2,379
1–57. a. Est. 40; Act. 39 c. Est. 10; Act. 9 e. Est. 300; Act. 294
1–59. a. $16,686 c. $17,828
e. Tot. $71,577

(LU 1–3)

1–61. a. 407,200 c. 91,200,000
1–63. a. 27 c. 36

Word Problems

1–65. A range of $265,800 to $318,000
1–67. $1,188
1–69. $26,390
1–71. 2,980 shares; $154,960
1–73. 84
1–75. 1km/L
1–77. 922; $54,398
1–79. 235 faculty; 7,050 students
1–81. $182,090
1–83. $28,745
1–85. 73
1–87. Sales = $22,047;
Gross Profit = $9,922
1–75. 1–89. 54,506
1–77. 1–91. $24

Additional Word Problems (LU 1–1)

1–93. $2,000
1–95. 1,587,000 *t*
1–97. 26,000,000
1–99. 40 thousands; 3 millions

(LU 1–2)

1–101. $19,973
1–103. 12,797 pounds
1–105. Est.: $9,400; actual $9,422
1–107. $746

(LU 1–3)

1–109. $640
1–111. 250 kilometres
1–113. 245,280
1–115. $12,900
1–117. a. seven million two hundred ninety-four thousand seven hundred two.
b. $1,105,298 c. $300,000

Challenge Problem

1–118.

Year	2003	Change	2004	
Income:				
Gross income	$69,000	times 2	$138,000	
Interest income	$ 450	$ −150	$ 300	
Total	$69,450		$138,300	
Expenses				
Living	$24,500	times 0.5	$12,250	
Insurance premiums	$ 350	times 3	$ 1,050	
Taxes	$14,800	$−250	$14,550	
Medical	$ 585	$+410	$ 995	
Investment	$ 4,000	$−1,000	$ 3,000	
Total	$44,235			
Year	**2003**		**2004**	
Assets				
Chequing account	$ 1,950	times 2	$ 3,900	
Savings account	$ 8,950	times 2	$17,900	
Auto	$ 1,800		$ –	
Personal property	$14,000	times 6/7	$12,000	
Total	$26,700		$33,800	
Assets rounded	**$30,000**		**$30,000**	
Liabilities				
Note to bank	$4,500	$−375	$4,125	
Liabilities rounded	$5,000		$4,000	
Net worth	$22,200		$29,675	Difference
Rounded net worth	$25,000		$26,000	$1,000

Summary Practice Test

1. a. 4,594 c. 17,594
2. Seven million, nine hundred forty-four thousand, five hundred eighty-one
3. a. 60 b. 600 c. 8,000 d. 20,000
4. 18,000; 18,648
5. 5,600,000; 5,995,352
6. 844,582,000
7. 260 R20
8. 100
9. $72
10. $700; no
11. $350

Calculator Use Practice Problems

a. 4,913 b. 101,208 c. 11 d. 59,794

CHAPTER 2

Drill Problems

2–1. Proper
2–3. Improper
2–5. $61\frac{2}{5}$
2–7. $\frac{59}{3}$
2–9. $\frac{11}{13}$
2–11. $60(2 \times 2 \times 3 \times 5)$
2–13. $96(2 \times 2 \times 2 \times 2 \times 2 \times 3)$
2–15. $\frac{13}{21}$
2–17. $15\frac{5}{12}$
2–19. $\frac{5}{6}$
2–21. $7\frac{4}{9}$
2–23. $\frac{5}{16}$
2–25. $\frac{3}{25}$
2–27. $\frac{1}{3}$
2–29. $\frac{7}{18}$

Additional Drill Problems (LU 2–1)

2–31. a. Improper c. Improper e. Improper
2–33. a. $\frac{36}{5}$ c. $\frac{31}{7}$ e. $\frac{131}{12}$
2–35. a. $\frac{6}{7}$ c. $\frac{1}{2}$ e. $\frac{8}{11}$

(LU 2–2)

2–37. a. 32 c. 480
2–39. a. $\frac{1}{3}$ c. $\frac{1}{18}$ e. $6\frac{1}{8}$ g. $5\frac{3}{4}$ i. $35\frac{7}{12}$

(LU 2–3)

2–41. a. $\frac{2}{3}$ b. $\frac{7}{26}$
2–42. a. $1\frac{1}{4}$ c. $1\frac{4}{21}$ e. 18 g. 24 i. $2\frac{2}{5}$ k. $\frac{2}{63}$

Word Problems

2–43. $1\frac{7}{12}$ metres needed
2–45. $25
2–47. $1,200
2–49. $63\frac{1}{4}$ inch; $11\frac{1}{2}$ inch remain
2–51. $29\frac{95}{128}$ kg per person
2–53. $121\frac{1}{12}$L
2–55. $525
2–57. $\frac{23}{36}$
2–59. $25
2–61. $3\frac{3}{4}$ lb apple; $8\frac{1}{8}$ cups flour; $\frac{5}{8}$ cup marg; $5\frac{15}{16}$ cups sugar; 5 tsp. cinn
2–63. 400 people
2–65. 20 pieces
2–67. 5,800 books
2–69. $200
2–71. $35\frac{7}{16}$ ft; $4\frac{9}{16}$ ft left
2–73. 55.47 km/h
2–75. $\frac{3}{8}$
2–77. $2\frac{3}{5}$ hours
2–79. $7,000

Additional Word Problems (LU 2–1)

2–81. $\frac{5}{12}$
2–83. $\frac{2}{3}$
2–85. $\frac{9}{12}$
2–87. $5\frac{3}{8}$

(LU 2–2)

2–89. $3\frac{1}{40}$ metres
2–91. $17\frac{5}{12}$ kms
2–93. $4\frac{8}{9}$ hours

(LU 2–3)

2–95. $39,000
2–97. 714
2–99. $20\frac{2}{3}$ kms

Challenge Problems

2–101. a. $261\frac{3}{4}$ cm b. 2 @ 2m boards or 400 cm c. $138\frac{1}{4}$ cm
2–102. a. 400 homes c. 3,000 people; 2,500 people d. $1,200,000

Summary Practice Test

1. Mixed number
2. Proper
3. Improper
4. $27\frac{3}{5}$
5. $\frac{31}{4}$
6. 14; $\frac{7}{10}$
7. 88
8. $28(2 \times 7 \times 2)$
9. $5\frac{17}{18}$
10. $\frac{3}{14}$
11. $6\frac{4}{19}$
12. $\frac{1}{4}$
13. $6\frac{4}{5}$ hours
14. 12,555 chairs
15. a. 24,000 soy b. 36,000 reg.
16. $36\frac{1}{4}$ hours
17. $15

CHAPTER 3

Drill Problems

3–1. Thousandths
3–3. .9; .95; .948
3–5. 6.9; 6.92; 6.925
3–7. 6.6; 6.56; 6.556
3–9. $2,011.67
3–11. .07
3–13. .09

3–15. .64
3–17. 14.91
3–19. $\frac{62}{100}$
3–21. $\frac{125}{10,000}$
3–23. $\frac{825}{1,000}$
3–25. $\frac{7,065}{10,000}$
3–27. $28\frac{48}{100}$
3–29. .004
3–31. .0085
3–33. 818.1279
3–35. 3.4
3–37. 2.32
3–39. 1.2; 1.26791
3–41. 4; 4.0425
3–43. 24,526.67
3–45. 161.29
3–47. 6,824.15
3–49. .04
3–51. .63
3–53. 2.585
3–55. .0086
3–57. 486
3–59. 3.950
3–61. 7,913.2

Additional Drill Problems (LU 13–1)

3–63. a. .433 c. 8.21 e. .5112
3–65. a. $\frac{83}{100}$ c. $2\frac{516}{1,000}$ e. $13\frac{7}{1,000}$
3–67. a. .13 c. .67 e. .56 g. .78 i. 2.38 k. 11.38 m. 4.86 o. 2.18

(LU 3–2)

3–69. a. .43 c. 10.735
3–71. a. 23.12 c. 8.66

Word Problems

3–73. .93
3–75. a. $7,360 c. $5,520
3–77. $225.90; $74.10
3–79. $353.54
3–81. 2.82 billion; 25.1 billion
3–83. $4,231.64
3–85. $6,650.28
3–87. Laundry detergent A; Mustard B; Canned tuna B
3–89. 40.24 dossages Yes
3–91. $5.70
3–93. $407.76
3–95. $258.25
3–97. a. $89 million
c. $15 million per month

Additional Word Problems (LU 3–1)

3–99. $118.96
3–101. $\frac{20}{73}$
3–103. $\frac{111}{122}$
3–105. .429

(LU 3–2)

3–107. $4.53
3–109. $111.25
3–111. 15

Challenge Problems

3–112. Total $386.08
3–113. 873.18

Summary Practice Test

1. 764.126
2. .6
3. .06
4. .006
5. $\frac{4}{10}$
6. $8\frac{95}{100}$
7. $\frac{951}{1,000}$
8. .14
9. .29
10. 4.63
11. .13
12. 288.8342
13. 10.3
14. 109.59
15. 22,453.6
16. 86,330
17. 705,518,978.1
18. $19.59
19. $531.56
20. $220.96
21. A $0.02/100 g
22. $276.79
23. $2.30

Cumulative Review—1–3

1. $405
2. 200,000
3. 50,560,000
4. $10
5. Yes; $4,740
6. $723.08
7. $369.56
8. $130,000,000
9. $51.73; $17.24; $68.97

CHAPTER 4

End of Chapter Problems

4–1. 16
4–2. 23.769
4–3. 0.0809
4–4. 75.35
4–5. 1.006183
4–6. 1.10356
4–7. 2.37102
4–8. 3,491
4–9. 3.29
4–10. 0.1298
4–11. 0.697
4–12. 4.297
4–13. 12.50
4–14. 189.33

CHAPTER 5

Drill Problems (1 of 3 sets)

5–1. $H = 55$
5–3. $N = 240$
5–5. $Y = 15$
5–7. $Y = 12$
5–9. $P = 25$

(2 of 3 sets)

5–11. $B = 70$
5–13. $N = 63$
5–15. $Y = 7$

(3 of 3 sets)

5–17. $B = 119$
5–19. $m = 60$

Additional Drill Problems

5–21. a. $3N = 70$ c. $N - 7 = 5$
e. $14 + \frac{1}{3}N = 18$ g. $\frac{3}{4}N = 9$

Word Problems (1 of 3 sets)

5–23. $m = \$80,000$
5–25. Hugh = 50; Joe = 250
5–27. 50 shorts; 200 t-shirts

(2 of 3 sets)

5–29. $P = \$429.50$
5–31. Pete = 90; Bill = 450
5–33. 48 boxes of pens; 240 batteries

(3 of 3 sets)

5–35. $D = \$134.9$ million
5–37. $W = 129$
5–39. Shift 1 = 3,360; Shift 2 = 2,240
5–41. 22 cartons of hammers; 18 cartons of wrenches

Additional Word Problems (LU 5–2)

5–43. 186
5–45. 180

5–47. $395
5–49. 36 watches; 12 necklaces; $252 watches; $48 necklaces
5–51. $4.5 million

Challenge Problems

5–52. a. 150 b. 300 c. $65,000 d. $217 e. $650
5–53. Before: $Bb = 4$; $B = 24$ After: $Bb = 10$; $B = 30$

Summary Practice Test

1. $300.99
2. $54,000
3. $FS = 30$; $BB = 180$
4. $F = 180$; $J = 720$
5. $D = 20$; $P = 80$
6. 950 hamburgers; 350 pizzas

CHAPTER 6

Drill Problems (1 of 2 sets)

6–1. 74%
6–3. 70%
6–5. 356.1%
6–7. .04
6–9. .643
6–11. 1.19
6–13. 8.3%
6–15. 87.5%
6–17. $\frac{1}{20}$
6–19. $\frac{19}{60}$
6–21. $\frac{27}{400}$
6–23. 7.2
6–25. 102.5
6–27. 156.5
6–29. 114.88
6–31. 16.2
6–33. 141.67
6–35. 10,000
6–37. 17,777.78
6–39. 108.2%
6–41. 110%
6–43. 400%
6–45. 59.4
6–47. 1,100
6–49. 40%
6–51. −6%

(2 of 2 sets)

6–53. $75; $135; $1,710
6–55. $24,528.30
6–57. $168,000
6–59. 9.56%; $9.56; 95.60; 95.60
6–61. $2,600
6–63. $10,937.50

Additional Drill Problems (LU 6–1)

6–65. a. 8% c. .9% e. 526% g. 1.1% i. 503.8% k. 26.2% m. 2.5%
6–67. a. 70% c. 162.5% e. 200% g. 16.7% i. 60% k. 31.3% m. 475%
6–69. a. $\frac{1}{4}$ c. 50% e. $\frac{2}{5}$ g. .7 i. $\frac{1}{12}$ k. $\frac{5}{16}$ m. .20

(LU 6–2)

6–71. a. 5.18 c. 100.8 e. 251 g. 45.32 i. .10 k. 30 m. 34
6–73. a. 210 c. 600 e. $17.50 g. 600 i. $75.00

Word Problems (1 of 5 sets)

6–75. 25%
6–77. $40,000
6–79. 10.06 L/100 km
6–81. 1,080,000
6–83. $1,111.11

(2 of 5 sets)

6–85. 10%
6–87. $30,000
6–89. Yes $15,480
6–91. 900
6–93. $742,500
6–95. $220,000
6–97. 33.3%

(3 of 5 sets)

6–99. 480
6–101. $39,063.83
6–103. $76.19
6–105. $1,900
6–107. $102.50

(4 of 5 sets)

6–109. 3.7%
6–111. $2,571
6–113. $8,000,000
6–115. 1,600
6–117. 28,000

(5 of 5 sets)

6–119. $920
6–121. 42%
6–123. a. $1,465.75 b. $143
6–125. a. .006 b. 640 mills
6–127. $1,480
6–129. $45,455

Additional Word Problems (LU 6–1)

6–131. $\frac{7}{10}$
6–133. .175
6–135. 188.4%
6–137. a. 0.075 b. $\frac{3}{40}$

(LU 6–2)

6–139. $9,000
6–141. $3,196
6–143. 329.5%

Challenge Problems

6–145. a. $1,380 b. $580 c. $626,271 d. $10,710,144
6–146. $38.74
6–147. a. $146,300,000 b. $333,100,000 c. .84%
6–148. $55,429

Summary Practice Test

1. 68.2%
2. 800%
3. 1,547%
4. 800%
5. .42
6. .0569
7. 6.0
8. .0025
9. 16.7%
10. 12.5%
11. $\frac{63}{400}$
12. $\frac{9}{125}$
13. $540,000
14. $2,166,667
15. 95%
16. 11.25%
17. $423.08
18. $426
19. $200,000
20. a. $221.74 b. 1,478.26
21. $5,767.25
22. $84,000
23. 5.3 mills
24. $2,436.85
25. $18,720

CHAPTER 7

Drill Problems

7–1. a. 23 : 25 : 26 b. 1 : 9 : 49
7–3. a. 1 : 2 : 10 b. 10 : 1 : 30
7–5. a. 5 : 3 b. 3 : 10
7–7. 1 : 2 : 1.357
7–9. 1 : 1.11 : 1.44
7–11. $c = 246.4$
7–13. $y = 2$; $x = 1.5$
7–15. $c = 24.00$; $d = 16.33$

Word Problems

7–17. 13.5 : 13.8 : 13.85 : 13.9
7–19. Mr. Peef: $127,272.73; Mr. Percival: $190,909.09; Mr. Stanley: $381,818.18
7–21. 50
7–23. $3,067.50 < $3,500 Yes

Summary Practice Test

1. 38 : 175
2. 690 : 570 : 1,801
3. 27 : 5
4. 45 : 34 : 9
5. 358,33
6. a = 608.00; c = 30.00
7. 2.22 h
8. $6,600

CHAPTER 8

Drill Problems

8–1. $1,572.87
8–3. $463.40

Additional Drill Problems (LU 8–1)

8–5. a. $430.64 c. $867.51
8–7. a. Neuner Realty Company c. The Royal Bank e. 14,0380
8–9. $37.79

Word Problems

8–11. $525.41
8–13. $1,560.40
8–15. $1,212.60
8–17. $1,535.15

Additional Word Problems

8–19. $1,435.42
8–21. Add: $3,000; Deduct: $22.25
8–23. $120.86
8–25. $1,315.20

Challenge Problems

8–27. $1,850.04
8–28. $3,061.67

Summary Practice Test

1. $199.88
2. $8,617.34
3. $7,685
4. $2,095.55
5. $6,976.70

CHAPTER 9

Drill Problems

9–1. .9114; .0886; $35.35; $363.65
9–3. .893079; .106921; $28.76; $240.24
9–5. $369.70; $80.30
9–7. $1,392.59; $457.41
9–9. June 28; July 18
9–11. June 15; July 5
9–13. July 10; July 30
9–15. $138; $6,862
9–17. $2; $198
9–19. $408.16; $291.84

Additional Drill Problems (LU 9–1)

9–21. a. $480 c. $50 e. $380
9–23. a. $75 c. $40.75
9–25. a. .7125; .2875 c. .72675; .27325
9–27. $3.51
9–29. $81.25
9–31. $315
9–33. 45%

(LU 9–2)

9–35. a. February 18; March 10 c. October 27; December 16 e. October 10; October 31
9–37. a. .98; $1,102.50 c. .98; $367.99
9–39. a. $16.79; $835.21 c. 0; $500

Word Problems

9–41. $48.38, $72.57
9–43. 9.80%
9–45. $576.06; $48.94
9–47. $5,100; $5,250
9–49. $5,850
9–51. $8,571.43
9–53. $8,173.20
9–55. $8,333.33; $11,666.67
9–57. $99.99
9–59. $489.90; $711.10
9–61. $4,658.97
9–63. $1,083.46; $116.54
9–65. $5,251.00
9–67. Save $4.27 with Verizon

Additional Word Problems (LU 9–2)

9–69. $12,230.40
9–71. a. $439.29 b. $491.21
9–73. $209.45
9–75. a. $765.31 (rounded) b. $386.99

Challenge Problems

9–77. $1,764; $252; 12.5%; $1,728.72
9–78. $4,891.42
9–79. $8,935.98
9–80. $1,526.88; January 15

Summary Practice Test

1. $210
2. $300
3. $284.23; $14.77
4. a. Oct 17; Nov 6 b. Aug 16; Sept 5 c. June 10; June 30 d. May 10; May 30
5. $270; $630
6. $11,960
7. B: 27.2%
8. $1,530.61; $4,469.39
9. 6,566.26

CHAPTER 10

Drill Problems

10–1. $40; $140
10–3. $4,285.71, $1,714.24
10–5. $6.90; 45.70%
10–7. $65.70; $153.30
10–9. $110.83
10–11. $34.20; 231%
10–13. 11%
10–15. $3,830.40; $1,169.60; 23.29%

Additional Drill Problems (LU 10–1)

10–17. a. $10 : 79 c. $4.35 e. $116.31
10–19. a. $2.00; 80% c. $0.28; 28.9% e. $24.99; 38.4%
10–21. a. $1.52 c. $372.92

(LU 10–2)

10–23. a. $4.80 c. $34.43 e. $0.15
10–25. a. $6.94 c. $30 e. $0.36
10–27. a. $28.57% c. 100% e. 66.67%

(LU 10–3)

10–29. a. $9.75; 50% c. $9.99; 25%
10–31. a. $3.59 b. $98.28

Word Problems

10–33. a. $3,000 b. 75%
10–35. $14.29
10–37. 5.997%
10–39. $84
10–41. 42.86%; No
10–43. $3.56
10–45. $1,245
10–47. 26.47%
10–49. a. $14 b. 350% c. 77.77%
10–51. $2.56
10–53. a. $359.60 b. 40% c. 28.57%
10–55. a. $210 b. 75%
10–57. 49%
10–59. $32.35
10–61. $29.98
10–63. a. $14.89 b. $10.87
10–65. a. $599 b. 85.57% c. 46.11%
10–67. $69.29
10–69. $230.30
10–71. 20%
10–73. $252.55
10–75. $3.64

Challenge Problems

10–77. a. 31.01% b. $3.43 c. $3.02
10–78. a. $94.98 b. $20.36 loss
10–79. a. $46 b. 11.392 c. $855,996 d. $510,996

10–80. a. $23.41 b. 166 c. $815
d. 272 e. $22.41; 173;
7 deliveries diff; $210 diff

Summary Practice Test

1. $448
2. 65.26%
3. $781.25; $468.75
4. $90; 38.9%
5. $228.57
6. $419.30
7. 37.42%
8. $80
9. 41.2%
10. $0.68

Cumulative Review—6–10

1. 650,000
2. $296.35
3. $133
4. $2,562.14
5. $48.75
6. $259.26
7. $1.96; $1.89

CHAPTER 11

Drill Problems

11–1. 35; $231
11–3. 40; 11; $12; $452
11–5. $1,071
11–7. $60
11–9. $13,000
11–11. $4,500
11–13. $11,900; $6,900; $138; $388

Based on 2003	Employee	Gross annual income, 2003	Payment frequency	Pays per year	Gross pay amount this period	Federal tax deductions	Ontario provincial tax deductions	Employee EI premiums	Employer's EI contributions in first quarter	CPP contributions (See Note 1)	Employer's CPP contributions in first quarter	Claim Code
								Factor × periodic pay	= 3 × 1.4 × Employee's contribution	Factor × periodic day	= 3 × Employee's contribution	
								$f = .021$		$f = .0495$		
11–14.	Clancey	$48,984	Biweekly	26	$1,884	$271.70	$107,95	$39.56	$166.17	$86.59	$259.78	2
11–15.	Sklar	$94,620	Monthly	12	$7,885	$1,510.40	$770.90	$165.59	$695.46	$375.87	$1,127.61	3
11–16.	Sanchez	$85,440	Monthly	12	$7,120	$1,292.00	$623.60	$149.52	$627.98	$338.00	$1,014.01	4
11–17.	Liung	$33,800	Weekly	52	$650	$56.65	$21.55	$13.65	$57.33	$28.84	$86.53	5
11–18.	Ali	$72,800	Weekly	52	$1,400	$221.60	$95.15	$29.40	$123.48	$65.97	$197.90	6
11–19.	Zubko	$51,246	Biweekly	26	$1,971	$229.30	$91.75	$41.39	$173.84	$90.90	$272.70	8

Additional Drill Problems (LU 11–1)

11–21. a. $324 c. $543.25
11–23. a. $124.80 c. $132

(LU 11–2)

11–25. a. $0 c. $479.55
11–27. a. $0 c. $146.35

Word Problems

11–29. a. $15.52 b. $56.58
11–31. $297
11–33. $825
11–35. $919.06 (2003)

Additional Word Problems (LU 11–1)

11–37. $723
11–39. $3,846.25
11–41. $2,032.48

(LU 11–2)

11–43. $223.85 (2003)

Challenge Problems

11–44. a. $191.98 b. $87.50
c. $1,044.65 (2003)

Summary Practice Test

1. 47; $474.50
2. $506
3. $14,200
4. $168.20 (2003)
5. $3,734.25 (2003)

CHAPTER 12

Drill Problems

12–1. $390; $9,390
12–3. $336.88; $7,336.88
12–5. 193; $27.84; $612.84
12–7. 93; $20.38; $1,020.38
12–9. 187; $73.78; $1,273.78
12–11. $1,904.76
12–13. $4,376.99

Additional Drill Problems (LU 12–2)

12–15. a. $8.05 c. $40.11

(LU 12–3)

12–17. a. $4,432.14 c. $3,481.02

(LU 12–4)

12–19.

FV	*t*	*I*	*r*	PV
$1,200	1	$120.00	0.10	$1,320.00
$600	1.5	$100.00	0.08	$700.00
$11,200	3	$1,344.00	0.04	$12,544.00

Word Problems

12–21. $4,000; $84,000
12–23. $2,377.70
12–25. 4.7 years
12–27. $21,596.11
12–29. $713.60; $44.25
12–31. $4.20; $5.60
12–33. $2,608.65
12–35. $18,980
12–37. 12.54%
12–39. 73 days
12–41. 5.7%

Additional Word Problems (LU 12–2)

12–43. a. $515.63 b. $6,015.63
12–44. 3%
12–45. $17.63; $659.12
12–47. $360

(LU 12–3)

12–51. $250
12–53. $3,041.67

Challenge Problems

12–55. a. $1,000 b. 8%
c. Debbie: $280; Jan: $1,400
12–56. a. $7.85 b. $275.33

Summary Practice Test

1. a. $32.22 b. $1,852.72
2. $235,200
3. $8,591.11
4. $8,583.01
5. $23,675.67
6. $134.80; $5,134.80 (see page 308)

CHAPTER 13

Drill Problems

13–1. $445.07; $17,554.93
13–3. 25 days
13–5. $51,431.51; 57; $722.86; $50,708.65
13–7. $9,841.46 (using 98 days)

Additional Drill Problems (LU 13–1)

13–9. a. $103.56; $6,896.44
c. $370.30; $18,979.70
e. $583.95; $12,906.05

(LU 13–2)

13–11. a. Sept 27; 91 days
c. July 13; 37 days

Word Problems

13–13. $8,543.84
13–15. $8,938.29
13–17. $9,893.74
13–19. $5,131.51; 56; $70.86; $5,060.65
13–21. $4,835.95

Additional Word Problems (LU 13–1)

13–23. $233.01; $15,966.99
13–25. $837.12; $8,862.88

(LU 13–2)

13–27. a. $357.44 b. $22,293.50
13–29. $721.43

Challenge Problems

13–31. a. $96.79 per $10,000 Bond
b. 177.01 per $10,000 Bond
c. 3.64% d. 3.61%
13–32. $2,127.66

Summary Practice Test

1. $130,000
2. a. $109.32 b. $6,890.68 c. $7,000
3. $30,312.11
4. $40,399.59
5. $19,342.47
6. $9,852.33; 5.58%

CHAPTER 14

Drill Problems

14–1. 4; 3%; $787.86; $87.86
14–3. $10,404; $404
14–5. 12.55%
14–7. 12; 2%; $2,050.09
14–9. 28; 3%; $7,692.55
14–11. 2,000 × (1 + .06) = 2,837.04

Additional Drill Problems (LU 14–2)

14–13. a. $920; $966; $46
c. $184.68; $198.30; $13.62

(LU 14–3)

14–15. a. $.6209 c. $.5513 e. $.3083
14–17. a. $5,142.65 c. $15,885.68

Word Problems

14–19. $19,960.65
14–21. Mystic $4,774.55 vs. $3,727.86
14–23. $25,735
14–25. $3,806.96
14–27. 5.06%
14–29. $37,644.74
14–31. Yes $17,908 (compounding)
14–33. $3,739
14–35. $13,883
14–37. 3.92%
14–39. 4.033%
14–41. 4.08%
14–43. $5,892.06
14–45. $442.39

Additional Word Problems (LU 14–2)

14–47. $5,978.09
14–49. $12,881.03
14–51. $3,207.09; $207.09
14–53. $13,152.42

(LU 14–3)

14–55. $13,356.94
14–57. $48,866.84

Challenge Problems

14–58. a. $143,921,614.40
b. $178,921,614.40
c. $160,921,614.40
14–59. Bank A has APY = 6.136% vs. Bank B APY = 6.5% choose B Need to deposit $663,908. Remainder in bank B of $36,092 will be worth $67,750 in 10 years

Summary Practice Test

1. $20,861.18
2. $22,077.81
3. $121,187.88
4. No $16,252 (compounding)
5. 9.2%
6. $18,324.46
7. $104,144.52
8. $39,837.47

CHAPTER 15

Drill Problems

15–1. $110,095.02
15–3. $111,196
15–5. $3,118.59
15–7. $3,118.60
15–9. $2,610.22

Additional Drill Problems (LU 15–2)

15–11. a. $1,000; $2,080; $3,246.40
c. $7,200; $15,120; $23,832
15–13. a. $6,888.60 c. $16,246.40

(LU 15–3)

15–15. a. $2,638.65 c. $7,217.10

(LU 15–4)

15–17*. a. $4,093.13
c. $1,395.59
e. $842.24
*Answers may differ due to methods used.

Word Problems

15–19. $3,797.79
15–21. $16,670.75
15–23. $22,354.67
15–25. $88,338.48
15–27. $27,855.71
15–29. $2,968.56
15–31. $128,492.97
15–33. Morton is $4,440.12 higher
15–35. $78,572.01
15–37. $325,525.91

Additional Word Problems (LU 15–2)

15–39. $13,412.10
15–41. $302,109.64; $2,715.54

(LU 15–3)

15–43. $24,251.80
15–45. $47,607.92
15–47. The cash value = $21,150.68 of 2000/quarter offer.
15–49. $136,431.06

(LU 15–4)

15–51. $17,615.52
15–53. $16,345.74

Challenge Problems

15–54.	Years to save	Rate	**Funds needed** Public Univ.	**Funds needed** Private Univ.
	11		$80,000.00	$240,000.00
			Annual Deposits	
	Bank A	6%	$5,343.44	$16,030.31
	Bank B	7%	$5,068.55	$15,205.66
15–55.			FV	$244,625.87
	Today investment		PV	$120,754.21
15–56.	$5,000			
	Per son	a. 1	Amount needed	$18,132.38
	Both sons	a. 2		$36,264.76
	For 10 years	b.	Monthly savings needed	$246.71

Summary Practice Test

1. $78,518.91
2. $30,455.67 vs. Q = $43,037.69
3. $78,803.40
4. $2,320
5. $2,605
6. $148,908
7. $38,747.10
8. $118,591.84
9. $486,578.40
10. $404,088.72

	PMT ($)	t (years)	j (%)	m_1	m_2	i_1	i_2	n	PV/FV
11.	$500	10	4	Semiannually	Monthly	**0.02**	**0.00330589**	**120**	FV = **$73,497.20**
12.	$2,000	25	6	Annually	Quarterly	**0.06**	**0.014673846**	**100**	PV = **$104,539.92**
13.	**$7,261.22**	6	5	Annually	Semiannually	**0.05**	**0.024695077**	**12**	FV = $100,000

CHAPTER 16

Drill Problems

16–1. $149,000; $6.6982; $998.03
16–3. $225,000; $7.9283; $1,783.87
16–5. $167,460.15
16–7. $159,000; $1,463.62; $978.57; $485.05; $158,154.95

Additional Drill Problems (LU 16–1)

16–9. a. $1,138.60 c. $4,002.13

(LU 16–2)

16–11. a. $1,408.21; $1,114.89; $293.31 c. $1,550.31; $1,430.27; $120.04

Word Problems

16–13. $263,441.32
16–15. $64,152.59
16–17. a. Pmt: $398.82; It. $79,647.27
c. Pmt = 455.21;
I_{tot} = $96,563.87
e. $34,033.98

Additional Word Problems (LU 16–1)

16–19. $2,443.36
16–21. a. $2,534.03 b. 2,465.33

(LU 16–2)

16–23. $13,660; $849.99

Challenge Problems

16–24. a. $84.75 b. Almost 24 months

Summary Practice Test

1. a. $770.29 b. $614.65; $155.65 c. $114,844.35
2. $504.30; $79,290
3. $993.51
4. $178,053

CHAPTER 17

Drill Problems

17–1. 6.50
17–3. $77.23
17–5. 2.7
17–7. 31.5
17–9. 8
17–11. 142.9
17–13. $200–$299.99 卌I
17–15. Traditional watch 183.6°

Additional Drill Problems (LU 17–1)

17–17. a. 6.78 b. 84.55
17–19. 35

(LU 17–2)

17–21. 18: 卌I II 7
17–23. 25–30: 卌I III 8
17–25. 7.2° for second class 7–12

Word Problems

17–27.

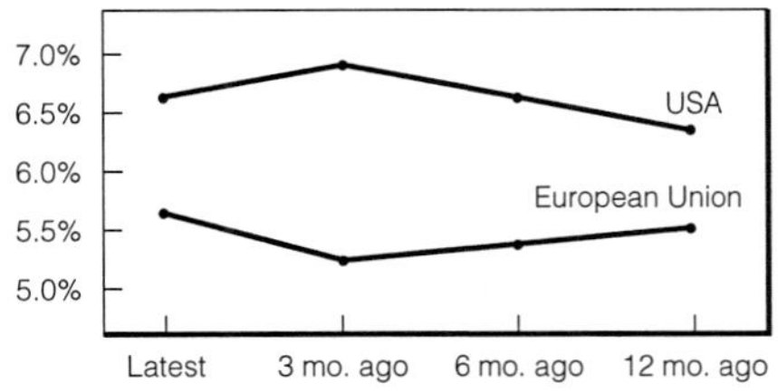

17–29.

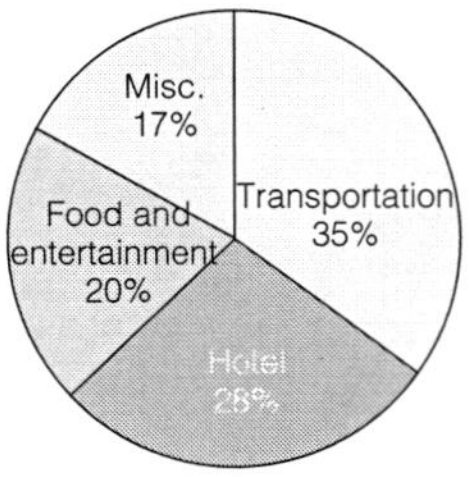

Transportation 126°
Hotel 100.8°
Food 72°
Miscellaneous 61.2°

17–31. 250

Additional Word Problems (LU 17–1)

17–33. $1,498,025.50
17–35. $10.75
17–37. $9.98

(LU 17–2)

17–39.

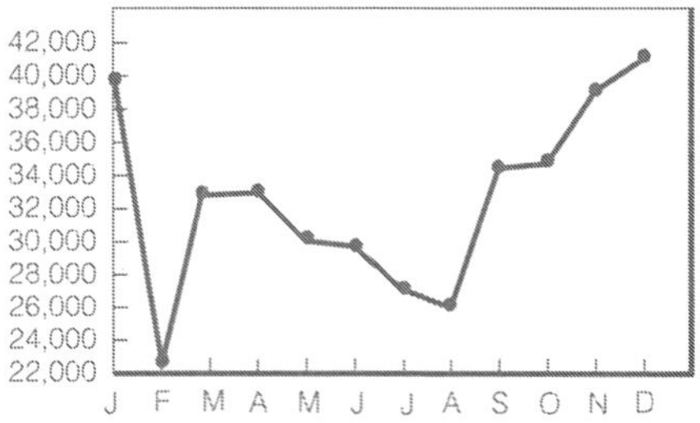

17–41.

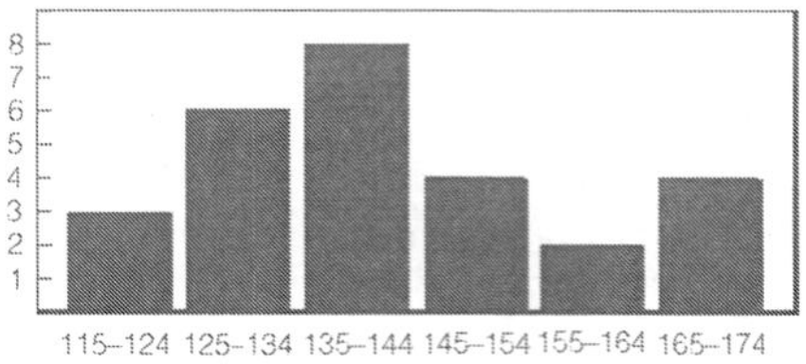

17–43. 555.6%

Challenge Problems

17–44. a. $57,000,000; 30.42%

	b.	c.
AAA	30.42%	109.51°
Riser	22.18%	79.85°
Casto	22.07%	79.45°
Balboa	12.7%	45.72°
Hunter	12.63%	45.47°

17–45.

Mortgage	24.94%;	89.78°
Taxes	15.42%;	55.51°
Insurance	10.88%;	39.71°
Miscellaneous	13.15%;	47.34°
Food	18.59%;	66.92°
Loan repairs	17.01%;	61.24°

Optional Assignment

17–46. 98
17–48. 4.3
17–50. 16%; 2.5%
17–52. 68%; 81.5%, 2.5%; 47.5%
17–54. Mean = 64.6
S = 5.02

Summary Practice Test

1. $144,200; $138,500
2. 1,300
3. 3.25
4. 400; 11; 2
5. Bar 3 on horizontal axis goes up to 300 on vertical axis
6. Profits 36°
   Cost of sales 144°
   Expense 180°

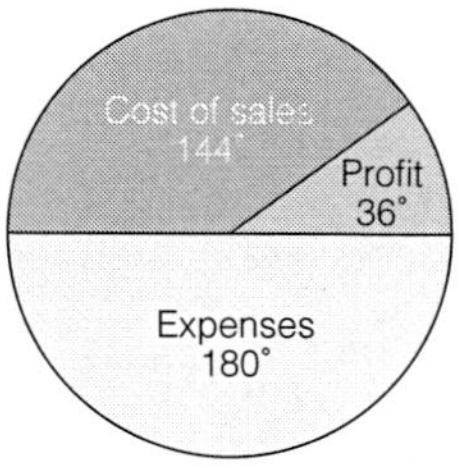

7. 177.3%
8. 9.0 standard deviation

GLOSSARY

This is a comprehensive list of the key terms used in the text. In many cases, examples are included in the definitions. Recall that key terms and their page references are listed in the Chapter Organizer and Reference Guide for each chapter.

Absolute loss What occurs when the company's price does not allow it to even recover the cost of buying.

Accelerated depreciation method A method of ***depreciation*** that computes more ***depreciation expense*** in the early years of the asset's life than in the later years.

Accounts payable Amounts owed to creditors for services or items purchased.

Accounts receivable Amounts owed by customers to a business from previous sales.

Accumulated depreciation The amount of ***depreciation*** that has accumulated on ***plant and equipment*** assets.

Acid test (***Current assets*** − Inventory − ***Prepaid expenses***) ÷ ***Current liabilities.***

Addend A number that is combined in the addition process. *Example:* 8 + 9 = 17, of which 8 and 9 are the addends.

Adjustable rate mortgage A ***mortgage*** whose ***interest*** rate is periodically adjusted over its term on the basis of an index such as the federal prime rate or the interest rate paid on government ***bonds.***

Adjusted bank balance The current balance of a chequebook after the reconciliation process.

Amortization The process of paying back a loan (***principal*** plus ***interest***) by equal periodic payments (see ***amortization schedule***).

Amortization schedule A timetable that shows the monthly payment to pay back a loan at maturity. The payment includes ***interest.*** Note that the payment is fixed at the same amount each month.

Amortization table A table showing the monthly payments necessary to amortize a loan at various rates and for various periods of time.

Amount of change (in a percent change calculation) The difference between the new value and the old value.

Amount financed Cash price − ***Down payment.***

Annual interest rate Same as ***nominal rate.***

Annual percentage rate (APR) The true or effective annual ***interest*** rate charged by sellers.

Annual percentage rate (APR) table A table with which one can look up the effective annual ***rate of interest*** on a loan or installment purchase.

Annual percentage yield (APY) An ***interest*** yield calculated on the actual number of days bank has the money.

Annuities certain Annuities that have stated beginning and ending dates.

Annuity A stream of equal payments made periodically.

Annuity due An ***annuity*** paid (or received) at the beginning of the time period.

Assessed value The value of a property that an assessor sets (usually a ***percent*** of the property's market value) that is used in calculating ***property tax.***

Asset cost The amount a company paid for an asset.

Assets Things of value owned by a business.

Asset turnover ***Net sales*** ÷ Total ***assets.***

ATM Automatic teller machine, a device that allows customers of a bank to transfer funds and make deposits or withdrawals without human assistance.

Automatic banking machine (ABM) Same as ***ATM*** (automatic teller machine).

Average daily balance The ***sum*** of daily balances divided by the number of days in the billing cycle.

Average inventory The total of all inventories divided by the number of times inventory is taken.

Balance sheet A financial report that lists ***assets, liabilities,*** and equity; it reflects the financial position of the company as of a particular date.

Bank discount The amount of ***interest*** charged by a bank on a note. (***Maturity value*** × Bank discount rate × Number of days bank holds note) ÷ 360.

Bank discount rate ***Percent*** of ***interest.***

Banker's Rule Time is exact days/360 in calculating ***simple interest.***

Bank reconciliation The process of comparing the bank balance to the chequebook balance so adjustments can be made regarding ***cheques*** outstanding, ***deposits in transit,*** and the like.

Bank statement Report sent by the bank to the owner of the chequing account indicating ***cheques*** processed, deposits made, and so on, along with beginning and ending balances.

Bar graph Visual representation using horizontal or vertical bars to make a comparison or to show the relationship between items of similar makeup. (See also ***histogram.***)

Base The number that represents the whole 100% to which something is being compared. Usually follows the word *of.*

BEDMAS A useful acronym for remembering the order of operations in complex calculations.

Beneficiary The person designated to receive the ***face value*** of the life insurance when the insured person dies.

Biweekly Every two weeks (26 times in a year).

Biweekly mortgage A ***mortgage*** whose payments are made every two weeks rather than monthly. This payment method takes years off the life of the mortgage and substantially reduces the cost of ***interest.***

Blank endorsement A signature of the current owner on the back of a ***cheque*** with the effect that whoever presents the cheque for payment receives the money.

Bodily injury A type of auto insurance that pays damages to people injured or killed by your auto.

Bond discount Selling ***bonds*** for less than the face value.

Bond premium Selling ***bonds*** for more than the face value.

Bonds A written promise by a company that borrows money to repay it, usually with fixed ***interest*** payment until maturity (repayment time).

Bond yield Total annual ***interest*** ÷ Total cost.

Book value Cost − ***Accumulated depreciation.***

Breakeven point The point at which costs and expenses are paid.

Canada Pension Plan (CPP) contribution A ***deduction*** from one's paycheque that goes toward one's participation in the Canada Pension Plan.

Cancellation A reducing process used to simplify the multiplication and division of ***fractions.*** *Example:*

$$\frac{\cancel{4}}{8} = \frac{1}{\cancel{4}}$$

Capital The owner's investment in a business.

Cash advance Money borrowed by the holder of a ***credit card.*** It is recorded as another purchase and used in the calculation of the ***average daily balance.***

Cash discount Savings that result from early payment by taking advantage of discounts offered by the seller; discount is not taken on freight or taxes.

Cash dividend Cash distribution of a company's profit to owners of its stock.

Cash value Except in the case of ***term*** insurance, this indicates the value of an insurance ***policy*** when terminated. Options fall under the heading of ***nonforfeiture values.***

Centi- Prefix indicating .01 of a basic metric unit. *Example:* 1 centimetre = .01 ***metre.***

Central measurements Averages and other measurements used by companies to guide business decisions. Examples are ***mean, median,*** and ***mode.***

Chain or series discount Two or more ***trade discounts*** that are applied to the balance remaining after the previous discount is taken. Often called a *series discount.*

Cheque Written document signed by an appropriate person that directs the bank to pay a specific amount of money to a certain other person or company.

Cheque register A record-keeping device that records ***cheques*** paid and deposits made by companies using a chequing account.

Cheque stub A slip attached to a ***cheque*** that provides a record of its having been written.

Circle graph A visual representation showing measures of the parts as compared to the whole.

Closing costs Costs incurred when property passes from seller to buyer such as for credit reports, recording costs, ***points,*** and so on.

CM Abbreviation for *credit memorandum.* A notice that the bank is adding funds to your account. The CM is found on your ***bank statement.*** *Example:* You might get a CM when the bank collects a note for you.

Coinsurance A type of ***fire insurance*** in which the ***insurer*** and the ***insured*** share the risk. Usually there is an 80% coinsurance clause.

Collision A type of optional auto insurance that pays for the repairs to your auto from an accident after a ***deductible*** is met. The insurance company will pay for repairs only up to the value of the auto (less the deductible).

Commission Payment for work done that is based on established performance criteria.

Common denominator To add two or more ***fractions,*** denominators must be the same.

Common stock Units of ownership called shares.

Comparative statement A statement showing data from two or more periods side by side.

Complement 100% less the stated ***percent.*** *Example:* 82% is the complement of 18% (100% − 18%).

Compound amount Same as ***future value.***

Compounded (annually, daily, monthly, quarterly, semi-annually) See ***compounding.***

Compounding Calculating the ***interest*** periodically over the life of a loan and adding it to the ***principal.***

Compounding frequency The number of times a year ***interest*** is compounded.

Compound interest ***Interest*** that is calculated periodically and then added to the ***principal.*** In the next period the interest is calculated on the adjusted principal (the old principal plus the added interest).

Comprehensive insurance A type of optional auto insurance that pays for damages to your auto by factors other than collision (for example, fire, vandalism, theft).

Compulsory insurance Insurance required by law—standard coverage.

Constants Numbers that have a fixed value such as 3 or 27. Placed on right side of an ***equation;*** also called *knowns.*

Contingent annuities Annuities whose beginning and ending dates are uncertain (not fixed).

Contingent liability A potential liability that may or may not result from ***discounting a note.***

Contribution rate (CR) Contribution margin expressed as a rate or as a percentage of the unit ***selling price.***

Conversion period How often (a period of time) the ***interest*** is calculated in the ***compounding*** process. *Example:* Daily every day; monthly twelve times a year; quarterly every three months; semiannually every six months.

Corporation A company with many owners or ***stockholders.*** The equity of these owners is called ***stockholders' equity.***

Cost The price retailers pay to the manufacturer or the supplier to bring merchandise into the store.

Cost of merchandise (goods) sold Beginning inventory + ***Net purchases*** − Ending inventory.

Credit card A piece of plastic that allows you to buy on credit.

Credit memo (CM) A bank form used to indicate a credit to one's bank account.

Credit period (end) Credit days that are counted from the date of an ***invoice.*** Has no relationship to ***discount period.***

Cross-multiplication rule A method of solving a ***proportion*** that consists of multiplying each ***numerator*** by the ***denominator*** from the other side of the ***equation.***

Cumulative frequency A running total of frequencies in a ***frequency distribution.***

Cumulative preferred stock ***Preferred stock*** whose holders must receive current-year ***dividends*** and any dividends in arrears before any dividends are paid out to the holders of ***common stock.***

Current assets ***Assets*** that are used up or converted into cash within one year or operating cycle.

Current liabilities Obligations of a company that are due within one year.

Current ratio ***Current assets*** ÷ ***Current liabilities.***

Daily balance Calculated to determine a customer's ***finance charge***: Previous balance + Any ***cash advances*** + Purchases − Payments.

Daily compounding ***Interest*** calculated on a balance each day.

Date The date that a ***promissory note*** was issued.

Debit card Card used for transactions that result in money being immediately deducted from a customer's chequing account.

Debit memo (DM) A bank form used to indicate a debit to one's bank account.

Deca- Prefix indicating 10 times a basic metric unit. *Example:* 1 decametre = 10 ***metres.***

Deci Prefix indicating .1 of a basic metric unit. *Example:* 1 decimetre = .1 ***metres.***

Decimal equivalent A decimal ***expression*** that represents the same value as a ***fraction.*** *Example:* .05 = $\frac{5}{100}$, so .05 is the decimal equivalent of $\frac{5}{100}$.

Decimal fraction A decimal ***expression*** representing a ***fraction*** whose denominator has a power of 10.

Decimal point A period—the centre of the ***decimal system***—located between the units and the tenths in a decimal number. ***Digits*** to the left of the decimal point stand for ***whole numbers***; digits to the right stand for ***fractions.***

Decimal system The U.S. base-10 numbering system that uses the 10 single-***digit*** numbers shown on a calculator.

Decimals Numbers written to the right of a ***decimal point.*** *Example:* The ".3" in 5.3, and the ".22" in 18.22.

Declining-balance method An accelerated method of ***depreciation.*** The depreciation each year is calculated by ***book value*** beginning each year times the rate.

Deductible An amount the ***insured*** pays before the insurance company pays. Usually the higher the deductible, the lower the ***premium.***

Deductions Amounts deducted from gross earnings to arrive at ***net pay.***

Deferred annuities An ***annuity*** that does not begin until after a certain time interval.

Deferred payment price The total of all monthly payments plus ***down payment.***

Denominator The number of a common ***fraction*** below the division line (bar). *Example:* The 9 in this fraction:

$$\frac{8}{9}$$

Deposit slip A document that shows date, name, account number, and items making up a deposit.

Deposits in transit Deposits not received or processed by bank at the time the ***bank statement*** is prepared.

Depreciation The process of allocating the cost of an asset (less ***residual value***) over its estimated life, during which it loses value due to normal use, product obsolescence, aging, and so on.

Depreciation expense A process involving ***asset cost,*** estimated ***useful life,*** and ***residual value*** (salvage or ***trade-in*** value).

Depreciation schedule A table showing amount of ***depreciation expense, accumulated depreciation,*** and ***book value*** for each period of time for a plant asset.

Difference The resulting answer from a subtraction problem. *Example:* ***Minuend*** less ***subtrahend*** equals difference: 215 − 15 = 200.

Differential pay schedule A pay rate based on a schedule of units completed.

Digit Any numeral from 0 to 9 considered as part of a number. For example, in 986, the "hundreds digit" is 9, the "tens digit" is 8, and the "ones digit" is 6.

Discounting a note Receiving cash from selling a note to a bank before the ***due date*** of a note. Steps to discount include: (1) calculate ***maturity value,*** (2) calculate number of days bank waits for money, (3) calculate ***bank discount,*** and (4) calculate ***proceeds.***

Discount period A span of time during which one can take advantage of a ***cash discount.***

Dispersion A number that expresses how information is scattered within a data set.

Distribution of overhead Companies distribute ***overhead*** by floor space or sales volume.

Dividend In the division process, the number that is being divided by another. *Example:* 15 is the dividend in the following:

$$5\overline{)15}$$

Dividends Distribution of company's profit in cash or stock to owners of stock.

Dividends in arrears ***Dividends*** that accumulate when a company fails to pay dividends to ***cumulative preferred stockholders.***

Divisor In the division process, the number that is dividing into another. *Example:*

$5\overline{)15}$, in which 5 is the divisor.

DM Abbreviation for *debit memorandum.* A notice found on your ***bank statement*** that the bank is charging your account. *Example:* "***NSF.***"

Dollar markdown Original ***selling price*** less the reduction to price. Markdown may be stated as a ***percent*** of the original selling price. *Example:*

$$\frac{\text{Dollar markdown}}{\text{Original selling price}}$$

Dollar markup Original ***selling price*** less ***cost.*** The ***difference*** is the amount of the ***markup.*** Markup may be stated as a ***percent*** of the original ***selling price.***

Dollar value of interest The ***interest*** on a ***principal*** expressed in dollars.

Down payment An initial cash payment made when something is purchased.

Draft A written order, such as a ***cheque,*** instructing a bank, credit union, or savings and loan institution to pay your money to a person or organization.

Draw The receiving of advance wages to cover business or personal expenses. Once wages are earned, a drawing amount reduces the actual amount received.

Drawee The person ordered to pay a ***cheque.***

Drawer The person who writes a ***cheque.***

Due date ***Maturity date*** or when a note will be repaid.

Earnings per share Annual earnings ÷ Total number of shares outstanding.

Effective rate True ***rate of interest.*** The more frequent the ***compounding,*** the higher the effective rate.

Electronic deposit What happens when a ***credit card*** is run through a terminal that approves (or disapproves) the amount and adds it to company's bank balance.

Electronic funds transfer (EFT) A computerized operation that electronically transfers funds among parties without the use of paper ***cheques***.

Employment Insurance (EI) contribution A ***deduction*** from one's paycheque that goes toward one's participation in Canada's unemployment insurance plan.

End of credit period The last day from the date of an ***invoice*** when the customer can take a ***cash discount***.

End of month (EOM) (*also* **proximo**) Credit terms offered by a seller that mean the ***cash discount*** period begins at the end of the month ***invoice*** is dated. After the 25th ***discount period***, an additional month results.

Endorse To sign the back of a ***cheque***, thus transferring ownership to another party.

Endowment life A form of insurance that pays at maturity a fixed amount of money to ***insured*** or to the ***beneficiary***. Insurance coverage would terminate when paid similarly to ***term life***.

Equation A mathematical statement that says two ***expressions*** or numbers are equal, putting an equal sign (=) between them.

Equation in one unknown An ***equation*** that contains only one ***variable***.

Equivalent equations ***Equations*** that have the same solution.

Equivalent (fractional) A ***fraction*** with the same final value as another fraction.

Equivalent interest rates Interest rates that result in the same ***future value*** on an investment or loan in one year's time.

Equivalent payment A single replacement value for payments at ***simple*** or ***compound interest***.

Equivalent payments A method of comparing two offers of interest payments by bringing the money values to the same point in time, either to today or to the point of one year from now.

Equivalent ratios ***Ratios*** that have the same meaning.

Escrow account A special account in which a lending institution requires each month of the insurance cost and real estate taxes be kept.

Exact interest ***Simple interest*** calculated using 365 days per year and the exact number of days in each month.

Excise tax A tax that government levies on particular products and services. A tax on specific luxury items or nonessentials.

Exponent A part of a ***power***, as in 7^3, where three is the exponent. See also ***base***.

Expression A meaningful combination of numbers and letters called *terms*.

Extended term insurance Insurance resulting from nonforfeiture, keeping the ***policy*** for the full ***face value*** going without further ***premium*** payments for a specific period of time.

Face amount The dollar amount stated in an insurance ***policy***.

Face value The amount of insurance stated on an insurance ***policy***—usually the maximum amount for which the insurance company is liable.

Federal tax deductions Monies deducted from one's paycheque by the federal government.

Finance charge Total payments − Actual loan cost.

Fire insurance Stipulated ***percent*** (normally 80%) of value that is required for an insurance company to pay to reimburse one's losses.

First-in, first-out (FIFO) method An inventory valuation method that assumes the first inventory brought into the store will be the first sold. Ending inventory is made up of goods most recently purchased.

Fixed costs (FC) Costs that don't change with increases or decreases in sales.

Fixed-rate mortgage A ***mortgage*** whose monthly payment is fixed over a number of years, usually 30.

FOB destination ***Freight terms*** by which the seller pays the cost of freight in getting the shipped goods to the buyer's location.

FOB shipping point ***Freight terms*** by which the buyer pays the cost of freight in getting the shipped goods to his or her location.

Formula An ***equation*** that expresses in symbols a general fact, rule, or principle.

Fraction A mathematical ***expression*** for a part of a ***whole number***. *Example:*

$\frac{5}{6}$ expresses 5 parts out of 6

Freight terms A statement of how freight charges will be paid. The most common freight terms are ***FOB shipping point*** and ***FOB destination***.

Frequency distribution A table showing how many times each of a number of items occurs.

Full endorsement A signature on the back of a ***cheque*** that identifies the next person or company to whom the cheque is to be transferred.

Future value (FV) The final amount of a loan or investment at the end of the last period. Also called *compound amount*.

Future value of annuity The future dollar amount of a series of payments plus ***interest***.

General annuity An ***annuity*** in which the ***compounding frequency*** and the frequency of payments are not equal.

Goods and Services Tax (GST) A value-added tax levied by the federal government on almost all goods and services.

Graduated-payment mortgage A ***mortgage*** in which the borrower pays less at beginning. As years go on, the payments increase.

Gram The basic unit of mass (similar to weight) in the ***metric system***. Twenty-eight grams equals about an ounce.

Greatest common divisor The largest possible number that will divide evenly into both the ***numerator*** and the ***denominator*** of a ***fraction***.

Gross pay Wages before ***deductions***.

Gross profit The ***difference*** between the ***cost*** of bringing goods into the store and the ***selling price*** of the goods.

Gross profit from sales ***Net sales*** − ***Cost of goods sold***.

Gross profit margin ***Markup*** expressed as ***percent markup on selling price***.

Gross profit method A method used to estimate value of inventory. It involves the company keeping track of the average ***gross profit*** rate, the ***net sales*** at retail, beginning inventory, and ***net purchases***.

Gross sales Total earned sales before ***sales returns and allowances*** or ***sales discounts***.

Hecto- A prefix indicating 100 times a basic metric unit.

Higher terms A form of a ***fraction*** with a new ***numerator*** and ***denominator*** that, although higher, is ***equivalent*** to the original. *Example:*

$\frac{2}{9} \rightarrow \frac{6}{27}$

Histogram A form of ***bar graph*** in which the possible values on one axis are divided into groups. These groups are treated as units whose measurement is indicated by the height of the bar.

Home equity loan A cheap and readily accessible ***line of credit*** backed by equity in your home; tax-deductible; rates can be locked in.

Horizontal analysis A method of analyzing financial reports in which each total this period is compared by amount of ***percent*** to the same total last period.

Improper fraction A ***fraction*** that has a value equal to or greater than 1; its ***numerator*** is equal to or greater than its ***denominator***. *Example:*

$\frac{6}{6}, \frac{14}{9}$

Income statement A financial report that lists the ***revenues*** and expenses for a specific period of time. It reflects how well the company is performing.

Income tax A tax that depends on allowances claimed, marital status, and wages earned.

Indemnity An insurance company's payment to the ***insured*** for loss.

Index numbers Numbers that express the relative changes in a ***variable*** compared with some ***base***, which is taken as 100.

Individual retirement account (IRA) An account established for retirement planning.

Installment cost ***Down payment*** + (Number of payments × Monthly payment). Also called *deferred payment.*

Installment loan A loan paid off with a series of equal periodic payments.

Installment purchases Purchases of an item(s) that require periodic payments for a specific period of time with usually a high ***rate of interest***.

Insured Customer or ***policyholder***.

Insurer The company that issues an insurance ***policy***.

Interest ***Principal*** × ***Rate*** × ***Time***.

Interest-bearing note A note whose ***maturity value*** is greater than the amount borrowed since ***interest*** is added on.

Interest rate ***Interest*** expressed as a percent.

Interval estimate An estimate that is a range of numerical values.

Inventory turnover A ratio that indicates how quickly inventory turns over:

$$\frac{\text{Cost of goods sold}}{\text{Average inventory at cost}}$$

Invoice A document recording purchase and sales transactions.

Just-in-time (JIT) inventory system A system that eliminates inventories. Suppliers provide materials daily as manufacturing company needs them.

Kilo A prefix indicating 1,000 times a basic metric unit.

Knowns Numbers in an ***equation*** that are specified, as opposed to the ***unknowns***.

Land transfer tax A tax payable to the provincial government by the purchaser upon the transfer of title to land from a seller to a buyer.

Last-in, first-out (LIFO) method An inventory valuation method that assumes the last inventory brought into the store will be the first sold. Ending inventory is made up of the oldest goods purchased.

Least common denominator (LCD) Smallest nonzero ***whole number*** into which all ***denominators*** of a ***fraction*** will divide evenly. *Example:*

$\frac{3}{2}$ and $\frac{1}{4}$

LCD = 12

Level premium term An insurance ***premium*** that is fixed, say for 50 years.

Liabilities Amounts a business owes to creditors.

Liability insurance Insurance for bodily injury to others and damage to someone else's property.

Like fractions ***Proper fractions*** with the same ***denominators***.

Like terms Terms that are all made up of the same ***variable***. *Example:* A + 2A + 3A = 6A.

Limited payment life (20-payment life) A type of insurance in which ***premiums*** are for 20 years (a fixed period) and provide ***paid-up insurance*** for the full ***face value*** of the ***policy***.

Line graphs Graphical presentations that involve a time element. Show trends, failures, backlogs, and the like.

Line of credit Credit that provides immediate financing up to an approved limit.

Linear equation An equation whose ***unknown*** is in the first ***power***.

Liquid assets Cash or other ***assets*** that can be converted quickly into cash.

List price Suggested retail price paid by customers.

Litre The basic unit of measure in the ***metric system*** for volume.

Loan amortization table A table used to calculate monthly payments on a loan.

Long-term liabilities Debts or obligations that a company does not have to pay within one year.

Lowest terms A form of a ***fraction*** in which no number divides evenly into the ***numerator*** and ***denominator*** except the number 1. *Example:*

$\frac{5}{10} \rightarrow \frac{1}{2}$

Maker The person who writes a note.

Manual deposit A way of making a charge sale in which the salesperson fills out charge slip and completes a ***merchant batch header slip*** at the end of the business day.

Margin The ***difference*** between ***cost*** of bringing goods into the store and the ***selling price*** of goods.

Markdown A reduction from original ***selling price*** caused by seasonal changes, special promotions, and so on.

Market price/value of T-bill A value obtained by discounting the ***face value*** at the bill's ***rate of return***.

Markup The amount retailers add to cost of goods to cover ***operating expenses*** and make a profit.

Markup percent calculation ***Markup*** percent on ***cost*** × ***Cost*** = ***Dollar markup***; or Markup ***percent*** on selling price × ***Selling price*** = ***Dollar markup***.

Maturity date The date the ***principal*** and ***interest*** are due on a loan.

Maturity value The value of a loan measured as the ***principal*** plus ***interest*** (if interest is charged). Represents the amount due on the ***due date***.

Maturity value of note The amount of cash paid on the ***due date*** of a note. If it is an ***interest***-bearing maturity, this value is greater than amount borrowed.

Mean Statistical quantity found by:

$$\frac{\text{Sum of all figures}}{\text{Number of all figures}}$$

Measure of dispersion A number that describes how the numbers of a set of data are spread out or dispersed.

Median A statistical term that represents the central point or midpoint of a series of numbers.

Members of an equation The mathematical expressions on either side of the equal sign in an ***equation.***

Merchandise inventory Cost of goods for resale.

Merchant batch header slip A slip used by a company to list and attach charge slips.

Metre The basic unit of length in the ***metric system.*** A metre is a little longer than a yard.

Metric system A ***decimal system*** of weights and measures. The basic units are ***metres, grams,*** and ***litres.***

Mill One-tenth of a cent or one-thousandth of a dollar. In the ***decimal system,*** it is .001. In application:

Property tax due = Mills × .001 × Assessed valuation.

Milli- A prefix indicating .001 of the basic metric unit.

Minuend In a subtraction problem, the larger number from which another is subtracted. *Example:*

$50 - 40 = 10$

Mixed decimal A combination of a ***whole number*** and decimal, such as 59.8, 810.85.

Mixed number The ***sum*** of a ***whole number*** greater than zero and a ***proper fraction:***

$2\frac{1}{4}, 3\frac{3}{9}$

Mode The value that occurs most often in a series of numbers.

Monthly One way of paying employees.

Mortgage The cost of a home less the ***down payment.***

Mortgage insurance Private or public insurance required by the lender if the down payment is less than 25% of the purchase price of the property.

Mortgage note payable The debt owed on a building that is a ***long-term liability;*** often the building is the collateral.

Multiplicand The first or top number being multiplied in a multiplication problem. *Example:*

Product = Multiplicand × ***Multiplier***

$40 = 20 \times 2$

Multiplier The second or bottom number doing the multiplication in a problem. *Example:*

Product = ***Multiplicand*** × Multiplier

$40 = 20 \times 2$

Mutual fund A group of ***stocks*** and/or ***bonds*** in which investors can buy shares.

Net asset value (NAV) The dollar value of one ***mutual fund*** share; calculated by subtracting ***current liabilities*** from the current market value of the fund's investments and dividing this by number of shares outstanding.

Net deposit ***Credit card*** sales − Returns.

Net income ***Gross profit*** − ***Operating expenses.***

Net pay See ***net wages.***

Net price ***List price*** − Amount of ***trade discount.*** The net price is before any ***cash discount.***

Net price equivalent rate A rate or factor that, when multiplied times the ***list price,*** produces the actual ***cost*** to the buyer. The rate is found by taking the ***complement*** of each term in the discount and multiplying them (do not round off).

Net proceeds ***Maturity value*** − ***Bank discount.***

Net profit (net income) ***Gross profit*** − ***Operating expenses.***

Net purchases Purchases − ***Purchase discounts*** − ***Purchase returns and allowances.***

Net sales ***Gross sales*** − ***Sales discounts*** − ***Sales returns and allowances.***

Net wages ***Gross pay*** − ***Deductions.***

Net worth ***Assets*** − ***Liabilities.***

No-fault insurance A type of insurance relating to bodily injury, in which damages (before a certain level) are paid by the insurance company no matter who is to blame.

Nominal interest rate A bank's stated ***rate of interest.***

Nonforfeiture values The value of a life insurance ***policy*** when it is terminated (except ***term***), represented by either (1) available ***cash value,*** (2) additional ***extended term,*** or (3) additional ***paid-up insurance.***

Non-interest-bearing note Note for which the ***maturity value*** will be equal to the amount of money borrowed since no additional ***interest*** is charged.

Nonsufficient funds (NSF) A situation in which the ***drawer's*** account lacked sufficient funds to pay the written amount of a ***cheque.***

Normal distribution A statistical situation in which data is spread symmetrically about the mean.

Number of periods (per term of an investment or loan) (*n*) Calculated as the number of years multiplied by the number of times the ***interest*** is compounded per year.

Numerator The part of a common ***fraction*** above the division line (bar). *Example:*

$\frac{8}{9}$, in which 8 is the numerator

Open-end credit A type of credit in which there is a set payment period. Also, additional credit amounts can be added up to a set limit. It is a ***revolving charge account.***

Operating expenses (overhead) Regular expenses of doing business. These are not ***costs.***

Operating loss The kind of loss that occurs when a company cannot recover total cost.

Ordinary annuities An ***annuity*** that is paid (or received) at end of the time period.

Ordinary dating A credit term offered by a seller in which there is a ***cash discount*** available within the ***discount period.*** The full amount is due by the end of the ***credit period*** if the discount is missed.

Ordinary interest A method of calculating ***simple interest*** using 360 days per year.

Ordinary life insurance See ***straight life insurance.***

Outstanding balance The amount left to be paid on a loan.

Outstanding cheques ***Cheques*** written but not yet processed by the bank before ***bank statement*** preparation.

Overdraft What occurs when a company or person writes a ***cheque*** without enough money in the bank to pay for it (an NFS cheque).

Overhead expenses ***Operating expenses*** not directly associated with a specific department or product.

Override A ***commission*** that managers receive due to sales by people whom they supervise.

Overtime Time-and-a-half pay for more than 40 hours of work.

Owner's equity See ***capital.***

Paid-up insurance Insurance in which a certain level of coverage can continue, although the ***premiums*** are terminated. This results from the nonforfeiture value (except ***term***). The result is a ***reduced paid-up insurance*** policy until death.

Partial payments Payments on a debt that are less than the total amount of the debt.

Partial products Numbers between the ***multiplier*** and the ***product.***

Partial quotient The result when a ***divisor*** doesn't divide evenly into a ***dividend.***

Partnership A business with two or more owners.

Payee One who is named to receive the amount of a ***cheque.***

Payment periods Spans of time over which payments are made on an ***annuity.***

Payroll register A multicolumn form to record payroll data.

PEMDAS A useful acronym for remembering the order of operations in complex calculations.

Percent A mathematical idea that stands for hundredths. *Example:* 4% is 4 parts of one hundred, or

$$\frac{4}{100}$$

Percentage method A method to calculate ***withholdings.*** Opposite of ***wage bracket method.***

Percent decrease The lowering of some amount expressed as a ***percent*** of the original amount.

Percent increase The increasing of some amount expressed as a ***percent*** of the original amount.

Percent markup on cost ***Dollar markup*** divided by the ***cost***; thus, ***markup*** is a ***percent*** of the cost.

Percent markup on selling price ***Dollar markup*** divided by the ***selling price***; thus, ***markup*** is a ***percent*** of the selling price.

Periodic interest rate The effective ***interest*** rate per compounding period.

Periodic inventory system Physical count of inventory taken at end of a time period. Inventory records are not continually updated.

Periodic payment A method of paying annual salaries to employees by which a certain amount is given at regular intervals, such as monthly, semimonthly, weekly, and biweekly.

Periodic payments Payments made at regular intervals of time.

Periods The number of years times the number of times compounded per year (see ***conversion period***).

Perishables Goods or services with a limited life.

Perpetual inventory system Inventory records are continually updated; opposite of periodic.

Personal property Items of possession, such as cars, home, furnishings, jewellery, and so on. These are taxed by the ***property tax*** (don't forget, ***real property*** is also taxed).

Piecework Compensation based on the number of items produced or completed.

Place value The part of the value of a ***digit*** in a number that results from its position.

Plant and equipment ***Assets*** that will last longer than one year.

Point of sale A type of terminal that accepts cards (like those used at ***ATMs***) to purchase items at retail outlets. No cash is physically exchanged.

Points A one-time payment made at closing when property passes from seller to seller. It is calculated as a ***percent*** of the ***mortgage*** and represents an additional cost of borrowing. Three points means 3% of the mortgage.

Policy A written insurance contract.

Policyholder The insured party of an insurance contract.

Portion The amount or part that results from multiplying the ***base*** times the rate. Not expressed as a ***percent*** but as a number.

Power An expression that signifies a number multiplied by itself a certain number of times. See also ***base*** and ***exponent.***

Power of the root What is expressed by an ***exponent.*** See also root.

Preferred stock A type of stock that has a preference regarding a ***corporation***'s profits and ***assets.***

Premium Periodic payments that one makes for various kinds of insurance protection.

Premium rates (payroll) Higher rates based on a quota system.

Prepaid expenses Items a company buys that have not been used and are shown as ***assets.***

Prepaid rent Rent paid in advance.

Present value of an ordinary annuity The amount of money needed today to receive a specified stream (***annuity***) of money in the future.

Present value (PV) The amount of money that will have to be deposited today (or at some date) to reach a specific amount of maturity (in the future).

Price-earnings (PE) ratio Closing price per share of stock ÷ ***Earnings per share.***

Price relative The ***quotient*** of the current price divided by some previous year's price—the ***base*** year—multiplied by 100.

Prime number A ***whole number*** greater than 1 that is only divisible by itself and 1. *Examples:* 2, 3, 5.

Principal The amount of money that is originally borrowed, loaned, or deposited.

Proceeds ***Maturity value*** less the bank charge.

Product The answer of a multiplication process, such as:

Product = ***Multiplicand*** × ***Multiplier***

$50 = 5 \times 10$

Promissory note A written unconditional promise to pay a certain sum (with or without ***interest***) at a fixed time in the future.

Proper fractions ***Fractions*** with a value less than 1; the ***numerator*** is smaller than the ***denominator***:

$$\frac{5}{9}$$

Property damage Auto insurance covering damages that are caused to the property of others.

Property tax Tax that raises revenue for school districts, cities, counties, and the like.

Property tax due ***Tax rate*** × Assessed valuation.

Proportion An equation of two ***ratios.***

Provincial Sales Tax (PST) A tax levied on sales to final customers that varies from province to province.

Provincial tax deductions Monies deducted from one's paycheque by the provincial government.

Proximo (*abbrev.* **prox**) Same as ***end of month* (*EOM*)**.

Purchase discounts Savings received by a buyer for paying for merchandise before a certain date.

Purchase returns and allowances The ***cost*** of merchandise returned to a store due to damage, defects, and so on. An allowance is a cost reduction that results when buyer keeps or buys damaged goods.

Pure decimal A decimal number that has no ***whole number***(s) to the left of the ***decimal point***, such as .45.

Quick assets ***Current assets*** − Inventory − ***Prepaid expenses***.

Quick ratio (***Current assets*** − Inventory − ***Prepaid expenses***) ÷ ***Current liabilities***.

Quotient The answer of a division operation.

Radical sign The symbol $\sqrt{\ }$ that signifies the operation of finding the root of a ***power***.

Radicand The number inside the ***radical*** sign.

Rate of markdown The markdown percent.

Rate of markup ***Markup*** expressed as percent markup on ***cost***.

Rate of return The difference between the value of a financial instrument now and its value at the time of purchase, divided by its value at the time of purchase. Same as ***yield***.

Range The ***difference*** between the highest and lowest values in a group of values or set of data.

Rate A ***percent*** that is multiplied times the ***base*** that indicates what part of the base we are trying to compare to. Rate is not a ***whole number***.

Rate of interest A ***percent*** of ***interest*** that is used to compute the interest charge on a loan for a specific time.

Ratio The relationship of one number to another found by division of two or more values.

Real property Land, buildings, and so on, which are taxed by the ***property tax***.

Rebate A ***finance charge*** that a customer receives for paying off a loan early.

Rebate fraction A ***sum*** of ***digits*** based on number of months to go divided by the sum of digits based on total number of months of loan.

Receipt of goods (ROG) Credit terms offered by sellers, such that the ***cash discount*** period begins the day that the goods are received.

Reciprocal of a fraction The interchanging of the ***numerator*** and the ***denominator*** of a ***fraction***. The inverted number is the reciprocal. *Example:*

$$\frac{6}{6} \longrightarrow \frac{7}{6}$$

Reduced paid-up insurance Insurance in which ***cash value*** is used to buy protection, the ***face amount*** is less than original ***policy***, and the policy continues for life.

Relative cumulative frequency The ***cumulative frequency*** in a ***frequency distribution*** divided by the total number of data points.

Relative frequency The ***ratio*** of the absolute frequency to the total number of data points in a frequency distribution.

Remainder Any left-over amount in a division operation.

Repeating decimals Decimal numbers made up of digits that repeat without end.

Residual value The estimated value of a plant asset after ***depreciation*** is taken (or at the end of its ***useful life***).

Restrictive endorsement An endorsement with the effect that the ***cheque*** must be deposited to the ***payee***'s account. This restricts anyone from cashing it.

Retail method A method to estimate cost of ending inventory. The cost ratio times ending inventory at retail equals the ending cost of inventory.

Retained earnings The amount of earnings that is kept in the business.

Return on equity ***Net income*** divided by ***stockholders' equity***.

Returns and allowances See ***purchases returns and allowances*** and ***sales returns and allowances***.

Revenues Total earned sales (cash or credit) less any ***sales discounts***, returns, or allowances (See ***purchases returns and allowances*** and ***sales returns and allowances***).

Reverse mortgage A type of mortgage that makes it possible for older homeowners to live in their homes and get cash or monthly income.

Revolving charge account A charge account in which charges for a customer are allowed up to a specified maximum, a minimum monthly payment is required, and ***interest*** is charged on balance outstanding.

ROG (receipt of goods) Credit terms offered by sellers according to which the ***cash discount*** period begins when goods are received, not ordered.

Root The number in a ***power*** that was multiplied by itself to produce the power.

Root (of an equation) The value of the ***unknown*** that makes the equation correct. Same as ***solution***.

Rounding decimals Reducing the number of ***decimals*** to an indicated position. For example, the number 59.59 becomes 59.6 when rounded to the nearest tenth.

Rounding whole numbers all the way A way of rounding so that only one nonzero ***digit*** is left. Rounding all the way gives the least degree of accuracy. *Example:* rounding 1,251 to 1,000; rounding 2,995 to 3,000.

Rule of 78 A method to compute ***rebates*** on consumer finance loans. Allows you to determine how much of a ***finance charge*** you are entitled to. A ***formula*** or table lookup may be used.

Safekeeping A bank procedure whereby a bank does not return ***cheques***. Cancelled cheques are photocopied.

Salary The compensation paid to employees if their workload is predictable and stable.

Salaries payable Obligations that a company must pay within 1 year for salaries earned but unpaid.

Sales (not trade) discounts Reductions in ***selling price*** of goods due to early customer payment.

Sales returns and allowances Reductions in price or reductions in revenue due to goods returned because of product defects, errors, and so on. When the buyer keeps the damaged goods, an allowance results.

Salvage value ***Cost*** − ***Accumulated depreciation***.

Selling price ***Cost*** + ***Markup*** = Selling price.

Semiannually Twice a year.

Semimonthly Twice a month.

Series discount See ***chain or series discount.***

Short-rate table A ***fire insurance*** rate table used when the ***insured*** cancels the ***policy.***

Short-term policy A ***fire insurance*** policy for less than 1 year.

Signature card An information card signed by a person opening a chequing account.

Simple annuity An ***annuity*** in which the compounding period coincides with the ***payment period.***

Simple discount note A note in which the bank deducts ***interest*** in advance.

Simple interest ***Interest*** that is only calculated on the ***principal.*** In $I = P \times r \times t$, the interest plus original principal equals the ***maturity value*** of an ***interest-bearing note.***

Simple interest formula:

Interest = Principal × Rate × Time

$$\text{Principal} = \frac{\text{Interest}}{\text{Rate} \times \text{Time}}$$

$$\text{Rate} = \frac{\text{Interest}}{\text{Principal} \times \text{Time}}$$

Single equivalent discount rate A ***rate*** or factor as a single discount that calculates the amount of the ***trade discount*** by multiplying the rate by the ***list price.*** This single equivalent discount replaces a series of ***chain discounts.*** The single equivalent rate is: 1 − ***Net price equivalent rate.***

Single trade discount What is offered when a company gives only one ***trade discount.***

Sinking fund An ***annuity*** in which the stream of deposits with appropriate ***interest*** will equal a specified amount in the future.

Sliding scale commission A differential ***commission*** in which the ***rates*** depend on different levels of sales.

Sole proprietorship A business owned by one person.

Solution (of an equation) The ***root*** of an ***equation.***

Solve an equation, to To find the value of the ***unknown*** of an ***equation.***

Specific identification method A method of calculating the cost of ending inventory by identifying each item remaining to ***invoice*** price.

Square root The number that when multiplied by itself once creates a ***power.***

Standard deviation A measure of the spread of data around the mean.

Stockbrokers People who with their representatives do the trading on the floor of the stock exchange.

Stock certificate A piece of paper that certifies ownership in a company.

Stockholder One who owns stock in a company.

Stockholders' equity ***Assets − Liabilities.***

Stocks Ownership shares in a company sold to buyers, who receive ***stock certificates.***

Stock yield percent Dividend per share ÷ Closing price per share.

Straight commission Wages calculated as a ***percent*** of the value of goods sold.

Straight life insurance (whole or ordinary) A form of insurance in which protection (full value of ***policy***) results from continual payment of ***premiums*** by the ***insured.*** Until death or retirement, ***nonforfeiture values*** exist for straight life.

Straight-line method A method of ***depreciation*** that spreads an equal amount of depreciation each year over the life of the ***assets.***

Straight-line rate (rate of depreciation) A ***rate*** of ***depreciation*** calculated by dividing 1 by the number of years of expected life.

Subtrahend In a subtraction problem, the smaller number that is being subtracted from another. *Example:* 30 in 150 − 30 = 120.

Sum The total in the adding process.

Sum-of-the-years-digits method An accelerated method of ***depreciation,*** whereby depreciation each year is calculated by multiplying cost (less ***residual value***) times a ***fraction.*** The ***numerator*** is the number of years of ***useful life*** remaining. The ***denominator*** is the ***sum*** of the years of estimated life.

Tax rate

$$\frac{\text{Budget needed}}{\text{Total assessed value}}$$

Term The length of time that money is borrowed.

Term of an annuity The time from the beginning of the first ***payment period*** to the end of the last ***payment period.***

Term life insurance Inexpensive life insurance that provides protection for a specific period of time. No ***nonforfeiture values*** exist for ***term.***

Term of a mortgage A period of time shorter than the amortization period for which the borrower and the lender make an agreement for a fixed ***interest*** rate.

Terms of payment Information about the payment of an ***invoice,*** which includes the ***credit period,*** the ***cash discount,*** and the date on which the credit or ***discount period*** begins.

Term policy The period of time that the ***policy*** is in effect.

Terms of the sale Information about the sale referred to by an ***invoice,*** which includes the ***credit period,*** the ***cash discount,*** the ***discount period,*** and the ***freight terms.***

Terms of the sale The criteria on an ***invoice*** showing when ***cash discounts*** are available, such as ***rate*** and time period.

Time A factor in the calculation of ***simple interest,*** expressed as years or fractional years.

Time line A graphical method of illustrating the ***time value of money.***

Time value of money The tendency of money to change its value over time.

Total cost ***Cost + Operating expenses.***

Trade discount Reduction off the original ***selling price*** (***list price***) not related to early payment.

Trade discount amount ***List price − Net price.***

Trade discount rate The ***trade discount amount*** given in ***percent.***

Trade-in (scrap) value The estimated value of a plant asset after ***depreciation*** is taken (or the end of its ***useful life***).

Tranche A new issue of a financial instrument.

Treasury bill A loan to the federal government for 91 days (13 weeks), 182 days (26 weeks), or 1 year.

Trend analysis A method of analyzing changes that occur in data by expressing each number as a ***percent*** of a ***base*** year.

20-payment life A type of insurance that provides permanent protection and ***cash value,*** but in which the ***insured*** pays ***premiums*** for first 20 years.

20-year endowment The most expensive type of life insurance ***policy.*** It is a combination of ***term*** insurance and ***cash value.***

Unemployment tax A tax paid by the employer that is used to aid unemployed persons.

Units-of-production method A ***depreciation*** method that estimates amount of depreciation on the basis of usage.

Universal life A ***whole life insurance*** plan with flexible ***premium*** and death benefits. This life plan has limited guarantees.

Unknown When solving ***equations***, the ***variable*** we are solving for.

Unlike fractions ***Proper fractions*** with different ***denominators***.

Useful life The estimated number of years the plant asset is used.

Value of an annuity The ***sum*** of a series of payments and ***interest*** (think of this as the ***maturity value*** of ***compounding***).

Variables Letters or symbols that represent ***unknowns***.

Variable commission scale A ***commission*** payment method whereby the company pays different commission ***rates*** for different levels of ***net sales***.

Variable costs (VC) Costs that change in response to changes in the volume of sales.

Variable rate A home ***mortgage*** rate that is not fixed over its lifetime.

Variable-rate mortgage A ***mortgage*** whose rate might be adjusted down without refinancing if rates fall.

Verification The process of checking the accuracy of the solutions of an ***equation***.

Vertical analysis A method of analyzing financial reports in which each total is compared to one total. *Example:* Cash is a ***percent*** of total ***assets***.

Weekly How some employers pay employees.

Weighted-average method A method of assigning costs to ending inventory that calculates the cost of ending inventory by applying an average unit cost to items remaining in inventory for that period of time.

Weighted mean A type of arithmetic average used to find an average when values appear more than once.

Whole life insurance See ***straight life insurance***.

Whole number Number that is 0 or larger and doesn't contain a decimal or a ***fraction***, such as 10, 55, 92.

Withholding The amount of a ***deduction*** from one's paycheque.

Workers' compensation Business insurance covering sickness or accidental injuries to employees that result from on-the-job activities.

Yield The percent ***rate of return*** on a financial instrument.

INDEX

A

absolute loss, 231
actual sales, calculation of, 136
addends, 8
addition
- addends, 8
- associative laws of, 10
- commutative laws of, 10
- decimals, 73–74
- estimate, by rounding, 9
- of fractions, 41–44
- horizontal, 9–10
- like fractions, 41
- mixed numbers, 43–44
- multiplication, as shortcut, 12
- organizer and reference guide, 19
- same number to both sides of equation, 103
- sum, 8
- unlike fractions, 41–43
- vertical, 9–10
- whole numbers, 8–10

age and activity circle graph, 403
algebraic operations. *See* addition; division; multiplication; subtraction
amortization schedule, 387, 388*t*
amortization table, 385, 385*t*
amount of change, 131
  see also percent change
Anheuser-Busch, 229
annual interest rate, 334
annual percentage yield (APY), 341–343
annuities
- annuity due, 357
  - *see also* annuity due
- basic concepts and types, 356–358
- deferred annuity, 357–358
- deferred period, 357
- described, 356–357
- end of the annuity, 357
- end of the payments, 357
- future value, 356*f*, 357, 359
- general annuity, 358
- *see also* general annuity
- *vs.* lump sum, 368
- ordinary annuity, 357
  - *see also* ordinary annuity
- organizer and reference guide, 370–372
- payment periods, 357
- periodic payments, 357, 366–367
- practice quizzes, 358, 363, 368, 370
- practice quizzes solutions, 378–380
- simple annuities, 358
  - *see also* simple annuities
- sinking funds, 366–367
- summary practice test, 377–378
- terms of, 357
- time line diagram, 357
- word problems, 375–377

annuity due
- described, 357
- future value, by table lookup, 362–363
- future value, manual calculation, 361–362
- *vs.* ordinary annuity, 363

approximate numbers, 4
arithmetic averages, 396–397
assessed value, 137
associative laws of addition, 10
associative laws of multiplication, 14
AT&T Corp., 298
automatic banking machine (ABM), 172
automatic teller machine (ATM), 172
averages
- *see also* central measurements
- arithmetic averages, 396–397
- grade point average (GPA), 397
- weighted mean, 397

B

bank discount, 322
Bank of Canada, 320
bank reconciliation
- completion of, 182
- deposits in transit, 180
- described, 179*f*, 180, 182*f*
- electronic funds transfer (EFT), 180
- nonsufficient funds (NSF), 181
- outstanding cheques, identification of, 180
- reconciliation process, 182*f*
- recording errors, 181
- steps, 180
- transactions not recorded, 180–181

bank statement, 178, 179*f*
Banker's Rule, 301
banking
- automatic banking machine (ABM), 172
- automatic teller machine (ATM), 172
- bank reconciliation, 179–182
- bank statement, 178, 179*f*
- chequing account, 172–175
- credit card transactions, 175–177
- debit card, 172
- enhanced ATM/ABM cards, 172
- online banking, 171, 183, 193
- organizer and reference guide, 183–184
- practice quizzes, 177–178, 183
- practice quizzes solutions, 191–192
- safekeeping procedure, 183
- summary practice test, 190–191
- and technology, 171
- word problems, 188–190

bar graphs, 401–402
base 10 system, 3
base (*B*), 127, 130–131
base of power, 92
BEDMAS, 18, 93
biotechnology, 100
biotechnology industry, 100
biweekly mortgage, 384
biweekly pay, 266
blank endorsement, 174, 175*f*
Bluefly Inc., 231
"borrowing," 10–11
breakeven analysis, 242–245, 261
breakeven point, 243
brownie recipe, 47
business cheques, 172–174, 174*f*
business math scrapbook
- banking, 193
- compound interest, 354
- decimals, 89
- discounts, 228
- equivalent prices and percentage changes, 418
- investments, 381
- linear equations, 120
- MDF Mouldings, 65
- online mortgages, 393
- percents and percent problems, 157
- pricing strategy, 262
- ratios and proportions, 169
- RRSPs, 381
- simple interest, 315
- solving for the unknown, 120
- Treasury bills, 330
- whole numbers, 33
- work for hire, 296

business statistics
- central measurements, 396–399
- frequency distribution, 400–401
- graphs. *See* graphs
- index numbers, 403–404
- interval estimate, 408
- mean, 396–397
- measures of dispersion, 405–408
- median, 398–399
- mode, 399
- normal distribution, 407–408
- organizer and reference guide, 408–411
- practice quizzes, 399, 404, 408
- practice quizzes solutions, 417
- range, 405
- standard deviation, 405–407
- summary practice test, 416
- use of, 396
- weighted mean, 397
- word problems, 414–416

C

calculator use
- compound amount and interest, 336
- decimals, operations with, 78
- fractions, 50–51
- future value of annuity due, 362
- future value of ordinary annuity, 360
- mixed numbers, 50–51
- one-step calculation, 225
- order of operations, 18
- percents, rounding, 124
- powers, evaluation of, 95–96
- present value, 339, 340
- present value of ordinary annuity, 366
- roots, evaluation of, 95–96
- sinking funds, 367

Canada
- beer production, 5
- biotechnology industry, 100
- brain drain worries, 100
- census, 159
- Chinese, as mother tongue, 132
- employment and unemployment, 7
- household spending, 9*t*
- international transactions, 318
- new motor vehicle production, 10
- rural communities, 159, 160
- taxes, levels of, 134

Canada-Mexico-United States merchandise trade reconciliation, 75
Canada Pension Plan (CPP) contributions, 273–274, 273*f*, 274*f*, 279–281
Canada Year Book 2001, 8
Canadian Banker, 183
Canadian Bankers Association, 183
Canadian Classification and Dictionary of Occupations (CCDO), 266
Canadian numbering system, 3
cancellation technique, 48
cash discounts
- *see also* discounts
- common credit terms, 206–211
- credit period, 203, 204
- days-in-a-month rule, 205
- days-in-a-year calendar, 206, 207
- described, 196
- discount period, 204
- due dates, 205–206
- end of credit periods, 205
- end of month (EOM), 210–211
- knuckle months, 205
- ordinary dating, 204–205, 206–209
- outstanding balance, 212
- partial payments, 211–213
- practice quiz, 214
- receipt of goods (ROG), 209
- terms of payment, 204
- terms of payment abbreviations, 204*f*
- terms of the sale, 205
- terms of trade, 203
- *vs.* trade discount, 204
- word problems, 211

central measurements
- described, 396
- mean, 396–397
- median, 398–399
- mode, 399
- weighted mean, 397

chain discounts, 200–203
cheque, 172
cheque register, 174, 181*f*
cheque stubs, 174
chequing accounts
- business cheques, 172–174, 174*f*
- cheque register, 174, 181*f*
- cheque stubs, 174
- deposit slips, 172, 173*f*
- described, 172
- drawee, 174
- drawer, 174
- elements of, 172–175
- endorsement, 174, 174*f*, 175*f*
- signature card, 172

circle graphs, 403
Cisco Systems Inc., 317
closing costs, 386
Coca-Cola Co., 124, 228
common denominator, 41
commutative laws of addition, 10
commutative laws of multiplication, 14
company policies, changes in, 2
complement, 199
compound amount, 333, 335–337
- *see also* future value (FV)

compound interest
- *see also* compounding
- annual interest rate, 334
- annuities. *See* annuities
- compounding frequency, 334
- described, 333
- equivalent interest rates, 343–345
- manual calculation, 335–337
- nominal interest rate, 334
- organizer and reference guide, 345–346
- practice quizzes, 337, 341, 343, 345
- practice quizzes solutions, 352–353
- present value, relationship to, 338
- quoted with two parts, 334
- *vs.* simple interest, 335–337
- summary practice test, 351–352
- time line diagrams, 332–333
- word problems, 349–351

compounded annually, 334
compounded daily, 334, 343
compounded quarterly, 334
compounded semi-annually, 334
compounding
- *see also* compound interest
- annually, 334
- daily, 334, 343
- described, 332, 333
- effective interest rate, 341–343
- frequency, 334
- number of periods (*n*), 334
- periodic interest rate, 334
- present value to future value, 333*f*
- quarterly, 334
- semiannually, 334

Conseco Inc., 331
constants, 101
construction industry, and imperial system, 92
Consumer Price Index, 271, 403, 404*t*
contingent liability, 322
contribution margin, 243, 244
contribution rate (CR), 244
cost
- closing costs, 386
- described, 230
- fixed costs (FC), 243
- known selling price and gross profit margin, 237–238
- known selling price and rate of markup, 234
- percent markup on cost. *See* percent markup on cost
- total cost, 231
- variable costs (VC), 243

cost-profit-volume, 242–245, 261
credit card transactions
deposit of, 175–177
electronic deposit statement, 177*f*
electronic deposits, 176–177
manual deposits, 175–176
merchant batch header slip, 176, 176*f*
net deposit, 176
credit memo (CM), 180–181
credit period, 203, 204
credit terms
end of month (EOM), 210–211
ordinary dating, 206–209
receipt of goods (ROG), 209
cross-multiplication rule, 162–163
cumulative frequency, 401
cumulative review, 90, 263

D

date (of promissory note), 318
days, calculation without table, 322
days-in-a-month rule, 205
days-in-a-year calendar, 206, 207
debit card, 172
debit memo (DM), 181
decimal fraction
conversion to decimals, 70
described, 70
mixed decimals, conversion from, 71–72
pure decimal, conversion from, 71–72
decimal numbers, 3, 68
see also decimals
decimal point, 3, 68
decimal system
described, 3
place-value system, 3
decimals
addition, 73–74
calculators, operations calculations with, 78
decimal fractions, conversion from, 70
described, 68
division, 74–75, 76
foreign currency applications, 75–76
fractional percents, conversion from, 124–125
mixed decimals, 71–72
mixed numbers, conversion from, 71
multiplication, 74, 76
organizer and reference guide, 78–80
percents, conversion from, 124–125
percents, conversion to, 123–124
place-value chart, 3, 4*f*, 68*f*
place values, relationship of, 68
practice quizzes, 72–73, 77
practice quizzes solutions, 87–88
proper fractions, conversion from, 71
pure decimal, 71–72
reading, 69
repeating decimal, 71
rounding to specified place value, 69–70
subtraction, 73–74
summary practice tests, 86
word problems, 83–85
deductions, 267
deferred annuity, 357–358
denominator, 36
deposit slips, 172, 173*f*
deposits in transit, 180
difference, 10
differential pay schedule, 269
discount period, 204
discount sheets, 197
discounting a note
bank discount, 322
contingent liability, 322
days, calculation without table, 322
described, 322
formulas, 322–323
interest-bearing note before maturity, 321–323
proceeds, 322
steps, 322
discounting Treasury bills (T-bills), 320–321
discounts
cash discount, 196, 203–214
chain discounts, 200–203
described, 196
multiple discounts, 201
off list price, 196
organizer and reference guide, 214–216
practice quizzes, 203, 214
practice quizzes solutions, 224–226
series discounts, 200–203
single trade discount, 199–200
summary practice test, 223–224
trade discounts, 196–203
word problems, 211, 221–223
Disney Stores, 106
dispersion, 405
see also measures of dispersion
distribution chain, 196
distributive laws of multiplication, 14
dividend, 14
division
both sides of equation by same number, 103–104
decimals, 74–75, 76
dividend, 14
divisor, 14
estimate, 15
even division, 15
fractions, 48–49
long division, 15
mixed numbers, 49
numbers ending in zeros, 16
organizer and reference guide, 20
partial quotient, 15
of powers, 93
proper fractions, 48–49
quotient, 14
remainder, 15
short division, 15
shortcuts for multiples of 10, 76
as subtraction shortcut, 14
symbols for, 14
uneven division with remainder, 15
whole numbers, 14–16
word problems, 16–17
divisor, 14
dollar markdown, 241
dollar markup, 231, 232, 235–236
dollar value of interest, 298
draft, 172
draw, 269
drawee, 174
drawer, 174
due dates
calculation of, 205–206
days-in-a-month rule, 205
days-in-a-year calendar, 206, 207
knuckle months, 205

E

effective interest rate, 319, 341–343
electronic deposit statement, 177*f*
electronic deposits, 176–177
electronic funds transfer (EFT), 180
employee pay. *See* pay
Employment Insurance (EI) premiums, 274–275, 274*f*, 275*f*, 282–286
end of credit periods, 205
end of month (EOM), 210–211
endorse, 174
endorsement, 174, 174*f*, 175*f*
enhanced ATM/ABM cards, 172
Enterprise Rent-A-Car, 196
equation
described, 101
equation in one unknown, 101
equivalent equations, 102
formula, 101
linear equation, 101
see also linear equation

members of an equation, 101
in one unknown, 101
proportions. *See* proportions
solution of the equation, 102
solving, 102
of two ratios. *See* proportions
verification, 102
equation equality rule, 103
equation in one unknown, 101
equivalent equations, 102
equivalent fractions, 39–40
equivalent interest rates
described, 343
shortcut formula, 344
substitution method, 343–344
equivalent markup, 240*t*
equivalent payments
compound interest, 340–341
described, 304
simple interest, 304–306
equivalent ratios, 160
estimate
see also rounding
addition, 9
division, 15
of market size or potential, 398
multiplication, 13–14
even division, 15
exact-days-in-a-year calendar, 300
exact interest method, 300
exponent, 92
expression, 101

F
face value
mortgages, 384
promissory notes, 318, 319, 321
federal tax deductions, 272, 272*f*, 287
fixed costs (FC), 243
fixed rate mortgage, 384
FOB destination, 198
FOB shipping point, 198
food processing industry, 36
Ford Motor Company, 402
foreign currency
decimal applications in, 75–76
key currency cross rates, 75*t*
formula (equation), 101
fraction conversions
to decimals, 70–73
improper fractions to whole or mixed numbers, 37–38
mixed numbers to improper fractions, 38
from percents, 125–126
raising to higher terms, 39–40
reducing to lowest terms, 38–39
fractional percents, conversion to decimals, 124–125
fractions
addition of, 41–44
$a^{b/c}$ button, 50–51
calculator use, 50–51
cancellation technique, 48
common denominator, 41
conversion procedures. *See* fraction conversions
decimal fractions, 70
denominator, 36
described, 36
division, 48–49
equivalent, 39–40
greatest common divisor, 38–39
higher terms, 39
improper fractions, 37–38
least common denominator (LCD), 41–43
like fractions, 40, 41, 44
lowest common denominator, 41*n*
lowest terms, 38–39
mixed numbers. *See* mixed numbers
multiplication, 47–48
numerator, 36
organizer and reference guide, 52–54
practice quizzes, 40, 46, 50, 51
practice quizzes solutions, 62–64
prime number method, 42
proper fractions, 37, 47–48, 48–49, 71
property of fractions, 40
reciprocal, 48–49
subtraction of, 44–45
summary practice test, 61
types of, 36–40
unlike fractions, 40, 41–43, 44
word problems, 49, 57–60
word problems and, 46
free trade, impact of, 73
freight terms, 198
frequency distribution, 400–401
full endorsement, 174, 175*f*
future value (FV)
see also compound amount; compound interest; maturity value (MV)
annuity, 356*f*, 357, 359
described, 298, 333
general annuity, 369
shortcut formula, 336
simple annuity due, by table lookup, 362–363
simple annuity due, manual calculation, 361–362
simple ordinary annuities, by table lookup, 360–361
simple ordinary annuities, manual calculation, 359–360
use of, 367

G
general annuity
described, 358, 369
future value, 369
maturity, 369
periodic payments, 369
present value, 369
sinking funds, 367
Goods and Services Tax (GST), 135–136
grade point average (GPA), 397
graphs
bar graphs, 401–402
circle graphs, 403
frequency distribution, 400–401
histogram, 401
intervals, 402
line graphs, 402
misleading graphics, 400
pie charts, 403
preparation, tips for, 402
greatest common divisor, 38–39
gross pay, 267–268
gross profit, 230
see also markup (*M*)
gross profit margin, 231*n*, 235
see also percent markup on selling price

H
higher terms, 39
Hispanic market, 229
histogram, 401
H.L. Heinz Company, 2
home equity loan, 384
home ownership
costs of, 386
mortgages. *See* mortgages
horizontal addition, 9–10
hourly rate, 267

I
imperial system of measurement, 92
improper fractions, 37–38
independent ABMs, 172
index, 95
index numbers, 403–404
India
Internet use in, 99
juice processors in, 120
interest
compound interest. *See* compound interest
compounding. *See* compounding
described, 298
dollar value of interest, 298
measurement of, 298
simple interest. *See* simple interest
and time value of money, 298
Interest Act, 384
interest-bearing promissory notes, 318*f*, 319

interest rate
- annual interest rate, 334
- described, 298, 302–303
- effective interest rate, 341–343
- equivalent interest rates, 343–345
- mortgages, 384
- nominal interest rate, 334, 342
- periodic interest rate, 334

Internet
- *see also* business math scrapbook
- banking, 171, 183, 193
- global usage, 122
- India, Internet use in, 99
- lower prices on, 196
- online activities, 122
- sales, and consumers, 40
- shopping, 198

interval estimate, 408
intervals, 402
investments
- compound amount, 333
- compounding, 332
- effective interest rate, 341–343
- equivalent interest rates, 343–345
- increase, in manufacturing industry, 1
- mathematics of, 332
- practice quiz, 333
- practice quiz solutions, 352
- residential values, by type of investment, 3*t*
- rule of 72, 332
- time line diagrams, 332–333

invoice, 196–197

J

Japan, loan problem in, 301–302
J.C. Penney Co., 240

K

knowns, 101
knuckle months, 205

L

La Casera, 228
land transfer tax, 386
least common denominator (LCD), 41–43
like fractions
- addition of, 41
- described, 40
- subtraction of, 44

like unknowns rule, 105
line graphs, 402
linear equation
- addition of same number to both sides, 103
- basic equation-solving procedures, 101–102
- described, 101
- division of both sides by same number, 103–104
- equation, 101
- equation equality rule, 103
- equation in one unknown, 101
- equivalent equations, 102
- formula, 101
- like unknowns rule, 105
- linear equation, 101
- mathematical expression, 101
- members of an equation, 101
- multiple processes rule, 104
- multiplication of both sides by same number, 104
- opposite process rule, 103
- organizer and reference guide, 110–113
- parentheses rule, 104–105
- practice quizzes, 105
- practice quizzes solutions, 117
- solution of the equation, 102
- solving an equation, 102
- solving for unknown, 102–105
- subtraction and multiplication to solve unknown, 104
- subtraction of same number from both sides, 103
- summary practice tests, 116
- terms of mathematical expressions, 101
- variables, use of, 101
- word problems, 105–110, 114–116

lines of credit, 323
list price, 196
list price calculation, 200
loans
- compound amount, 333
- interest. *See* interest
- interest rate, 298, 302–303
- maturity value (MV), 298, 299–301
- partial payments, 305
- present value of simple interest, 304–306
- principal, 298, 302
- time, 300, 303

long division, 15
loss
- absolute loss, 231
- operating loss, 231

lowest common denominator, 41*n*
lowest terms, 38–39
lump sum, *vs.* annuities, 368

M

MacLean's, 100, 160, 196
magazine free issues, 228
maker, 318
manual deposits, 175–176
margin, 230
- *see also* markup (M)

markdowns
- described, 240
- dollar markdown, 241
- organizer and reference guide, 246–247
- practice quiz, 242
- practice quiz solution, 260
- rate of markdown, 241
- sale price, 241
- series, calculation of, 241

market price/market value of T-bill, 321
markup (M)
- described, 230
- dollar markup, 231, 232, 235–236
- equivalent markup, 240*t*
- markdowns, 256
- organizer and reference guide, 246–247
- percent, expression in, 231
- percent markup on cost, 231–235
- percent markup on selling price, 235–240
- practice quiz, 235
- practice quizzes, 240
- practice quizzes solutions, 257–260
- rate of markup (R_M), 231–235, 231*n*
- series, calculation of, 241
- summary practice test, 256

mass-market retailers, 35
mathematical expression, 101
maturity date, 318
maturity value (MV)
- *see also* future value (FV)
- calculation of, 299–301
- described, 298, 319
- simple interest, 335

McDonald's Corp., 2, 262
measures of central tendency. *See* central measurements
measures of dispersion
- described, 405
- normal distribution, 407–408
- range, 405
- standard deviation, 405–407

median, 398–399
members of an equation, 101
merchant batch header slip, 176, 176*f*
metric system of measurement, 92
mill, 138
minuend, 10
misleading graphics, 400
mixed decimals
- conversion to decimal fractions, 71–72
- described, 71

mixed numbers
- addition of, 43–44
- calculator use, 50–51

conversion from improper fractions, 37–38
conversion to decimals, 71
conversion to improper fractions, 38
described, 37
division, 49
as improper fractions, and subtraction, 45
multiplication, 48
subtraction of, 44–45
M&M's®, 36, 68, 122–123
mode, 399
monthly pay, 266
mortgage insurance, 386
mortgages
amortization schedule, 387, 388*t*
amortization table, 385, 385*t*
biweekly mortgage, 384
described, 384
effect of interest rate, 386
face value, 384
fixed rate mortgage, 384
home equity loan, 384
interest, calculation of, 387
interest rate, 384
monthly payment, computation of, 385
new balance of monthly payment, 387
organizer and reference guide, 388
practice quizzes, 386, 388
practice quizzes solutions, 392
principal, calculation of, 387
reverse mortgage, 384
summary practice tests, 391
term of a mortgage, 384
total cost of interest, 386
types of, 384
variable rate mortgage, 384
word problems, 390–391
multiple discounts, 201
multiple processes rule, 104
multiplicand, 12
multiplication
associative laws of, 14
both sides of equation by same number, 104
cancellation technique, 48
checking, 13–14
commutative laws of, 14
cross-multiplication rule, 162–163
decimals, 74, 76
distributive laws of, 14
estimating, 13–14
fractions, 47–48
mixed numbers, 48
multiplicand, 12
multiplier, 12
numbers ending in zeros, 13
organizer and reference guide, 20
partial products, 12
by power of 10, 14
of powers, 93
product, 12
proper fractions, 47–48
as shortcut to addition, 12
shortcuts for multiples of 10, 76
to solve for unknown, 104
whole numbers, 12–14
whole numbers with two or more digits, 13
word problems, 16–17
multiplier, 12
Municipal Property Assessment Corporation (mpac), 138–139

N

NAFTA, 73
negative power, raising to, 94
net deposit, 176
net income (*P*)
calculation of, 243
described, 230
net pay, 275
net price
calculation, 199
described, 197
formula, 197
net price equivalent rate, 201–202
net price equivalent rate, 201–202
net profit (*P*), 230
see also net income (*P*)
nominal interest rate, 334, 342
non-interest-bearing promissory notes, 319
nonsufficient funds (NSF), 181
normal distribution, 407–408
number of periods (*n*), 334
numbers, *vs.* variables, 101
numerator, 36

O

online banking, 171, 183, 193
operating expenses (*E*), 230
operating loss, 231
operational signs, 101
operations, order of. *See* order of operations
Oplink, 317
opposite process rule, 103
order of operations
acronym for, 18
BEDMAS, 18
calculator use, 18
examples, 18
exponent operations, 93
organizer and reference guide, 20
PEMDAS, 18
ordinary annuity
vs. annuity due, 363
described, 357
general annuity, 358, 369–370
present value, 363–366
simple annuities, 358
see also simple annuities
ordinary dating, 204–205, 206–209
ordinary interest method, 301
organizer and reference guide
annuities, 370–372
banking, 183–184
business statistics, 408–411
compound interest, 345–346
decimals, 78–80
discounts, 214–216
fractions, 52–54
linear equations, 110–113
markups and markdowns, 246–247
mortgages, 388
payroll, 289–290
percents and percent problems, 139–142
perishables, 248
powers, 96–97
promissory notes, 324
proportions, 164–165
ratios, 164–165
roots, 96–97
simple interest, 306–308
solving for the unknown, 110–113
whole numbers, 19–21
outstanding balance, 212
outstanding cheques, 180
overdrafts, 179*f*
overhead (*E*), 230
overrides, 270
overtime, 267–268

P

parentheses rule, 104–105
partial payments, 211–213, 305
partial products, 12
partial quotient, 15
patents, and rodents, 100
pay
biweekly pay, 266
gross pay, 267–268
hourly rate, 267–268
monthly pay, 266
net pay, 275
overrides, 270
overtime, 267–268
periodic payments, 266
salaries, 266
semimonthly pay, 266
straight-time earnings, 267
weekly pay, 266
pay slip, 270*f*
payee, 318
payment periods, 357

payroll calculations
- differential pay schedule, 269
- organizer and reference guide, 289–290
- overtime calculation, 267–268
- piecework rate, 268
- practice quiz, 270
- practice quiz solutions, 295
- salary plus commission, 270
- straight commission with draw, 269
- straight piece rate pay, 268
- summary practice test, 295
- variable commission scale, 269
- word problems, 294

payroll deductions
- calculation of, 271–275
- CCRA payroll deduction tables, 271, 272*f*
- CPP contributions, 273–274, 273*f*, 274*f*, 279–281
- Employment Insurance (EI) premiums, 274–275, 274*f*, 275*f*, 282–286
- federal tax deductions, 272, 272*f*, 287
- income tax rates for, 271*f*
- organizer and reference guide, 289–290
- practice quiz, 275–288
- practice quiz solutions, 295
- provincial deductions, 273, 273*f*, 288
- summary practice test, 295
- TD1 ("2003 Personal Tax Credits Return"), 271, 276
- TD1ON ("2003 Ontario Personal Tax Credits Return"), 277–278
- total tax deductions, 271–273
- word problems, 294

PEMDAS, 18, 93

percent change
- formula for, 132
- order of numbers in numerator, 132
- percent decrease, rate of, 132
- percent increase, rate of, 132–134
- positive amount of change, 132
- practice quiz, 134
- practice quiz solution, 155–156

percent decrease, 132

percent increase, 132–134

percent markup on cost
- calculation of, 232
- cost, with known selling price and rate of markup, 234
- described, 231
- dollar markup calculation, 232
- *vs.* percent markup on selling price, 239*t*
- percent markup on selling price, conversion from, 239–240
- percent markup on selling price, conversion to, 238–239
- rate of markup, 231
- selling price, with known cost and rate of markup, 233–234
- summary of calculations, 240

percent markup on selling price
- calculation of, 235–236
- cost, with known selling price and gross profit margin, 237–238
- described, 235
- dollar markup calculation, 235–236
- *vs.* percent markup on cost, 239*t*
- percent markup on cost, conversion from, 238–239
- percent markup on cost, conversion to, 239–240
- selling price, with known cost and gross profit margin, 236–237
- summary of calculations, 240

percent problems
- actual sales, calculation of, 136
- base, solving for, 130–131
- base (*B*), 127
- organizer and reference guide, 139–142
- percent change, 131–134
- portion, solving for, 128–129
- portion formula, 126–131
- portion (*P*), 127
- practice quizzes, 131, 134, 137
- rate, solving for, 129–130
- rate (*R*), 127
- summary practice test, 152
- taxes, 134–139
- word problems, 148–151

percents
- applications of. *See* percent problems
- decimal percent, conversion to fraction, 126
- decimals, conversion from, 123–124
- decimals, conversion to, 124–125
- described, 122
- fractional percents, conversion to decimals, 124–125
- fractions, conversion to, 125–126
- information provided by, 122
- markup, 231
- mixed percent, conversion to fraction, 126
- organizer and reference guide, 139–142
- practice quizzes, 126
- practice quizzes solutions, 153–156
- rounding, 124
- summary practice test, 152
- word problems, 148–151

periodic interest rate, 334

periodic payments, 266, 357, 366–367, 369

perishable items, 242, 248, 260

personal property, 137

pie charts, 403

piecework rate, 268

place-value chart, 3, 4*f*, 68*f*

place-value system, 3

plasma-based flat TVs, 396

portion formula
- base, solving for, 130–131
- base (*B*), 127
- portion, solving for, 128–129
- portion (*P*), 127
- practice quiz, 131
- practice quiz solutions, 153–155
- rate, solving for, 129–130
- rate (*R*), 127
- solving percents with, 127–131

portion (*P*), 127–129

powers
- base, 92
- calculator use, 95–96
- described, 92
- division, 93
- exponent, 92
- expressions of, 92
- multiplication, 93
- order of operations, 93
- organizer and reference guide, 96–97
- power of 10, multiplication by, 14
- power of the root, 95
- practice quizzes, 94, 96
- practice quizzes solutions, 98
- raising a power to a power, 93
- raising a product or quotient to a power, 94
- raising to negative power, 94
- raising to power of 0, 94

practice quizzes
- annuities, 358, 363, 368, 370
- banking, 177–178, 183
- breakeven analysis, 245
- business statistics, 399, 404, 408
- compound interest, 337, 341, 343, 345
- cost-profit-volume, 245
- decimals, 72–73, 77
- discounts, 203, 214
- fractions, 40, 46, 50, 51
- investments, 333
- linear equations, 105

markdown, 242
markup, 235, 240
mortgages, 386, 388
payroll, 270, 275–288
percent problems, 131, 134, 137
percents, 126
perishable items, 242
powers, 94, 96
present-value formula, 340
promissory notes, 321, 323
proportions, 164
ratios, 161
roots, 95, 96
simple interest, 298, 301, 303, 306
solutions. *See* practice quizzes solutions
solving for unknown, 105, 110
whole numbers, 7, 11–12, 17, 19

practice quizzes solutions
annuities, 378–380
banking, 191–192
breakeven analysis, 261
business statistics, 417
compound interest, 352–353
cost-profit-volume, 261
decimals, 87–88
discounts, 224–226
fractions, 62–64
investments, 352
linear equations, 117
markdowns, 260
markups, 257–260
mortgages, 392
payroll, 295
percents and percent problems, 153–156
perishable items, 260
powers, 98
promissory notes, 328
proportions, 167–168
ratios, 167
roots, 98
simple interest, 313–314
solving for the unknown, 117–119
whole numbers, 30–31

present value (PV),
compound interest, relationship to, 338
described, 333, 337
general annuity, 369
money value movement to the left of time line, 341
ordinary annuities, 363–366
ordinary annuities, by formula, 365–366
ordinary annuities, by table lookup, 364–365
practice quiz, 340
of simple interest, 304–306
use of, 367
using, 338–340

price relative, 403

pricing
basic selling price formula, 230
cost (*C*), 230
markdowns, 240–242
markup (*M*), 230
net profit (*P*), 230
operating expenses (*E*), 230
overhead (*E*), 230
percent markup on cost, 231–235
percent markup on selling price, 235–240
perishable items, 242
sale price, 241
selling price (*S*), 230
visualizing image, 230

prime number, 42

principal, 298, 302, 304

problem solving
company policy, initiation of change in, 2
proportions, use of, 162–164

proceeds, 319, 322

product
described, 12
raising to a power, 94

promissory notes
date, 318
described, 318
discounting, 321–323
face value, 318, 319
interest-bearing, 318*f*, 319
maker, 318
maturity date, 318
non-interest-bearing, 319
organizer and reference guide, 324
payee, 318
practice quizzes, 321, 323
practice quizzes solutions, 328
proceeds, 322
rate, 318
simple discount note, 319–321
simple interest note, 319
structure of, 318–319
summary practice test, 328
term, 318
word problems, 326–327

proper fractions
conversion to decimals, 71
described, 37
division, 48–49
multiplication, 47–48
reciprocal, 48–49

property tax
assessed value, determination of, 137
calculation of, 138–139
described, 137
formula, 139
practice quiz, 139
tax rate, 137–138

proportions
cross-multiplication rule, 162–163
described, 162
organizer and reference guide, 164–165
practice quiz, 164
practice quiz solutions, 167–168
problem solving, use in, 162–164
standard form, 162
summary practice test, 166
word problems, 166

provincial deductions, 273, 273*f*, 288

Provincial Sales Tax (PST), 136–137

proximo, 210*n*

pure decimal
conversion to decimal fractions, 71–72
described, 71

Q

quotient
described, 14
raising to a power, 94

R

radicals, 95

radicand, 95

raising a power to a power, 93

raising a product or quotient to a power, 94

raising to negative power, 94

raising to power of 0, 94

range, 405

rate of markdown, 241

rate of markup (R_M), 231, 231*n*
see also percent markup on cost

rate (of promissory note), 318

rate (*R*), 127, 129–130

rates of return, 320, 321*t*

ratios
comparisons with, 161
described, 160
equation of two ratios. *See* proportions
equivalent ratios, 160
operations with, 161
organizer and reference guide, 164–165
practice quiz, 161
practice quiz solutions, 167
properties of, 160–161
summary practice test, 166
use of, 160
word problems, 166

reading
decimals, 69
whole numbers, 3–4
real estate industry, and imperial system, 92
real property, 137
receipt of goods (ROG), 209
reciprocal, 48–49
reducing fractions, 38–39
reference guide. *See* organizer and reference guide
"register rage," 35
relative cumulative frequency, 401
relative frequency, 401
remainder, 15
remodeling, 121
repairs and maintenance, 386
repeating decimal, 71
restrictive endorsement, 174, 175*f*
retirement savings, 356
revenue
contribution margin, 243, 244
described, 243
per unit (*S*), 243
reverse mortgage, 384
rodents, and patents, 100
root of the equation, 102
roots
calculator use, 95–96
described, 96
index, 95
organizer and reference guide, 96–97
power of the root, 95
practice quizzes, 95, 96
practice quizzes solutions, 98
radicals, 95
radicand, 95
square root, 95
rounding
see also estimate
addition, estimate of, 9
approximate numbers, 4
decimals, to specified place value, 69–70
illustration of, 5–6
organizer and reference guide, 19
percents, 124
whole numbers, 4–6
rule of 72, 332

S

safekeeping procedure, 183
salaries, 266
sale price, 241
selling price (*S*)
basic selling price formula, 230
described, 230
known cost and gross profit margin, 236–237
known cost and rate of markup, 233–234
percent markup on selling price. *See* percent markup on selling price
semimonthly pay, 266
series discounts, 200–203
short division, 15
signature card, 172
simple annuities
described, 358
future value, by table lookup, 360–361
future value, manual calculation, 359–361
present value, 363–366
present value, by formula, 365–366
present value, by table lookup, 364–365
sinking funds, 367
simple annuity due
future value, by table lookup, 362–363
future value, manual calculation, 361–362
simple discount note, 319–321
simple interest
calculation of, 299–301, 319, 335
vs. compound interest, 335–337
described, 299
exact-days-in-a-year calendar, 300
exact interest method, 300
ordinary interest method, 301
organizer and reference guide, 306–308
practice quizzes, 298, 301, 306
practice quizzes solutions, 313–314
present value of, 304–306
simple interest formula, 299–300
solving for the unknown, 301–303
summary practice test, 313
word problems, 310–312
simple interest note, 319
single equivalent discount rate, 202
single trade discount, 199–200
sinking funds, 366–367
slotting fees, 203
solution of the equation, 102
solving an equation, 102
solving for the unknown
basic linear equations, 101–105
difference problems, 108
equation equality rule, 103
finding the whole when part is known, 107
like unknowns rule, 105
multiple processes rule, 104
number problems, 107
opposite process rule, 103
organizer and reference guide, 110–113
parentheses rule, 104–105
practice quizzes, 105, 110
practice quizzes solutions, 117–119
rule, 102
simple interest formula, 301–303
with subtraction and multiplication, 104
summary practice tests, 116
unit and dollar sales, with total units known, 109
unit and dollar sales, with total units unknown, 109
unit sales, calculation of, 108
unknown, described, 101
word problems, 105–110, 114–116
square root, 95
standard deviation, 405–407
statistics. *See* business statistics
straight commission, 269
straight piece rate pay, 268
straight-time earnings, 267
substitution method, 343–344
subtraction
"borrowing," 10–11
decimals, 73–74
difference, 10
division, as shortcut, 14
of fractions, 44–45
illustration, 10
like fractions, 44
minuend, 10
mixed numbers, 44–45
organizer and reference guide, 20
same number from both sides of equation, 103
to solve for unknown, 104
subtrahend, 10
unlike fractions, 44
whole numbers, 10–11
word problems, 11
subtrahend, 10
sum, 8
summary practice tests
annuities, 377–378
banking, 190–191
business statistics, 416
compound interest, 351–352
decimals, 86
discounts, 223–224
fractions, 61
linear equation, 116
markups and markdowns, 256
mortgages, 391
payroll, 295

percents and percent problems, 152
promissory notes, 328
proportions, 166
ratios, 166
simple interest, 313
solving for the unknown, 116
whole numbers, 29–30

T

taxes
actual sales, calculation of, 136
on discounted prices, 136
Goods and Services Tax (GST), 135–136
levels of, in Canada, 134
mill, 138
practice quiz solutions, 156
practice quizzes, 137, 139
property tax, 137–139
Provincial Sales Tax (PST), 136–137
tax rate (property tax), 137–138
TD1 ("2003 Personal Tax Credits Return"), 271, 276
TD1ON ("2003 Ontario Personal Tax Credits Return"), 277–278
technology
banking industry, 171
food processing industry, 36
term of a mortgage, 384
term of loan or deposit, 298
term (of promissory note), 318
terms of mathematical expressions, 101
terms of payment, 204
terms of payment abbreviations, 204*f*
terms of the sale, 205
terms of trade, 203
time, 300, 303
time line, 298
time value of money, 298, 304
total cost, 231
trade discounts
see also discounts
vs. cash discounts, 204
chain discounts, 200–203
complement, 199
described, 196
distribution chain, 196
examples of, 196
freight terms, 198
list price calculation, 200
multiple discounts, 201
net price calculation, 199
net price equivalent rate, 201–202
net price formula, 197
practice quiz, 203
restrictions on, 198
series discounts, 200–203
single equivalent discount rate, 202
single trade discount, 199–200
trade discount amount, 196
trade discount amount formula, 197
trade discount rate, 197
word problems, 211
trade reconciliation study, 75
tranche, 321
Treasury bills (T-bills), 320–321, 330

U

uneven division with remainder, 15
United States
annual percentage yield (APY), 341–342
Banker's Rule, 301
ordinary interest method, 301
property taxes in, 138*n*
Truth in Savings Law, 342
Univision Communications, 229
unknown, 101
see also solving for the unknown
unlike fractions
addition of, 41–43
described, 40
subtraction of, 44

V

variable commission scale, 269
variable costs (VC), 243
variable rate mortgage, 384
variables, 101
verification, 102
vertical addition, 9–10

W

"Wage Rates, Salaries and Hours of Labour," 266
Wal-Mart Stores Inc., 195
weekly pay, 266
weighted mean, 397
White Label ABMs, 172
whole numbers
addition of, 8–10
described, 3
division, 14–16
improper fractions, conversion from, 37–38
multiplication, 12–14
numeric, 3–4
organizer and reference guide, 19–21
practice quizzes, 7, 11–12, 17, 19
practice quizzes solutions, 30–31
reading and writing whole numbers, 3–4
rounding, 4–6
subtraction, 10–11
summary practice test, 29–30
verbal form, 4
word problems
annuities, 375–377
banking, 188–190
blueprint aid for dissection and solving, 6–7
business statistics, 414–416
compound interest, 349–351
decimals, 77, 83–85
difference problems, 108
discounts, 211, 221–223
dissection and solving, 6–7
division, 16–17
finding the whole when part is known, 107
fractions, 46, 49, 57–60
linear equations, 114–116
mortgages, 390–391
multiplication, 16–17
number problems, 107
payroll, 294
percent increase, rate of, 132–134
percents and percent problems, 148–151
portion, solving for, 128–129
promissory notes, 326–327
proportions, 166
ratios, 166
simple interest, 310–312
solving for the unknown, 114–116
solving for unknown, 105–110
steps to solving, 7
subtraction, 11
unit and dollar sales, with total units known, 109
unit and dollar sales, with total units unknown, 109
unit sales, calculation of, 108
whole numbers, 25–30
writing whole numbers, 3–4

X

Xerox Corp., 323

Y

yields, 320, 321*t*

EXACT DAYS-IN-A-YEAR CALENDAR (EXCLUDING LEAP YEAR)												
Day of month	31 Jan.	28 Feb.	31 Mar.	30 Apr.	31 May	30 June	31 July	31 Aug.	30 Sept.	31 Oct.	30 Nov.	31 Dec.
1	1	32	60	91	121	152	182	213	244	274	305	335
2	2	33	61	92	122	153	183	214	245	275	306	336
3	3	34	62	93	123	154	184	215	246	276	307	337
4	4	35	63	94	124	155	185	216	247	277	308	338
5	5	36	64	95	125	156	186	217	248	278	309	339
6	6	37	65	96	126	157	187	218	249	279	310	340
7	7	38	66	97	127	158	188	219	250	280	311	341
8	8	39	67	98	128	159	189	220	251	281	312	342
9	9	40	68	99	129	160	190	221	252	282	313	343
10	10	41	69	100	130	161	191	222	253	283	314	344
11	11	42	70	101	131	162	192	223	254	284	315	345
12	12	43	71	102	132	163	193	224	255	285	316	346
13	13	44	72	103	133	164	194	225	256	286	317	347
14	14	45	73	104	134	165	195	226	257	287	318	348
15	15	46	74	105	135	166	196	227	258	288	319	349
16	16	47	75	106	136	167	197	228	259	289	320	350
17	17	48	76	107	137	168	198	229	260	290	321	351
18	18	49	77	108	138	169	199	230	261	291	322	352
19	19	50	78	109	139	170	200	231	262	292	323	353
20	20	51	79	110	140	171	201	232	263	293	324	354
21	21	52	80	111	141	172	202	233	264	294	325	355
22	22	53	81	112	142	173	203	234	265	295	326	356
23	23	54	82	113	143	174	204	235	266	296	327	357
24	24	55	83	114	144	175	205	236	267	297	328	358
25	25	56	84	115	145	176	206	237	268	298	329	359
26	26	57	85	116	146	177	207	238	269	299	330	360
27	27	58	86	117	147	178	208	239	270	300	331	361
28	28	59	87	118	148	179	209	240	271	301	332	362
29	29	—	88	119	149	180	210	241	272	302	333	363
30	30	—	89	120	150	181	211	242	273	303	334	364
31	31	—	90	—	151	—	212	243	—	304	—	365

Note: If a leap year, add 1 day to table if February 29 falls between two dates.

Metric/Imperial Unit Conversion Table

Imperial → Metric

Linear Measure (Length/Distance)

Imperial	Metric
1 inch	25.4 millimetres
1 foot (= 12 inches)	0.3048 metre
1 yard (= 3 feet)	0.9144 metre
1 (statute) mile (= 1,760 yards)	1.6093 kilometres
1 (nautical) mile (= 1.150779 miles)	1.852 kilometres

Square Measure (Area)

Imperial	Metric
1 square inch	6.4516 sq. centimetres
1 square foot (= 144 square inches)	9.29 square decimetres
1 square yard (= 9 square feet)	0.8361 square metre
1 acre (= 4,840 square yards)	0.40469 hectare
1 square mile (= 640 acres)	259 hectares

Cubic Measure (Volume)

Imperial	Metric
1 cubic inch	16.4 cubic centimetres
1 cubic foot (= 1,728 cubic inches)	0.0283 cubic metre
1 cubic yard (= 27 cubic feet)	0.765 cubic metre

Capacity Measure (Volume)

Imperial	Metric
1 (imperial) fl. oz. (= 1/20 imperial pint)	28.41 ml
1 (US liquid) fl. oz. (= 1/16 US pint)	29.57 ml
1 (imperial) gill (= 1/4 imperial pint)	142.07 ml
1 (US liquid) gill (= 1/4 US pint)	118.29 ml
1 (imperial) pint (= 20 fl. imperial oz.)	568.26 ml
1 (US liquid) pint (= 16 fl. US oz.)	473.18 ml
1 (US dry) pint (= 1/2 quart)	550.61 ml
1 (imperial) gallon (= 4 quarts)	4.546 litres
1 (US liquid) gallon (= 4 quarts)	3.785 litres
1 (imperial) peck (= 2 gallons)	9.092 litres
1 (US dry) peck (= 8 quarts)	8.810 litres
1 (imperial) bushel (= 4 pecks)	36.369 litres
1 (US dry) bushel (= 4 pecks)	35.239 litres

Mass (Weight)

Imperial	Metric
1 grain	0.065 gram
1 dram	1.772 grams
1 ounce (= 16 drams)	28.35 grams
1 pound (= 16 ounces = 7,000 grains)	0.45359237 kilogram
1 stone (= 14 pounds)	6.35 kilograms
1 quarter (= 2 stones)	12.70 kilograms
1 hundredweight (= 4 quarters = 112 lb.)	50.80 kilograms
1 (long) ton (= 2,240 lbs.)	1.016 tons
1 (short) ton (= 2,000 lbs.)	0.907 ton

Metric → Imperial

Linear Measure (Length/Distance)

Metric	Imperial
1 millimetre	0.0394 inch
1 centimetre (= 10 mm)	0.3937 inch
1 decimetre (= 10 cm)	3.937 inches
1 metre (= 100 cm)	1.0936 yards
1 decametre (= 10 m)	10.936 yards
1 hectometre (= 100 m)	109.36 yards
1 kilometre (= 1,000 m)	0.6214 mile

Square Measure (Area)

Metric	Imperial
1 square centimetre	0.1550 sq. inch
1 square metre (= 10,000 sq. cm)	1.1960 sq. yards
1 acre (= 100 sq. metres)	119.60 sq. yards
1 hectare (= 100 acres)	2.4711 acres
1 square kilometre (= 100 hectares)	0.3861 sq. mile

Cubic Measure (Volume)

Metric	Imperial
1 cubic centimetre	0.0610 cubic inch
1 cubic metre (one million cu. cm)	1.308 cubic yards

Capacity Measure (Volume)

Metric	Imperial
1 millilitre	0.002 (imperial) pint
1 centilitre (= 10 ml)	0.018 pint
1 decilitre (= 100 ml)	0.176 pint
1 litre (= 1,000 ml)	1.76 pints
1 decalitre (= 10 l)	2.20 (imperial) gallons
1 hectolitre (= 100 l)	2.75 (imperial) bushels

Mass (Weight)

Metric	Imperial
1 milligram	0.015 grain
1 centigram (= 10 mg)	0.154 grain
1 decigram (= 100 mg)	1.543 grains
1 gram (= 1,000 mg)	15.43 grains
1 decagram (= 10 g)	5.64 drams
1 hectogram (= 100 g)	3.527 ounces
1 kilogram (= 1,000 g)	2.205 pounds
1 ton (= 1,000 kg)	0.984 (long) ton

Calculator Reference Guide

A QUICK REFERENCE GUIDE TO USING YOUR POCKET CALCULATOR*

[+] Plus key to add.
[−] Minus key to subtract.
[×] Multiplication key.
[÷] Dividend key.
[=] Completes calculation.

Topic	Manual example	Using your calculator	Display answer
Addition/subtraction	15.842 + 3.2 − 24.642	15.842 [+] 3.2 [−] 24.642 [=]	−5.6
Multiplication/division	$\frac{24 \times 26}{12}$	24 [×] 26 [÷] 12 [=]	52
Using a minus sign in multiplication	−14 × 46	14 [+/−] [×] 46 [=]	−644
Find the portion (using the percent key)	What is 35% of $800?	800 [×] 35 [%] *Note:* No equal sign is punched.	280
Find the rate	$280 is what percent of $800?	280 [÷] 800 [%]	35
Find the base	$280 is 35% of what number?	280 [÷] 35 [%]	800
Discounts	$500 less 5%	500 [−] 5 [%]	475
Adding on sales tax	$600 plus a 5% tax	600 [+] 5 [%]	630
A discount and a tax	$150 less 30% plus a 6% tax	150 [−] 30 [%] [+] 6 [%]	111.30
Simple interest	$\$1{,}200 \times 8\% \times \frac{60}{365}$	1200 [×] 8 [%] [×] 60 [÷] 365 [=]	15.780821
Using memory	$\frac{45}{3 \times 3}$	3 [×] 3 [=] [M +] 45 [÷] [MR] [=]	5
Memory used to solve principal using % key	$\frac{\$180}{11.5\% \times \frac{30}{360}}$	30 [×] 11.5 [%] [÷] 360 [=] [M+] 180 [÷] [MR][=]	18782.674
Same example without % key	$\frac{\$180}{.115 \times \frac{30}{360}}$	.115 [×] 30 [÷] 360 [=] [M+] 180 [÷] [MR][=]	18782.674

*Each calculator has variations—check your instruction booklet:

[+/−] Changes sign of number from positive to negative or negative to positive.

[CE] Clears last entry and NOT total.

[MC] Clears memory.

[%] Multiply by percent of the amount.

[M+] Stored in memory (added).

[M−] Subtracted from memory.

[MR] Recalls what is stored in memory.

Reprinted by permission of Texas Instruments Incorporated.

TI BA II PLUS™ is a financial calculator that solves time-value-of-money calculations such as annuities, mortgages, and savings, and generates amortization schedules.

See the Texas Instruments Web site for features and Quick Guide at http://www.ti.com/calc/docs/baiip.htm

SAMPLE QUICK GUIDE REFERENCE

Payment and Compounding Settings (P/Y, C/Y)

The BA II Plus defaults to 12 payments per year (P/Y) and 12 compounding periods per year (C/Y). You can change one or both of the settings to any number. The examples below assume the BA II Plus is set to four decimal places.

To set both the P/Y and the C/Y to 1:

Press	Display	
[2nd] [P/Y] 1 [ENTER]	P/Y =	1.0000
[↓]	C/Y =	1.0000
[2nd] [QUIT]		0.0000

The above example shows annual compounding. You may want to set the P/Y to a different number than the C/Y. The following example shows how to set the BA II Plus for a monthly payment that is compounded quarterly.

To set the P/Y to 12 and the C/Y to 4:

Press	Display	
[2nd] [P/Y] 12 [ENTER]	P/Y =	12.0000
[↓]	C/Y =	12.0000
4 [ENTER]	C/Y =	4.0000
[2nd] [QUIT]		0.0000

The P/Y and C/Y settings continue indefinitely (even though the calculator is turned off and on), until you change them.

To calculate the future value of a dollar:

What is the future value of $1.00 invested for five years at an interest rate of 7% compounded annually? For this example, set P/Y and C/Y to 1.

Press	Display	
[2nd] [CLR TVM]		0.0000
1 [+/−] [PV]	PV =	−1.0000
5 [N]	N =	5.0000
7 [I/Y]	I/Y =	7.0000
[CPT] [FV]	FV =	1.4026

Clearing the Calculator

Clearing the calculator is different from resetting it. You can clear one or more values while retaining other data, whereas resetting the calculator clears all data and restores all settings to factory defaults.

To clear the calculator:

Press	To clear
[→]	One character at a time (including decimal points)
[CE/C]	An incorrect entry, an error condition, or error message
[2nd] [QUIT]	All pending operations in standard-calculator mode — or — Out of a prompted worksheet and return to standard-calculator mode (values previously entered remain in the prompted worksheet)
[CE/C] [CE/C]	An unfinished calculation — or — A keyed, but not yet entered, variable value in a prompted worksheet — or — Out of a prompted worksheet and return to standard-calculator mode (values previously entered remain in the prompted worksheet)
[CE/C] [2nd] [CLR TVM]	All values (N, I/Y, PV, PMT, FV) in the TVM (Time-Value-of-Money) worksheet
[2nd] [CLR Work]*	A prompted worksheet (other than TVM) Also returns you to the first variable in the worksheet
[2nd] [MEM] [2nd] [CLR Work]*	All values stored in all 10 memories
O [STO] and the key for the number of the memory (0–9)	One memory

*You must be in the worksheet you want to clear before using [2nd] [CLR Work]. Refer to the Notes section for each worksheet in the BA II Plus Guidebook to see how clearing affects specific worksheets.